THE WISDOM OF THE CROSS

John Howard Yoder

THE WISDOM OF THE CROSS

Essays in Honor of
JOHN HOWARD YODER

Edited by

Stanley Hauerwas, Chris K. Huebner,
Harry J. Huebner, and Mark Thiessen Nation

WILLIAM B. EERDMANS PUBLISHING COMPANY
GRAND RAPIDS, MICHIGAN / CAMBRIDGE, U.K.

© 1999 Wm. B. Eerdmans Publishing Co.
255 Jefferson Ave. S.E., Grand Rapids, Michigan 49503 /
P.O. Box 163, Cambridge CB3 9PU U.K.

Printed in the United States of America

04 03 02 01 00 99   7 6 5 4 3 2 1

ISBN 0-8028-4398-0

To Anne Marie Guth Yoder

Contents

Preface   x

John H. Yoder, Ecumenical Neo-Anabaptist:
A Biographical Sketch   1
   Mark Thiessen Nation

"Patience" as Method in Moral Reasoning:
Is an Ethic of Discipleship "Absolute"?   24
   John Howard Yoder

NEVERTHELESS

John Howard Yoder's Systematic Defence of Christian Pacifism   45
   Nancey Murphy

Be Honest in Just War Thinking! Lutherans, the Just War
Tradition, and Selective Conscientious Objection   69
   Reinhard Hütter

From Police Officers to Peace Officers   84
   Tobias Winright

Christian Spirituality of Nonviolence as Reconciliation   115
   Ernest W. Ranly

vii

CONTENTS

THE POLITICS OF JESUS REVISITED

Jesus and the Zealot Option   131
  William Klassen

The Politics of Jesus in the Sermon on the Plain   150
  Glen H. Stassen

The Biblical Concept of "the Principalities and Powers":
John Yoder Points to Jacques Ellul   168
  Marva J. Dawn

ALTERNATIVES TO METHODOLOGISM

Moral Agency as Embodiment: How the Church Acts   189
  Harry J. Huebner

Historicizing the Historicist: Ernst Troeltsch and
Recent Mennonite Theology   213
  Arne Rasmusson

Discipleship in a World Full of Nazis: Dietrich Bonhoeffer's
Polyphonic Pacifism as Social Ethics   249
  Mark Thiessen Nation

Tradition and Truth in Christian Ethics: John Yoder
and the Bases of Biblical Realism   278
  Grady Scott Davis

THE OTHERNESS OF THE CHURCH

The Believers Church in Theological Perspective   309
  James Wm. McClendon, Jr.

Meeting in the Power of the Spirit: Ecclesiology, Ethics,
and the Practice of Discernment   327
  Gayle Gerber Koontz

Contents

Sorting the Wheat from the Tares: Reinterpreting
Reinhold Niebuhr's *Interpretation of Christian Ethics*   349
  Michael G. Cartwright

Love Your Enemies: The Church as Community of Nonviolence   373
  Jane Elyse Russell, OSF

TERTIUM DATUR

History, Theory, and Anabaptism: A Conversation
on Theology after John Howard Yoder   391
  Stanley Hauerwas and Chris K. Huebner

Theology in the Mirror of the Martyred and Oppressed:
Reflections on the Intersections of Yoder and Cone   409
  J. Denny Weaver

Theological Orthodoxy and Jewish Christianity:
A Personal Tribute to John Howard Yoder   430
  A. James Reimer

Deuteronomic or Constantinian: What Is the Most
Basic Problem for Christian Social Ethics?   449
  Gerald W. Schlabach

Supplement to "A Comprehensive Bibliography of the
Writings of John Howard Yoder"   472
  Mark Thiessen Nation

Contributors   492

Preface

John Howard Yoder, good Mennonite that he was, did not honor honor. How do you honor a man who does not honor honor when his work has been so important to so many? We do not pretend that this book answers that question. Rather this book testifies to our indebtedness to John Howard Yoder, but also, we hope, to our love of him. John sought neither to be honored nor loved. Rather, in all that he wrote and did, John directed us to the Crucified who is alone worthy of love and honor. That he did so, of course, is the reason we cannot ignore his significance in our lives.

This book has been a long time in the making. It was first conceived ten years ago but then aborted because of matters between John and the church which needed to be processed. At the time we felt that it was inappropriate for one arm of the church to celebrate the work of a scholar while another arm "disciplined" him. We therefore postponed the celebration to a time when that process was completed. Hence in 1997 the project was revived.

From the outset it was our intention that we would present the book to John at an appropriate occasion such as a meeting of the Society of Christian Ethics. We were apprehensive about such a presentation because we knew that John was going to be, as we say in the South, "none too pleased" that the book had been done. God has obviously relieved us of that worry, which at once makes us sad and happy. We are happy that John now enjoys the fellowship of the saints and, in particular, conversation with the early Anabaptists he so loved. But we are sad that this extraordinary Christian whose work so challenged our received ways of thinking and living is now gone.

Yet as we hope this book testifies, we have only begun to learn the lessons John's work represented. John did not provide new answers to old questions;

but rather, like Wittgenstein, he changed the questions. We suspect we are just beginning to appreciate the significance of how John taught us to think theologically. We hope, therefore, that this book represents a beginning through which we can help one another better understand how to go on after John Howard Yoder.

We are particularly grateful for all those who have written essays for this book. They may appear to be something of a ragtag bunch, ranging from Mennonite "insiders" to free-floating intellectuals. Yet they all share a common appreciation for John and what John cared about. We are all students of John, but some of these authors had the privilege to be his doctoral students. We are extremely pleased that this book provides the occasion for John's students to express their debt to John, but even more what they learned from him.

The other editors of this volume need to give a special word of thanks to the person that was the driving force that made this book a reality, that is, Mark Thiessen Nation. No one knows — as will be clear from the biographical essay Mark provides in this book — more about the life and work of John than Mark. Mark provided not only the imagination for the book, but also did most of the work. Harry and Chris Huebner did more than their share. I fear my role was largely that of a cheerleader.

Yet I confess I am extremely proud of this book. For the essays are not only of high quality, but I think John would have enjoyed reading them. He would have done so because the essays are not really about him, but instead they witness to the kind of work his work made possible. John had no interest in establishing a "new theological position," but rather he sought to foster a community of discussion that would do better what he had tried to do. We hope this book at least in some small way represents that kind of development.

I once observed to John how illuminating I found the list he provides at the beginning of *The Politics of Jesus* of the ways the mainstream has to insure that Jesus is not the norm for Christian living and, in particular, "social ethics." He was not impressed that I was impressed by his analysis. Instead he asked me if I could extend the list. John loved lists, he loved revising his lists, like the different kinds of nonviolence he characterized in *Nevertheless*, but most of all he loved it when others found a way to do better what he had tried to do. We do not pretend to be able to do John's work better than he has done it, but we hope at least this book has added one or two items to John's lists.

We are particularly grateful to Eerdmans Publishing and, in particular, to Jon Pott not only for publishing this book but for their support of John's work. Eerdmans published not only John's last book, *For the Nations: Essays Public and Evangelical*, but also *The Royal Priesthood* and *The Politics of Jesus*. The latter is particularly noteworthy since at the time they published *The Politics of Je-*

sus, John was not well known and the book was, to say the least, unique. John took great pleasure that a Reformed publishing house had so supported his work. That Eerdmans did so at least suggested that John represented something more than a voice from a minority tradition.

I suggested above that no one knows more about John's life and work than Mark Nation. That is not true. There is one other person who knew John better than any of us — Annie Yoder. It gives us great pleasure, therefore, to dedicate this book to Annie, who is every bit as formidable a person as was John. We admire not only Annie's love and loyalty to John, but her love of God which is manifest, like John's was, in her willingness never to say less than the truth. No one misses and mourns John more than Annie. May this book at least gesture to her that we too miss and mourn John, and that we do so because of his and her witness to God's nonviolent cross.

Stanley Hauerwas

John H. Yoder, Ecumenical
Neo-Anabaptist: A Biographical Sketch[1]

Mark Thiessen Nation

I

Stanley Hauerwas is right that if there was anything that could make John Yoder "testy" it was to be "pigeonholed" as a "Mennonite thinker."[2] That was because John knew that such "pigeonholing" was done to dismiss or, at least, to marginalize what he had to say. This marginalization had happened often enough that when he wrote the introduction to *The Priestly Kingdom* in the early 1980s, he sought to make it clear that "these pages do not describe a Mennonite vision." "Without disavowing my ethnic and denominational origins, I deny that this view is limited to people of that same culture or derived in its detail from that experience." Rather, he made the "claim that the vision of discipleship projected in this collection is founded in Scripture and catholic tradition, and is pertinent today as a call for all Christian believers."[3]

There are many ways to describe John Howard Yoder. These quotations

---

1. I want to thank Albert J. Meyer, John Yoder's brother-in-law and longtime friend, and Mary Ellen (Yoder) Meyer, John's sister, for their helpful responses to several earlier drafts of this essay. I also want to thank Marlene Epp, editor of *Conrad Grebel Review*, for permission to use portions of my essay, "He Came Preaching Peace: The Ecumenical Peace Witness of John H. Yoder," *Conrad Grebel Review* 16 (Spring 1998): 65-76.

2. Stanley Hauerwas, "When the Politics of Jesus Makes a Difference," *Christian Century* 110 (October 13, 1993): 984.

3. John Howard Yoder, *The Priestly Kingdom* (Notre Dame: University of Notre Dame Press, 1984), 4, 8.

from *The Priestly Kingdom* provide one. He was a broadly ecumenical neo-Anabaptist.[4] He never tried to disown his own denominational inheritance; everyone knew he was Mennonite. He was an heir to the Anabaptist heritage. But far be it from him to take that inheritance for granted. He worked and reworked the tradition that was his. Using that tradition as a hermeneutic, he sought to provide a compelling voice for a catholic, radically reforming way of understanding the Christian faith that he hoped would, in its main outlines, be embraced by all Christians.[5] Simultaneously, knowing that not everyone would embrace his form of the Christian faith, he sought to call Christians (and others who would listen) to live disciplined lives in relation to violence. This brief biographical sketch will show how he came to be who he was and how he expressed his ecumenical neo-Anabaptism. We first look at the local church and the ancestry that were the inheritance of John H. Yoder.

II

"Biography begins with parents and ancestors."[6]

"Without disavowing my ethnic and denominational origins . . ."

John Yoder was reared in Oak Grove Mennonite Church, just outside of Smithville, in northern Ohio. This Mennonite church was founded around 1816.[7]

---

4. Yoder used the term "neo-Anabaptist movement" to refer to the recent revival of interest in sixteenth-century Anabaptists in his quickly written summary of an April 1952 meeting of Mennonite graduate students, "'Reflections on the Irrelevance of Certain Slogans to the Historical Movements They Represent' or 'The Cooking of the Anabaptist Goose' or 'Ye Garnish the Sepulchres of the Righteous,'" 1.

5. See John Howard Yoder, "Anabaptist Vision and Mennonite Reality," in *Consultation on Anabaptist-Mennonite Theology*, ed. A. J. Klassen (Fresno, CA: Council of Mennonite Seminaries, 1970), 5: "What is meant here by the label 'Anabaptist' is not a century but a hermeneutic."

6. John Howard Yoder, "1980 Autobiography," Unpublished transcript of an autobiographical tape made by Yoder for James Wm. McClendon, Jr., and Karen Lebacqz in 1980, 1.

7. For a history of Oak Grove Mennonite Church see James O. Lehman, *Creative Congregationalism: A History of the Oak Grove Mennonite Church in Wayne County, Ohio.* (Smithville, OH: Oak Grove Mennonite Church, 1978). Also see John Umble, "The Oak Grove-Pleasant Hill Amish Mennonite Church in Wayne County, Ohio, in the Nineteenth Century (1815-1900)," *The Mennonite Quarterly Review* 31 (July 1957): 156-219.

Strictly speaking, until the 1920s, the church was Amish Mennonite. However, to refer to Oak Grove as Amish Mennonite is confusing for those unfamiliar with American Mennonite (and Amish) history. Oak Grove was founded by those standing within Anabaptist/Mennonite

2

John Howard Yoder's great-great-grandfather, his great-grandfather, and his father together provided leadership at Oak Grove for over one hundred years.[8]

John K. Yoder (1824-1906) and his family moved to Wayne County, Ohio from Mifflin County, Pennsylvania in the spring of 1855, five years after John K.'s ordination to the ministry. He would come to be "one of the most powerful, influential, and widely known bishops in the Amish Mennonite church during the last four decades of the 19th century."[9] He provided significant leadership in Amish Mennonite churchwide meetings, meetings that would help determine the direction of the Amish Mennonites. Early in his ministry John K. was seen to be "forward-looking in his progressiveness, but his deep respect for meaningful patterns and traditions of the past gave him restraint and caution. . . . [He] always insisted upon a strong congregationalism in the government of his church, even if it meant leaving the older ways considerably. . . . He preached and taught powerfully and led his congregation to discipline rigorously. Yet he had a very democratic spirit. And he displayed unusual confidence

history who are descended from the followers of Jakob Ammann, who separated from other Mennonites in the late seventeenth century. In the third quarter of the nineteenth century in the U.S., the followers of Ammann found two different ways of appropriating their tradition. One way — the way many Americans now associate simply with the term "Amish" — came to be designated by the term "Old Order Amish" and the other as "Amish Mennonite." John Howard Yoder's great-great-grandfather, John K. Yoder, was one of the leaders who helped to lead one segment of the descendants of Ammann in the progressive direction to become Amish Mennonites. (On the beginnings of the Amish branch of the Mennonite tradition see Steven M. Nolt, *A History of the Amish* [Intercourse, PA: Good Books, 1992], 23-41 and John D. Roth, trans. and ed., *Letters of the Amish Division: A Sourcebook* [Goshen, IN: Mennonite Historical Society, 1993]. On the divisions that developed in the second half of the nineteenth century, see Paton Yoder, *Tradition & Transition: Amish Mennonites and Old Order Amish, 1800-1900* [Scottdale, PA: Herald Press, 1991].)

8. Lehman, *Creative Congregationalism*, 78-127, 237-78. I am conscious, as I write this, that men figure much more prominently in this biographical sketch than do women. This is partly because of the biases of the sources from which I draw. It is also because of the more public nature of the roles of men during the time being covered by this sketch. However, it is important that it be stated that, besides the ones named, many women had significant roles in shaping the worlds that were the tradition John H. Yoder inherited.

9. Umble, "Oak Grove Church," 206. A note on the word "bishop" here: "It does not mean a person exercising responsibility over a diocese. [A bishop] was considered a sufficiently mature and responsible leader that he sometimes became a resource to other congregations in matters of reconciliation and ordination of leadership" (Lehman, *Creative Congregationalism*, 25). It is also worth noting that ministry was not how John K. earned a living. He was a businessman. However, Theron Schlabach is right that "quite probably he did business mainly to carry on his larger role as religious and moral leader in church and community" (Theron F. Schlabach, *Peace, Faith, Nation: Mennonites and Amish in Nineteenth-Century America*, The Mennonite Experience in America, Vol. 2 [Scottdale, PA: Herald Press, 1988], 53).

in the involvement of lay members in church matters."[10] "Amid the changing pattern of church activity and organization two principles determined his policies: the maintenance of the fundamentals of the Dordrecht Confession as laid down in the Eighteen Articles; and the unity and peace of the brotherhood."[11] This approach to the church influenced his style as he provided leadership within his own congregation, in offering counsel to other congregations, and in the nationwide meetings.

Christian Z. Yoder ("C. Z.," 1845-1939), the youngest son of John K., did not become a minister until age fifty-eight.[12] This was because ministers at this time in the Amish Mennonite church were chosen by lot.[13] Nine times he had been through the lot. It finally fell to him in 1904. By this time C. Z. was already a successful farmer and very actively involved in the Oak Grove church. Long before he was a minister he had organized the Oak Grove Sunday School, serving as its superintendent for thirty-three years. He also assisted in the organization of the Ohio Sunday School Conference, beginning in 1895. For many years he served on the music committee of the Mennonite general conference.[14] "It will readily be observed by any student of American Mennonite hymnology that C. Z. Yoder assisted in compiling the most major hymnbooks covering over a half century of hymnology for the Mennonite Church."[15] He was on the board of directors for the Elkhart Institute and, later, Goshen College.[16] He served in several capacities with Mennonite mission agencies in the very em-

10. Lehman, *Creative Congregationalism,* 78.

11. Umble, "Oak Grove Church," 205. The Dordrecht Confession, from 1632, has been called "the mother among Mennonite confessions": Howard John Loewen, *One Lord, One Church, One Hope, and One God: Mennonite Confessions of Faith* (Elkhart, IN: Institute of Mennonite Studies, 1985), 24. The confession appears on pp. 63-70. Also see Gerald C. Studer, "The Dordrecht Confession of Faith, 1632-1982," *The Mennonite Quarterly Review* 58 (October 1984): 503-19.

12. See especially Umble, "Oak Grove Church," 196 and Lehman, *Creative Congregationalism,* 78-127. C. Z. Yoder provides much of the information that is known about the Oak Grove church. That is because he kept a diary for more than seventy-five years, from 1862 to 1939! (Lehman, 71)

13. On the Amish Mennonites see note seven, above.

14. The Mennonite general conference was the general governing body for the ("Old") Mennonite Church. This general governing body came into existence around 1900 (James J. Juhnke, *Vision, Doctrine, War: Mennonite Identity and Organization in America, 1890-1930,* The Mennonite Experience in America, Vol. 3 [Scottdale, PA: Herald Press, 1989], 124-30). This governing body is not to be confused with the General Conference Mennonite Church, a separate Mennonite branch that began in 1860 (see Schlabach, *Peace, Faith, Nation,* 117-40).

15. Lehman, *Creative Congregationalism,* 227.

16. Lehman, *Creative Congregationalism,* 131, 140. Elkhart Institute was the predecessor of Goshen College, the ("Old") Mennonite college founded in Goshen, Indiana in 1903.

bryonic stage of those agencies. He served as the first vice president and then for nine years as the president of the Mennonite Board of Missions and Charities and for another eight years as chairman of the Missions Committee of the Board. "For many years he [also] served as an evangelist, his preaching and singing ministry taking him to Amish and Mennonite communities in all sections of the country until C. Z. Yoder became a household name throughout the church."[17]

One of the states in which Christian Z. Yoder evangelized was Virginia. While there, he did some evangelism work with another Christian, Christian Good (1842-1916), a Mennonite minister from Harrisonburg. This man would be John H. Yoder's other great-grandfather.[18] Among the facts that had been passed down to John Yoder about his great-grandfather Good was that he was a conscientious objector during the Civil War. "When commanded to shoot he said 'but those are people. I don't shoot people' so that the confederate army put him in the kitchen."[19]

Christian Good and Anna Heatwole Good (1841-1889) had nine children. Four of their sons moved to Sterling, Illinois and became a part of the Science Ridge Mennonite Church. One of their sons was Samuel. Samuel Good (1878-1905), John H. Yoder's grandfather, became a leader in the church, but died of tuberculosis at the age of twenty-seven.[20] Ethel (1903-1992) was born to Samuel and Mary Ellen ("Mamie" Reisner) Good (1881-1973) two and a half years before Samuel died.[21] Thus "Mamie" was a widow at a very young age. Family members helped them as they could; but it was difficult for Mamie. She was first an apprentice to a dressmaker and then a doctor's helper, assisting when babies were born. When Ethel was ten years old she and her mother moved to Chicago where her mother became a (volunteer) worker in the Mennonite city mission in Chicago. Mamie married Amos Neff (1887-1951) when Ethel was twelve. Ethel spent the rest of her childhood in Chicago, until she moved to Indiana to attend Goshen College in the fall of 1920. There she, the

17. Umble, "Oak Grove Church," 196.

18. Lewis Christian Good, *A Good Tree Grew in the Valley: The Family Record of Christian Good, 1842-1916* (Baltimore: Gateway Press, Inc., 1974).

19. J. H. Yoder, "Memo to Mark Nation," November 28, 1995, 1. Also see Lewis Christian Good, *A Good Tree Grew in the Valley*, 1-3.

20. John Yoder mentioned on more than one occasion that Samuel's brother, Aaron C., "for the next sixty years [following Samuel's death] was one of the most visible (Old) Mennonite ministers, a much traveled evangelist." (Yoder, "Memo to Mark Nation," 1. Also see index, under Aaron C. Good, of Willard H. Smith, *Mennonites in Illinois* [Scottdale, PA: Herald Press, 1983].)

21. The following information is from Ethel G. Yoder, "My Story," unpublished autobiographical essay, written in installments between April 11, 1987 and May 25, 1992.

granddaughter of Christian Good, met Howard C. Yoder (1897-1983), the grandson of Christian Yoder. By October 7, 1925 they were married and moved to the Smithville area, worshiping in Howard's home church, Oak Grove Mennonite Church.

To pick up the thread again of the Oak Grove Mennonite Church: for our purposes, John S. Yoder, John H. Yoder's grandfather, is significant for one particular reason. C.Z. had seven sons. Only one of them remained in the Mennonite church, that is, John S. One of John S.'s sons, Howard C. (John H.'s father), served with Mennonite Central Committee for two terms — one in the 1920s and one in the 1940s — first in Russia and then in Western Europe.[22] Howard was for many years a leader in the Oak Grove congregation and was an "influential and highly respected layman." At several critical junctures he offered what was considered to be wise counsel, some of it given during his years of service as chair of the church council. In fact his widow, Ethel Yoder, was probably right that "at one time in the middle 40s it was his gift as a mediator that held the church together." It was suggested that he should be the bishop for the congregation. However, Howard responded from London, where he was serving in relief work: "I do not feel in the least that that is where God wants me. I do not see what I could do for the congregation in that office that I can not do as a member."[23]

In 1927 the eastern Amish Mennonite conference of Pennsylvania and Ohio, of which Oak Grove was a part, merged with the Ohio Mennonite Conference of the ("Old") Mennonite Church.[24] At that time "some Amish congregations, such as the Oak Grove congregation in Wayne County, Ohio, were more progressive in matters of education and dress than were the 'old' Mennonite conferences they joined."[25] This progressivism was manifested in numerous ways within the congregation and within the Yoder family. Without question it shaped John H. Yoder to be profoundly Mennonite. It also gave him a sense of freedom. As he put it:

22. Mennonite Central Committee (MCC), founded in 1920, is the joint relief and service agency of nearly all North American Mennonites. (See Harold S. Bender et al., eds., *The Mennonite Encyclopedia*, vol. 3 (Scottdale, PA: The Mennonite Publishing House, 1957), and Cornelius J. Dyck and Dennis D. Martin, eds., *The Mennonite Encyclopedia*, vol. 5 (Scottdale, PA: Herald Press, 1990), both s.v. "Mennonite Central Committee."

23. Lehman, *Creative Congregationalism*, 247; Ethel G. Yoder, "My Story," 11. For the situation in the Oak Grove church in the 1940s see Lehman, *Creative Congregationalism*, 237-55.

24. The "Old" Mennonite Church (sometimes simply called The Mennonite Church) is the oldest (founded ca. 1683) and largest of the Mennonite bodies in North America. As I write this, the "Old" Mennonite Church and the General Conference Mennonite Church (the second largest Mennonite body in North America, founded in 1860) are moving toward becoming one body.

25. Juhnke, *Vision, Doctrine, War*, 121.

I grew up in a relaxed relationship to that culture, never needing, as many do, to prove my independence of it. Never sensing any coercion to stay within it. So that my choice to stay within it, although predisposed obviously by generations of ethnic continuity and by the church faithfulness of my parents, was by no means a matter of bowing to superior pressure but was rather a willing choice made in small stages in young adulthood. That makes it difficult to this day for many Mennonites, especially younger ones, to understand me when they, although chronologically younger than I, are, in a sense, representative of an earlier phase of the denominational quarrel with culture because they still had to fight Mennonitism in its more conservative forms to prove their independence of it. Whereas I had greater freedom and was therefore able progressively to accept that as my story without being coerced to do so.[26]

But, of course, Oak Grove was only one Mennonite Church. It was also related to the larger Mennonite world.[27] It is to that world that we now turn.

III

"In [Harold S. Bender's] work, for the first time, the renewal concern reached all the way back to the sixteenth-century sources."[28]

"I deny that this view is limited to people of that same culture or derived in its detail from that experience."

For most nineteenth-century North American Mennonites, German was the language of worship, of religion, and dominated everyday life. The peculiarities of dress, nonresistance, and other ways of living in a nonconformed manner were reinforced by the barrier of language. As with the Amish today, so with most nineteenth-century Mennonites, they knew and accepted that they were

---

26. Yoder, "1980 Autobiography," 3-4.
27. Of course there were really a number of "Mennonite worlds." For the sake of brevity we will look at one relevant slice of one of those worlds, the first larger Mennonite world to which John Yoder related outside of his home church. This is the world of the "Old" Mennonite Church. Some of what I am saying in the next section would apply to the world of other Mennonite bodies, but I don't assume that it all would. (For a picture of something of the various Mennonite worlds throughout the first forty years of Yoder's life, see Paul Toews, *Mennonites in American Society, 1930-1970: Modernity and the Persistence of Religious Community*, The Mennonite Experience in America, Vol. 4 [Scottdale, PA: Herald Press, 1996].)
28. Yoder, "Anabaptist Vision and Mennonite Reality," 25.

different from "the English." Put positively, their language connected them with their history. The *Ausbund*[29] from which they derived their hymns, the *Martyrs Mirror*[30] from which they derived models of discipleship, all reminded them that *Gelassenheit* (yieldedness) and *Demuth* (humility) were the way for them, even if not for "the English." They were Mennonites, stemming from an honored tradition of Anabaptists, who spoke the same language they did, language meaning not simply German but, more importantly, a pattern of life.

Around the turn of the century, change that was already well under way was to accelerate. "The moment when Mennonites in general turned 'English' came around 1898-1900."[31] Leonard Gross has dubbed the almost half-century from 1898 to 1944 "the doctrinal era of the Mennonite Church": "The uniqueness of this era lay in its ahistorical nature, in its doctrinal center and in the fact that it was an extended interlude, the likes of which were not experienced in preceding centuries nor in the decades after 1944."[32]

In 1864 John F. Funk had begun a Mennonite paper in English and German editions: *Herald of Truth* and *Der Herold der Wahrheit.* According to Leonard Gross, "John Funk did not rock the boat theologically, culturally or socially. He provided, in effect, a journalistic forum for the many voices from almost every corner of the Mennonite Church."[33] "Overnight Daniel Kauffman replaced John F. Funk as the leader granting direction, giving definition and leading the way into a brave new Mennonite world. The death in 1899 of John S. Coffman, the only other major church wide figure, helped impel Daniel Kauffman into

29. On the *Ausbund* see Harold S. Bender et al., eds., *The Mennonite Encyclopedia,* Vol. 1 (Scottdale, PA: The Mennonite Publishing House, 1955), s.v. "*Ausbund.*" On its waning influence after 1800 see Schlabach, *Peace, Faith, Nation,* 91ff.

30. Thieleman J. van Braght, *Martyrs Mirror,* third English edition (Scottdale, PA: Herald Press, 1886 [from 1660 Dutch edition]), still in print. According to Robert S. Kreider and John S. Oyer, "for Mennonites in their 465 years of history, no book except the Bible has been more influential in perpetuating and nurturing their faith than the *Martyrs Mirror.*" (John S. Oyer and Robert S. Kreider, *Mirror of the Martyrs* [Intercourse, PA: Good Books, 1990], 7.) See also James W. Lowry, *The Martyrs' Mirror Made Plain* (Lagrange, IN: Pathway Publishers, 1997).

31. Leonard Gross, "The Doctrinal Era of the Mennonite Church," *The Mennonite Quarterly Review* 60 (January 1986): 86. James Lehman says about Oak Grove (*Creative Congregationalism,* 98): "German continued as the basic language of the Sunday school even until the turn of the century."

32. Gross, "The Doctrinal Era," 83. See also J. Denny Weaver, "The Quickening of Soteriology: Atonement From Christian Burkholder to Daniel Kauffman," *The Mennonite Quarterly Review* 61 (January 1987): 5-45 and J. Denny Weaver, *Keeping Salvation Ethical: Mennonite and Amish Atonement Theology in the Late Nineteenth Century* (Scottdale, PA: Herald Press, 1997).

33. Gross, "The Doctrinal Era," 84.

8

the Mennonite limelight to bridge what otherwise would have been a void in the Mennonite Church."[34] In 1898 the Mennonite General Conference was formed. That same year Daniel Kauffman published his book, *Manual of Bible Doctrines*.[35]

> Earlier there had been a complementarity of doctrines, based on the corporate faith of disciples who gathered in the name of the Prince of Peace and continued consciously in the faith of their forbears. In contrast, Mennonitism with Daniel Kauffman turned virtually ahistorical, with an imposed unity of doctrine brought to bear upon the Mennonite Church from a newly organized center, the results of which were supposed to unify all believers within the Mennonite Church. The new doctrinal approach, combined with a new authoritarianism of church polity, resulted, however, in a definite narrowing of the theological scope and precipitated as well a radical shift in the Mennonite group dynamic.[36]

In 1901 the German Mennonite paper, *Herold der Wahrheit*, came to an end. 1908 saw the birth of a new Mennonite magazine, the *Gospel Herald*, of which Daniel Kauffman was editor from 1908 until 1943.[37] In addition to his 1898 book, Kauffman also edited a 1914 book, entitled *Bible Doctrines*. This was revised by Kauffman in 1928 and renamed *Doctrines of the Bible*. As James Juhnke says, these books "did not enjoy the status of an official creed. But they provided an accepted standard for 'old' Mennonite congregations, Bible conferences, winter Bible schools, and other forums. They also bore the marks of the escalating American Protestant debate between Modernists and Fundamentalists. In his 1898 volume Kauffman had simply assumed the authority of the Bible without worrying much about a theory of inspiration. . . . However, the 1914 book included a thirty-page chapter on 'The Bible' . . . [that] set forth a conservative theory of biblical revelation."[38]

Kauffman died in 1944. The two decades before his death saw considerable turmoil in the Mennonite Church, much of it related to the debates between Modernists and Fundamentalists. "In 1923-1924," for example, "the board of Goshen College closed the school for a year largely because many of its constituents feared for its orthodoxy. In the 1920s, among [Mennonite Church]

34. Gross, "The Doctrinal Era," 91.

35. Daniel Kauffman, *A Manual of Bible Doctrines* (Elkhart, IN: Mennonite Publishing House, 1898).

36. Gross, "The Doctrinal Era," 92.

37. J. Daniel Hess, "One Magazine, Five Editors, and 90 Years of Journalism," *Gospel Herald* 90 (January 27, 1998): 2.

38. Juhnke, *Vision, Doctrine, War*, 129.

district conferences, Indiana-Michigan (at whose center the college sat) lost four congregations, six ministers, and an eighth of its members due to quarrels over what some thought was 'liberalism.'"[39] When Goshen College began hiring new faculty for the reopening in the fall of 1924 it hired H. S. Bender. However, Bender was hired to teach history and sociology rather than theology because "he was not considered 'safe' theologically."[40]

This was a time of transition, a time of opportunity to set new directions for the Mennonite Church. Dates are in some ways arbitrary ways of establishing turning points in the lives of individuals, movements, or churches. But perhaps 1927 can be seen as a significant year within the history of the Mennonite church for the twentieth century. It was 1927 when Harold Bender began *The Mennonite Quarterly Review,* making it easier for Bender and his many students to "search for a usable past."[41] It was in 1927 when Guy Hershberger suggested that focusing on peace theology might be a way to avoid becoming mired down in the debates then raging about doctrine.[42] And it was 1927 when John Howard Yoder was born. He would both make the most of the "usable past" and, out of that past, spend many fruitful years articulating a peace theology.

IV

"I . . . was . . . able progressively to accept that as my story without being coerced to do so."

"[This] vision of discipleship . . . is founded in Scripture and catholic tradition, and is pertinent today as a call for all Christian believers."

John Howard was born on December 29, 1927 in Smithville, Ohio. On February 8, 1931, when John was three years old, a brother, named Charles Good, was born into the family. When Charles was barely more than a year old he became sick and died within three days. March 11, 1933, one year — to the day — after he died, a sister, Mary Ellen, was born into the family.

We err if we imagine that John Yoder was born into some backwater,

39. Toews, *Mennonites in American Society,* 71. On the general struggle see pp. 64-83.

40. Al Keim, "The Anabaptist Vision: The History of a New Paradigm," *Conrad Grebel Review* 12 (Fall 1994): 241.

41. I am borrowing the title of a chapter, the first part of which is on Bender, from Toews, *Mennonites in American Society,* 84-106.

42. Toews, *Mennonites in American Society,* 64.

rural ethnic Mennonite world.[43] For one thing John was right that he "came . . . from one of the most liberal and acculturated Mennonite communities. The Oak Grove Mennonite Church, when I was growing up there, probably had more college graduates in its membership than any other Mennonite Church, except the ones at the colleges."[44] But, also, in the summer of 1935 John's family moved from Smithville to Wooster, because they were dissatisfied with the schools in Smithville.[45] Thus John spent most of his childhood in a community and in a school that were not populated by ethnic Mennonites. He was the only Mennonite in his classes. As a child John went to Fellowship of Reconciliation meetings with his parents in Wooster, Ohio.[46] In high school John participated in extemporaneous speech competition and was on a debate team that won the state championship. Among other topics, John debated the issue of pacifism. He played French horn in band and had the male lead in operettas during his last two years of school. During his last year in high school he took a few classes at the College of Wooster, a Presbyterian college.

John did not want to attend a Mennonite college. He looked into other possibilities. He wanted to attend one of the two universities he knew of that had programs centered around a "great books" curriculum. He had secured acceptance and scholarships in special programs at the University of Chicago and St. John's College, Annapolis, Maryland. Both of these programs would have allowed him to begin study after finishing only two years of high school. However, his parents, especially his mother, very much wanted him to go to Goshen College. Out of respect for his parents he went. However, if he had to go to Goshen College he had decided he would spend no more than two years there. So he made arrangements with the college to complete all of his requirements for a B.A. in Bible within two years, which he did.[47]

43. For the biographical information that follows I am chiefly indebted to two curricula vitae for John Yoder (one compiled by me, with John's assistance; the other by John); an untitled transcript of a 1980 autobiographical tape made by John Yoder for James Wm. McClendon, Jr., and Karen Lebacqz ("1980 Autobiography"); a June 12, 1991 interview with John Yoder by the author ("1991 Interview"); and a July 14, 1991 supplement to this interview, given to the author by John Yoder ("1991 Interview Supplement"), as well as Ethel G. Yoder, "My Story." All of these are unpublished.

44. John H. Yoder, "1991 Interview Supplement," 6.

45. This is the reason John's mother gives. John, in 1980, says it was "because of family greenhouse interest" ("1980 Autobiography," 4).

46. At that time the Fellowship of Reconciliation was an international Christian pacifist organization, with local chapters.

47. He did this in the midst of, at various times throughout the two years, participation in the A Cappella Chorus, the French club, the German club, the Mennonite Historical Society,

John began college at Goshen in the fall of 1945. This was an exciting time to be at Goshen College. Among John's teachers were Guy F. Hershberger and H. S. Bender. Hershberger had, only one year earlier, published *War, Peace, and Nonresistance,* a major statement among Mennonites on the issue of war.[48] As Leo Driedger and Donald Kraybill say: "*War, Peace, and Nonresistance* . . . became a benchmark in the legacy of Mennonite peacemaking."[49] In speaking of the content and significance of the book, Paul Toews says:

> If Hershberger presented his approach as nonpolitical, it nevertheless embodied a prophetic witness that gave it pragmatic relevance. As nobody had before him, Hershberger positioned historic Mennonite understandings to make them relevant for the larger ecumenical world and even for the nation at large. He was traditionally Mennonite in his argument that Christian ethics was for Christians only, yet he enlarged the boundaries in which nonresistance had effect. . . . Hershberger offered a radically two-kingdom theology but one in which Christians clearly contributed to the social order.[50]

However, it was Harold S. Bender who had the more profound influence on John Yoder. Bender's area of expertise was church history, but he taught widely. "As for Bender, in 1945-1946 he taught eleven hours each semester, in addition to being dean [of the new seminary] and all his church work. His courses that year included church history, Mennonite history, apostolic history, Romans, Ethics, biblical introduction and biblical archaeology."[51] Bender's seminal essay, "The Anabaptist Vision," had also only been published little

---

the Devotional Life Committee, the college debate team, and editorship of the college newspaper. He also won the peace oratorical contest. His second year of college he was taking thirty-three hours per term. According to one of his roommates he rose at 4 A.M. and went to bed at about 10 P.M. virtually every day.

48. Guy F. Hershberger, *War, Peace, and Nonresistance* (Scottdale, PA: Herald Press, 1944). This book was revised, first in 1953 and, for a second time, in 1969.

49. Leo Driedger and Donald B. Kraybill, *Mennonite Peacemaking: From Quietism to Activism* (Scottdale, PA: Herald Press, 1994), 72.

50. Toews, *Mennonites in American Society,* 127.

51. Keim, *H. S. Bender,* 342. "Bender's faculty colleague, Olive Wyse, once told him, 'I have often heard students say that when you give yourself to teaching, you are one of the best teachers they have ever known'" (Keim, *Harold S. Bender, 1897-1962* [Scottdale, PA: Herald Press, 1998], 343). My thanks to Al Keim for e-mailing prepublication versions of some of the chapters of this book to me. We are in his debt for his fine work on Bender. Albert J. Meyer, John's roommate during John's second year at Goshen, said: "I would say that [Bender's] influence on John, as well as many others, was profound" ("Al Meyer Interview, 1990," 8).

more than a year earlier.[52] This essay was indicative of a "dramatic shift among historians from ignoring or excoriating Anabaptists to taking them seriously as a subject for Reformation research."[53] But it also encapsulated key elements of a vision he transmitted to his eager students, a vision that would provide impetus for years of research, wrestling, and writing. These basic elements were discipleship as "a concept which meant the transformation of the entire way of life of the individual believer and of society so that it should be fashioned after the teachings and example of Christ;" "a new concept of the church as created by the central principle of newness of life and applied Christianity;" and "the third great element in the Anabaptist vision was the ethic of love and nonresistance as applied to all human relationships."[54] "It was Bender's luck to articulate a new interpretation of history which influenced how historians understood the Anabaptists. Only after the fact did he come to understand that he had also provided his fellow Mennonites with a new self-definition of who they were and where they came from. He gave Mennonites a 'usable past.'"[55] It was John Yoder's luck (and ours) that he was one of those "fellow Mennonites" to study with Bender in his prime, later to be recognized by some as "the most gifted theologian of that gifted generation of Bender's protégés."[56]

In the summer of 1946 John went on an assignment with the Mennonites and Brethren to help care for a shipload of horses to be transported to Europe.[57] His ship, the *S.S. Virginian,* docked for a few days in Poland. While there John decided to search for a Mennonite church in Gdansk. He was arrested and brought before the mayor of the town as a spy. With the help of a Russian-English dictionary he convinced them he was not a spy and was released.

After graduating from Goshen College in 1947, Yoder returned to Ohio to work as a research assistant in the field of plant nutrition at the "Yoder Brothers" greenhouse in Barberton. He did this until the summer of 1948 when

52. Harold S. Bender, "The Anabaptist Vision," *Church History* 13 (March 1944): 3-24; reprinted, with slight revisions, in *The Mennonite Quarterly Review* 18 (April 1944): 67-88. On the history and context surrounding this influential address see *The Conrad Grebel Review* 12 (Fall 1994): 233-82 and Keim, *H. S. Bender,* ch. 14.

53. Keim, *H. S. Bender,* 321.

54. H. S. Bender, "The Anabaptist Vision," in *The Recovery of the Anabaptist Vision,* edited by Guy F. Hershberger (Scottdale, PA: Herald Press, 1957), 42-43, 47, 51.

55. Keim, *H. S. Bender,* 327; "Bender's luck" was the expression Keim used in an earlier version of this chapter. The published version has the expression "Bender's calling."

56. Keim, *H. S. Bender,* 506.

57. "Brethren" is a term connected to numerous Christian groups. These particular Brethren trace their roots to 1708 in Germany. They have, from their beginnings, had a close tie to Mennonites. See Donald F. Durnbaugh, *Fruit of the Vine: A History of the Brethren, 1708-1995* (Elgin, IL: Brethren Press, 1997).

he traveled from eastern Iowa to western Pennsylvania on a "peace team," speaking about peacemaking in various Mennonite churches and camps. This gave him experience in speaking about peace and exposure to a broader range of Mennonites.

He had applied to do overseas service with Mennonite Central Committee. The processing of his request took time. While waiting, he took some religious studies courses at the College of Wooster, studied Hebrew at Goshen College, and researched and wrote his first scholarly essay for publication, on the legal status of church discipline among the Old Order Amish.[58]

On April 1st of 1949, John Yoder arrived in France to begin a Mennonite Central Committee assignment. H. S. Bender had said to Yoder: "We are assigning you to France to do youth work and to give a peace testimony." But it was more than that.

> In the late 1940s and the early 1950s, the French Mennonites were being split between a conservative majority and a group (primarily of young people) who sought a deeper, more expressive spiritual experience. A key part of Yoder's assignment was to help mediate the tensions between the two groups. . . . It was a measure of the high regard Bender and Orie Miller had for Yoder that they would send such a youthful and inexperienced worker to such a difficult assignment.[59]

Apparently their confidence was well-placed. For Jean Séguy, in his masterful history of French Mennonites, says: "One can say that along with Pierre Widmer, he [J. H. Yoder] was one of the most effective instruments of the reorganization of the [French Mennonite] churches after 1945. . . . Few men will have exercised such a profound influence in [the churches'] transformation in this post-war period."[60]

Yoder's daily work was overseeing a network of children's homes. For the next five years he oversaw the transformation of the relief program there from being one of primarily feeding people to one with a network of children's homes, based "on the notion that stranded children are the people most in need

58. John Howard Yoder, "Caesar and the Meidung," *The Mennonite Quarterly Review* 23 (April 1949): 76-98.

59. Keim, *H. S. Bender,* 458-59.

60. Jean Séguy, *Les Assemblées Anabaptistes-Mennonites de France.* (Paris: Mouton & Co. and Ecole des Hautes Etudes en Sciences Sociales, 1977), 637. The first sentence is a slightly altered translation of the one provided in the quotation in Neal Blough, "The Anabaptist Vision and Its Impact Among French Mennonites," *The Mennonite Quarterly Review* 69 (July 1995): 383. The second sentence is based on a translation provided by David Fielden at the London Mennonite Centre.

of being fed and the best way to feed them is also to house them."[61] Working in one of these children's homes was the French Mennonite, Anne Marie Guth. On July 12th of 1952 John and Anne were married. Between 1953 and 1969 they would have seven children, six of whom survived infancy.

From the beginning of his time in Europe Yoder was involved in ecumenical conversations about pacifism. "Harold Bender took me along to the International Mennonite Peace Committee, and the people who represented the Mennonites ecumenically took me along very soon in 1950."[62] Some of these conversations were in the context of formal conferences, among them the ones that came to be called the "Puidoux theological conferences." Albert J. Meyer highlights the significance of these encounters. He says, "the Puidoux theological conferences of the fifties and sixties were the first extended theological conversations in over four hundred years between the Historic Peace Churches . . . and the official churches of Central Europe."[63] John Yoder played a central role in these events, delivering significant lectures at most of them.[64] During his last three years in Europe he was a member of the ecumenical committee of the German Protestant *Kirchentag* and the Europe Council of the International Fellowship of Reconciliation.

While in Europe Yoder also pursued graduate studies, receiving a Dr. Theol. *(insigne cum laude)* from the University of Basel (1962). He studied with a number of the luminaries there, including Walter Eichrodt and Walter Baumgartner in Old Testament, Oscar Cullmann in New Testament,[65] Karl Jaspers in philosophy, and Karl Barth in dogmatics.[66] Under the supervision of Ernst Staehelin he wrote his doctoral thesis (and a subsequent volume) on the disputations between the magisterial Reformers and the Anabaptists in early sixteenth-century Switzerland.[67]

Additionally, it was during his time in Europe that he was, as an academic, articulating what it meant to engage the larger world in relation to peace. He wrote essays about Karl Barth and Reinhold Niebuhr, two of the ma-

61. John H. Yoder, "1980 Autobiography," 11.

62. John H. Yoder, "1991 Interview Supplement," 1.

63. Albert J. Meyer, "Mennonites," in *On Earth Peace: Discussions on War/Peace Issues Between Friends, Mennonites, Brethren and European Churches, 1935-1975*, edited by Donald F. Durnbaugh (Elgin, IL: The Brethren Press, 1978), 14.

64. See the appropriate sections of Donald F. Durnbaugh, *On Earth Peace*.

65. He heard Cullmann give the lectures that became Cullmann's books on Peter, Christology, and the state in the New Testament.

66. Yoder attended a number of Barth seminars offered in both French and English. Among other lectures Yoder heard Barth present what became volumes III/iv (dealing with war) and IV/ii (dealing with sanctification/discipleship/peace) of *Church Dogmatics*.

67. See Mark Thiessen Nation, *A Comprehensive Bibliography of the Writings of John Howard Yoder* (Goshen, IN: Mennonite Historical Society, 1997), 20, 24.

jor theological voices of the day who had addressed themselves to the question of violence.[68] He also made his first efforts at formulating a theological rationale for why Christians should be actively involved in the world, something he would continue to write about for the rest of his life.[69]

During his last three years in Europe, while a full-time student at the University of Basel (1954-1957), Yoder oversaw the Mennonite Board of Missions and Charities relief program that had begun in Algeria in response to the earthquake there in 1954. He wrote a series of five articles about his experiences in Algeria, reflecting on Islam, the war, and the relief efforts.[70]

Much has been written about the "Concern" group that grew out of the gathering of some Mennonites who were doing graduate studies in Europe.[71] This group began, innocently enough, with a "European Study Conference of American Mennonite Students in Europe," April 14-25, 1952. The core "Concern" group consisted of seven Mennonite men doing graduate studies. "Sociologically, the group begins with people who shared in some degree the experiences of CPS,[72] MCC, study of history and theology, travel abroad, evangelism and the peace witness. Not all are (Old) Mennonite but most have had contact with the revival of interest in Anabaptist studies and many have been at Goshen."[73] What they had in common was that they had been energized by the rediscovery of the Anabaptist heritage of the Mennonite tradition. Because of their own studies of the Anabaptist tradition these students came to be critical of those, such as H. S. Bender, who had led them to these studies in the first place. They had been led to the conclusion, as John Yoder put it, "that if we were to make sense of North American Mennonitism, it would have to become more Anabaptist, more radical, more self-critical, less mainstream Evangelical, less institution centered."[74]

---

68. John Howard Yoder, "Reinhold Niebuhr and Christian Pacifism," *The Mennonite Quarterly Review* 29 (April 1955): 101-17 (original pamphlet, 1954); John Howard Yoder, *Karl Barth and the Problem of War* (Nashville: Abingdon Press, 1970) (greatly expanded from a 1954 essay).

69. Portions of one of these lectures are published as "The Theological Basis of the Christian Witness to the State," in *On Earth Peace,* edited by Durnbaugh, 136-43.

70. See Nation, *A Comprehensive Bibliography,* 16-17.

71. See *Conrad Grebel Review* 8 (Spring 1990). Also see Keim, *Harold S. Bender,* ch. 21.

72. CPS stands for Civilian Public Service, which was "a plan of service provided under the United States Selective Service and Training Act of 1940 for conscientious objectors who were unwilling to perform any kind of military service whatsoever" (*The Mennonite Encyclopedia,* "Civilian Public Service," vol. 1, 604); also see Albert N. Keim, *The CPS Story: An Illustrated History of Civilian Public Service* (Intercourse, PA: Good Books, 1990).

73. John Howard Yoder, "What Are Our Concerns?" *Concern* 4 (June 1957): 20.

74. Yoder, "1980 Autobiography," 18-19.

As John Yoder said in a letter to Bender: "What has happened to me is that in the process of growing up I have put together an interest in anabaptism, which you gave me, an MCC experience to which you were instrumental in assigning me, and theological study to which you directed me, to come out with what is a more logical fruition of your own convictions than you yourself realize."[75] One could look on some of these responses as an adolescent knocking of elders' points of view.[76] John Yoder is probably right that "creating this group gave us a young Turk image within the Mennonite institutions back home. And young Turks were not yet welcome."[77] However, this group was certainly not an adolescent flash in the pan. It convened a number of meetings over the next six years and edited a pamphlet series from 1954 to 1971.[78] The purpose of the pamphlet series was announced in the first issue: "to stimulate informal discussion and common searching within the brotherhood for a strengthening of prophetic Christian faith and conduct."[79] By issue number three the statement of purpose had changed to "an independent pamphlet series published by a group of Mennonites, dealing with questions of Christian renewal."[80]

Yoder finished his graduate studies in 1957 and returned to the U.S. For the first year he worked at the "J. S. Yoder and Son" greenhouses in Wooster, Ohio. During the summer of 1958 he was one of the resource people to speak on Mennonite theology to the faculty of the three Mennonite Church colleges. It was here for the first time that he addressed himself to the concept of Christ and culture. Beginning with the academic year 1958-1959 he was a sabbatical replacement for J. C. Wenger at Goshen College Biblical Seminary, teaching New Testament Greek and contemporary theology, as well as doing theological

---

75. Yoder letter to Bender (1952), quoted in Keim, *H. S. Bender,* 456.

76. John Yoder himself reflects on adolescence and maturation in the "Addendum to Cooking the Anabaptist Goose," Unpublished paper, Mennonite Church Archives, Goshen, Indiana, July 27, 1952, 1-2. However much there may have been some "adolescent" reaction to their elders on the part of the "Concern" group, it should not be imagined that there was loss of respect. It was apparently John Yoder's idea to compile a *Festschrift* for H. S. Bender (see Letter from Paul Peachey to John Howard Yoder, April 1, 1955 [year unclear], Mennonite Church Archives, Goshen, Indiana). Paul Peachey and John Yoder were part of the planning committee of what became *The Recovery of the Anabaptist Vision: A Sixtieth Anniversary Tribute to Harold S. Bender,* ed. Guy F. Hershberger (Scottdale, PA: Herald Press, 1957). Yoder also, many years later, dedicated a book to the memory of H. S. Bender: *He Came Preaching Peace* (Scottdale, PA: Herald Press, 1985), 5.

77. Yoder, "1980 Autobiography," 19.

78. See the "Concern Chronology," *Conrad Grebel Review* 8 (Spring 1990): 201-4.

79. "Editorial note," *Concern* 1 (June 1954): inside front cover.

80. "Concern," *Concern* 3 (1956): inside front cover.

research and writing regarding Christian attitudes toward the state for the Institute of Mennonite Studies.[81]

From 1959 to 1965, he worked full-time as an administrative assistant for overseas missions at the Mennonite Board of Missions. From the beginning of his tenure with the mission board he initiated contacts with Evangelical leaders, the National Association of Evangelicals, and the National Council of Churches. For a period of nine years, beginning in 1960, he worked in several official roles with the National Council of Churches and over a period of more than twenty years, beginning in 1963, he worked in various capacities with the World Council of Churches. With the WCC this included being a member of the study commission on the Theology of Mission, a member of the Faith and Order Colloquium, an adjunct staff member of the Commission on World Missions and Evangelism, and a consultation speaker for the Commission on Justice, Peace, and the Integrity of Creation. Also while he was with the mission board, John, while serving on the Mennonite Student Services Committee, helped create the university campus ministry program. Through the student services program a summer educational experience was organized to provide college-quality theological education for those studying at non-Mennonite colleges. Yoder's papers on H. Richard Niebuhr and biblical realism had their beginnings as presentations at these sessions. He also was instrumental in creating patterns of conference affiliation that permitted a congregation to be affiliated with both the ("Old") Mennonite Church and the General Conference Mennonite Church. The mission board also provided him the channels through which to actively continue both his Mennonite and ecumenical contacts in Europe, including, but not limited to, pushing the peace issue when he could.

Yoder was also a part-time instructor at the Mennonite Biblical Seminary in Elkhart from 1960 to 1965.[82] During this time he was often called on to be the faculty spokesperson for inter-seminary meetings, meetings that were held with representatives from various seminaries in the region. At some of these meetings he spoke on baptism, ministry, and just war theory.

81. This culminated in the publication of *The Christian Witness to the State* (Newton, KS: Faith and Life Press, 1964) and *The Christian and Capital Punishment* (pamphlet) (Newton, KS: Faith and Life Press, 1961).

82. Goshen College Biblical Seminary (later Goshen Biblical Seminary) was, at this point, the ("Old") Mennonite Church seminary, located in Goshen, Indiana. The Mennonite Biblical Seminary was the General Conference Mennonite Church seminary, located in Elkhart, about ten miles from Goshen. They merged onto one campus in the fall of 1970 in Elkhart, but still with two separately identified staff (with Yoder the first president for Goshen Biblical Seminary after the move). Together they formed the Associated Mennonite Biblical Seminaries. They currently have one president and one staff.

Beginning in 1965, Yoder became a full-time professor with Goshen Biblical Seminary (1965-1977) and became an associate consultant with the Mission Board (1965-1970). From 1970 to 1973 he was president of Goshen Biblical Seminary (although he was teaching in Argentina from 1970-1971) and was acting dean from 1972 to 1973. Among other courses at the seminary, Yoder taught "Systematic Theology," "Anabaptist Theology," "Issues in Ecclesiology," "Christology and Theological Method," "Christian Attitudes to War, Peace, and Revolution," "History and Theology of Ecumenical Renewal,"[83] and "Theology of Christian World Mission."

Yoder taught an occasional course at Notre Dame as early as 1967, but beginning with the autumn of 1977 he became a full-time professor at the University of Notre Dame, with Goshen Biblical Seminary buying a portion of his time from Notre Dame until the spring of 1984. Already in 1973, Yoder was chair of the program in nonviolence at Notre Dame as well as (starting in 1986) a Fellow of the Joan Kroc Institute for International Peace Studies. As a Fellow of the Peace Institute John gave a number of lectures and wrote a number of occasional papers.[84] While at Notre Dame he regularly taught three courses to undergraduates: "Voices in Non-Violence," "Christian Attitudes to War, Peace, and Revolution," and (team taught) "The Legality and Morality of War." Among his graduate level courses were "History of Christian Social Ethics," "Method in Christian Social Ethics," "Christian Social Ethics," "Radical Reformation,"[85] "Religious Roots of Non-Violence," "The Theology of the Churches' Social Ministry," and (on ethical method) "The Just War Tradition." In addition, he coordinated a multi-departmental course that was offered twice on the Catholic Bishops' pastoral letter, *The Challenge of Peace*.[86]

Over the years Yoder conducted lecture tours in approximately twenty countries, including various Latin American, Asian, and Western European countries, as well as South Africa, Poland, and Australia. He taught for a year in Argentina (1970-71), France (1974-75), and Jerusalem (1975-76). His fluency in French, German, and Spanish helped in many of these situations. He also taught intensive courses at New College, Berkeley, California; Regent College, Vancouver, B.C.; and Asia Theological Seminary, Manila. Of course,

---

83. This interest was also expressed through his involvement, at various points, as a consultant for several intentional Christian communities, including Reba Place Fellowship, Fellowship of Hope, and Sojourners Community and the network, Community of Communities.

84. See Nation, *A Comprehensive Bibliography*, especially unpublished listings 1990-1996.

85. Another expression of this interest was his service as co-convener for the committee on continuing conversations for the Believers Church Conferences from 1967 until his death.

86. National Conference of Catholic Bishops, *The Challenge of Peace: God's Promise and Our Response* (Washington, D.C.: United States Catholic Conference, 1983).

this is to say nothing of the many, many speaking engagements Yoder gladly accepted over the years in the U.S. These speaking engagements ranged from the most prestigious schools in the country to the most humble venues, from conservative Evangelical to liberal Protestant, from mainstream Catholic to fringe, radical Catholic, from religious to nonreligious, and from pacifist to nonpacifist.

There were various other professional involvements on the part of Yoder. He was a member, at various times, of about nine professional organizations. He was associate director of the Institute of Mennonite Studies from 1965 to 1973. He was on the board of directors of the Mennonite Historical Society in 1947 and then from 1965 to 1986. He was the president of the Society of Christian Ethics from 1987 to 1988, after serving a term as a member of the board of directors. For the same organization he was the cochair of the special interest group on war, religion, and society from approximately 1970 to 1992. He was a member of the board of editors of the *Journal of Religious Ethics* from approximately 1978 to 1990, a member of the board of editors of *The Mennonite Quarterly Review* from 1961 to 1992, and he was a contributing editor of *Sojourners* (formerly *Post-American*) from approximately 1973 to 1988.

No summary of John Yoder's life and work would be complete without mention of his writings. Stanley Hauerwas has said "that when Christians look back on this century of theology in America *The Politics of Jesus* will be seen as a new beginning."[87] Without question *The Politics of Jesus* was a peak in John Yoder's career; it is what he will always be known for. As David Weiss puts it:

> His thesis, simply put but thoroughly and eloquently argued, was that Christian ethics begins not by finding ways to set aside the radicalness of Jesus' ethics, but rather by finding ways in community to take those ethics seriously. In other words, the church is to bear the message of the gospel by *being* that message. If the gospel of God's reconciling love had political implications for the community of followers called into being by Jesus — if it decisively shaped the pattern of their life together — then it will continue to have such implications among those of us who link ourselves to that heritage and that calling.[88]

87. Stanley Hauerwas, "When the Politics of Jesus Makes a Difference," 982. J. Philip Wogaman, in his *Christian Ethics: A Historical Introduction* (Louisville: Westminster/John Knox Press, 1993), 233-35, in naming only a handful of people who deserved their own section in his chapter on "Formative Christian Moral Thinkers," entitled one of the sections, "John Howard Yoder and the 'Politics of Jesus.'"

88. David Weiss, "In Memory of John Yoder: Scholar, Professor, Friend," *The Observer* (January 27, 1998): 9.

This message touched a nerve. The first edition sold roughly 75,500 copies. The second edition, published in 1994, had sold 11,000 by April of 1998.[89] It has been translated into nine languages. But none of these figures — as impressive as they are — begin to adequately convey the influence of this book. In 1970 Brevard Childs indicated that there was no "outstanding modern work . . . in English that even attempts to deal adequately with the biblical material as it relates to ethics."[90] Two years later, reported Bruce Birch and Larry Rasmussen, John Yoder, in *The Politics of Jesus,* presented a "welcome and glowing exception" to this omission.[91] By the early 1980s Edward LeRoy Long, Jr., stated that *The Politics of Jesus* "has become as frequently cited in discussions of social ethics as Paul Ramsey's *Deeds and Rules* in the discussion of norm and context."[92] *The Politics of Jesus* has in various ways helped reshape the field of Christian ethics over the last twenty-five years. And it continues to receive acclaim. Richard Hays, in an imposing 1996 work says:

> Yoder's hermeneutic represents an impressive challenge to the church to remain faithful to its calling of discipleship, modeling its life after the example of the Jesus whom it confesses as Lord. As Christian theologians increasingly are forced to come to grips with the demise of Christendom and to acknowledge their minority status in a pluralistic world, Yoder's vision offers a compelling account of how the New Testament might reshape the life of the church.[93]

But the influence of *The Politics of Jesus* and Yoder has reached far beyond the academy. As Jim Wallis said, "John Yoder inspired a whole generation of Christians to follow the way of Jesus into social action and peacemaking."[94]

I never heard John complain that many wrote and talked almost as if *The Politics of Jesus* was the only thing he ever wrote. I, for one, am grateful that the book has had — and continues to have — such a tremendous influence. However, it is important to note that John wrote seventeen books, hundreds of articles, and hundreds of unpublished essays.[95] He wrote them in five languages.

89. Letter from Anne Salsich, Wm. B. Eerdmans Publishing Co., April 16, 1998.
90. Quoted by Bruce C. Birch and Larry L. Rasmussen, *Bible and Ethics in the Christian Life* (Minneapolis: Augsburg Publishing House, 1976), 16.
91. Birch and Rasmussen, *Bible and Ethics*, 18.
92. Edward LeRoy Long, Jr., *A Survey of Recent Christian Ethics* (New York: Oxford University Press, 1982), 90.
93. Richard B. Hays, *The Moral Vision of the New Testament: A Contemporary Introduction to New Testament Ethics* (New York: HarperSanFrancisco, 1996), 253.
94. Jim Wallis, "Lives of Peacemaking," *Sojourners* 27 (March-April 1998), 8.
95. See Nation, *A Comprehensive Bibliography* and the supplementary bibliography included in this volume.

They cover a wide range of subjects. For the average person or even the average theologian it is certainly not necessary that they master the bulk of John Yoder's writings. However, it is not fair to imagine that one has "read" Yoder when one has barely begun to read the mass of material he produced over a period of more than fifty years.

No topic received more of Yoder's time and attention than the subject of peace.[96] The breadth, depth, and variety of his writings on peace are astounding. Walter Wink is undoubtedly right that "more than any other person, Yoder has labored to bring the Peace Church witness against violence into the mainstream of theological discussion."[97] This labor included "the seriousness with which he has carried out his role as a friendly critic of just-war thinking."[98]

V

Two things are tempting as I bring this essay to a close. One is to engage in a lengthy interpretation of what the above narrative means. That temptation I will totally forgo at this stage; I will let the narrative stand on its own. The other is to make the ending overly personal. I will leave it up to the readers to determine whether I have been "overly" personal; I hope not. But I do want to end on a personal note.

I was stunned when I received a phone call from Stanley Hauerwas on the afternoon of Tuesday, December 30th, informing me that John Yoder was dead. The day before John had celebrated his seventieth birthday with his extended family. He went to his office at Notre Dame, as usual, at about 6:00 A.M. Tuesday. He sent e-mail messages to me and others that Tuesday morning. Before noon he died of an aortic aneurysm, in the hall just outside his office.

None of us expected John would be absent from us this soon. Had I thought that would have been the case I would have asked him many questions about his life and family that I did not ask. Many times during the course of working on this essay I have felt a profound sadness deep in my soul. John is gone; it is hard to believe. For months after he was gone I often caught myself considering e-mailing John about this or that. He was a wealth of information and, if he thought he could offer some help, was almost always more than will-

96. See Mark Thiessen Nation, "He Came Preaching Peace: The Ecumenical Peace Witness of John H. Yoder," *Conrad Grebel Review* 16 (Spring 1998): 65-76.

97. Walter Wink, *The Powers That Be* (New York: Doubleday, 1998), 204.

98. Drew Christiansen, S.J., "A Roman Catholic Response," in *When War Is Unjust*, revised edition, by John Howard Yoder (Maryknoll, NY: Orbis Books, 1996), 102.

ing to respond to a question — or shoot off a letter or e-mail to one of the many people he knew around the world.

Anyone who has heard John Yoder speak knows that he had one of the sharpest analytical minds imaginable. Anyone who was around him much also knows that he was, well, interpersonally awkward. As David Weiss put it, "Though academically brilliant, John was not similarly gifted in social graces. . . . Perceived by some as either arrogant or indifferent, I think it is truer to say that his powerful intellect was matched by a hardy shyness."[99] This is a nice, and appropriate, way to put it. One could also put it more harshly. At the memorial service for John at College Mennonite Church in Goshen, Indiana, John's son-in-law, Tom Yoder Neufeld, used what I thought was the perfect image for John's life (as, really, for any of our lives), the one drawn from 2 Corinthians 4:7: "We have this treasure in clay jars."[100] John, like all of us, was a clay jar. And clay jars — all of them — have their flaws. As Tom Yoder Neufeld put it: "At the best of times [clay jars] have rough and chipped edges. And at the worst of times they fall and break; and the sharp edges of the shards can cut and wound, and wound deeply."[101] Sometimes John wounded, sometimes deeply. I am convinced that he was genuinely sorrowful when he was made aware of having wounded someone, though he probably was not good at expressing such sorrow.

Clay jar he certainly was. But there was, without question, treasure in that very human vessel. Peter Steinfels, in the *New York Times* obituary of Yoder, reported a conversation between Yoder and Glen Stassen. Stassen was telling Yoder how some scholarly papers showed the influence of Yoder's thought. "'Your influence must really be spreading,' Mr. Stassen recalled saying. 'Not mine,' Mr. Yoder replied. 'Jesus.'"[102] "John Yoder inspired a whole generation of Christians to follow the way of Jesus into social action and peacemaking," said Jim Wallis.[103] Nothing could have pleased John more. May his witness continue; may his gifts of writing and teaching continue to shape our lives, our churches, and our world.

---

99. David Weiss, "In Memory of John Yoder: Scholar, Professor, Friend," 9.

100. Tom Yoder Neufeld, "Meditation at the Memorial Service for John Howard Yoder," College Mennonite Church, January 3, 1998, published in *Conrad Grebel Review* 16 (Spring 1998): 93-96.

101. Neufeld, "Meditation," 95.

102. Peter Steinfels, "John H. Yoder, Theologian at Notre Dame, Is Dead at 70," *The New York Times* (January 7, 1998).

103. Jim Wallis, "Lives of Peacemaking," *Sojourners* 27 (March-April 1998): 8.

"Patience" as Method in Moral Reasoning: Is an Ethic of Discipleship "Absolute"?[1]

John Howard Yoder

The challenge:
Being careful about the difference between good and bad
kinds of "compromise"
or good and bad kinds of "absolutes."

A. Itemizing the Ways in Which "Absolutes" Are Qualified

It is not always meant as a term of abuse, but it is always inaccurate, when the views I represent are called "absolutist."

I do hold (a) that the authority of Jesus in moral matters is greater than that of other teachers, or of "reason," or of "intuition."
I do hold (b) that the prima facie burden of proof lies with those who would advocate exceptions to the general guidelines of Christian morality, rather than with those who advocate respecting them.

1. [Eds: This essay has a history. It began on September 7, 1982 as a four-page memo in response to an inquiry by Gayle Gerber Koontz, now Professor at Associated Mennonite Biblical Seminaries, entitled "Two (or a Dozen) Ways Moral 'Absolutes' are Qualified." It has been expanded several times since and circulated to students as "Methodological Miscellany, Moral Theology #1: Is an Ethic of Discipleship 'Absolute'?" Then when Yoder made many of his unpublished articles available on his website, he gave it its current title. It was last revised in August 1997. Permission to publish this essay here was granted by his wife, Annie Yoder.]

I do argue (c) that certain of the looser kinds of "situational" and "consequential" moral reasoning, and certain loose forms of exception-making which have been fashionable in the last generation are irresponsible.

Yet none of these positions (a through c) can properly be called "absolutist," if that term is meant as a distinguishing characteristic. In each of those debates (a through c) the other value, which according to others should override my commitment, is no less subject to be called an "absolute."

These following considerations, itemized and distinguished from one another for the sake of clarity, may tend to coincide or to overlap in their application more often than they will contradict one another. It is nevertheless important to be able to distinguish among the different kinds of reasons for what I here call "patience," i.e., considerations which call for purported "absolutes" to be mitigated, yet without justifying the dominant alternative constructions, usually called "relativist" or "realist," of moral logic.

The term "absolute" (which I used above in scare quotes, to signal its power to mislead) is misleading. I accept it only under protest and in order to get on with the real debate. It is not in itself appropriate. (A few other comments of a prefatory or contextualizing nature are added at the end of the text.)

1. Pedagogical patience takes account of the fact that human learning takes place in sequences and stages. Usually it is difficult for a learner to learn D before learning A, B, and C. Sometimes the alignment of the elements in the series has to do with the logic of the matter to be learned, as in a sequence of theorems in geometry. Sometimes other information, or skills, like language knowledge, must precede new learning. Sometimes it has to do with the neurological or psychological readiness of the learner. Sometimes the very structure of a field (e.g., spiritual direction in the contemplative life, or professional training, or engineering based on mathematics), calls for sequential stages in learning a set of skills or insights. Thus, for example, I cannot expect someone to discuss with care the meaning of discipleship who has never entertained the possibility that church and world might not be identical, or that Jesus was Jewish, or that God is person-like.

The last decades have seen a proliferation of quasi-scientific approaches to the pedagogy of moral and spiritual insight. Building on the theories of early childhood learning associated with Jean Piaget, Lawrence Kohlberg in "moral development" and James Fowler in "spiritual development" have constructed scales of stages into which a person does (or should, or may, or is assumed to) grow. The limits of this approach are numerous. This is not the place to spell them out at any length.[2] Yet the basic insight contains a serious element of truth. We cannot deny that some important understandings and operations are possible in the human mind only after certain prerequisite capacities (neurological, linguistic, intellectual, cultural) have been acquired.[3]

A similar kind of teachability sequencing applies to societies. A state which plays fast and loose with habeas corpus can hardly be asked to forgo the death penalty. A culture which despises the just war constraints need not be invited to rise to the challenge of nuclear pacifism. Jesus' words about pearls and pigs represent not *speciesist antiporcinism* but realistic audience criticism. There can well be persons or audiences where I will not expect to be able to communicate all that I need to say about the sacredness of life.

2. I called the above kind of "patience" "pedagogical" because the "stages" in question are located in the learning trajectory of the subject, for whom certain "truths" (or perhaps certain "skills") which are valid in themselves would be premature. There is another, different category of reasons for timing and spacing different truths, which we might name "corrective," whose locus is in a dialogical social setting. Many needed arguments are true in their context but not finally. They use concepts which if absolutized become false, yet serve as part of a valid process. Examples:

(a) Sixteenth-century Protestant criticism of what had come of medieval Christianity appealed to "The Scriptures" in a way that was needed, although when systematized it became wooden and epistemologically naive.

(b) The exact meaning of a text (most significantly of a biblical text) in its original context can never be known with absolute certainty: if once completely grasped its meaning *for now* would still be unclear. Nonetheless it is worth seeking to approximate a basically correct interpretation.

(c) Nineteenth-century historicism thought that with proper critical use of sources one could establish the record of events "as they really happened"; this offered a necessary correction for legend-formation and self-serving readings. Yet there is no really accessible fully solid "factual" ground floor.

2. For example: Lawrence Kohlberg's scale (a) mixes empirical and ethical valuation claims in a challengeable way; (b) is gender and culture specific; (c) considers the moral agent to be the individual, with only glancing account taken of community dimensions.

3. The obverse seems also to be true. After a certain age some learnings seem no longer to be possible. A child reared for years without human society becomes incapable of learning language. A duckling after a certain age cannot learn to swim.

(d) More recently, twentieth-century relativism has overcorrected in the other direction, claiming that all meanings are community-dependent. This too is an overdone corrective. I deny that my views are in that sense arbitrary or unverifiable. The fact that all meanings are community-dependent does not mean that all views are equally valid.

(e) The awareness of the dangers of subjective bias led people to try to reach "objectivity" or a "view from nowhere." The idea is deceptive; yet the effort is valuable.

(f) Most theological systems distinguish at some point or other between "religious" and "secular," or between "individual" and "social," or between "inward" and "outward." Often these dichotomies are ultimately abusive. In the substance of moral discourse the splits they impose are usually wrong. Yet along the way they sometimes have a positive corrective function.

(g) Many moral systems distinguish between "levels" of generality or specificity, such as "rules," "policy," and "pastoral application," or between "ideals" and "realism," or between "norms" and "justified exceptions." Such distinctions are often used to cover up irresponsibility or disobedience, or as trump cards, but they can be illuminating.

Thus there will often be proper *corrective* uses of arguments that are not ultimately valid. We might call this "the right use of wrong theology."[4] There are valid points needing to be made whose validity should not be negated on the ground that in a given setting the only way available to make them is subject to criticism from some other level.

3. Pastoral patience takes account of other dynamic dimensions, likewise located within the person learning, which may hinder or facilitate the appropriation of normative truth. They are matters of the will, of trauma and healing, of trust and commitment. Some points cannot be made in certain settings, or to certain persons, or by certain persons, because of those dynamics. For example, I have long argued that certain intrinsically valid points about some limitations of Latin "liberation theology" as a system cannot credibly be argued by gringos. The ecumenical notion of the "epistemological privilege of the oppressed" articulates such a corrective. Some concerns about overdoing feminist victim language, although intrinsically valid, cannot credibly be argued by a stronger older man.

4. ". . . a decision made for the wrong conscious reasons may yet by the grace of God be the right decision." In my *Karl Barth and the Problem of War* (Nashville: Abingdon Press, 1970), 26.

4. Ecumenical patience is the result of our accepting willingly and not just grudgingly the fact that we are conversing with people who have been educated otherwise than ourselves, in ways that we think theologically wrong, yet which are for them for the present the framework of their integrity and accountability. In most cases where my own convictions, or some distinctive confessional Christian position which I might hold (which are not the same), must be argued, the other people whom I differ with not only have been taught their position, which already rejects mine, solidly and accept it sincerely; they are also in most cases in the majority numerically and historically.

What I have said thus far should be true for everyone. For me personally, this dimension is further reinforced by a special ecumenical vocation, sometimes operative in interconfessional institutions and sometimes in teaching the history of Christian thought, in which it has often been my role to interpret empathetically other views than my own, and to articulate the present pertinence of my view by using the concepts of others.[5]

5. There is a multicultural or cosmopolitan dimension to this "patience." In contrast to most of the contemporary moral theology and philosophy which are overwhelmingly anglophone, carried on by a network of people in Oxbridge, New England, Durham, and Berkeley, I am more at home in other languages, other worlds, and therefore other formulations of what is to be debated. That would be even more the case had I been privileged to learn Slavic or Semitic or Asian languages.

6. David Neville has reminded me that such "patience" is at work as well in my suspicion of the drive of many for a single master method[6] and of the "foundationalist" claim to a privileged point of departure.[7] My meeting the interlocutor on his own terms is not merely a matter of accepting the minority's conversational handicap[8] although it is that. It is also a spirituality and a lifestyle.[9] So I discuss war in just-war terms with nonpacifists. I discuss exception

5. For several years in the work of the Faith and Order Colloquium of the National Council of Churches, I was assigned to serve as secretary of the findings committee.

6. David Neville edits the Australian (largely Baptist) journal *Faith and Freedom*. Cf. my "Walk and Word: Alternatives to Methodologism," in *Theology Without Foundations: Religious Practice and the Future of Theological Truth,* ed. Nancey Murphy, Stanley Hauerwas, and Mark Nation (Nashville: Abingdon Press, 1994), 77-90; a point also made in *The Priestly Kingdom: Social Ethics as Gospel* (Notre Dame: University of Notre Dame Press, 1984), 111-15.

7. Cf. my "Meaning after Babble: With Jeffrey Stout Beyond Relativism," *Journal of Religious Ethics* 24 (Spring 1996): 125-39.

8. Cf. *Priestly Kingdom,* 111.

9. Like the early Quakers, Gandhi and Martin Luther King both recognized how nonviolence is not only an ethic about power but also an epistemology about how to let truth speak for itself.

making with the casuists, rather than sweepingly denouncing casuistry as do Karl Barth, Jacques Ellul, and some Lutherans.

7. There is a (psycho) therapeutic patience which goes even farther in yielding (for a time, for a reason) to the other. The language of individual self-fulfillment, although ultimately semantically vacuous and destructive, may be functional transitionally to free a person victimized by wrongly authoritarian structures. Similarly the notions of pluralism, value-freedom, "rights," "contract," "empowerment," may serve in transitional corrective ways, without their being ultimately tested for their truth value. This differs from the general "right use of wrong theology" (2 above) in that the particular abuse for which it corrects is one peculiar to the realm of doctrinal authority. It differs from "pastoral patience" (3 above) in that the offense to which one grudgingly yields is located in intellectual history, not only in intra- or interpersonal dynamics.

8. There is the patience of the "subject," which the New Testament calls "subordination," as it applies to the state or to any other superordinate power.[10] We accept it as a fact, without accepting it as the best, that we live in a society ruled by the sword, in which, as long as the fallen state of things persists, the only alternative to being ruled by the sword of one violent party is to be ruled by the sword of another party whose power is greater and whose injustice may at best (we hope) be (at least marginally) less. We thus accept it, let it be, subordinate ourselves to the fact of the sword, without its being morally normative for ourselves, either in the sense of divine institution or in that of a call to us to guide our discipleship. In this broad acceptance of what is in principle unacceptable, there is no formal or fundamental difference between the pacifist and the nonpacifist; it is only that the pacifist has had more occasion to think about it. Neither the Protestant "radical right" nor the "politically correct" postmodern left has wholeheartedly accepted this component of modern civility.

9. There is a special kind of "corporate" patience dictated by respect for the roles of others. As a member of a (parish) congregation, or of any other living institution whose values I do not dictate, and which has not called me as a teaching elder, I am not responsible to bring my academic "better wisdom" as theologian to bear to evaluate whether the preacher (or the amateur theologian teaching Sunday school) uses terms rightly. Nor am I called, as social process thinker, to evaluate how the congregation as institution makes its decisions.

---

10. Everyone does this, but in our age of empowerment rhetoric few would be caught admitting that they do it. The chapter in my *The Politics of Jesus* on the place of this theme in the moral thought of the early church has been found objectionable by most readers, even though such different readers as Eduard Schweizer and Elisabeth Schüssler-Fiorenza agree with its thesis (cf. 188ff in the second edition of *The Politics of Jesus*).

This is the special point of some of the literal imperatives in Romans 12 and 1 Corinthians 12.

In fact, my focused role as academic *didascalos* makes me less, not more, responsible to intervene in the "lay" processes which carry the week-by-week freight of intellectual and social community formation. There is here again such a thing as a "right use of wrong theology," i.e., the acceptance as legitimate, within their "lay" settings, of formulations with which academic rigor or ecumenical sensitivity will find fault.

10. There is the "collegial" patience of the outvoted theologian. On numerous subjects, not only on the issue of the morality of war, being outvoted by the majority and sustaining my views "against the stream" is my accustomed stance. Other examples in my own experience are abortion, authority roles, feminism, the dignity of singleness, divorce and remarriage, homosexuality, "the pastorate," war, how to structure a denomination, how to administer a university, or the social use of punitive process. Coming to terms with being hopelessly outvoted is quite different from being convinced.

11. There can be a cumulation of the "ecumenical" setting (4 above), the "political one"(6), and the "disciplinary" one,[11] whereby one settles into the need to use over the long haul the alien categories of those who rule the society. This is what Jeremiah (ch. 29) told the Jewish exiles to do in Babylon.[12] I have been called on more than some others to make this kind of grudging obeisance,[13] most notably:

- in the numerous conferences, papers, courses, and a book in which I have interpreted, refined, and challenged respectfully the just war tradition;
- in the tactical acceptance of the place in the University of Notre Dame of Reserve Officer Training programs, and in collegially recognizing the men who lead them. Catholic pacifists, who although nonviolent still feel more magisterial about how to teach morality, generally are less "patient"

11. Cf. my very early essay "Witness to the State" (1964). [Eds.: the current version is *The Christian Witness to the State* (Eugene, OR: Wipf & Stock Publications, 1997).] I do not know of many other authors making the ecumenical effort to communicate within a system which they fundamentally challenge.

12. Cf. my papers on the exile and similar writings *inter alia* Daniel L. Smith, *The Religion of the Landless: A Sociology of the Babylonian Exile* (Bloomington, IN: Meyer-Stone Books, 1989). [Eds.: Yoder wrote several essays discussing the theme of the exile. Two of them are: "Exile and Exodus: Two Faces of Liberation," *Cross Currents* (Fall 1973): 297-309; and "See How They Go with Their Face to the Sun," *For the Nations: Essays Public and Evangelical* (Grand Rapids: Eerdmans, 1997), 51-78.]

13. Above par. 6 this was described as a spirituality and lifestyle. Here the same examples are noted as matters of vocationally assigned tasks.

with the Reserve Officer Training Corps (ROTC) on a Catholic campus than I am. They have a right to be.

12. There is the "contrite" patience of repentance. Assuming that our position is the correct position, we must recognize that it has often been represented inadequately or even unfaithfully, by persons whose claim to represent it has therefore decreased its credibility, including ourselves. Sometimes these inadequacies were mere human frailty, personally irreproachable. Other times (e.g., empire, paternalism, sexism, the abuse of office, racism), they were worse than that, and call for outright condemnation and for repentance in the full sense of the term. In either case we have to recognize that it is not simply through the faults or ignorance of those other people that they do not accept what we think we know to be correct. Recognizing our own complicity (e.g., in colonial exploitation, even if I never personally owned a slave or took anything away from an "Indian") is grounds for real guilt, and thereby also for patience in advocacy. Even more strongly should this obtain if/as one recognizes having in fact culpably participated in the wrong.

13. There is the "modest" patience of sobriety in finitude. Although we have good grounds (if we have adequately studied a matter) to believe that in its main lines the things we are sure of are worthy of that assurance, we must always keep open spaces where sometimes our ignorance and at other times our sinfulness will have kept us from seeing all the truth. This modesty is not a reason to yield on specific points to others whose positions are no better. It is no grounds for our affirming the opposite of what we are now sure of, nor for relativizing the concrete accountability of our concrete decision making,[14] which must always take place under conditions of finite knowledge; but the certainty in which we have to act one day at a time must never claim finality. Our recognition that we may be wrong must always be visible.[15] One way to say this would be to begin every statement one ever makes with "as far as I know" or "until further notice." That I do not begin every paragraph this way does not mean that I do not mean it.[16] This is

---

14. This is what H. R. Niebuhr seems to me to have been doing with the notion of divine sovereignty. Because our knowledge is finite and we cannot second-guess the divine wisdom, therefore we should not be too sure of our sense of being called by Jesus, so we should be less critical of the claims of our environing "culture." His pupil James Gustafson carries the same logic farther, by using the label "theocentric" to undercut all value claims except his own anthropocentric vision.

15. Balthasar Hubmaier and Hans Denck, among the most gifted witnesses of the first generation of sixteenth-century Anabaptism, both used the proverbial "I may be wrong but I cannot be a heretic, since I am asking you to correct me."

16. I said this of my *Karl Barth and the Problem of War*, 72. In principle it applies to anything an honest intellectual says, but to begin every sentence that way would be tedious.

or ought to be true for any statement true of any honest intellectual, all the more so when the subject matter under discussion is contested. It is in no way either more or less pertinent to my views than to everyone else's.

14. There is the *gelassen* patience of yieldedness in response to justification by grace alone. My attitude to views/actions I disagree with, which I nonetheless "let be," does not constitute a judgment on whether those persons may be saved, or may be loved. Much popular religion, much of fundamentalism, and much of premodern Roman Catholicism, do deal with disagreement in those terms, as if my integrity called me to deny the salvation of those who differ with me; thus this does need to be said. Agreement is not a condition of salvation or of honor.

15. There is the "honest" patience of ignorance. In any moral system, a part of the determination of the values at stake is based upon empirically derived information, known with various degrees of certainty, about the values at stake and about how different lines of action will produce different costs and benefits. Positions calling themselves "utilitarian" or "consequentialist" tend to count on this information to be relatively knowable and, when known, to be decisive, and usually to be self-serving. That does not mean that other views give to such data no weight at all. The knowledge that all such data is knowable only to a finite degree of accuracy, and that in some cases too little is known for a cost/benefit calculation to help to tip the scales of decision, is one further element of uncertainty in any view, and of course in my own view.

16. There is the "resigned" patience with which one faces honestly the authentically insoluble tragic dilemma. There can be situations in which there is no visible acceptable way out, where prima facie binding obligations evidently cannot all be satisfied at once. More "casuistic" approaches try to resolve these matters with a lexical ordering to be followed in case of collision:

- rather lie than be killed
- rather kill than be raped
- rather kill an enemy than let him kill a friend

and more of the kind. Once the hard cases have been resolved by such a casuistic answer one can claim to be "right" after all. I am less easily convinced by such arguments, from which it follows that I am more "patient" than such confident casuists. As I spelled it out in *What Would You Do?*,[17] there are more options than the evident ones; miracle and martyrdom are possibilities not to be excluded. Thus consequentialist argument can never be leakproof. But I do *not*

---

17. *What Would You Do? A Serious Answer to a Standard Question*, 2nd ed. (Scottdale, PA: Herald Press, 1992).

32

claim to know *ahead of time* that either miracle or martyrdom is promised or commanded.[18] I know I can never *justify* killing, or adultery, or blasphemy. I know I can never approve institutionally and in principle of preparations *before the fact* to be in a position to do those things, as war does. Some may call this position of clearly not knowing "absolute," though I think it a wrong use of the term. I do *not* know, however, that life will spare me (or anyone or everyone else) needing to face any situations where I may be part of a process whereby such things happen, and nothing about my ethical approach makes such a promise, or claims that God has made it.[19] I make no claims for my capacity either a priori or in the situation to find an acceptable solution to every dilemma; it is the mainstream traditions which make that claim.[20] Nor is it my business (nor the business of ethics) to set limits to what God can or will forgive (or to promise that He will) in such situations (or in any others).

17. There is the "apocalyptic" patience of waiting in hope (Rev. 6:10). Liberation ethics speaks of the "power of fragility" to accredit the people, in their own eyes and in those of the oppressors. Part of the reason for not pressing my case comes from the overlap between the ethos of advocacy and the ethos of social struggle. To argue one's case too aggressively may forsake the grace which is "made perfect in weakness" (2 Cor. 12:9).

18. There is the "audience-sensitive" patience of not making a point which in a given setting a given audience is not willing or not able to hear. This brings together several of the above strands:

(a) The gringo may be burdened with postcolonial guilt, and may not feel credible in making a critical point of a liberation theologian, even though the point is intrinsically valid, because in that setting, "coming from me," it would not be respected.[21] This might be called the reflexive form of the ad hominem argument. It can be that the only honest way to represent what I stand for is not to speak just now. In this connection I have some-

---

18. Cf. Gayle Gerber Koontz's dissertation "Confessional Theology in a Pluralistic Context: A Study of the Theological Ethics of H. Richard Niebuhr and John Howard Yoder," Boston University Dissertation (University Microfilms) 1985, 106f. This point is further elucidated in part B below.

19. This disavowal is not redundant or trivial. There are people who promise a miraculous way out as validation of apparently risky right action. I have heard such testimonies with regard to doing without military violence. Some who reject abortion when the mother's health or life is threatened make such claims.

20. That is the whole point of the casuistic method.

21. This is a more complex form of the "readiness" considerations with which I began in (1) above.

times offended Mennonite pacifists by not arguing back at Latin liberationists.

(b) There may be dialogical settings where the culture-dependent meaning systems of two interlocutors are so far apart, so incompatible, that the only honest thing to say is nothing, until one can come closer to finding a common language. Until a "higher court" or a "common language" can be found, there may, in certain settings, be no way to do apologetics. Classical "natural law" or "reason" arguments make (or presuppose tacitly) the claim that the person arguing has the right and the power to dictate what the common language is; a nonviolent epistemology cannot do that. Sometimes the only nonviolent response to a skewed dialogical situation is silence, as a refusal to collaborate in epistemological tyranny.

(c) The total symbol system is skewed. This is true in general by virtue of the fallenness of reason and nature; it is true even more dramatically in a setting where a particular ideology dictates the only way to reason. There may be settings where there is no coherent way to make some specific point because of the way in which one grammar has been imposed.

19. There is the "political" patience of the outvoted citizen or subject (like, but different from 6 and 8 above, moving on from 9). As pacifist citizen in a nonpacifist civil community I can participate discerningly, conscientiously, in public discourse and decision making when the terms of reference are not my own. Some (pacifists and nonpacifists) think this is excluded; the person who is outvoted should emigrate, they think.[22] The question obviously has more complexity for a person for whom being outvoted is likely than for someone whose expectations are Constantinian.[23] People otherwise as discerning as Paul Ramsey, Richard Miller, and Russel Sizemore have claimed the right to forbid my using their just war language to converse with them, since (in their view) for the pacifist all wars must be equally bad. They thus demonstrate their lack of imagination for how moral discourse may have to be done in a *kairos* or *status confessionis* whereby the nature of the case the moral truth can count on no fair public hearing.

This kind of patience is beginning to become understandable to some Roman Catholics who, without considering abortion morally acceptable, no longer advocate seeking to criminalize it against the will of the majority of a population.

---

22. I addressed this already in 1955 in the text which later became *The Christian Witness to the State.*

23. I also dealt with the problem of using others' language in "The Christian Case for Democracy" in *The Priestly Kingdom,* 158ff.

Summary of Part A

As far as I can see, all of these considerations will apply to any kind of decent person taking a position on the grounds of moral conviction on any important subject. There is nothing peculiarly Christian or Mennonite or (God forbid!) "Yoderian" about these considerations. Any honest Catholic or Methodist or Jewish or atheist ethicist should say the same, although for one or the other of those persons different priorities or frequencies might obtain among the nineteen types. If my formulation of these above arguments is fuller or more careful than what some others might offer, that may itself bear witness to the "patience" which I am discussing, or to the fact that my location in a Catholic university or my participation in ecumenical dialogue aid me toward being more self-aware in these matters. Yet the "Catholic or Methodist or Jew or atheist" *could* make all the same points. There is nothing "sectarian" about them. They are by definition radically ecumenical.

- The weight of some of these considerations might, however, tend to be heightened if one held, as I do, to the view that the dignity of the enemy is such that one should especially love one's enemy and not do violence to his or her dignity.
- They would be especially weighty if one were convinced, as I am, that membership in a believing community is voluntary rather than imposed by a parental covenant.
- They would be especially appropriate if one believed, as I do, that decision making in the church should be free from manipulation by the power of the civil order.
- They would be especially appropriate if one believed, as I do, that authority in the faith community is decentralized and consensual, rather than pontifical.

Thus while none of these considerations is unique to me or to advocates of "radical discipleship," they should and do have a special degree of cogency for us. That is, people holding views like mine should by the nature of things be (and in some cases with God's help may be) more "patient" in these ways and less "absolutist" than the advocates of other views.

B. The Ways in Which Anti-Absolutist Arguments Are Nonetheless Wrong

Those who hold anti-absolutist arguments (which one usually qualifies as "realist" or "relativist"), while by calling me "absolutist" they are incorrect, they are right in recognizing that I challenge them in a way they are not comfortable with.

It is, as the above demonstrates, not at all clear why the ascription (usually pejorative) of "absolutism" should be addressed any more to my position than to others. Yet it does seem to be the case that it is addressed to those who challenge violence more than to people who advocate costly discipleship in other realms, addressed to advocates of discipleship more than to advocates of other principled ethical modes, addressed to pacifists more than to principled nonpacifists, and to christological pacifists more than to pragmatic ones.

Before entering seriously into conversation with this reproach, I must insist that it is structurally illogical and unfair. There is nothing more absolute (for the person involved) than the claim that it is my business to terminate someone else's life. There is nothing more legalistic than the statement in principle that the government of any state has the authority to order me to kill people. The fact that someone may be intellectually flexible or fuzzy about stating the conditions under which they plan to do that killing does not make the lethal act any less absolute in its impact upon the neighbor or the enemy. I thus object to the term "absolute," if it is held to be a description of my view as it differs from others. The term in that usage is an inept and deceptive instrument of ethical deliberation.

Another term sometimes used as a near-synonym is "exceptionless." That does not clarify as much as one thinks. It may mean the claim that no situation will arise where that norm cannot be satisfied. Such a negation may be understood as a social-statistical prediction or as a cosmological confession of faith. Or it may mean that one cannot conceive ahead of time of any case in which one could justify disregarding that norm.

I do not claim that sinless or harmless perfection is humanly possible. I do not deny that there can be specific decision situations in which it will be impossible to avoid falling short of the demands of some of one's firm moral commitments. I spelled this out in number 16 of part A above. I shall call these, for the purpose of this outline, "casuistic crunch situations." Classical Catholic casuistry called them situations of "collision" between prima facie duties, and resolved them with a set of lexical rules about which values come first in which cases.[24] Above I called such cases "tragic dilemmas."

---

24. "Double effect" rules are one subset of this approach. Cf. my packet *"Exceptio Probat"* (Shalom Desktop Publication, 1995), on the varieties of such arguments.

What I do deny is (1) that such hard cases should be made, as they tend to be, the *center* of ethical deliberation, as if the fundamental moral question were ever simply either (a) whether in an imperfect world we can't have everything we want or (b) in case of collision which values take priority.

What I do deny is (2) that such crunch decisions are prototypical: i.e., that they represent the essential nature of ethical deliberation, so that it is by lining up crunch cases that one can prove a point, with regard, for instance, to the morality of war or abortion or lying, or that it is by listing hard cases that one can best teach and learn ethics. As has been said more fully by a roster of colleagues (Stanley Hauerwas, James McClendon, Alasdair MacIntyre . . .) in the fields of philosophical and Christian ethics recently, such "quandarism," or "decisionism," or "punctualism" sets aside precisely those elements of moral discourse which are the most fundamental, those where the specificity of a Christian perspective counts the most, and those where there is the most room for improvement.

What I do deny is (3) that such casuistic crunch decisions are typical: i.e., that most people most of the time are making decisions of that kind, which test at their outer edges the applicability of basic rules. Most of the time the basic rules do suffice, once one has identified an issue honestly. To concentrate only on where the basic rules do not quite reach, or on hard cases where two basic rules are in inevitable collision, is precisely to concentrate on the atypical. "Hard cases make bad law." Preoccupation with looking for loopholes is one of the most insidious ways to undermine the claims of ordinary moral obligation, and the viability of ordinary community relationships.

What I do deny is (4) that powerful people have more crunch decisions than weak people or victimized people or middle-level people do. It is usually such questions as "what would you do if you were the president?" which people use to test how far general rules about love of the enemy can reach. Making the ruler the prototypic moral decider in that way is part of the Constantinian legacy to which our culture is heir. But the person in a position of much power is less torn between conflicting pressures and obligations than is the subordinate: the middle-level bureaucrat, the lieutenant or noncommissioned officer, the member of a team who shares equally in discussion but not in decision, the member of a minority whose priority wishes are never heard. Such middle-level people, who know enough to dissent but have less authority, are in the worse moral bind.

What I do deny is (5) that such casuistic crunch decisions are the definition of tragedy. Since Reinhold Niebuhr, the notion of "tragedy" has been cheapened by appealing to it as a way of self-justification when a person in political responsibility decides he must hurt someone (regularly an adversary; not himself) in order to serve someone else or some cause. Those are hard choices, although it is because of his desire to be able to make them his way (this usually is a masculine stance), rather than letting someone else make them otherwise, that the person in political responsibility got himself into that difficult position: to call them "tragedy" (or sometimes "courage") domesticates and exploits the concept. Its basic assumption, that moral obligation usually takes the form of a prohibition, in such a way that moral courage most of the time is a question of justifying exceptions, is itself anti-Judaic and unevangelical. To claim the label of "tragedy" for regularized and justified arrangements, whereby the defense of one's own interests is favored over the dignity or life of others, and further to claim, tacitly or overtly, that being "tragic" is itself a mark of being true, is a self-righteous abuse of language. It adds blasphemy to injury. It too is part of what has given "casuistry" a bad name.

We would do better to retain the word "tragic" for situations truly beyond our wisdom or beyond our control, rather than using it in self-justification for those cases where we think we have figured out the right though painful thing to do. We should save the adjective for situations where the powers of evil are overwhelming or incalculable, rather than claiming it for situations which are subject to our own sovereign control and which we ourselves then declare less evil than another and therefore right for us to impose on others. We should reserve the label "tragedy" for cases where there is less reason to trust in our own capacity (in terms of information, will, and virtue, as well as power) to do the right even when we think we know it.

What I do deny is (6) that my critics are any more temperate or moderate, any less "absolute" than I, in what they consider decisive for obedience. They challenge my values because they prefer other values; but those other values are no less determining for them. After all, what they want to convince me of is that in the crunch case their values should overrule mine. They are willing to kill for their other values, as I am not. In the light of this fact about the lay of the land in the debate, the very popular use of terms like "ambiguity" or "ambivalence" to describe their view is misleading. Such terms seem to suggest fine differences of shading, debatable readings in complicated situations — but in fact the real choices usually being talked about are something very decisive and simple like bombing or not bombing a city.

What I do deny is (7) that these borderline cases are so probable, so frequent, and so predictable that we ought institutionally to honor them by planning ahead of time to be ready to respond to a worst-case projection of how bad it might be. To institutionalize readiness for war is already to deny that it is, as the theorists claim, an extreme last resort. One does not prepare ahead of time to be able to inflict overkill in a situation of last resort. Especially one does not delegate the decision about the cases which meet the logical requirements for the extreme case to professional Pentagon people running through the provisions of their briefing books.

Thus the very fact of institutionalizing the readiness to do something extreme means that it is no longer truly being considered extreme. It has been brought into the realm of the thinkable and therefore of the likely. Not only has it been built into an hypothetical scenario; it has been written up as an authorized "standard operating procedure" in the officers' manuals. This can be demonstrated by the fact that the real historical cases in which cities and populations have been destroyed in war have not been like the extreme imaginable borderline crunch cases with which the speculative debate of ethicists seeks to demonstrate that not all killing can be avoided. They are worse, less justifiable, and could have been more avoidable, but they were not avoided, because readiness for them was institutionalized, as the restraints were not.

What I do deny is (8) that an ethic responding to the Gospel of Jesus Christ is any more open to be strained, tested, challenged, or called into doubt, by facing "hard cases," than is an ethic claiming to possess as a warrant a nondialogical knowledge derived from "nature" or "reason" or even realistic self-interest. In fact, an ethic claiming to be founded in "nature" or "reason" is by definition less able to be "patient" in the sense I am talking about. It must *by the nature of its argument* claim that those values are defined self-evidently i.e., nondialogically.

What I do deny is (9), deepening the point of 2 above, that the question "can there be an exception?" ought to be one of the primary ways to test and exposit a rule. This is the methodological error of "quandarism." To look for exceptions, especially to be driven, before the hard case and as a general exercise in method, by the concern that there must be an exception to every rule, is the mirror image of the legalism it rejects.[25] To use the general formal statement that "there may be exceptions" as a basis to institutionalize the infractions, as Daniel Maguire does with abortions, as *The Challenge of Peace* does with deterrence, and as the just war tradition does with killing, is ultimately dishonest, since it clothes as an exception to one rule what is in fact a commitment to the greater authority of a different rule.

What I do deny is (10), extending 9, the appropriateness of the special tilt toward permissiveness which once gave to the adjective "jesuitical" (not to

---

25. Cf. the place of the Grenzfall in Karl Barth's writing on killing. Barth ticks off the kinds of killing and the reasons, asking each time "is an exception justified here?" The question "is this a moral absolute?" with which this outline began skews even the most careful theologian's approach.

Ignatius of Loyola himself) a bad name. Casuistry is not wrong, but essential. The same is true for exception making, an indispensable part of casuistry. But when the analysis, either in the actual practice of the sacrament of absolution or in the intellectual ground laid in manuals of moral theology for the exercise of that ministry, is tilted toward the individual convenience of the penitent and away from the values borne by (or in modern parlance the "rights of") the other parties to the case, with the result that one invests more ingenuity in authorizing exceptions than in helping to keep the rules, then the discipline has gone wrong.[26]

What I do deny is (11) that, in holding to the priority of the prima facie duty more strongly than others do, I am thereby either in thought or in action more "pure" than others.[27] It is the Augustana Confession XVI, not a "sectarian" or "puritan" document, which says of war that it can be waged "without sin," whereas there are other things that one may be asked to do which cannot be done without sin and which one should therefore not do. It is the Catholic casuistry which by cleanly distinguishing between physical and moral evils fosters the notion that moral purity is possible.[28] The Niebuhrian or the Sartrian has no corner on dirty hands. The question is not whether one can have clean hands but which kind of complicity in which kind of inevitable evil is preferable.

Summary to Part B

Both of the sections of the above survey are appropriate when I defend myself against the easy accusation of not taking account of the fallenness and the limited potential of the real world situation. It is, however, strange to see it suggested in the first place either that my position would not make such adjustments, or that the need to recognize such matters would be peculiar to my

26. My notes from a session of the Society of Christian Ethics, where Charles Curran and I were assigned to respond to Albert R. Jonsen and Stephen Toulmin, *The Abuse of Casuistry: A History of Moral Reasoning* (Berkeley, CA: University of California Press, 1988), are now in the packet *"Exceptio Probat."* Curran and I largely agreed.

27. This misapprehension is spelled out at special length by Leslie Griffin when she unfairly uses me as a target in her "The Problem of Dirty Hands," *Journal of Religious Ethics* 17 (Spring 1989): 31ff. After beginning by referring to me, Griffin later admits that what she is dealing with is not my position. That does not keep her kind of argument from belonging in this picture.

28. This is what is going on when the classical "double effect" theory says that there are some "intrinsically evil" acts which must never be committed.

position. All of the above adjustments are made or implied as far as I can see in any systematic ethical tradition, if honestly held. They are not peculiar to pacifism or to discipleship ethics. If others who make the same moves describe them less fully or less clearly than I have tried to do here, it may be because their being in a majority situation (or their assumption that they are) enables them to get away with being less careful, taking less account of their critics.

Likewise the negation of these dimensions of adjustment is not something that may fairly be attributed specifically to me or to Anabaptists or to discipleship ethics: "absolutisms" which deny such "patience" can be found no less in Catholic, Lutheran, Reformed, and humanistic forms.

Prefatory Comments

The following considerations were presupposed in the preparation of the above text. They are placed here at the end rather than at the beginning, because to place them first would have appeared diversionary.

(a) The first draft of the following outline was prepared in response to a request from Gayle Gerber Koontz, now Professor of Theology and sometime Dean and Acting President at the Associated Mennonite Biblical Seminaries, years ago as a part of her dissertation preparation. I am grateful to Gayle for that prodding. My first effort, part of which she cited in her dissertation,[29] was quite incomplete. I therefore have returned here to the attempt to itemize the series of different kinds of "patience" which qualify, modify, mitigate, or nuance the application of any ethical standard, in the shift from the stance of normative exposition, which is the duty of the teacher, to the level of applications in concrete ministry and decision.

(b) One reader characterized the above exposition as claiming that I am "right."[30] Certainly no one would bother to exposit a position that they thought wrong; yet the stylistic or psychodynamic overtones of the criticism are off the mark. The authorial "I" here speaks for the coherence of a mode of moral discourse, a position, not for a person. I as the person John Yoder am not generous, or consistent, or transparent, or adequate. If

---

29. Koontz, "Confessional Theology in a Pluralistic Context," 272.

30. The grounds for reproach are not clear. Obviously she thought that in so characterizing me she was right.

I were to claim certain other virtues there would be something wrong with making the claim.

(c) Because that decision was made for me by the environing intellectual culture, it has been easiest to make the wrongness of killing and the obligation of enemy-love the simplest test specimens along the way through the argument. I have accepted that frame of reference for the sake of discussion. That does not mean my granting that the moral issues of truth telling, promise keeping, bread sharing, sexual integrity or honoring parents would be shaped in a fundamentally different way.[31]

(d) Because that decision was made for me by the environing ecumenical intellectual culture, I have acceded in this entire survey to the moralizing mode which asks "is this obligation binding?" As anyone who has read my less methodologically focused publications knows, that very mode is alien to my own convictions. Normal Christian moral discourse should be about enablement more than prohibition; about law as a form of grace, not a polar alternative to it; about pardon more than duty. Yet if I had put this paragraph at the head, it could have been misread as an effort to trump the debate by reaching for other warrants than those admitted in rigorous moral discourse, or asking for a softer style of accountability.

31. It is however oddly the case that not all those other themes are subject to the same kind of modification which mainstream positions impose on the Gospel command of enemy-love. There is no "just" or "holy" alternative seriously advocated to monogamy, or to promise keeping, or to monotheism, as there are to not killing. There are exceptions made by some systems to the obligation of truth telling, but even in that realm there is no counterpart of the Pentagon and the War Colleges to institutionalize unavoidable lying.

NEVERTHELESS

John Howard Yoder's Systematic Defense of Christian Pacifism

Nancey Murphy

1. Introduction

Christian pacifists are often disadvantaged in debates with other Christians by not having the prestige of systematic theologians to back up their claims, showing them to be essential to Christian life and thought. However, the writings of John Howard Yoder constitute a fairly complete, systematic account of Christian theology, in which Christian nonviolence is shown to be not an optional extra for the heroic Christian, but the very substance of Christian faithfulness. Yoder disclaimed being a systematic theologian. He believed (rightly, I think) that theology should be written in the service of the church, addressing issues as they arise, and not driven by any philosophical or systematic motivations. However, this perspective on the nature of theology does not prevent others from looking at Yoder's many writings and perceiving the organization and coherence of the whole.

My method for displaying the systematic coherence of Yoder's theology will seem peculiar to some. I have written previously on the similarities in structure between scientific reasoning (the structure of "scientific research programs") and the structure of systematic theologies.[1] I believe it was my immersion in philosophy of science that attuned me to the sophisticated reasoning and use of evidence in Yoder's works. Thus, I hope I may be excused for import-

---

1. Nancey Murphy, *Theology in the Age of Scientific Reasoning* (Ithaca, NY, and London: Cornell University Press, 1990).

ing jargon from philosophy of science for ordering my presentation of Yoder's thought.

2. Scientific Research Programs

The philosopher of science Thomas Kuhn is well known in a variety of disciplines today for his theory of paradigms and revolutions in science — the Newtonian paradigm supplanting the Aristotelian, and being supplanted in turn by relativistic physics.[2] However, it has proved surprisingly difficult to pin down exactly what Kuhn meant by a paradigm. Imre Lakatos, less well known outside of philosophy of science, has provided a much simpler and clearer account of the logical structure of science.[3] He describes the history of science in terms of competing research programs.

A research program has the following structure: It includes a core theory, which unifies the program by providing a general view of the nature of the entities being investigated. For this reason, and because the core theory is not directly testable, it is called metaphysical. For example, the ancient metaphysical theory of atomism became the core of early modern physics and chemistry.

The core is surrounded by a "protective belt" of "auxiliary hypotheses." These are lower-level theories, which both define and support the core theory. The auxiliary hypotheses are referred to as a protective belt since potentially falsifying data are accounted for by making changes here rather than in the core theory, called the "hard core" since it cannot be abandoned without rejecting the entire research program. Included among the auxiliary hypotheses are theories of instrumentation — the theories involved in the construction of experimental apparatus (e.g., electron microscopes) and needed for interpreting the data they produce.

Finally, assorted data support the auxiliary hypotheses. That is, the auxiliary hypotheses nearest the edges explain the data and are thereby confirmed by those data; higher level hypotheses — that is, theories nearer the center — explain lower-level theories. The core theory itself is the ultimate explanatory principle.

It would be more accurate to say that a research program is a temporal *series* of such networks of theory, along with supporting data, since the core theory stays the same but the belt of auxiliary hypotheses must be changed over time to account for new data.

2. Thomas Kuhn, *The Structure of Scientific Revolutions*, 2nd ed. (Chicago: University of Chicago Press, 1970).
3. Imre Lakatos, "Falsification and the Methodology of Scientific Research Programmes," in Lakatos, *The Methodology of Scientific Research Programmes: Philosophical Papers Vol. 1*, ed. John Worrall and Gregory Currie (Cambridge: Cambridge University Press, 1978).

A mature program also involves what Lakatos calls a positive heuristic, which is a plan for systematic development of the program in order to take account of an increasingly broad array of data. An important development in recent philosophy of science has been the recognition of the role of models in science. Scientists use a variety of kinds of models, from mathematical models to physical models of various sorts. Another way to describe the positive heuristic is to say that it envisions the development of a series of increasingly accurate and sophisticated models of the process or entities under study.

For example, the hard core of Newton's program consisted of his three laws of dynamics and his law of gravitation. Auxiliary hypotheses included initial conditions and applications of the laws to specific problems. The positive heuristic was the plan to work out increasingly sophisticated solutions for the orbits of the planets: first, calculations for a one-planet system with the sun as a point-mass, then solutions for more planets, and so on.

3. Yoder's Research Program

I have argued that by making appropriate substitutions we can see that theological programs have the same structure as scientific research programs. Here, doctrinal theories will take the place of scientific theories; data will come from scriptural texts, and perhaps from religious experience, from historical events, and elsewhere.[4]

The task of the rest of this paper, then, will be to show that Yoder's theology fits the form of a scientific research program. This means that we must be able to isolate a core theory — a central thesis from which all the rest of the theoretical structure (the network of auxiliary hypotheses) follows. These lower-level theories must be supported by appropriate sorts of data. In addition the system as a whole must show development over time; and ideally that development ought to be governed by a positive heuristic, a coherent plan for elaborations and refinements of the theoretical content.

3.1. The Hard Core

David Kelsey has written that the use one makes of Scripture in grounding theological claims depends on a prior "single, synoptic judgment" in which one

4. See Murphy, *Theology in the Age of Scientific Reasoning.*

attempts to "catch up what Christianity is basically all about."[5] Yoder's best-known work is *The Politics of Jesus.* In the preface to the second edition he writes that the book is intended to show that the total moral witness of the New Testament texts is political.[6] I believe one could go further and say that, for Yoder, the point of the New Testament witness, *tout court,* is first of all moral and political (as opposed to metaphysical, doctrinal, mystical). I venture to sum up Yoder's program as follows:

> The moral character of God is revealed in Jesus' vulnerable enemy love and renunciation of dominion. Imitation of Jesus in this regard constitutes a *social* ethic.

I shall take this to be the hard core of Yoder's theology. In the following subsections I present auxiliary hypotheses that fill out the program.

3.2. Relating the Core to Ethics

The first aspect of the program that I shall examine is the line of reasoning by which Yoder's social ethic is developed and related to the description of God in the hard core.

The rationale for ethics, not only for Yoder but for many Christian ethicists, is the requirement to imitate the character of God. Yoder claims that sharing in the divine nature is "the definition of Christian existence"[7] and cites texts from throughout the New Testament as grounds — Matt. 5:43-48; 6:12, 14-15; Luke 6:32-36; 11:4; Eph. 4:24; Col. 3:9, 13; 1 John 1:5-7; 3:1-3; 4:17; 1 Pet. 1:15-16.

Because the moral character of God is revealed in Jesus, the definition of Christian existence can also be expressed as "being in Christ": loving as he loved, serving as he served. However, Yoder argues that there is only one respect in which Christians are specifically called to *imitate* Christ, and that is in taking up the cross.[8] So a crucial question is how to interpret the cross. The Christian's cross, Yoder argues, does not represent any and every kind of suffering; it is exactly the price of social nonconformity. Jesus' warning to expect persecution is a statement about

---

5. David Kelsey, *The Uses of Scripture in Recent Theology* (Philadelphia: Fortress Press, 1975), 159.
6. John Yoder, *The Politics of Jesus,* 2nd ed. (Grand Rapids: Eerdmans, 1994), vii.
7. Yoder, *Politics,* 115.
8. Yoder, *Politics,* 94-95.

the relation of our social obedience to the messianity of Jesus. Representing as he did the divine order now at hand, accessible; renouncing as he did the legitimate use of violence and the accrediting of the existing authorities; renouncing as well the ritual purity of noninvolvement, his people will encounter in ways analogous to his own the hostility of the old order.[9]

Yoder's arguments in elaborating his ethical views involve drawing conclusions from his core theory in conjunction with sociopolitical insights. One of the ways in which Yoder's work contrasts with that of many other Christian ethicists is in the requirement he places upon himself to draw his sociopolitical analyses themselves from Scripture.

The most significant contribution that Yoder's reading of Scripture makes to political analysis is his use of the Pauline doctrine of the "principalities and powers." Yoder raises the question: if Jesus' ministry is to be understood in political terms, where in the New Testament do we find the equivalent of the concepts of *power* or *structures* as these are used by contemporary social scientists? It happens that in the 1950s and 60s New Testament research by G. B. Caird, Hendrik Berkhof, and others began to build a body of exegetical literature turning upon a set of terms used by Paul and his school: "principalities and powers," "thrones and dominions," "angels and archangels," "elements," "heights and depths," "law" and "knowledge." In the intervening centuries many of these terms were taken to apply to demons and angelic beings, and thus came to be ignored in the modern period.

Apparently, the New Testament concept of the powers developed from concepts of the alien gods of other nations in Old Testament understanding — hence there is a lingering sense of their being spiritual realities. However, the most significant function of the terms is to signify what we would now call power structures: human traditions, the state, class and economic structures, and religious institutions, to name a few.[10]

If we can make this connection between Paul's peculiar set of powers and our contemporary concept of power structures, then we are in a position to appreciate Paul's sociopolitical theory and to see Jesus' relation to the power structures. The powers were created by God for good purposes, since human social life is impossible without them. However, they are "fallen" in the sense that they do not serve the good of humankind for which they were

---

9. Yoder, *Politics*, 96.

10. Walter Wink has written extensively on the powers. He claims that the spiritual realities are the "interiorities" (we might say, the analogue of personalities) of sociopolitical entities. See *Naming the Powers* (Minneapolis: Fortress Press, 1984); *Unmasking the Powers* (Minneapolis: Fortress Press, 1986); and *Engaging the Powers* (Minneapolis: Fortress Press, 1992).

created, but seek instead their own self-aggrandizement. They have become idols in that they require individuals to serve them as though they are of absolute value.

Christ's role in relation to the powers was to destroy their idolatrous claims. In his public ministry he showed that it was possible to live a genuinely free life in spite of the powers. He conquered the powers through his death, in that the most worthy representatives of Jewish religion and the Roman state conspired to put him to death and thus revealed their true colors. Christ "disarmed the principalities and powers" by stripping them of their ability to create an illusion of absolute legitimacy; he made a public spectacle of them and thereby triumphed over them (cf. Col. 2:15).

In the time between Christ's victory on the cross and the eschaton, the powers linger on, but their absolute sway over Christians is broken. With our Western heritage of freedom of dissent (a legacy partly of the Radical Reformation, or Free Church, tradition) it is difficult for us to imagine the liberating effect that Jesus' "defeat" of the powers must have had in a traditional society in which social class, gender roles, family, religion, and nation placed absolute demands on the individual.

The ethical conclusions that follow from this analysis, along with the injunction derived from Yoder's core hypothesis to follow Christ to the cross are as follows: Power structures are a reality, and they serve essential purposes in human life. However, their claims cannot be granted ultimacy because the powers are "fallen." Thus, the Christian must sometimes refuse cooperation. The refusal to cooperate is a *sign* of the (truly) ultimate claim of God on human life, and helps to liberate others from slavish obedience to the powers. The cost of defying the powers, especially when it effectively undercuts their idolatrous claims, is suffering — sometimes even to the point of death. This, precisely, is the meaning of bearing one's cross.

> What Jesus refers to in his call to cross-bearing is rather the seeming defeat of that strategy of obedience which is no strategy, the inevitable suffering of those whose only goal is to be faithful to that love which puts one at the mercy of one's neighbor, which abandons claims to justice for oneself and for one's own in an overriding concern for the reconciling of the adversary and the estranged.[11]

---

11. Yoder, *Politics*, 236.

3.3. Methodological Auxiliary Hypotheses

I have already alluded to an auxiliary hypothesis of a methodological sort that shapes Yoder's program: the requirement to make use of the sociopolitical analyses that can be found in Scripture, rather than analyses based on other sources.

Another methodological auxiliary is Yoder's systematic rejection of individualism. The ethical tradition tells us that we must choose between the individual and the social. "But Jesus doesn't know anything about radical personalism." The personhood Jesus proclaims is instead a call to be integrated into a new, healing sort of community. "[T]he idea of Jesus as an individualist or a teacher of radical personalism could arise only in the (Protestant, post-Pietist, rationalist) context that it did."[12]

Notice that Yoder's preference for the understanding of the relation of individual to community that he attributes to Jesus, in preference to that of Modern Protestantism, is an *instance* of preferring the sociological analysis of Scripture over that of other sources.

3.4. The Positive Heuristic

Lakatos invented the term 'positive heuristic' in order to allow him to discriminate between scientific research programs that develop a unified vision of their subject matter from those that progress by means of accidental accretion of theoretical insights. The positive heuristic, then, is a plan, either consciously formulated or implicit, that directs the growth of a scientific research program. I have suggested elsewhere that the positive heuristic of a theological program will be the plan to elaborate the central vision in such a way as to cover all of the traditional theological loci in a manner consistent with the hard core of the program and in accordance with any other binding constraints.[13] For example, the positive heuristic of an existentialist theological program would be to reinterpret the traditional Christian doctrines in terms of the existentialist account of the nature of human existence.

The positive heuristic of Yoder's program would be the plan to interpret the standard Christian doctrines in a way consistent with his core theory and with his political reading of Jesus' ministry, and subject to the methodological assumptions just mentioned. A more thorough account of Yoder's program would also address his more technical exegetical assumptions. As mentioned

12. Yoder, *Politics,* 108.
13. Murphy, *Theology in the Age of Scientific Reasoning,* 185-86.

above, Yoder does not intend to write as a systematic theologian, so he would disavow any such conscious plan. I argue, though, that no one could hope to promote a view of Jesus that differs so radically from the standard account without expecting it to be possible to work out the theological consequences of this view within the usual theological battlegrounds (loci).

In the following subsections we see the fruit of this heuristic for Christian doctrine.

3.5. Doctrinal Auxiliary Hypotheses

One way to interpret the epistemological status of theological doctrines is to see them as auxiliary hypotheses contributing to a research program in theology. Accordingly, I now proceed to examine the doctrinal positions that make up the theological content of Yoder's program.

3.5.1. Christology and Trinity

Yoder's accounts of the *content* of Christology and the doctrine of the Trinity are close to the historic orthodoxy of the ancient creeds and councils. Where his account differs from the standard account is in his justification of these doctrines. Both are justified insofar as they attribute to Jesus the "metaphysical" status he must have in order that the church be justified in worshiping *and obeying* him as absolute LORD. So the doctrinal affirmations are justified because they explain *why* the ethic taught by Jesus is morally binding.

> When the later, more "theological" New Testament writings formulated the claim to preexistence and cosmic preeminence for the divine Son or Word (John 1:1-4; Col. 1:15ff.; Heb. 1:2ff.) the intent of this language was not to consecrate beside Jesus some other way of perceiving the eternal Word, through reason or history or nature, but rather to affirm the exclusivity of the revelation claim they were making for Jesus. The same must be said of the later development of the classic ideas of the Trinity and the Incarnation. "Incarnation" does not originally mean (as it tends to today in some theologies of history, and in some kinds of Anglican theology) that God took all of human nature as it was, put his seal of approval on it, and thereby ratified nature as revelation. The point is just the opposite; that God broke through the borders of our standard definition of what is human, and gave a new, formative definition in Jesus. "Trinity" did not originally mean, as it does for some later, that there are three kinds of revelation, the Father speaking through creation and the Spirit through experience, by which the

52

words and example of the Son must be corrected; it meant rather that language must be found and definitions created so that Christians, who believe in only one God, can affirm that that God is most adequately and bindingly known in Jesus.[14]

So the doctrine of Christ's divinity and the unity of the Son with the Father function as guarantees that no other claims can be more binding on humankind than those of Jesus. There is no other redeemer figure whose claims take precedence over those of Jesus Messiah; there can be no other source of divine revelation that contradicts Jesus' teaching. Conversely, doctrinal heresies are defective insofar as they lead to the rejection of Jesus' ethic. Ebionitic heresies (denying Christ's divinity) thereby deny his right to moral lordship. Docetism (denying the full humanity of Christ) calls into question the possibility, and thus the requirement for, mere humans to imitate Jesus' faithfulness.

3.5.2. Atonement, Sin, and Justification

When we come to the doctrines of atonement and justification, Christian anthropology and sin, we reach the point where Yoder's theology is most clearly divergent from the standard account of Christian doctrine. By the standard account, I mean to refer especially to Reformation and post-Reformation forms of Christianity, owing much to Augustine. The features of the standard account include a doctrine of the Fall as a key to understanding human nature, a major emphasis on substitutionary atonement, and justification as imputed righteousness.

It has become common since the publication of Gustaf Aulén's *Christus Victor*[15] to speak of three types of atonement theories: the Anselmian or substitutionary theories; the Abelardian or moral influence theories; and the "classical" ransom or conflict theories, according to which the work of Christ is interpreted in terms of conflict with and triumph over cosmic evil powers. Several versions of the latter were developed during the early centuries of the Church: Christ as a ransom paid to the Devil; a transaction wherein God used Christ as "bait" to deceive the Devil; and a political form in which the Devil lost his rightful dominion over sinful humankind by abusing the sinless Christ.

While the classical theory clearly has New Testament support, it has been seen as objectionable because it involves the concept of the Devil, which many now take to require "demythologization." Aulén had argued that the

---

14. Yoder, *Politics*, 99.
15. Gustaf Aulén, *Christus Victor*, trans. A. G. Herbert (New York: Macmillan, 1931).

mythological language of the conflict theory could simply be dropped, leaving the theory intact. But then it is no longer clear what is meant by "cosmic evil powers."

Yoder's central understanding of atonement fits the classical model, and fills the gap left by the excision of a mythical Devil by means of the interpretation of the "principalities and powers" described above. These superhuman power structures are the forces with which Jesus came into conflict, and from which he has freed humankind, both by his example (and here the moral influence theory gets its due) and by stripping them of the illusion of absolute legitimacy, precisely because their most worthy representatives abused him in his innocence. The cross has as much significance in this theory as it does in the substitution theory, but for different reasons. Yoder does not ignore personal sinfulness, but he gives it neither the significance nor the inevitability that it has in Augustinian Christianity. His focus instead is on institutionalized sin; the remedy for it is found in freedom from bondage to the principalities and powers, and especially in the creation of a new social order, the church.

Yoder's account of justification, also, is sociopolitical.

> Let us set aside for purposes of discussion the assumption that the righteousness of God and the righteousness of humanity are most fundamentally located on the individual level. . . . Let us posit as at least thinkable the alternate hypothesis that for Paul righteousness, either in God or in human beings, might more appropriately be conceived of as having cosmic or social dimensions. Such larger dimensions would not negate the personal character of the righteousness God imputes to those who believe; but by englobing the personal salvation in a fuller reality they would negate the individualism with which we understand such reconciliation.[16]

Yoder argues that justification (being set right with God) is accomplished when Christians are set right with one another. In Paul's ministry, the reconciling of Jews and Gentiles was primary. The "new creation" is a new "race" of humans where the Jewish law no longer forms a barrier between Jew and Gentile, and where gender and economic differences are reconciled as well.

> But it is *par excellence* with reference to enmity between peoples, the extension of neighbor love to the enemy, and the renunciation of violence even in the most righteous cause, that this promise takes on flesh in the most original, the most authentic, and most frightening and scandalous, and therefore the most evangelical way. It is the Good News that my enemy and

16. Yoder, *Politics*, 215.

I are united, through no merit or work of our own, in a new humanity that forbids henceforth my ever taking his or her life in my hands.[17]

All of this — a primarily social concept of sin and justification, and a conflict view of atonement suitably politicized — contributes to a complete reinterpretation of the main features of New Testament theology, especially of the Pauline corpus, which, since Luther, has been taken to focus instead on imputed personal righteousness before God on the grounds of faith.

3.5.3. Excursus: Walter Wink on the Domination System

New Testament scholar Walter Wink has expanded on Yoder's claim that the principalities and powers form a system. In its fallen state, Wink calls this the Domination System. Wink's analysis strengthens Yoder's position in several ways.

First, this conceptual move explains the integral relationship between an ethic of nonviolence and an ethic of social and economic justice. That is, Yoder and many others recognize that social justice and nonviolence "go together." Why? Wink provides a sociological-historical explanation.

The Domination System arose in the Middle East sometime between 4000 and 3000 BCE. Before this period, archaeological evidence shows, there were many peaceful civilizations — cities with no walls, no armies, no weapons for battle. After 3000 BCE, warfare proliferates dramatically.[18] By this same date, autocracy was the accepted order of things: the social system was rigidly hierarchical, authoritarian, and patriarchal. Power lost by men through submission to the ruling elite was compensated by power over women, children, hired workers, slaves, and the land. Power inequalities permitted economic inequalities, and the amassing of wealth became necessary for the support of large armies.

The Domination System has its own myth of origins in the *Enuma Elish* (from around 1250 BCE, but based on much older traditions). Here the universe is said to have been created out of the body of a murdered goddess. The gods themselves set the pattern of domination and warfare. The implication is that the very substance of which humans are created is tinged with violence. Furthermore, warfare and domination are necessary to prevent the cosmos from reverting to the chaos from which it was created.

So here is the story that gives meaning to mainline Western culture. It was

17. Yoder, *Politics*, 226.
18. Wink, *Engaging the Powers*, 36.

repeated in Greek and Roman mythology. It continues today in nearly all of the literature and television programming used to socialize children: it is the story of the good guy preserving order by means of violence. It lies behind the social-scientific research programs unmasked by Milbank, whose deep thesis is an "ontology of violence."[19] Unfortunately it has had all too deep an influence on mainstream Christianity, showing up thinly disguised in the 'just war' tradition from Augustine to the present.

The contribution that Wink's historical research makes to Yoder's theological program, then, is first to explain historically and sociologically the intrinsic connections between social justice and nonviolence: they are related in virtue of that which they oppose.

The second strength of the Domination System theory is that it makes all the more plausible Yoder's claim that God's response to evil must be at the social level, not just the level of personal sin. Once a single society falls prey to the mythology of the Domination System, it forces its neighbors to do likewise, and individuals within the societies lose their freedom to object. Consequently, the solution must be to instigate (or reinstigate) a whole new model of sociality (the church); to unmask the idolatrous pretensions of the Domination System (cf. Col. 2:15); and to teach individuals that resistance to the system is possible (the example of Jesus).

Finally, Wink's claim that domination is not coeval with civilization provides strong evidence against theological positions that root it in a constant human sinfulness extending all the way back to the Fall at the beginning of human history. This, in turn, makes more plausible the claim that there is hope for progressively decreasing the levels of violence, coercion, and economic inequality in contemporary societies.

3.5.4. Excursus: René Girard and Atonement Theory

René Girard has published a study on the relation between violence and religious ritual that can be used to eliminate an anomaly from Yoder's program. Yoder claims that he does not intend to reject the standard account of the work of Christ, but only to place it in a social and cosmic setting. Yet readers are likely to object that he needs to give some positive account of New Testament passages that use the language of temple sacrifice to interpret the atoning work of Christ. Girard's conclusions regarding religious sacrifice allow us to do just

19. See Stanley Hauerwas, "Creation, Contingency, and Truthful Nonviolence: Reflections on John Milbank's *Theology and Social Theory*," *Faith and Freedom* 4 (June 1995): 12-17.

that. I argue that, properly interpreted, the sacrificial atonement motifs exactly reinforce Yoder's own interpretation of what Christianity is basically all about.

Girard's thesis is that religious rites of sacrifice, both animal and human, are devices to quell violence among members of a community.

> [I]f left unappeased, violence will accumulate until it overflows its confines and floods the surrounding area. The role of sacrifice is to stem this rising tide of indiscriminate substitutions and redirect violence into "proper" channels.[20]

Thus, the ritual restores the harmony of the community, reinforces its social fabric. The victim used for the sacrifice is a surrogate for members of the community who have excited the animosity of their fellows. The victim, Girard points out, always shares some characteristics identifying it with the community. For example, the Nuer, who sacrifice cattle, describe the "society" of the herd in the same terms that they use for their own human relations. Yet the victims cannot be of the same class as the community itself — human victims are always marginal or distinguished in some way — so that their death does not incur any responsibility for vengeance on the part of community members. Thus, ritual sacrifice allows for the venting of aggression without the "interminable, infinitely repetitive process" of vengeance, which, whenever it turns up in some part of the community, "threatens to involve the whole social body" (14-15). Girard notes that sacrifice is generally seen as an act of mediation between a sacrificer and a deity, and argues that the sacrificial process requires a degree of *misunderstanding*. If the celebrants comprehended the true role of the sacrificial act (as Girard describes it) then it would lose its effectiveness. The participants must suppose that it is the god who demands the victim. The reason, Girard speculates, is that "men can dispose of their violence more efficiently if they regard the process not as something emanating from within themselves, but as a necessity imposed from without" (14).

If Girard's anthropology can help us think our way back to a society ordered by a code of vengeance, rather than by a modern legal system,[21] it becomes clear that the sacrificial atonement motif is not an alternative to Yoder's account of Christian theology in terms of nonviolence and reconciliation. Now

---

20. René Girard, *Violence and the Sacred*, trans. Patrick Gregory (Baltimore: Johns Hopkins University Press, 1977), 10.

21. And both Old and New Testament societies were still largely of this type; see Bruce J. Malina, *The New Testament World: Insights from Cultural Anthropology* (Atlanta: John Knox, 1981).

we can see Christ, the lamb of God, as the one victim whose sacrificial death is permanently efficacious for ridding the community of violence (cf. Heb. 7:27).

The parallels with Girard's account of ritual sacrifice are startling: The victim must be similar enough to suffer on behalf of community members, yet different enough not to be confused with other, non-sacrificeable members. So Jesus is described as both fully human and as the unique Son of God. The moral ambiguity of the sacrificial victim is found here as well. Jesus is described as the wholly sinless one, yet "reckoned among the transgressors." The symbolism of the Last Supper even maintains a hint of the cannibalism that is so often incorporated in sacrifice.

We even find in cruder versions of this atonement theology the "necessary degree of misunderstanding": the claim that God the Father required the death of his Son as satisfaction for sin.

So if Girard is correct, the point of the interpretation of Christ's death as the once-for-all sacrifice for sin, for communities in which ritual sacrifice was still an effective control on the cycle of vengeance and violence, would have been to say that violence and vengeance within the community is henceforth prohibited. And against this background we can see more clearly the importance of Paul's (and Yoder's) emphasis on the new humanity that refuses to count any class of people as outside of the community thus protected from violence by the sacrifice of the Lamb. What does the sacrificial imagery mean, then, for us who are far removed from cultures where propitiatory sacrifice makes sense? For us, Girard suggests, war and the legal system with its punishments are the primary means of redirecting violence away from protected community members. I would add, as well, that civil religion with its explicit description of loss of life in battle as "sacrifice" maintains the necessary degree of misunderstanding — the illusion that the innocent lives lost on the battlefield are not victims of the citizens' own aggression but are demanded by a righteous god. It may not be pure cynicism when commentators attribute America's small wars to the need to unify the citizens at home for the *domestic* political agenda.

The obvious application of sacrificial atonement imagery to our contemporary situation is to call for a permanent end to violence, both spontaneous and institutionalized. Christ for us, too, is the one victim whose death should be permanently efficacious in ridding our present-day communities of violence. Yoder's image for the work of Christ and of his followers is that of *absorbing evil;* stopping the "eternal, infinitely repetitive process" of violence (Girard) by refusing to retaliate. And, we would add, by refusing as well to find a scapegoat from the margins of our community.

The misunderstanding that it is God who required the death of Jesus as scapegoat for sinners has all too often contributed to the view that God also demands the death of others as payment for sin. Demythologization of atonement imagery requires recognition that it is not God, but our own human principalities and powers that demand the death of criminals, the "sacrifice" of young men on the battlefield. High Christology demands that we recognize God's voice not in the powers demanding sacrificial death, but rather in the one whose life was sacrificed on the cross.

Thus, the addition of Girard's anthropology to this theological program allows for the overcoming of what would be called an anomaly in science — a datum that cannot be reconciled with the theory. The anomaly here is the sacrificial language used in the New Testament to interpret the death of Jesus. This language has led to the development of theories of the work of Christ that are at least different from Yoder's interpretation, and in some cases actually opposed to it. I have used Girard's thesis regarding the social function of ritual sacrifice as an auxiliary hypothesis to interpret the anomalous data in a way that is not only consistent with Yoder's program, but adds additional confirmation.[22]

3.5.5. Church, World, and Eschatology

An important thesis for Yoder, as well as for other theologians in the Anabaptist tradition, is the recognition that "the church is not the world." The sixteenth-century Anabaptists' most distinctive feature was their rejection of the state-church arrangement, which identified the boundaries of the church first with the empire and then with the nation state. The "ana-baptists" (that is, rebaptizers) rejected infant baptism in part because it was the means by which the incorporation of all citizens into the state church was effected.

When Yoder distinguishes the church from the world, he means to say that there is a system — a set of interconnected power structures — that is opposed to the work of Christ. An important question dividing Christian ethicists is whether there is any possibility for moral improvement in social institutions. This question, Yoder would argue, needs to be recast as a set of questions regarding the possibilities for change within both the church and the world, and especially how the church can affect the world.

The church is an alternative social reality in the midst of the world. By its very existence it unmasks the principalities and powers, exposing the illegitimate claims of family, privileged social class, and nation. In a variety of

---

22. Yoder commented on an earlier version of this essay. He endorsed the use made here of both Wink and Girard, but cautioned that he would not want to endorse some of the further moves they make.

ways this unmasking frees church members to lead agapeistic lives. For example, Christians are *freed from* requirements to avenge injuries to family members' honor.

The church is a laboratory for imagining and practicing new forms of social life. Where it had once been unimaginable that Jews could live in community with pagans, within a generation that "new creature" became a reality. Christians are even now trying to imagine a community in which there is no such thing as male and female (cf. Gal. 3:28).

Within the church social practices are, to a degree, healed of their sinfulness. The powers themselves can be redeemed — they can accept their role as servants of God in support of human sociality. For example, leadership becomes a form of service. Economic practices are not primarily for the amassing of wealth, but for the production of something to share. Housekeeping aims at hospitality to the stranger.

In addition, the church has developed unique social practices that aim at maintaining and improving the moral character of the community. One of these is the practice of "binding and loosing" that Jesus is reported to have taught his disciples:

> "If your brother does wrong, go and take the matter up with him, strictly between yourselves. If he listens to you, you have won your brother over. But if he will not listen, take one or two others with you, so that every case may be settled on the evidence of two or three witnesses. If he refuses to listen to them, report the matter to the congregation; and if he will not listen even to the congregation, then treat him as you would a pagan or a tax-collector. Truly I tell you: Whatever you forbid on earth shall be forbidden in heaven, and whatever you allow on earth shall be allowed in heaven."
> (Matt. 18:15-18)

This practice has the potential not only for supporting individuals in their faithfulness to the community's teaching, but also offers opportunity both for healing personal grievances and for productive discussions on matters of conduct.[23] When it does involve reevaluation of the community's moral standards it becomes an instance of a second Christian practice, that of communal discernment. Yoder calls this practice the rule of Paul, since its justification in all of the new Protestant movements during the Reformation referred to Paul's first letter to the Corinthians (chap. 14).

The idea behind this practice is that God's Spirit will lead the community

---

23. See Yoder, *Body Politics: Five Practices of the Christian Community Before the Watching World* (Nashville, TN: Discipleship Resources, 1992), ch. 1.

in making decisions about doctrine and moral issues through the consensus that arises out of open conversation. The Quakers have worked out most thoroughly and self-consciously an understanding of how the Spirit shapes and guides the church.[24] The practice of discernment can be a powerful tool for cumulative moral development within the church.

All of these features of the church suggest that conscientious pursuit of the good can and will lead to cumulative moral development, both of Christ-like character among the members and of noncoercive, virtue-enhancing institutions and practices.

However, religious institutions themselves easily become quite powerful and they are especially prone to become idolatrous. So there can be no smug expectation of inevitable moral progress. The prophet will always be needed to call the church to focus critical moral discernment on itself.

The church acts as an agent of change in the world by showing the world alternatives to its coercive practices. While it is simply a fact that the world does not and cannot operate as the church does, there are still vast differences among the powers in terms of the degree to which they approximate the will of God. The church, as an ethical laboratory, can teach the world better ways. For instance, many attribute modern forms of democratic government to skill and lessons learned in free-church polity. The ideas of public education and hospitals came from church institutions.

Yoder's hope for partial realization of God's social will for humankind in history sets him in opposition to Reinhold Niebuhr's "Christian realism." Niebuhr claimed that all human social groups are necessarily less moral than the individuals that comprise them. Yet it would be difficult to say that Yoder's analysis of social institutions is any less *realistic* than Niebuhr's. What accounts for the difference is different views of eschatology (i.e., doctrine of the last things). More specifically, these two theorists have different views of the relation between history and the Kingdom of God.

Niebuhr points out that while all Christians look forward to the *parousia,* the triumphant return of Christ, some interpret this event as a future happening *within* the temporal-historical process; others as necessarily outside of or *beyond* history. Because he sets up the question in terms of the problem of the temporal and the eternal (the claim is that the eternal can never be actualized in the temporal) Niebuhr is forced to side with those whose eschatology transcends history. This, in turn, leads to the conclusion that guilt and moral ambiguity are permanent features of the interim. Christ's overcoming of the world can only mean that Christians know the meaning of history, not that history it-

---

24. Yoder, *Body Politics,* ch. 5.

self is transformed.[25] Yoder claims that the New Testament sees our present age, from Pentecost to the *parousia,* as a period of the overlapping of two aeons. These are not distinct periods of time, for they exist simultaneously.

> They differ rather in nature or in direction; one points backwards to human history outside of (before) Christ; the other points forward to the fullness of the kingdom of God, of which it is a foretaste. Each aeon has a social manifestation: the former in the "world," the latter in the church or the body of Christ.[26]

The new aeon was inaugurated by Jesus; Jesus is a mover of history, not merely a teacher of how to understand history's moral ambiguity.[27] The meaning of history is found in the work of the church;[28] the church by its obedience is used by God to bring about the fullness of the Kingdom, of which the church is a foretaste.

The resurrection of Jesus is God's guarantee that the new aeon will ultimately prevail. This entails that the means Jesus chose for participation in history are the right ones: the cross and not the sword, suffering and not brute power determine the meaning of history. One need not choose between *agape* and effectiveness.[29]

So the ultimate effectiveness of self-sacrificing love is guaranteed; but its rightness is not based on effectiveness, but rather on the fact that it anticipates the victory of the Lamb.[30] This ethic makes sense only if Jesus' choice not to rule violently is the surfacing of an eternal divine decision; if self-emptying is not only what Jesus did, but is the very nature of God.[31]

> This conception of participation in the character of God's struggle with a rebellious world, which early Quakerism referred to as "the war of the lamb," has the peculiar disadvantage — or advantage, depending upon one's point of view — of being meaningful only if Christ be he who Christians claim him to be, the Master. Almost every other kind of ethical approach espoused by Christians, pacifist or otherwise, will continue to make

25. Reinhold Niebuhr, *Moral Man and Immoral Society* (New York: Charles Scribner's Sons, 1932).

26. Yoder, *The Original Revolution: Essays on Christian Pacifism* (Scottdale, PA: Herald Press, 1971), 55.

27. Yoder, *Politics,* 233.

28. Yoder, *Original Revolution,* 61.

29. Yoder, *Politics,* 232, 109.

30. Yoder, *Original Revolution,* 61.

31. Yoder, *He Came Preaching Peace* (Scottdale, PA: Herald Press, 1985), 93.

sense to the non-Christian as well. Whether Jesus be the Christ or not, whether Jesus the Christ be Lord or not, whether this kind of religious language be meaningful or not, most types of ethical approach will keep on functioning just the same. For their true foundation is in some reading of the human situation or some ethical insight which is claimed to be generally accessible to all people of good-will. The same is not true for this vision of "completing in our bodies that which was lacking in the suffering of Christ" (Col. 1:24). If Jesus Christ was not who historical Christianity confesses he was, the revelation in the life of a real man of the character of God himself, then this one argument for pacifism collapses.[32]

3.6. Confirmation

Different theological research programs call for different kinds of data to support them. This is analogous to the different kinds of support that are relevant to, say, different schools of thought in psychology: B. F. Skinner's reinforcement schedules versus Freud's dream analyses and slips of the tongue. Yoder's central thesis is about the proper interpretation of the meaning of Jesus, and about what Jesus means for history and ethics.

Since the Scriptures are the only significant source of information about Jesus, it stands to reason that these texts should provide an important body of data for Yoder, along with other historical texts and traces that are relevant for assisting in their interpretation. Yoder's more systematic works such as *The Politics of Jesus* contain sophisticated arguments to the effect that his line of interpretation is more faithful to the texts, more fruitful for interpreting obscure passages, than others. Yoder has provided additional scriptural confirmation of his program in published sermons and occasional essays. In this body of literature he has worked through a surprising variety of texts, in each case providing a reading that confirms his interpretation of the life and teaching of Jesus.

However, the other aspect of Yoder's thesis, that Jesus (thus understood) is the ultimate revelation of the character of God and thus of the meaning and purpose of human history, cannot be confirmed merely by Scripture studies without begging the question. The purely theological thesis, the theory about the character of God, can only be fully confirmed eschatologically, although it can acquire some plausibility for Christians from their relations with God in prayer. However, there is a thesis about history embedded in Yoder's theology that may be testable in the interim. Yoder has stated it as follows:

---

32. Yoder, *Politics*, 237.

[I]f *kenosis* [Jesus' renunciation of worldly prerogatives] is the shape of God's own self-sending, then any strategy of Lordship, like that of the kings of this world, is . . . a strategic mistake, likely to backfire.[33]

Yoder pays some attention to the relative effectiveness of nonviolent versus violent means of social and political action. However, his more intriguing contribution here is the suggestion that his version of ethics leads to (what I would call) a new research program in the study of history, part of which is the examination of the effects of violence and nonviolence.

We now turn to asking . . . whether this "messianic" orientation will have particular implications for history as an intellectual discipline, i.e., for historiography, the recounting of events and the discerning of meanings. Can one gain new light upon the relevance of a Free Church vision of ethics by claiming that it also leads to a new way of interpreting events in the past? Decision in the present is often very much the product of how the past has been recounted to us. If we are then to open up a new future it must be the extension of a rereading of the past. Historiography must be rehabilitated by being taken back from the grasp of the military historians and the chroniclers of battles and dynasties, and informed by other criteria to judge a society's sickness or health.

Instead of reading history as proof of a theory of political science, i.e., the definition *sine qua non* of the state as its monopoly of physical coercion, could we study the story with some openness to the hypothesis that genuine power is always correlated with the consent of the governed or legitimized in some other way? Is there such a thing as a "peace church historiography"?[34]

Yoder mentions a variety of hypotheses that follow from this reorientation of assumptions about history.

1. The sword is not the source of creativity.
   1.1 Theological considerations make a major contribution to the spirit of an age and to political developments.
   1.2 History may be more affected by quiet ministry than by princes.
2. Manhood is not brutality.
   2.1 History and conflict cannot be understood on a simple model of good guys and bad guys.

33. Yoder, *The Priestly Kingdom: Social Ethics as Gospel* (Notre Dame: University of Notre Dame Press, 1984), 145.
34. Yoder, *Original Revolution*, 160-61.

3. If you wish peace, prepare for it.
    3.1 Preparing for war brings conflict.
    3.2 Practice of constructive methods of conflict resolution will help to undermine unjust institutions and build healthy ones.
4. War is not a way to save a culture.
5. Social creativity is a minority function.
    5.1 The person in power is not always free or strong.
    5.2 Minority groups have more freedom to experiment with new forms of social life.
6. Rulers are not necessarily society's benefactors.[35]

In short, Yoder's claim is that "world history," the historiography of "the world" (in the theological sense defined above) produces a distortion of the past, which then provides justification for further coercive practices. Perhaps an equally credible narrative could be constructed, a narrative that is in fact more accurate, which will make it clear that the real historical force is suffering love.

3.7. Rebutting Counterevidence

Two sorts of possible counterevidence could be particularly damaging to the theological program sketched here: the complicity of the church in the worst evils of history, and biblical passages that appear to condone or require violence.

The well-known sins not only of individual Christians but especially of the institutional churches themselves rightly raise doubts about Christianity's truth claims, although this is not straightforward falsification, owing to the fact that one of Christianity's central claims has always been its doctrine of sin. The more appropriate approach is to ask whether the observed patterns of goodness and evil are roughly what theological teaching should lead us to expect, and here we have to distinguish among theological traditions. For the Catholic tradition, with its teaching on the non-defectability of the church, sinful church practices constitute a major anomaly; this is much less the case for the Protestant tradition, according to which the church must be *semper reformanda* (always needing reforming).

Yoder's version of the Anabaptist tradition is even less damaged by the sin of the church: not only can he predict it, he can specify its main cause. The church is a power; all powers are subject to corruption when they seek their own good over that of service to God. When the churches become involved in

35. Yoder, *Original Revolution*, 162-76.

Constantinian arrangements with the great powers of empire or state, they have much more to protect and will inevitably become corrupted. Thus, the church itself must always be on guard against grasping for power (as the Protestant tradition emphasizes) and *in particular* it must eschew state-church status.

A second advantage of the Anabaptist tradition for answering the problem of corruption in the church is its teaching on church discipline. Much discredit is brought upon Christian teaching by the behavior of individual members of churches (Mafiosi at Mass, for example). However, Anabaptist church discipline was founded on Matthew 18, and when this practice is followed, members' conduct is either brought into accord with church teaching or they are excluded from worship.

So I claim that while evil within and by the churches is indeed a terrible scandal, it presents less of an anomaly for the Anabaptist tradition than for others. Persistently sinful individuals do not count as church members in "believers' churches"; the most heinous institutional sins of Christendom (predictably, according to the Anabaptists) have been committed by churches that have made compromises with the empire or the state.

In the second strategy of counterevidence, several passages in the New Testament are regularly used to attempt to rebut pacifist interpretations of Jesus' mission and teaching: "Every person must submit to the authorities in power, for all authority comes from God, and the existing authorities are instituted by him" (Romans 13:1) is often cited as proof that Christians have a responsibility to serve in the military. However, such a reading ignores the context of the text, both the preceding and subsequent verses, and the social setting of the original readers. Romans 13 follows a passage which calls for peace and nonresistance to evil:

> Never pay back evil for evil. Let your aims be such as all count honourable. If possible, so far as it lies with you, live at peace with all. My dear friends, do not seek revenge, but leave a place for divine retribution; for there is a text which reads, "Vengeance is mine, says the Lord, I will repay." But there is another text: "If your enemy is hungry, feed him; if he is thirsty, give him a drink; by doing this you will heap live coals on his head." Do not let evil conquer you, but use good to conquer evil. (Rom. 12:17-21)

We should not be deceived by chapter breaks, added much later, into separating this passage from Romans 13:1, which immediately follows it. The Revised English Bible's translation of the next verse is: "It follows that anyone who rebels against authority is resisting a divine institution. . . ." It is very unlikely that Paul meant to send his Roman readers to join the army, since most Christians then were not Roman citizens and thus were ineligible for military service. All of this makes it much more likely that Paul is cautioning the Roman Christians *against* taking up arms, that is, against joining in the armed rebellion against the government!

Secondly, there is a puzzling passage in Luke's Gospel in which Jesus, on the way to his arrest, tells his disciples to provide swords:

> He said to them, "when I sent you out barefoot without purse or pack, were you ever short of anything?" "No," they answered. "It is different now," he said; "whoever has a purse had better take it with him, and his pack, too; and if he has no sword, let him sell his cloak and buy one. For scripture says, 'And he was reckoned among transgressors,' and this, I tell you, must be fulfilled in me; indeed, all that is written of me is reaching its fulfilment." "Lord," they said, "we have two swords here." "Enough!" he replied. (Luke 22:35-38)

This passage has been used frequently in the pacifism debate: If Jesus had not meant his disciples to kill, why would he have told them now to arm themselves? Is he not preparing them for legitimate self-defense after Pentecost? But, Yoder asks, how could two swords be "enough" for twelve disciples travelling two by two?[36]

One possible reading of Jesus' motives in arming his disciples, of course, is to take him at his word — it is to fulfill the prophecy found in Isaiah 53:12:

> Therefore I shall allot him a portion with the great, and he will share the spoil with the mighty, because he exposed himself to death and was reckoned among transgressors, for he bore the sins of many and interceded for transgressors.

If Jesus was to be taken as a criminal, to be executed by crucifixion, the punishment for insurrection, the symbols of armed rebellion in the hands of his followers would be appropriate. Two swords might not be enough for defense, but plenty for conviction.

Another passage often used is the Johannine story of Jesus "cleansing the temple" (John 2:13-17). The usefulness of this text for justifying violence depends on a once common but now generally rejected translation. According to the King James Version, Jesus, "when he had made a scourge of small cords, he drove them all [the money changers and those that sold oxen, sheep, and doves] out of the temple, and the sheep and the oxen . . ." (v. 15). This act of physical violence by Jesus is then said to set a precedent for his followers.

However, more recent translations make it only the animals that are driven out: "Making a whip of cords, he drove all of them out of the temple,

---

36. Yoder, *Politics*, 45 n. 44.

both the sheep and the cattle" (NRSV).[37] Thus, the story is better read as a non-violent action campaign against the temple authorities.

So these passages, long used as proof texts against pacifists, support contrary readings that are at least as plausible, and perhaps more so.

4. Conclusion: Theology and Cosmology

Yoder claims that the ministry of Jesus has not only social-ethical and historical significance, but *cosmic* significance:

> Then to follow Jesus does not mean renouncing effectiveness. . . . It means that in Jesus we have a clue to which kinds of causation, which kinds of community-building, which kinds of conflict management, go with the grain of the cosmos, of which we know, as Caesar does not, that Jesus is both the Word (the inner logic of things) and the Lord ("sitting at the right hand"). It is not that we begin with a mechanistic universe and then look for cracks and chinks where a little creative freedom might sneak in (for which we would then give God credit): it is that we confess the deterministic world to be enclosed within, smaller than, the sovereignty of the God of the Resurrection and Ascension.[38]

> "[C]ross and resurrection" designates not only a few days' events in first-century Jerusalem but also the shape of the cosmos.[39]

Recall that the core theory of a research program is said to be metaphysical — it tells us about the nature of the reality with which the science is concerned. So here we see the metaphysical claim standing behind Yoder's nonviolent ethic, but also unifying and making sense of the whole of Christian teaching, of Yoder's doctrinal "research program."

In Yoder's works, then, written over the course of his career as historian, theologian, and ethicist, Christian pacifists find the systematic theological justification for their stance: it is a reflection of the very nature of the cosmos.[40]

37. For a discussion of the problematic aspects of the Greek grammar, see Yoder, *Politics*, ch. 10.

38. Yoder, *Politics*, 246.

39. Yoder, *Politics*, 160.

40. Much of this article is a slight revision of material excerpted from Nancey Murphy and George F. R. Ellis, *On the Moral Nature of the Universe: Theology, Cosmology, and Ethics* (Minneapolis: Fortress Press, 1996), ch. 8. I thank the press for permission to publish it here. A much shorter version was published in *Faith and Freedom* (March 1996): 3-11.

I also thank James Wm. McClendon, Jr., for helpful suggestions for the revision.

Be Honest in Just War Thinking!
Lutherans, the Just War Tradition,
and Selective Conscientious Objection

Reinhard Hütter

While I had the privilege to learn from many areas of Professor Yoder's rich and multifaceted theological work, it undoubtedly was his forceful reframing of the just war tradition from a Christian pacifist stance that had the deepest influence on me. Therefore, it is only appropriate for me as part of the "magisterial Reformation tradition" to express my deep gratitude for and indebtedness to John H. Yoder's work by showing how I see myself forced to address my own theological tradition in this new light.

Discussions of the just war tradition among Lutherans have an odd character.[1] They are similar to reinventing the wheel whenever we need a car. The last extended discussion of the just war tradition among Lutherans in this country took place during the Vietnam War.[2] In the following years the discus-

---

1. The use of the term "tradition" over against "doctrine" or "theory" is to signal that the Christian just war tradition has been an ongoing discourse, in which there has been a consensus on the main criteria, yet in which constant accommodations to new circumstances have had to be made, and in which there are ongoing disputes about the interpretation of some criteria. The term "doctrine" would wrongly imply that the just war tradition has been formulated in just one official or permanently valid form, while the term "theory" would imply a static set of unchangeable rules and principles to be applied to all cases.

2. An important document we need to retrieve from this time is Richard J. Niebanck's *Conscience, War, and the Selective Objector*, Studies in Justice, Peace and Freedom 1 (Board of Social Ministry, Lutheran Church in America, 1968). In light of the recent Gulf war this document is still highly relevant, yet the fact that it is completely forgotten clearly documents Lutheranism's ongoing amnesia in regard to the just war tradition.

sion ended and the whole notion disappeared in the closet of outmoded tools of the theological tradition.[3] Thus, unsurprisingly, late in 1990 Lutherans were again caught unprepared by the public debate about "just war" criteria in rela-

3. Yet it is important to note the one outstanding exception, namely Charles P. Lutz, *Conscription and Conscience: Ethical Dilemma for Lutherans,* ELCA, 1990 and his introduction to John H. Yoder, *When War Is Unjust: Being Honest in Just-War Thinking,* 2nd ed. (Maryknoll, NY: Orbis, 1996), xi-xx. It is also important to note the Church statements during the Vietnam War and in the years after. It is only deeply troublesome how little these statements have fueled an ongoing discourse about the just war tradition, selective conscientious objection, and Christian pacifism in American Lutheranism.

War, Peace, and Freedom, adopted by ALC General Convention, October 1966.

Conscientious Objection, adopted by LCA Biennial Convention, June 1968.

Selective Conscientious Objection, adopted by ALC General Convention, October 1968.

National Service and Selective Service Reform, adopted by ALC General Convention, October 1970.

Military Service: Conscientious Participation and Conscientious Objection, adopted by AELC Delegate Assembly, October 1980.

Compliance with Registration Law, adopted by ALC General Convention, October 1980.

Mandate for Peacemaking, adopted by ALC General Convention, September 1982.

Peace and Politics, adopted by LCA Biennial Convention, June/July 1984.

See the interesting account of the intense struggle around the LCA's 1968 Social Statement *Conscientious Objection* in Christa R. Klein with Christian D. von Dehsen, *Politics and Policy: The Genesis and Theology of Social Statements in the Lutheran Church of America* (Minneapolis: Fortress Press, 1989), 86-89 and 199-201, and also the account on the social statement *Peace and Politics,* op. cit., 161-69 and 247-58.

In addition, there is the noteworthy case of the Augustana Synod which resolved in 1941: "In view of the present situation which calls for serious and prayerful thought concerning the problem of war, *Be it resolved:* That the Lutheran Augustana Synod recognizes the authority of properly constituted government. However, we respect the attitude of the conscientious objector relative to war. We believe the government should not violate the Christian conscience by seeking to compel conscientious objectors to engage in combatant military service. We ask exemption from all forms of combatant military service for all conscientious objectors who may be members of the Augustana Synod" (*Social Pronouncements of the Augustana Lutheran Church 1937-1962* [Board of Social Ministry, Lutheran Church in America], 19).

In 1942 part of the minutes say: "The Synod urges its members to remain loyal to Christ; to be on guard lest the sanction of the Church be given to anything which is contrary to the spirit of Christ; to seek to maintain civil and religious liberties during this period when passion can so easily be aroused; to withstand all propaganda of hatred and revenge; to manifest a spirit of good will toward those among us who spring from nations with which our country is now at war; to manifest generosity to those who suffer because of the war, including prisoners of war; to support the work of ministering to the spiritual needs of the men in the armed forces of our country; to work for justice and good will among groups and nations; to seek and support national policies in harmony with the will of God and to work for a just and lasting peace" (op. cit., 19-20). The resolution from 1941 was not reconfirmed, yet neither was it revoked.

I owe the information about the Augustana Lutheran Church to Ms. Joanne Pearson.

tionship to the Kuwait crisis. The sudden reemergence of another impending war and the lingering memories of a previous debate caused a scramble for the closet, just to find a rusty, outmoded, and ineffective tool among a lot of spider webs.

Maybe my imagery is problematic since it seems to suggest that the just war tradition has been used in the past by, and is a traditional option for, Lutherans.[4] Yet far from it. My claim is that Lutherans never really owned the just war tradition in the form of an ongoing discourse as, for example, the Roman Catholics did until recently.[5] To continue the imagery, many Lutherans might think we have a lawn mower in the garage, yet we have still to discover that the motor is missing! This wrong assumption about the just war tradition makes Lutherans especially vulnerable to public debates about "just war," as the most recent one showed.[6]

There are at least three reasons why Lutherans are especially vulnerable to

4. It therefore is somewhat problematic to refer to what presently often are called the "classic just war criteria" without being embedded in an ongoing theological and ethical tradition, in which these criteria are constantly discussed, accommodated to new political and military developments, and applied in an ongoing discriminative practice of the Church. Just for the sake of basic information I list the broader consensus of the "classic just war criteria," which have presently more to do with international law than the Church's peace mandate. The criteria to be met before war *(ius ad bellum)* comprise (1) last resort, (2) just cause, (3) declaration by a lawful authority, and (4) prospect of success. The criteria to be met during war *(ius in bello)* are (1) proportionality of means and ends, (2) just conduct (i.e., immunity of noncombatants). The criterion to be met after war is mercy to the vanquished, which means that no demands for punitive reparations or unconditional surrender are made. Each of these criteria is in need of further specified interpretation and application depending on the convictions of the interpreting community and on the political and technological circumstances. In other words, the just war tradition has never worked as a "theory" to be applied to specific situations, rather it only works as an ongoing discourse-tradition.

5. For the most detailed and comprehensive discussion of the just war tradition in American Catholic thought see George Weigel, *Tranquillitas Ordinis: The Present Failure and Future Promise of American Catholic Thought on War and Peace* (Oxford/New York: Oxford University Press, 1987).

6. For detailed argumentation on why the use of "just war" rhetoric in relation to the Gulf war by the administration and the media was a misuse of the just war tradition see Alan Geyer, "Just War and the Burdens of History," *The Christian Century* (Feb. 6-13, 1991): 135; John H. Yoder, "Just War Tradition: Is It Credible?" *The Christian Century* (March 13, 1991): 295-98; Rosemary Radford Ruether, "The Dangerous Illusions of Victory," *The Christian Century* (March 20-27, 1991): 318-19; Stanley Hauerwas, "Whose 'Just' War? Which Peace?" in *But Was It Just?*, ed. David DeCosse (New York: Doubleday, 1992), 83-105. For voices arguing the opposite position see James T. Johnson, "The Use of Force: A Justified Response," *The Christian Century* (Feb. 6-13, 1991): 134-35 and Richard John Neuhaus, "Just War and This War," in the *Wall Street Journal* (January 23, 1991).

the self-deceptive character of a highly media-influenced public debate about "just war."

First, "just war" is mentioned in the confessional writings: to be precise, in article XVI of the Augsburg Confession. Article XVI deals with civil government and states in the main section the following:

> It is taught among us that all government in the world and all established rule and laws were instituted and ordained by God for the sake of good order, and that Christians may without sin occupy civil offices or serve as princes and judges, render decisions and pass sentence according to imperial and other existing laws, punish evildoers with the sword, engage in just wars, serve as soldiers, buy and sell, take required oaths, possess property, be married, etc.[7]

The article ends with the following remark: "But when commands of the civil authority cannot be obeyed *without sin*, we must obey God rather than men (Acts 5:29)."[8] Since article XVI tacitly presupposes the existing just war tradition as developed by Western Catholicism and therefore does not specify anything in detail, Lutherans are in danger of identifying the two words *iure bellare*, the engaging in "just wars," with the present just war rhetoric as employed by the government and the media.

Second, while the just war tradition seems to have a binding nature for Lutherans on the grounds of article XVI of the Augsburg Confession, there has

---

7. *The Book of Concord*, trans. and ed. by Theodore G. Tappert (Philadelphia: Muhlenberg Press, 1959), 37.

8. My emphasis. In a letter to the author, John H. Yoder has made the very interesting and thought-provoking point that in CA XVI the phrase "without sin" is being used both positively and negatively, in one way as designating what is permitted, in the other as determining when one should disobey government! The phrase seems to be used here on a casuistic level which is not identical with the fundamental theological designation of the human person as *"simul iustus et peccator."* The phrase seems to imply that while all our actions remain the actions of sinners, we can act in faithful obedience and in faithless disobedience to God's commandments. (Cf. Luther's opening paragraph in his "Treatise on Good Works" (1520), *Luther's Works,* vol. 44 [Philadelphia: Fortress Press, 1966], p. 23!) Yet with losing the confessional of Roman Catholicism and without sharing something similar to the community context of common discernment and mutual accountability of the "left-wing" Reformation, Lutheranism seems to have lost over time the very context in which the "without sin" could make any discriminative sense between concrete obedience and concrete disobedience. By leaving the captivity of legalism and works-righteousness, later Lutheranism, especially after the modern "turn to the subject," entered the new captivity of private subjugation to respective cultural *ethoi* (presently libertinism) and public subjugation to patriotisms and the relative autonomy of all public spheres of life (presently especially "economy").

been no ongoing catechetical, theological, and magisterial discussion on the topic as, for example, has been the case among Roman Catholics, for whom the just war tradition ironically never became a binding doctrine! Thus Lutherans are in the odd position of being bound to a just war tradition in our confessional writings whose toughness, inner complexity, detailed argumentation, and implicit condemnation of modern warfare have sunk into oblivion. Therefore, the present half-hearted adherence to the just war tradition by Lutherans seems largely to be an unconvincing lip service to a forgotten tradition. Subscribing to a broad just war understanding under present conditions only eases one's conscience and earns a questionable respectability in the public arena of modern nation-states.

Third, the history of the involvement of Lutherans in all kinds of wars both on this continent and in Europe is a sad one. Maybe further historical research will develop different results, but I do not know of any prominent war since the Reformation waged by a state to which a Lutheran Church belonged, and which that Lutheran Church body declared as inherently unjust and therefore the participation of Christians in the war as offensive to God's will and contradictory to the Christian vocation. I think one of the basic problems in this regard was the fact that the respective state was always bigger than the Lutheran Church in it; in addition, the Lutheran Church often was dependent on the state in a variety of ways. Therefore, what happened over time in Lutheranism was that the highly developed critical concept of the just war tradition, which Luther in his treatises and also article XVI of the Augsburg Confession tacitly presuppose as a given of the Catholic tradition, quietly disappeared and instead a normative concept of the state as one of the orders of creation gained increasingly in importance. In this context warfare was construed as a legitimate and unavoidable element of conflict-resolution among nation-states, and the Christian was to serve as a soldier, this being a normal element of at least every male Christian's vocation under the conditions of general draft practices in modern nation-states. Thus, Lutheran Churches provided the states in which they found themselves with a theological rationale for warfare in the state's interest. In other words, while continuing to pay lip service to the just war tradition Lutherans have, in fact, generally become nation-state realists, on both sides of the Atlantic.

Now, we could accept this as a given and go on from here, especially if we were to assume that we live in an inherently good nation, which means a nation that principally fights only "good wars." Yet for a variety of good theological reasons we might be slightly reluctant to fully subscribe to this core assumption of the nationalistic myth. In addition, taking openly the position of nation-state realists, we get into serious tension with both Martin Luther and the confessional writings. And this is problematic in at least two respects.

For if Lutherans want to argue against Christian pacifism on grounds of the confessional writings and Luther's own position, they have to subscribe to the just war tradition. If Lutherans do that, we must, first, recognize that national-interest warfare clearly contradicts the whole just war tradition.[9] Secondly, to accept the just war tradition seriously, we must subscribe to the *whole* just war tradition, which means also accepting selective conscientious objection! Only by taking selective conscientious objection seriously both in theory and in practice are we taking the just war tradition seriously.

In order to warrant this claim let me remind you of two passages out of Luther's works. Of course, they were written in a predemocratic context. Yet they are far from irrelevant for our present situation, especially in light of the recent Gulf war. In both instances Luther makes a strong case for selective conscientious objection in the context of a clearly presupposed and accepted Just War Tradition:

> But if, as often happens, the temporal power and authorities, or whatever they call themselves, would compel a subject to do something contrary to the command of God, or hinder him from doing God's commands, a man has to say what St. Peter said to the rulers of the Jews, "We must obey God rather than men" [Acts 5:29]. He did not say, "We must not obey men," for that would be wrong. He said, "God rather than men." [It is] as if a prince desired to go to war, and his cause was clearly unrighteous; we should neither follow nor help such a prince, because God had commanded us not to kill our neighbor or do him a wrong. Likewise, if the prince were to order us to bear false witness, steal, lie or deceive, and the like [we should refuse]. In such cases we should indeed give up our property and honor, our life and limb, so that God's commandments remain.[10]

A second question: "Suppose my lord were wrong in going to war," I reply: If you know for sure that he is wrong, then you should fear God rather than

---

9. National-interest warfare presupposes the autonomy of the national interest. Machiavelli was the first theoretician of this concept, which is presently embodied in the whole notion of the "national security state." As Yoder says, "[The autonomy of the national interest] denies either explicitly or implicitly the possibility that the military operations of the state could or should be judged in the light of objective criteria other than self-interest. That means a rejection of just war in the strict sense" (*When War Is Unjust*, 14). For a detailed and fascinating analysis of the modern nation-state see Anthony Giddens, *The Nation-State and Violence* (Berkeley and Los Angeles: University of California Press, 1987).

10. Martin Luther, "Treatise on Good Works," 100.

men, Acts 5:29, and you should neither fight nor serve, for you cannot have a good conscience before God. "Oh no," you say, "my lord would force me to do it; he would take away my fief and would not give me my money, pay, and wages. Besides, I would be despised and put to shame as a coward, even worse, as a man who did not keep his word and deserted his lord in need." I answer: You must take that risk and, with God's help, let whatever happens, happen. He can restore it to you a hundredfold, as he promises in the gospel, "Whoever leaves house, farm, wife [spouse], and property, will receive a hundredfold," etc. [Matt. 19:29].[11]

As I mentioned earlier, article XVI of the Augsburg Confession only talks about the Christian civil government's right to *iure bellare,* to wage "just wars." If we take Luther's above comments as a hermeneutical key for the very short passage in the Augsburg Confession it is not the administration which decides whether a given war is a just war, but the Christian individual in the context of the Christian community![12]

The central issue with which we have to come to terms again is the question whether the just war tradition belongs to the church or to the state. In other words, is the state's claim to wage a just war and the state's warranting the claim by using this or that criterion authoritative for Christians or is the church's own deliberation, discernment, and judgment the decisive point of orientation for the Christian's conscience? For Lutherans since the Reformation it has been predominantly the state which decided authoritatively on this question, with the result that Lutherans, after having left the Babylonian captivity of a distorted church, entered the Babylonian captivity of the emerging modern nation-state. The just war tradition could be regarded as a test case for this fatal transition from the fire into the frying pan.[13] Why? If the arbiter of the just war tradition is, in the broadest

---

11. Martin Luther, "Whether Soldiers, Too, Can Be Saved" (1526), in *Luther's Works,* vol. 46 (Philadelphia: Fortress Press, 1967), 130.

12. Of course, one could argue that Luther emphasized that in the case of doubt the soldier should always trust the government's good judgment. While this was a questionable yet still reasonable qualification in the sixteenth-century context of citizenship, diplomacy, and warfare, it has become an increasingly problematic qualification in the context of modern warfare and especially in the context of modern public-relation politics. The qualifier "in the case of doubt for the government" might have contributed to the eclipse of the just war tradition in Lutheran areas in the post-Reformation period. Under modern conditions of cynical "spin control" by governments and control and manipulation of information by militaries, Luther's qualification becomes completely counterproductive by invalidating the practical and discriminatory nature of the just war tradition.

13. See Yoder's outstanding essay "The Reception of the Just War Tradition by the Magis-

sense, the church, then this means that there are always ecclesial voices out-side the given nation-state which provide a differing reading of that na-tion's "just cause," or "just war." It is easier for Christians from other na-tions to unmask the pretensions of a given nation-state than for the Christians who are part of that respective nation![14] It is not socialism which failed as the first international movement, it is the church which failed and continues to fail as a transnational community. Do we regard the question whether the body of Christ or the nation-state has the prior claim on us and our solidarity as a legitimate and pressing question? If we do, then the just war tradition (and selective conscientious objection) becomes the test case for how we answer this question. If we regard it as a repulsive alternative since it creates a tension between two realities which belong inherently to-gether, it only shows the power of the nation-state's construal of reality in the minds of post-Reformation, i.e., modern, Christians. The Lutheran de-velopment of Romans 13 into an isolated metaphysics of the state in direct immediacy to God can be understood as our theological burnt offering in the nineteenth and early twentieth centuries to the "myth of the state." A serious reclaiming of the just war tradition involves nothing else than a

---

terial Reformers," *History of European Ideas* 9 (1988): 1-23, for an excellent discussion of this "forgotten," yet crucial aspect in the Reformation tradition. Yoder summarizes his detailed his-torical discussion with the following conclusion (20-21):

> Before the Reformation, the just war tradition was an inchoate body of distinctions and rules of thumb whereby confessors, canon lawyers and moralists hoped to restrain war, once it was clear (since the Constantinian establishment) that they could not forbid it. The intent to restrain was sincere. It could issue in penitential disciplines. For the early Martin Luther it could (hypothetically) demand selective conscientious objection.
>
> *After* the Reformation, the ordinary meaning of the mention of the "just war" in the creeds, to the ordinary Protestant, clerical or lay, was the opposite. War is all right. Those who reject it are condemned by name. The sovereign who sends his subjects to war is *prima facie* trustworthy as a judge of cause and means. The way is open for citizen-soldiers and for uncritical Protestant patriotism. There should be no surprise that the first strong modern objections to total war in the light of the just war tradition should have come from Roman Catholics.

14. This is the reason why in the 1930s for Dietrich Bonhoeffer the ecumenical context was so crucial for his peace activities! Yet he remained a lonely voice in the desert. Had the theo-logians in Germany not been so overly parochial and in complete identification with their own nation, but had instead acknowledged the primary bond of the Church as gathered from all na-tions, there might have taken place another development in the German churches during the 1930s. Had the Christians in all nations before World War I been more connected with each other than with their respective nation-states, World War I might not have received the relent-less Christian backing and justification as it did from all sides.

theological rereading of the modern nation-states since the Reformation, their wars (including the Revolutionary War!), and their imperialistic conquests of North and South America, Africa,[15] and parts of Asia, which was too often backed by the motive of spreading "Christianity" — a justification which was always unacceptable for the just war tradition![16]

As John H. Yoder has reminded us, the just war tradition — if it works — should be discriminatory from the outset between wars to be fought and

15. For a fascinating account of the way in which a Social Darwinistic racism and the technology of the machine gun were the two core factors in the nineteenth-century conquest of Africa by European imperialist nation-states, see John Ellis, *The Social History of the Machine Gun* (London: The Cresset Library, 1975), 79-110: "Making the Map Red." This account witnesses indirectly to the total eclipse of the Christian just war tradition in the nineteenth-century's pervasive ideological climate of Social Darwinistic imperialism among so-called "Christian" nation-states. The imperialistic modern nation-state does not have any interest in administering the just war tradition justly because the latter completely undercuts that nation's "missionary" outreach to include other nations in the overarching "peace" or "order" of its empire. Thus, for example, the U.S. occupation of the Philippines, Cuba, and Puerto Rico after the Spanish-American War was a clear form of expansionism covered by "manifest destiny," yet completely unjustifiable from the perspective of the just war tradition. Protestant denominations which were themselves captives of the nationalistic "mission of America" were, of course, utterly unable to witness to the just war tradition over against the government's expansionist policy. See Roger G. Betsworth, *Social Ethics: An Examination of American Moral Traditions*, (Louisville: Westminster/John Knox, 1990), 107-37 ("The Mission of America"), for a very accessible account of the ideological forces which undermined the just war tradition in the American context.

16. A difference of religion is not a legitimate cause in the just war tradition! In other words, a "crusade" is not a justifiable war. For the clear distinction between "crusade" and the *iure bellare* in the sixteenth century see especially Martin Luther, "On the War against the Turk" (1529), in *Luther's Works*, vol. 46, pp. 161ff., and Francesco de Vitoria OP (1480-1546), *De Indiis et de Iure Belli Reflectiones*, trans. J. P. Bate, in J. B. Scott, ed., *Classics of International Law* (1944). The eclipse of this crucial insight took place in the religious wars of the sixteenth and seventeenth centuries in Europe. As John H. Yoder put it: "Just at a time when Catholic tradition had begun to disentangle the no-holds-barred crusade from the civilly justifiable but also restrainable war, internecine confessional battles repatriated to Christendom the reality of the crusade, without the name. Half of the middle of Europe was destroyed in the name of God. . . . In the seventeenth century, European Christians fought European Christians about whether to have a Roman Catholic priest or a Lutheran pastor in each parish. Religion itself, i.e., doctrine and ritual, the fine points of sacramental theology, is what they fought about; not simply that there were two different religions behind the battle and that the battles were religiously motivated. The 'infidel' was one's own cousin across the next river" ("The Reception of the Just War Tradition by the Magisterial Reformers," 17). The early Reformation principle *"sine vi, sed verbo"* (without force, but through the word) was forgotten, and the defense of ultimate truth through warfare became a possibility again. The eclipse of the distinction between "crusade" and the just war tradition marks the beginning of modern ideological warfare in an increasingly post-Christian world.

those to be rejected.[17] If we say "just war tradition" we say willy-nilly also "selective conscientious objection." If we are not willing to subscribe to the latter, we are not really talking about the just war tradition. In other words, selective conscientious objection is a logical implication of the just war tradition, and it should have been applied from time to time if we assume that some of the wars around the world Lutherans (and other Christians, of course) were and are involved in were and are unjust wars. I do not know of any collective case in which Lutheran Churches even attempted something like a collective selective conscientious objection or openly supported selective conscientious objection in response to the state's waging an unjust war. Yet it is only selective conscientious objection which makes the just war tradition a justifiable concept, because it provides a discriminatory device to place the burden of proof on those in the Christian community who advocate for the need of warfare in a particular case.

Thus, if selective conscientious objection is the decisive test for how seriously Lutherans have taken the just war tradition, we have utterly failed. To rebut pacifists with the remark that we are bound by our confessional heritage to the just war tradition can only be understood as either hypocrisy or as just another element of our presently pervasive historical amnesia.

An additional delicacy is that selective conscientious objection is not a constitutionally guaranteed right of each citizen. Thus, as Charles Lutz has rightly pointed out,[18] the Lutheran dilemma is either to take the just war tradi-

---

17. Cf. Yoder, *When War Is Unjust*, 70-79.

18. Cf. Charles P. Lutz, *Conscription and Conscience: Ethical Dilemma for Lutherans*, 3-10. For a thorough discussion of the constitutional and legal implications of selective conscientious objection, see John A. Rohr, *Prophets Without Honor: Public Policy and the Selective Conscientious Objector* (Nashville: Abingdon Press, 1971), esp. 17-99. This study is a very valuable discussion of the whole issue from public policy and the legislator's perspective. In addition, it discusses individual cases of importance. Yet its strength is also its decisive weakness, since Rohr seems to suggest with his whole approach that a discussion of selective conscientious objection is possible without its embeddedness in a comprehensive and living just war tradition which is itself located in a theological and Church-related discourse. Rohr's construal only knows two central realities, the individual selective objector with his or her individual conscience on the one side and a liberal legislation/public community on the other side. While this is a legitimate self-construal of liberalism it is a theologically problematic one because of its complete lack of reflection upon the primary importance of God's call and claim on us and the related centrality of the Church in the light of whose constitutive narrative the Christian person, including her/ his conscience, and the "world" are construed. In other words, it is of decisive importance whether selective conscientious objection is construed as a right, a privilege, or an impossibility in the context of a liberal constitution or whether it is construed as a potential and always present ingredient of the Christian just war tradition. The two construals do not necessarily have to be in conflict with each other, yet it is crucial to remember that decisions in the constitutionality

tion seriously in all of its implications and therefore to subscribe fully to selective conscientious objection and thereby support a position that is in potential conflict with the existing law, or to operate from the outset within the present legal framework. The second option would force us either to submit to the administration's judgments about the given nature of any war (and I am still waiting for that government in the world which declares its own present activities as unjust) or to become part of the Christian pacifist witness that on theological grounds rejects participation in *all* warfare in principle, and who are not eligible for draft. So the choice we have to face as Lutherans in the United States of America is either to support a presently illegal option or to drop even our official adherence to the just war tradition and openly declare what many already do, namely either our adherence to national-interest warfare or to Christian pacifism.

If there is any way to rescue the just war tradition in its originally intended sense, then it has to be radically reclaimed by the church's magisterial teaching and has to become an inherent part of the catechetical instruction on the congregational level, and then a part of the moral formation of all of us in our Christian vocation. In other words, the real test for our seriousness about the just war tradition will be selective conscientious objection. Only if we support selective conscientious objection publicly, provide support structures for it, and count on the possibility that we may have to follow that path are we starting to take the just war tradition seriously again. Only if the congregation were the training ground for Christian citizenship and its peculiar character would there be a concrete practice-context in which the just war tradition could make sense. Outside of the ecclesial practice-context the just war tradition is nothing less than a dangerous remnant of a Christian past which only can be misused for propaganda purposes camouflaging the state's real interests.[19] In other words, by superficially and half-heartedly subscribing to the just war tradition Lutherans do nothing else than, in fact, support national-interest warfare fueled by the emotions of a nationalistic crusade mentality. Yet according to the just war tradition this is utterly unacceptable: to condone war in principle as a "tragic" yet always unavoidable means for the good end of collective self-interest or "national security" according to the jargon of the modern nation-state.

In this respect, it is of crucial importance to understand clearly what we mean when we claim that a war is "justifiable." One meaning belongs to the

---

and legality of selective conscientious objection do not at all effect selective conscientious objection as an integral element of the just war tradition.

19. For a penetrating analysis and critique of this kind of use of the just war concept, see Hauerwas, "Whose 'Just' War? Which Peace?", 83-105.

very core of the just war tradition, the other meaning has recoined the term to make it suitable for usage in the context of national-interest warfare. John H. Yoder has given a succinct description of a "justifiable war" in the sense of the just war tradition: "The concept is never that war is an act of positive righteousness or a duty: it is rather a lesser evil, for which a case can be made under defined circumstances."[20] In other words, when it can be demonstrated by appealing to the central criteria of the just war tradition that it is the lesser evil, then warfare is "justified." It is exactly nothing else than an exceptionally justified last resort for defending the neighbor for the neighbor's sake.[21] This concept of justifiability has been the meaning of "just war" throughout this essay.

Yet there is a decisively different understanding of "justifiable" war, which presently enjoys a high currency. This "realist" argument runs the following way: While wars in cases of last resort may be necessary, and in that sense "justifiable," no war can, of course, be ever "just" in the strict sense due to the very nature of warfare as such. War might, at certain times, be a tragic necessity, and it is better to get it over with quickly by winning it with the highest accessible use of military force than to prolong it unnecessarily. While this understanding attempts to mitigate the inherent cruelty of any form of warfare, which can never be an unqualified implementation of "justice," it has a decisive weakness. This is the fact that it is utterly vulnerable to any claims of "military necessity" or other utilitarian rationales based on military or national self-interest. According to this logic of "justifiable war," the bombings of Hiroshima and Nagasaki and the counterbombing of German cities during World War II,[22] the use

20. Yoder, "The Reception of the Just War Tradition by the Magisterial Reformation," 21.

21. Warfare under all the conditions of the just war tradition in its earlier period never meant that it was an inherently good practice, an inherently good aspect of the Christian vocation. Rather, according to Augustine, Christians who participated in a "justified" war had to go through a process of repentance which included being barred from participating in the Eucharist for a limited time span. It is only with the Reformation that soldiering is accepted as an inherently unproblematic profession. It seems that the just war tradition was decisively weakened with the loss of unity in the Western Church. In addition, the fact that most of the curses focused on God, Heaven, Christ, the Cross, and the Sacraments can be traced to the soldiery of the post-Reformation wars, especially to the Thirty Years War, which not only devastated Central Europe but also the credibility of Christianity in its very core, should give us Lutherans some food for reflection in light of our relatively uncritical acceptance of soldiering as a normal aspect of the Christian vocation! For a more detailed historical account see Yoder, "The Reception of the Just War Tradition by the Magisterial Reformers," especially 9-18.

22. On this question see the very interesting article by Stephen E. Lammers, "William Temple and the Bombing of Germany: An Exploration in the Just War Tradition," *Journal of Religious Ethics* 19 (Spring 1991): 71-92.

of napalm, Agent Orange, and the bombings of Laos and North Vietnam during the Vietnam War, and the counter-city targeting during the Cold War were legitimate measures since they were called for by "military necessity."[23] This understanding of "justifiable war" has become the substitute for the Christian just war tradition and broadly governs the considerations of warfare among modern nation-states. Selective conscientious objection is an alien concept for this utilitarian reasoning about warfare.

Selective conscientious objection presupposes a community of moral formation and deliberation in which the just war tradition is alive and a matter of ongoing discussion and refinement. Only in the context of communities of moral deliberation and formation can we reclaim the just war tradition and its inherent principle of selective conscientious objection. This could provide the context in which we could remember that the denunciation of unjust wars is an inherent element of the truth-telling mandate of proclaiming God's Word!

Should this prove to be impossible for a variety of good or bad reasons, Lutherans and other "mainline" churches will have nothing convincing with which to respond to the ongoing witness of Christian pacifism as presented to us by Mennonites, the Church of the Brethren, the Amish, Hutterites, Quakers, and other Christian communities as, for example, the Catholic Worker and the Lutheran Peace Fellowship, for whom nonviolence is an inherent aspect of the Christian's vocation. If it should be the case that the Christian just war tradition has in effect disintegrated in the religious wars in the post-Reformation era and has become increasingly meaningless with the rise of imperialistic modern nation-states and their expectation of all citizens to submit unqualified support in the case of war, pacifism as an essential aspect of the Christian vocation in the old aeon seems to be the only alternative to maintain the original intention of the just war tradition.[24] In other words, we are faced with the alternative either to make selective conscientious objection a workable and viable reality in our churches or to become Christian pacifists. These seem to be the only alterna-

23. In the terminology of the just war tradition the aspect of *ius ad bellum*, the criteria for the justifiability of war, is maintained and the *ius in bello* has been given up in light of the "military necessities" of modern warfare. Paul Ramsey's stressing of the immunity of noncombatants as a crucial and integral aspect of the just war tradition was aimed at overcoming this decisive weakness at the core of the Niebuhrian notion of "justifiable" warfare. By vigorously reinstating the whole concept of *ius in bello* Ramsey overcame the most problematic aspect in the concept of "justifiable" warfare. Cf. Paul Ramsey, *War and the Christian Conscience* (Durham, NC: Duke University Press, 1961), esp. 34-59 and 171-91.

24. It is no accident that the just war tradition appears in Yoder's *Nevertheless: Varieties of Religious Pacifism* (Scottdale, PA: Herald Press, 1992) under the heading "The Pacifism of the Honest Study of Cases," 22-28.

tives faithful to the peace mandate of the Christian vocation as expressed over a millennium in the just war tradition.

A reclaiming of the just war tradition would, of course, also have to imply a critical analysis and challenge of at least three crucial issues. The first one is the presently illegal nature of selective conscientious objection in a nation-state that supposedly subscribes publicly to the just war tradition.

The second and at least equally important issue is the nature of a professionalized military, a "standing army" primarily made up of the nation's poor and marginalized minorities whose "free service" is only a disguise of economic necessities forcing an underclass and lower middle class into a profession that serves in the long run only the economic interests of those who will never have to serve themselves because of vastly superior economic opportunities.[25]

Thirdly, if it is true that the just war tradition has been co-opted by the modern nation-state and serves as a camouflage of national-interest wars, then the institution of military chaplaincy has become highly questionable. Only if chaplains could be a truly independent presence in the military free to call a spade a spade, free to counsel, free to support pastorally and theologically selective conscientious objectors, and free to witness rigorously to the church's just war tradition could it be a credible institution. Yet in modern highly professionalized military machines chaplains are as much part of the "green machine," the killing machine, as any other support personnel. Military chaplaincy as presently practiced in modern armies in the Western world primarily serves the interests of the military, namely to stabilize spiritually and psychologically and support those who are involved in the frightening reality of killing and getting killed. While there are good reasons for the church not to leave Christians alone in this awful reality, the structural institution of military chaplaincy only suggests an uncritical condoning of modern warfare by the church and ultimately by God to whom we are called to witness.[26]

25. For a fascinating account of one of the "invisible" aspects of the Vietnam War in this regard, see Wallace Terry *Bloods: An Oral History of the Vietnam War by Black Veterans* (New York: Ballantine Books, 1984).

26. See especially the chapter "God and the Chaplains" in William P. Mahedy's outstanding book *Out of the Night: The Spiritual Journey of Vietnam Vets* (New York: Ballantine Books, 1986), 111-17. Mahedy, who had been a chaplain in Vietnam during the Vietnam war, says: "Symbols speak loudly: while the chaplain wears his religious insignia on the left collar of his battle dress, he displays on his right shoulder the insignia of military rank. He is an officer in the army, navy, or air force. He is, like the soldiers themselves and their military commanders, an integral part of the 'green machine,' the army. He is seen as inseparable from the basic function of the green machine, which is killing" (112). "I believe the essential failure of the chaplaincy in

These comments might not give us an easy perspective in the present context but they should at least continue a good tradition which Martin Luther has initiated for us, namely to examine the true just war criteria rigorously and truthfully. Either we begin to be honest with just war thinking by again seriously attending to *all* the implications of the just war tradition, or we should begin to consider that Christian pacifists have something essential to teach us about the Christian vocation in a world of competing nation-states![27]

Vietnam was its inability to name the reality for what it was. We should first have called it sin, admitted that we were in a morally ambiguous and religiously tenuous situation, and then gone on to deal with the harsh reality of the soldier's life. I do not believe that a Christian chaplain can legitimately go beyond the toleration of killing in immediate self-defense. He errs if he tries in any way beyond that to supply religious motivation for the soldier to 'carry on the struggle'" (114). In the context of any modern war, this admirable understanding of Christian chaplaincy in the military would be unacceptable from the military's side since it would constantly undermine the military's alternative narrative of "military necessity," which is essential for justifying the killing of human beings on a massive scale.

27. I am indebted to Bonnie Block, Michael G. Cartwright, Lowell O. Erdahl, George Forell, Nancy Heitzenrater Hütter, and especially John H. Yoder for reading and commenting on an earlier draft of this essay.

From Police Officers to Peace Officers

Tobias Winright

Quis custodiet ipsos custodes . . . ?

Juvenal[1]

Introduction

In his biography of the pacifist Leo Tolstoy, Ernest J. Simmons relates a humorous story about a response that Tolstoy gave to a question regarding the possible inconsistency of those Russian Revolutionists and Social Democrats who, on the one hand, detested violence, but, on the other hand, advocated its use against opponents to the revolution. Because the inquirer's sympathies lay with the revolutionists rather than the Russian secret police, he asked, "Is there not a difference between the killing that a revolutionist does and that which a policeman does?" In reply, however, Tolstoy tersely opined, "There is as much difference as between cat-shit and dog-shit. But I don't like the smell of either one or the other."[2]

I can imagine Tolstoy, were he living in the United States today, giving a similarly critical evaluation of police violence. Indeed, several highly publicized cases involving excessive force by police in recent years promptly come to mind. The well-known Rodney King case is one example. While driving on the eve-

1. Juvenal, *Sixteen Satires*, trans. Steven Robinson (Manchester, U.K.: Carcanet New Press, 1983), satire 6, lines 31-32, p. 122: "But who will keep guard on the guardians . . . ?"

2. Ernest J. Simmons, *Leo Tolstoy* (Boston: Little, Brown and Company, 1946), 651. I am grateful to Lee Camp for bringing this story to my attention.

ning of March 3, 1991, this African-American male was pulled over and confronted by Los Angeles police officers, who proceeded to arrest him on a number of charges. On the surface this sort of incident occurs frequently and could have been reported as a routine traffic arrest, except for the additional fact that it was filmed by a bystander with a video camera. All who saw the replays on the network news watched fifteen uniformed officers repeatedly bludgeon, bruise, and lacerate King. Although shocking to the consciences of the American public, one criminal justice expert has observed: "That beating was not unique in the history of policing. It probably has kin in every state in the Union, in every country, and indeed in every significant police force as far back as we can trace the police function."[3]

Another example is the bombing of the radical African-American group, MOVE, by Philadelphia police in 1985. Founded in the early 1970s, members of MOVE adopted the surname "Africa," advocated animal rights, opposed technology, and communally lived together, usually in friction with neighbors and police. When a shoot-out occurred in 1978 with the Philadelphia police, the result was one officer's death and the imprisonment of several MOVE members. Relocating in another house, the remaining members installed loudspeakers outside that they used to demand the reopening of their fellow members' legal cases. When neighbors complained about the noise, trash, and evidence of weapons, the Philadelphia police decided to take action. On May 13, 1985, five hundred heavily armed police officers surrounded the house, demanding the surrender of four members on charges including harassment, rioting, and possessing explosives. A ninety-minute gun battle ensued that ended in stalemate. Thereupon, the police resorted to dropping a bomb on MOVE's house. It ignited a tremendous fire, however, that quickly consumed the building. The blaze, that the police allowed to burn, ultimately engulfed and destroyed sixty-one other houses in the neighborhood and killed eleven MOVE members, including six adults and five children.[4]

Other recent examples of excessive use of force by law enforcement include the beating of illegal Mexican aliens by deputies in California (videotaped by a news helicopter), the ATF and FBI assault on the Branch Davidians at Waco, and the 1992 FBI shooting of Vicki Weaver, using rewritten rules of engagement, deviating from standard operating procedure, ordering "shoot to kill" at Ruby Ridge. In fact, researchers estimate that police officers kill approxi-

3. Michael Davis, "Do Cops Really Need a Code of Ethics?" *Criminal Justice Ethics* 10 (Summer/Fall 1991): 14.
4. Robin Wagner-Pacifici, *Discourse and Destruction: The City of Philadelphia v. MOVE* (Chicago: University of Chicago Press, 1994).

mately six hundred criminal suspects annually, shoot and wound an additional twelve hundred, and fire at and miss another eighteen hundred.[5] Considering the prevalence of violence in American culture, and given the rote adoption of the "war" or "crimefighting" paradigm for law enforcement, similar incidents continue to be likely.

One need not be a Tolstoyan pacifist, however, in order to criticize such instances of police violence. Most of the scholarly literature pertaining to the topic of police use of force addresses the matter from one of a variety of disciplines: criminology, political science, sociology, or philosophy. One of the first scholars to philosophically scrutinize police use of force, criminal justice expert Lawrence Sherman, suggests that, on the one hand, many issues in police ethics are "in fact clear-cut, and hold little room for serious philosophical analysis," while on the other hand, the use of force deserves sober study since it is "very complex, with many shades of gray."[6] Getting to the crux of the matter, Sherman claims, "The most basic question of all criminal justice ethics, of course, is whether and under what conditions one can reconcile doing harm to others with our widespread norms against harm." In passing, he muses that the literature on pacifism, nonviolence, and conscientious objection may be relevant, but adds that he has unfortunately not seen such an approach applied to the domestic use of force by police. So, sincerely curious, he forthrightly asks: "Can a pacifist be a police officer or a judge? Can a Christian? Can a Rawlsian? What is the ethical defense for saying that killing is wrong and then urging killing in response to killing?"[7]

5. Irene Prior Loftus et al., "The 'Reasonable' Approach to Excessive Force Cases Under Section 1983," *Notre Dame Law Review* 64 (1989): 136. See also William A. Geller, "Officer Restraint in the Use of Deadly Force: The Next Frontier in Police Shooting Research," *Journal of Police Science* 13 (1985): 153-71; and "Police and Deadly Force: A Look at the Empirical Literature," in *Moral Issues in Police Work*, ed. Frederick A. Elliston and Michael Feldberg (Totowa, NJ: Rowman and Allanheld, 1985), 197-235. A more recent survey and analysis of the empirical studies on "appropriate force and inappropriate force" is provided by Kenneth Adams, "Measuring the Prevalence of Abuse of Force," in *Police Violence: Understanding and Controlling Police Abuse of Force*, ed. William A. Geller and Hans Toch (New Haven and London: Yale University Press, 1996), 52-93. According to Adams, the data indicate that six percent of arrests involve the use of force by police, although observational research suggests that it occurs at least twice as often as official use-of-force reports indicate (61-62).

6. Lawrence Sherman, "Learning Police Ethics," *Criminal Justice Ethics* 1 (1982): 19.

7. Lawrence Sherman, *Ethics in Criminal Justice Education* (New York: The Hasting Center, 1982), 38. Cf. Geller, "Officer Restraint in the Use of Deadly Force: The Next Frontier," 160, where he similarly asks, "What is the bearing of an officer's personal moral code concerning when and whom it is proper to shoot on his or her actual use of deadly force? Insight into this question . . . will be useful in anticipating the extent to which administrative policy and training can effectively override — or harness — individual officer predilections."

In what follows, I shall treat Sherman's question about "the ethical defense for saying that killing is wrong and then urging killing in response to killing," which he addresses specifically to the three groups (i.e., pacifists, Christians, Rawlsians), though my investigation will proceed in reverse order. Most of my attention, however, will focus on the question about whether a pacifist can be a police officer, for as Lisa Cahill has observed with a hint of curiosity: "Pacifists generally are opposed not only to war, but to any form of direct physical violence, although they may make exceptions to this bias by permitting police action."[8] In view of this, J. Philip Wogaman suggests that pacifists' mere *acceptance* of — in addition to the issue of possible *participation* in — police actions, including violence, in order to maintain the state may "in one sense . . . be equivocation."[9] Therefore, in the pacifist section I shall survey the various pacifist responses that might lead Wogaman to draw such a conclusion. Finally, because the subject of policing was of much interest to my teacher, John Howard Yoder, I shall attempt to offer a Christian pacifist perspective on police use of force, drawing and building on the few, brief reflections he wrote on the subject.[10]

Can a Rawlsian Be a Police Officer?

The so-called Rawlsians, for their part, have not been reluctant to offer their views, in response to Sherman's question, on this issue. Indeed, almost every contribution in the public debate, although not always self-identified as "Rawlsian," arises from a social contractarian perspective. This is probably the case due to the fact that policing, as we know it, is a modern institution that coincided with the rise of the liberal democratic nation-state.

8. Lisa Sowle Cahill, *Love Your Enemies: Discipleship, Pacifism, and Just War Theory* (Minneapolis: Fortress, 1994), 2.

9. J. Philip Wogaman, *Christian Ethics: A Historical Introduction* (Louisville: Westminster/John Knox Press, 1993), 280.

10. As for Yoder's interest in this subject, the last memo that I received from him, dated 24 December 1997, was a three-page critique of a local police department for a coerced confession that it conducted, which was videotaped and later featured on the NBC news program *Dateline.* Yoder suggested that I give "further visibility" to this event in a "police ethics periodical . . . for some moral pressure on local police." One of the reasons why he directed this memo, and others like it, to me is that some members of my family — including my mother — and I have previous experience in the field of law enforcement, with personal stories that Yoder often enjoyed discussing. As for why I say "attempt to offer a Christian pacifist perspective," I must confess that I, myself, am not currently a pacifist, although Yoder's life and work has influenced me tremendously.

Though *functional* origins may be traced to ancient communal self-policing, modern policing began *institutionally* at the urging of Sir Robert Peel in 1829 with the "New Police" of Metropolitan London. Due to increasing crime and riots, against which the earlier, decentralized constables were ineffective and the military was excessively forceful, Peel organized the first modern police department, in which policing came to be understood as "a distinctive career, with a specific ideology of service, professional identity and craft skills. . . ."[11] Indeed, Peel intended to distinguish police officers from soldiers, but ended up appropriating heavily from the military organizational model in order to convince critics that his New Police would perform its duties as impeccably as the British military. Nevertheless, the New Police differed from the military in that the police did not carry swords and firearms, though they did sometimes have truncheons. To be sure, opposition to an established police department existed, but it was based on the anxiety that the New Police would serve as a political puppet and tool of the upper class.[12] Over the span of the next century, however, the Metropolitan Police gradually gained widespread acceptance.

The transplanting of the police onto American soil began similarly. In 1834, Boston policemen were also unarmed and "restrained from committing brutal acts by the prior warning of their superiors, by their own good judgment, and by fear of physical retaliation."[13] But even at this stage, as an unarmed force, police in the United States aroused misgivings among the people, many of whom labeled these departments as "un-American," "undemocratic," and "militaristic."[14] Such accusations were aggravated as the police began wearing uniforms and often obtained their jobs through a spoils systems for supporting certain politicians. For these reasons, the American people perceived police as a threat to their personal liberties.

The supposedly "un-American" police soon diverged from the British

11. Robert Reiner, *The Politics of the Police,* 2nd ed. (Toronto: University of Toronto Press, 1992), 45. This historical sketch draws from Reiner, who provides a balanced account of both "orthodox" and "revisionist" interpretations of the rise and development of modern policing; see especially pp. 9-51.

12. Reiner, *Politics of the Police,* 16-17. Cf. George Berkley, *The Democratic Policeman* (Boston: Beacon Press, 1969), 5. Interestingly, no reference is made of any church or theological reaction, except for a brief mention by Steve Uglow that Quakers and working classes initially opposed police forces. He does not delve into the Quaker criticism however. See *Policing Liberal Society* (New York: Oxford University Press, 1988), 15.

13. Roger Lane, *Policing the City: Boston 1822-1885* (Cambridge, MA: Harvard University Press, 1967), 187.

14. Berkley, *Democratic Policeman,* 5. Cf. Raymond B. Fosdick, *American Police Systems* (New York: The Century Co., 1920), 70-71.

model, however, and became distinctively American with the use of firearms to enforce the law. Police in increasingly violent American cities began carrying revolvers in the 1850s for their own protection after criminals began using firearms. And after the Civil War, the availability of thousands of army revolvers on the surplus market hastened the widespread rearmament of the general society, resulting in official acceptance of police use of revolvers.[15] The Boston police, for instance, acquired firearms in the aftermath of the Draft Riot of 1863. Roger Lane suggests that, as a result, "the fact that most policemen carried their revolvers tipped the physical balance in their favor, making them more formidable but also increasing the danger of brutality on their part."[16] Obviously, the American version of Peel's vision has experienced over the years more police violence, probably due to "some combination of American social and historical forces [which have] blended with the military model to produce a volatile mix."[17]

Given that policing as we know it developed in Western liberal democracies, I suspect it should be no surprise that most philosophers and criminologists who address the subject — and in particular the use of force — turn to social contract theory. Jeffrey Reiman, for example, draws from classical social contract thinkers in order to construct an ethical approach to police use of force which emphasizes individual rights, personal freedom, and government through consent.[18] According to this view, since the problem of some hypothetical "state of nature" is that "everyone's freedom to use force at his [or her] own discretion undermines everyone else's freedom to work and live as he [or she] wishes, it becomes rational for freedom-loving people to renounce their freedom to use force at their own discretion . . . if (and only to the extent that) the sacrifice of this freedom results in a gain in real and secure freedom to live as one wants."[19] In other words, instead of the insecurity of some "state of nature," in which each person must protect his or her own interests, and in which there is a danger of unlimited coercion, citizens in the social contract consent to

15. Lawrence Sherman, "Execution Without Trial: Police Homicide and the Constitution," in *Police Deviance*, ed. Thomas Barker and David L. Carter (Cincinnati: Pilgrimage, 1986), 190.

16. Lane, *Policing the City*, 187-88.

17. Jerome H. Skolnick and James J. Fyfe, *Above the Law: Police and the Excessive Use of Force* (New York: The Free Press, 1993), 128.

18. Jeffrey H. Reiman, "The Social Contract and the Police Use of Deadly Force," in *Moral Issues in Police Work*, ed. Frederick A. Elliston and Michael Feldberg (Totowa, NJ: Rowman and Allanheld, 1985); Reiman relies on John Locke's *Second Treatise of Government*, Thomas Hobbes's *Leviathan*, Jean-Jacques Rousseau's *The Social Contract*, and John Rawls's *A Theory of Justice*.

19. Reiman, "Social Contract," 239.

an exchange of some of their freedoms to a civil government authorized to have the power to protect their fundamental rights. The institution of law enforcement is a manifestation of government authority and power, functioning as an executor of the legislative will. At the same time, however, the right to use force, which is deposited in the police, according to this social contract perspective is not without limits.

Indeed, for liberalism there remains a normative cutting edge that hinges on "whether renouncing a private use of force and allowing a public agency to enforce this renunciation results in greater concrete freedom for everyone."[20] The liberal emphasis on freedom thus provides a general guide with which to distinguish between legitimate and illegitimate exercises of power. That is, coercive action by police that restricts or endangers citizen freedom, instead of securing and broadening it, undermines the authority of the police by reproducing the conditions of the state of nature that the police are supposed to remedy. Accordingly, Steve Uglow interprets Peel's careful organization of the police in contradistinction from the military as seeking to abide by the prohibition on the arbitrary use of physical force by the state, a core concept within liberalism, with its view that the rights of the person are inalienable over and against state coercion. In addition, Uglow writes:

> The capacity to use force crystallizes the relationship between individual and state, defining the measure of control that citizens are granted over their own lives. . . . The guiding principle developed within liberal societies has been that such force must be *essential* and *minimum*. The former implies that state violence is a tactic of last resort, the latter that the violence must be no more than is needed to prevent the anticipated harm.[21]

Social contractarians, therefore, usually limit police use of force, first, to self-defense (private citizens actually retain this right in the absence of a police officer) and, second, to protect the lives of private citizens. Until recently, this approach justified police use of force, including lethal force, to protect property or to stop a fleeing felon who may or may not have posed a physical threat. It seems to me, however, that the social contract approach does not necessarily rule out these latter possibilities.

To be sure, this philosophical perspective regards coercive power as the *raison d'être* of policing. As Vance McLaughlin puts it, "[Police] routinely use force to carry out their role as enforcers — the use of force is inherent in the

20. Reiman, "Social Contract," 240.
21. Uglow, *Policing Liberal Society*, 53, 12; cf. Reiman, "Social Contract," 237-38, 240-43; Berkley, *Democratic Policeman*, 2-4, 107-9.

profession. . . ."[22] Although they are supposed to minimize the use of force, police nevertheless are referred to by Reiner as "specialists in coercion."[23] This is why philosopher John Kleinig observes — I think rightly — that the predominant paradigm for policing associated with a liberal contractarian approach is the "crimefighter" or "war" model. As he puts it, "Classical social contract theory perceives such a role for police. Just as an army is needed to protect us from the barbarian without, a police force is required to protect us from the barbarian within."[24] Yet, although Kleinig acknowledges that "any model of policing that fails to take into account their authority to employ force will be inadequate," he correctly argues that there are "serious practical and moral problems" with the crimefighter model. Quite simply, it encourages an "us" versus "them" mentality, in which the police view their role punitively, so that they are inclined to be cynical in their attitudes toward the public and treat suspects as though they are guilty criminals. More problematic, most police officers *like* to see themselves as crimefighters, even though their actual work is diversified, with such activities as helping injured accident victims, searching for lost children, calming quarreling spouses, or coaching a youth basketball team. Kleinig, therefore, believes that the crimefighter model "runs a risk of excess." And ethical perspectives on the use of force that are based on social contract theory, he suggests, are too minimalistic and attenuated to rein in this model.

Can a Christian Be a Police Officer?

In spite of Sherman's query to Christians, their voice is conspicuously absent in the public discussion regarding police use of force.[25] To be sure, this omis-

---

22. Vance McLaughlin, *Police and the Use of Force: The Savannah Study* (Westport, CT: Praeger, 1992), 1.

23. Reiner, *Politics of the Police*, 2, 59-60.

24. John Kleinig, *The Ethics of Policing* (New York: Cambridge University Press, 1996), 24-25.

25. The lack of a Christian or theological contribution to the debate is evident in a recent collection of essays edited by William A. Geller and Hans Toch, who observe that the book's contributors all share a common concern about this controversial subject even while representing "many diverse perspectives." See *Police Violence: Understanding and Controlling Police Abuse of Force* (New Haven and London: Yale University Press, 1996), viii. This volume contains mostly social science contributions which — although representing a variety of disciplines and genuinely aiming to help police avert or at least mitigate their use of force — continue to presuppose, philosophically and politically, a liberal democratic or social contractarian perspective. See the essays by David H. Bayley, "Police Brutality Abroad," 273-91; William A. Geller and Hans Toch, "Understanding and Controlling Police Abuse of Force," 292-328.

sion may be attributed to the fact that the question of the use of force by law enforcement officers has basically been a lacuna in the literature of Christian social ethics. This state of affairs is curious given the long and rich history of Christian theological reflection on violence. As Lisa Cahill observes, "The challenge to decide about violence, especially state-supported and institutionally perpetuated violence, has been with Christians from the beginning."[26] More incisively, Stanley Hauerwas claims that "the question of violence is the central issue for any Christian social ethic."[27] And yet, while much theological attention has been given to whether or how Christians should participate in international conflicts and warfare, Edward Malloy accurately perceives "a noticeable deficiency in applying such analysis to the domestic context of crime" and police use of force in response to it.[28] Again, this is interesting given that many law enforcement officers are also Christians, who presumably struggle on a regular basis with the issue of violence or force.[29] Of course, Sherman's questions about whether a Christian and whether a pacifist can be a police officer are not necessarily the same question. For not all Christians are pacifists.

One nonpacifist Christian ethicist who mentions at least in passing the use of force by police is Ralph Potter. In his book, *War and Moral Discourse*, Potter writes that the "mode of thinking" associated with the just war tradition pertains "to all situations in which the use of force must be contemplated. . . ."[30] Beginning with a "debt of love that Christians owe to their

26. Cahill, *Love Your Enemies*, ix.

27. Stanley Hauerwas, *The Peaceable Kingdom: A Primer in Christian Ethics* (Notre Dame: University of Notre Dame Press, 1983), 114.

28. Edward A. Malloy, *The Ethics of Law Enforcement and Criminal Punishment* (Lanham, MD: University Press of America, 1982), 2.

29. Anecdotal evidence of this daily struggle concerning violence and faith is provided in a book aimed at a popular audience and edited by Judith A. Kowalski and Dean J. Collins, *To Serve and Protect: Law Enforcement Officers Reflect on Their Faith and Work* (Minneapolis and Chicago: Augsburg/ACTA, 1992). Vividly etched in my memory is a question posed by a panelist during my own oral board interview within the application process: "Would your Christian faith hinder or prevent you from a performance of duty, such as shooting to kill an alleged perpetrator?" I was at a loss as to how to respond, for it seemed to me that scripture and church teaching may not directly apply to this question. Thus, I instinctively assumed that the basic logic of the church's just war teaching was analogous enough to the department's policies when I responded "no" to the question. But over the years the question haunted me.

30. Ralph B. Potter, *War and Moral Discourse* (Richmond: John Knox Press, 1973), 49-50. Interestingly, Paul Ramsey also touches on the subject of policing when he grounds his version of just war theory in the duty to love. As an illustration of this, he embellishes the story of the Good Samaritan from Luke 10:25-37, suggesting that it would have been better to prevent the violent robbery by having a police force on the road to Jericho. Indeed, Ramsey asks what would

neighbors," he identifies two claims that are at "opposite poles of the continuum of Christian attitudes toward war and violence."[31] At one end is the claim to "contend for justice" or "protect the innocent," and at the other end rests the claim "that we should not harm any neighbor." Both claims, Potter insists, must be held in tandem through the "framework" of the just war tradition. Because of the latter claim of nonmaleficence, there exists a "burden of proof" upon those who attempt to justify the use of force. In other words, there is a "strong presumption against the use of violence, a presumption established for the Christian by the nonresistant example of Jesus and for the rational non-Christian by prudent concern for order and mutual security."[32] This presumption may be overridden only by the other strong claim, namely, to do justice and protect the innocent against unjust aggressors. As an example, Potter appeals to the role of the police, "as servant[s] of the community," who "promise to risk [their] own life in defense of . . . any who need protection from unjust attack."[33] Thus, according to Potter, if a Memphis police officer had seen the rifle aimed at Martin Luther King, Jr., the claim to protect the innocent would have overridden the claim to do no harm, thereby obligating the officer to fire upon the assailant. Indeed, Potter is one of the few Christian ethicists who specifically addresses the role of police, calling on other Christian scholars to help officers, who "deserve counsel and instruction," to carefully "reflect upon the mode of reasoning appropriate to their office that would guide them in determining when they should act, how they should act, and why."[34]

The only other Christian ethicist, to my knowledge, who offers a fairly substantial treatment of police use of force is Edward Malloy, who, like Potter, writes from a just war perspective. The first chapter of his *The Ethics of Law Enforcement and Criminal Punishment* stands as one of the few theological

---

Jesus have made the Samaritan do "if he had come upon the scene while the robbers were still at their fell work?" Answer: act like a police officer. Whenever a choice must be made between "the perpetrator of injustice and the many victims of it," the latter are to be preferred out of Christian charity. See Paul Ramsey, *The Just War: Force and Political Responsibility* (New York: Charles Scribner's Sons, 1968), 142-43; *Basic Christian Ethics* (Louisville: Westminster/John Knox, 1950, 1993), 165, 169-71; *War and the Christian Conscience: How Shall Modern War Be Conducted Justly?* (Durham, NC: Duke, 1961), xvi-xvii. In contrast to Ramsey, Gordon Kaufman suggests that, whenever Cain is threatening to kill Abel, perhaps Cain is in greater need of redemptive love, which may be more important for Christians than protection of the innocent. See *The Context of Decision* (New York: Abingdon, 1961), 98, 105.

31. Potter, *War and Moral Discourse*, 53-54.
32. Potter, *War and Moral Discourse*, 61; see also 32.
33. Potter, *War and Moral Discourse*, 55-56.
34. Potter, *War and Moral Discourse*, 60.

treatments of the topic of police use of force that, although preliminary and brief, deals with this issue as a subject worthy of attention itself. Malloy writes:

> At the theoretical level, most ethical reflection about the problem of violence has centered on difficulties in personal relations or on the horror of warfare. In between these two extremes stands the role of the police in a contemporary setting.[35]

Thus homing in on the neglected role of police, Malloy recommends the just war tradition as a "helpful ethical framework for analysis." With it he conducts "an exercise of analogical interpretation" that he trusts "has not stretched the just war tradition too far," in which each criterion of the just war tradition is analyzed vis-à-vis guidelines for the use of force in policing, resulting in a coherent, restrained ethical grid for application in the latter context.[36] Malloy hopes that his "modest venture in a field which is ripe for interdisciplinary cooperation might encourage other Christian ethicists to grapple with this problem of the control of, and response to, domestic violence."[37]

The first criterion with which Malloy deals, therefore, is "legitimate authority," i.e., war may be waged only by a recognized government. Adapting this to the police context, the police officer may use coercive force only when he or she truly represents the body politic.[38] Though sworn to uphold the law, police possess an enormous amount of discretion and cannot always consult with a superior or make a decision in advance; in many cases, therefore, they are authorized under oath to determine on the spot when to use force. Yet, such authority is derivative and is thereby withdrawn when other

---

35. Malloy, *Ethics of Law Enforcement*, 10.

36. Malloy, *Ethics of Law Enforcement*, 24.

37. Malloy, *Ethics of Law Enforcement*, ix. Malloy initially considered the problem of police use of force in a paper, "Ethics and Police Intervention in Domestic Violence," that he presented at the 1979 annual meeting of the Society of Christian Ethics. See Edward LeRoy Long, Jr., *Academic Bonding and Social Concern: The Society of Christian Ethics 1959-1983* (Notre Dame: Religious Ethics Incorporated, 1984), 117. Other Christian ethicists, however, have not answered Malloy's (or Potter's) clarion call for contributions on this issue. For an updated expansion of Malloy's work, see Tobias L. Winright, "The Perpetrator as Person: Theological Reflections on the Just War Tradition and the Use of Force by Police," *Criminal Justice Ethics* 14 (Summer/Fall 1995): 37-56 (a version of my first paper for Professor Yoder). A fuller analysis of the historical, jurisprudential, philosophical, and theological treatments of the use of force in policing may be found in my dissertation, which is under the direction of Todd David Whitmore and currently in progress, "The Challenge of Policing: An Analysis in Christian Social Ethics" (Ph.D. diss., University of Notre Dame).

38. Malloy, *Ethics of Law Enforcement*, 12.

criteria for justifiable use of force are not satisfied. Criminologists Jerome Skolnick and James Fyfe corroborate this view: "[W]here police derive their authority from law and take an oath to support the Constitution they are obliged to acknowledge the law's moral force and to be constrained by it," and if an officer uses force in an inappropriate way, "he or she undermines the very source of police authority."[39]

Another criterion is that war may be fought only for a "just cause."[40] Because the object of the just war tradition, in Malloy's account, includes both vindicating justice and restoring peace, traditional examples that he mentions are national defense and protecting allies. Importantly, Malloy does not include punishment here. So, adapting this criterion of just cause to the context of policing requires the existence of an operative legal code from which can be derived any situation where police use of force may be warranted. This, of course, presupposes the justice of the code as a whole. Therefore, when a just law is broken (i.e., injustice or crime), intervention by police is justified.

Since the response, moreover, must be "proportionate" to the offense, police officers possess the discretionary ability to perhaps issue a warning for many infractions, or help persons in a conflict to talk and work things out, rather than make a forceful arrest. The pivotal role of the criteria of "proportionality" and "last resort" especially comes into view by considering the use of lethal force. According to Malloy, a police officer may fire a weapon only to protect life (one's own or someone else's), for a "life may be taken only when a life is at stake."[41] To kill someone unjustly is to judge him or her "guilty in an irrevocable manner," which is the reason that Malloy does not include punishment as an example of just cause. For him, the role of the police is not to punish but to apprehend or incapacitate the perpetrator. Thus, it should be a "reluctant decision to employ" force, especially lethal force, which is why it is a last resort. The police should exhaust all other possible methods, in other words, for handling a situation before resorting to force. Again, Malloy's view finds corroboration in what Kleinig describes as a process of the "tightening up of state legislative permissions or, in many cases, departmental policies and practices."[42] In the wake of a monumental Supreme Court decision in 1985, the justifiable use of deadly force has been limited to two categories: (1) the officer may shoot to defend herself or himself from grievous bodily injury, and (2) the officer may

---

39. Skolnick and Fyfe, *Above the Law,* xvi.
40. Malloy, *Ethics of Law Enforcement,* 12-13.
41. Malloy, *Ethics of Law Enforcement,* 17-18; 13, 22.
42. Kleinig, *Ethics of Policing,* 112, 114-18.

shoot to save another person from grievous bodily injury.[43] Departments no longer allow their officers to shoot fleeing felons under any circumstances, especially in situations in which the perpetrator no longer poses an immediate threat to anyone's life.[44]

It should be readily apparent that, for Malloy, the criteria coalesce as an interlocking framework, which is perhaps why he identifies himself as a "strict constructionist" just war theorist.[45] That is, he requires that each and every criterion be met before justifying war, or in this case, the use of force by police. If any of the criteria cannot be satisfied, a "no" to the use of force must be the result. Still, it is Malloy's view that the classic criteria for the justified use of force are easier to observe and conform to in the domestic context of police work than they are in the international setting of military conflict.

Can a Pacifist Be a Police Officer?

What about Sherman's question to the pacifists? Can a pacifist be a police officer? The short, and common, answer is given by Potter: "If to be a Christian one must be nonviolent, then no Christian should assume the office of policeman, soldier, or magistrate."[46] Returning to his hypothetical Memphis police officer who has an opportunity to forestall the assassination of Martin Luther King, Jr., Potter determines that "adherence to nonviolent ideals" by this officer "would not have marked a triumph of high morality; it would have been a suspicious and serious dereliction of duty." Similarly, Malloy writes, "Anyone who rules out categorically firing a gun in the course of their work should not enter police work in the first place."[47] According to Malloy, a pacifist police officer, who is unwilling to shoot a weapon under any circumstances, would endanger fellow officers and civilians.

Pacifism, however, *has* been a viable and consistent tradition in the history of the Christian church. It was especially dominant in the first three centu-

43. Geller, "Police and Deadly Force: A Look at the Empirical Literature," 218. Geller calls this a "defense-of-life" shooting policy. See *Tennessee v. Garner,* 471 U.S. 1, 105 Supreme Court 1694, 85 L. Ed. 2nd 1 (decided 27 March 1985).

44. Whereas in the eighteenth century the English jurist, William Blackstone, justified deadly force in stopping a felon who was fleeing, in recent years "the rationale for the rule is gone; that while all felonies were capital crimes in the eighteenth century, relatively few are in the twentieth." See John C. Hall, "Deadly Force, the Common Law and the Constitution," *FBI Law Enforcement Bulletin* 53 (April 1984): 27.

45. Malloy, *Ethics of Law Enforcement,* 28 n. 23; cf. p. 11.

46. Potter, *War and Moral Discourse,* 56.

47. Malloy, *Ethics of Law Enforcement,* 17; cf. 29 n. 31.

ries when Christian writers opposed participation in the military for a variety of reasons, including prohibitions against killing itself and/or prohibitions against idolatry and emperor worship.[48] Over subsequent centuries, pacifism was a mark of such Christians as the desert monks, St. Francis, the historic peace churches of the Radical Reformation (e.g., Mennonites), and the Quakers. This being the case, what do *pacifists themselves* have to say in response to Sherman's query?

Actually, a variety of answers may be found among pacifists, most likely because pacifism comes in a variety of forms.[49] For example, a pacifist may oppose violence but not necessarily all force, or another pacifist may reject war but tolerate some violence short of war. The latter pacifist, that is, may claim that whereas all war involves violence, not all violence involves war. So, although most pacifists oppose all war, their miscellany of stances on violence, coercion, and force leads their views on policing to diverge into four discernible but overlapping positions. First, some pacifists, who reject all war and participation in war, likewise renounce all policing and participation in policing. Second, many pacifists exclude policing as a career for themselves while they accept policing as a valid and necessary institution in the wider society. Third, a growing number of pacifists accept "police actions" in the international arena, which indicates that they probably accept policing in the domestic arena. And fourth, some pacifists reject war although they accept policing — especially restrained, nonlethal policing — as a role for both others and themselves. I shall now turn to each of these pacifisms vis-à-vis Sherman's question.

Pacifists Who Answer "No"

To begin, some pacifists renounce violence in any form. Just as they reject all war and participation in war, so too do they repudiate all policing and partici-

---

48. See David G. Hunter, "The Christian Church and the Roman Army in the First Three Centuries," in *The Church's Peace Witness,* ed. Marlin E. Miller and Barbara Nelson Gingerich (Grand Rapids: Eerdmans, 1994).

49. See John Howard Yoder, *Nevertheless: The Varieties and Shortcomings of Religious Pacifism* (Scottdale, PA: Herald Press, 1971), where he identifies at least eighteen types or subtypes of pacifism. Cf. Duane L. Cady, *From Warism to Pacifism: A Moral Continuum* (Philadelphia: Temple University Press, 1989), 61-62; also, James W. Child and Donald Scherer, *Two Paths Toward Peace* (Philadelphia: Temple University Press, 1992), 68-71, where they identify a variety of pacifisms, including, for example, (1) "nonresistance"; (2) those who strictly prohibit all violence; (3) those who prohibit lethal violence; and (4) those who reject organized violence between nations.

pation in policing. This version of pacifism opposes killing in all circumstances. There is, in other words, an absolute (i.e., without exception) prohibition against killing. The sixteenth-century Anabaptists and Tolstoy represent this perspective, which has been identified as "nonresistance."[50] Out of obedience to the way of Jesus, these pacifists abdicate involvement in the coercive politics of civil society, thereby conceding the ongoing existence of evil in the wider world. Thus, while Tolstoy's answer that police violence is not much different from revolutionary violence could be attributed to the fact that he had in mind the Russian secret police, it ultimately arises from his interpretation of Jesus' Sermon on the Mount as calling for nonresistance. This grounds Tolstoy's opposition to all violence, including police violence. As he puts it with regard to military service: "It is not only Christians but all just people who must refuse to become soldiers — that is, to be ready at another's command (for this is what a soldier's duty actually consists of) to kill all those one is ordered to kill."[51] Even if employing violence as a soldier is done to protect one's own people or self, Tolstoy maintains that Jesus' call to nonresistant forgiveness and love of one's enemies nevertheless excludes soldiering. And, because Tolstoy denounces all violence as intrinsically contrary to Jesus' teaching on nonresistance, by extension, pacifists themselves ought neither to participate as police, nor to legitimate policing in the wider society.

Pacifists Who Answer "No" and "Yes"

A second group of pacifists waive policing as a career for themselves while they condone policing as a valid and necessary institution in the wider society. For example, writing in response to some Mennonites at mid-century who approved of participation in international police-type forces instead of the mili-

---

50. See Reinhold Niebuhr, "Why the Christian Church Is Not Pacifist," in *Christianity and Power Politics* (New York: Charles Scribner's Sons, 1940), 1-32. Niebuhr acknowledges that this version of pacifism genuinely possesses internal integrity and corresponds faithfully to Jesus' teaching, but he (wrongly, I think) also claims that it is socially irresponsible. He contrasts this "genuine pacifism" against "heretical pacifism" which neglects sin and holds an overoptimistic view of human nature. On the influence of Niebuhr's grid of pacifisms (and how it is mistaken with regard to the question of responsibility) see John Howard Yoder, "How Many Ways Are There to Think Morally About War?" *The Journal of Law and Religion* 11 (1994-95): 104-6; and "Reinhold Niebuhr and Christian Pacifism," *Mennonite Quarterly Review* 29 (April 1955): 101-17.

51. Leo Tolstoy, "Advice to a Draftee," in *War and the Christian Conscience: From Augustine to Martin Luther King, Jr.*, ed. Albert Marrin (Chicago: Henry Regnery Company, 1971), 212.

tary, Guy Franklin Hershberger deems that the coercion and violence of both the police and the military are not acceptable for pacifist Christians themselves. Even if the violence of policing involves more restraint and less bloodshed, he criticizes any "sanguine Mennonite with sufficient optimism to argue for political participation" in such state capacities as "sheriffs and policemen who use the gun sparingly. . . ."[52]

At the same time, however, Hershberger acknowledges that the police function, according to Romans 13, is a necessary one — for the maintenance of order and to execute God's wrath on wrongdoers — in society and in, if there is one, international society. But such a role remains "forbidden to nonresistant Christians who seek to follow Christ who taught men when smitten on the one cheek to turn the other also."[53] This is why, Hershberger suspects, the early Christians refused to perform the "police or punitive functions of the state." Moreover, while he concedes that the modern state possesses positive functions rather than only coercive police power, and while he acknowledges the necessity of the state and its police for the order of society, Hershberger nevertheless maintains that the state monopoly on coercion remains central. Indeed, although differences exist in degree between the police and the military, "the two are the same in kind."[54] Such being the case, "the nonresistant Christian cannot consistently serve as a policeman any more than he can as a soldier." This answer echoes Tolstoy's, but it differs in that Hershberger tolerates policing in the wider society by those who are not pacifist Christians like himself.

A similar point of view is offered more recently by Howard Zehr, who avows that the question about how Christian pacifists respond to crime is central to their "faith and experience." Specifically, he believes that the pacifist's response of calling the police for protection or to make an arrest is "problematic." There is recognized in Romans 13, he thinks, a need for police — "some people do indeed need to be restrained, some need the shock of apprehension" — but society, Zehr adds, relies excessively on the state's forceful response.[55] Of course, Zehr assumes in his analysis a "no" to the question about whether paci-

52. Guy Franklin Hershberger, *The Way of the Cross in Human Relations* (Scottdale, PA: Herald Press, 1958), 181-83. Today Hershberger would have to include police*women* in his discussion.

53. Guy Franklin Hershberger, *War, Peace, and Nonresistance* (Scottdale, PA: Herald Press, 1946), 205.

54. Hershberger, *War, Peace, and Nonresistance* 363-64.

55. Howard Zehr, *The Christian as Victim* (Akron, OH: Office of Criminal Justice, Mennonite Central Committee, 1982), 3, 5, 20, and 22, respectively. For a similar view, see Dave Jackson, *Dial 911: Peaceful Christians and Urban Violence* (Scottdale, PA: Herald Press, 1981), 50-52, 107-11.

fist Christians themselves may be police. Given this, though, the next question that follows is whether pacifists may rely on nonpacifists to serve as police officers for their protection. For if the police are called, Zehr cautions, those pacifists who called them share some complicity in what they do, which is especially problematic if the police employ lethal force. Be that as it may, he declines to provide either a universal positive or negative answer to whether pacifist Christians should call the police. Zehr does advocate, after all is said and done, that pacifist Christians at least encourage the police to pursue more nonviolent methods and restraint "without necessarily expecting them never to use force."

It is particularly in view of positions such as Hershberger's and Zehr's, which forbid policing by pacifists but accept it by nonpacifists for the good of society, that Wogaman's worry about possible equivocation initially surfaces. As James Child phrases it, "A consistent pacifist . . . must believe that calling the police, who will then come and use violent force, is a vicarious exercise of violent force on his own part."[56] Yet, when asked whether such pacifist Christians do not *de facto* depend upon other citizens to restrain criminal evil while refusing to do so themselves, a recent exponent of this variation of pacifism offers a common retort: "To this we may answer *Yes*, but without embarrassment. After all we do not *ask* anyone to act in ways in which we disapprove."[57]

Pacifists Who Answer "Yes" to International Policing

As alluded to in Hershberger's critical response against them, there is a third, growing set of pacifists who accept "police actions" in the international arena. For them, policing is a legitimate and desirable function in the wider, international sphere, and they accept possible pacifist participation in it. These pacifists hold that the differences between the traditional military and police models are significant enough for pacifists to accept police-type actions on the international level. For example, with historical precedent in the intervention of the United Nations in Korea, U.S. troops in recent years have undertaken humanitarian interventions into other nations including Somalia and Bosnia. Such activity is often classified as a "police action" instead of warfare, I suspect, because the former activity is understood as drawing on the analogy of the putatively more acceptable use of force in the civic realm. As Duane Cady astutely observes, "The point is that the smaller-scale acts of war have greater likelihood

56. Child, *Two Paths Toward Peace*, 88.
57. Robert E. D. Clark, "The Case for All-Out Pacifism," in *Pacifism and War: When Christians Disagree*, ed. Oliver R. Barclay (Leicester, England: Inter-Varsity Press, 1984), 97.

of being justified because the relevant factors are more manageable. This is why scale-reducing analogies are used, to persuade (oneself and others) that a given act of war is morally acceptable."[58]

Thus, many pacifists, out of genuine concern for justice and the welfare of others, now express an openness — however reluctantly — to forceful actions resembling police use of force: "The paradigm of police action, allowing for the use of violence in order to stop criminal activity, may enable some pacifists to accept military action, even killing, as a means of order."[59] Although they reject war, some pacifists apparently endorse a form of policing as a function in the international arena, assuming that there is a recognized international authority which will hold its police forces accountable to strict guidelines of restraint (in other words, actually, to the criteria of the just war tradition). They believe that an international police power would differ in degree and kind from military power as we know it.

Potter, however, takes issue with this form of pacifism. Indeed, he finds it "logically odd" that some "who call themselves pacifists" accept the notion of an international police force and would even "bear arms in a peacekeeping venture under international authority."[60] For Potter, as for Hershberger, the coercion intrinsic to both policing and military activity is not essentially different, which is why the violent functions of each context is considered analogous. In contrast to Potter, those pacifists who accept international policing emphasize the analogy between domestic policing and international policing, not the one Potter identifies between domestic policing and international *warfare*. These pacifists maintain that the difference between policing and war is not simply a matter of degree, but a difference that is profound and structural. In Potter's view, however, a "thoroughgoing pacifist, bound by an absolute rejection of killing under any and all circumstances," should participate neither in war nor in any policing capacity.

58. Cady, *From Warism to Pacifism*, 36.

59. Richard B. Miller, "Casuistry, Pacifism, and the Just-War Tradition in the Post-Cold War Era," in *Peacemaking: Moral and Policy Challenges for a New World*, ed. Gerard F. Powers, Drew Christiansen, SJ, and Robert T. Hennemeyer (Washington, DC: U.S. Catholic Conference, 1994), 207. For another essay in the same volume that makes this observation, see Kenneth R. Himes, OFM, "Catholic Social Thought and Humanitarian Intervention," 224-25. Examples of pacifists who have expressed a receptiveness to considering humanitarian interventions may be found in *Sojourners* 22 (April 1993): 4-5, 10-26. See especially Jack Nelson-Pallmeyer, "Wise as Serpents, Gentle as Doves?" (10-13). At mid-century, James Thayer Addison suggested that the U.N. intervention in Korea was "rightly viewed . . . as the international equivalent of police work," in *War, Peace, and the Christian Mind: A Review of Recent Thought* (Greenwich, CT: Seabury, 1953), 19.

60. Potter, *War and Moral Discourse*, 66.

Potter's assumption that the external violence of the state is analogous to its internal violence may be found in James Martineau's 1855 anti-pacifism sermon, described as "perhaps the best modern example of the 'police analogy' as a justification of war."[61] Just as the state, on behalf of its individual citizens, must use police to keep the peace and to protect threatened citizens against criminals, so too the state is responsible in the international sphere. In this view, the use of force in each sphere may differ in degree but not in kind. Given this analogy, therefore, if a Christian "has availed himself of the services of the police to arrest and the courts to try the offender against his person or goods; if, in short, he consents to have a place in civil society at all; he has engaged himself, by active coercion, in resistance to evil, and in his private capacity *gone to war* with the delinquencies he meets."[62] In Martineau's thinking, such pacifists either must rule out policing along with war, or, if they continue to accept policing, must honestly discontinue describing their ethical stance as pacifism and accept war as well.

But is Martineau's claim about the existence of this analogy valid? Perhaps a brief *excursus* would be appropriate at this point, for both pacifists and nonpacifists stand divided — even within their own camps — on this question. Of course, analogies are neither univocal nor equivocal; rather, they involve attributes which are neither precisely the same nor yet simply different. Therefore, both the similarities and the dissimilarities between policing and war have been noted by various writers.[63] On the one hand, the analogy seems plausible for various reasons. To begin, it is commonly agreed that the state possesses a monopoly of physical power at its disposal to maintain peace both internally and externally. Moreover, nations are viewed as existing in relationship to other nations, just as persons do with other persons. Accordingly, they interact either justly or unjustly, thereby also holding moral agency and culpability. By the same token, in their interactions, the use of force, or the potential thereof, often

61. Albert Marrin, *War and the Christian Conscience*, 119.

62. James Martineau, "Rights of War," in Marrin, *War and the Christian Conscience*, 121.

63. See Addison, *War, Peace, and the Christian Mind*, 17-19; Cecil John Cadoux, *Christian Pacifism Re-examined* (Oxford: Basil Blackwell, 1940), 40-45; Charles E. Raven, *War and the Christian* (New York: Macmillan, 1938), 116, 150-52; Robert Lowry Calhoun, *God and the Common Life* (New York: Charles Scribner's Sons, 1935, 1954), 234; Roland H. Bainton, *Christian Attitudes Toward War and Peace: A Historical Survey and Critical Re-evaluation* (New York: Abingdon, 1960), 240-41. For more recent accounts of the differences between the civil use of force and warfare, see Cady, *From Warism to Pacifism*, 36; and Jenny Teichman's *Pacifism and the Just War: A Study in Applied Philosophy* (Oxford and New York: Basil Blackwell, 1986), 38-46. Also, see John Howard Yoder, *The Politics of Jesus: Vicit Agnus Noster*, rev. 2nd ed. (Grand Rapids: Eerdmans, 1994), 204; and Stanley Hauerwas, *Dispatches from the Front: Theological Engagements with the Secular* (Durham, NC: Duke University Press, 1994), 131-32.

compels nations to abide by international law, much like the use of force, or the potential thereof, compels individuals to abide by domestic law.

On the other hand, the analogy seems to break down in a number of ways. First, the "civic sense" that can be presupposed between nations such as Canada, England, and the United States does not exist among nations generally. There is no true community of nations. Second, the plausibility of the analogy hinges upon the existence of a recognized international authority with an international police force, neither of which as of yet exist. Simply put, there is no world federation similar to the federal system of the United States or any other national federal system. Third, the analogy appears to crumble when, given the absence of an impartial international authority and police force, and given the absence of universally recognized laws, one nation undertakes upon itself the role of the world's police officer. Within a nation, police must enforce the law within the parameters or limits of the laws themselves (laws that are known by the criminal to be applicable to him or her as well). Thus, the violence employed by police officers is subject to review by the authorities and often by civilian review boards. Fourth, the police are only one component in a criminal justice system. Their role is to apprehend criminals for trial, not to act as judge, jailer, or executioner (i.e., not to punish) — all of which are not distinguished so neatly in warfare. Fourth and closely related to this, in the police function the violence is applied only to the alleged perpetrator of a crime, whereas in warfare the violence is directed more broadly at armies and populations rather than, for example, only against a criminal dictator. Finally, there are significant differences in degree, and "questions of degree in matters of practical conduct often make all the difference between what is right and what is wrong."[64] For instance, the extent of damage, especially with regard to harming innocent civilians, is much greater in the international sphere; whereas domestic police use of force, at least in theory (the Philadelphia bombing of MOVE is counterevidence), tends to be more discriminating and controlled.

Because of these incongruities between policing and warfare, Robert C. Calhoun submits: "To approve police duty, even when it involves unavoidable violence, does not commit one to approval of . . . international or civil war."[65] For Calhoun, police are responsible to the law, proportionate in the application of force, and discriminating when distinguishing between criminal and innocent civilians. As a result, the police prefer to attempt any possible peaceful means before resorting to lethal force. Therefore, disagreeing with Martineau, Calhoun discerns the analogy to be more appropriate between domestic polic-

---

64. Cadoux, *Christian Pacifism Re-examined,* 43.
65. Calhoun, *God and the Common Life,* 234.

ing and international *policing*, rather than between policing and international *war*. And, acceptance of policing, be it domestic or international, he asserts, does not necessarily require acceptance of war, be it civil or international. Or, as Cadoux puts it, the analogy is "real and possibly even close, and must therefore be allowed for in any ethical assessment we may frame, but . . . it is not sufficiently close to constitute . . . a demonstration that, if one [i.e., domestic or international policing] is to be ethically justified, there cannot be any fault to find with the other [i.e., civil or international war]."[66]

I think it important to note that the ethical criteria employed here to evaluate the similarities and differences in both contexts of war and policing include such principles as just authority, just cause, last resort, proportionality, and discrimination. When, for example, Raven declares that his "duty as a Christian citizen to arrest a burglar or to protect a lonely woman from rape has no sort of bearing upon [his] duty to smash up the homes and torture the families" of an enemy nation, he implicitly assumes traditional just war criteria rather than a principled pacifist point of view.[67] So, the question may legitimately be asked of these pacifists who accept international policing, does admitting the real differences between policing and warfare mean pacifists are legitimate in approving of the violence in policing? For police action itself, just like war, is not always justifiable or right.[68] Even if the analogy between war and policing has both strengths and weaknesses, the use of force in either context requires justification. And the *ethical logic or framework* used to evaluate the justifiability of the use of force in either case, as Potter and Malloy claim, does seem to be analogous. Even Teichman, who emphasizes the dissimilarities between police violence and external state violence, concedes that the basic logic of restraint in the just war tradition begins from the premise that the state's limited use of violence in a just war "is similar to its exercise of force in internal jurisdiction."[69] I suspect that this is why many pacifists converge with just war advocates with regard to international police actions and humanitarian interventions.

Pacifists Who Answer "Yes"

Some of the pacifists who are now open to international police actions obviously presuppose a favorable disposition, on their part, toward domestic polic-

66. Cadoux, *Christian Pacifism Re-examined*, 43-44; cf. Addison, *War, Peace, and the Christian Mind*, 19.

67. Raven, *War and the Christian*, 152.

68. Teichman, *Pacifism and the Just War*, 46.

69. Teichman, *Pacifism and the Just War*, 46.

ing itself. This group, however, is not homogenous on this topic either. On the one hand, some of these pacifists reject war but accept police use of force, including the lethal use of force. On the other hand, however, some of these pacifists also reject war and accept policing, but only policing that is nonviolent and nonlethal.

An example of the former sort of pacifism is the current mayor of South Bend, Indiana. Although a conscientious objector during the Vietnam war (citing religious and personal reasons of conscience), he made it clear to the local newspaper (when he was under consideration for the office) that he believes the use of force "sometimes is necessary" in society. And, anticipating the possible questions about his pacifism and how it might affect his mayoral decisions, he points to his "strong support of the police department as an example of his understanding of that."[70] This seemingly contradictory stance really is not new. Indeed, Quaker founder George Fox, for example, accepted the sword as a legitimate component of the police function of the state that when properly employed responds to the Light of Christ that the criminal violates within herself or himself.[71] For Fox, violence is not equivalent to *any* use of the sword, but is rather the unjust use of the sword. In view of this, pacifists along this vein hold that the lethal force justifiably used by police is not violence and certainly not violent like killing in war. As one exponent of this version of pacifism puts it, these pacifists cannot commit themselves to an "absolute rejection of killing in all circumstances."[72]

Like Fox, some pacifists, therefore, do not understand force as wrong or evil *per se*. Unlike Fox, however, other pacifists distinguish force from *lethal* force, with the latter often deemed as violence. Cady, for instance, argues that a pacifist may oppose violence, which is or could be lethal, but not necessarily exclude force, particularly nonlethal force. He objects to the view of pacifism that sees it as a monolithic, absolutist position holding "that it is wrong, always, everywhere, for anyone to use force against another human being."[73] Although this absolutist version is certainly one kind of pacifism, Cady notes that it is not the most commonly held version. As an alternative, he suggests that most pacifists today distinguish between violence, force, coercion, and power.

---

70. "Ex-POW Kernan backs objector," *South Bend Tribune*, December 2, 1996.

71. James F. Childress, "Answering That of God in Every Man," *Quaker Religious Thought* 15 (1974): 25.

72. Lowell Erdahl, *Pro-Life/Pro-Choice: Life-Affirming Alternatives to Abortion, War, Mercy Killing, and the Death Penalty* (Minneapolis: Augsburg, 1986), 28, 82-83.

73. Cady, *From Warism to Pacifism*, 13, 61-62. Cf. Teichman, *Pacifism and the Just War*, 4-5, 40; and Addison, *War, Peace, and the Christian Mind*, 17-18, notes that not all pacifists are Tolstoyan, seeing force as intrinsically evil, especially those pacifists who accept force as exercised by police.

For this reason, a number of Christian pacifists describe their stance as *nonviolent resistance* rather than as Hershberger's or Tolstoy's *nonresistance*. Of course, parenthetically, it should be noted that Hershberger's understanding of pacifism as an absolute refusal to kill does not, by definition, rule out nonviolent resistance, although he himself may reject this. The reckoning of pacifism as nonviolent resistance, however, *has* gained acceptance as the twentieth century has proceeded, especially with the examples of Gandhi, Martin Luther King, Jr., and others.[74] With this type of pacifism in mind, then, the efficacy of violence in policing, generally assumed by nearly everyone considered to this point, is called into question. That is, when the greater efficacy of nonviolence is granted, policing itself can be envisioned in a completely different way.

Accordingly, when pacifists are pressed, "*What if* you were in a police counterterrorism unit and you were trying to stop a sniper on a roof about to fire into a crowd of people?", Walter Wink responds that this scenario already assumes "a framework that virtually *requires* violence as its response." And it is this framework itself that he calls into question.[75] As an advocate of nonviolent resistance rather than passive nonresistance, Wink brings to our attention another way to resolve the police "what if" dilemma that coheres with the proposed distinction between force and violence.[76] According to Wink, *force* refers to "a truly legiti-

74. For cases of nonviolent resistance, see William R. Miller, *Nonviolence: A Christian Interpretation* (New York: Association Press, 1964); Gene Sharp, *The Politics of Nonviolent Action* (Boston: Porter Sargent, 1973); and Ronald J. Sider, *Nonviolence: The Invincible Weapon?* (Dallas: Word, 1989). It should be briefly noted that the distinction between nonviolent resistance and nonresistance is viewed differently by nonpacifists like Reinhold Niebuhr and Paul Ramsey. They reject the view that nonviolent resistance is a Christian pacifist stance; that is, they see *nonresistance* as faithful to Christ's teachings. See Niebuhr, "Why the Christian Church Is Not Pacifist," 10; and Ramsey, *Basic Christian Ethics,* 69. Although Niebuhr criticized the nonviolent resistance methods as being not genuinely Christian, he did anticipate that the Gandhian methods would work in the American setting, for example, with regard to what would become the civil rights movement; see Niebuhr, *Moral Man and Immoral Society* (New York: Charles Scribner's Sons, 1932), 252.

75. Walter Wink, *Engaging the Powers* (Minneapolis: Fortress, 1992), 236. My thanks goes again to Lee Camp for bringing Wink's point to my attention. Similarly, Donald Scherer, *Two Paths Toward Peace,* 113-14, asks whether police *must* be armed as they are, citing counterexamples of the English "bobbies" and the nonviolent martial art of *aikido* as a method of protection and defense. See also Ronald J. Sider and Richard R. Taylor, "Jesus and Violence: Some Critical Objections," in *Nuclear Holocaust and Christian Hope* (Downers Grove, IL: InterVarsity, 1982), 117, 149-50; also Ronald J. Sider, *Nonviolence: The Invincible Weapon?* 3-4; Daniel A. Dombrowski, *Christian Pacifism* (Philadelphia: Temple University Press, 1991), 96-97; and Jackson, *Dial 911,* 50, says of the British "bobbies": "They truly looked like *peace*-keepers and helpers."

76. Wink, *Engaging the Powers,* 227, 236, and 384 n. 16.

mate, socially authorized, and morally defensible use of restraint to prevent harm being done to innocent people," whereas *violence* is excessive, injurious, or lethal force. In order to promote policing that accords with his nonviolent perspective, Wink suggests that the just war criteria be renamed "violence-reduction criteria" so that both just war advocates and pacifists can cooperate in countering the police's current and "routine use of unnecessary violence."[77]

Therefore, contrary to the assumption behind the "what if" question, Wink demonstrates that policing does not necessarily *have* to be violent in order to be effective. After all, other options exist, including, for example, the strict gun control policy of Canada, the unarmed or minimally armed "bobbies" of the British police departments, and the improved training of police in nonviolent, less-than-lethal methods of control and restraint. Thus, for instance, in the case of a crazed gunman, the criminal can be immobilized and apprehended with a sedative dart or a jolt of electricity instead of a deadly bullet. And besides, most police work already is nonviolent, for police spend much of their time in a service capacity to the community, helping at an accident, or educating children about the dangers of drugs. For these reasons, some pacifists who share Wink's perspective conclude, "Nothing we have said implies or requires that Christians should not participate in police activity."[78]

Yet, do they think that Christians may use greater force as police officers when it sometimes may be required? For police work, as it is currently performed, continues to potentially require the resort to lethal force. Indeed, less-than-lethal tactics and methods sometimes turn out to be lethal (which is why such methods are referred to as less-than-lethal rather than nonlethal). In view of this, perhaps it boils down to the following stance for these pacifists:

> In many societies, we will not be able to serve as judges or police [officers], because these occupations have been ruled out by the obligations which they have been given either to take life or to sanction the taking of life. However, in those societies (such as the UK) which have rejected the death penalty and have a largely unarmed police force, these may be appropriate avenues of Christian involvement.[79]

And, similarly, Wink's parting thought on the question about whether a pacifist Christian can do police work is: "The answers are not self-evident, and are as

77. Wink, *Engaging the Powers,* 224, 227, 236-41.

78. Sider and Taylor, "Jesus and Violence," 117.

79. Willard Swartley and Alan Krieder, "Pacifist Christianity: The Kingdom Way," in *Pacifism and War: When Christians Disagree,* ed. Oliver R. Barclay (Leicester, England: Inter-Varsity Press, 1984), 57.

much a matter of individual vocation and national location as of moral norms."[80]

In sum, it should by now be apparent that there is an assortment of pacifist perspectives, with overlap among them, on the issue of police and the use of force — and not all pacifists would agree with Tolstoy's implied evaluation of policing. Yet, these versions of pacifism may or may not be *Christian*. Some of the pacifist voices above identify themselves as Christian, but others do not. And, actually, there are representatives of both Christians and non-Christians in each type of pacifist perspective on policing covered to this point. Yet, while Sherman's questions about Rawlsians, Christians, and pacifists have been addressed, another voice that is specifically Christian and pacifist has not yet been heard in response to the question about policing.

Conclusion: A Yoderian Point of Departure

"The exposition I have chosen is to let the panorama of diverse theories unfold progressively, from the dialogue already in process, rather than proceeding 'foundationally' on the ground of what someone might claim as 'first principles.'"[81] Such was John Howard Yoder's approach when interpreting and treating ethical issues, and this is what I have endeavored to accomplish up to this point in the essay. For Yoder's concern about concrete moral questions usually involved a survey and analysis of the plurality of methods and positions represented in a particular discussion. Approaches that are teleological, deontological, virtue-oriented, contract-based, or narrative-dependent all fell within the scope of his careful consideration, and Yoder, in turn, would attempt some "mixing and matching according to the shape of a particular debate."[82] In doing so, Yoder perceived himself as not representing one method or "position" but, rather, a posture of love and creative witness. As he put it, "My conviction that war is wrong is not derived from a metaethical commitment to exceptionless prohibitions or to any other one mode of reasoning. I honor the people who have expressed themselves in those terms, while pointing out for present purposes that it is not the only way to argue."[83]

80. Wink, *Engaging the Powers*, 238-39; cf. Stanley Hauerwas, "Who Is 'We'?" *Sojourners* 22 (April 1993): 15.

81. John Howard Yoder, "How Many Ways Are There to Think Morally About War?" 84.

82. John Howard Yoder, "Walk and Word: The Alternatives to Methodologism," in *Theology Without Foundations*, ed. Stanley Hauerwas, Nancey Murphy, and Mark Nation (Nashville: Abingdon, 1994), 87.

83. John Howard Yoder, "'What Would You Do . . . ?' Revisited," unpublished memo "for interested ethics students," dated December 1996, p. 2.

For Yoder, Christian pacifism or nonviolence is inseparable from the very life of the community of Christians formed and shaped by Jesus Christ's life, death, and resurrection. Such Christian nonviolence stems from the person and work of Jesus Christ, and it is the only example of pacifism up to this point in the essay for which Jesus Christ is indispensable. Its theological basis is in "the character of God and the work of Jesus Christ," whose death and resurrection "reveals how God deals with evil; here is the only valid starting point for Christian pacifism or nonresistance."[84] The new life inaugurated by Jesus Christ is not some ideal or absolute principle that requires Christian adherence to pacifism as a legalistic position. Rather, because of the Spirit present in the church since Pentecost, Christian pacifism, for Yoder, is not a "legalistic and absolutist sectarian pacifism" but, instead, part and parcel of the embodied Christian life of discipleship in the church.[85]

Yoder's Christian pacifism, therefore, at times overlapped with or encompassed elements of the other versions of pacifism, and the question of policing brings these points of contact into view. For example, like some of the pacifists surveyed above, Yoder acknowledged the biblical legitimacy of the police function by nonpacifists within the wider society.[86] Romans 13 (along with 1 Timothy 2 and 1 Peter 2), in his interpretation, recognizes the state's function as preserver of order and tranquility, which "obtain when the innocent are protected" in order that "all [people] might come to knowledge of the truth." In this way, the state's policing function within society receives legitimation; however, Yoder was quick to point out that Romans 13 does *not* apply at the international level of warfare. For, in policing, the innocent can be distinguished from the perpetrator, and a semblance of order can be maintained; whereas, in war neither of these are possible. Nevertheless, even with regard to policing itself, Yoder concluded that the state never possesses a blanket authorization to use force: "The use of force must be limited to the police function, i.e., guided by fair judicial processes, subject to recognized legislative regulation, and safe-

84. Yoder, *Politics of Jesus,* 239; and *The Original Revolution: Essays on Christian Pacifism* (Scottdale, PA: Herald Press, 1971, 1977), 56, respectively.

85. Joel Andrew Zimbelman correctly notes this in "The Contribution of John Howard Yoder to Recent Discussions in Christian Social Ethics," *Scottish Journal of Theology* 45 (September 1992): 371, 378-79. See also Stanley Hauerwas, *Dispatches from the Front,* 117-118, 120. Cf. Lisa Sowle Cahill, *Love Your Enemies,* 2, where she accurately observes that many pacifists do not begin so much with an ethical reply to the violence question, but also p. 35, where she incorrectly surmises that Yoder "arrives at a negative judgment on any Christian use of violence in any situation."

86. John Howard Yoder, *The Christian Witness to the State* (Newton, KS: Faith and Life Press, 1964), 36-37, 46-48; *Original Revolution,* 60. Cf. Bainton, *Christian Attitudes Toward War and Peace,* 13, 60.

guarded in practice against its running away with the situation. Only the absolute minimum of violence is therefore in any way excusable."[87] To discern whether a state's police force complies with this standard from Romans 13, Yoder suggested that we evaluate "one case at a time" and that we be on constant alert for the state's demonic side, when it succumbs to the temptation to overdo the police function, about which Revelation 13 warns.

In addition, similar to those pacifists who generally opposed policing by pacifists, Yoder made reference to the example of the early Christians, who believed that "the Christian as an agent of God for reconciliation has other things to do than to be in police service."[88] Yet by 170 CE some soldiers who were Christians did not get excommunicated, for rather than fighting in war, the actual work of most soldiers during the *Pax Romana* consisted in road protection against bandits, transportation of mail, guarding prisoners, or fire-fighting service. As long as the Christian soldier had not killed anyone or burnt incense to Caesar, he was permitted to continue his living as a Christian and as a soldier. Indeed, Yoder considered the just war tradition, developed initially by Ambrose and Augustine, as derived from this "function of the police in domestic peace-keeping."[89] Nevertheless, in both his scriptural interpretation and his reference to the practices of the early Christians, Yoder seemed to converge with those pacifists, like Hershberger and Zehr, who reject policing by Christian pacifists themselves, but accept it by nonpacifists for the sake of society.

At the same time, though, Yoder's reflections on pacifism and policing appeared to share more in common with those pacifists who express an openness to nonviolent policing, even by pacifists. Although earlier Yoder mentioned pacifism and nonresistance as synonymous terms, he came to see Christian pacifism as entailing nonviolent resistance. As Joel Zimbelman has observed: "In some later works (among those published after 1974), Yoder often employs the term 'nonviolent resistance' (rather than 'nonresistance') to specify the fundamental imperative of the Christian community."[90] Indeed,

87. Yoder, *Christian Witness to the State*, 36-37.

88. Yoder, *Christian Attitudes to War, Peace, and Revolution: A Companion to Bainton* (Elkhart, IN: Co-Op Bookstore, 1983), 31, 34; *Christian Witness to the State*, 56; "War as a Moral Problem in the Early Church," unpublished paper, dated 4 June 1991, pp. 8-9. Cf. Wink, *Engaging the Powers*, 211; Bainton, *Christian Attitudes Toward War and Peace*, 79-81; Swartley and Krieder, "Pacifist Christianity," 57; Clark, "Case for All-Out Pacifism," 110; and James F. Childress, "Moral Discourse About War in the Early Church," in *Peace, Politics, and the People of God*, ed. Paul Peachey (Philadelphia: Fortress, 1986), 131 n. 5.

89. John Howard Yoder, *The Priestly Kingdom: Social Ethics as Gospel* (Notre Dame: University of Notre Dame Press, 1984), 75; *Politics of Jesus*, 204.

90. Zimbelman, "Contribution of John Howard Yoder," 388.

Yoder often stressed the fact that nonviolent resistance *can* be a way of effective Christian response, although he also pointed out that Christians do not measure the value of such resistance by its effectiveness. For him, given the numerous examples of successful nonviolently resistant movements and persons — including Gandhi and the civil rights movement led by Martin Luther King, Jr. — "the door is open for nonviolent procedures of maintaining order" in a society.[91] And Yoder believed that more could be done along this vein.

Hence, on one occasion when he was asked about what to do in the face of crime and violence, Yoder replied with a question of his own: "Have you ever wondered whether some nonlethal method would be consistent with Jesus' teaching?"[92] And as an example of what he had in mind, Yoder followed up with another question: "Have you ever thought about *judo?*" Indeed, he sometimes suggested *judo* rather than *karate* as a method of defense, since the former involves grabs and holds rather than the latter's punches and kicks. On this distinction, Yoder echoed Scherer's advocacy of *aikido,* which is a "soft" martial art that emphasizes defense through guiding an aggressor in a way that his aggressive force works against him.[93] In this willingness to consider soft martial arts as examples of legitimate nonviolent force, Yoder appeared to be in agreement with those pacifists who advocate nonviolent resistance and who accept policing, either by themselves or by others, that employs less-than-lethal methods. But, again, Yoder cautioned such Christian pacifists to remember that pacifism should not deal with only the *means* question, for the claim that they can achieve without violence what violence usually promises to achieve, while sometimes true, is not necessarily the case. But this does not mean, in turn, that violence would be okay in such instances. Christian pacifism, for Yoder, "is one in which the calculating link between our obedience and ultimate efficacy has been broken, since the triumph of God comes through resurrection and not through effective sovereignty or assured survival."[94] So, although he evinced an openness to nonviolently resistant methods of defense, Yoder refused to see this as exhaustive of what it means to be a Christian pacifist.

Although Yoder was a prolific, though taciturn, nestor among Christian pacifists, he endeavored to critically and sympathetically engage in conversation with just war interlocutors, giving them the benefit of the doubt and employing their moral language to whatever extent possible. His willingness to go

91. Yoder, *Christian Attitudes to War, Peace, and Revolution: A Companion to Bainton,* 279. Also in this volume, p. 255, he outlined four possible pacifist answers, without indicating his own view, to whether it is permissible to serve in an international police force.
92. Reported by Jackson, *Dial 911,* 51.
93. Scherer, *Two Paths Toward Peace,* 111-13.
94. Yoder, *Politics of Jesus,* 239.

the second mile to ecumenically engage just war proponents was, in the final analysis, an expression of love of enemy, turning the other cheek, and affirming the dignity of the adversary. Indeed, Yoder had "greater respect" for those nonpacifists who view violence as evil (in contrast to nonpacifists who see violence as good, e.g., Rambo in war or Dirty Harry in policing), but who undertake responsibility for the protection of innocent neighbors against aggressive neighbors — "in short, what we have seen to be the police function of the state."[95] Thus, he considered himself as striving to honor the human dignity, the *imago Dei*, of those who adhere to, or at least verbally assent to, the just war tradition, by inviting them to be honest with the restraints that the tradition purports to place upon the use of lethal force.[96] And he would, I think, do the same for those — like just war theorists Potter and Malloy, or criminal justice philosopher Kleinig — who are concerned about the ethics of the use of force in policing: "Wherever any new opening for the moral criticism of the use of violence arises, it is in some way a use of the just war logic, and should be welcomed as at least an opening for possible moral judgment."[97]

That being the case, Yoder indicated an interest in Kleinig's "social peacekeeper" model as an alternative to the "crimefighter" model. The social peacekeeper model couches policing within a wider framework of community and social practices of service, thereby hopefully curtailing the use of violence. As Kleinig puts it, "So understood, the peacekeeper model is broad enough to encompass most of the work that police do, whether it is crimefighting, crime control, or interventions in crisis situations. But what is more important is the irenic cast that it gives to police work."[98] Indeed, Kleinig confesses his respect for pacifists and their critiques of violence, which is why he maintains that there is a *prima facie* "presumption against the use of force."[99] To be sure, the peacekeeper paradigm does not rule out the use of force altogether, but through the social and community practices the model involves, the social-

95. Yoder, *The Original Revolution*, 76.

96. Yoder, "Gordon Zahn Is Right," unpublished draft of a paper, dated January 1997, pp. 1, 5, 9; see also Yoder's *When War Is Unjust*, rev. ed. 5; and "On Not Being Ashamed of the Gospel: Particularity, Pluralism, and Validation," *Faith and Philosophy* 9 (July 1992): 285-300. Yoder also believed that when just war proponents seriously adhere to the criteria of the tradition, fewer lives and values are destroyed.

97. Yoder, *The Original Revolution*, 132.

98. Kleinig, *Ethics of Policing*, 28-29.

99. Kleinig, *Ethics of Policing*, 96-98, 101. Yoder once asked me if I knew the provenance of Kleinig's perspective on the *prima facie* presumption against the use of force. It seems to echo Potter's understanding of the just war logic. Cf. Child, *Two Paths Toward Peace*, 27-30, where he similarly advocates a "Minimal Justified Violence View" that involves a "presumption against violence."

contractarian rules regarding the use of force are reinforced. Accordingly, Kleinig provides several criteria for justifying the use of force, criteria that clearly have functional analogs in the criteria of the just war tradition. In the end, Kleinig hopes that the peacekeeper model will facilitate efforts to make police use of force "a last (albeit sometimes necessary) resort rather than their dominant *modus operandi*."[100] And I think that Yoder would have welcomed Kleinig's work as an opening for holding police accountable in their use of force.

In sum, Yoder once asked, "If it is granted that nonresistant love is the way of the disciple, and if it is said at the same time that police force, within definite limits, is legitimate in the fallen world, can the Christian be the policeman?"[101] I have attempted to show how Yoder unpacked the two premises of this Sherman-like question. After all is said and done, however, Yoder refused to accept the straightforward "no" of Tolstoy, which is not to say that he gave an automatic "yes" either. Indeed, I suspect that Yoder would have expressed, in the end, a dissatisfaction with the way Sherman's questions at the beginning of this essay are phrased. For the question about whether a Christian or a pacifist can be a police officer is posed in legalistic terms. Yoder once suggested rephrasing the question: "Is the Christian *called* to be a police officer?" He speculated that if such a Christian believed that he or she truly possessed a calling to be both an agent of reconciliation as a Christian and an "agent of the wrath of God" as a police officer, then he or she must provide evidence — since the latter responsibility of using force "requires exceptional justification" — to the church of "such a special calling." At the time that he wrote these reflections, Yoder confessed that he had not met anyone "testifying to such an exceptional call."[102]

I think that Yoder's reflections were on the mark, especially given the present violent condition of American society and the current character of its police. For now and for the foreseeable future, "what is still the most salient fact about the police, the very thing that calls for special justification and for special accountability, namely, [is] that the police have the authority to order us around and to use violence to back those orders up."[103] Yet, *in principle*, policing by Christians — perhaps even by pacifist Christians — cannot be excluded. If, on the one hand, the peacekeeping model proposed by Kleinig and, on the

100. Kleinig, *Ethics of Policing*, 29.
101. Yoder, *Christian Witness to the State*, 56-57.
102. Yoder, *Christian Witness to the State*, 56-57.
103. Jeffrey Reiman, "The Scope and Limits of Police Ethics," review of *The Ethics of Policing*, by John Kleinig, *Criminal Justice Ethics* 16 (Summer/Fall 1997): 45; cf. Child, *Two Paths Toward Peace*, 85-87.

other hand, if stricter guidelines for the use of force are both implemented and followed — in other words, if we move from police officers to peace officers — it may become more possible for Christians and pacifists to serve such a calling.[104]

---

104. I owe a special debt to Lee Camp and David Weiss who commented on drafts of this essay. As our professor invited us: *Vicit agnus noster, eum sequamur.*

Christian Spirituality of Nonviolence as Reconciliation: An Essay in Honor of John Howard Yoder

Ernest W. Ranly

Nonviolence and Reconciliation

For the winter semester of 1989 I was on campus at the University of Notre Dame as a visiting fellow at the Helen Kellogg Institute for International Studies. Since 1973 I had been in full-time pastoral ministry in the central Andes of Peru and now I was reimmersing myself in the intellectual waters of academia. As a Catholic priest/instructor in philosophy I had studied, taught, and written on nonviolence, but now the Maoist revolutionary group in Peru, *Sendero Luminoso* ("Shining Path"), had destroyed my theories and strategies of active nonviolence. Slowly, while at the Catholic campus of Notre Dame, I tried making contact with theologians, philosophers, and "peace people" to seek help for the impasse I was in.

One night the pacifist Colman McCarthy, a columnist for the *Washington Post*, gave a talk on nonviolence. Informally, he recounted various anecdotes and personal experiences in his positive exhortation for peace and nonviolence. When he ended there was a time for questions. There were one or two simple comments. Then a long silence. To my own surprise I found myself explaining publicly the situation of total violence which we had in Peru and asked the speaker his counsel. To my embarrassment, the man lost his composure. He could hardly talk. He mumbled a few things about "doing what you could do" and then the person in charge mercifully declared the evening's program closed.

I returned to my quarters that night at a loss to know where to turn.

Early the next morning I found in my faculty box on the Notre Dame campus a note saying in effect that Colman McCarthy waffled on my question and that, *yes*, there *is* something one can say and one can *do* in such a situation as we had in Peru. The note was signed by John Howard Yoder. I looked him up immediately. And while I had read his work *The Politics of Jesus,* I now took on Professor Yoder as a loving mentor, a colleague and, over the years, a challenging correspondent. So when I, priest-missionary, needed help in nonviolence on the campus of a Catholic university, I found the needed advice and companionship in the person and the wisdom of the Mennonite theologian, John Howard Yoder.

This essay is written in grateful acknowledgment of the loving service and the Socratic questioning which I have received over the past few years.

The development of my own understanding of nonviolence has coincided with very distinct periods of my life. But when I make autobiographical references, I do not want to reduce what I have to say to a mere retelling of an individual story so that it is just one more witness or testimony. My thesis is that there is a very definite logic and structure (a metaphysics, if you will) to the theory and practice of nonviolence and that it is well worth our time and effort to articulate, define, and make explicit that logical structure. I present this paper with the hope that John Howard Yoder would be the first to agree.

1. The Need of a Metaphysics for Nonviolence

To some the term "metaphysics" may seem somewhat quaint. But for a Catholic priest trained in Thomistic philosophy (Ph.D., Saint Louis University, 1964), who in the sixties taught at a liberal arts Catholic college (Saint Joseph's College, Rensselaer, Indiana) "metaphysics" referred to some permanent underlying structure of ultimate reality. One can speak of "logical structure," "grounding consequences," "guiding principles," "criteria and strategies." In any case, nonviolence is not simply being a "nice guy" or "turning the other cheek" or an excuse for an outing at some munitions plant or for doing a groupie thing at Woodstock.

I worked at defining nonviolence. One must overcome the obvious semantic difficulty that the form of the word is negative. Also one must address the popular notion that only violence achieves results. Violence marks the whole of human history. Frantz Fanon, a student of Sartre, declared that oppressed peoples can acquire self-identity and dignity only by "creative" violent action. After the assassination of Dr. Martin Luther King, Jr., the Students' Nonviolent Coordinating Committee (SNCC) lost its sense of nonviolence and took up Mao's Little Red Book to say that "Power comes only through the barrel of a gun!" The new buzz word was *Power*. And it may appear that only the violent person is active, powerful, dominating, creative, in control of things.

Yet, along with J. Glenn Gray, my analysis is that violence belongs much more to the Aristotelian logical category of passion than to the category of action. In violence, one looks first at the victim who has suffered by an action of another, an action which is both external to and destructive of the victim's own inner being. A person has an individual rational nature, which is the source and center of its own free acts. Violence is destructive of that very personhood. Gray goes on to study the person actively involved in violent action. The very agent of such violence, Gray states, is no longer a free, creative, responsible person. The violent agent is enraged, overcome by emotion, reacting blindly from resentment, from frustration, from powerlessness. The first victim of violence is really the violent person who is no longer in free, responsible possession of his own being.

If *violence* is passive, then its opposite, *nonviolence,* becomes deeply personalistically active. Reflecting on the language of J. Glenn Gray, one can say that only in nonviolence can a free person, through memory, imagination, and language, possess her own inner being in consciousness and conscience. But active nonviolence must be situated in the world of real history. Since Cain killed his brother Abel, human history is a history of blood. It pervades more than just military history of wars and battles, goes further than psychologically latent aggressive instincts. Our poetry, our songs, our heroes, our dreams are filled with violence. It was Paul Ricoeur who helped me sense the narrative dimensions of violence. One who prepares to be nonviolent must realistically assess the deeply human roots of violence. And one must possess an adequate rationale in defense of nonviolence. This is what I mean by a need for a metaphysics of nonviolence.

All theories of nonviolence must start with the one master and father of nonviolence: Mohandas Karamchand Gandhi, known universally as "The Great Souled One," Mahatma Gandhi. In his early "experiments with truth," Gandhi was searching desperately for the proper word to describe what he was about. He devised the word *satyagraha. Graha* means "clinging to"; *satya* is a form of the ancient Hindu formula for the Godhead. *Sat* can mean *truth* or *being.* It is the all-pervasive and all-powerful presence of the Divine in things. (In Zen the word is *Tao.) Satyagraha,* then, is "clinging to truth," "truth force," or, as Gandhi sometimes playfully referred to it, "soul force."

Sat can be realized only in the peaceful, deeply reflective abiding with the inner force of things. In other words, nonviolence *(ahimsa)* is the very mode or

117

manner in which the true inner being of the divine presence is realized. Gandhi's experiments with truth led him to transfer and translate *satyagraha* from religious contemplation into social/political activism relevant to the historical process of India's political independence from England. One cannot separate the discipline, training, strategy, and tactics of Gandhi's active nonviolent noncooperation from his religious metaphysics. Nonviolence cannot stand alone as an independent principle or as its own goal. Gandhi spoke of *ahimsa* (nonviolence) only in the context of *satya,* only in his Hindu faith that truth, love, and goodness are present in a living unity in the world.

Dr. Martin Luther King, Jr., a Christian minister, explicitly made the Christian faith the theoretical basis for his strategy and practice of nonviolence. That is, faith in the redemptive character of Christ's death and resurrection gave King grounds for nonviolence. Obviously, as a Catholic priest-professor I accepted enthusiastically King's reinterpretation of Gandhi, but, as I will point out, I still had a lot to learn about what I later came to call the Christian spirituality of nonviolence.

Religious faith need not be the only foundation for nonviolence. Natural and human values such as family, love, peace, freedom, and justice may serve as the supporting foundation. But these words cannot be empty slogans; they must have their own profound and universal metaphysical reality. Oddly, the Marxist thesis that history inevitably will take humanity to the utopia of a perfect classless society in itself could serve as a basis for nonviolence, except that for Marx the very process is one of dialectical violence. This is the exact opposite of the *satya* or the *Tao* or some benign providence making present the Reign of God. Recent theories of the planet Earth as the Great Mother or *Gaia* could well serve as the basis for an ecological theory of nonviolence.

Upon the certainty that *satyagraha* will ultimately prevail, Gandhi could discipline his followers into "active noncooperation," or "militant-active nonviolence" to engage in protests, demonstrations, strikes, and boycotts, even using Thoreau's theories and strategies of civil disobedience. These strategies, separated from their metaphysical context, were transplanted to the United States where social activists, such as Saul Alinski, converted them into strategies for community development. Suddenly there was a new slogan for nonviolence. "It works!" The social scientists came to the defense of nonviolence. Gene Sharp (among others) demonstrated exhaustively by many specific historical examples that, in fact, nonviolence has often been a very practical and successful strategy. So nonviolence was incorporated into political strategies and in worldwide nongovernmental organizations as a pragmatic tool, totally abstracted from all metaphysics. Obviously, as a pure method, it could be employed towards any end: for or against abortion; for or against assisted suicide;

for or against the rights of Native Americans to the land. Gandhi, who always identified the means with the end as one sole entity, would be aghast at the new applications of nonviolence as pure technique. Only through my Peruvian experience did I come to realize that both Gandhi and the pragmatic social scientists presumed a great number of prior conditions necessary to make active nonviolence feasible.

At this point of my growth in nonviolence I became intrigued by liberation theology, which said that the fundamental posture of Christian theology (and philosophy?) was not academic, abstract orthodoxy but Christian orthopraxis. So I packed up my books and writings on nonviolence and carried them to the central Andes of Peru. There I became engaged in full-time pastoral ministry with miners, peasants, and shepherds for some twenty years.

It was a time of great social turmoil in Peru. After twelve years of military rule, in May 1980, a general election gave Peru a democratically elected President and Congress. But in a small, remote mountain village (Chuscchis) in the Department of Ayacucho, armed men took the ballot boxes and burned them. It was the first public act of *Sendero Luminoso* (to be commemorated every year thereafter with planned acts of terrorism). And slowly my theory and practice of active nonviolence began to unravel.

2. Prior Sociopolitical Conditions for Nonviolence

During the 1970s, the political left made some dramatic displays of strength in Peru, although it was internally divided. I watched church groups toy with different aspects of Marxism. I always found myself on the outside.

First of all, I was turned off by the shallowness of empty sloganeering. Also, I was working within the mining section, with Marxist-indoctrinated labor unions, and I saw no serious program that could change the fate of our people for the better. But mostly, I retained the intellectual ideals of nonviolence. I didn't want to think about the possible meaning of slogans such as "Armed conflict to the ultimate consequences!"

I heard about academic disputes among Marxists in the provincial universities. Marxism was a foregone conclusion. But the rising power groups talked about a pure Maoism, using the Peruvian peasant class as its base. The charismatic leader was Abimael Guzman, a philosophy teacher at the National University of San Cristobal of Huamanga in Ayacucho. After years of training small cells of university students, "President Gonzalo" sent well-indoctrinated teachers to all parts of the Sierra teaching a pure Maoist ideology of violence.

When the open violence began, I accepted the fact very slowly and be-

119

came simply aghast at what was happening. I knew the people of the peasant villages, and I could not imagine how they had been motivated into such brutal violence. In time, the Peruvian government sent in its armed forces and a classic "dirty war" began. To my horror I came to realize that what we had so blithely studied in the sixties in Mao's *Little Red Book* was being replayed right here in Peru. Guzman's revolution was a textbook example of Maoist strategy: A general environment of terror was created. Dynamite explosions in front of public buildings become regular features. Bridges, railroads, and high tension electric lines are destroyed. Towns and major cities — even Lima — have frequent blackouts. The military arrive in force. They are sniped at, ambushed, demoralized. Far back into the mountains, a small armed band comes upon an isolated peasant village. They hold all-day, all-night classes in consciousness-raising. Attendance and compliance are obligatory. Especially the youth are easily converted and conscripted into the revolutionary movement.

The armed forces hear about the Senderista presence in the village. Who informed the police? The Senderistas perform summary execution of all the "squealers" ("soplones"). The army arrives. But secretly the Senderistas return and kill a few army troops. The army searches the village for the killers and make "disappear" a few villagers. The armed forces, of course, cannot stay at every little village all through the Sierra. Weeks later common graves are uncovered. Families identify the missing people. The Senderistas return to the village. "See," they say. "There is the enemy. The army are the ones that kill."

In time, all ordinary public officials — the mayor, the notaries, the representatives of government bureaucracies — have either been executed or have long since left. In the vacuum of all law and order, common criminals begin their own operations, especially through blackmail and threats. In some cases, old family feuds break out anew. In some areas, drug lords operate brazenly, either defying or collaborating with Sendero or with would-be law-enforcing officials. This is what we call the situation of *total violence*.

Slowly I came to realize that the strategy of active nonviolence was no longer germane. To stage a protest march in such an environment would be like lighting a candle in a hurricane. Civil disobedience was unthinkable: there were no courts, judges, or trials. I came to realize that active nonviolence — even that of Gandhi — depended upon a number of prior social, political conditions.

Gandhi was familiar with the law in England and trusted the English common law court system. Gandhi could depend upon a favorable world press. Gandhi could argue, plead (even from prison), to a public realm of common ideals and values. Even more was this the case for Martin Luther King, Jr., Thoreau, and my old colleagues in the peace movements in the United States.

120

Active nonviolence requires for its success a number of essential conditions: a well-established state, a functioning government, a legal system (including independent courts and judges) that generates a reasonable degree of confidence and respect. And, underlying all of this, there is a general consensus on the meaning of life, on human rights, and on basic ethical values. None of this was present with us in Peru (or in many other parts of the world today) in what is a situation of *total violence*. Nonviolence no longer promised pragmatic social success. So what were we to do? This was my question to Colman McCarthy that night at Notre Dame.

3. A Christian Spirituality of Nonviolence

As a Catholic priest, I was active within the Peruvian Conference of Religious Superiors. We were very sensitive to the suffering of our people. Through the years of 1986-89 we formed inter-congregational teams to give traditional missions in those "emergency zones" where there were no longer resident pastors or religious Sisters. In preparing the mission teams we briefed them on the psychology of fear and on knowing the precise nature of the dangers they would face from the various violent elements in the area. Of course, all this was done within a context of deep Christian faith and commitment. Gingerly, we addressed the issue of possible martyrdom.

The violence unleashed in the high Andes spread rapidly to all parts of Peru. Now the role of the Religious Conference was not to prepare people to go to the areas of violence, but to prepare them to confront and withstand the violence as it came upon them in their own communities. The first question was: Do we stay or do we leave? Overwhelmingly, the religious agreed to stay with their suffering people. But *why* do we stay and *what* do we do if we stay? We came upon the famous question of John Howard Yoder: What to do when there is nothing to do? How were we to be nonviolent?

We were all Christians, so, of course, our basic sense of faith, prayer, commitment, and hope were centered on Christ and the Gospels. The metaphysical underpinnings of our nonviolence would be Christian, a Christian nonviolence. But that sounds too theoretical and abstract. We needed a spirituality.

I define spirituality as an ordered, disciplined transformation of life according to clearly defined principles and values. The *life* I transform can be my own or it can be the life of society or of the whole planet. It is an ordered and disciplined process, not a fly-by-night onetime experience. A *Christian* spirituality finds its "principles and values" in the following of Jesus of Nazareth.

Jesus is the same yesterday, today, and forever. But as the science of her-

121

ERNEST W. RANLY

meneutics teaches, when the observer's whole world changes, the very objects of observation also change. Our new world of total violence made us look upon the Scriptures in a new light. We began to comb the Scriptures to discover the nonviolent Jesus.

First of all, we discovered that Jesus was born into a century of rebellions, massacres, terror, class conflicts, religious fanaticism, official corruption, assaults, and robberies. Many of his parables speak to the surrounding realities of injustice and cruelty: the Good Samaritan, the unjust judge, the vineyard worker-assassins. The vaunted *Pax Romana* was a cruel peace imposed by the Roman Empire through force of arms. In one instance, the Romans crucified two thousand insurgents. Matthew tells the story of Herod ordering the death of children less than two years old born in Bethlehem and its surroundings. Violence touched Jesus very closely when at the whim of a drunken king the head of John the Baptist was served on a platter during a feast of the royal court. Today's barbarities can hardly surpass that! John's disciples lovingly buried his remains and the Gospels say that Jesus withdrew alone to pray. But as John Howard Yoder had pointed out years before, the "politics" of Jesus was to return to his people and confront his adversaries. He did not retreat to a monastery or hermitage.

Jesus understood the violence of his own time. Three times he announced in detail the manner of his own death. We say, then, that it is in the spirit of Jesus to study and understand the specific tactics and strategies of the violence that is around us. Liberation theology always starts from our own *realidad*. Therefore, we studied Mao's *Little Red Book* as well as the tactics of National Security. For many this was a new kind of retreat: studying in bloody detail the strategies of the violent elements operative in our world. Our question was: How to follow Christ in situations of violence?

We felt the need to face up to the common phenomenon of fear. A Christian spirituality must build upon solid health of mind and body. Open violence brings on extraordinary stress and anxiety. Fear is a powerful, gripping, wrenching emotion that is not easily kept under control of mind or will. Rising as it does out of that most basic instinct of self-preservation, fear is not only irrepressible but it is also useful — essential, in fact — in helping the prudent person assess real dangers. It can be pragmatically and psychologically dangerous to deny or hide the fact of fear or to regard it as a sign of weakness. Fear joined with guilt becomes an unbearable burden.

So, again, within the context of a retreat, there were group dynamics over fear. A Christian spirituality of nonviolence presupposes a community environment of support that allows all to share openly their feelings of fear, anxiety, frustration, and helplessness. Superiors must become very sensitive and doubly considerate when dealing with subjects suffering under such stress. Some persons should simply be transferred from the more conflictive areas. Those who stay must make a free, deeply personal option in favor of nonviolence (as we have seen in the very definition of nonviolence). Meanwhile, those who stay in violent zones feel the need for more free time, more recreation, more times to share their feelings. Grace presupposes and builds upon the natural. In times of violence we need new ways to follow the nonviolent Christ.

4. A Spirituality of Presence

We began to formulate what we called "a spirituality of presence." What to do when there is nothing to do? All social works, such as soup kitchens, people's cooperatives, and distribution of food and clothing, had to be stopped. In some places, even church services, the sacraments, public ceremonies were severely limited. In other words, we openly acknowledged that there were no immediate social goals to be gained by our presence.

Was the nonviolence of Jesus a strategy to gain other social, political goals? The life, teaching, and praxis of Jesus must be understood in its totality within his world of unrestrained violence. Jesus, the beloved Son, always felt close intimacy with the Father, Abba. He came preaching peace. The message of his life is the Good News that God is present in human history in the love of Jesus, poor, humble, and meek. The kingdom of God is not to be won by the sword, as Jesus clearly states at the time of his arrest. The final vindication is only to be had by the kerygmatic proclamation of the resurrection.

We look for different signs to attest to the presence of the kingdom. In spite of our professed faith, we Christians are still very much pagans, or at best Pelagians, trusting in our own works or thinking that economic or social advances are major criteria of the kingdom of heaven. Total violence strips away all such delusions. Simply staying in areas of conflict helps make manifest the continuing presence of the kingdom of God. This humble, quiet, valiant presence, in solidarity with the victims of violence, is the presence of Christ among us.

There are wakes and burials to attend, with all the turbulent emotions when the dead are victims of mindless violence. While we avoid specific suggestions or formulas for action, yet our presence should be *visible*. All the people — the suffering residents of the area, the military, the various subversive groups — should know that the church has remained in the region. During armed general strikes, walking with the people, visiting homes, playing soccer with the youth create a wonderful sense of solidarity.

When we have nothing to do we finally do what Christ did so simply and effectively: a prayerful, faith-filled spirituality of presence. This becomes a reconciling, peacemaking presence. Some of us see this as a sacramental presence where the Eucharist takes on a broader sacramental, communitarian effectiveness. Women may turn to Mary, the Mother of Jesus, at the foot of the Cross, along with other women. Again, the silent presence of those women is a powerful political statement, denouncing sin and injustice and announcing hope in God.

The Christian spirituality of nonviolent presence should not be construed as an expression of mere passive resignation, of quietism or fatalism. Our presence was a concrete form of political/historical praxis. As we have seen, nonviolence is not an escape to the desert far from the world's problems. We chose to stay with our people and share with them their sufferings.

We were not able to denounce cases of torture and the like to the public authorities (who were often the very culprits), or to protest such acts by subversive groups, or even to report them to the media, since such accounts were distorted and manipulated by irresponsible elements in the media. But we visited the tortured and we welcomed them to share their stories with us. Christian witness must always be a witness to truth. A presence that knows and preserves the truth is a powerful restraint against the Father of Lies and the destructive forces of darkness. Recent history has demonstrated the great value of documented case histories once violence passes and a country seeks reconciliation. There is much to do through a spirituality of presence.

What of martyrdom? Yes, we had to face that question. Before the violence passed, two religious Sisters and three priests had been explicitly assassinated as victims of the political violence. Several others died because of the complex circumstances of those times. No one looks upon physical death as an end in itself. As one priest testified in a group exchange: "It's easy to be killed. Any day I can join a protest, flaunt a terrorist order, denounce a public authority and I will become the direct object of a death threat." In all our testimony no one ever said that she or he was ready to die for eternal life. But many answered: "We will not abandon our people." "We will stay in our communities in service to our people." "We do not stay out of a whim to be martyrs, but to serve the people." No one has greater love than this, to give a life for friends. The nonviolent Christ died a violent death. The ultimate norm of a Christian spirituality is the following of Christ as proposed in the Gospels. The following of (the nonviolent) Christ is the supreme rule. Through our stubborn persistence and dogged reflection we had formulated and lived out a Christian spirituality of nonviolence.

5. Nonviolence as Reconciliation

In 1992 Robert Schreiter, C.PP.S., sent me his book *Reconciliation: Mission and Ministry in a Changing Social Order.*[1] Within a worldwide context of violence, Schreiter studies the relation of violence and reconciliation, outlines very succinctly the genuine Christian understanding of reconciliation and describes the church's role in mission and in ministry in the service of reconciliation. I now understand Schreiter's ideas on reconciliation as a natural (almost necessary) complement to what we had left incomplete when we defined the Christian spirituality of nonviolence as a spirituality of presence. Yes, Christian nonviolence is an ongoing presence, which then allows and invites the power of God to realize a deeper spiritual reconciliation.

Schreiter carefully defines what Christian reconciliation *is not*. Needless to say, it is not pacification imposed upon a people by military power or by more subtle political or economic measures. Consonant with what we have explained above, reconciliation is *not* conflict resolution; it is not arbitration; it is not a skill to be mastered to manage the cessation of hostilities. These are all very positive elements, parallel to how active nonviolence can achieve positive social effects, but this is not Christian reconciliation. Nor is reconciliation a hasty peace declared by some civil authorities, often the same authorities responsible for the violence in the first place. Perpetrators of violence, once they stop the active violence, cannot simply absolve themselves and declare some kind of peace or ask for "Christian forgiveness." Nor should church people meddle too quickly in the process, especially if they have not suffered with the victims. There is the danger that they will trivialize the suffering of the victims, not seek out the underlying causes of the violence, and will too hastily conclude with a superficial peace.

Schreiter points out that although the word *reconciliation* never occurs in the Hebrew Scriptures, it is a key concept in divine revelation and especially in Christian soteriology. According to 2 Corinthians 5:18-19, it is God who initiates and brings about reconciliation. Violence is so great an evil, the emotions of enmity and resentment so strong, that only Christ, who has suffered all the degradations of being a victim, can bring it about. The Christian story as told in Romans and Second Corinthians is that reconciliation is the work of God achieved in the blood and cross of Christ. Reconciliation is a free, unmerited gift from God.

---

1. Robert Schreiter, *Reconciliation: Mission and Ministry in a Changing Social Order* (Maryknoll, NY: Orbis Books, 1992). I also have copies of his articles "Reconciliation as a Missionary Task," *Missiology* 20 (1992): 3-10 and "Reconciliation as a Model of Mission," *Neue Zeitschrift für Missionswissenschaft* 52 (1996): 243-50.

Reconciliation is a process we discover already active in God through Christ. Yet the process begins only with the victim, with that victim who in the depth of his wrath and impotence has felt the presence of Christ "who proves his love for us in that while we were still sinners, he died for us" (Rom. 5:8-9). Reconciliation is not simply a new resolution on the part of the victim. It is discovered in the justifying and reconciling grace of God welling up within the very throes of violence. God in Christ enters into the depths of the experience of human suffering, of conflict and of violence which, through the resurrection of Christ, is a new story of deliverance and life. Christian reconciliation is a new creation which embraces all dimensions of reality, even the cosmic. In this new reality, both the victim and the oppressor must begin to see themselves and their world in a new light. The victim does not "forgive and forget." The victim is asked to remember in great detail his sufferings; as we have seen, he must give witness to the full truth of what has happened. But in the full mercy of God, the victim begins to understand that in Christ God would want to forgive the oppressor. And in this moment of grace, the victim begins to realize anew his own inner dignity and self-worth. This all-too-brief summary of Schreiter's thesis on Christian reconciliation squares perfectly with our experiences in Peru both during and after the times of active violence.

A major point made by Schreiter is how we can become (should become) *ministers* of reconciliation. He writes within the theology of mission and sees reconciliation as a missionary task in the contemporary world of change and conflict. But I want to add that a ministry of reconciliation is the culminating task of a spirituality of nonviolence. In other words, what we were content to call simply a spirituality of presence will have a much deeper human and mystical fulfillment in the ministry of reconciliation.

Only the victim in God's good time can come to experience how in Christ God also loves the oppressor, is willing to forgive the oppressor and can effect a new creation between the victim and the oppressor, which is called Christian reconciliation. The shattered victim discovers God's offer of healing grace and accepts God's favor as a restoration of an abused and broken humanity. Others can become ministers of reconciliation only by being in solidarity with the victim and being invited and allowed to be ministers of reconciliation by the victim. The spirituality of presence now becomes a ministry of reconciliation. In staying faithful to the Jesus story both in proclamation and in witness, nonviolent persons become conduits of the saving and reconciling grace of Christ, who by his blood makes of diverse groups one people. They allow the victims to express in cries and prayers the anguish of their sufferings, in union with Christ and with so many of the Psalms. They never hide the full truth of humanity's crimes but they offer — in Schreiter's words — "a ministry in which one can

126

hold on to hope against the apparent odds of broken lives and communities. . . . In which the human community can be imagined from a new place: this is surely the Good News of Jesus Christ in our time. News of one who has known our suffering, who now knows glory but still bears the scars of his torture and death."

THE POLITICS OF JESUS
REVISITED

Jesus and the Zealot Option

William Klassen

This occasion of honoring the memory of my friend, neighbor, and colleague provides an opportunity to assess again the Zealot option of Jesus, a hypothesis seriously challenged by a number of writers. For John Howard Yoder, "the very core of [Jesus'] originality was his rejection (sympathetic, but a clear rejection nonetheless) of the Zealot option."[1] The fundamental questions he has raised about historical Jesus research deserve a critical discussion. If indeed there was no Zealot option, because, as we are repeatedly told, there was no Zealot party and no Zealots at the time of Jesus, then Yoder's thesis loses its cogency and logical strength.

It is my hypothesis that Yoder's thesis is as strong as ever as a historical postulate and that virtually all modern scholars who reject it have been duped into an untenable position, largely because of the vigor with which Morton Smith could argue a point and the icy ridicule, if not contempt, with which he dismissed all those who disagreed with him. The republication of Smith's major essay on the Zealots in his collected essays twenty-six years later, without any critical assessment,[2] is, I suggest, a disservice to all scholars, not least to Smith himself, who enjoyed critical response. For if his thesis was flawed when the essay was first published, it is even more discredited today.

To be sure, senior historians of the early church at times assumed that the Zealots were an insignificant fringe sect of Judaism, with little to add to our un-

---

1. *The Politics of Jesus* (Grand Rapids: Eerdmans, 1972), 100. This remains unchanged in the second edition (1994), p. 98. On pages 56-59 of the later book, Yoder addresses, with his usual acuity, the argument of Horsley and others.

2. Morton Smith, *Studies in the Cult of Yahweh, Vol. 1: Studies in Historical Method, Ancient Israel, Ancient Judaism*, ed. Shaye Cohen (Leiden: E. J. Brill, 1996), 211-26.

derstanding of Judaism in the Second Temple period, of the life of Jesus of Nazareth, or of the literature of the early Christian movement. The Zealots were mostly neglected in treatments of early Christian history and background. Robert M. Grant, for example, ignores them almost completely in spite of his recognition that the relationship of Jesus to the revolutionary movements of his time deserves careful attention.[3]

By contrast, most treatments of the sects and parties of Judaism, and virtually all Jewish scholars, deal with the Zealots as a subgroup of the Pharisees. Marcel Simon even declares it

> certain that the milieu in which Jesus lived and acted was saturated with the Zealot spirit. Jesus himself, put to death by the Romans as a Zealot, constantly had to make clear his position over against this militant wing of Jewish nationalism. He disavowed this movement, being no more attached to it than he was to Pharisaism.[4]

Simon is a case of a Jewish scholar studying his own history, who was not able to avoid an encounter with the phenomenon of zeal and the role it played in the first century.[5] Although liberal Protestants who studied Judaism, like George Foot Moore in his classic study of Judaism,[6] virtually ignored zeal, David Flusser sees Jesus' teaching about the kingdom of heaven as an idea taken from the Rabbis and directed against the Zealots, and he concludes that "the main

---

3. Robert M. Grant, *A Historical Introduction to the New Testament* (New York: Harper, 1963), 277.

4. Marcel Simon, *Jewish Sects at the Time of Jesus* (Philadelphia: Fortress, 1967), 43-46. For this quote, see 138. The standard accusations of bias in favor of a Zealot hypothesis driven by theological interests were begun by Kirsopp Lake (in his article "The Zealots," in F. J. Foakes Jackson and Kirsopp Lake, *The Beginnings of Christianity, Vol. 1: The Acts of the Apostles* [London: Macmillan, 1920], 424) and echoed by Smith against Schürer and by Horsley against Schlatter and Hengel. They hardly apply to Simon.

5. Most remarkable, perhaps, is the role attributed to the Zealots by Joseph Klausner in his book *Jesus of Nazareth: His Life, Times, and Teaching,* trans Herbert Danby (New York: Macmillan, 1929). He considers Jesus close to the Zealots in his early ministry. The Zealots were hotheaded enthusiasts (222): "the finest patriots Israel knew from the rise of the Maccabeans to the defeat of Bar Kokhba . . . their one crime . . . they acted according to their conscience" (204). "Simply active and extremist Pharisees" . . . "they merely added to their love for the written and oral law of God the duty of protecting it with the sword" (205). The majority of Jewish interpreters appear to conclude either that Judas Iscariot was a Zealot or had leanings in their direction. E.g., see Irving Zeitlin, *Jesus and the Judaism of His Time* (Cambridge: Polity Press, 1988).

6. George Foot Moore, *Judaism in the First Centuries of the Christian Era* (Cambridge, MA: Harvard University Press, 1954), 3 vols. The index does not even list the Zealots, although Phineas is mentioned on two occasions under "Expiatory Suffering," (I, 549, also cf. vol. III, 165) and as being like Elijah the typical zealot, "the incarnation of zeal for the Lord," (II, 358).

guilt of Jesus' generation was its apocalyptic fever which found its dangerous expression in Zealotism."[7]

Kaufman Kohler,[8] perhaps more than any other one person, opened our eyes to the existence of the Zealots as a distinct group. Adolph Schlatter, who showed such a superb knowledge of and sensitivity to the fact that early Christians were first of all Jews, in his history of Judaism and of the early church,[9] used all of the sources and made some very astute observations about the Zealots and their relation to Christianity and to Judaism.

This is also true of the excellent article on ζέλος in Kittel's *Theological Wordbook* written by Albrecht Stumpff.[10] One of the difficulties in dealing with the Zealots is the variety of terms used to describe them. Thus we have the generic term "robbers," the term "Sicarii" from the Latin word "sica" meaning dagger, and even the term Galileans[11] may refer to this group.

Since Robert Eisler wrote his two-volume work *Jesus King, Not Ruling* (1929/30) and his book *Messiah Jesus and John the Baptist* (1931) in which he tried to show that Jesus was a Zealot, this party has been given more consideration and more concentrated study. Eisler's thesis was partially accepted by S. G. F. Brandon in his book *The Fall of Jerusalem and the Christian Church* (1951), and in the later book on *Jesus and the Zealots: A Study of the Political Factor in Primitive Christianity* (1967), and since then the importance of the Zealots has been recognized. But in spite of that, there are still people, following Kirsopp Lake who wrote in 1920, who argue that the movement must be seen only as a tendency and not as a party; that since Josephus does not use the word "Zealot" to describe a political party until he describes the events of 66 C.E., this indicates that the party did not exist until the period of the Jewish war.[12]

---

7. See Flusser's book *Jesus* (1968; now available in a good expanded English translation [Jerusalem: Magnes Press, 1997]): 105-7. The quote is from David Flusser, *Judaism and the Origins of Christianity* (Jerusalem: Magnes Press, 1988): 531.

8. See Kohler's article, "Zealots," in the *Jewish Encyclopedia* 12 (1906): 639-43.

9. See, e.g., Adolph Schlatter, *The Church in the New Testament Period*, trans. Paul P. Levertoff (London: SPCK, 1955), especially 55, 84-85, 198-200, 256, 268-69.

10. Gerhard Kittel, *Theologisches Wörterbuch zum Neuen Testament* (Stuttgart: W. Kohlhammer, 1949-1979), 2: 879-90, especially 886-90. See also the articles on ληστής by Karl Heinrich Rengstorf in 4:262-68 and on "sicarius" by Otto Betz in 7:277-81.

11. Seán Freyne, *Galilee from Alexander the Great to Hadrian 323 B.C.E. to 135 C.E.: A Study of Second Temple Judaism* (Notre Dame: University of Notre Dame Press, 1980) cautions not to impute too much Zealot influence into Galilee per se, but deals extensively with the role of the Zealots and concludes that the differences among Smith, Rhoads, and Hengel "may to some extent be a difference of emphasis" (219).

12. See his essay "The Zealots" in *The Beginnings of Christianity*. His first sentence reads: "It is somewhat of a shock to discover from Josephus that, if his evidence be correct, the use of

Kirsopp Lake, who first cited this evidence, treated Josephus quite uncritically and drew very interesting evidence from it. He also displayed considerable animus against theologians. He was followed by Morton Smith,[13] who drew the most astonishing conclusions, most of which are quite naively accepted by Richard Horsley in his crusade to remove the Zealots from consideration as a foil for our understanding of Jesus. And it has worked. Seldom, I suggest, have so many people been seduced by such frothy evidence.[14]

Even an exacting scholar like Raymond Brown concludes that "the evidence in Josephus places *the first existence* of the sicarii and the Zealots in Palestine two or three decades after Judas' death."[15] In the light of this somewhat confusing picture we address the question: Were the Zealots a voluntary association at the time of Jesus? Or where they a "coalition" instead of a party?[16] Or perhaps a "community"?[17] a network?[18]

Whatever may be the exact relationship between Jesus and the Zealots, if such a group existed during his life, the pressure to study his relationship to them has come from two directions:

---

the name Zealot to describe a Jewish sect or party cannot be earlier than A.D. 66." What is not often observed is that Kirsopp and Sylvia Lake recognized the strength of the "Patriotic party" and that "part of the teaching of Jesus was a strong polemic against the Zealots . . . and in favour of the Poor and the Meek" (*Introduction to the New Testament* [London, 1938]:198, 229).

13. Smith, "Zealots and Sicarii: Their Origins and Relation," *Harvard Theological Review* 64: (1971): 1-19; see above footnote 2 and Marcus Borg, "The Currency of the Term 'Zealot,'" *Journal of Theological Studies* 22 (1971): 504-12.

14. That this view has become a part of NT dogma is clear from such statements as: "The Zealot party did not yet exist, but there were already some who thought in terms of a real war" (E. P. Sanders, *The Historical Figure of Jesus* [London: Penguin, 1993], 190) and "It is now impossible, however, to link Jesus with the Zealots, because they did not appear as a major party in Judaism until the Great Revolt against Rome which began in 66 C.E." (James Charlesworth, *Jews and Christians* [New York, Crossroad, 1990], 44). Note that Sanders says only the "party" did not yet exist, while for Charlesworth since it was not a "major" party, it could not be linked to Jesus. Presumably Jesus would be linked only to "major" parties.

15. Raymond Brown, *The Death of the Messiah* (New York: Anchor, 1992) 2:1415 (my italics). See also 1:689-93. He also accepts Smith's position that the usage in Josephus defines when a group came into existence and began to be an option.

16. As suggested by Torrey Seland, *Establishment Violence in Philo and Luke: Study of Non-Conformity to the Torah and Jewish Vigilante Reactions* (Leiden: Brill, 1995). His study of zeal and Phineas is especially important, pp. 42-74.

17. So David Rhoads, *Israel in Revolution 6-74 C.E.* (Philadelphia, 1976), 55. "A community with a tradition of devotion to this point of view," and "a connection between Judas the Galilean and the later Sicarii."

18. As suggested by Harold Remus. I am grateful to the Waterloo Biblical Colloquium for many helpful suggestions in discussing an earlier draft.

(1) a wider study of the relationship of Jesus and the early church to the state in the first century. Oscar Cullmann, in his work *The State in the New Testament* (1956), particularly advocated the thesis that Jesus was in active touch with the political movements of his time. This was also supported by W. R. Farmer in his book, published during the same year, entitled *Maccabees, Zealots and Josephus* (1956). John Howard Yoder's book, *The Politics of Jesus*, closely examined this relationship and is the most capable attempt yet to see Jesus as a human being who had political options before him.

(2) The second source is the burgeoning studies in the makeup of Judaism in the first century and therefore the relationship of each group to the early Christians. The best work in this area comes from Martin Hengel, whose fundamental thesis was that

> the history of Palestinian Judaism from the time of Pompey's conquest of Jerusalem until the Revolt of Bar Koseba about two hundred years later is deeply marked by the Jews' struggle for religious and political freedom. It was during the middle period of these two centuries — from the time when Judea became a Roman province until the destruction of Jerusalem — that the so-called 'Zealots' appeared as exponents of that struggle for freedom.[19]

What appears obvious is that Jesus and the emerging Christianity never joined in the Sadducean unreserved submission to the Roman state, for this submission was born out of religious indifference. More important and perhaps more attractive to emerging Christianity was the theoretical solution of the problem of the state as represented by the Pharisees, the Essenes, and especially by the Zealots.

The Zealots clearly represent the sharpest expression of the theocratic ideal. It is firmly based in the Hebrew Scriptures, particularly in the story of Phineas in Numbers 25:10-13. The narrative there reports that when Israel had settled at Shittim the people gave themselves over to debauchery with the daughters of Moab. They joined in the sacrifices to their gods and as a result of this the anger of Yahweh blazed out against them. Yahweh tells Moses that he is to take all the leaders of the people, impale them before Yahweh in the sun; then the burning anger of Yahweh will turn away from Israel. Moses is then reported as saying to the judges of Israel: "Everyone of you must put to death those of his people who have committed themselves to the Baal of Peor." The narrative then goes on:

19. Martin Hengel, *The Zealots*, trans. David Smith (Edinburgh: T. & T. Clark, 1989), 1.

A man of the sons of Israel came along, bringing the Moabite woman into his family, under the very eyes of Moses and the whole community of the sons of Israel as they wept at the door of the tent of the meeting. When he saw this, Phineas the priest, son of Eleazar son of Aaron, stood up and left the assembly, seized a lance, followed the Israelite into the alcove, and there rammed them both through, the Israelite and the woman, right through the groin. (Num. 25:6-8)

The narrator reports that thus the plague was arrested after twenty-four thousand people had died.

In addition, Yahweh now speaks to Moses and commends Phineas for having turned away the wrath of Yahweh from the sons of Israel:

Because he was the only one among them to have the same zeal as I have; for this I did not make an end in my zeal, of the sons of Israel. Proclaim this, therefore: to him I now grant my covenant of peace. For him and his descendants after him, this covenant shall ensure the priesthood forever. In reward for his zeal for his God, he shall have the right to perform the ritual of atonement over the sons of Israel.[20]

In Psalm 106:30 recognition is given to Phineas for his intervention and for his checking of the plague and reference is made to his "reputation for virtue through successive generations forever."

The central factor in the story of Phineas is that Phineas is commended above all for his zeal. The word which is used to describe this refers to someone who is passionately active for Yahweh. It is someone who becomes an agent for God's righteous wrath and judgment against idolatry, or who commits to any action which will stem the tide of transgression of the law which could excite God's jealousy. In the studies of the Holy War in the Hebrew Scriptures it has been concluded that the Holy War is a cultic event, an institution in which the Godself acts. This zeal is itself, according to Hengel, an eschatological sharpening of the law and indicates the heightened demands of the law in moments of eschatological urgency.

Perhaps more significant for the study of the origins of the Zealot party is the reference made to him in 1 Maccabees 2:54 where Phineas is described as a forerunner of the Maccabees. The incident is similar to Numbers 25 in that the people of

---

20. "The episode became a paradigmatic example in perpetuity," writes George Mendenhall in his treatment of this incident in "The Incident at Beth Baal Peor," in *The Tenth Generation: The Origins of the Biblical Tradition* (Baltimore: Johns Hopkins University Press, 1974), 105-21, present quote from 106. In "Jesus and Phineas: A Rejected First Century Role Model," in *SBL Seminar Papers* (1986): 490-500, I trace the pervasive influence of this incident and especially of Phineas in the first century.

Israel are unfaithful to God and Mattathias "showed his fervent zeal for the law just as Phinehas had done by killing Zimri" (1 Macc. 2:24). Later he is described as "our Father, who never flagged in zeal, and his was the covenant of an everlasting priesthood" (1 Macc. 2:54). It seems clear now that zeal was also a phenomenon at Qumran and even that Phineas may be mentioned in their documents. [21]

But where do early Christianity and zealotism intersect? With respect to Paul, Johannes Weiss was convinced that Paul would have had an intense aversion to the zealotism of Palestine and suggests that for Paul it was a dark force of iniquity.[22] More recently, Terry Donaldson explores the interesting hypothesis that the pre-conversion Paul was motivated by zeal in his persecution of the church. He describes as "thoroughly discredited" "the popular view, in which the 'Zealots' existed as a party agitating for rebellion from the time of its founding by Judas of Galilee until it was finally successful in 66 c.e."[23] Thus he is clear that Paul was driven by zeal "but he was not a member of an identifiable Zealot party." What is perhaps most remarkable about Donaldson's paper is that it does not once refer to Hengel's book on the Zealots but Smith is quoted as an almost canonical figure in this connection. This omission is not corrected in his recent book on Paul.[24]

More important is the question of the intersection of Jesus with this religious attitude of zeal. It has been a topic of considerable discussion.[25] Uro, for example, notes that

21. Paul Garnet finds a number of references and allusions to Phineas. See his *Salvation and Atonement in the Qumran Scrolls,* (WUNT 2 reihe #3) (Tübingen: Siebeck, 1977), 59-60; 66-68; 80, 100-102; 110-11.

22. Johannes Weiss, *Earliest Christianity,* trans. F. C. Grant (New York: Harper Torch, 1959), 2:591, 614.

23. In his article, "Zealot and Convert: The Origin of Paul's Christ-Torah Antithesis," *Catholic Biblical Quarterly* 51 (1989): 673 n. 66.

24. T. Donaldson, *Paul and the Gentiles* (Philadelphia: Fortress, 1997). In his article, "Zealots," in *International Standard Biblical Encyclopedia,* ed. Geoffrey Bromiley (Grand Rapids: Eerdmans, 1988), he lists Hengel but does not discuss him (4:1175-79). In an article, "Rural Bandits, City Mobs and the Zealots," *Journal for the Study of Judaism* 21 (1990): 19-40, Donaldson deals with Hengel as he provides a critical analysis of Horsley's theory on the relationship between social banditry and the Zealots. Stephen Westerholm considers a "full-scale study both of Zealots and Sicarii and their legal understanding a desideratum." In Peter Richardson and Stephen Westerholm, eds., *Law in Religious Communities in the Roman Period* (Waterloo, ON: Wilfred Laurier University Press, 1991), 3.

25. See among others Risto Uro, *Sheep Among Wolves: A Study of the Mission Instructions of Q* (Helsinki, 1987), who on pages 139ff. deals with the zealots. Hoffmann, "Die Versuchungsgeschichte in der Logien Quelle, Zur Auseinandersetzung der Judenchristen mit dem politischen Messianismus," *Biblische Zeitschrift* 13 (1969): 207-23; William Klassen, "A 'Child of Peace' (Luke 10:6) in First Century Context," *New Testament Studies* 27 (1981): 488-506.

The form of the salutation, "peace to this house" is in accordance with the normal Jewish greeting. But the description of this *shalom* makes it clear that the salutation reaches a significance which goes beyond the everyday use . . . [S]ome call it magical effect (Hoffmann, Käsemann, Bosold, and Schottroff-Stegemann).[26]

He suggests that to put it more accurately, "the greeting of the messengers relies on the dynamistic power of the uttered word manifested, e.g., in the blessings and curses. This view is strange to the modern Western mind but is common in most primitive and ancient cultures." Uro cites von Rad:

These and countless other examples to be found in comparative religion rest on a conception of language which we may call dynamistic, since here the word (or a symbolic action) is thought to possess a power which extends beyond the realm of the mind and may be effective in the spatial and material world also.[27]

He criticizes Hoffmann for using a "great deal of energy to argue that the obscure 'men of violence' (Matt. 11:12) should be read to mean Zealots for the anti-Zealotic interpretation of Q materials has been widely accepted and is plausible." The mission of the Q group then would have been closely connected with the political situation of the time. The Christian missionaries, who were opposed to the military plans of the Zealots, propagated their own more peaceful message by recruiting "sons of peace" in the decades before the outbreak of the war (cf. the "peace party" depicted by Josephus in *Wars* 4:128-34).

But according to Uro, "Such a reading of the 'house instructions' does not carry the day. It gives to 'peace' a one-sided meaning, placing the emphasis on the anti-military content of this word and leaving aside the many other religious as well as social connotations that *shalom* and *eirene* could have in the Jewish and Christian usage."[28] He sees no reason to assume that "at the time when the early instructions were formulated there was a division between war and peace parties. Indeed, he suggests: "It is questionable whether we should speak of a Zealot *party* before 66 CE at all."[29]

Uro also concludes that "[n]either does 'peace' signify a political program but is, as elsewhere in the New Testament, an essential aspect of the Christian life.

26. Uro, *Sheep Among Wolves*, 136.
27. G. von Rad, *Old Testament Theology*, vol. 2: *The Theology of Israel's Prophetic Traditions* (London: SCM Press, 1975), 85; quoted in Uro, *Sheep Among Wolves*, 137.
28. He footnotes von Rad and Förster in Kittel but fails to observe that they include all those connotations.
29. Uro, *Sheep Among Wolves*, 140 n. 95.

This means that 'son of peace' denotes one who has a share in the new faith or at least sympathizes with it. . . . [They] are local sympathizers with the Jesus movement . . . although the 'peace' probably has a specifically Christian connotation and in the mouth of a wandering charismatic functioned as an effective blessing providing magical protection to the household."[30] Uro seems to have no appreciation for the uniqueness of this formulation, whether coined by Jesus or his followers. He provides an intriguing example of how a historical distortion can cause us to lose our way in trying to understand the Jesus movement.

I select for more extensive review, Morton Smith, the most influential, and Richard Horsley, the most prolific of those who maintain that historical truth is not served by pressing the Zealot hypothesis. Since the late seventies Horsley has published at least three books (one of which, *Bandits, Prophets and Messiahs*, with J. S. Hanson, received a prize [1985]) and at least eleven articles in refereed journals on the subject of the Zealots, the Sicarii, and on the popular Jewish resistance in Roman Palestine.[31]

One major historical puzzle will be reviewed here: Who were the Zealots, were they a voluntary society, and when did they become a movement or party to be reckoned with? This is especially important since Horsley continues to insist that "'The Zealots' as a long-standing movement advocating armed rebellion against Roman rule can now clearly be seen as a modern scholarly construct based on a confusion or conflation of the 'Fourth Philosophy' or brigands. . . ." He maintains further that Josephus "clearly distinguishes the Fourth Philosophy led by Pharisees who (apparently nonviolently) resisted the Roman tribute of 6 C.E." He further argues that the "Zealots proper" formed as a group or coalition only after the revolt against Rome was well underway in the winter of 67-68 C.E. This "convenient foil" against which to portray Jesus as an apolitical teacher of nonviolence is a "scholarly construct."[32]

The Historical Question

Horsley approaches the historical question, "Were there zealots or was there a Zealot 'party' in the first three decades of the common era?", as one who has to correct the dominant theological obsession of scholars. He offers a more "real-

30. Uro, *Sheep Among Wolves*, 141. See also Gerd Theissen, *The First Followers of Jesus: A Sociological Anaylysis of the Earliest Christianity*, trans. John Bowden (London: SCM Press, 1978), 14.

31. Richard A. Horsley, *Jesus and the Spiral of Violence: Popular Jewish Resistance in Roman Palestine* (New York: Harper and Row, 1987).

32. See Horsley, "The Death of Jesus," in *Studying the Historical Jesus*, ed. Craig Evans and Bruce Chilton (Leiden: Brill, 1994), 395-422. This quote from 408.

istic" approach but he also seeks to correct "structural-functionalist social science, especially influential in Anglo-American scholarship . . . based on the assumption of a stable social system which undergoes certain tensions and adjustments while it is maintained basically intact." Instead he suggests viewing the events of the first century in Palestine as a colonial or imperial situation which "by its very structure of dynamic tensions and conflictual relationships requires a more historically conscious and dialectical approach."[33] He seeks to make precise distinctions between *sicarii* and *lēstai* and Zealots, and follows Morton Smith in arguing that the "Zealots" did not exist as a party during the life of Jesus and that they do not figure in the popular Jewish resistance against Rome until the year 66.

This important historical question was posed most sharply by Martin Hengel in the first edition of his work, *Die Zeloten* (1961). Hengel has steadfastly held the position that the Zealots were identical to the *sicarii*, that they "formed a relatively exclusive and unified movement with its own distinctive religious views and that they had a crucial influence on the history of Palestinian Judaism in the decisive period between 6 and 70 A.D." Although he does not provide a detailed investigation of the relationship between Zealotism and the New Testament he deals with a number of "points of contact," generally revealing an "authentically anti-Zealot tendency in the New Testament."[34]

Morton Smith, ten years later, challenged Hengel's position, and although Horsley[35] follows Smith in most essentials, Smith takes, at times, a quite differ-

---

33. Horsley, *Spiral,* 19. See also Horsley, "Ethics and Exegesis: 'Love Your Enemies' and the Doctrine of Non-Violence," *Journal of the American Academy of Religion* 54, 1 (1986): 9-10. He concludes that "the 'dagger men' were apparently dormant during the ministry of Jesus. Neither they, nor the Zealots proper, who originated during the Revolt in 67-68, nor any other Jewish group for which we have evidence, provides an opposition against which Jesus would have been formulating his injunction to love one's enemies." The concept of the Zealots he describes as "the most determinative false assumption."

34. Hengel, *The Zealots,* 5, 309, 378-79.

35. See especially Horsley's articles, "The Zealots: Their Origin, Relationship and Importance in the Jewish Revolt," *Novum Testamentum* 28, 2 (1986): 159-92, and "The Sicarii: Ancient Jewish 'Terrorists,'" *Journal of Religion* 59 (1979): 435-58. In the first article he says that he will "presuppose Smith's critique" and offers the opinion that "one would think that Morton Smith's sharp rebuttal would have laid these misconceptions to rest" (435). Smith has, according to Horsley, "made abundantly clear that Josephus knows the Sicarii and Zealots as totally different groups, involved at different times and places during the Jewish revolt" (436). This in spite of Smith's recognition that zeal was influential in shaping the resistance to Rome in which resistance Judas of Galilee was a prominent figure: "Judas's (of Galilee) sect survived, continued its opposition to the Romans, was led by his descendants, and in the mid-fifties, when Roman control of the country began to disintegrate, made itself notorious by a series of murders of distinguished individuals. These won this party the name of sicarii" (Smith, "Zealots and Sicarii," 18).

ent position than Horsley does. But since the former is so frequently quoted, especially in Horsley's earlier works, we will begin our discussion by retracing Smith's arguments in his oft-cited article of 1971.[36]

Smith, in reviewing the literature, praises Kohler for having isolated the admiration of zeal which leads to murder, as in the case of Phineas and Elijah, and describes zeal as widespread from Maccabean times on. He recognizes that the imitation of Phineas and Elijah was often invited and that "such thought and practice was closely connected with resistance to foreign rule." He applauds Kohler's treatment of zeal as a "major contribution, most important because it indicated that *private individuals* (my italics) might often have adopted the ideal on their own. Accordingly we cannot suppose that every individual who claimed to be a 'zealot,' or was called so by his neighbours, *was a member of an organization*."[37] It is fascinating to see how important this "individualistic" point is. Is it really conceivable that individual zealots existed in many parts of Palestine and over a number of decades without forming any sort of group?[38]

Smith also has high praise for Farmer, who worked out in detail the relationship between the Maccabees and later representatives of the tradition of zeal. He likes especially Farmer's ability to distinguish such individual zealots from "the political party that took that name."[39] Klausner is praised for having seen that the incidents of revolt against Rome in the first century "were not organized by one party" but would probably mean *only* that "Judas [of Galilee c.e. 6] was the first to make resistance to alien rulers a religious duty and to set an example of the fanaticism which later led to disaster, *not* that Judas started an organization which produced all the later incidents."[40]

---

36. Smith, "Zealots and Sicarii," 1-19. P. W. Barnett states, "It is now widely held that the Zealots emerged as a party only after the war with Rome had begun" ("The Jewish Sign Prophets," *New Testament Studies* 27 [1981]: 686) and footnotes only Smith.

37. Smith, "Zealots and Sicarii," 2, 3.

38. An idea apparently first suggested by B. Salomonsen, "Some Remarks on the Zealots with Special Regard to the term 'Qannaim' in Rabbinic Literature," *New Testament Studies* 13 (1965/67): 164-76. He credits the idea to R. Edelmann (168), and himself concludes that "the *qannaim* . . . were most likely private persons without any official position in the Jewish community . . . they had nothing to do with the patriotic Zealots of the first century" (176).

39. Farmer prefers to use the term "group" whose history we do not know and thus avoids some of the difficulties raised by Smith; see "Zealot," in *IDB* (1962) 4:936-39. H. Merkel in his article, "Zealot" in *IDB* (1976): suppl. 979-82 uses the term Zealot to refer to a "movement founded in a.d. 6-7," a "relatively unified movement" (980). Unfortunately Merkel does not discuss Brandon's thesis at all, although he rejects Smith's thesis. David Rhoads, "Zealots" in *ABD* (1992): 1043-54 suggests on the origins and goals of the Zealot coalition that "the truth may be a combination of both views" (1049).

40. Smith, "Zealots and Sicarii," 3, 5.

Josephus' statements about Judas indicate to Smith only that "he set the example and provided the rationale for resistance to Rome, not that he founded the Zealot party. . . ." It is therefore immaterial whether Judas led a considerable revolt. Smith indeed argues that because the notion of zeal was so popular it is quite unjustified to take an isolated reference to a "zealot" as evidence that the individual referred to "was a member of the party."[41]

This obsession with the idea of a "party" leads Smith to refer to "Judas' party" — "Josephus has no hesitation about referring to this party *(Sicarii)*" — but the passage he cites from Josephus (*Ant.* 20.102) has no reference to a party at all! "The social conditions would not favour the growth of a single organized, ideologically motivated party . . . there was no strong motive for submitting to a central organization, and there was a natural disinclination to do so. . . . Consequently it is not surprising that there is no evidence of any major, country-wide resistance organization, even down to the beginning of the war." Repeatedly Smith refers to "representatives of any organization," or an "extensive revolutionary organization." Smith then appeals to these "facts," dismissing Hengel's account of the development of the Zealot party as a work of fantasy.[42]

But is Smith's own description any less fantastic? Smith states that after the passage in *War* (4.161) when Josephus first introduces the name, he "frequently refers to this party." Although its composition and leadership change, it is "to judge from Josephus's expressions — always a recognizable group."[43] What those "expressions" are we are not told, and my reading of Josephus, which finds no such expressions, leads me to a conclusion directly opposite to that of Smith's.

When Smith attributes to Josephus "an account of the organization of *the*

---

41. Smith, "Zealots and Sicarii," 6. See the basic study by H. A. Brongers, "Der Eifer des Herrn Zebaoth," *Vetus Testamentum* 13 (1976): 269-84. He observes that in the religiously colored uses of the Hebrew original the person of zeal intervenes for the sake of God in order to vindicate God's sovereignty. "Proven *chasidim* come to expression here; people who identify totally with the cause of Yahweh and who take action with the same energy for God's honour as if their own were assailed. It is an expression of the deepest union with Yahweh which does not seek to avert sacrificing one's own life. Characteristic words are 'zeal for your house eats me up' (LXX *katesthio*); NEB: 'bitter enemies of your temple tear me in pieces' (Psa 69:9); 'Zeal for your house devours me for my enemies have forgotten your words' (Psa 119:139)."

42. Smith, "Zealots and Sicarii," 13-15.

43. Smith, "Zealots and Sicarii," 16. By my count Josephus uses the term "Zealot" sixty-one times; four times before 4.161 and fifty times after that. At the same time he uses the term "leaders of the Zealots" only once (4.224) and never provides a hint on how they were elected or even how they organized. In all the words of praise heaped upon the strength of the Zealots nothing is ever said about organization. The narrative of Josephus rather impresses their disorganization upon us.

Zealots as a party" (his italics), which we are invited to accept at face value, I am even more baffled. As Smith sees it, Judas of Galilee was influenced by the admiration of "zeal" and by the zealot models of Phineas and Elijah. The party of Judas resisted the Roman government as Phineas and Elijah had resisted their rulers. He then proceeds, "It seems unlikely however that the organization Judas founded . . . called itself the Zealots." The reason he gives is highly suspect: "Had it done so, the same title could hardly have been taken, as it was in the revolt, by a quite different party."[44] He thinks rather that they may have called themselves "Israel."

Surely such a conclusion is drawn without any evidence or any firsthand knowledge of how various dissident groups organize and how they go about naming themselves. Has he never heard of more than one Mennonite or Lutheran church? Indeed is there only one group which calls itself Christian? Surely exactly those who are zealous about the practice of their religion have the least compunction about using an honorific title. Precisely because it is such an honorific title, Josephus refrains from using it any more than he has to.[45] Indeed it can and has been argued that Saul also considered himself a zealot (Gal. 1:14: "extreme zealot"; Phil. 3:6; cf. Acts 21:20; 22:3).[46]

Smith, however, concluded:

> Whatever it called itself, Judas's sect survived, continued its opposition to the Romans, was led by his descendants, and in the mid-fifties, when Roman control of the country began to disintegrate, made itself notorious by a series of murders of distinguished individuals. These won this party the name of

44. Smith, "Zealots and Sicarii," 17-18.

45. The term appears some sixty times in Josephus but once it is even applied to Josiah's intense desire to follow David. Most often when it refers to a recognizable group, Josephus seeks to discredit them by using the term "so-called Zealots" (twice) or "people who called themselves Zealots." Clearly he is out to discredit what happened when zeal was wedded to violence and commitment to overthrow the Romans by force. He considered them zealous not for virtue but "in the cause of vice in its basest and most extravagant form" (4.161). "The name quite obviously refers to the ideal of zeal in the service of the Lord to which the Maccabees earlier had been loyal. The Zealots regarded themselves as soldiers of God and believed that, as such, they were entitled to special protection. Whence their ardour and intransigence." Mireille Hadas-Lebel, *Flavius Josephus: Eye Witness* (New York: Macmillan, 1993), 128-29, 166-67.

46. Jerome Murphy-O'Connor, *Paul: A Critical Life* (Oxford: Clarendon Press, 1996), 65. cites Justin Taylor (in a forthcoming publication) as considering Paul to be a Zealot, i.e., a religious nationalist during the time he persecuted Christians. Murphy-O'Connor considers the weakness of this "attractive hypothesis" that it may exaggerate the importance of "zealot" in Galatians 1:14 and "zeal" in Philippians 3:6. One of the strongest features of James Dunn's *The Theology of Paul the Apostle* (Grand Rapids: Eerdmans, 1998) is the attention he pays to "zeal as being a feature of being in Judaism" during the second temple period (350).

'sicarii' by which Josephus consistently refers to it from this time on, but we cannot suppose that every assassin in Palestine was a party member.[47]

Smith is at pains to point out that "[i]n all this history there is no evidence of any connection of these *sicarii* with the Zealots." His reason: The Zealots *"as a party"* (my italics) did not exist until the winter of 67-68 — individuals, yes, "but there is no clear evidence that they yet formed a definite party, and Josephus in *War* 4.130-161 gives a full description of the formation of the party in Jerusalem."[48] Yet surely it is possible for "connections" to exist without there being a "party."

Anyone who reads this section in Josephus will look in vain for any such description, much less a "full" one, but the idea that the Zealots became a major organized party after 66 C.E. has nevertheless been widely accepted, especially by Horsley, whose whole case rests on Smith.[49] But the impression Josephus leaves of this group is one of chaos, not of an orderly party with a clearly defined membership, a platform, a leadership responsible to membership, or whatever else we may mean by the term "party" these days. To be sure, some of the brigands collaborated in what Josephus calls their "wrecking of liberty" (*Wars* 4:159), but Josephus obviously describes them as lacking all organization or party status, although they do consider themselves zealous for vice.[50]

We need to take seriously Smith's statement that zealot values and models and strategy were alive and well from the time of the Maccabees until at least Bar Kochba. But to try to establish Smith's corollary position that these were individuals and not adherents to an organized party and that therefore no connections exist between the events of 6 C.E. and 66 C.E. is, it seems, historically naive and too closely allied with an American definition of "parties." Moreover to insist that you have to be a "party" to have influence is to betray one's existence in the ivory towers of academia, political science departments, or media organizations. The most problematic aspect of this position is that it is historically a pure construct and makes it more difficult to see the interlocking political and religious dimensions of the Zealot movement and also, of course, of the Jesus movement. In short it works against one of Horsley's major goals, especially his insistence on "concrete social context" or "social-historical context."[51]

47. Smith, "Zealots and Sicarii," 18.

48. Smith, "Zealots and Sicarii," 19.

49. See footnote 25 above. That also accounts perhaps for the fact that Smith is only once (in error it seems) referred to in Horsley's book, *Jesus and the Spiral of Violence*, 336.

50. It should be noted that Josephus does not once call them zealots until the very end of this section. For him there are two groups, the "friends of peace" and the revolutionaries who are really "wreckers of liberty."

51. Horsley, "Ethics and Exegesis," 9-10.

Horsley and Smith take a similar, very literal, indeed a biblicist, approach to this historical question. Both are interested in the word Josephus used for the zealot party and when he first used it. They make little or no allowance for Josephus' own agenda and the possibility that his selection of words promotes his own values and propaganda purposes more than they strive for historical accuracy. Josephus takes, for example, the Phineas narrative, disconnects it from its relation to the Zealots, and expands it as a narrative in defence of the rights of pagan women.[52]

Unfortunately, Horsley follows Smith in his obsession with the word "party," and when they use it they mean "political" party. Presumably unless one can demonstrate that the Zealots met every four or five years to elect a leader and had a membership list, we are not allowed to use the term "party" to designate them. That argument is obviously considerably below the level one would expect from such distinguished academics.[53] One would certainly need to question whether it has any resemblance to what was going on in first-century Palestine. Moreover it is not consistently carried out at all. Smith states, for example, that "Josephus speaks of the *sicarii* as uniting to form a definite organization in the days of Judas the Galilean — and the presumption is strong that this was the organization founded by Judas and led by his descendants."[54] Presumably one can speak of Judas forming a "sect" but not of a Zealot party in those days.

Thus both Horsley and Smith base their position on Josephus and him alone. If Josephus does not use the word to describe anyone who lived during the time of Jesus, then we must conclude that there were no "zealotic" temptations for Jesus. Little attention is paid to the reasons why Josephus may have avoided this term or indeed about possible motives he might have for avoiding it. Anyone who suggests that Jesus was tempted by zealot options or by violence used in the name of Yahweh in order to purify the people along the lines of

---

52. *Ant.* IV.131-55. His main interest seems to be the speech of the Midianite women (134-39), modeled apparently on a similar story of the Scythians and the Amazons in Herodotus iv.111-14 (so H. St. J. Thackeray in Loeb Classical Library). See Klassen, "Phineas," and Seland, *Establishment Violence*, but above all W. C. van Unnik, "Josephus' Account of the Story of Israel's Sin with Alien Women in the Country of Midian (Num 25:11)" in *Travels in the World of the Old Testament: Studies Presented to M. A. Beek*, ed. H. van Voss et al. (Assen: van Gorcum, 1974), 241-61.

53. It began, apparently with Kirsopp Lake, whom Smith quotes with approval: "No doubt the Fourth Philosophy supplied the intellectual attitude from which the Zealots and the Sicarii [logically] started, but there is no possibility of clearness in historical writing if the name of a political party be given to its logical antecedents" (Smith, "Zealots and Sicarii," 3 n. 21; word in bracket omitted by Smith, see Lake, "The Zealots," 422).

54. Smith, "Zealots and Sicarii," 10-11 n. 58.

Phineas, the original zealot, is using the zealots as a "foil" to interpret Jesus, a method Horsley has consistently rejected. Smith, at least, recognized that the zealot model, as I prefer to call it, was widespread in first-century Judaism. It could not be simply turned off from the years C.E. 6 till C.E. 66. As long as Jews read the Hebrew Bible, had it read to them, or retold their stories, the option of Phineas was available to them.

Smith at least recognized the value of Hengel's work on the theological level. Does not Horsley owe us a more detailed rebuttal of the important work done by Martin Hengel? It cannot be dismissed with the words, "it seems a model of solid scholarship — that is the great German facade," as Smith does.[55] Smith is, however, not so biased against German scholarship that he cannot recognize in Hengel "a full and richly documented exposition of theological positions *which may plausibly be attributed to the Zealots or to the Sicarii or to both* — and even if the attribution should be incorrect, the exposition would be valuable as an account of themes which were of great importance in the thought of first-century Judaism" (my italics). Smith also admits that all he is concerned with is the "distinction and external history of the sects."[56]

Surely Hengel's nationality has nothing to do with the question; nor does Horsley advance the discussion when he decries "the wilful literalism and metaphysical tendencies of the hostile German (Lutheran) theologians."[57] That is as useful as dismissing Horsley's or Smith's position simply because they are Americans and tend to reject the word "party" because they appear to think of it as analogous to the Republican or Democratic party of the country they call home.[58]

It is a supreme irony that Horsley, who has invested so much in sociological and cultural research, would ultimately base his position so much on the ap-

55. Smith, "Zealots and Sicarii": "All these hoary howlers are embedded in a mass of learned data about even more dubious details which add nothing of importance to the discussion" (11); "In sum [Hengel's] collection of arguments is worthless" (12); "Hengel's account of the development of the Zealot party is mainly a work of fantasy" (15); Daniel's work is dismissed as "ignorant nonsense" (17 n. 91).

56. Smith, "Zealots and Sicarii," 12-13.

57. Horsley, *Spiral*, 337 n. 26. This thrashing of German theologians begins with Lake who, in "The Zealots," objects to Schürer's statement that Judas ben Hezekiah is *"sicherlich"* the same as Judas of Galilee, "except in so far as the use of *"sicherlich"* in theological writing indicates the combination of insufficient evidence with strongly held opinion" (424). Curiously the same conclusion is reached in the new edition of Schürer (1973) by Jewish scholars who could hardly be accused of theological bias. The editors of the new edition state: "He is no doubt identical with Judas son of Hezekiah" (I, 381).

58. Horsley, *Spiral*, 17 where he wonders whether the Pharisees should even be called a "party," "with its connotations of political organization."

pearance of one word, and that he shows so little interest in doing the careful sociological and textual study of Josephus which is demanded. A reality can, after all, exist without certain code words being used. 1 Peter has a profound concept of the church even though the word *ecclesia* is never used. Does the fact that certain historical writers do not mention Jesus of Nazareth mean that he did not exist? Or because Josephus never mentions the Christians, does that mean they did not exist?

Horsley's invitation to consider the first-century Palestinian situation as one of occupation is welcome. Having lived for some three years under Israeli occupation among Palestinians I am confident that anyone who lives under occupation knows that both the occupier and the occupied can be influenced by religious zeal and that it is very difficult to analyze parties or groups. Above all it is difficult to make neat distinctions between political parties and religious confraternities. Guerrilla groups such as the current *sicarii* in Israel strike with devastating effect; the authorities have, however, a very difficult time even today determining who did what. Even the bombing of the King David Hotel after more than four decades defies a description with any degree of historical accuracy.

More important for our discussion, Jews who lived under the mandate prior to 1948 did not need to be told who the "enemy" was, and certainly Palestinians who have lived under occupation since 1967 when reminded of the "love your enemies" teaching have no trouble knowing who that is for them. It seems hard to believe that it would have been difficult for first-century Jews — Jesus had no need to define for his listeners who the "enemy" was.

In revolutionary or protest situations one of the strongest and wisest techniques is to keep organizational matters to an absolute minimum. One of the most effective in recent times, the association known as "Women in Black," an anti-occupation protest group, meets regularly in many cities and towns in Israel. They have no organization, you cannot join them, but they have functioned over several years in a very effective way by silently meeting in public areas and calling attention to the injustice of the occupation. Jew, Arab, or expatriate, male or female may join their meeting. Whether Smith would consider them an "organization" is hard to say, but they surely are a voluntary association. Any historian wishing to tell the story of protest in current Israel will have grave difficulties getting minutes of their meetings or reviewing their membership lists. Still, they exist and make their presence known.

To reject the zealots as a "foil" is, of course, Horsley's right. But he must, in order to merit our respect, accept Judaism as a foil, otherwise Jesus is not a human being living in history. Furthermore, we need to know whether it is zeal as a quasi-religious political phenomenon or even a movement of Zealots that

147

he rejects or just an organized party so named, as Smith clearly does. We must work more carefully through the Jewish sources of the first century and attempt to reconstruct what life was like for Jesus as a young man growing up and getting his education in the synagogue. Would he not have heard the stories of Phineas and Mattathias? And with his keen sensitivity might he not have some stirrings of religious zeal in him?

Once we agree that there were zealots throughout the days of Jesus' life, indeed that at least one of his disciples was a zealot before he met Jesus (Luke 6:16), that Jesus had contact with them and no doubt found their devotion for Yahweh attractive, and that there is a continuous thread between the *lēstai* of the first decade of the Common Era and the *sicarii* and Zealots of Masada, it is no longer suspect to use Zealotism as a foil. In historical research a foil serves merely to heighten the distinctness of a person's position by seeing it in the light of the context from which that person came. And it is clear that the context of first-century Judaism included a widespread and significant number of people who held to an ideal of zealotism that may be described as follows:

1. An unconditional commitment to maintain Israel's distinctiveness, her pure covenant uniqueness, and to maintain her religious and political borders, a commitment which makes them distinct from the Pharisees (or shall we say from those Hasidim who did not believe in a Jewish state?).
2. The willingness to follow Phineas' example in using force to obtain these objectives, to the death if need be. The paradigm for action, in particular killing fellow Jews who had offended God and thus establishing a covenant of peace, had been provided by Phineas the priest and followed by Elijah the prophet, but the crowning achievement had been carried out by Mattathias, who had acted against a foreign occupier. He led the way in providing them with a distinctive model of how zeal expresses itself in relationship to the convergence of paganism and Judaism.[59]
3. A depth of commitment that was based ultimately in the zeal of God, who alone is King, who passionately loves the people of Israel.

As a first-century Jew, Jesus would have received inspiration from Jewish stories and ideals. He would have had before him as an attractive option the model of Phineas to demonstrate Yahweh's zeal by killing those who transgressed God's laws. That he refused that option cost him in the end his life, but it also pointed

59. Paula Frederiksen, *From Jesus to Christ: The Origins of the New Testament Images of Jesus* (New Haven: Yale University Press, 1988), 70-93, provides a good portrait of the "idea of Israel" in the Judaism of Jesus' time.

to another way in which zeal could be expressed in faithfulness to the covenant of God.

The zealot option did exist for Jesus, but also for Paul, and we must ask whether in Paul's case remnants of zeal did not continue to manifest themselves after his conversion. Dunn is correct in applying the features of zeal to Paul's life.[60] Surprisingly though, he fails to deal with the most relevant text of Paul in which he says: "I am zealous for you with a divine zeal" (2 Cor. 11:2-3). Not only has Paul spoken of their zeal on his behalf (2 Cor. 7:7) and the zeal of the Macedonians to give money (2 Cor. 9:2), but he also refers to zeal in connection with vindication (7:11). In all of this we see Paul redefining the way in which zeal, the zeal of the Lord, is defined in the new life in Christ. What Paul did was to redefine the armor of God so that he could still press for the purity of God's people and passionately be zealous for God's people with God's own zeal.[61] He wanted, even more than Phineas wanted for his people, to present the Corinthians "as a chaste virgin to her true and only husband" (2 Cor. 11:2).

But Paul also used the whole armor of God, and that meant that the God of peace worked through the community of the faithful to "crush Satan under their feet" (Rom. 16:20). Paul and the early Christians rejected violence and military strength to bring about the Kingdom of God. The Zealots did not, and in so doing signified their unfaithfulness to God, and although Zealots continue to this day to assert themselves under the guise of faithfulness to Jahweh and even to Jesus Christ, they end inevitably as did the defenders of Masada in mass murder on mountains which they vow "will never fall again." Jesus could have chosen to live as a zealot and die with them on Masada, had he played out his life differently. So could have Paul.

Jesus chose instead the option to declare his platform as "love your enemies" on the Mount of the Beatitudes and invite his followers to do so just as Paul announced it with singular clarity, even if not in the precise words in Romans 12 and even if, as is recognized today, he leans on Jewish teachers to do so. Both faced the Zealot option squarely; both rejected it firmly and without equivocation. It remains one of the lasting legacies of John Howard Yoder that he helped many people to see that.

60. Dunn, *Theology of Paul*, 350-53.
61. It is especially significant that zeal is an important part of God's armor, except in the New Testament. See the excellent treatment of this theme in Tom Yoder Neufeld, *Put on the Armour of God: The Divine Warrior from Isaiah to Ephesians*, JSNT Supplement Series No. 140 (Sheffield: Sheffield Academic Press, 1997).

The Politics of Jesus in the
Sermon on the Plain

Glen H. Stassen[1]

Whenever I gave John Howard Yoder credit for what I had learned from him, he retorted with modest, detached objectivity that I was already writing in these directions before his influence; or that it didn't really come from him, but from Jesus. But Yoder's clarity and articulateness created the space and gave the confidence for many of us to have the courage to write what we were sensing more profoundly, and to be more faithful followers of Jesus. In addition to that, I really have learned much from him.

John gave me encouragement not to segregate social ethics from serious biblical study but to try "to throw a cable across the chasm which usually separates the disciplines of New Testament exegesis and contemporary social ethics."[2] After the MCC conference on *The Politics of Jesus* in Kansas City, Yoder suggested we take the paper I presented and do a series of dialogue lectures in different locations. (Thus began our book with Diane Yeager, *Authentic Transformation* [Nashville: Abingdon Press, 1996].) On our flight to Sioux Falls for our lectures at the North American Baptist Theological Seminary, he sat across the aisle and behind me, where he could watch what I was doing, and function as my conscience. (I have often imagined him looking over my shoulder at what I do. It has made my ethics more faithful.) What I was doing was studying the

1. I am grateful to David Neville, editor of *Faith and Freedom*, for helpful editorial improvements, and to Donald Hagner for incisive New Testament suggestions, without implying his agreement with the chiastic structure. This is a somewhat revised version of an essay published in *Faith and Freedom* (June 1996) in honor of John Howard Yoder.

2. John Howard Yoder, *The Politics of Jesus*, 2nd ed. (Grand Rapids: Eerdmans, 1994), 4-8.

prophet Isaiah, which I placed alongside John's points about the jubilee to strengthen the base for what he and I were both saying. When we disembarked, he feigned a puzzled look and asked, "You mean you are a Christian ethicist who studies the Bible?" I should have been quick enough to answer, "Yes, when I am about to do a dialogue with you."

Like Yoder, I believe Christian ethics is stronger when we dig into biblical scholarship. Not that ethics may be simply read straight from the Bible; there are many historical and methodological variables to discuss. But without attention to the results of critical biblical research Christian ethics is impoverished at its base.

The learning might even be a two-way street. What biblical scholars and all of us see depends in part on the social-ethical assumptions that have crept into our perception of our own historical context. Far more misinterpretation happens because of uncriticized ethical loyalties, practices, and assumptions than because of errors in Greek grammar. By shining light on these odd-shaped splinters and logs that bias biblical interpretation, Christian ethics can be a critical tool for biblical interpreters.[3] It can be an instrument of the Holy Spirit to correct misreadings and suggest alternative interpretations.

I miss John's continuing dialogue greatly. Now I feel the call for many of us to extend his pioneering work. In gratitude for what I have learned from Yoder, I offer here one small piece in that direction. He bases the first half of *The Politics of Jesus* on the Gospel of Luke, yet does not discuss the Sermon on the Plain in Luke 6:20-49, which fits his ethics of enemy-love and politics of peacemaking well.

At present, the outstanding commentary on Luke by François Bovon is not available in English. Bovon has proposed that the Sermon on the Plain is structured as a chiasm: The second half is the mirror image of the first half, just like the letter X or Greek Chi. The first and last elements (1 and 1′ in Table 1) mirror each other; as do the second and second to last (2 and 2′), and so on. The parallel elements mirror each other not only in form but also in meaning, so we can learn new insights about the meaning of each element by consulting its mirror image. Furthermore, the central members (7 and 7′ below) are at the heart of the meaning of the whole chiasm. Therefore we can sharpen our understanding of the sermon by examining the parallels, and the pivotal center.[4]

---

3. See Yoder's comment in *The Politics of Jesus*: "Once we are sensitized by those questions, we might begin . . . by seeking to read one portion of the New Testament without making the usual prior negative assumptions about its relevance . . ." (11). See also his criticisms of the false dichotomies interpreters assume, "the many ways . . . of avoiding the normativeness of Jesus" (102-9).

4. François Bovon, *Evangelisch-Katholischer Kommentar zum Neuen Testament, III$_1$ Das Evangelium Nach Lukas (Lk. 1:1–9:50)* (Zurich: Benziger und Neukirchener Verlag, 1989), 309.

Prior to Bovon, scholars had not noticed the chiastic structure of the Sermon on the Plain. For example, in his Anchor Bible commentary on the Gospel of Luke, published eight years before Bovon's, Joseph Fitzmyer wrote: "In contrast to the relatively well-constructed Matthean Sermon on the Mount, the Lukan sermon is loose and rambling."[5]

I suggest Bovon's discovery may be extended to incorporate the introductory blessings and woes and the concluding teachings on the speck and log and on doing Jesus' words (1, 2, 2', 1' in Table 1). I also suggest other minor modifications to Bovon's analysis. And I shall suggest implications for Christian ethics.

Chiastic Structure of the Sermon on the Plain

1. Four Beatitudes (6:20-23).
   2 pairs of parallel blessings:
   Blessed are you poor, hungry, weeping, persecuted; your reward is great.
2. Four Woes (6:24-26).
   2 pairs of parallel woes:
   Woe to you rich, full, laughing, praised; your state will be reversed.
3. Transition/Introduction (6:27a).
   Assonant rhyme in the Greek:
   I say to ye; who listen to me.
4. Love your enemies (6:27b-28).
   2 pairs of commands:
   Love your enemies & do good to them; bless & pray for them.
5. Take Transforming Initiatives (6:29-30).
   2 pairs of commands:
   Offer cheek & don't withhold shirt; give & don't ask back.
6. Golden Rule (6:31).
   One imperative:
   Do to others as you'd have them do to you.
7. Compare with Sinners; No Reward from God (6:32-34).
   3 symmetrical sentences imply alienation from God:
   If you love, do good, lend only to those who love,

5. Joseph Fitzmyer, *The Gospel According to Luke (I–IX)* (Garden City, NY: Doubleday, 1981), 628.

do good, repay back, what reward do you get?
Even sinners do that.

7′   Character of Christians & Grace of God (6:35).
3 symmetrical commands imply grace from God:
Love, do good, lend, expecting nothing back;
Great reward, adopted by God, who is merciful.

6′   Call for Mercy (6:36).
One imperative related to Golden Rule:
Be merciful, just as your Father is merciful.

5′ Do Not Judge (6:37a-b).
2 reciprocities with negative commands:
Don't judge, don't condemn & you won't be judged, condemned.

4′ Forgive & Give (6:37c-38a).
2 reciprocities with positive commands:
Forgive & you'll be forgiven; give & you'll be given.

3′ Conclusion/Transition: Measures of Grace (6:38b-c).
2 rhyming lines beginning with *measure* in the Greek and ending with *to ye:*
Measure overflowing to you; measure you give will be given to you.

2′ Four Proverbial Hypocrisies (6:39-42).
2 pairs of proverbs in parallel:
Blind man can't lead a blind man. Disciple not above master.
Why see speck but not log? First remove your log, then see speck.

1′ Four Admonitions on Producing Good Fruit & Doing My Words (6:43-49).
2 pairs of contrasts:
Good & bad tree. Figs & grapes.
Hears & does words. Hears & does them not.

1. Grace and Bondage; 2. Jubilee and Justice

Even before the chiasm begins, grace is emphasized. Jesus has just proclaimed the program of his ministry as empowerment by the Holy Spirit to preach good news to the poor, release to the captives, recovery of sight for the blind, liberty to those who are oppressed, and the jubilee year of the Lord (Luke 4:18-19, quoting Isaiah 61). This is the good news of God's grace, acting to deliver those in bondage. Then Jesus restores social outcasts to community (5:12-14) and forgives sinners and heals the paralyzed (5:17-26). Levi, a despised tax collector, responds to Jesus' forgiving and restoring to community (5:27-28). "In 5:29-32 Jesus is depicted as one who not only restores and forgives an individual but as one who associates with the many who are in need," foreshadowing the church's learning to associate with the poor and with Gentiles.[6] These social outcasts in 5:12-32 are then pronounced blessed in the beatitudes. The joyous celebration of this deliverance is a sign that the bridegroom is with us; God is acting now to deliver us (5:33-39). Jesus feeds the hungry and heals the paralyzed on the Sabbath, then spends the whole night in prayer, a clear sign that points to God's grace, God's presence, God's deliverance (6:1-12).

Grace and mercy mean not only wiping out past sin, but restoring to community. Levi is not only forgiven but made a member of the disciples who follow Jesus, including a Zealot who hates tax collectors.

Grace and mercy mean not only forgiveness, but deliverance for the poor, the blind, the paralyzed, the oppressed. The beatitudes and woes focus especially on deliverance from economic injustice — the jubilee/justice theme that Yoder has highlighted for us.[7] To invest ourselves in the struggle for justice for the world's oppressed is an essential practice in peacemaking. In fact, the jubilee passage, Isaiah 61, "has influenced both the Matthean beatitudes and the Lukan woes."[8]

The British New Testament scholar, C. F. Evans, points out that "you poor," Greek *ptochos*, "means a beggar, one who is destitute . . . , 'the poor ones' (Ps. 149:4). Their poverty is often a scandal, especially when the result of oppression or dispossession by the wealthy, and it is to be removed by God (Psalm 9:18; 10; 72:2-4, 12-13; 82:2-4 . . .)."[9] Similarly, Eduard Schweizer comments: "Jesus addressed himself unconditionally to the poor and never allowed fanaticism to ignore earthly suffering as though the believer were already dwelling in heaven. . . . The disciples . . . are intended to move others to make their possessions available to the poor. Luke is therefore especially fond of telling about the rich and respected who respond to this call (19:1-10; Acts 4:36-37; 10; 16:14-15, 27-34; 18:18). . . ."[10]

6. Charles H. Talbert, *Reading Luke* (New York: Crossroad, 1982), 63.

7. Yoder, *The Politics of Jesus,* ch. 3.

8. Eduard Schweizer, *The Good News According to Luke* (Atlanta: John Knox Press, 1984), 122. See J. Dupont, *Les Béatitudes,* vol. II: *La Bonne Nouvelle* (Paris: H. Gabalda et Compagnie, 1969), 114ff., 122, and passim.

9. C. F. Evans, *Saint Luke* (London and Philadelphia: SCM Press and Trinity Press International, 1990), 329.

10. Schweizer, *Good News,* 120. Talbert, *Reading Luke,* 71, somewhat spiritualizes the meaning on the thin basis that Luke 1:51-53 (Mary's Magnificat) proclaims that God scatters

So in Luke 6:20-23, the first member of the chiasm, the beatitudes are grace. They "are not exhortations but congratulations and condolences based on eschatological blessings not apparent on the surface.[11] The present tense in Luke 6:20, "blessed are you, for yours is the kingdom of God," means that justice is about to be given to the poor; those who suffer injustice in the present age are already in process of receiving just compensation.[12] It is redress, deliverance, intervention, jubilee, as in Isaiah 61. You are poor, hungry, mourning, and persecuted now, but you are participating in God's action of delivering. Yours is already the reign of God, and you will be filled, laughing and rejoicing, for great will be your reward.

Correspondingly, the woes (6:24-26) are realistic recognitions of bondage based on a frequently repeated theme in Luke: Wealth and boasting keep people from entering the reign of God. They trap us. They distort our vision. They prevent us from seeing the reign of God, from seeing the neighbor's need, from acting with compassion.

The Sermon on the Plain ends with four teachings on hypocrisy and blindness, corresponding to the four woes in the introduction; and four teachings on doing the words Jesus teaches, corresponding to the four beatitudes. The hypocrisies are signs of bondage akin to the woes. Doing the words of Jesus is participation in the blessings of the reign of God. Commenting on the eight teachings at the end of the sermon, Joel Green says "these apparently disparate sayings have puzzled commentators."[13] Seeing that they parallel the eight blessings and woes makes their order and intent clear. The beatitudes celebrated delivering grace; the woes judgment. Doing the deeds of Jesus is participation in delivering grace; the hypocrisy of not doing them while claiming goodness is participation in judgment. The grace that Jesus teaches in Luke is not cheap grace. "Jesus' practices of healing, his table fellowship with toll collectors and sinners, and now the inclusive nature of this audience — these and other aspects of his ministry symbolize the wide reach of God's grace. All are welcome, but to stay, to be able to name Jesus as 'Lord,' Jesus' gracious invitation must be joined by obedience."[14]

---

the proud as well as the mighty and the rich, while exalting the lowly and hungry. But Luke 1:51ff. is in fact a paraphrase of 1 Samuel 2:1ff., which speaks of the poor and hungry, and rich and proud, with the usual Old Testament realism that the poor are oppressed by the powerful. The point is not *either* religious *or* socioeconomic; the socioeconomic injustice is a religious problem since God cares for and delivers the oppressed.

11. Talbert, *Reading Luke,* 69-70.

12. Dupont, *Les Béatitudes,* vol. II, 106, 115, 122, and passim.

13. Joel Green, *The Gospel of Luke,* The New International Commentary on the New Testament (Grand Rapids: Eerdmans, 1997), 276, citing Nolland and Bock.

14. Cf. Dietrich Bonhoeffer, *The Cost of Discipleship* (New York: Macmillan, 1963), 47ff.; and Green, *The Gospel of Luke,* 261.

As hypocrites, merely pretending to be faithful, we are blinded by un-faithfulness, and our seeing is distorted. Throughout the gospels Jesus repeatedly emphasizes recovering sight, seeing with compassionate, single-minded, and sound vision as opposed to blindness and double vision. This suggests we need an ethics of perception, not only an ethics of principles or virtues. How we see depends on our loyalties, expectations, and practices. Seeing clearly takes more than situational open-mindedness; it takes repentance, removing barriers between ourselves and others, and removing the investments, practices, and greed that distort our vision the way a magnet bends the flow of electricity. In the Sermon on the Mount, Jesus connects the eye that is not sound with greed, with hoarding treasures and serving mammon (Matt. 6:19-24). Bovon says the problem here is not only evil intent; we are in bondage to self-deception and cannot correct ourselves. We need God's grace in Jesus Christ. Bovon identifies five steps in Jesus' way of correction:

(a) avoiding putting ourselves as judge over others;
(b) truly hearing the words of Jesus, which address us with love and hope;
(c) recognizing our serious errors (log, not splinter);
(d) readiness to become new persons (removing the log);
(e) only then can we be like Jesus (6:40b) and become teachers for others.[15]

The first practice in peacemaking is to acknowledge that it is participation in God's delivering grace. It is eschatological joy. If we practice peacemaking as our own virtue, we become self-righteous and judgmental. We alienate those with whom we want to make peace. We miss the joy of giving thanks for God's deliverance. And we end up with burnout.

The second practice in peacemaking is to acknowledge that we are powerless to deliver ourselves from vicious cycles of injustice and hostility. Our alienation is far deeper than we can comprehend or control alone. We are stuck in alienating processes, mechanisms of bondage, vicious cycles beyond our power to reverse alone. Only such realism enables us to appreciate the joyous significance of the small steps of recovery, the mustard seeds, that we do experience.

Peace people often fail to celebrate interim victories. Someone always says, "Sure, but the government did it only because they wanted political advantages. There are still thirty thousand more nuclear weapons in the arsenal. Torture and death squads still roam in Latin America. How can you celebrate when there is still so much sin around?" (Cf. Luke 6:33ff.) Only when we acknowledge that we are stuck in mechanisms of bondage from which we cannot deliver ourselves, and

15. Bovon, *Evangelisch-Katholischer Kommentar*, 335.

cannot expect perfect recovery, can we appreciate the joy of the significant gifts of grace in which we are allowed to participate. Thank God for the mustard seeds!

Surely a similar problem of self-righteousness and arrogance infests governments and foreign-policy elites. The need to acknowledge grace and bondage, and possession-driven blindness to the economic needs of the poor, is just as great for prime ministers, presidents, senators, and national security advisors. John Yoder has taught us to make our Christian witness to the state, for the shalom of the city where we dwell.

3. The Community of Those Who Listen, Including Enemies

Luke 6:17-20 notes that Jesus came down from a mountain and stood on a level place, "with a great crowd of his disciples and a great multitude of people from all Judea, Jerusalem, and the coast of Tyre and Sidon.... They had come to hear him.... And all in the crowd were trying to touch him.... Then he looked up at his disciples and said...." In 6:27 he says, "I say to ye who listen to me."[16] At the end of the sermon, in 7:1, we read, "After Jesus had finished all his sayings in the hearing of the people, he entered Capernaum." Jesus proclaims God's will not only for his few disciples, but for the multitudes, for humankind. (Not that we all obey; but this is God's will, and God is Lord over all.)[17]

Yoder has taught us that Jesus not only addressed individuals, but gathered an alternative community of disciples who would hear (and do) what he taught. We see this in the sermon. Peacemaking requires a group, a community, a church; alone we feel powerless. In a group that listens to God together, we begin to feel grace. Forming church-based or grassroots peacemaking groups is the climactic practice of the consensus-based just peacemaking theory developed by twenty-three interdisciplinary scholars in *Just Peacemaking: Ten Practices to Abolish War*.[18]

16. My translation is only half-successful in reflecting the rhyming vowels in the Greek: "*alla humin . . . akouousin.*" The parallel verse in 6:38 rhymes similarly, both halves beginning with *metro/metron* and ending in *humin*.

17. Green, *The Gospel of Luke*, 261. The sermon on the mount also begins in Matthew 5:1 with "When Jesus saw the crowds, he went up the mountain; and . . . his disciples came to him." And it ends in 7:28, "the crowds were astounded at his teaching. . . ." A recurrent theme throughout Bonhoeffer's *Ethics* is the Lordship of Christ over all of life, rather than a two-realms split in which Christ is lord over only the inner life. Bonhoeffer bore the fruit, stood the test in the laboratory of history, when others who limited Christ's concrete lordship to the inner church realm failed.

18. *Just Peacemaking: Ten Practices to Abolish War*, ed. Glen Stassen (Cleveland: Pilgrim Press, 1998). It is also the climactic practice in my earlier *Just Peacemaking: Transforming Initiatives for Justice and Peace* (Louisville: Westminster/John Knox, 1992), 86ff. 109ff., and passim.

Yoder has also pointed out that a central theme in Luke is the inclusion of Gentiles, outcasts, and enemies. Jesus is addressing those in the "great" crowds, "all" who will hear, "the multitude," including Gentiles from outside the Jewish region, from the coast of Tyre and Sidon.[19] A central theme throughout Luke and Acts is the struggle to include foreigners who are rejected by the inner community. This is a peacemaking theme. One characteristic that makes the alternative community different from the world is its inclusion of foreigners and outcasts. As Jacques Dupont emphasizes, the last beatitude says four times that the faithful community has itself experienced exclusion, rejection, ostracism; it knows what exclusion feels like.[20] He suggests this echoes the community's experience of rejection in Isaiah 66:5. The Christian community listens to the outcast and the enemy. How could it be otherwise? The community follows Jesus, whose message is compassion and mercy toward outcasts and enemies.

We may not distort the theme of alternative community to become exclusivistic. The community of Jesus and the Spirit keeps reaching out to embrace those who are foreign to it, and witnessing to the powers about who is the real Lord and what is His real will. It seeks the shalom of the city to which we have been dispersed.[21]

The parallel verse near the end of the chiasm (6:38b-c) wraps up Jesus' teaching on not judging but forgiving. Practicing forgiveness shapes the kind of community that embraces foreigners, outcasts, the marginalized. The community is based on grace, not exclusivity. Jesus' teaching promises this community God's grace-based generosity:

A good measure, pressed down, shaken together, running over,
   will be put into your lap;
for the measure you give will be the measure you get back.

"The measure you give" does not mean that God will give us back the same amount that we gave. Our measure will be running over. Grace will overflow our container. The meaning is that if we relate to others with grace, mercy, transforming initiatives, forgiveness, God will relate to us with grace, mercy, transforming initiatives, and forgiveness. We will be surprised and overwhelmed by God's goodness.[22]

---

19. Green, *The Gospel of Luke*, 262-63; 266.

20. Dupont, *Les Béattitudes*, vol. II, 288; see also 285-94.

21. Yoder, *For the Nations* (Grand Rapids: Eerdmans, 1997), 33, 41, 52ff., 65n, 136, 237.

22. Therefore I have slightly altered Bovon here, placing both lines about grace overflowing the measure into item 12, instead of splitting the first line about the good measure overflowing into item 11. I have also added the title, "Measures of Grace."

Church members — and governments — often refuse to talk with antagonists they judge not to be righteous enough. Jesus' witness is that we must talk with precisely such adversaries. This is the Christian practice of making peace with others, binding and loosing, which Yoder says spills over into the world as conflict resolution. If we don't talk and seek reconciliation, we are not peacemakers. As Yitzhak Rabin said, "You don't make peace with friends, you make peace with your bitterest enemies."

4. The Love That Acts to Affirm Enemies' Valid Interests

William Klassen and John Piper have shown that Jesus' teaching on loving our enemies echoes throughout the New Testament and early Christian writings. In the early church, "it was the most quoted saying of Jesus."[23] Jesus' early followers understood this command as central to what it meant to follow Jesus.

Luke gives us the command, "Love your enemies," in parallel with the words, "do good to them, bless them, and pray for them." The parallel format gives us a clue to the meaning. New Testament scholars widely agree that "the love commanded by Jesus is no sentiment but rather the active pursuance of the enemies' good, and that not grudgingly or only in an exterior manner but from the heart. . . . 'Do good' indicates the active tenor of the love called for."[24] Just as the Good Samaritan did nine deeds of deliverance for the victim in the ditch — going to him, pouring oil and wine in his wounds, then bandaging them, putting him on his donkey, bringing him to an inn, caring for him, paying for him, and promising to return — so love in the New Testament is characterized by deeds of deliverance.

Love also means to pray for and to bless. "To bless" in the New Testament is not merely to utter a word, but to pray that God will act for our enemy's good. Jesus did not affirm all the interests of his enemies; he often confronted his adversaries, calling for repentance. But he calls us to affirm and pray for our enemy's valid interests.

If love is merely a sentiment, it lacks realistic relevance to the politics of peacemaking. But the international relations theorist, Robert Jervis, demonstrates how the psychological propensity to perceive *all* the enemy's assertions

23. William Klassen, *Love of Enemies: The Way to Peace* (Philadelphia: Fortress Press, 1984), 43, 84, and passim. John Piper, *"Love Your Enemies": Jesus' Love Command in the Synoptic Gospels and in the Early Christian Paranesis* (Cambridge: Cambridge University Press, 1979), 27ff. and passim.

24. John Nolland, *Luke 1–9:20*, Word Biblical Commentary, vol. 35A (Dallas: Word Books, 1989), 294. See also Green, *The Gospel of Luke*, 272.

as antagonistic and untrue causes serious distortions of perception, failure to make use of opportunities to make peace, and unnecessary war and destruction.[25] The same distortion afflicts our adversaries' perceptions. Therefore it takes deeds, demonstrations, to break through their distorted perceptions of distrust.

Jesus' concrete teachings of practices in peacemaking should not be reduced to mere illustrations of a general point. When he teaches that we are to pray for our enemies, it is not merely a random illustration, to be discarded if we get the main point about love. Just before delivering the Sermon on the Plain, Jesus went up into the mountain to pray (6:12). In Matthew 5:44, Luke 6:28, Romans 12:14, and 1 Corinthians 4:12, we are asked to pray for our enemies. In Luke 22:31-34 Jesus discloses that Satan will use Peter to deny him, but that he has been praying for Peter. In Luke 23:34 Jesus prayed for his enemies as he died on the cross, in Acts 7:60 Stephen did likewise as he was being martyred, and in Romans 15:30ff., Paul appealed urgently that his brothers and sisters in Rome would pray for his deliverance from his enemies in Judea. Praying for our enemies is an essential New Testament practice in peacemaking, echoing through the New Testament, not a throwaway option.

5. The Grace That Takes Transforming Initiatives

Some label the theme of Luke 6:29-30 "nonviolence," "nonresistance," "nonretaliation," or "renunciation of rights." But "transforming initiatives" is a better label. Renunciation does not accurately capture the theme of the four teachings — a positive, creative alternative, rather than merely not doing something.[26] Yoder writes, "The 'resistance' which we renounce is a response in kind, returning evil for evil. But the alternative is not complicity in [the evil one's] designs. The alternative is creative concern for the person who is bent on evil, coupled with the refusal of his goals."[27]

In the Greek there are four parallel teachings in two pairs:

If anyone strikes you on the cheek, offer the other also;
and if anyone takes away your coat do not refuse even your shirt.

25. Robert Jervis, *Perception and Misperception in International Relations* (Princeton: Princeton University Press, 1976), ch. 4.

26. Green, *The Gospel of Luke*, 272.

27. John Howard Yoder, *The Original Revolution: Essays on Christian Pacifism* (Scottdale, PA: Herald Press, 1972), 48.

> If anyone begs from you, give;
> and if anyone takes away your goods, do not ask them back.

None of the lines tells us *not* to do something, but to venture a creative initiative that was not asked for: offer the other cheek, offer the shirt, give, do not ask them back.[28] Combined with Luke 6:35, the pivot of the whole chiasm, these suggest that we take the initiative of giving without expecting anything in return.

Jesus' emphasis is not only on what we are not to do, but on the initiative we are to take beyond what is demanded. Renunciation is surely implied — a renunciation of violent, evil means. But Jesus' teaching goes beyond that — to a transforming initiative. The teaching fits the emphasis on grace with which the beatitudes begin: God does not merely renounce punishing us, but takes the initiative to deliver us. Grace is not merely renunciation; it is transforming initiative.

Yoder points to the theme of "revolutionary subordination" in the epistles. The subordination is the renunciation part of the drama; the revolution is the assertive initiative. "The pattern is thus uniformly one of creative transformation."[29]

The term "nonresistance" comes from our translation of the Greek *antistenai* in Matthew 5:39, as "do not resist evil." Walter Wink has shown that the Greek means "do not be violently resisting."[30] Clarence Jordan has established that the Greek (*to ponero*) does not mean "evil," but the instrumental "by evil means," just as Paul reports in Romans 12:21. Jesus certainly resisted evil, in the sense Yoder specifies — not complying with the evil goals of one who is evil. But he did not resist violently, or by evil means. Nor did he set himself in a judging, condemning, hateful relationship that points toward violence (Luke 6:37, the bottom part of the chiasm that mirrors Luke 6:29-30).

Nor do these teachings mean we should not be assertive. Jesus surely was assertive. The assertiveness that Jesus teaches here is the assertiveness of surprising initiatives that may transform the enemy's judging and condemning into openness and peace. It is an evangelistic strategy of transformation.

---

28. See Walter Wink, *Engaging the Powers* (Minneapolis: Fortress Press, 1992), ch. 9, for an explanation of the meaning of these four teachings as transforming initiatives, not a doormat strategy. See also Stassen, *Just Peacemaking*, ch. 2 and 3, for an interpretation of the sermon on the mount and its structure consistent with the present interpretation of the sermon on the plain. Nolland, 296, points out that "do not refuse" is a figure of speech which "stands for the positive urging of the course of action. So "do not refuse" means "offer." Similarly with "do not ask them back."

29. Yoder, *The Politics of Jesus*, 185.

30. Walter Wink, "Beyond Just War and Pacifism: Jesus' Nonviolent Way," *Review and Expositor* 89 (1992): 197-214.

The transforming initiatives interpretation is confirmed if we look at the symmetrically corresponding teachings in the chiasm. Items 4 and 5 are parallel with each other; and their form is two pairs of parallel commands, just as items 4' and 5' are two pairs of parallel commands. Their content is positive transforming initiatives. Item 4 points to love not merely as renunciation or not doing something, but as positive actions, initiatives: love, do good to them, bless and pray for them. Items 4' and 5' teach us that we should not judge but instead take positive initiatives of forgiving and giving.

Jesus' command not to "judge" means not to "condemn," not to adopt an attitude of censoriousness, not to fail to show mercy to the guilty, not to criticize and find fault with one's neighbor. It does not forbid making an honest and realistic assessment. Jesus often assessed and confronted others.[31]

Jesus teaches not only what we are not to do, but gives us the pattern to substitute for it. Instead of judging and condemning, we are to forgive and give. Once again, initiatives of mercy are the creative pattern. Bovon calls these two sets of teachings "reciprocities":

> Do not judge, and you will not be judged;
> do not condemn, and you will not be condemned.
> Forgive, and you will be forgiven;
> give, and it will be given to you.

The reciprocal consequences (you will not be judged, you will be forgiven, etc.) are in a passive form, signalling action by God. God's grace gives us the initiative to forgive and give rather than judge and condemn. As we take these initiatives we participate in God's reign and receive an eschatological promise.

Alert Christians discern the peacemaking relevance of forgiving rather than judging.[32] Everyone has experienced the culture of blame that seems to possess some persons most of the time and all of us some of the time. It destroys relationships, families, and churches. We have discerned governments paying official public relations specialists high salaries to assert with a straight face and a censorious voice that the fault is all the other side's; that when the other side decides that it is serious about peacemaking, we might consider taking a different position; that their initiatives toward us thus far have all been selfishly motivated, or intended to divide us, or nothing new; and therefore we

---

31. I. H. Marshall, *The Gospel of Luke* (Grand Rapids: Eerdmans, 1978), 265-66. Fitzmyer, *The Gospel According to Luke,* 641.

32. See the chapter by Alan Geyer on the practice of repentance and forgiveness as essential to peacemaking in *Just Peacemaking: Ten Practices for Abolishing War;* and Donald W. Shriver Jr., *An Ethic for Enemies: Forgiveness in Politics* (New York: Oxford University Press, 1995).

will take no initiatives ourselves. Meanwhile the other side also does its share of condemning. People die, oppression continues, and we are all told to feel righteous. Breakthroughs come when somebody quits condemning and takes the initiative of forgiving, or at least listening. When this happens, Christians should applaud noisily.

6. Love Others as Your Father Loves You

Furthermore, the transforming initiatives interpretation gives new meaning to the Golden Rule, "Do to others as you would have others do to you" (item 6 in the chiasm). Some scholars are puzzled by its presence here; it seems to contradict Jesus' emphasis on mercy and compassion. As Nolland says, it seems to echo the reciprocity ethic found in some Greek and Roman sources: treat others as you would like to be treated *so that* they will then do good to you.[33] But as he rightly observes, Jesus tried to overcome a reciprocity ethic. We are not supposed to do good things for others merely to get them to do good things for us.

If we see the Golden Rule within the context of an understanding of love as transforming initiatives, it does not mean reciprocity but rather, "Take the transforming initiative of doing for them what you would appreciate if it were done for you." Understood this way, the Golden Rule is more grace-based, and fits the context better. It is symmetrical with Luke 6:36, "Be merciful, just as your Father is merciful." Bovon comments that Luke bases Christian ethics on God's mercy rather than God's holiness, and understands God's mercy as initiative-taking. So in the parable of the lost sheep in Luke 15:4-7, Luke "declares the initiative full of love that Jesus takes toward sinners and thereby the prevenience of God toward humankind (with the goal of rehabilitation of humans as God's children (cf. 6:35 and 15:11-32)."[34] "The disciples seize the ethical initiative as God's love does in relation to humankind."[35] Commenting on Jesus' teaching of love for the enemy in 6:27-28, Nolland remarks, "It is certainly an imitation of God (Luke 6:35). . . . Jesus calls for an aggressive pitting of good against evil. This is a thoroughgoing evangelistic strategy which denies the social reality of two mutually exclusive groups . . . ; it takes up and radicalizes the highest demands group solidarity might impose and asks for these to be practiced in relation to the enemy."[36] Exactly.

---

33. Nolland, *Luke 1–9:20*, 297f.
34. Bovon, *Evangelisch-Katholischer Kommentar*, 323. See also Green, *Gospel of Luke*, 271.
35. Bovon, *Evangelisch-Katholischer Kommentar*, 322.
36. Nolland, *Luke 1–9:20*, 296.

7. Transforming Initiatives of Love

In a chiasm, the central elements are the heart of the meaning of the whole teaching. The point of items 7 and 7′ is to contrast a love of grace-based initiative with the mere reciprocity of sinners who love, do good, and lend only to persons who will give back in return.[37] Jesus asks, what reward or credit is this to you? "Reward" in 6:35 is the same word as in 6:23, which is speaking of eschatological reward in heaven. "Credit" is a translation of the Greek *charis,* which normally means grace. Both words point to reward from God. And the three positive teachings of item 7′ each point to God's gracious reward and mercy when we love, do good, and lend to the unjust and ungrateful, as God does. Thus the chiastic structure helps us see the centrality of love as initiatives, and the centrality of God's mercy as the basis for the whole teaching. The two central members of the chiasm point us to God's kindness toward sinners, the ungrateful, and the selfish as well as toward us, the disciples. Therefore I have modified Bovon's titles for 7 and 7′ to emphasize God's grace. Grace is basic to the whole sermon. As Fitzmyer comments, "The motivation for such love is the love or mercy of God, the father of Christian existence, which is to be imitated."[38]

Conclusions

First, our analysis of the Sermon on the Plain has yielded themes that recur throughout the New Testament and are central to the gospel: grace and bondage, justice and deliverance of the poor, Christian community and the inclusion of outcasts and enemies, the love that is disclosed in Christ, the grace that takes transforming initiatives, prayer, forgiveness, and repentance. These same themes recur in New Testament passages on peacemaking, such as Matthew 5, Romans 12, 1 Corinthians 4, also Philemon and 1 Peter. Yoder is right that peacemaking is found not merely in one isolated passage in Luke's Gospel. It is

37. Green, *The Gospel of Luke,* 273, sees part of the chiastic mirroring that Bovon has proposed, apparently without having read Bovon's commentary: In verses 35-36, "Jesus summarizes the message of vv. 27-34 by repeating the triad of love, doing good, and lending/giving, and by contending that all three must be exercised freely, without calculation, without expectation of return." The parallels to verses 27-34 that he cites actually include verse 37 as well as 35-36, so in fact he has seen the repetition of 27-34 in 35-37 that is the heart of Bovon's insight. Darrel L. Bock, *Luke,* Volume 1, Baker Exegetical Commentary on the New Testament (Grand Rapids: Baker Books, 1994), 602, sees the parallel between 6:32-34 and 6:35 just as here proposed.

38. Fitzmyer, *The Gospel According to Luke,* 630.

deeply rooted in God's grace, whose character is revealed in a history of transforming initiatives, culminating in Christ. Peacemaking as transforming initiatives is at the heart of the gospel.

Second, the strategy of "transforming initiatives" points to God's grace, God's transforming initiatives of mercy to the unjust and ungrateful. Each practice invites us to participate in God's grace and mercy, God's peacemaking. We are not merely obeying a law, but being adopted as God's children. Therefore, "joyful are the peacemakers, for they shall be called children of God" (Matt. 5:9).

Third, the practices of peacemaking are not meant legalistically. As Bovon says, the same mechanisms work *analogously* in different contexts. Therefore the practices of peacemaking require discernment, detecting imaginatively how they may occur in each new context. Each practice should be understood in its social context, with special attention to the politics of Jesus' day, to the political context of the early church around the time of the disastrous Jewish War against Rome, to Jesus' Bible, the Hebrew Scriptures, and to the political context of our day.

Fourth, the practices of dynamic peacemaking that Jesus points to are essential to all relationships — individual, family, church, and international. The seven criteria do not point only to an inner subjective spiritual process, or to a distant apocalyptic end, but to a dynamic personal and social process of peacemaking now. Bovon calls this a systemic interpretation. He argues that it is preferable to the subjective-individualist interpretation of Rudolf Bultmann and Herbert Braun. "The mechanisms of love and hate function analogously between individuals, social groups, and even nations. The command of enemy-love is a practical alternative to the other systems of recurring violence and oppression." It is based on "the initiative of God who first loves us, God's enemies. . . . God's initiative gives us the possibility and the strength to carry out God's command. Without God's love it would be as weak and powerless as Paul says the law is. The imitation of God is the consequence of this initiative of God's." It is based on following the way of Jesus, on the promise of becoming children of God (Luke 6:35b and Matt. 5:45), and on the promise that the enemy may be converted. In receiving love from God, "we can love the enemy. So we move out of the closed deadly system of retaliation, and a changing relationship to Jesus and to the enemy is made possible."[39] The image of the enemy we hold causes distorted perceptions, prepares for war, and causes us to miss opportunities for resolving conflicts of interest. The skill of imagining initiatives

---

39. Bovon, *Evangelisch-Katholischer Kommentar,* 320. This systemic interpretation fits Yoder's emphasis on the powers and authorities, and his argument throughout *For the Nations* that the gospel concerns not only the inwardness of the community but also the will of God for the nations.

or solutions that affirm both sides' valid interests requires the dynamic of love — to identify with and affirm the enemy's valid interests.

Similarly, Yoder points out that justice/jubilee is not an unattainable ideal irrelevant to the social order. "The jubilee which Jesus proclaims is not the end of time, pure event without duration, unconnected to either yesterday or tomorrow. The jubilee is precisely an *institution* whose functioning within history will have a precise, practicable, limited impact."[40] It is politically relevant.

Fifth, a transforming initiatives strategy means we are not to wait for the government, but to take initiatives ahead of what the government does. It makes clear to the church that we practice peacemaking initiatives out of obedience to Christ and in response to the world's need, independent of whether governments seek peace. If we aren't practicing peace, to urge others to do so is hypocrisy. George Williamson, past president of the Baptist Peace Fellowship of North America, was asked whether his going with a Fellowship of Reconciliation group to Iraq, bringing gifts of medicine and messages of peace while the U.S. government was preparing for war, might not undermine the government's peacemaking efforts. He answered: "I hope my government is making the same kind of peacemaking efforts we are making. If it is, I can't imagine how our peacemaking efforts could possibly undermine what they are doing. And if my government is not making peacemaking efforts, then as a Christian disciple I need to be taking this initiative anyway."

Sixth, Duane K. Friesen has described how a nonviolent strategy of positive peacemaking initiatives and a step-by-step functional approach can be effective in conflict resolution and international peacemaking.[41] Daniel Buttry has described the dramatic international impact of the peacemaking strategy of nonviolent direct action developed by Mahatma Gandhi, Martin Luther King, Jr., and others. Similarly, the strategy of independent initiatives that runs from Charles Osgood's *An Alternative to War or Surrender* through the strategies of the Nuclear Weapons Freeze Campaign and the European peace movement, to the Catholic Bishops' pastoral letter, *The Challenge of Peace,* finally was adopted in modified form by governments in "confidence-building measures" and in initiatives by Mikhail Gorbachev, the U.S. Congress, and George Bush that reduced nuclear weapons dramatically.[42]

Finally, why not join the initiatives in the Sermon on the Plain to form a

40. Yoder, *The Politics of Jesus,* 107-8.

41. Duane Friesen, *Christian Peacemaking & International Conflict: A Realist Pacifist Perspective* (Scottdale, PA: Herald Press, 1986); and his concluding chapter of *Just Peacemaking: Ten Practices to Abolish War.*

42. See Daniel Buttry, *Christian Peacemaking: From Heritage to Hope* (Valley Forge, PA: Judson Press, 1994). See also *Just Peacemaking,* ch. 1 and 2.

"just peacemaking theory"? After sixteen centuries of "just war theory," whose criteria are usually applied *after* forces preparing for war have built such momentum that they cannot be diverted, might we finally be ready to define ten peacemaking practices that are already abolishing war here and there, and that can spread further when Christians join in supporting them? Can these shape our Christian witness to the state about essential practices of making peace? Can we then begin applying the criteria early in a potential conflict while there is still time? Can we do our part for the shalom of the world in which we live, and actually seek to abolish war? This will not initially stop governments from every war, but it is already stopping many wars, and it is spreading. And it can at least help Christians not to be hoodwinked into believing the government's assertions that it is doing all it can to make peace, when it is in fact avoiding the essential practices.[43]

---

43. This is the argument of *Just Peacemaking: Ten Practices to Abolish War.*

The Biblical Concept of "the Principalities and Powers": John Yoder Points to Jacques Ellul[1]

Marva J. Dawn

Throughout the ages of Christianity the biblical notion of "the principalities and powers" has influenced systematic theology, liturgy, and ethics. Beginning with the basic texts about the powers in Romans, 1 Corinthians, Philippians, Colossians, and Ephesians, much of the self-understanding of the early church and individuals within it derived from the notion that union with Christ led to conflict with other values and entities.

According to Visser 't Hooft, an understanding of the cosmic Christ and the significance of his victory over the principalities and powers was lost during the time of the Reformation, when Luther's and Calvin's struggles against different apocalyptic sects necessitated cautious interpretation of the cosmic aspects of biblical eschatology. Friedrich Schleiermacher expressed clearly the trend toward a non-cosmic and subjective conception of Christ's kingdom, and Adolf von Harnack, Ernst Troeltsch, Johannes Weisz, and Albert Schweitzer continued the progression.[2]

One widely influential leader in restoring the vocabulary of the powers in

---

1. An abbreviated edition of this article first appeared as "Principalities and Powers: Yoder Points to Ellul" in the Australian Baptist Peace Fellowship journal, *Faith and Freedom* 5 (June 1996): 54-59. My thanks to editor David Neville for permission to use the expanded version here.

2. W. A. Visser 't Hooft, *The Kingship of Christ: An Interpretation of Recent European Theology* (New York: Harper and Brothers, 1948), 15-31.

theological discussion was John H. Yoder's teacher, Karl Barth. In the 1953 lectures which formed the basis for *Church Dogmatics* IV.2, Barth describes the powers as "spirits with a life and activity of their own, lordless indwelling forces . . . [which] are entities with their own right and dignity . . . as absolutes. . . ." He comments on "the obscurity, ambivalence, and unintelligibility of their reality and efficacy," their "wraith-like transitoriness," and "the variety of the forms in which they arise in the different periods and cultural circles of human life and in the lives of individuals," but Barth insists that their reality and efficaciousness cannot be ignored.

Barth refuses to accept the criticism that the view of the New Testament authors was "magical." Instead, he claims that they were less hindered by the worldview of their contemporaries than we are and thus "have in fact . . . seen more, seen more clearly, and come much closer to the reality in their thought and speech, than those of us who are happy possessors of a rational and scientific view of things." They were able, consequently, to take into account freely "the strange reality and efficacy of the lordless powers." What is necessary, Barth concludes, is a demythologizing not of the concept of "the principalities and powers," but of the myths of the powers, such as the State or Mammon. By means of their myths — e.g., political illusions — the powers are able to exert their tyranny.[3]

A major impetus for this return of the language of the powers was the extremity of events in the years surrounding World Wars I and II. Persons trying to find language to describe the horrors of the times returned to the concept of "the principalities and powers" to explain that which went beyond modern psychological explanations. Similarly, in the era of nuclear weapons and the cold war, the vocabulary of "the powers" began to be used to describe the world's precarious situation. As Amos Wilder of Harvard asserts, the concept, rather than obfuscating or impeding the relevance of New Testament eschatology or Christology, instead emphasizes the urgency of applying the gospel to the world of power structures in which we live.[4] Contemporary ethicists fail to deal adequately with the problems of our times if they treat only on a material level evils that require a spiritual response.

3. Karl Barth, *The Christian Life: Church Dogmatics IV*, trans. Geoffrey W. Bromiley (Grand Rapids: Eerdmans, 1981), 214-33.

4. Amos N. Wilder, *Kerygma, Eschatology, and Social Ethics* (Philadelphia: Fortress Press, 1966), 23-34.

John Howard Yoder and the Concept of "the Powers"

John Howard Yoder was a leader in explicating and responsibly using the biblical notion of "the principalities and powers" — not only by his own writing, but also by making available to English readers the works of others who unfold the reality of the powers. He assisted the Hutterian Society of Brothers in editing *God's Revolution: The Witness of Eberhard Arnold,* who, along with Karl Barth and others, followed in the line of Johann Christoph Blumhardt and his son, Christoph Friedrich. These men, whose emphasis that Christ's lordship includes also the social and political aspects of life, had been largely unheard or misunderstood in their own time (the 1800s), but began to be comprehended in the aftermath of World War I.[5]

John Yoder also discovered and translated Dutch theologian Hendrik Berkhof's *Christus en de Machten;*[6] this book is foundational for much of the contemporary studies of the biblical concept of "the principalities and powers." In his preface to the second edition, Berkhof thanks Yoder for making his work available to English readers just a few years after Karl Barth reneged on his original intention to issue a German translation in the series *Theologische Studien,* which he edited. Berkhof recounts that Barth later apologized for not doing so because he felt that Berkhof "mythologized" the powers too much and "that he could not approve of such a publication at a time when his own theology was under the crossfire of Bultmann and his disciples." However, Berkhof notes, in his comments on "The Rebellious Powers" in the last lectures of *Church Dogmatics* Barth joins him in "combating the modern spirit whose rational-scientific world view has no eye left for the power of the Powers."[7]

Making extensive use of Berkhof's work, John Yoder discusses the biblical concept of "the principalities and powers" most thoroughly in "Christ and Power," the eighth chapter of *The Politics of Jesus.*[8] Yoder demonstrates the complexity of modern uses of the word *structure* to illustrate the "clarity and ambiguity" of the language of power (136-38). Then he summarizes the biblical concept of the powers as originating in the creative purpose of God and remaining

---

5. See *God's Revolution: The Witness of Eberhard Arnold,* ed. The Hutterian Society of Brothers and John Howard Yoder (New York: Paulist Press, 1984).

6. Hendrik Berkhof, *Christ and the Powers,* trans. John H. Yoder (Scottdale, PA: Herald Press, 1977). Berkhof's Dutch work appeared in 1953, was first translated by Yoder in 1962, and was reissued by Herald Press fifteen years later.

7. Berkhof, *Christ and the Powers,* 10.

8. John Howard Yoder, *The Politics of Jesus,* 2nd. ed. (Grand Rapids: Eerdmans, 1994), 134-61. (Originally published in 1972.) Page references are given parenthetically in the following text.

under God's sovereignty even though they have fallen (140-44). Following Berkhof, Yoder suggests that certain concrete modern phenomena are "structurally analogous to the Powers" (142), rather than equated with them. To show the broad range of such analogous phenomena, he lists religious, intellectual ("'ologies and 'isms"), moral ("codes and customs"), and political structures ("the tyrant, the market, the school, the courts, race, and nation") and claims that such an understanding enables the concept of "the principalities and powers" to provide a more refined analysis of the problems of society and history than is possible in theological descriptions that emphasize the "personality" of the powers (142-44).

Next, Yoder asks what the meaning of the work of Christ is "if our lostness consists in our subjection to the rebellious powers of a fallen world." He answers that, since "subordination to these Powers is what makes us human," then, if "God is going to save his creatures *in their humanity,* the Powers cannot simply be destroyed or set aside or ignored. Their sovereignty must be broken. This is what Jesus did, concretely and historically . . ." (144). The work of the church, then, is to proclaim the message of Christ's victory over the powers by being a community liberated from their dominion. Consequently, the church's role is a "revolutionary subordination" (162-92), which serves the world rather than seeking to dominate it. It is the community of those who seek to follow Jesus which will be the primary social structure through which other structures can be changed (154-55). The pattern is one of "creative transformation" (185). One example to demonstrate such creative transformation is John Yoder's superb analysis in *The Christian Witness to the State,* which discusses, in its second chapter, Christ's lordship over the powers as "The Ground for the Witness to the State."[9]

Yoder emphasizes that the lordship of Christ is a structural fact, not at all limited to those who have accepted it. He summarizes the significance of this fact by introducing us to Johann Christoph Blumhardt, who

> rediscovered for German Protestantism a century ago the wondrous power of the gospel in individual lives and at the same time the eschatological foundation of Christian involvement in politics. We may echo his battle cry: "Dass Jesus siegt ist ewig ausgemacht. Sein ist die ganze Welt!" "That Jesus is conqueror is eternally settled: the universe is his!" This is not a statement concerning the benevolent disposition of certain individuals to listen or of certain powers to be submissive. It is a declaration about the nature of the cosmos and the significance of history, within which both our

9. See John H. Yoder, *The Christian Witness to the State* (Newton, KS: Faith and Life Press, 1964), 8-14.

conscientious participation and our conscientious objection find their authority and their promise. (157)

It is not Yoder's purpose in *The Politics of Jesus* to "spell out at length samples of the relevance of this kind of approach for concrete social and ethical thought." Instead, he points to Jacques Ellul and insists that in the latter's writing on money, the law, violence, and technology, he "probably . . . thinks the most consistently within the framework of this approach, though often without direct allusion to the Pauline vocabulary" (157).

Because Jacques Ellul rarely alludes directly to the biblical vocabulary, scholars do not usually recognize how pervasive the biblical concept of "the principalities and powers" is in his thought. My chance remark to John Yoder about noticing Ellul's deep commitment to the subject and his responding affirmation of the need to study the concept in Ellul's work led to many years of fruitful research with Yoder as my dissertation director. As Yoder's *Politics* suggests, in Ellul can be found the most thorough fleshing out of the significance of the biblical concept of "the powers" for contemporary ethical reflection.

Jacques Ellul's Scattered References to the Powers and His Place in the Spectrum of the Disciplines

French lay theologian, social critic, and professor of law and institutions, Jacques Ellul was one of the first to apply the concept of "the principalities and powers" to domains other than the state. In a series of three foundational articles on "Problèmes de civilisation" published in *Foi et Vie* in 1946 and 1947, Ellul laid out his basic assumptions concerning the "structures" of the world and the need for Christian realism to recognize the workings of these "forces." Throughout his fifty-year career in social criticism, biblical studies, and ethics, Ellul continued to unfold an extensive analysis of the nature of these "forces," the powers. However, his programmatic essays of 1946-47 had not been previously translated into English, and most of his other works fall into distinctive tracks of social criticism or theology; consequently, few of his readers are aware of the significance of the concept of "the principalities and powers" in Ellul's thinking. With John Yoder's invaluable advice and foundational assistance, I prepared a translation of, and commentary on, Ellul's early articles.[10] This book details the structure and functioning of the powers as enunciated by Ellul in his earliest work in *Foi et Vie*.

10. See Marva J. Dawn, trans. and ed., *Sources and Trajectories: Eight Early Articles by Jacques Ellul That Set the Stage* (Grand Rapids: Eerdmans, 1997).

Ellul first became known in the English-speaking world in 1964 when *The Technological Society* was translated into English ten years after its appearance in French. Two important sequels to this work were *The Technological System* of 1977 (1980 in English) and *The Technological Bluff* (1988/90). Related books study propaganda (1962/65), political illusions (1965/67), clichés (*A Critique of the New Commonplaces* — 1966/68), revolutions (1969/71), violence (published in English first, 1969), and modern forms of the sacred (*The New Demons* — 1973/75). Hundreds of his articles detail various observations about the technological society. These works, which philosophize about large moral issues and deal centrally with the problem of power, are named *sociologie* in Europe, but would be labeled "critical social thought" in the United States. They expose the functioning of the principalities, for Ellul's thorough consciousness of the influence of the demonic powers upon social realities undergirds his sociological assessments, though he avoids the biblical terminology in order not to cloud the issues.

Though Ellul might be considered one example of a particularly eminent line of social theorists (including such people as Marcuse and Durkheim), he goes against the tide in the field of biblical hermeneutics. His criticism of some modern methods of biblical exegesis is severe, and sometimes his own methods seem to lack essential rigor. His biblical works include volumes on Ecclesiastes (1989/90), Jonah (1952/71), II Kings (*The Politics of God and the Politics of Man* — 1966/72), and Revelation (1975/77) and biblical treatments of the subjects of money (*Money and Power* — 1954/85) and the city (*The Meaning of the City* — in English first, 1970). The latter three contain extensive references to the biblical notion of "the principalities and powers."

In the field of ethics, the influence of both Kierkegaard and Barth is evident. Rather than outlining a system of ethics along the classical deontological or teleological lines, Ellul posits an *Ethics of Freedom* (1973/76), which is radically christocentric and practically applied to such issues as the use of money (*Money and Power* — 1954/85), the practice of prayer (*Prayer and Modern Man* — in English first, 1970), and the way our culture destroys language by misuse and its emphasis on the visual (*The Humiliation of the Word* — 1981/86). All of these works emphasize the ways in which Christians should deal with the principalities and powers. As will be seen below, Ellul insists that he speaks out of a lifelong confrontation with the question of the powers.

His claim must not be taken lightly. His severe sociological analyses of the all-encompassing influence of the powers undergird his intensity and reinforce our recognition that his call to Christians to be aware of the working of the powers and of the need for battle against them is a warning that must be heeded. That is a major motivation for my attempts to demonstrate that the

173

concept of "the powers" links Ellul's tracks, for the importance of the concept in his thinking is usually overlooked by those who study his works.

The Concept of "the Principalities and Powers" as a Common Core in Ellul's Theology and His Social Criticism

That the concept of "the principalities and powers" provides a bridge between Ellul's *sociologie* and his theology first came to my attention[11] because of the section on "the powers" in *The Ethics of Freedom,* in which Ellul lists the following possibilities of interpretation for the biblical notion:

> Are they demons in the most elemental and traditional sense? Are they less precise powers (thrones and dominions) which still have an existence, reality, and, as one might say, objectivity of their own? Or do we simply have a disposition of man which constitutes this or that human factor a power by exalting it as such . . . ? In this case the powers are not objective realities which influence man from without. They exist only as the determination of man which allows them to exist in their subjugating otherness and transcendence. Or finally, at the far end of the scale, are the powers simply a figure of speech common to the Jewish-Hellenistic world, so that they merely represent cultural beliefs and have no true validity?

Ellul situates himself somewhere between the second and third interpretations for these reasons:

> On the one side, I am fully convinced with Barth and Cullmann that the New Testament *exousiai* and the power of money personified as Mammon correspond to authentic, if spiritual, realities which are independent of man's decision and inclination and whose force does not reside in the man who constitutes them. Nothing that I have read to the contrary has had any great cogency for me. Neither the appeal to Gnosticism nor reference to the cultural background seems to me to explain the force and emphasis of the New Testament writers in this area. In particular the opposite view has to follow the common practice of ignoring certain essential passages where Paul cannot be adequately demythologized.
>
> On the other side, however, the powers do not act simply from outside after the manner of Gnostic destiny or a *deus ex machina.* They are characterized by their relation to the concrete world of man. According to the bib-

---

11. This connection was first explicated in Marva J. Dawn, "An Introduction to the Work of Jacques Ellul," *Word and World* 9 (Fall 1989): 386-93.

lical references they find expression in human, social realities, in the enterprises of man. In this sense the occasion of their intervention is human decision and action. . . . [T]he world of which the New Testament speaks is not just a spiritual and abstract reality but one which is identical with what man in general calls the world, i.e., society.[12]

This passage is especially important because throughout most of his career Ellul maintained that position between the second and third options he listed above. Specifically, he asserts that the way in which the powers transform "a natural, social, intellectual, or economic reality into a force which man has no ability either to resist or to control" and the way in which this force "gives life and autonomy to institutions and structures" or "attacks man both inwardly and outwardly" and "alienates man by bringing him into the possession of objects" correspond to biblical passages such as Ephesians 6:12 (152-53). Then, in his most personal comments on the subject, Ellul describes this connection between the powers and social realities:

> Political power has many dimensions, e.g., social, economic, psychological, ethical, psycho-analytical, and legal. But when we have scrutinized them all, we have still not apprehended its reality. *I am not speaking hastily or lightly here but as one who has passed most of his life in confrontation with their question and in their power.* We cannot say with Marx that the power is an ideological superstructure, for it is always there. *The disproportion noted above leads me to the unavoidable conclusion that another power intervenes and indwells and uses political power, thus giving it a range and force that it does not have in itself.* The same is true of money . . . [and] technology. (153-54, emphasis added)

These were the sentences that led to my chance remark to John Yoder and his consequent invitation to make their import the subject of my doctoral research. The dissertation demonstrates that this consciousness of the powers and their relationship to social realities undergirds Ellul's critical social assessments, though he has avoided the Pauline terminology because of his firm conviction that to bring traditional religious references into the academic milieu of

---

12. Jacques Ellul, *The Ethics of Freedom*, trans. and ed. Geoffrey W. Bromiley (Grand Rapids: Eerdmans, 1976), 151-52. Page references to this book in the following discussion are given parenthetically in the text. I have chosen not to muddy quotations by changing Ellul's use of "man" to inclusive language; because of Ellul's emphasis on the person, his abhorrence of violence, and his very great kindness to visitors (myself included), I think he would be using inclusive language by now, though his resistance to cultural fads would prevent him from some of the follies to which political correctness sometimes leads.

sociologie is inappropriate. His insistence that he speaks out of a lifelong confrontation with the question of the powers shows us that the concept provides
an important key for interpreting his work.

The dialectic of Ellul's two tracks of work is linked by the powers in that
he wants to relate the hope and grace of his theology to the concrete situation
of the powers at work in the world. On the other hand, he insists that only on
the basis of true freedom through faith is he "able to hold at arm's length these
powers which condition and crush me . . . [and to] view them with an objective
eye that freezes and externalizes and measures them . . ." (228-33). Among those
powers that he can freely assess objectively Ellul specifically includes in *The
Ethics of Freedom* the modern state, social utility, money, and the technological
society (234, 256).[13]

The Structure and Functioning of the Powers
as Enunciated by Ellul's Earliest Articles in *Foi et Vie*

The foundation for Ellul's work was explicitly laid in his earliest articles in *Foi et
Vie* in 1946 and 1947. Because the series was previously untranslated, however,
few who read Ellul understood how his career began with such an outlining of
his basic understanding of the "principalities and powers," which he then undertook to assess more thoroughly in his larger works of *sociologie*.

In the series' first article, "Chronique des Problèmes de Civilisation I: En
Guise d'Avertissement," written shortly after World War II, Ellul concludes his
introductory remarks by warning that people of 1946 must make a decision on
the question of the *structures* of society.[14] Then, fundamentally, he responds as
follows to the inevitable criticism that his work is pessimistic:

> [W]hat I do know is that the world in which I live is the domain of *Satan;*
> that human beings, myself included, are radically sinful, and that God, mi-
> raculously, allows them to live. . . . But God does more than preserve. He

13. My dissertation, "The Concept of 'The Principalities and Powers' in the Works of
Jacques Ellul" (University of Notre Dame, 1992), maps Ellul's sociological assessments of these
entities on pp. 166-251. Hereafter cited as "Concept."

14. Jacques Ellul, "Chronique des Problèmes de Civilisation: En Guise d'Avertissement," *Foi et Vie* 44 (September/October 1946): 678-80; English translations given here, rendered to make them inclusive, are from Dawn, *Sources*, 13-22 ("Chronicle of the Problems of
Civilization: I. By Way of a Brief Preface"). Page references to this English version in the following discussion are given parenthetically in the text. Emphasis will be added to note key
words used by Ellul to signify the powers; the term *structures* is Ellul's earliest designation for
them.

saves. . . . And God saves in such a way that *the prince of this world*[15] is sub-ordinated to the salvation of humankind by virtue of the victory of the Savior who becomes Lord. (16, emphasis added)

In this article of 1946 Ellul explains the connection of the two tracks of his future work by calling himself a citizen of two cities who must by means of the discernment of spirits examine different facts and examine them differently. His work is to seek the final roots of the present situation (in the workings of the powers of Satan and the prince of this world) and to judge these daily facts spiritually — i.e., with true Christian realism. Only such a judgment can give intelligible continuity for political and social events (18). Work to understand the *structures* of the world in light of the revelation must be constantly redone, for it can never be enclosed in a theological, political, or economic system, since the world is always changing.

Ellul's purpose is to make an inventory of *forces,* beyond their social and economic forms, which condition life in modern times (19). These *forces* are identical throughout the world; they are common in all of civilization; they are independent of human will; they have a reality not easily separable from their temporary form; and they give to the present age a radically new character. This description is immensely important, for this is Ellul's initial understanding — written in 1946 — of the structure and functioning of the powers which undergirds all of his sociological, biblical, and ethical work.

Indeed, Ellul asserts that his inventory of *forces* is not intended to exhaust the question nor to give solutions, for each of the points that he indicates will merit a scientific study of one or several volumes (as the unfolding of his career has demonstrated). Moreover, to give solutions for the problems of civilization would be impossible. He declares that before a solution can be sought, a method must be found, and, before that, the problem must be accurately posed. The folly of our times, he insists, is that one pretends to give solutions without seeing the problem of these *forces.*

Ellul asserts that we live in an age that is essentially materialistic — or, more accurately, that is characterized by a radical separation of the material and spiritual domains. This societal separation prohibits seeking fundamental *spiritual causes* for economic or political problems (20).

The major fault of Christianity is that it has sought to deal with social problems with charity, which does not fulfill the necessary spiritual conditions for it to be effective (21). Consequently, Ellul proposes that the inventory which

15. Not until forty years later in his *The Subversion of Christianity* (Grand Rapids: Eerdmans, 1986) does Ellul specifically *name* "Satan" and "the Prince of this world" as among the "principalities and powers."

he will give in future articles will have as its goal to give elements for thinking sanely in our times so that Christianity can be lived in a concrete fashion in the midst of our society's difficulties (22).

Ellul concludes the second article of the series, "Problèmes de Civilisation II: On Demande un Nouveau Karl Marx" (1947), with the inventory he promised in the first article and warns that it is necessary to pay attention to the *structures* of our society.[16] Ellul's main theme in this article is that social problems were being badly posed because they are isolated from the rest. Thus, the utopians make two medical errors; they choose remedies without diagnosing the malady, and they treat the exterior symptoms and not the true disease they express (36-37). (These comments especially point to the need for the kind of wholistic assessment which Ellul attempted seven years later in *The Technological Society,* thirty years later in *The Technological System,* and more than forty years later in *The Technological Bluff.*)

Ellul exclaims that there is need for a new Karl Marx to pose questions in their entirety (38-40). He insists that only an analysis that leads to the discovery of the *particular underlying principles* common to all of civilization (the *forces* of his first article) will be sufficient.

In this second article, Ellul clarifies as follows his use of the term *structures* or *données fondamentales,* which again provides a foundational description of some of the elements of his understanding of the powers:

> Underneath the phenomena which we are able to see in the social, political, economic realms, there are some permanent *forces* of which the tracks are found in each of the phenomena considered, and which ensure its unity to our times beneath its chaotic and disordered appearance. Exactly as in a tapestry, there is an unseen warp which ensures the unity of the fabric and which is the foundational element upon which is developed the outward designs and ornaments. (42)

The word *structure* has become watered down to signify merely the temporary superstructures of the economy or politics, which can be changed without changing society itself. On the other hand, the *structures* are not eternal, as philosophy would name permanent elements. Rather, Ellul is concerned about those *structures* which authentically characterize modern society.

The second characteristic of the *structures* is that they are common to

16. Jacques Ellul, "Problèmes de Civilisation: On Demande un Nouveau Karl Marx," *Foi et Vie* 45 (May/June 1947): 374; translation in Dawn, *Sources,* 45 ("Needed: A New Karl Marx [Problems of Civilization II]"). Page references to the English version in the following discussion are given parenthetically in the text.

many phenomena of our society, and, therefore, give a certain unity to its total-ity (43). The third characteristic is that if they were modified, all of civilization would be put in question. Because these *structures* have been misunderstood, techniques and utopias have been equally inefficacious.

Finally, a *structure* concerns the individual life of persons. It is a decisive *force* in the organization of their lives, the order of their thoughts, their behav-ior, their habits, and, at the same time, such *power* tends precisely to annihilate them (44). Ellul concludes, then, with a list of the essential *structures* which he proposes to study in future articles: "Technique, Production, the State, the City, and War" (45).

That list outlines much of Ellul's work in hundreds of articles and scores of books over the next fifty years. The third article of the initial series, "Problèmes de Civilisation III: Le Realisme Politique" (1947), deals specifically with the *structure* of politics, focuses especially on its realism, which Ellul calls "an enormous corrupting power," and offers a different sort of realism as the Christian response to the powers.[17]

Most significantly, this article thoroughly describes Ellul's fundamental perception of the opposition between political realism, which actually is an il-lusion, and Christian realism, which enables the believer to recognize the func-tioning of the powers in the world. The article thereby summarizes the major motivations for most of the work of Ellul's various tracks — viz., to grow in Christian realism by means of his biblical studies, to see the world more realis-tically in his social criticism, and to challenge the church to take up more effec-tively its task of Christian realism in his ethical works.

It is not possible here to map Ellul's thorough exposition of political and Christian realism. He discusses nationalism as dominated by the *spirit of power* (55) and political realism in the economic domain as representing an *enormous corrupting power* (66). Ellul shows the workings of the principalities when po-litical realism and its "law of things" lead to the vanishing of the real person and of humanity (67). The powers' functioning is also evident because a character-istic of political realism is the trait of illusion (67-69).

Many details in Ellul's 1947 description prefigure much of his later work in *sociologie* — his criticism of nationalism; of (non-Christian) realism's crite-ria of success and utility; of how a morality of means necessitates the use of propaganda to arouse the support of the masses; of the reduction of politics to

---

17. Jacques Ellul, "Problèmes de Civilisation III: Le Realisme Politique," *Foi et Vie* 45 (November/December 1947): 714 and 720-34; translation in *Sources*, 66 and 71-84 ("Political Realism [Problems of Civilization III]"). Page references to the English version in the following discussion are given parenthetically in the text.

imperialisms, leading fatally to conflicts more and more vast; of the moral hypocrisy inherent in realism of action; of the law of things in the economic domain and the consequent vanishing of the real person; of political realism's
trait of illusion. These ideas were all expanded especially in *Propaganda: The
Formation of Men's Attitudes, The Political Illusion, Violence: Reflections from a
Christian Perspective,* and in *Autopsy of Revolution.*

Ellul's next section begins, then, with the clarification that realism is anti-
Christian not at all because Christianity is a spiritualism, but because it is itself
a realism, but of another kind. Christianity's realism begins with the recognition of the state of total and irremediable sin in which a human being is
plunged (72). Sociological studies of our civilization are only the actualization
of the fact that our world is the domain of *the Prince of this world* (73). Ellul asserts that the concordance between our sociological investigations and the
Word of God (the two tracks of his work) is central to Christian realism, for
God does not detach us from reality, but rather plunges us into all of it — both
the material and the eternal (73-74).

Revelation alone is not sufficient, nor is the Revelation irrelevant to the
real problem of humanity and society. In the realm of politics, for example,
theological affirmations are insufficient; it is necessary to study the facts to see
the biblical truth incarnated. Then this recognition of the facts and the application of Scripture to the facts (74) lead necessarily to a decisive position. If the
world appears in its reality as the domain of *the Prince of this world,* we are
brought to a revolt by our nonacceptance of the concrete reality as it is and by
the necessity of snatching the domination from this usurper. Compared to political realism, which is conformism because its criterion is the unrolling of history, the realism of Christianity is revolutionary (in the sense of changing the
course of history), because its criterion is the lordship of Jesus Christ, which
must be incarnated in contradistinction to the constantly observable incarnation of *the principality of Satan.* The deplorable conformity of Christians shows
not a lack of virtues or of courage, but of true realism, and an abstraction of
their spiritual life (75).

Ellul calls not for placing facts into a theory more or less Christian, but
for utilizing the revelation to have a view of the phenomena more profound
and more true than experience or sense or reason is able to give us (which is
what Ellul attempts to do in all his *sociologie*). The revelation teaches us that the
phenomena are signs of a deeper reality — that of the *powers.* Thus, Christian
realism always stands in opposition to political realism, for Christian realism
constantly puts political, economic, and social phenomena in their place (76).

The liberty of faith enables us to know when to revolt against the world
and when to accept it, depending on which spirit animates something — that

of *Satan* or the Holy Spirit. Ellul especially emphasizes as the purpose of his study that we must ruin the consensus of political realism and attack especially the *demonic spirit* of our society's enormous means, by affirming Christian realism through the thought and life of the members of Christ (79).

This early discussion is especially important because Ellul juxtaposes the way of Christian realism with political realism, the way of the demonic powers, which are defeated only in Christ. His insistence that the former *must* be the perspective of Christians for their work to be of service shows us the reason for his own work — an attempt realistically to recognize in social reality the working of the powers and to offer the alternative of Christian freedom.

Ellul's Perspectives on the Nature and Being of the Powers

In *The Politics of Jesus,* John Yoder does not explicate the Pauline doctrine of the powers, but accepts the exegesis of others working in "the mood of 'biblical realism'" and insists that their exposition "is by now widely understood and accepted by scholars in the field."[18] In contrast to Yoder's pointing to others, Ellul claims to explicate the biblical concept, though he never does any specific exegesis of the Pauline passages and his perspective has changed in significant ways.[19]

Ellul's descriptions of the principality of Mammon in *Money and Power* especially illustrate his usual position on the spectrum of four interpretations sketched in *The Ethics of Freedom* (quoted above). He insists that wealth in itself is an economic power and, as such, must be rejected as the opposite of Jesus' path of humility. Consequently, New Testament authors write of money with "severe realism"; rather than thinking about money in economic or moral terms, they discuss it in spiritual terms.[20] Compared to the Targums and Talmud, Jesus gives the term *Mammon* greater force and precision; his personifica-

---

18. Yoder, *Politics,* 136. My extensive survey of exegetical literature on the biblical notion of "the principalities and powers" showed a wider diversity of interpretations, which Yoder acknowledges on p. 160. Chapter 3 of my dissertation demonstrates the vast terrain covered in discussions of the biblical concept of "the powers." There is no agreement as to their existence, and the debates between exegetes concerning many of the terms and passages fall into no consistent patterns. There is not so much disagreement on how to deal with the powers, however, though particular ethicists highlight various aspects of the ongoing struggle. See Dawn, "Concept," 36-83.

19. An exposition of Ellul's understanding of the being of the powers and how to deal with them can be found in Dawn, "Concept," 84-165 and 252-375.

20. Jacques Ellul, *Money and Power,* trans. LaVonne Neff (Downers Grove, IL: InterVarsity Press, 1984), 69-72. Page references to this book in the following discussion are given parenthetically in the text.

tion of money as the power Mammon is a unique deification that indicates its importance in his teaching. Such personification was not taken from the cultural milieu, but appears to be a special creation of Jesus — exceptional since he is not in the habit of using deifications and personifications. Ellul explicates this power as follows:

> This term should be understood not in its vague meaning, "force," but in the specific sense in which it is used in the New Testament. Power is something that acts by itself, is capable of moving other things, is autonomous (or claims to be), is a law unto itself, and presents itself as an active agent. That is its first characteristic. Its second is that power has a spiritual value. It is not only of the material world, although this is where it acts. It has spiritual meaning and direction. Power is never neutral. It is oriented; it also orients people. Finally power is more or less personal. And just as death often appears in the Bible as a personal force so here with money. Money is not a power because man uses it, because it is the means of wealth or because accumulating money makes things possible. It is a power *before* all that, and those exterior signs are only the manifestations of this power which has, or claims to have, a reality of its own.
>
> We absolutely must not minimize the parallel Jesus draws between God and Mammon. He is not using a rhetorical figure but pointing out a reality. God as a person and Mammon as a person find themselves in conflict. Jesus describes the relation between us and one or the other the same way: it is the relationship between servant and master. Mammon can be a master the same way God is: that is, Mammon can be a personal master.
>
> . . . Jesus is not describing a relationship between us and an object, but between us and an active agent. He is not suggesting that we use money wisely or earn it honestly. He is speaking of a power which tries to be like God, which makes itself our master and which has specific goals. (75-76, emphasis Ellul's)

This passage has been quoted extensively because it thoroughly reveals Ellul's position, similar to his perspectives on other powers in most of his works, that Mammon is not a power because of humanity's relation to it or use of it, but that "it is a power *before* all that." Furthermore, these paragraphs seem to indicate a separate existence in that the power functions, as does God, "as a person" and establishes its own purposes and mastery, though phrases such as "more or less personal" and "autonomous (or claims to be)" preserve the biblical ambiguity concerning the being of the powers. Ellul asserts that Jesus' teaching shows that money as a power is not a vague force, but he certainly leaves vague the nature of the force that it is.

Ellul names Mammon as a power by means of this phenomenological approach:

> We are not free to direct the use of money one way or another, for we are in the hands of this controlling power. Money is only an outward manifestation of this power, a mode of being, a form to be used in relating to man — exactly as governments, kings and dictators are only forms and appearances of another power clearly described in the Bible, political power. This comparison does not necessarily mean that money can be ranked with the "rule and authority and power and dominion" of which Paul speaks (Eph. 1:21). But neither does anything require us to challenge this interpretation. Without proof to the contrary, it would seem reasonable to accept this identification. (76-77)

Ellul's description of the parallelism of characteristics and function of Mammon and political power not only suggests that both are pertinent exemplars of the workings of "the powers" in the twentieth century, but also emphasizes that it is not the outward manifestations of the principalities but the authority behind these forms that gives them their controlling power over us.

Ellul's section on the powers in *The Ethics of Freedom* begins by explaining that the name "the powers" biblically refers to the "forces which subjugate" human beings. Ellul contends that we have to take the term in its broadest sense and include not just the evil and rebellious powers, not just powers "which scripture has rightly or wrongly, realistically or mythically, personalized," but also such things as the law and religion.[21] Earlier in the book Ellul specifically says that "every manifestation of power is an expression of the might of Satan," who controls the power and through it causes human beings to subjugate one another. "In [his] devaluation of force and government, Jesus shows very clearly that he attributes both their orientation and also their exercise to him who is always the prince of this world" (55). This position is a significant one, for it names the powers as entities outside of human beings and yet closely linked with human and social realities.

Ellul moves from this position in one of his last books, *The Subversion of Christianity,* which also categorizes Satan and the Prince of this World as distinct principalities and associates the function of Power only with the latter. In contrast to his "unavoidable conclusion" in *The Ethics of Freedom,* "that another power intervenes and indwells and uses political power [and money and technology], thus giving [them] a range and force that [they do] not have in

---

21. Ellul, *Ethics,* 144-45. Page references to this book in the following paragraphs are given parenthetically in the text.

[themselves]" (153), he insists in *Subversion* that the powers are "not a kind of reality of their own."[22] In contrast to most of Ellul's works, *The Subversion of Christianity* leans toward the third and entirely human possibility for interpretation and away from the biblical ambiguity concerning the nature of the principalities and powers.

Rather than Ellul's earlier ambiguous naming of powers and their functions, *Subversion* explicitly delineates the powers in the following typology:

> The Bible refers to six evil powers: Mammon, the prince of this world, the prince of lies, Satan, the devil, and death. . . . Concerning these six, one might remark that if we compare them we find that they are all characterized by their functions: money, power, deception, accusation, division, and destruction. In other words, they are not a kind of reality of their own. They do not exist as people do with their infinite complexity, multiple applications, evolutions and diversities, relations and inner mystery. What seems to me to be important in this vision of anticreation is precisely that there is no mystery about it, no opening up of a further world of evil. There is no infernal world or hierarchy of fallen angels with superimposed eons. There is nothing behind it. We are told about powers that are concretely at work in the human world and have no other reality or mystery. . . . [T]hey are expressions of chaos. . . . They exist only as this chaos . . . a force for disorder. . . . (174-76)

This passage illustrates a decisive shift away from Ellul's earlier conviction "that the New Testament *exousiai* and the power of money personified as Mammon correspond to authentic, if spiritual, realities" which "are independent of man's decision and inclination and whose force does not reside in the man who constitutes them."[23] Ellul's earlier and more ambiguous stance corresponds more closely with the biblical picture.

In spite of Ellul's shift in understanding the nature of the powers, his application of the concept to social realities remains the same. His entire career underscores his insistence in *The Ethics of Freedom* that his comments about the principalities and powers are not spoken "hastily or lightly," for he "*has passed most of his life in confrontation with their question and in their power*" (153). This assertion reminds us that Ellul's many works in *sociologie* are intended to expose the workings of the powers and to offer an excellent example of the

---

22. Jacques Ellul, *The Subversion of Christianity*, trans. Geoffrey W. Bromiley (Grand Rapids: Eerdmans, 1986), 176. Page references to this book in the following discussion are given parenthetically in the text.

23. Ellul, *Ethics*, 152. The following page reference to this book is given parenthetically in the text.

Christian realism to which he calls Christians in his ethics. All the gifts of Ellul's long career challenge contemporary ethicists to take seriously the functioning of the biblical powers in such social realities as politics, economics, and technology, and to deal with them on the spiritual level at which alone they can truly be engaged.

Postscript

Now with the unexpected death of John Yoder, part of me wants to rewrite my contribution to this *festschrift* to concentrate more on John's insights into the powers and the way his constant and faithful nonviolence was a profound demonstration of resisting the powers. However, I realize that what was already written would be what John would want — that my efforts would point beyond him to others and especially to God. Nevertheless, I must add here a postscript to note how John's mentoring both before and during the writing of my dissertation on Ellul's understanding of the powers embodied what I was learning from Ellul.

First and most important for my life's work, John did not let the academic institution become a "power" in his life. When I visited Notre Dame prior to moving there for doctoral work with him and Stanley Hauerwas, John asked what I did — and when I told him about my work in congregations under "Christians Equipped for Ministry," he responded, "Then what do you need a Ph.D. for? You're already doing what the church needs." I explained that I had become both a pacifist and one concerned about character formation by reading the Bible and that, as a result of my teaching, lots of people were turning to me with questions for which I had no answers, so I knew I needed mentors to teach me. John accepted that, but his initial questions continued to goad me during my doctoral work not to let the push for "credentials" become a "power" in my life.

This remained important when my dissertation ran into the "power" of institutional departmental politics. John kept reminding me that I was doing this work to learn and not necessarily for the credentials. He refused to react to the politics with the violence of power plays, but urged me continuously to respond with efforts at new understanding and reconciliation.

Though several persons in the academy discounted my choice to continue working for the larger church after receiving the Ph.D. as less worthy of my attention than being an academic, John consistently affirmed that decision, which became for me a resistance to many "powers," including Mammon. John also lauded my efforts to turn my dissertation research into a book that could serve lay people, too, by introducing them to Jacques Ellul's insights,[24] and, though the project would have been impossible without his help in understanding both Ellul's French phrasings and the European situation in which Ellul wrote, he refused to take credit for his assistance.

John Howard Yoder must be thanked for the many ways he pointed English readers to the great significance of Jacques Ellul's sociological assessments and the value of his ethical call — and for the many ways he himself incarnated the kinds of opposition to the powers both he and Ellul described.

24. See Dawn, trans. and ed., *Sources and Trajectories.*

ALTERNATIVES TO METHODOLOGISM

Moral Agency as Embodiment:
How the Church Acts

Harry J. Huebner

The relationship between the obedience of God's people and the tri-
umph of God's cause is not a relationship of cause and effect but one of
cross and resurrection.

J. H. Yoder

Introduction

The attempt in this century to assess the moral significance of the church has focused largely on the Troeltschian typology, "church-sect," and the Niebuhrian "made in America" addendum category, "denomination," the latter being but a minor variant of the former. This di(tri)chotomy may well have placed the church at the center of the discussion; it may even have facilitated the sociological appreciation of the church for some scholars. It has nonetheless managed to obfuscate the ethics debate in a manner that has undermined the role of the church for faithful Christian living.[1] Witness, for example, that the term "sectarian," pace Troeltsch and Niebuhr, has become a pejorative term. To call a position "sectarian" today not merely describes it, but labels it morally untenable. While this in itself may not be that serious, the problem is that it permits critics of so-called sectarian ethics to feel justi-

---

1. For a helpful essay which sorts out the limits of the Troeltschian categories see Duane Friesen, "Normative Factors in Troeltsch's Typology of Religious Association," *Journal of Religious Ethics* 3 (Fall 1975): 271-83.

fied in not taking seriously their underlying claims about Christology, eschatology, and Trinity.[2]

Upon rereading some of the literature on the subject, it has become apparent to me that the recourse to name-calling is rooted in the lack of agreement on theological language and hence on what is required to resolve the matter. Principally it is a debate over Christian moral agency. After all, the significant issue is not really *that* so-called sectarians "separate" themselves from society or *that* church-types "compromise" the Christian "principles" of love and peace, but rather how can we give theological clarity to our being and acting in the world. So-called sectarians would not concede to social irresponsibility in distancing themselves from mainstream society. They would argue that their way of being "church" constitutes precisely the way serious Christians ought to be socially involved. By the same token, those accused of compromise would maintain that unless you are willing to adapt your means to concrete social possibilities, you cannot responsibly exercise God's incarnated mandate in social-historical reality. Both would maintain their convictions about Christian ethics because of their beliefs about other claims.

This dispute has yet another level which calls into question the very structure of the debate itself. For example, those often accused of sectarianism (Yoder, Hauerwas, et al.) refuse to concede the value of the standard categories governing the debate. The contention is that these are products of a modernist imagination which has taught us that we must choose, as Alasdair MacIntyre puts it, between encyclopaedic and genealogical modes of moral inquiry.[3] Here the effort is to reject the underpinnings of the debate altogether because they do not fit the imagination of the biblical/theological tradition. In other words, they argue that there is a need to find alternative metaphors which do not enslave us to the shortcomings of the modern dualisms.

This essay will take one particular thread of the dispute, namely, moral agency — God's and ours — and suggest an alternative paradigm. I am, of course,

2. An example of just this problem is found in the discussion between James Gustafson, "The Sectarian Temptation: Reflections on Theology, the Church and the University" in *Proceedings of the Catholic Theological Society* 40 (1985): 83-94, and Stanley Hauerwas, "Introduction," in *Christian Existence Today: Essays of Church, World and Living in Between* (Durham, NC: The Labyrinth Press, 1988), 1-21. Gustafson criticizes Hauerwas et al. for yielding to the sectarian temptation, and Hauerwas replies: "What I find unfair, however, is the assumption that my critic has a hold on my task by calling me 'sectarian.' Show me where I am wrong about God, Jesus, the limits of liberalism, the nature of the virtues, or the doctrine of the church — but do not shortcut that task by calling me a sectarian" (8).

3. See Alasdair MacIntyre, *Three Rival Versions of Moral Inquiry: Encyclopaedia, Genealogy, and Tradition* (Notre Dame: University of Notre Dame Press, 1990).

aware that there are some who contend that the notion of moral agency is itself a product of modernist logic and hence is language better avoided. Hauerwas, for example, states that moral agency as used in contemporary ethics rests on questionable notions of the self, actions, and freedom.[4] I do not disagree with Hauerwas here. Yet that particular sense of moral agency has no exclusive claim on governing how we speak of our actions. Christians need to think carefully about how social change happens and how we understand ourselves and our practices in the larger context of God's work in the world. It may well be that just as we lack the courage of our convictions we also lack the wisdom to know how to participate positively within social reality and its tragedies.

When we change the context for moral agency from the self to the church, or from freedom to acting within tradition, we are thrown headlong into the "sectarian debate." And over the past few decades there have been two distinct yet intersecting foci to this debate. One might be called epistemological sectarianism and the other sociological sectarianism.[5] Each ascribes a differently nuanced meaning to "sectarianism." According to the first, as we will see, "sectarian" means community dependence; according to the second it means withdrawal from mainstream society.

Epistemological Sectarianism

In a recent article Anthony Battaglia makes the by now familiar claim that the reason sectarian epistemology is gaining appeal in our day is because Cartesian foundationalism has fallen on hard times. Nowadays honest scholarship forces us to recognize that we must relegate all thought and reason to particular social contexts. As Battaglia puts it, "Since we cannot know that our truth claims are objectively true, we fall back on what we do know: that they are considered true in our community and have been proven workable there."[6] Yet Battaglia is careful not to relegate postmodern ethics to a Nietzschean nihilism.

I will not here discuss the issue of foundationalism versus antifoundationalism. In fact, to do so would, according to scholars like Yoder and Hauerwas, be paying too much homage to theory. While they reject a foundationalism that assumes access to truth via a disembodied universal reason, what is far more in-

---

4. See Hauerwas, "Agency: Going Forwards by Looking Back," in *Christian Ethics*, ed. Lisa Sowle Cahill and James F. Childress (Cleveland: The Pilgrim Press, 1996), 185-95.

5. Stanley Hauerwas identifies the matter in this way, in his "Will the Real Sectarian Stand Up?" *Theology Today* 44 (April 1987): 87.

6. Anthony Battaglia, "Sect or Denomination: The Place of Religious Ethics in a Post-Churchly Culture," *The Journal of Religious Ethics* 16 (Spring 1988): 133.

teresting is the claim that their "antifoundationalism" renders the church-sect dichotomy itself obsolete. No longer is there an indubitable truth to reject; no longer a universal society to dissent from.[7] It is also interesting that, historically speaking, Radical Reformer churches have displayed a proclivity for pluralism and communitarianism because both readily accompany a countercultural/religious self-understanding. They have not pretended to be doing theology for everyone in the sense that they shared a common viewpoint with everyone. Nor were they thinking for everyone in the sense that they accepted an account of universal reason. And yet they believed their position to be grounded in the truth. This is why it is not a contradiction for these churches to say that although it might well make sense for someone to have a certain war fought, nevertheless they will not fight in it. For them it makes no sense on the basis of their reading of the Jesus story. They believe that Christian ethics is for Christians and "not for everyone," and the ethic that is "for everyone" (Kant's categorical imperative) is not necessarily binding for faithful Christians.

The issue here is authority. How can we know? How can we see? And the claim is that we must resist making the choice between knowing from the standpoint of Jesus Christ and knowing from the standpoint of culture, as Niebuhr does in his Christ/culture paradigms.[8] The Christian challenge is to come to know the world (culture) from the standpoint of Jesus Christ. This means that there is an epistemological bias towards the biblical/ecclesial tradition. Yoder states the matter succinctly when he says that "the church precedes the world epistemologically. We know more fully from Jesus Christ and in the context of confessed faith than we know in other ways."[9] For theologians like

7. Hauerwas states in his response to Wilson D. Miscamble and Michael J. Quirk (see *Theology Today* 44 [April 1987]: 69-94): "It makes no sense to continue to talk of 'sectarianism' or even 'kinds of sectarianism' after you have allowed, as Quirk has done, the essential rightness of the antifoundationalist critique. There is no universal society and/or knowledge from which the so-called sect can dissent" (88). And a little later in the same article, referring to Alasdair MacIntyre and other modern scholars, he says, ". . . I generally share their historicist starting point as well as their more communitarian and antiliberal political and social theory" (92). See also his introduction to *Christian Existence Today*.

8. See H. Richard Niebuhr, *Christ and Culture* (New York: Harper and Row, 1951).

9. See especially John Howard Yoder, *The Priestly Kingdom: Social Ethics as Gospel* (Notre Dame: University of Notre Dame, 1984), 11. Stanley Hauerwas echoes this theme throughout his writings. See also Vigen Guroian, "Bible and Ethics: An Ecclesial and Liturgical Interpretation," *The Journal of Religious Ethics* 18 (Spring 1990): 129-57, and his *Ethics After Christendom: Towards an Ecclesial Christian Ethic* (Grand Rapids: Eerdmans, 1994), and Anthony Battaglia, "Sect or Denomination: The Place of Religious Ethics in a Post-Churchly Culture," *The Journal of Religious Ethics* 16 (Spring 1988): 128-42. All embrace religious epistemologies which are said to be "sectarian," albeit not all for the same reasons.

Yoder and Hauerwas, who are often called sectarian ethicists, it is the faithful church community which makes it possible for us to understand the world around us and to do the will of God within that world. "World" is therefore a theological category. Christian knowledge and action cannot be abstracted from the lives of real people because neither is properly understood abstractly. Both presuppose a concrete social community which, as a discipleship training base, is a prerequisite for knowing God and the world. The assumption is that you cannot properly know God and world unless you have been instructed in the art of knowing and living by Christian practices. Yoder therefore continues by saying that "the church precedes the world as well axiologically, in that the lordship of Christ is the center which must guide critical value choices. . . ."[10]

In summary, ethicists like Yoder and Hauerwas make the "sectarian" epistemological claim not because of their philosophical reservations about foundationalism. That is, it is not as though they begin with postmodern philosophy and choose to view the Christian faith from that "epistemologically grounded" perspective. This is precisely what they do not do. The coincidence, whatever it may be, between their approach and certain postmodern options, can only be explained by a coming together to some common insight via vastly different journeys. Their "sectarian epistemology" is first of all rooted in the conviction regarding how God works in the lives of the community and in history and the personal/revelational nature of religious knowledge.[11] They believe that in Christ we see Creator God and that Jesus meant it when he said that the key to the knowledge of God is entering into God's dramatic story in Christ.[12] This implies a way of knowing commensurate with the incarnation of God in Christ and the subsequent invitation for all to claim a particular way of life. They are not sectarian epistemologists if by that is meant a separatist communitarianism unconcerned about matters of the world. Indeed Yoder has no special interest in theories of knowledge — foundational or otherwise — or, for that matter, theory of any kind.[13] He instead

---

10. Yoder, *The Priestly Kingdom*, 11.

11. This can be seen in Yoder's early writings such as *Peace Without Eschatology?* (Scottdale, PA: Herald Press, 1961) as well as in his more recent work such as "'Patience' as Method in Moral Reasoning: Is an Ethic of Discipleship 'Absolute'?" in this volume, 24-42; and "Discerning the Kingdom of God in the Struggles of the World," in *For the Nations: Essays Public and Evangelical* (Grand Rapids: Eerdmans, 1997), 237-45.

12. This is a common theme in scripture. A specific reference is Luke 11:52: "Woe to you lawyers! for you have taken away the key of knowledge; you did not enter yourselves, and you hindered those who were entering" (NRSV).

13. Yoder says, in an unpublished article, "Absolute Philosophical Relativism Is an Oxymoron" (1993) that "To make an issue of foundationalism is a form of foundationalism" (1).

suggests a specific mode of being in the world; a specific way of knowing the world through the eyes of the confessing community. Hence what one knows and how one lives cannot be separated. In fact, we come to know by doing. Notice how the issue is really not epistemology: no longer is it a matter of knowing either universally or perspectivally, but how to live in order to come to know the truth. To say it still differently, what drives scholars like Yoder and Hauerwas is not first of all the dominant Western epistemological quest at all, but rather the very desire to wrest theology from the epistemologists. In this respect both are more in tune with Stanley Fish, who has suggested that Western thought has long (falsely) believed that theories are the driving forces and communities the objects of change. He proposes that we see community as "the engine of change" and theories as important only insofar as communities have them.[14] In this way, the characteristic drive to first get our epistemology straight before important things can happen is vitiated, and epistemology gives way to sociology.

Sociological Sectarianism

An example of this side of the dispute is found in the debate between Hauerwas on one side and on the other Wilson Miscamble and James Gustafson, who charge him with a "withdrawal ethic" sectarianism.[15] Miscamble responds to Hauerwas's statement that "the claim that the first social task of the church is to be herself is not sectarian if by that is meant a retreat or withdrawal from the world." Says Miscamble:

> Let us be frank. Although he has denied the appellation, Hauerwas' ecclesiology is quite sectarian. Although he needs to develop further and focus his ecclesial stance, it is clear from what he has outlined to this point that Hauerwas sees the mission of the church as one of standing apart from

14. See, for example, the dialogue between Gary A. Olson and Fish in "Fish Tales: A Conversation with 'The Contemporary Sophist," in Stanley Fish, *There's No Such Thing as Free Speech and It's a Good Thing, Too* (New York: Oxford University Press, 1994), 281-307. Speaking of the role of abnormal discourse as a catalyst for change, Fish says, "One of my arguments is that strong-theory proponents attribute to theory a unique capacity for producing change and often believe (and this is perhaps a parody) if we can only get our epistemology straight, or get straight our account of the subject, then important political and material things will follow. It's that sense of the kind of change that will follow from a new theoretical argument that I reject" (288-89).

15. See "Symposium," *Theology Today* 44 (April 1987): 69-94, and Gustafson, "The Sectarian Temptation," 83-94.

society and witnessing to it. The church certainly stands "against culture," to borrow from H. Richard Niebuhr's categories. His approach runs counter to traditional Catholic ecclesiology which places the church directly in history and sees the church as having an integral role in the development and defense of societies and cultures. And in doing so, Hauerwas effectively removes the church from the life and death policy issues of the human community.[16]

To this Hauerwas replies:

> Miscamble accuses me of sectarianism because I have argued that the church ought to stand apart in order to witness to society. For the life of me, I do not understand why that position ought to be understood as sectarian. Such a witness does not prevent the church from speaking out on such issues as nuclear war, capital punishment, poverty, or the degradation of the family. What it does is position the church in a manner such that the church can serve society imaginatively by not being captured by societal options or corresponding governmental policy.[17]

Note that Miscamble assumes that unless you place the church "directly in history" and as "having an integral role in the development and defence of societies and cultures," it is sectarian in the pejorative sense, i.e., not morally responsible. Hauerwas sees this as precisely the way the church ought to exercise its responsibility toward society. Note that Hauerwas is not retreating from his claim that the church should "separate" itself from the "world." What he is challenging is the assumption that a proper kind of separation from the world (i.e., one which keeps the church from becoming world) makes the church morally irresponsible and/or morally irrelevant to the world. In addition, he resists allowing his challenger to define for him what the world and the church are that should remain separate.

Gustafson states the critique more radically and I believe more aptly. He accuses Hauerwas of lacking a doctrine of creation. He goes on to say:

> Faithful witness to Jesus is not a sufficient theological and moral basis for addressing the moral and social problems of the twentieth century. The theologian addressing many issues — nuclear, social justice, ecology, and so forth — must do so as an outcome of a theology that develops God's relation to all aspects of life in the world, and develops those relations in terms which are not exclusively Christian in a sectarian form. Jesus is not God.[18]

16. Wilson Miscamble, "Sectarian Passivism," *Theology Today* 44 (April 1987): 73 n. 22.
17. Hauerwas, "Will the Real Sectarian Stand Up?" 90.
18. Gustafson, "The Sectarian Temptation," 93.

Gustafson has stated the issue succinctly. We note that it gets us right back to the problems of Christology and Trinity. The implicit assumption for Gustafson appears to be that Jesus was morally misguided or naive (in any event, cannot be our sole moral foundation) and that when we go back to God we discover another "ethic" which is more "friendly" to, or inclusive of, the structures of society.

The issue is stated with unusual candor by saying that "Jesus is not God." Of course, if he is right then we need to go elsewhere, to the creation story, for instance, for a basis to ethics. But in what sense could that position be called Christian given that he puts it over against, or at least in tension with, the ethic of Jesus? Is not Christian ethics by definition rooted in Christ?[19]

It is important to note that the doctrines of the divinity of Christ and the Trinity are not inventions of the so-called sectarians. Hauerwas and Yoder, as I read them, are merely spelling out the *moral* implication of Chalcedon and Nicea for the church. After all, they are both "catholic" theologians. For them discipleship and pacifism are normative not only for a minority which wishes to live "radical" Christian lives, but for the universal church.[20] To "develop God's relation to all aspects of life in the world" (Gustafson) may well be the way to state the mandate for the Christian church, but why the assumption that a christologically based ethic necessarily truncates this mandate? Affirming that "in Christ all things are created" (Colossians 1:16; Ephesians 3:9) surely cannot mean that we understand Christ by looking at creation. Its intent is exactly the opposite, namely, the person of Christ requires us to take a fresh look at how we understand creation.[21] If Jesus is the Christ, as the Christian church has always taught, then for those of us who claim his name in our own self-characterization, knowing and following him in daily life become self-evident

19. Gustafson himself defends the close connection between creator God and Jesus in his earlier writings like *Can Ethics Be Christian?* (Chicago: University of Chicago Press, 1975). See particularly 169ff. It is all the more difficult to understand why he is now driving a wedge between the two when earlier he emphasized the connection. See also *Christ and the Moral Life* (New York: Harper and Row, 1968), especially the chapter entitled "Jesus Christ, the Lord Who Is Creator and Redeemer," 11-60.

20. Yoder makes this same point in his "'But We Do See Jesus': The Particularity of Incarnation and the Universality of Truth" in *The Priestly Kingdom: Social Ethics as Gospel* (Notre Dame: University of Notre Dame Press, 1984), 46-62.

21. Yoder puts the matter this way: "'Incarnation' does not originally mean (as it tends to today in some theologies of history, and in some kinds of Anglican theology) that God took all of human nature as it was, put his stamp of approval on it, and thereby ratified nature as revelation. The point is just the opposite; that God broke through the borders of man's definition of what is human, and gave a new, formative definition in Jesus." *The Politics of Jesus* (Grand Rapids: Eerdmans, 1972), 101.

aspirations because we believe that to do so is to enter into the very intent of creator God.

Both foci of the sectarian dispute then, the epistemological as well as the sociological, raise the fundamental issue of how, in the construction of a Christian ethic, we speak of God, Jesus Christ, and the church, especially as we unpack the notion of "bringing about" God's kingdom. This is the point of disagreement among Christian ethicists today and this is where the effort at clarification should focus. The ethic of Yoder and Hauerwas is sometimes seen as resting on a narrow Jesuology and a command-obedience, God-church relationship which has nothing to do with "bringing about" the kingdom on earth, because the church is only preoccupied with itself. This ethic is considered socially irrelevant because it is thought to be interested only in a biblical fidelity where faithfulness and effectiveness are seen as irreconcilable. But this is an unnecessarily myopic interpretation of their view of the church as moral agent.

The Church as Moral Witness

Reinhard L. Hütter has written a helpful article on the church as moral agent in which he contrasts what he calls two "sect-type" models of moral agency for the church. He uses as the two poles the theologies of Yoder and Rauschenbusch. It is interesting that Hütter sees both theologians in the "sect-type" tradition, and the reason is their mutual reliance on Jesus for an ethical base. The issue between them is not who Jesus is and how he can be understood as a moral source — on this there is significant agreement — but on what view of agency this implies for the church. The latter, says Hütter, has historically been the main issue for ethicists who wish to base their ethic on Jesus.

Hütter argues that Yoder and Rauschenbusch represent two quite different views of the church as moral agent because they have different views of the relationship between history and eschatology. "Rauschenbusch understands *history as universal eschatology* whereas Yoder understands *eschatology as particular history*. Their respective ecclesiologies reflect this basic divergence, and it shapes the unfolding of their ecclesial ethics." What Hütter means by this becomes clear as we read on:

> For Rauschenbusch the church is responsible for the course of history, since history itself has the potential of its own fulfillment and is in need of competent and motivated agents to press it in that very direction. The church has to take the crucial function of a socio-political "midwife" helping to bring to birth that very "Kingdom of God" which "history" carries in its

womb. The fulfillment of history lies in its intrinsic telos of a universal society of brotherhood and cooperative fellowship. . . . In such a setting "effectiveness" has priority and might imply the use of violence for the sake of the goal to be reached. . . . For Yoder it is exactly the opposite: *eschatology turns into history* in the form of the concrete and particular history of the visible "new order" of the church. For those who can say "Vicit agnus noster, eum sequamur" (*The Politics of Jesus*, 250) the eschaton became history. . . . Therefore not "effectiveness" but rather "obedient faithfulness" represents for Yoder the decisive criterion for the church's activity.[22]

I believe that Hütter is essentially correct in stating the difference between these two models of ecclesial moral agency. He shows that their difference is derived from different ways of bringing together four important elements, God, Jesus Christ, the church, and the kingdom of God.

Rauschenbusch's understanding of this relationship could be illustrated as follows:

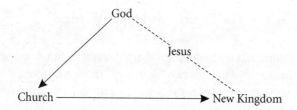

He argues that God wills the church to be the agential instrument in establishing the kingdom of God on earth. Hence we have a solid line between God and church as well as between the church and the kingdom of God. In other words, the social gospel mandates the church to "christianize the social order" and in so doing it is to bring to birth the kingdom of God. He argues that in the life, death, and resurrection of Jesus Christ, God has defined for us the elements of this new social order which we are now called upon to establish: a community of social justice, where the sick are healed and poverty is eradicated. All of this only makes sense if Jesus, although pointing to the nature of the kingdom, nevertheless did not himself bring it about — hence, the dotted connection between God through Jesus to the kingdom of God.

We notice that Rauschenbusch's ethic is a form of teleology where the telos is disclosed to us by Jesus, and it is now our task to bring it to fruition. The moral agency of the church is not in principle different from the model of

22. Reinhard Hütter, "The Church: Midwife of History or Witness of the Eschaton?" *Journal of Religious Ethics* 18 (Spring 1990): 47.

Millian teleology — the telos once clearly seen is to be realized through human agency.

Yoder sees the relationship among these elements differently as follows:

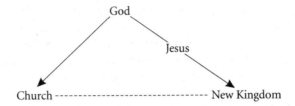

Yoder does not significantly disagree with Rauschenbusch's analysis of the characterization of the kingdom of God as seen in Jesus Christ. The point of disagreement is over the way in which Jesus "brings about" this kingdom and the implications this has for the church. For Yoder the central paradigm for understanding ecclesial moral agency is the cross/resurrection because it is the way God works and hence the way God's actions can be understood. Jesus did not bring about the kingdom by "christianizing the social order," he brought it about by bearing witness to the truth of God's grace and then allowing its power to blossom into a new reality in spite of the powers of evil which opposed it. It is God alone who gives life and God's justice which alone can prevail against the forces of evil. Hence the solid line between God through Jesus to the kingdom of God. Yoder explains it as follows:

> The key to the obedience of God's people is not their effectiveness but their patience. The triumph of the right is assured not by the might that comes to the aid of the right, which is of course the justification of the use of violence and other kinds of power in every human conflict; the triumph of the right, although it is assured, is sure because of the power of the resurrection and not because of any calculation of causes and effects, nor because of the inherently greater strength of the good guys. The relationship between the obedience of God's people and the triumph of God's cause is not a relationship of cause and effect but one of cross and resurrection.[23]

Hence also the dotted line between the church and the new kingdom. The church's task is to be a sign of the new, but the realization of the new is a gift from God. The relationship between cross and resurrection is one of blessing. That is, while faithfulness does not produce God's blessing, nor is it irrelevant. Blessing remains gift.

23. Yoder, *Politics*, 238.

Applying this image to the "church as body of Christ," we can see that, like Jesus, the church is also not to make the world Christian but to concentrate on being the church: on being witnesses to God's truth. The church is to focus on giving power to that which was first given, namely, the way of God in Jesus Christ. But this does not suggest any lack of concern for the world. In fact, the assumption is that on this model, since it is the occasioning of God's redemption, the most radical social change of all is potentially possible. After all, it happened in the resurrection of Jesus. Biblical fidelity is not for the benefit of the community alone — although it is that — but for the world. The transforming power of God can, through God's faithful, be an embodied sign of God's redemption of the world.[24]

There is an important difference between the two models precisely at the point of the moral agency of the church. Yoder's view demands that the church be seen as moral agent in the same way that Jesus was; that is, the moral significance of Jesus lies not only in his pointing to the nature of the kingdom of God, but also in his embodiment of that to which he pointed.[25] His faith was that the incarnation of God's truth was power enough to effect whatever change God willed. God's power alone brings about new life — resurrection. Hence, you cannot separate that towards which you move and your moving there. Hütter describes this by saying that for Yoder eschatology becomes particular history. That is, the presentation of God's truth in Jesus Christ and the faithful improvisation of the same by the "body of Christ," is the embodiment of the rule of Christ.

For Yoder the essential preoccupation of the church is to concentrate on being the church.[26] If it fails in this task, it will fail in all efforts to "bring about" the kingdom. Its being the church is the way concrete social change happens. For like Christ, its "body" will actively express redemptive ways of healing relationships, of liberating people, of providing enough for physical well-being, of resolving conflict, of forgiving sinners, of assisting the dying, of welcoming new life, etc., just like it will embody new Christ-like ways of celebrating God's redemptive presence among us. Rauschenbusch, on the other hand, who maintained that Jesus did not bring about the kingdom, assumed that precisely be-

---

24. Yoder puts it this way: "'Sign,' rather than 'instrument,' describes more properly how our words and deeds 'work'. We proclaim; our humanizing deeds signify" ("Discerning the Kingdom of God in the Struggles of the World," 240).

25. Hauerwas also makes this point by calling Jesus the "Autobasilia," a term borrowed from Origen. See *A Community of Character: Toward a Constructive Christian Social Ethic* (Notre Dame: University of Notre Dame Press, 1983), 44.

26. See, for example, "Let the Church Be the Church," in *The Original Revolution: Essays on Christian Pacifism* (Scottdale, PA: Herald Press, 1971), 107-24.

cause Jesus did not, we must. How else is it to happen? But since Jesus did not bring about that to which he pointed, he can also not be of much guidance in showing us *how* this is to happen. Here we are left to our own creativity. Therefore we set for ourselves whatever attainable goals we can that move us closer to the kingdom and seek to attain them. The work of God is achieved in small steps taken by God's faithful. Rauschenbusch's view of the engine of social change is made clear in the following words:

> It was only when concrete material interests entered into a working alliance with Truth that enough force was rallied to break down the frowning walls of error. On the other hand, the classes within which Anabaptism gained lodgement lacked that concrete power, and so the Anabaptist movement, which promised for a short time to be the real Reformation of Germany . . . died a useless and despised death. In the French Revolution the ideal of democracy won a great victory, not simply because the ideal was so fair, but because it represented the concrete interest of the strong, wealthy, and intelligent business class, and that class was able to wrest political control from the king, the aristocracy, and the clergy.[27]

The difference between Yoder and Rauschenbusch lies at the center of the contemporary Christian ethics debate on the role of the church. This difference, however, is not so much about what Jesus did or said or even what he pointed to, but instead with how the church re-narrates the story of Christ and how that re-narration functions in the shaping of the Christian community and thereby the world. To say this differently, the question is what was God doing in Jesus Christ and what is God doing through us?

Moral Agency in the Image of the Trinity

Gustafson is certainly correct in his contention that Christian ethics must ultimately be rooted in God the creator, sustainer, and culminator of the universe. If it is not, we would have no way of justifying the Christian view of moral goodness as definitive. Then it would be utterly particular and as Christians we would at most be responding to a command which we feel obligated to obey because we bear allegiance to the commander. Nevertheless, the conclusions which Gustafson draws from this contention and the theological presuppositions behind it are much less convincing. He says:

27. Walter Rauschenbusch, *Christianity and the Social Crisis* (New York: Macmillan, 1920), 402.

If God is the source of how things really and ultimately are, if God is the sustainer and even the destroyer of aspects of life in the world, if God is the determiner of the destiny of things, then whatever one says about how God is related to the world demands theological attention to ways in which nature, history and culture are interpreted and understood by investigations appropriate to them. Put boldly, if God is sovereign over all things then knowledge of nature, and so forth, as informed by investigations proper to nature, have to be taken into account in order to say something about God.

On this basis he critiques "sectarians" for an exclusively "historical" approach to an understanding of God, i.e., one derived solely from the historical Jesus. He goes on to say:

In Christian sectarian form God becomes a Christian God for Christian people; to put it most pejoratively, God is assumed to be the tribal God of a minority of the earth's population. Or, if God is not a tribal God there is only one community in the world that has access to knowledge of God because God has revealed himself only in the life of that community. Or still another possible assumption, and worse from my perspective than the other two, Christian theology and ethics really are not concerned so much about God as they are about maintaining fidelity to the biblical narrative about Jesus or about maintaining the "biblical view" as a historical vocation that demands fidelity without further external justification, or idolatrously maintaining historic social identity.[28]

It is hard to understand why Gustafson rejects out of hand the possibility that there can be moral continuity between creator/sustainer/culminator God and Jesus, the Christ. In so doing, he breaks apart the moral unity within the Trinity, a basic doctrine of orthodoxy. On this point the so-called sectarians align themselves more closely with biblical/orthodoxy theology. For them "God was in Christ reconciling the world [not just one small community] to himself" (2 Corinthians 5:19). The assumption is that the way of Jesus and the way of God are not two ways but one.

"Trinity" did not originally mean, as it does for some later, that there are three kinds of revelation, the Father speaking through creation and the Spirit through experience, by which the words and example of the Son must be corrected; it meant rather that language must be found and defini-

28. Gustafson, "Sectarian Temptation," 92-93.

tions created so that Christians, who believe in only one God, can affirm that he is most adequately and bindingly known in Jesus.[29]

Fidelity to Jesus does not imply a disregard for nature and culture; it just means that nature and culture should not be held as independent and unintegrated moral and theological sources. Whenever they are, cultural and religious pluralism are extrapolated into a theological pluralism. Historically this has been the real idolatry.

It is disconcerting that Gustafson so matter-of-factly advocates "investigations appropriate to (nature)" and "investigations proper to nature" as if everyone simply understands and accepts that this cannot possibly include theology and the biblical story. I see two problems here. Firstly, it credits the natural and social sciences with a foundationalist privileged status, a view which is seriously put in question by some current philosophers of science,[30] and secondly, one with perhaps more serious consequences for the Christian faith, it implies the sharpest of disjunctions between science and theology, a position which is also being questioned.[31] His comments in the second quotation about a tribal God for a tribal people are equally unwarranted. It misrepresents the calling of Christ to his followers. He did not call his disciples to an inner spirituality or tribal club leaving everything social, historical, and natural in place. It was far more radical and encompassing. Yoder extrapolates:

> The calling of the people of God is thus no different from the calling of all humanity. The difference between the human community as a whole and the faith community is a matter of awareness or knowledge or commitment or celebration, but not of ultimate destiny. What believers are called to is no different from what all humanity is called to. That Jesus Christ is Lord is a statement not about my inner piety or my intellect or ideas but about the cosmos. Thus the fact that the rest of the world does not yet see or know or acknowledge that destiny to which it is called is not a reason for us to broker some wider or thinner vision, some lower common denominator or halfway meeting point, in order to make the world's destination more acceptable or more accessible.[32]

29. Yoder, *Politics,* 101.

30. See, for example, Paul Feyerabend, *Against Method,* 3rd ed. (London: Verso, 1993) where he argues that "neither science nor rationality are universal measures of excellence. They are particular traditions, unaware of their historical grounding" 214.

31. See Nancey Murphy, *Reconciling Theology and Science: A Radical Reformation Perspective* (Kitchener, ON: Pandora Press, 1997).

32. Yoder, "Firstfruits: The Paradigmatic Public Role of God's People," in *For the Nations,* 24.

A deep-seated impediment for accepting the moral unity of God is the normativity, in contemporary theology, of the distinction between history and nature.[33] Emphasis on the former supposedly gives priority to Jesus and a consequent "ethic of the kingdom" while emphasis on the latter gives priority to God and an "ethic of creation." But this dichotomy can only be maintained from outside the Christian narrative, one more at home in Enlightenment rationality.[34] Choosing between the two makes the story of Jesus, and indeed the life of his followers, unintelligible and morally intolerable. From within the narrative, however, where God raises Jesus from the dead, the dualism collapses. In the resurrection, creator God asserts power over creation. Hence, in driving a wedge between creator God — the God of history and the created order — and the God of Jesus, we make the redemption of God morally irrelevant and "fallen" nature morally normative. Worse still, we make the biblical narrative morally unintelligible. Put simply, the Christian narrative tells us that the God of creation continues to create and recreate in light of the fallenness and sinfulness of original creation. God wills the restoration of all creation. Hence an "ethic of the kingdom" and an "ethic of creation" must be one and the same ethic. If not, God was not significantly in Christ.

Yoder and Hauerwas have recognized the untenability of the history/nature distinction and have attempted to empower an alternative language. Of course their theology is based on the historical revelation of God in Israel and in Christ, but they can do this precisely because they hold that the God of creation is at work in our time. Their approach demands that we give new consideration to the story of how God acted in creation/history and how through that process we can come to see the character of God as relevant for our own moral understanding and action. Hence the Bible is normative for them in a way which it is not for Gustafson.

But this divergence of ethical views may well have another basis. Perhaps behind the discomfort with a discipleship ethic lies the dislike for what so much of the Jesus story makes normative, namely, nonviolence and an appreciation for the normally considered powerless ones in our society, the poor and the weak. Yet this is so much part of the story itself, from Genesis through Revelation, that an appeal to the orders of creation over against this motif does violence to it. Even a superficial glance at the story shows us this.

The normal assumptions of the actions of kings is that they act with auto-

---

33. Yoder critiques several different versions of this dichotomy in his *Politics*, 94-114.

34. See, e.g., Alasdair MacIntyre, "Why the Enlightenment Project of Justifying Morality Had to Fail," in *After Virtue: A Study in Moral Theory* (Notre Dame: University of Notre Dame Press, 1984).

cratic authority which is usually mediated through the most powerful social institutions available. However, the God of Israel initiates the kingdom-building process with actions of lowliness and simplicity. In choosing one faithful person (clan) and promising that faithfulness will have its harvest, God's hand is tipped in the direction of "minority power," instead of dominant social structures (Rauschenbusch), as the medium of kingdom agency.[35] The statistical and sociological odds for failure were extremely high. Yet "salvation" happens. This is a mustard seed view of moral agency. It need not happen immediately, not even finally, but it does happen beyond reasonable expectation when ordinary people do God's will.

The story goes out of its way to make the point that its happening combines both divine and human agency in a specific way. Abraham's faithfulness is neither the primary cause nor is it irrelevant in the establishment of the kingdom. Yet God's faithfulness always remains at the center. The story tells us that when Abraham opens himself to the faithfulness of God's grace the kingdom comes. Abraham's improvisations become the expression of the kingdom, only when God blesses his efforts.

This model of divine agency is seen throughout the biblical account. In the Exodus God again works with the lowliest of people, namely the slaves, moving them towards liberation. And again its "working" is seen as rooted in the giftedness of God's grace. After all, the slaves themselves had virtually no social power. God *gave* the children of Israel liberation from Egypt. God *gave* them food in the desert, *gave* them the law, the land, etc. And when they finally came into possession of the land, God *gave* them a prophet to remind them that they owe their identity as liberated ones to the giftedness of God since with the possession of land they became particularly vulnerable to misunderstanding themselves as achievers and conquerors, as living by their own hand. And therein lay the temptation to idolatry and the inevitability of their demise. Their own power was simply not as great as God's and hence it could not save them.

This same model of God's moral agency is seen in the life, death, and resurrection of Jesus. Jesus acted in total openness to the God he had come to know and whom he saw at work in the story of his people. He understood the workings of God this way when he likened it to a mustard seed and told the story of the prodigal son. Yet most significantly he exemplified it by refusing to resort to an instrumental ethic in order to avoid his own death. Jesus' relinquishment of instrumentality was an expression of faith in the ultimate redemptive power of God. It was a participation in God's work.

---

35. See Yoder, "If Abraham Is Our Father," in *The Original Revolution*, 85-104.

It is instructive, albeit somewhat dangerous, to reflect on why the biblical narrative sees God acting so much from the standpoint of the powerless and the poor. But when we do, we are pushed to reflect on the difference between the two social groupings. It is characteristic of the rich to rely on their own power and control. After all, they have the means to do so. But from this perspective, how could the story of the graciousness of God come to be known? The biblical story shows God to be the ultimate moral force, because within God's being lies the ground of moral truth. How else then can we come to know the good except in our openness and reliance upon God? And this means training ourselves in faithfulness rather than manipulating outcomes to our own limited, even if well-intentioned, moral ends. This process alone can guard us against the temptation to impatience and moral detours which inevitably short-circuit the redemptive power of God.

A Story

Ludwig Wittgenstein once said in response to C. D. Broad's presentation of three different theories of truth that "Philosophy is not a choice between different 'theories.'" Similarly we could say that "theological ethics" is also not a choice between different theories. But what replaces theory? "Grammar" and story, according to Wittgenstein. He continues in response to Broad's theories of truth as follows:

> We can say that the word ['truth'] has at least three different meanings; but it is mistaken to assume that any one of these theories can give the whole grammar of how we use the word, or endeavour to fit into a single theory cases which do not seem to agree with it.[36]

To speak of moral agency as embodiment is not an attempt to develop a new theory of agency, but to present another "grammar" with which we can tell our stories. If anything, it is an alternative way of seeing — alternative not in the sense that one must choose between it and, say, other ways like deontology and teleology, but in the sense that it can accommodate both the obvious duty aspects and the goals aspects of moral living which neither of the other two approaches can. Moreover, with such a grammar, the very moral notions of duty and goal get transformed.

I cannot think of a more appropriate way to illustrate what happens when

36. Quoted in Ray Monk, *Ludwig Wittgenstein: The Duty of Genius* (New York: Penguin Books, 1990), 322.

people change their "grammar" and their way of seeing things than to tell a story. This particular story, the beginnings of the Palestinian Intifadah,[37] is a good example of a shift in thinking away from a primary focus on moral agency as calculated instrumentality or as obedience to commands, to one rooted in an expression of and participation in a reality that points beyond available social possibilities. For the Palestinians it meant that they could express (embody) a peace they could not achieve. Although they were used to not being in charge, through the Intifadah experience, they found that "not being in charge" did not mean noninvolvement in social change.

An accident in Gaza on December 8, 1987, in which an Israeli vehicle drove into a van filled with Palestinian workers, is often cited as the trigger event for the Intifadah.[38] Several Palestinians were killed in the collision. This, in itself, is not an unusual occurrence in the Occupied Territories, but, together with several other social factors, it sparked the beginning of an effort towards social change the likes of which surprised even the Palestinian people.

What is fascinating about this struggle from our vantage point is that it radically altered the people's perception of how social change can happen. During the early 1980s, one heard them blame their plight on external factors like the American government funding of the Israeli military and the lack of concern by the United Nations about Israeli settlement building in the occupied territories. Since the causes of their problems were external, hope for change also resided there. The Intifadah changed this way of thinking about how society can change.[39]

The immediate response to the accident was a series of protests and demonstrations in the Gaza strip. But this time, when the Israeli military came to

---

37. Another illustration of moral agency as embodiment which space limitations will not permit us to discuss here, is the recent social upheaval in former USSR countries. Who could have predicted the awesome social changes which have taken place there in such a short period of time? Moreover, who would have predicted that the breakup of this empire would be relatively peaceful? The manner in which social change normally happens was defied. The people "brought things about" which were previously not conceived possible. It requires a new language (grammar) for understanding such events.

38. The term "Intifadah," although usually translated "uprising," literally means "shaking off." For a helpful summary of the causes of the Intifadah, see Gail Pressberg, "The Uprising: Causes and Consequences," *Journal of Palestine Studies* 67 (Spring 1988): 38-50.

39. I lived in Jerusalem and worked as a Mennonite Central Committee volunteer in the West Bank from 1981 to 1983. During this time I had the occasion to talk with many Palestinians, academics, and others. I was impressed with how consistently they blamed others for their problems. On a return visit to the region (August 1990) it was hard to believe that I was speaking with the same people about the same topic. Their analysis of their plight and their understanding of solutions had changed so much.

put down the protest, the Palestinians acted in concert out of a new sense of moral outrage and a determination to steadfastly withstand all efforts to squelch their radical "NO." At first it was the children who refused to obey the military orders to disperse. When faced with military jeeps, instead of retreating to their homes they threw stones at them. This was an act of defiance and noncomplicity with what they considered evil being done to them.[40] It was the embodiment of a moral claim focused not only on the particular act that killed several of their people, but on the status quo of injustice which had existed since 1948. Their response did not grow out of any calculation of possible outcome. It was instead an expression of the conviction that the status quo itself was deeply immoral and that their task was to make this known by upholding the counterclaim of moral truth.

This new "language" of what they were doing revolutionized the Palestinian people's struggle. Jonathan Kuttab, a Palestinian lawyer, put it this way shortly after the event:

> What has occurred in the Palestinian communities living under Israeli occupation is nothing short of revolutionary. The revolt has so transformed and radicalized the way people act and interact that it has produced a new consciousness in Palestinian thinking and relationships. One can now speak about pre-intifadah (the uprising) and post-intifadah thinking, perceptions, and behaviour. Certain trends that began more than five months ago in the streets with the naive, uninformed, and unrealistic children have now been generalized. The children possessed a new spirit that challenged the occupation, and they have been able not only to sustain this movement, but also to infuse the rest of Palestinian society — their elders, institutions, leaders, and even the Palestinian communities outside — with the same spirit.[41]

Kuttab appropriately identifies the significance of children in transforming the peoples' new understanding of social change. This is reminiscent of the way Jesus spoke about the role of the weak ones, including children, in "sign-

---

40. For Muslims throwing stones is a ritualistic symbol of self-cleansing from the powers of evil. During the pilgrimage to Mecca part of the ceremony entails throwing stones at an object which symbolically portrays evil. As such it is an act of purification and self-discipline. (I gained this insight from a lecture delivered in Jerusalem, August 20, 1990, by Nafuz Azaili, a Muslim pacifist working with the Political Center for the Study of Non-violence in Jerusalem.) Nevertheless, one should be cautious not to confuse this ritual with throwing a stone at a human being in order to maim. That, of course, is an act of violence.

41. Jonathan Kuttab, "The Children's Revolt," *Journal of Palestine Studies* 68 (Summer 1988): 26.

ing" the kingdom. When moral agency is understood as embodiment, children can have a significant moral function. They are able to give expression to a higher morality more simply and clearly than encumbered adults are. The only social power children have is the power to point with naivete beyond themselves to another power — moral integrity, or truth, or God. But this is precisely what they can often do better than adults because they naturally realize that they are not in charge and can only have power by participating in another's power. If we see social change as occurring only via the powerful ones, or those in control, or the majority, the inevitability of relatively minor modifications is almost assured, and children most certainly will be morally excluded.

What are the concrete social achievements of the Intifadah? In the spring of 1988 Kuttab listed six. The first achievement he identified is empowerment towards action. It "shattered the barrier of fear, in removing the internal inhibitions that the occupation had planted and cultivated in the individual and collective thought processes of every Palestinian." Second, it united the people into one body that worked together for a single cause of justice. Third, the understanding of moral agency itself was altered. Instead of seeing social change as coming from the outside, it was now seen as rooted within the people themselves as they participate in a power beyond themselves. "We believe that history is on our side, time is on our side, and, certainly, God is on our side." Fourth, it changed the Palestinian people into a more self-consciously moral people. "[A] new sense of generosity and spirit of giving has emerged in Palestinian society." They changed from a "nation of beggars" to a people who experienced the "joy, the beauty, the wonder of giving, contributing, sacrificing." Fifth, it led to a whole new way of organizing their society. On all levels they began to operate on the assumption that what they were striving for — an independent homeland — is already present in their hearts and imaginations. Its realization needs only to be given concrete expression. On this basis they restructured their entire social existence. Education, economics, health, public security — virtually every social structure and practice has been reconsidered and is now in the hands of local grassroots committees. This required tremendous discipline, self-restraint, and commitment to a common vision. Kuttab gives an example. When the Palestinian police resigned, predictions of anarchy abounded. Instead, the crime rate fell. "There have been no cases of looting, harassment of girls on the street is almost unheard of, and instances of theft and burglary have dropped to almost zero since the uprising." Moreover, their rather simple expression of a vision gave them awesome power. It rendered the Israeli military virtually powerless against them. Sixth, through this process, the people adopted a stance of openness to receiving from beyond themselves. "This new openness and spirit . . . reflect[s] the fact that the challenge that was first issued by the children is now being accepted throughout society by every person, institution, socio-economic class, and sector."[42]

The Intifadah has cost the Palestinians well over one thousand lives to date, primarily in clashes with the Israeli military. And indeed the changes in the past ten years have been many to discuss here. Yet they discovered something new and profound: that the power of their actions lies not primarily in their instrumental value, but in their ability to embody what is morally good. I have told their story here as an example of a shift in the language of moral agency from one of instrumentality/command to embodiment.

Conclusion

In this essay I have endeavored to show how focusing on God, which I believe every Christian is called to, need not compel us to a "creation ethic" in tension with the ethic of Jesus. The two must be kept together. After all, it is precisely the belief that God wills to redeem this world and that we are invited to participate in the victory which characterizes the biblical imagination.

My claim assumes that the Christian life is more akin to a pianist learning to play a Chopin Polonaise than to a computer programmer writing a new program. A computer programmer is dependent upon his/her own imagination in both what is projected as valuable as well as how it is brought about. A pianist is dependent upon much training to acquire the skills necessary to make the master's music for which a script has already been written. Here the pupil is invited to "imitate" the music of the master with her/his own interpretation and improvisation. Both the pianist and the computer programmer may be producing something good. You cannot argue that one model is effective and the other not. Nevertheless, how each is "effective" depends upon an entirely different "grammar." The computer programmer is measured against his/her own goals and objectives, and the musician against how well he/she has learned the skills which alone can enliven the music of the master.

Let me refer again to an earlier diagram, only this time to a more expanded version of it.

42. Kuttab, "Children's Revolt," 25-31.

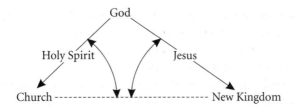

I have argued with Yoder and Hauerwas that Jesus is the revelation of God who points to and embodies the kingdom. I also agree that the church's relationship to the new kingdom is best seen as witness or sign. In this way there is no less a connection between the church and the new kingdom than there is between the way of Jesus and the way of the church. This is symbolized by a connecting arrow between them. Yet the dotted line relationship between church and new kingdom shows that the relationship is one of blessing and not cause and effect. That is to say, although God brings the kingdom about, we participate in it (bear witness to it).

The relationship between God and the church needs fuller articulation. This is not appropriately described as a command-obedience relationship. A preferable metaphor here is that of invitation-participation. We are invited to open ourselves to God's graciousness and empowerment — hence the openness symbol to God. This entails our willingness to have God transform our lives individually and collectively into a whole new reality. It emphasizes the need for us to cultivate the skills (virtues, practices) which are necessary in order for us to be people capable of following Jesus.

I suggest that on this understanding of moral agency we can more readily resist the seduction of thinking that we must choose between sect and church-type models of faithfulness. After all, both models fail to do justice to the resurrection power of God and both rely too heavily for their self-definition upon the world around them, even if one does so positively and the other negatively.

The claim I am making here is not a novel one. Examples of contemporary scholars who speak of the church in a similar way come readily to mind, to wit, Susan Thistlewaite and Paul Hanson. "We have to rethink the whole approach to peace and justice issues in the churches and reject the concept that justice is an issue. It is not an issue. It is an identity for the church,"[43] says Thistlewaite. And Hanson: "The church's purpose is not its own. The church is present in the world on behalf of the God by whose grace it has been called

---

43. Susan Brooks Thistlewaite, "Peace and Justice, Not Issues but Identities for the Church (Interview)," *Engage/Social Action* 15 (January 1987): 33-37.

into existence. Thus at the heart of the church's act of self-definition is a basic theological question: What is the nature of God's presence in the world?"[44]

When all is said and done, the issue for Christian living is not sectarian versus church-type nor is it an ethic of creation versus an ethic of the kingdom. Christians cannot make a choice between Jesus and God. The issue for us is coming to know the God of Israel and of Jesus Christ to be true God, and finding the strength to act in accordance with these convictions. This strength comes, as we saw in the Intifadah story, when people stop distinguishing between that which they struggle to achieve and their achieving it. The strength comes in living it. When people open themselves to God, i.e., when they worship together, they open themselves to become people who can live the moral life, not for themselves but for the glory of God.

> So then brothers and sisters, stand firm and hold fast to the traditions that you were taught by us, either by word of mouth or by letter. (2 Thess. 2:15, NRSV)

---

44. Paul D. Hanson, "The Identity and Purpose of the Church," *Theology Today* 42 (October 1985): 342-52.

Historicizing the Historicist: Ernst Troeltsch and Recent Mennonite Theology

Arne Rasmusson

In an odd way, twentieth-century Mennonite theology, through its newly recovered relationship with mainstream Protestant theology, let itself be forced into a distorted and unfruitful contrast between faithfulness and responsibility that partly concealed some of its richest resources and put it into a no-win situation in relation to precisely this mainstream theology. We see this in two decisive mistakes, here represented by Guy Hershberger and J. Lawrence Burkholder; namely, that they let mainstream Protestantism determine, firstly, who they should be (Hershberger) and, secondly, what social responsibility means (Burkholder). Behind both these developments, or temptations, stands (directly and indirectly) that towering figure of early twentieth-century theology, Ernst Troeltsch.

This essay consists of three main parts. In the first, I will discuss this development by contrasting Hershberger and Burkholder, who respond in opposite ways to the Troeltschian temptations. However, I will use them more as types, rather than offer a close reading of them. Therefore, I am basically using only a couple of their texts.[1] I will try to show how the way they state the issues is dependent on categories developed by Troeltsch's very different theology. This is one main theme in the second part of this essay. The brothers Niebuhr are, of course, important for mediating this type of theology to the American

---

1. This may be most unfair to Hershberger, as his views seem to have developed quite a bit. I do not, for example, use his large book *The Way of the Cross in Human Relations* (Scottdale, PA: Herald Press, 1958) or any other later writings. Burkholder's views in the 1950s and today seem, concerning the issues this essay deals with, more or less identical.

213

context, but both Burkholder and Hershberger were, although to a different extent, also directly influenced by Troeltsch. In the case of Burkholder, Troeltsch is the major influence. Troeltsch, together with Max Weber, is his methodological mentor. Moreover, he says that he is also indebted to Troeltsch "for his interpretations of the general problem of social responsibility and for his understanding of the history of Christian social policy."[2] Hershberger is likewise influenced directly by Troeltsch, whose "excellent" work he recommends,[3] although here the mediation through Reinhold Niebuhr may be more important.

But the aim of the second part, on Troeltsch, is not only to show this dependence; I will also analyze and criticize Troeltsch's theology and some governing assumptions behind his views. Beyond the fact that my reading of Troeltsch, which I am doing much more extensively elsewhere, ought to make us somewhat surprised that he could be so influential among Mennonites, I will try to show how these assumptions distort, or even create, the way the so-called issue of faithfulness and responsibility is set up and understood. And this opens up the third and final part of the essay, in which I will show how John Howard Yoder's theology provides rich resources for overcoming this unhappy situation.

Hershberger versus Burkholder

Christian Nonresistance and the Violent State

I take Hershberger's book *War, Peace, and Non-Resistance* as an example of an approach that gives primacy to faithfulness to the gospel. I will not give a full description of his views, nor will I take into account how he later modified his views, but will only highlight a few strands of his thought that are important for my purposes.

Discipleship as nonresistance is central in Hershberger's thought. What is notable is the thin biblical and theological basis on which this is built. He is highly biblicist. Nonresistance has to be followed out of obedience to Christ, though he does not want it to be described as blind obedience.[4] But the biblical basis he gives is Jesus' Sermon on the Mount, which is read as a series of general commands almost devoid of any wider theological context, other than that Jesus speaks with

2. J. Lawrence Burkholder, *The Problem of Social Responsibility from the Perspective of the Mennonite Church* (Elkhart 1989), 6. See also p. 3.

3. Guy Hershberger, *War, Peace, and Non-Resistance* (1944; Scottdale, PA: Herald Press, 1991), 75, 80, and 171.

4. Hershberger, *War, Peace, and Non-Resistance*, 241f.

divine authority and that discipleship is only possible for the regenerated. Jesus is here seen mainly as a teacher, and discipleship is construed as following his commands. Hershberger, of course, has a wider theology, but it is not operative when he discusses the Christian life, or so it seems to me. How is the Sermon on the Mount related to Jesus' life, death, and resurrection as a whole? Furthermore, how is it related to creation, redemption, eschatology, and so on?[5]

His approach is related to an individualistic understanding of salvation. The mission of Christ, according to Hershberger, is to gather individuals into the kingdom of God and give them eternal life. "The man of the new covenant is saved by grace, and with the indwelling Spirit of God to direct his steps he is enabled to keep the moral law."[6] The kingdom of God, and by implication the church, is thus described as a "brotherhood of saved individuals," and it is to this brotherhood that the Sermon on the Mount is directed. This understanding of individual salvation is then contrasted to the concept of social salvation in the thought of the social gospel movement. Regeneration and discipleship are contrasted with education and reform.[7]

Even if he seems to have a rather individualistic concept of salvation, Hershberger has a strongly communal understanding of the church. But he fails in this book to develop adequately the connections between this understanding of church and his conception of salvation. The result is that he also fails to develop the connections between salvation, church, and Christian social ethics.[8]

If the church of saved individuals is one pole of his dualistic system, the state is the other. Here his thought tends to be essentialist and ahistorical. He defines the state in the following way:

> The state is an agency for the administration of justice with the aid of force, in an evil society, and it is not motivated by Christian love. Therefore the

5. This is a critique rightly emphasized especially by James Reimer. Saying this, however, opens the question of how this should be done. See, for example, his "Towards a Theocentric Christology: Christ in the World," in *The Limits of Perfection: A Conversation with J. Lawrence Burkholder*, ed. Rodney J. Sawatsky and Scott Holland, 2nd ed. (Kitchener, ON: Pandora Press, 1996), 95-109. I disagree, however, with Reimer's description of Yoder in this article.

6. Hershberger, *War, Peace, and Non-Resistance*, 46.

7. Hershberger, *War, Peace, and Non-Resistance*, 180, 238.

8. Theron Schlabach thinks this may be a result of a lingering influence in Hershberger's thought from the dichotomizing of ethics and soteriology that occurred in the late nineteenth-century "Mennonite Quickening," in which Mennonites were influenced by Protestant evangelicalism, and which Hershberger failed consistently to overcome. See Schlabach, "Reveille for *Die Stillen Im Lande*: A Stir Among Mennonites in the Late Nineteenth Century," *Mennonite Quarterly Review* 51 (1977): 213-26. According to Schlabach, Hershberger himself accepted this analysis. I owe this information to an e-mail from Schlabach (24 August 1997).

outlook of the New Testament is entirely unpolitical. It has nothing to say about how the affairs of the state should be conducted. It does not suggest that the Christian should play any role in the state itself, and everywhere it assumes that he is not part of the state.[9]

He does, however, recognize that the modern welfare state has assumed many functions in which Christians can participate, like education, public health service, and the building of roads. These possibilities imply a more historical understanding of the state, but he does not elaborate on this.[10]

Central in his ethic is a literal understanding of love as absolute nonresistance. This nonresistance is sharply distinguished from mere nonviolence. Here he agrees with critics such as Reinhold Niebuhr and can therefore write: "No one has done better than Reinhold Niebuhr in showing the sharp distinction between non-violence and New Testament non-resistance."[11] So the most important moral distinction is drawn between nonresistance and every form of resistance and not between, say, nonviolence and violence. The result is that he not only does not see any important moral distinction between the police and the military,[12] but also that he describes the struggle against slavery, Gandhi's nonviolent strategy, or the civil rights campaign as a form of warfare.[13] He does, however, admit that because the world cannot exist without force, there is, of course, good reason to prefer the nonviolent tactics of a Gandhi over violent strategies.[14]

So Christians cannot participate in the state, nor in labor unions. This does not mean that Christians are not interested in the wider society. He thinks that the church can be more influential in other ways than through direct participation in politics. The church can, through its own life, witness to the truth. He thinks the best way may be to develop planned Mennonite rural communities with their own economic and social life. This would include Mennonite factories, "banking" systems, and social institutions, working on a nonresistant

9. Hershberger, *War, Peace, and Non-Resistance,* 53.

10. Hershberger, *War, Peace, and Non-Resistance,* 164f.

11. Hershberger, *War, Peace, and Non-Resistance,* 195. See also 207, 240-42.

12. Hershberger, *War, Peace, and Non-Resistance,* 175f.

13. On slavery, see Hershberger, *War, Peace, and Non-Resistance,* 188f., on Gandhi, 1, 190-97, and 253, and on the struggle for civil rights, 198-200.

14. Two decades later, however, he could express himself very positively about Martin Luther King, Jr., and civil rights activity. John Howard Yoder says: "He did not reject it because it was active, nor because it called for social change, nor because it appealed to the American vision. He saw it as church based, as loving, as willing to bear the cross, as evangelical in spirit and mood and hymnology." (*Christian Attitudes to War, Peace, and Revolution* [Elkhart, IN: Co-Op Bookstore, 1983], 366.) How this should be related to his earlier thought I leave aside.

way of life.[15] He thinks this form of example can also lead to changes in the world. But he also defends prophetic critique, and different forms of peace work and social work. More generally he argues what we today might call the communitarian thesis: "The health of our entire civilization depends upon the health, the vigor, and the solidarity of the small community."[16] Historically he refers to the role of Anabaptism and Baptism in the creation of modern religious freedom, which is at the heart of democracy.[17] And generally, one can say that Hershberger is in no way politically and sociologically naive. Rather, his book is sociologically quite sophisticated.

In summary, one might say that Hershberger has a form of social theology based on the Sermon on the Mount and lived in the Christian community by saved individuals. But his individualistic account of salvation, the thin general theological framework for this social theology, and his essentialist understanding of the state, as well as of resistance and nonresistance, make it difficult for him to relate this to the wider society. However, as I have also indicated, his theology is not a closed system, but rather unstable and open-ended and could be drawn in different ways and thereby transformed.

Social Responsibility in an Ambiguous World

Burkholder wrote his dissertation, which much later became the book *The Problem of Social Responsibility from the Perspective of the Mennonite Church,* in sharp reaction to the view Hershberger represents. However, what strikes the outsider is the similarity of their thought. In a later text (the text on which I will build much of the following),[18] Burkholder recounts how he found his Mennonite theology inadequate when confronted with the Second World War and his experiences in China. Nonresistance does not work in concrete political life. Life is by nature morally ambiguous and compromise is necessary. Ted Koontz writes that what is surprising is that Burkholder is surprised that he could not live his Mennonite ethic in China.[19] Is not that exactly what Hershberger would say is the case? That the world cannot be run on the principles of nonresistant life is a crucial conviction of Hershberger's theology. One gets the impression

15. Hershberger, *War, Peace, and Non-Resistance,* 224-28.
16. Hershberger, *War, Peace, and Non-Resistance,* 250. See further 249-53.
17. Hershberger, *War, Peace, and Non-Resistance,* 244-49.
18. Burkholder, "The Limits of Perfection: Autobiographical Reflections," in *The Limits of Perfection,* 1-54.
19. Ted Koontz, "Goshen College not China: Challenges to Mennonite Ethics," in *The Limits of Perfection,* 113-17.

that Burkholder was more a "liberal pacifist" than an advocate of a Mennonite ethic of nonresistance.

However, as Koontz also notes, it is more important to see that Burkholder's dualisms are not primarily between church and world, but between the absolute demands of Jesus and actual life, and "between a person, free from the encumbrances of social roles and responsibilities which imply conflicting obligations, and a person encumbered by them and, along with that person so encumbered, organizations of all sorts."[20] So we have a double duality. First, between ideals and actuality, and, second, between abstract, absolute individuality and actual social life on both individual and collective levels. The result is that the usual dualism between church and world is undermined. Christian love, *agape*,[21] is simply ontologically impossible to live in a concrete social life. This is as true inside the church as outside it, and in family life as much as in bureaucracy.

This contrast between ideal and actuality is made necessary by his view of *agape*. He defines this love as "disinterested love, unmixed with anticipated rewards, reciprocations, mutual gratification, and preferences based upon merit." He continues to say "that all human relationships must be judged by their approximation to *agape*, just as the relative must be measured by its relation to the absolute, the temporal to the eternal, and the partial to the complete." From this definition of love follows the rather obvious conclusion. "Life, especially collective life, could not be run by *agape* alone. *Agape* may, however, serve as an ideal point of reference."[22] He does, however, go on giving examples from his own experiences why *agape* cannot be lived by itself. Yet, as he defines Christian love, this is superfluous, as it goes without saying that it is an absolute ideal that cannot be lived in pure form.[23]

This contrast between ideal and actuality makes the concept of compromise central in his thought, as social reality is by necessity ambiguous.[24] He sees "the failure to actualize pure love perfectly" as "the main problem of Christian social ethics. But only through compromise can love be objectified socially, however imperfectly."[25]

This also shows that the impossibility of living pure love does not make the ideal of *agape* superfluous. He thinks that this radical form of what he calls

20. Koontz, "Goshen College not China," 116.
21. About the relation between nonresistance and *agape*, Burkholder says the following: "Non-resistance is applied *agape*" (*Social Responsibility*, 64).
22. Burkholder, "The Limits of Perfection," 8-9.
23. Burkholder, "The Limits of Perfection," 11, 18f., 26.
24. Burkholder, "The Limits of Perfection," 37-39.
25. Burkholder, "The Limits of Perfection," 49.

sectarian theology is necessary and an authentic component of all Christianity. But it cannot be the whole story. However, instead of making an accommodating synthesis of ideal and reality, he wants to relate them dialectically. He even argues that "reality is dialectically structured."[26] The demands of the gospel should not be watered down, but lived in the concrete, which by necessity means compromise.

One easily gets the impression that his concept of *agape*, more than Jesus, is his authority. And he actually says, in response to Gordon Kaufman, that "even if there were no Jesus of Nazareth, I would still regard agape love as the pinnacle besides which all else are lesser values."[27] Furthermore, by his definition, Jesus, as a bodily and social being, cannot be a pure incarnation of *agape*, although Burkholder sometimes gives the impression that he was. He then refers this to the fact that Jesus was single, lived a short life, had no organizational responsibilities, and anyhow awaited the imminent coming of the kingdom of God.[28] Consequently his question for Christian ethics is as follows: "What do we do with a perfectionist ethic born amid the particularity of Israel, taught and modelled by a single person in an eschatological setting where it was presumed that the end of history is imminent?"[29]

If this is true, Mennonite theology is not only impossible to live in the world, as Hershberger also would say, it is also inadequate for corporate Mennonite life. The problem becomes, however, especially acute in politics, by which he means "participation in government as a responsible decision maker, legislator, judge, department head, ambassador, or high level executive."[30] Politics is about power, and politicians have to make many hard and difficult decisions. Compromise is necessary, and one often has to act on tragic necessities. All this is for the sake of the general well-being. Here the idea of justice will be more important than love. He can also say: "Justice is love come to terms with multiplicity and institutional organization."[31]

Burkholder notes that contemporary Mennonitism has strayed far away from Hershberger's vision and that it is now much more implicated in the structures of the wider society than when its center was agrarian communities. He thinks that this now has led Mennonites to the same challenges that once were at the roots of the theologies of Ernst Troeltsch and Reinhold Niebuhr:

26. Burkholder, "The Limits of Perfection," 35. See further 33-35, and 41f.
27. Burkholder, "Concluding Postscript," *The Limits of Perfection*, 144.
28. Burkholder, "The Limits of Perfection," 19-21, 28f.
29. Burkholder, "The Limits of Perfection," 28.
30. Burkholder, "The Limits of Perfection," 43.
31. Burkholder, "The Limits of Perfection," 36.

the social and economic revolutions of modern times, which have turned the basically agrarian economy into a highly organized industrial and technical society, are challenging Mennonite ethics in much the same way that the thought of Ernst Troeltsch and Reinhold Niebuhr was challenged earlier. The question which Troeltsch and Niebuhr asked was, "How can Christ's absolute ethic of love become relevant to the structure of modern life?"[32]

So we will now turn to the thought of Troeltsch. It is not only true that there is a parallelism between the challenges; the way the challenge is formulated is also very much influenced by the way Troeltsch (and Niebuhr) formulated the issues.

But before that, just a question. Burkholder writes that Mennonite ethics is impossible to live. Of course it is, so construed. But is that Mennonite ethics? For me, his account of love sounds more like Kant and German idealism than Jesus and the New Testament, or, I would guess, Mennonite theology. Matthew 18 has always been a key text for Mennonites, as Burkholder shows.[33] That can hardly be reconciled with his account of absolute nonresistance.

The Background of Ernst Troeltsch's Thought

Christianity's Lack of Social Theology

Troeltsch's direct and indirect influence on Mennonite theology is quite easy to see. Most well-known is his church/sect typology, which is still very often used not only by outsiders, but also by Mennonites themselves. In some ways Troeltsch's description of the sect-type as a necessary component of Christianity and his description of its quite extraordinary sociohistorical importance give a more positive evaluation of the Radical Reformation tradition than had been usual before Troeltsch. And it is interesting to see how his church/sect typology has become part of the self-understanding of Mennonite theology, as well as an instrument in internal Mennonite controversy. I have elsewhere analyzed and criticized this whole conception at length, as well as H. R. Niebuhr's church/culture model.[34] These categories mislead much more than they help understanding. It would be best if people stopped using them, but I suppose

32. Burkholder, "The Limits of Perfection," 52.

33. Burkholder, *Social Responsibility,* 111-13.

34. Arne Rasmusson, *The Church as "Polis": From Political Theology to Theological Politics as Exemplified by Jürgen Moltmann and Stanley Hauerwas* (Notre Dame: University of Notre Dame, 1995), ch. 11.

that is a futile hope. These concepts have become cultural institutions, just as, say, the fact/value distinction; they live on in spite of all criticism directed against them. However, here I will tackle the problem from another direction.

According to Troeltsch, the church does not have any social theology. The reason is that the gospel is wholly apolitical. The message of Jesus and the early church is purely religious and directed at the personal plane and the Christian community. Jesus proclaims an eschatological order of love that cannot be a basis for Christian social theology. By social theology he means a specifically Christian theory about the state and the secular or natural order.[35] When the church yet develops what he calls a "social philosophy," this is done through borrowing from other sources, mainly Stoic philosophy. Stoicism, he thinks, gave the church categories that could mediate the absolute ideals of the gospel and relative historical reality. One might say that a better description is that Troeltsch uses Stoic categories for describing what has happened.[36]

Here we already have the idea of the necessary compromise between ideal and reality with which especially Burkholder works. Troeltsch and Burkholder, but also Hershberger, assume that "reality" is given. On the one side you have ethical ideals and on the other "reality," and to be able to practice the ideals in the limited reality you have to compromise. At least political reality is finally governed by power relations. That is how reality is constituted. Whatever one thinks about it, it has to be accepted. Christian love can, at best, only be a sort of intrusion into this power reality and thereby perhaps change it at the margins. For Burkholder and Troeltsch, Christian love, as absolute nonresistance or self-sacrifice, is only understood as an ideal and can only be present on an individual and immediate level. On the social level it can only be present through instrumental reason in the form of justice. It has to be adjusted to social reality.

This view presupposes some strong form of the fact/value distinction. There is a neutral reality on which we can agree. How we "value" this and how we try to relate our values to this world is a secondary question. But this is surely wrong. Social and political "reality" is, first of all, historically constituted. It is contingent. It could (of course, within limits of various sorts) be different in many ways, and we do not know how different. A historicist such as Troeltsch does recognize this, but he fails to see some of its consequences. Secondly, we do not perceive reality "directly." What we see is dependent on the language we use, the stories we tell, the practices we live with, and so on. Our perception is in it-

---

35. See for example Ernst Troeltsch, *The Social Teaching of the Christian Churches* (London: George Allen & Unwin, 1931), ch. 1, and idem, *Religion in History* (Edinburgh: T. & T. Clark, 1991), 160, 190, 200f., 205, 212, 218, 344, 351.

36. So, for instance, in Troeltsch, *Religion in History*, 159-67 (esp. 160-62) and 321-42.

self evaluative. And this is important, because we live in the world we see. It is thus misleading to think of ethics in terms of relating ideals to reality. We have to understand that ethics has to do with our common imagination, something Troeltschian "realism" tends to obscure.[37] Instead of arguing this point theoretically, I shall exemplify it through Troeltsch's writings.

The Rise of the Modern Nation-State
and the Privatization of the Gospel

Troeltsch recognizes that Christianity has played an important role in the formation of the Western world. But he is much more skeptical about its role in modernity. Modernity, which partly has Christian roots and partly emerged in radical conflict with the churches, has released forces with which a Christian social philosophy cannot contend. The forces he refers to are primarily the modern state, capitalism, science, and faith in science. These forces are not only too strong for a Christian social philosophy, they also radically change the conditions for the life of the churches.

Troeltsch recognizes that the modern state "as the unitary and sovereign organization for exercising the total will of the community" is a modern phenomenon that did not exist during the Middle Ages. Europe of the Middle Ages was a very complex network of authorities in different relations to each other. Above all this was "the spiritual world-empire of the church,"[38] a sort of "Christian community of peoples."[39] This means that the politics of the medieval world was influenced by a form of Christian morality of rights and duties for individuals, classes, and communities. As Troeltsch writes: "The effect of this in theory, and to a large extent also in practice, was a form of politics religiously inspired and religiously controlled, the religion retaining all the time its supernatural and humanitarian quality." Failure to realize these ideals was explained by sin (and sin was something to fight against), not by problems in the theory.[40]

The modern state in the form of the nation-state (developed through the phase of absolutism) is a very different phenomenon and emerges partly in conflict with the church. It is, Troeltsch argues, autonomy and power that characterize this state. "Organized as a centralized power and supported by a mod-

37. Cf. John Milbank, *The Word Made Strange* (Oxford: Blackwell, 1997), ch. 10.

38. Troeltsch, *Religion in History,* 241.

39. Troeltsch, *Christian Thought: Its History and Application* (London: University of London Press, 1923), 140.

40. Troeltsch, *Christian Thought,* 139-41.

ern military force, the state discovers the logic of the idea of power, which implies a thoroughgoing internal organization and a capacity for external defense that is accountable to no one." Two principles characterize this state: secularity and rationality. The state's secularity refers to the idea of the state as the highest moral value. It gives no space to any transcendent purpose. Its rationality refers to the idea of the state as created by human intelligence. "The state replaces the irrational divine providence by a rational secular one."[41]

Machiavelli gives a theoretical expression to this new emerging situation. Troeltsch describes his doctrine as "a declaration of the emancipation of politics from the religious ethics and the religious universalism," and therefore as a return to paganism.[42] The state is sovereign and no values have supremacy over the state.

It is important to see the centrality of force and violence in this conception of the state. Inasmuch as there is no instance above the state, it is not accountable to anyone. Its own interests are supreme, and its base is its internal and external power. Troeltsch has a basically agonistic understanding of history; history is a struggle for existence, for power, for survival. The influence of the language of social Darwinism is evident, as Troeltsch recognizes.[43] "We can and must frankly acknowledge the natural process with its consequences, the struggle for existence, natural selection, and the formation of power, as the natural order — as a positive ordinance of God based on the very nature of things."[44] If this is the case, "it becomes apparent why the state must be power and cannot be anything else. In the struggle for existence, only that intensified and ruthless power survives which increases by the absorption of all that it has vanquished. [This power] can entertain sentimentalities and general principles only at the price of its own perdition."[45]

It is not difficult to see why Christianity in Troeltsch's view cannot have more than marginal effects on modern politics. The principles of the gospel have very little to do with this reality. This is aggravated by the nature of Christianity as understood by Troeltsch. A further reason that Troeltsch so strongly separates Christianity and politics is that he sees religious life as something primarily personal and individual. The gospel of Jesus is a combination of absolute individualism and absolute universalism; that is, a universalism that goes beyond any particular community.[46] Religious institutions and doctrines are

41. Troeltsch, *Religion in History*, 241-42.
42. Troeltsch, *Christian Thought*, 144; so also in Troeltsch, "Imperialismus," *Die Neue Rundschau*, 26:1 (1915): 12.
43. Troeltsch, *Religion in History*, 174; and idem, "Imperialismus," 7.
44. Troeltsch, *Religion in History*, 200.
45. Troeltsch, *Religion in History*, 175.
46. Troeltsch, *The Social Teaching*, 55-58.

necessary but religiously secondary. So the social nature of the church is seen as not a part of its religious essence.

Troeltsch's view of Christianity is intimately connected to his understanding of the modern state, as his own writings implicitly show. This understanding of religion is a correlate to the emergence of the modern state's claim to absolute sovereignty. Troeltsch argues that the modern state in the *same process* unites people into nation-states and individualizes them. To be able to make people into Germans, Frenchmen, Swedes, and so on, for whom their own nation-state is sovereign and their own nationality is primary, other particular and traditional identities and loyalties have to be made secondary to the nation-state, be it, for example, regional identities, kinship, estates, or church. He thus thinks that the absolutist state, with its centralization of power and struggle against the public power of the church, was a necessary step in the formation of modern nation-states. "Absolutism fused the peoples into nations and imbued them with this feeling for the state. But by leveling the old social structure based on states, and by radiating a secular and rationalistic spirit, absolutism ended by pulverizing the peoples into individuals."[47] So the supremacy of the nation-state and the autonomy of the individual are intimately connected. By reducing the person to an abstract individual in the name of freedom, it gave legitimacy to the state's struggle against alternative loyalties and especially the church. As the sociologist Zygmunt Bauman writes:

> 'Man as such' was, of course, a code name for a human being subordinated to, and moved by, one power only — the legislating power of the state; while the emancipation that had to be performed so that 'the essence' could shine in all its pristine purity stood for the destruction or neutralization of all *pouvoirs intermédiaires* — 'particularizing' powers sabotaging the job the 'universalizing' power of the modern state strove to perform.[48]

In this process Christianity, especially in the form of Protestantism, changed its self-understanding from a socio-theological practice that could not be distinguished from its bodily and social manifestation in the church to a set of basically private and subjective convictions and experiences of individuals. So understood, the church could easily coexist with the state's claims of absolute supremacy.[49]

---

47. Troeltsch, *Religion in History,* 244.

48. Baumann, *Postmodern Ethics* (Oxford: Blackwell, 1993), 82.

49. For a very good historical discussion of this issue, see William T. Cavanaugh, "'A Fire Strong Enough to Consume the House': The Wars of Religion and the Rise of the State," *Modern Theology* 11 (1995): 397-420.

In his reading of the New Testament, Troeltsch then projects this subjectivist Protestantism of modernity onto Jesus and the early church. He could sometimes criticize this individualistic concept of religion and Christianity as a product of the Enlightenment that leads one to misunderstand the historical Christian social philosophy. But he fails to see that his own perspective is still imprisoned in these categories.

Although the Mennonite tradition seems to be strongly anti-individualistic, it is striking how much both Hershberger and Burkholder in different ways work in these categories. Burkholder is in this respect the most clearly Troeltschian of the two. For him the center of Christianity seems to be the absolute ideal of *agape* which has to be embodied (and thereby compromised) in social reality. The essence of Christianity is thus a disembodied and asocial ideal. Like Troeltsch, he defends this view in terms of universalism. The church is by necessity particular and therefore a secondary expression of the gospel, which in its purity can be present only in the abstract individual. Hershberger on his side works with an individualistic concept of salvation, which therefore seems disconnected from his social ethics, and tends to come in conflict with his otherwise strongly communal ecclesiology.

All three have great difficulties seeing any connection between politics as a sphere of force and power and the Gospel of absolute love. They have different solutions to this problem, but their basic imagination is quite similar. And this imagination has effects, because — as I have said — we live in the world we see. I will show this by discussing Troeltsch's understanding of a subject matter central for Mennonites, namely the issue of war. This is interesting because Troeltsch is usually seen as the good liberal in German theology in contradiction with contemporary conservatives such as Reinhold Seeberg.

War, Nationalism, and Christianity

I do not think it is difficult to see why Troeltsch's view of the state described above makes war an unavoidable element of history in general and of the modern period in particular. The modern international system consists of rival independent states in constant conflict with each other. Because there is nothing above the state, force is the final — though not the only — arbiter. States are born in war, and war is a continuing expression of the struggle for existence. War is thus an essential part of history. That has to be accepted, whatever we think about it.

> There is no doubt: war belongs to the natural and unavoidable phenomena among peoples, to the struggle of survival of the big organizations of power, which they can avoid only with great difficulty and often not at all.

He goes even further. The struggle between states is an expression of "the law of the ascendancy of healthy and future-thrusting states and the law of the decline of aged and internally weakened states."[50]

What makes Troeltsch especially interesting is that he clearly recognizes the consequences of his view. Most recent moral philosophy and theology simply take existing nation-states as they are today for granted, ignoring that they are results of war. This is difficult for Troeltsch to do, as the unification of Germany was a very recent development. War was a primary means in this unification process. These wars were not wars of defense. And Troeltsch thinks it is impossible to say that only wars of defense are justified. The theory of just war is thus also impossible to hold. That would be to deny the legitimacy of Germany, as of most other nation-states.

> This big artifice of a people and a state, which we defend, has come about and has grown only through fighting and war. The unity of the German tribes is the result slowly achieved through countless wars and fights among ourselves, wars and fights which have not at all been pure wars of defense.[51]

He thus bestows war with a great moral and religious value. It is one of life's greatest duties.[52] He certainly does recognize how this view of state, history, and war contradicts much of Christian faith. But for him the power state and the international system of antagonistic states is a fact that has to be accepted.

In the end he defends a politics of "practical compromise," compromise between political reality and ideals, between naturalism and ethical values, between Machiavellian nationalism and humanitarian ideas. Although force is an unavoidable component of politics, to a certain extent humanitarian ideals can modify both domestic and foreign policy. "How this can be accomplished will depend in each case upon the special circumstances, and must thus be left to the genius of statesmen of imagination and insight."[53] How this imagination is

---

50. Troeltsch, "Der Völkerkrieg und das Christentum," *Die Christliche Welt*, 15 (1915): 296-97.

51. Troeltsch, *Deutscher Glaube und Deutsche Sitte in unserem groen Kriege* (Berlin 1914), 18. See also "Der Völkerkrieg," 296f.

52. "Undertaken for genuine necessities of life and future, war is a people's holy, divine duty" (Troeltsch, "Der Völkerkrieg," 297).

53. Troeltsch, *Christian Thought*, 159-60.

formed and disciplined is thus presumably extremely important, but Troeltsch has as little to say about that as does Burkholder.

It is thus not surprising that Troeltsch's thought is very nationalistic. Whatever the origin of a specific nationalism, and even if the description of one's own country in part is built on less than historical truth, nationalism in itself is real, and is, he thinks, the primary ethical principle of the nation-state and a strong ethical force or passion that creates its own reality.[54] Nationalism is the basic principle of the modern nation-state.[55] He acknowledges that this principle "has absolutely nothing to do with the Christian ethic." However, it has to be accepted, just as war has to be accepted. It is an essential part of the modern nation-state system. One cannot, in Troeltsch's view, really choose.

> The state has an independent moral idea, the idea of nationalism, patriotism, and political honor, which is given with it and stems from its very nature. Experience indicates that not even Christianity is able to do anything directly with this idea. It must presuppose this moral idea as implicit in the state.[56]

The issues of the supremacy of the nation-state and the importance of nationalism became especially acute during World War I. The nationalistic frenzy, especially during the beginning of this war, is well-known. This is true also for Troeltsch.[57] However, it is important to see that what Troeltsch writes during the war is basically consistent with the view he had defended for a long time, although the way he expresses his views during the beginning of the war is

54. Nationalism "constitutes the ethical orientation of innumerable people for whom religion is no longer a serious reality but who nevertheless wish to devote their little ego to some great cause. Love of country, as the devotion of the individual to the glory of the whole, is its great ethical passion" (Troeltsch, *Religion in History*, 178).

55. "There can be no doubt that nationalism represents a genuine ethical principle; in fact, the most direct, the most elemental, the most powerful principle of political ethics" (*Religion in History*, 179).

56. Troeltsch, *Religion in History*, 191-201.

57. "Oh, if the speaker of this hour only were able to transform each word into a bayonet, a rifle, a canon!" However, he realizes that also the "word" is extremely important for the warfare. It is here he can contribute. (Troeltsch, *Nach Erklärung der Mobilmachung* [Heidelberg 1914], 6.) There is a difference between Troeltsch's more "edifying" and political war writings and his more scholarly writings on the same issue. Sometimes this is used to excuse him from some of his more strident celebrations of the war. To understand him we should concentrate on his more scholarly writings, it is said. To this, two remarks are in order. First, the basic view I have described is the same in both cases. Second, his more popular writings are politically and culturally at least as important as his more scholarly work. All writing is a form of action.

naturally more extreme.[58] His views before, during, and after the war are basically the same.

It is, however, noteworthy that his war texts are more religiously passion-
ate than most (if not all) of Troeltsch's other writings. According to Troeltsch,
war reveals the irrational nature of reality, which draws people to religion.[59]
However, it is religion in the service of the nation-state of Germany. In his discussions of the German army he uses a rather strong religious language. First of
all, he describes the German army as a tool that the God of history uses.[60] In a
discussion of how to correlate faith in Germany with the Christian faith, he says
that intrinsic in a belief in the kingdom of God is belief in the earthly means
God uses for fulfilling his will on earth. Among these means are the German
state and the German army. He does not, at this time at least, believe that this
faith in Germany and its army is in contradiction with Christianity. A belief in
the God-given mission of Germany necessarily brings with it a faith in a living,
communicating God who " — through his governance of the world — protects
and asserts the national incarnations of the divine spirit."[61] For one who can
describe the German nation-state as a historical incarnation of the Spirit of
God, it is not surprising that he also talks about how he, together with the German people, loves from the heart the German army to which its hope of salvation is directed. "And even when we love it [i.e., the army] already in peace time
where it only is the symbol of our state's strength and readiness, so we pour
down on it with streams of love now during the war, where our salvation rests
in its hand and where its hardships, renunciations, its heroism and persever-
ance are saving us." He thinks that this sort of military spirit is *morally* much
superior to the Anglo-Saxon "merchants' spirit."[62]

But does not Christianity transcend the love of one's own country?
Troeltsch answers that Christianity goes beyond any faith in one's nation-state,
but that it is on an individual level. The center of Christian faith is about God
and the soul, about sin, forgiveness, and eternal life. But that does not say any-

58. He writes in 1922, commenting on his situation of being close to the center of power
and the people of power through living in Berlin. "This led to a rather full participation in war-
time journalism. The fact that I was able to observe the great historical events, at least in part,
very close to their source afforded me a deep and vital impression of the nature of historical
destinies, developments, and catastrophes in a way that no study of books and documents could
give" (Troeltsch, *Religion in History,* 374).

59. Troeltsch, *Mobilmachung,* 12. Cf. Troeltsch, *Unser Volksheer* (Heidelberg 1914), 21.

60. Troeltsch, *Unser Volksheer,* 7.

61. Troeltsch, *Deutscher Glaube,* 25.

62. Troeltsch, *Unser Volksheer,* 17-20. The quotes are from 18f. In "Der Völkerkrieg," 301,
he writes about the inner relationship between "the national Gospel and the Gospel of Christ-
mas."

thing about the questions of politics and war, more than that for, say, the individual soldier. This is God's ultimate word, but God's first and immediate word in the current situation is about "the love for state and fatherland as the embodiment of the divine thought in the German essence." He ends this discussion with the following words: "We hear God's voice in this, our struggle imposed by fate, and follow it with strong faith, innerly at one with fate's will, which is imposing these fights on us. We will stay and remain as it [i.e., fate's will] does."[63]

Troeltsch thus assumes a basically agonistic metaphysics. The struggle for existence is the most basic force in history, a fact which makes violence and war unavoidable components of history. History is more than violence, and the struggle can be modified in different ways, but it is not less. The gospel peace cannot change this situation. Troeltsch sees instead God as behind this violent struggle. Because this is the way reality is, we have to prepare for war, for war is unavoidable. Similarly, politics in general is struggle for power.

The outbreak of the First World War was thus very understandable for Troeltsch, just as he in his last text (written in 1922) wrote that he soon expected a new war in Europe.[64] He was, of course, not alone in his views on the nation-state and war. The necessity of war was a central part of the cultural imagination of the German elites as well as of the elites of many other nations. This war-culture was to a large extent responsible for this war. The leading war historian John Keegan has written:

> Politics played no part in the conduct of the First World War worth mentioning. The First World War was, on the contrary, an extraordinary, a monstrous cultural aberration, the outcome of an unwitting decision by Europeans in the century of Clausewitz to turn Europe into a warrior society.[65]

63. Troeltsch, *Deutscher Glaube*, 25-30. The quotes are from 28 and 30.

64. Because war is an unavoidable ingredient in the nation-state system, he thinks that the recent World War "has not proved a turning-point in history, but simply *one episode among others*. This sinister phrase indicates, I fear, the destiny that awaits us at the present time" (*Christian Thought*, 150).

65. John Keegan, *A History of Warfare* (New York: Alfred A. Knopf, 1993), 33. "By 1914 an entirely unprecedented cultural mood was dominating European society, one which accepted the right of the state to demand and the duty of every fit, male individual to render military service, which perceived in the performance of military service a necessary training in civic virtue and which rejected the age-old social distinction between the warrior — as a man set apart whether by rank or no rank at all — and the rest, as an outdated prejudice" (355). For another interesting discussion of the emergence of this type of morality, see Norbert Elias, *The Germans: Power Struggles and the Development of Habitus in the Nineteenth and Twentieth Cen-*

ARNE RASMUSSON

It is this "monstrous cultural aberration" that Troeltsch calls "realism." It was a culture that was supported by both church and university. Both maintained a theology of the nation-state. The type of theology and sociology Troeltsch represented made alternative views and possibilities culturally invisible. The type of disciplined churches and the convictions, common practices, and virtues which would have been required if the church should have been able to offer any form of resistance, even for being able to describe reality in alternative ways, was lacking. Moreover, Troeltsch himself was very much responsible for this state of affairs as he himself strongly supported and further developed these views and worked against any form of church and theology that might have been a source of opposition. So it should be noted that this culture was not only backed up by social and political reactionaries, but by leading liberal scholars such as Troeltsch and Max Weber, scholars whose intellectual categories since then have had an immense influence on twentieth-century intellectual life.[66]

---

turies, ed. Michael Schroter (New York: Columbia University Press, 1996). He writes: "In a world of dynastic states . . . a policy of unrestrained self-interest in inter-state relations was a personal policy of rulers who . . . stood in the line of succession of a warrior tradition. The code they followed in inter-state relations was largely an extension of the code which they followed in personal relations" (148). However, when this morality becomes part of increasingly democratized nation-states and when it is combined with a very different sort of moral code arising from other classes of society, we both see a division between personal and state morality and a change in the "emotional color" of the latter. The nationalist outlook obtains a new degree of moral absolutism. Elias writes that "most of the sovereign interdependent nation-states which together form the balance of power figuration in the twentieth century produce a two-fold code of norms whose demands are inherently contradictory: a moral code descended from that of rising sections of the *tiers état,* egalitarian in character, and whose highest value is 'man' — the human individual as such; and a nationalist code descended from the Machiavellian code of princes and ruling aristocracies, inegalitarian in character, and whose highest value is a collectivity — the state, the country, the nation to which an individual belongs" (154f.).

66. Usually Troeltsch and, even more, Weber (who was more skeptical about this war than Troeltsch, although he often sounded like Troeltsch), are described as being leaders in the moderate forces in contrast to the type of thinking represented by the conservative Lutheran theologian Reinhold Seeberg. (See, e.g., Seeberg, *Geschichte, Krieg und Seele. Reden und Aufsätze aus den Tagen des Weltkrieges,* [Leipzig 1916], and Günther Brakelmann, *Protestantische Kriegstheologie im 1. Weltkrieg. Reinhold Seeberg als Theologe des deutschen Imperialismus* [Bielefeld 1974].) We see this especially in the debate over the war aims. Troeltsch and Weber were sharply critical of Seeberg's grand annexationist dreams, though they were not in principle against all forms of annexations. (Weber wanted to make part of eastern Europe into a sort of vassal state to Germany.) However, this is a difference on the level of realistic politics, not concerning the basic views on state, nationalism, and war in general. Troeltsch and Weber, partly because of their closeness to the centers of power, were much more realistic, though not realistic enough, about the possibilities of Germany than Seeberg. One of the reasons for Weber's oppo-

230

The result of this war-culture was the catastrophe we call the First World War and some years later the even greater catastrophe of the Second World War. The question is often asked of pacifists what should one have done against Hitler. But Hitler was a result of this culture and the history it created. He did not come from nowhere. It was a culture strongly supported and partly created by the church. Hitler was, after all, voted into power and enthusiastically supported by millions of Protestants and by many of the most brilliant of German theologians. What would have happened if the German church had been different?

The Different Imagination of the Church

I know no book that exemplifies my thesis better than Jean Bethke Elshtain's *Women and War.*[67] In this book she discusses the languages and narratives through which war has been interpreted and enacted in the history of the West, and shows in the process why understanding this is more important than understanding the principles used for judging war. She describes on the one hand the history of armed civic virtue from the Greeks by way of Machiavelli and the French revolution to the compulsory military service systems of the militarized nation-states of the nineteenth and twentieth centuries (so warmly celebrated by Troeltsch). These national service systems are, together with the national school systems, the two basic tools for creating a national consciousness (in addition, of course, to war itself).

But she describes also, on the other hand, the Christian attempt to disarm this civic virtue. "Finding in the 'paths of peace' the most natural as well as the

---

sition to German annexationism in Europe was that this, because of the destroyed relations to other European powers and the strength it would take to keep, would destroy the possibilities of German overseas imperialism. On this, see Wolfgang J. Mommsen, *Max Weber and German Politics 1890-1920* (Chicago: University of Chicago Press, 1984). For an informative account of the immediate historical and political context for Troeltsch's writings during the war, see Bernd Sösemann, "Das 'erneuerte Deutschland'. Ernst Troeltschs politisches Engagement im Ersten Weltkrieg," *Troeltsch-Studien. Band 3: Protestantismus und Neuzeit,* ed. Horst Renz and Friedrich Wilhelm Graf (Gütersloh 1984), 120-44. For a good overview of this period in German religion, see Thomas Nipperdey, *Religion im Umbruch: Deutschland 1870-1918* (München 1988).

67. Jean Bethke Elshtain, *Women and War,* 2nd ed. (Chicago: University of Chicago Press, 1995). Cf. Rasmusson, *The Church as "Polis,"* 306-13. See also Elshtain's book *Public Man, Private Woman* (Princeton: Princeton University Press, 1991), ch. 2, for a similar discussion of the role of Christianity for the understanding of the relationship between the public and the private, and thus the role of women.

most desirable way of being, Christian pioneers exalted a pacific ontology." She depicts this as an entering of something new in history, a sort of counter-politics. "This sort of principled resistance to public power was something new under the sun, opening up a range of options, duties, responsibilities, dilemmas, and reassessments not available in classical antiquity, bearing implications for men and women alike."[68] By making peace primary the burden of proof was given to the ones who wanted to use violence. Even later when the church as a whole had abandoned its earlier pacifism, this ontology of peace still had a restraining effect during the Middle Ages in spite of its uneasy coexistence with the warrior codes of the political elites.

Elshtain also argues that the Reformation, especially in its Lutheran form, in effect went hand in hand with the emergence of the absolute state and thereby legitimated the release of the political regimes from the constraints of the medieval church. She therefore contends that "Luther prepares the way for the political theology that underlies the emergence of the nation-state. . . . Centuries scarred by religious wars are one result of the turn." She furthermore maintains that this crusading ethos does not disappear with the Enlightenment and the coming secularization, but reappears as the militarism of the nation-states — often strongly supported by the established national churches as well as by the not formally established American churches.

> The discourse of armed civic virtue and the ferocious excesses of holy war pursued for the state rather than for God came together in a way that fused undisguised *machtpolitik* with assumptions of state divinity, canalizing popular sentiment into collective enthusiasm for the 'state ideal' as the self-identity and definition of 'a people'; integrating whole populations into mobilized political patterns; producing young men prepared to make the 'supreme sacrifice' and young women prepared to see to it that they did.[69]

I have told these stories to show that neither ethics nor politics is primarily a question of relating abstract principles to concrete reality. What we see as reality is an enacted narrative. Troeltsch is trying to mediate the theologies of modernity with his Christian faith, rather than trying to mediate Christianity with "reality." Troeltsch describes, and Burkholder's language implies the same view, the process of modernization as the release of the secular spheres from the authority of the church. The secular is always there in latent form. The history of the West consequently becomes the history of the gradual liberation of in-

---

68. Elshtain, *Women and War*, 122-26.

69. Elshtain, *Women and War*, 136-37. See further on this, Elshtain, *Meditations on Modern Political Thought* (New York: Praeger, 1986), 5-20.

strumental reason from different sorts of restrictions: "The secular motives that had previously been inhibited but never ceased to exert influence were now set free."[70] Sociology is thus a "dispassionate analysis"[71] of social reality itself independent of theological premises. For Burkholder theology is then added on to a sociological analysis.

This view has recently been sharply criticized from many different directions. The most ambitious theological criticism is John Milbank's *Theology and Social Theory*. Contra Troeltsch, he argues that the "secular" is historically constituted and thus something contingent. "Once, there was no 'secular.'"[72] In this book he thus traces the emergence of the secular. He shows how the emergence of a secular domain is closely related to the rise of the absolute state (which was the forerunner to the modern nation-state) and the new conception of the secular sphere as the space for pure power, pure instrumentality. We have seen how Troeltsch himself describes this development, but then not as a specific and contingent cultural development, but as a liberation of the natural. The natural is the struggle for existence, which then has to be disciplined in different ways. It is precisely by imagining politics as a sphere of pure power that the new discipline political science is given an object to study. Behind these developments are also, according to Milbank, changes in late medieval theology. It is nominalist and voluntarist theology that provides the new discipline with conceptual categories.[73]

Milbank goes on doing similar analyses of economics and sociology, including the sociology of Weber and Troeltsch. But I cannot develop that here. The point is that these disciplines are not only empirical disciplines, but are also carriers of political, moral, and theological understandings of reality. They represent the self-description of modernity, the theology of modernity and its main actor, the nation-state. If this is right, and many philosophers, sociologists, and even some economists would agree, then sociology or political science cannot depict "reality" in a neutral way.[74] For theology to build on sociology, understood as dispassionate analysis, is to betray its own task. Theology

---

70. Troeltsch, *Religion in History,* 266.

71. Burkholder, *Social Responsibility,* 3.

72. John Milbank, *Theology and Social Theory* (Oxford: Blackwell, 1990), 9.

73. Milbank, *Theology and Social Theory,* ch. 1.

74. Cf., for instance, Alasdair MacIntyre, *After Virtue* (Notre Dame: University of Notre Dame Press, 1981), Margareta Bertilsson, *Slaget om det moderna* (Stockholm 1987), Dorothy Ross, *The Origins of American Social Science* (Cambridge: Cambridge University Press, 1991), Arthur J. Vidich and Stanford M. Lyman, *American Sociology: Worldly Rejections of Religion and Their Directions* (New Haven: Yale University Press, 1985), and Robert Nelson, *Reaching for Heaven on Earth: The Theological Meaning of Economics* (Savage, MD: Rowman & Littlefield, 1991).

can, of course, learn a lot from sociology, but it cannot give sociology, or any other social discipline, a privileged position.

This is important, because what is understood as "realism" depends on how the world is seen, which in its turn is related to one's communal practice. An alternative discourse-practice helps the moral imagination and vice versa. It is this that makes ecclesiology so theologically important. Therefore, Milbank can say that "theology has to reconceive itself as a kind of 'Christian sociology': that is to say, as the explication of a socio-linguistic practice, or as the constant re-narration of this practice as it has historically developed." Behind this assertion is his long argument in his book that "there can be no sociology in the sense of a universal 'rational' account of the 'social' character of all societies, and Christian sociology is distinctive simply because it explicates, and adopts the vantage point of, a distinct society, the Church."[75] An alternative sociolinguistic practice provides possibilities to see the world from another perspective. This includes for Milbank a counter-history, that critically rereads history with the help of the perspective and the categories provided by the narrative of Jesus Christ and its continuation in the church. This requires a counter-ethics that describes the practice of the church in its continuity and discontinuity with its antique and modern context. Milbank deals, among other things, with the Christian understanding of love and forgiveness, the reconciliation of difference and virtue, and the conviction that peace, not violence, is the first and final reality. Such a rereading of history and such a counter-ethics involves a counter-ontology, a trinitarian ontology or metaphysics of the cross of Christ that makes peace final. This gives him a perspective from which he can deconstruct the agonistic ontologies that permeate both modern and postmodern thought.[76]

Cultural Imagination, Realism, and Responsibility

How you conceive responsibility has much to do with the sort of metaphysics you assume. You cannot be responsible in general. Troeltsch's thought was formed by an agonistic cultural imagination that made alternative possibilities invisible. Hershberger's ahistorical and essentialist understanding of the state and his view of love as absolute nonresistance too easily lead to the same result. But the state can take many different forms. Even the modern nation-state system, which is now nearly universal and outside of which it is extremely difficult

75. Milbank, *Theology and Social Theory*, 380-81.
76. Milbank, *Theology and Social Theory*, ch. 12.

to think, is a contingent development. It was not a necessary development and it was helped along by the church.[77] A major hindrance for at least some changes at the margin is that our imagination is imprisoned in frozen categories. There are other streams in Hershberger's thought that point in this direction. One of many ways the church can be of service to the world is to nurture alternative ways of seeing the world that question what are thought to be necessities.

It is also important to note that insofar as Burkholder's moral and political imagination is different from Troeltsch's, as it often is — he is after all a pacifist — this cannot be explained in terms of their common model of compromise between ideal and reality. This model makes the process behind how reality is read invisible. Burkholder's vision is influenced by the faith and practices of his Mennonite context, as Troeltsch's is by his context of a Protestant *Volkskirche* in a post-Bismarckian intellectual milieu. Troeltsch was certainly realistic, given his reading of reality. I agree with Burkholder that there are real moral dilemmas, that compromises are necessary, and so on. But that recognition does not help us very much, nor would it have helped Troeltsch.

To be able, at least to some extent, to think outside a given hegemonic cultural imagination you need an alternative community that tells another narrative, forms other practices, extols other virtues. Thinking is a bodily and social activity. Troeltsch was thinking out of the centers of German intellectual and political life: first, the university, which of course is one of the central institutions of the nation-state, and, second, political life in Berlin. He was not a very active churchgoer,[78] but that would not have helped anyhow, because German Protestantism, both liberal and conservative, was more or less completely identified with German nationalism. There were no alternatives around. This shows the importance of ecclesiology, and an ecclesiology of a specific sort.

---

77. Cf., for instance, Charles Tilly, *Coercion, Capital, and European States AD 990-1992*, rev. ed. (Cambridge, MA: Basil Blackwell, 1992); Hagen Schulze, *States, Nations and Nationalism: From the Middle Ages to the Present* (Oxford: Blackwell, 1996); Liah Greenfeld, *Nationalism: Five Roads to Modernity* (Cambridge, MA: Harvard University Press, 1992); and Adrian Hastings, *The Construction of Nationhood: Ethnicity, Religion and Nationalism* (Cambridge: Cambridge University Press, 1997).

78. His biographer Hans-Georg Drescher writes: "It is almost impossible to imagine Troeltsch in close contact with church life, say as a regular churchgoer" (*Ernst Troeltsch: His Life and Work* [Minneapolis: Fortress Press, 1993], 116).

John Howard Yoder's Transformation
of Christian Social Theology

On Reconstructing Mennonite Theology

In order to state such an ecclesiology convincingly, we have to overcome the individualistic and disembodied Protestant reading of Jesus, the church, and salvation that Troeltsch represents, but that we also tend to find in a weaker form in the writings of Hershberger and Burkholder. If the church has inaugurated an alternative history, a counter discourse and practice, the disembodied and asocial view of religion espoused by Troeltsch and modernity in general is disastrous. What is needed is a recovery of the bodily and social nature of human life and therefore of salvation.

One of the most powerful resources for doing this has been developed in precisely the same Mennonite context that created the theologies we have been considering. I am, of course, thinking of the remarkable work of John Howard Yoder.[79] One way of reading him is as an attempt constructively to liberate American Christian theology (and not just Mennonite theology) from the distorting categories of Troeltsch and the brothers Niebuhr. Although he most often deals directly with the Niebuhrs, he knows very well that behind them we find Troeltsch. As he says, "Troeltsch has obtained a wide following in American thought through the brothers Niebuhr; it is very difficult for an American Protestant ethicist even to conceive that questions might be posed in other terms."[80] That this is true is seen not least in the fact that Yoder himself so very often is read, both by the "mainstream" and by other Mennonites, in precisely these terms and thus as an updated form of the type of theology that Hershberger has represented in my discussion. Although Yoder so often has described and criticized this unhappy dichotomy, many of his readers seem unable to think outside this dichotomy, which gives no place to the alternative type of theology that Yoder has tried to develop.[81] But that he represents an al-

---

79. In more recent Mennonite theology, many have tried another way out of the dilemma that I have been describing — namely, the roads of the various political theologies, including liberation theology, that have been developed from the 1960s forward. I have in *The Church as "Polis"* tried to show why this is a mistake. Cf. also Milbank's discussion of the Catholic tradition of political and liberation theology in ch. 8 of *Theology and Social Theory*.

80. Yoder, *The Politics of Jesus*, 2nd ed. (Grand Rapids: Eerdmans, 1994), 105 n. 11.

81. See, for example, Yoder's books *Christian Attitudes to War, Peace, and Revolution: A Companion to Bainton* (Elkhart, IN: Co-Op Bookstore, 1983), 372-420, *The Christian Witness to the State* (Newton, KA: Faith and Life Press, 1964), 88-90, and *Nevertheless: The Varieties and Shortcomings of Religious Pacifism*, rev. and exp. ed. (Scottdale, PA: Herald Press, 1992).

ternative is clear (although closer to Hershberger than Burkholder), and that may be easier to see today than when Yoder first formulated his constructive proposals. It should be remembered that the basic contours of both his critique and his constructive approach were developed already during the 1950s.[82] I cannot here discuss Yoder's position fully. I will limit myself to a brief overview of some of the themes most relevant to our discussion.

Of course, Yoder's entire mature position was not completed at once, although it is remarkable how much was in place already in the 1950s. He started inside the then dominant discourse in Mennonitism and remade it from within.[83] While Burkholder in part simply turns Hershberger upside down, Yoder develops and transforms a Hershberger-type discourse in a way that helps him get out of the conceptual restrictions of this debate and develop a much more fruitful approach. It is interesting to read his early book *The Christian Witness to the State* from this perspective.[84] In the beginning of the book we find a lot of the conceptual apparatus that Hershberger and Burkholder work with. But as one reads on, it becomes clear how Yoder breaks through and transforms this conceptual structure.

Yoder does sometimes use essentialist-sounding language. For example: "The very nature of the state is force."[85] And he accepts Hershberger's and other contemporary Mennonites' criticisms of liberal pacifism and its assumption that the state could follow some sort of Christian pacifism.[86] But it soon becomes clear that he does not intend with the statement we have cited to state a doctrine or a general theory of the state. It is simply an empirical statement. "Whatever the state is or should be in theory, in fact every state wields the sword, and it is that fact that sets the theme for this study."[87] Moreover, this lack

82. See esp. the essay "Peace Without Eschatology" from 1954, now in Yoder, *The Royal Priesthood: Essays Ecclesiological and Ecumenical* (Grand Rapids: Eerdmans, 1994), 143-67.

83. On the background of the early development of Yoder's theology, see Paul Toews, "The Concern Movement: Its Origins and Early History," *Conrad Grebel Review* 8 (1990): 109-26. Albert N. Keim also gives an interesting account of the early Yoder's relationship with Mennonitism in his recent biography *Harold S. Bender, 1897-1962* (Scottdale, PA: Herald Press, 1998), 450-71.

84. The material for the book *The Christian Witness to the State* was originally presented in 1955, and then reworked 1958-59 (in partial collaboration with an advisory group that included both Hershberger and Burkholder as well as another famous Mennonite theologian, Gordon Kaufman), but it was not published until 1964. See p. 4.

85. Yoder, *Witness*, 7. In a text originally from 1954, he can similarly write that "the purpose of the state [is] that of achieving a 'tolerable balance of egoisms' (an expression borrowed with gratitude from Reinhold Niebuhr)" (*The Royal Priesthood*, 153. Cf. his comments on 147 n. 3).

86. Yoder, *Witness*, 6f. See esp. n. 3.

87. Yoder, *Witness*, 12 n. 6.

of a doctrine of the state means that Yoder does not have a theory of the ideal state which could function as a criterion for criticism of the actual state. This has one important consequence. There is no given upper level above which a state cannot be expected to rise. For example, the type of "realpolitik" Troeltsch assumed is not necessary. "There is no level of attainment to which a state could rise, beyond which the Christian critique would have nothing more to ask; such an ideal level would be none other than the kingdom of God." He can also say, using the sort of language I have used, that "the essentialist approach is in itself foreign to the historical thrust of the biblical witness."[88] On the other hand, from this it does not follow that anything can be asked of the state. One has to begin with the actually existing states. But there is no general theory telling us what we can expect. Historical, social, cultural, and political circumstances change.[89] "We do not ask of the government that it be nonresistant; we do, however, ask that it take the most just and the least violent action possible."[90]

If we go to Yoder's other writings it becomes even clearer that the way he develops his approach calls into question Troeltsch's account both theologically and sociologically. Moreover, for Yoder theology and sociology are interconnected. His theology, and the ecclesial discourse-practice on which it depends, helps him, so he thinks, construe social and political reality in a truer way.

Above all, his description of Jesus and the early church is very different from Troeltsch's. His book *The Politics of Jesus* can be read as a deconstruction of the assumptions behind a Troeltschian reading of the New Testament. He questions, for example, Troeltsch's division between individual and social ethics. Emphasizing the Jewishness of Jesus, he writes: "Jesus doesn't know anything about radical personalism. The personhood which he proclaims as a healing, forgiving call to all is integrated into the social novelty of the healing community." He continues: "The idea of Jesus as an individualist or a teacher of radical personalism could arise only in the (Protestant, post-Pietist, rationalist)

---

88. Yoder, *Witness*, 32, 34. In a later analysis of Romans 13 he writes: "Instead of a stable institution, dating from creation, the 'state as such,' this text tells us to think of a dynamic process related to and reflecting the saving work of Christ, as this work reaches even beyond the realm of the church" (*The Politics of Jesus*, 195).

89. That even the modern state can take drastically different shapes is seen not least in the development of the German state(s) during the last hundred years: from the Wilhelmine state, via the Weimar-state and Nazi-state, and the communist East Germany and the liberal West Germany, to the modern unified liberal German state inside the European Community. This shows that, even if we limit ourselves to one country during one century, it is not helpful to ask about the relationship between church and state in general.

90. Yoder, *Witness*, 42. He further develops these ideas on pp. 74-83.

context that it did; that is, in a context which, if not intentionally anti-Semitic, was at least sweepingly a-Semitic, stranger to the Jewish Jesus."[91]

Yoder's Jesus is instead the proclaimer and inaugurator of a new eschatological social order. In his life, message, and destiny, the kingdom of God has come near, and it takes an anticipatory concrete shape in the people that answer his call by following him. In him they meet at the same time God and God's purpose for human life. In his life and destiny, and climactically in his death and resurrection, they learn to know God's way with the world, and through following him they learn to know what they are called by God to be. The difference between church and world is thus a question of posture — some embrace and some reject the lordship of Christ.[92]

The Church and the Powers

Several things follow from this account. First, the church, and not the state, is the primary, but not the only, locus for God's redeeming work in the world. This does not mean that the world outside the church is empty of God's creative action. The model Yoder uses for talking about this, and which he thinks preferable to the idea of "the orders of creation" and later similar approaches as well as to the "Thomist" nature-grace model, is the New Testament concept of the "powers."[93] With "powers" he refers to religious, intellectual, moral, social, and political structures. He describes these structures as created by God (they

91. Yoder, *The Politics of Jesus*, 108f.

92. For an interesting discussion of Yoder's use of Scripture, see Richard Hays, *The Moral Vision of the New Testament* (New York: HarperCollins, 1996), 239-53. Discussing Yoder's *The Politics of Jesus*, he says: "At numerous points, his reading reflects an astute — indeed, almost prescient — grasp of important developments in the field of New Testament studies" (245). It is quite remarkable to which extent a perspective like Yoder's today finds support in some recent biblical scholarship. In addition to Hays, see for instance Luke Timothy Johnson, "The Social Dimension of *Soteria* in Luke-Acts and Paul," *Society of Biblical Literature 1993 Seminar Papers*, 520-36; Gerhard Lohfink, *Wie hat Jesus Gemeinde gewollt? Zur gesellschaftlichen Dimension des christlichen Glaubens* (Freiburg 1982); idem, *Wem gilt die Bergpredigt? Beiträge zu einer christlichen Ethik* (Freiburg 1988); idem, "Jesus und die Kirche," *Theologisches Jahrbuch* (1990): 64-106; idem, "Die Not der Exegese mit der Reich-Gottes-Verkündigung Jesu," *Theologische Quartalschrift* 168 (1988): 1-15; Wayne A. Meeks, *The Moral World of the First Christians* (Philadelphia: Westminster Press, 1986); Ben F. Meyer, *The Aims of Jesus* (London: SCM Press, 1979); Jürgen Roloff, *Die Kirche im Neuen Testament* (Göttingen 1993); Peter Stuhlmacher, "Kirche nach dem Neuen Testament," *Theologische Beiträge* 26 (1995): 301-25; N. T. Wright, *The New Testament and the People of God* (Minneapolis: Fortress, 1992); and idem, *Jesus and the Victory of God* (Minneapolis: Fortress, 1996).

93. See Yoder, *The Politics of Jesus*, ch. 8.

are an essential and unavoidable part of human life), but also as fallen (they have made themselves absolute, and therefore enslave people). However, even as fallen they are used by God for preserving human life.

Yoder does not develop a precise account of what these powers are, because he conceives them in very general terms. That is, any human life is lived in some form of moral, social, and political structures, etc., although the form this takes varies enormously. What is called the state is one central expression of the political structuring of social life. In this sense the state is used by God for preserving human life. The state is also fallen, as seen by its claim to absolute supremacy and its demand for final loyalty. It is in this sense that Yoder would claim that Troeltsch's attitude to the German nation-state was idolatry, an idolatry that enslaves and distorts one's understanding of reality and its priorities and that seriously harms human life.

If these powers, understood in the loose sense I indicated above, are part of God's good creation and an inevitable part of human life, salvation cannot be understood apart from them. As Yoder says:

> If then God is going to save his creatures *in their humanity,* the Powers cannot simply be destroyed or set aside or ignored. Their sovereignty must be broken. This is what Jesus did, concretely and historically, by living a genuinely free and human existence. This life brought him, as any genuinely human existence will bring anyone, to the cross. . . . Like everyone, he too was subject . . . to these powers. He accepted his own status of submission. But morally he broke their rules by refusing to support them in their self-glorification; and that is why they killed him.[94]

Thus the powers are unmasked through Christ's death on the cross and his vindication by the resurrection. This very unmasking, showing their modest reality, that they are not ultimate realities, is their defeat. Nothing but the triune God has ultimate value. Christ is Lord, not these powers.

This is then also what the church has to proclaim and live, which means that the church through its own life brings something new to history. Elshtain's discussion of the early church's inauguration of a new understanding of power, state, and violence is thus a good description of this process. This unmasking of the powers then also influences the way the powers themselves work. From this perspective, one of the great tragedies of history is the fact that the church instead of exposing the powers (for example, the state and the nation) has sacralized them and made them into God's direct and primary instruments in history. As German Protestantism, Troeltsch in-

94. Yoder, *The Politics of Jesus,* 144f.

cluded, did with the German people and the German state, so does the church always when it is thinking more about on whose side it should be (which power — which state, ideology, movement, class — it should support), than on how most faithfully it can be the church in its present circumstances. In other words, this perspective helps Yoder look at history and at social and political reality in a different way from those who see states and nations as the central actors in history.

A second thing that follows from this account is that it leads Yoder to stress the bodily and social nature of Christian life and theology. The previous discussion of the powers that structure human life shows this. "In this view of things the condition of the creature, our fallen state, the continual providential care of God which preserves us as human, the saving work of Christ, and the specific position of the Christian community in the midst of history are all described in terms of social structures and their inherent dynamics."[95] The Christian message is thus not a set of disembodied general truths or philosophical or moral principles. It is instead a communal life embodied in concrete ecclesial practices such as baptism, the eucharist, fraternal admonition, the exercise of the gifts of the Spirit, and the discernment process of the common meeting.[96] In this sense it is a sort of politics; it has to do with "the common life of human beings."[97]

Trinitarian Metaphysics and Political Interpretation

Third, this account also implies what might be called an eschatological and trinitarian metaphysics. By metaphysics I mean an account of reality implied in Yoder's theology. He does not, and would not, develop a detailed and general metaphysics, but he does claim that we can understand something of the ultimate shape of reality through God's history with the world, with its center in the cross and resurrection. Someone might object that this account is more christocentric than trinitarian. Yoder would rightly answer that this objection builds on a misunderstanding of the doctrine of the Trinity. What this doctrine says is that we must talk about God so that God the Creator is none other than God as we meet God in the life and destiny of Jesus Christ and in the continua-

95. Yoder, *The Politics of Jesus*, 149f.
96. On this see esp. Yoder, *Body Politics: Five Practices of the Christian Community Before the Watching World* (Nashville: Discipleship Resources, 1992), and idem, *The Royal Priesthood*, 359-73.
97. Yoder, *The Royal Priesthood*, 147 n. 3. On the definition of "politics," see Rasmusson, *The Church as "Polis,"* 187-89.

tion of Christ's life through the Spirit in the existence of the church. There is no other God behind this God.[98]

It is an eschatological metaphysics in the sense that it is not a description of a homogenous unchanging reality, but of a historical and social process. Not only the world as created by God, but also sin, the cross and resurrection, the conflict between church and world, and the work of the Spirit in the church are elements of this understanding of reality.

It is only in reality so understood that Yoder's politics makes sense. Thus, at the end of *The Politics of Jesus*, he says that the biblical apocalypses (and it might also be said about the Christian gospel in general) "are about how the crucified Jesus is a more adequate key to understanding what God is about in the real world of empires and armies and markets than is the ruler in Rome, with all his supporting military, commercial, and sacerdotal networks." The consequences of this are of immense importance. "Then to follow Jesus does not mean renouncing effectiveness. . . . It means that in Jesus we have a clue to which kinds of causation, which kinds of community-building, which kinds of conflict management, go with the grain of the cosmos, of which we know, as Caesar does not, that Jesus is both the Word (the inner logic of things) and the Lord ('sitting at the right hand')."[99]

In other words, this kind of metaphysics, embedded and implied in an ecclesial discourse-practice, creates a framework for historical, social, and political interpretation and practice. It cannot simply be read off the surface of history, because the trinitarian understanding of reality is implicit in it, but Yoder thinks it can generate new readings of history and social and political reality whose fruitfulness can be tested "empirically." But it is also important to observe that Yoder does not think that, from this, we can develop a general theory that provides a handle on history and its direction, so that we might calculate what is effective political action. This is not a deficiency in his "theory"; rather, it is intrinsic to his Christian metaphysic that this type of calculation is impossible. In his perspective, "the calculating link between our obedience and ultimate efficacy has been broken, since the triumph of God comes through resurrection and not through effective sovereignty or assured results." He is therefore critical of social and political theories (like Marxism, liberal social engineering, much economic theory) that assume that there is a "visible, understandable, and manageable"[100]

98. See, e.g., Yoder, *The Politics of Jesus*, 99, 100f., and idem, "How H. Richard Niebuhr Reasoned: A Critique of *Christ and Culture*," in Glen H. Stassen, D. M. Yeager, and John Howard Yoder, *Authentic Transformation: A New Vision of Christ and Culture* (Nashville: Abingdon Press, 1996), 61-65.

99. Yoder, *The Politics of Jesus*, 246.

100. Yoder, *The Politics of Jesus*, 239, 229.

relationship between cause and effect, so that if we have adequate information and the means of power we can move society in the "desired" or "necessary" direction. This idea tends to make "effectiveness" in itself into a moral value ("responsibility"), so that the means are justified by the ends to which they are used. In contrast, Yoder defends the final inseparability of means from ends.

So instead of a sort of utilitarian approach, Yoder defends a form of practical reason that includes a finally unformalizable discernment formed by an ecclesial discourse-practice. He thus does not defend some blind obedience to rules, nor the idea that ethics and politics can be directly derived from Scripture. But the church thinks and lives inside this Christian discourse-practice (or so it should), although she employs knowledge derived from many different sources.[101] Even if the Christian understanding of reality does not give him the means to calculate, it still gives an empirically meaningful perspective from which to think. Yoder thus reads reality theologically. And he thinks his metaphysics is more true than, say, Troeltsch's.[102]

---

101. Yoder, *The Priestly Kingdom: Social Ethics as Gospel* (Notre Dame: Notre Dame Press, 1984), 11.

102. Nancey Murphy has, in several very interesting writings, tried to develop this aspect of Yoder's theology, or maybe rather to integrate Yoder's theology into her project of understanding theology as a science. She tends to make his theology into a general theory "about everything," with a central "hardcore," methodological auxiliary hypotheses, and a positive heuristic. See Murphy's chapter in this volume, as well as Nancey Murphy and George F. R. Ellis, *On the Moral Nature of the Universe* (Minneapolis: Fortress Press, 1996), esp. ch. 8, and Nancey Murphy, *Reconciling Theology and Science: A Radical Reformation Perspective* (Kitchener, ON: Pandora Press, 1997). However, I think this misstates what Yoder is about. For a very good (although appreciative) criticism of Murphy and Ellis, see Roland Spjuth's not yet published article "Is Ethics Also Among the Sciences?" He writes, e.g.: "In Yoder's conception of the Anabaptist moral tradition, Christianity is not all about something basic that can be condensed in a theoretical core but is rather the life of Jesus and the social embodiment of discipleship within the church. That is, at its heart there is a 'practical moral reasoning.' Such a practical moral reasoning functions differently than a research-program. It is not a deduction from some central core or value within a coherent system (or an application of universally valid rules and neither is it simply doing 'what the scripture says'). For Yoder, practical moral reasoning is rather the skill of 'binding and loosing' described in Matthew 18:15-18. A particular moral choice is made in communal conversation (where two or three are present), in a context of forgiveness, reconciliation and listening to witnesses." He also questions the meaningfulness and the appropriateness of the sort of general theory or unified worldview they develop. "The task is not to provide a whole world-view but rather to keep science humble by deconstructing present structures of dominion, giving hints of another possible social construction of morality and bringing surprises and questions to rigid systems."

Responsibility Reconsidered

Consequently, he has continually criticized the sharp dualisms posited between faithfulness and responsibility, "absolutism" and realism, *agape* and effectiveness, although again and again he himself is described in these terms. If Yoder is right, there is no final contradiction between *agape* and effectiveness. We do not have to choose one or the other, because *agape,* understood in the light of the cross and resurrection, is the way God's salvation works in history.[103] The conflict between Yoder and Troeltsch or Niebuhr is thus misdescribed when it is said to concern moral purism contra political responsibility, or absolutism contra compromise. Instead it is a conflict between different construals of reality and between different moralities. Yoder understands the necessity of compromise and of casuistry, if it means that you often cannot do what in an ideal situation would be the best. In one text, for example, he lists, in a typically Yoderian analytic way, nineteen *different* types of "considerations which call for purported 'absolutes' to be mitigated."[104]

One may also describe it as a question of different moralities (though the description of reality is a determinative part of a morality). Troeltsch puts the principle of nationalism on the top or near the top of his "scale of values," although he knows that this is in conflict with Christian morality. For Yoder, following Jesus Christ is much more important than defending the American nation-state. Thus he denies "that my critics are any more temperate or moderate, any less 'absolute' than I, in what they consider decisive for obedience. They challenge my values because they prefer other values; but those other values are no less determining for them."[105] In Yoder's view, Troeltsch's nationalism violated the commandment against idolatry.[106] The same then is true concerning the issue of "responsibility." As Yoder says:

> The strong emotional appeal of the word *responsibility* and the extreme pejorative ring of the epithet *irresponsible* have avoided the need for precise definition of the virtue in question. Rigorous analysis of the function the term discharges in the ethical argument of the Niebuhrian school would probably confirm that there is no more exact meaning than that *responsibility signifies a commitment to consider the survival, the interest, or the power of one's own nation, state, or class as taking priority over the survival, interest*

103. Yoder, *The Politics of Jesus,* 109.
104. Yoder, "'Patience' as Method in Moral Reasoning: Is an Ethic of Discipleship 'Absolute'?," ch. 2 in this volume, 24-42.
105. Yoder, "'Patience.'"
106. Yoder, *Witness,* 15f.

or power of other persons or groups, of all of humanity, of the "enemy," or of the church. If it does *not* mean this, the concept of responsibility cannot prove what it is being used to prove in current debate. If it *does* mean this, it is clearly questionable at two points: a) the priority of state over church; b) the priority of oneself and one's own group over others or the "enemy," as the locus both of value and of decision. This basic egotism of the responsibility argument is clothed as a form of altruism.[107]

Troeltsch and Yoder interpret social and political reality differently because they construe reality differently. They defend different social metaphysics: in simplified terms, Yoder a metaphysics of peace and Troeltsch a metaphysics of violence. And as we have seen, Yoder would also deny that the contrast between him and Troeltsch is that of a faith-based versus an empirically-based account. In retrospect, it is easy to see that Troeltsch's reading of social and political reality was formed by and integrated into a general cultural imagination with its specific metaphysics, an imagination that itself participated in creating the specific political reality it imagined. It was not a description of political reality as such. Moreover, it was also influenced by his specific form of Protestant theology and metaphysics. A Christian discourse-practice of the sort Yoder defends could have given another perspective from which history and social and political reality could have been read *and* thereby supplied the church a concrete basis for resistance, in a way Troeltsch's type of theology could not.

Our actions are to a great extent determined by our reading of history. A rereading of our history may therefore help us see new possibilities in the present.[108] Yoder himself provides quite a few examples of both possible rereadings of history and of the actual social and political importance of the church's life for the world. He describes them as hypotheses whose empirical fruitfulness you can analyze and discuss. In this sense, they do not differ from Troeltsch's parallel historical and sociological descriptions.

One example is Yoder's criticism of the importance given to political leaders, naked power, and force in much conventional history writing. The importance of control of the centers of political decision-making is central for Troeltsch, as well as for much current Christian thinking. To be able to get things done, one has to control or directly influence the state. The consequence is that the struggle to gain power and to be on the "right side" becomes central, and a theology of Yoder's type is easily seen as irrelevant. Yoder has often questioned this view and the idea that social change primarily has to do with the control of the center. Economic, cultural, and religious factors are at least as im-

107. Yoder, *Witness,* 36 n. 1.
108. Yoder, *The Royal Priesthood,* 208.

portant. Moreover, the power of political leaders is very limited by the structures and processes that brought them to power as well as by cultural and economic forces. Another aspect is Yoder's claim that "social creativity is a minority function." For example, he suggests that "[t]he creativity of the 'pilot project' or the critic is more significant for a social change than is the coercive power that generalizes a new idea."[109] And this is more often provided by minorities and dissenters than by the power elite occupied by running the current order.[110] This is also related to the fact that social and political reality look different if seen from "below" or from the "margin" than from "above." If this is right, it follows that "there are other more useful ways to contribute to the course of society than attempting to 'rule'."[111]

Put differently, what Yoder with this and many other examples wants to emphasize is that the social theory behind views like those of Troeltsch and Burkholder, and to a lesser extent Hershberger,[112] is built on a faulty dichotomistic view of society. In this view society consists of, on the one hand, autonomous individuals and, on the other, of a political sphere determined by an autonomous political rationality, often (as with Troeltsch) understood in basically Machiavellian terms. In this understanding there is little space left for a Christian social practice and Christian social theology. On the one hand, the autonomy of individual preferences will be in conflict with any idea of a common ecclesial discipleship. On the other hand, the political sphere, so understood, does not give any space for a substantial social theology. But if this social theory is questioned, the relevance of the type of Christian ecclesial discourse-practice he defends is highly relevant.[113]

Moreover, for Yoder this does not primarily take the form of an abstract social theory, but of visible ecclesial practices. The existence and practice of the church is in itself good news that other ways of being a society are possi-

---

109. Yoder, *The Royal Priesthood*, 215.

110. This view is also in part defended by Troeltsch historically, although he does not draw the same conclusions. See my discussion of this in *The Church as "Polis,"* 234-42, 245-47.

111. Yoder, *The Royal Priesthood*, 210.

112. In part Hershberger develops, as we have seen, ideas similar to Yoder's, but he fails to see the full implications of them.

113. Most recent political theology presupposes the criticized form of sociopolitical imagination. In contrast to this, Milbank claims that "the key distinguishing mark of Christian social teaching in the nineteenth and twentieth centuries — whether Catholic, Calvinist or Anglican" is "the advocacy of complex space" (*The Word Made Strange*, 271). With the idea of complex space he has in mind a society of "'intermediate associations' which variegate the monotonous harmony of sovereign state and sovereign individual" (271). Cf. Rasmusson, *The Church as "Polis,"* ch. 15.

ble. He mentions, for example, the egalitarianism built into Christian baptism, the political importance of forgiveness, the economic reality implied in the eucharist, the practices of the open church meeting, and the role of each individual in the common life of the church owing to the universality of the gifts of the Spirit.[114] Because they are not only elements of a theory, but concrete social practices, he thinks they have a degree of general intelligibility that an abstract Christian theory lacks.[115] It is also his claim that these types of practices, in various ways, historically have influenced general society and still have that potential.

To sum up, Yoder argues that cultures, societies, and states are not unified and mono-causal systems and that there are many different sorts of power and different ways of resisting, influencing, and relating to societies and states. It is never, and this is true for any interesting moral position, only a question of involvement versus withdrawal in general, but of a discriminating attitude and practice, which means different relations to different parts of societies and states. And because societies and states are different, the possible relations between them and the church will also differ greatly. Being in control of the central power system is not the only and not even the most important and especially not the most creative way of being "responsible" for the society one lives in. To flesh out this claim, and his correlative assertion about the interpretative power of the Christian discourse-practice, I would need to discuss concrete historical cases and in some detail show how a Christian interpretation makes a difference, but there is no space for that in this essay. I have elsewhere at some length and with the help of modern social theory tried to show the plausibility of the understanding of social change Yoder defends.[116] His own writings are also filled with examples, although one would have wished that he had developed some of these examples at much further length. He mentions the many books of the late French sociologist, historian, and theologian Jacques Ellul as perhaps the best example of a social theorist interpreting the modern world in

114. Yoder, *For the Nations: Essays Public and Evangelical* (Grand Rapids: Eerdmans, 1997), 43-46.

115. "The challenge to the faith community should not be to dilute or filter or translate its witness, so that the 'public' community can handle it without believing, but so to purify and clarify and exemplify it that the world can perceive it to be good news without having to learn a foreign language" (Yoder, *For the Nations,* 24).

116. See esp. Rasmusson, *The Church as "Polis,"* ch. 15, and "Kristen social teologi och modernitetens villkor. Från Ernst Troeltsch till John Milbank," *Tidsskrift for teologi og kirke,* 68:4, 1997, 243-71. In addition to the literature mentioned there, see now also James C. Scott, *Seeing Like a State: How Certain Schemes to Improve the Human Condition Have Failed* (New Haven: Yale University Press, 1998).

ARNE RASMUSSON

terms of the powers.[117] The fruitfulness of this perspective is also seen in the work of people like Stanley Hauerwas,[118] John Milbank, Nancey Murphy, and David Toole.[119] And much of this recent fruitful theological work is directly or indirectly heavily influenced by the work of Yoder — and in particular Yoder's overcoming of Troeltsch's dichotomistic understanding of social theology.[120]

117. Yoder, *The Politics of Jesus*, 157, 159. See also Marva Dawn's article in this volume, 168-86.

118. Yoder's relation to Hauerwas is an interesting issue that I cannot deal with here. Only one observation is in order. Hauerwas's theology, as we know it, is unthinkable without the influence of Yoder. But Yoder was not always happy with how he was used by Hauerwas. (See Hauerwas's wonderful tribute to Yoder, "Remembering John Howard Yoder," in *First Things* 82 [April 1998]: 15-16.) The last book Yoder published during his lifetime has the title *For the Nations*, and its first sentence reads: "The theme of this book is the tone of voice, or the style and stance, of the people of God in the dispersion" (1). That this partly was aimed at Hauerwas is obvious, whose "contrarian" style (one of Hauerwas's books has the title *Against the Nations*) Yoder seemed less than happy with. Yoder seemed more interested in discovering commonalities and possibilities than Hauerwas. This leads to an obvious difference in writing style. Yoder could, e.g., write an essay called "The Christian Case for Democracy" (in Yoder, *The Priestly Kingdom*, ch. 8), while Hauerwas writes things like "The Democratic Policing of Christianity" (in Hauerwas, *Dispatches from the Front: Theological Engagements with the Secular* [Durham 1994], ch. 4) with subtitles such as "Democracy and the Death of Protestantism." And Hauerwas, on his side, sometimes criticizes Yoder, e.g., for his positive use of the idea of the "voluntary church," which Hauerwas thinks is imbued with liberal assumptions. I think Yoder would answer that it is not helpful to criticize the language of "voluntary" (or "democracy," "egalitarianism," "human rights," and so on) in general. Instead you have analytically to differentiate between different uses of this language. One can imagine him writing a memo "To whom it may concern" with, say, twelve different uses of the word "voluntary," some of which are helpful, some of which are neutral, and some of which are harmful. Although Hauerwas's suspicions often are well-founded, I think Yoder is right on the need for this type of analytical distinctions. Making such distinctions may also be a way of creating a free space for different uses, while sweeping rejections easily make one into a prisoner of the dominant language. Cf. my own discussion of Hauerwas's indiscriminate rejection of the language of public and private in Rasmusson, *The Church as "Polis,"* 296-98. So although Yoder's analytical style sometimes can be exasperating, and Hauerwas's rhetoric often is enjoyable and powerful, Hauerwas could often strengthen and clarify his case if at times he also in this learned something from Yoder.

119. See Toole, *Waiting for Godot in Sarajevo: Theological Reflections on Nihilism, Tragedy, and Apocalypse* (Boulder: Westview Press, 1998).

120. Many thanks to Jim Fodor, Stanley Hauerwas, Chris Huebner, Harry Huebner, Reinhard Hütter (who also translated the German citations into English), Theron Schlabach, and Ross Wagner for helpful comments on earlier drafts.

Discipleship in a World Full of Nazis: Dietrich Bonhoeffer's Polyphonic Pacifism as Social Ethics

Mark Thiessen Nation

Preface

In 1984 I had the privilege of attending a significant conference in Seattle, Washington commemorating the fiftieth anniversary of the Barmen Declaration of Faith, the document that served as the rallying point for the Confessing Church movement in Nazi Germany.[1] Among many notable speakers was Dietrich Bonhoeffer's first very close friend, Franz Hildebrandt. In the course of his lecture Hildebrandt extemporaneously remarked "if there is any one book every pastor should read it is *The Politics of Jesus* by John Howard Yoder."[2] Twenty-five years earlier Hildebrandt had written a foreword to the booklet version of Yoder's essay, "Peace Without Eschatology:"

---

1. The confession is included as an appendix in Arthur C. Cochrane, *The Church's Confession Under Hitler*, 2nd ed. (Pittsburgh: Pickwick Press, 1976), 230-34. For a discussion of the confession in its historical context, see Klaus Scholder, *The Churches and the Third Reich, Volume Two: The Year of Disillusionment 1934, Barmen and Rome*, 2nd ed., trans. John Bowden (Philadelphia: Fortress Press, 1988).

2. This is not an exact quote, but my memory of what he said. Yoder was in the audience when this was said. (He was referring to John Howard Yoder, *The Politics of Jesus* [Grand Rapids: Eerdmans, 1972].) In the published version of his lecture Hildebrandt simply lists *The Politics of Jesus* as "essential literature" in a footnote to a comment affirming pacifism: Franz Hildebrandt, "Barmen: What to Learn and What Not to Learn," in *The Barmen Confession: Papers from the Seattle Assembly*, ed. Hubert G. Locke (Lewiston, NY: The Edwin Mellen Press, 1986), 302.

What is commonly said from the pulpits about this subject [peace], if it is mentioned at all, would, as Dr. Yoder points out, "be just as possible, if Christ had never become incarnate, died, risen, ascended to heaven, and sent His Spirit." We are ineffective precisely because we are disobedient. In a theological and ecclesiastical climate where "otherworldliness" is banished from the New Testament, where any literal application of the Gospel is suspect of "Schwärmertum" and where only the ex-pacifist is respectable, it will take some time and not a little humility to admit, especially for those trained in the school of the great Reformers, that at this point in question the Mennonite minority has been, and still is right: "not because it (nonresistance) works, but because it anticipates the triumph of the Lamb that was slain."[3]

What is intriguing to me is that Hildebrandt's comments apply, rather precisely, to what has often happened to the legacy of his dear friend, Dietrich Bonhoeffer. Bonhoeffer is deemed respectable precisely because he is perceived to be an "ex-pacifist." That he was, in his youth, a pacifist makes him admirable, in that it shows he was morally serious. That, in his maturity, he outgrew his pacifism, makes him a model for many interpreters of Bonhoeffer's social ethics legacy.

These interpreters make of Bonhoeffer's complicity in plotting for a projected tyrannicide an ethical paradigm, and see the later writings as Bonhoeffer's apology for that involvement. Since tyrannicide is not what the Sermon on the Mount commands, the interpretation goes, of course *Nachfolge* had to be left behind. If the conspiracy were to be taken as a prime paradigm, then truly there would have to be a "shift" somewhere. Bonhoeffer would then have to be seen as turning away from the reality of the visible church even though the Tegel letters testify to the contrary. He must be seen as forsaking the continuity of faith, even though the "nonreligious interpretation of biblical concepts" had the announced precise intent of reaffirming that continuity in a changing world. The — unsuccessful — plotting on Hitler's life must be seen as the crowning work of his life even though he was not at its center and it did more harm than good.[4]

Bonhoeffer is perceived as moving through stages that led to his eventual mature position wherein he realizes the necessity of violence.[5] In this way the

3. Franz Hildebrandt, foreword to John H. Yoder *Peace Without Eschatology?* (A Concern Reprint) (Scottdale, PA: Herald Press, 1961), 3-4.
4. John H. Yoder, "The Christological Presuppositions of Discipleship," Paper presented to the Bonhoeffer Society at the American Academy of Religion meeting, November 1987, 25, Mark Thiessen Nation Collection.
5. All of us who appreciate the legacy of Bonhoeffer cannot help but be grateful for the

Bonhoeffer social ethics legacy avoids the taint of association with the "Schwärmertum."[6] Having thus freed the Bonhoeffer legacy from his immature "phase" of a preoccupation with the Sermon on the Mount and discipleship, we are in a position to see that this ex-pacifist's central teaching regarding social ethics is to be "responsible," even if that way of living would "be just as possible, if Christ had never become incarnate, died, risen, ascended to heaven, and sent His Spirit."

However, it is as difficult for me as for John Yoder or Franz Hildebrandt to believe that "responsibility" is appropriate as a centrally defining term for a Christian understanding of peace. And unless I totally misread the life and writings of Dietrich Bonhoeffer, this is not an appropriate grid through which to read his central teaching. All of this is to say, Bonhoeffer's legacy regarding social ethics and the use of violence is often far too captive to a Niebuhrian[7] (and Troeltschian) scheme wherein "pacifism comes to appear a naive luxury, dependent on secure circumstances and gentlemanly enemies. It concedes that 'realism' requires unscrupulous force to be met by force."[8]

In 1989 I first attempted to address what I believed to be the distorted reading of Bonhoeffer's pacifism through writing an almost fifty-page essay fo-

---

great labor of his friend Eberhard Bethge in preserving and promoting that legacy. And yet, after reading Bethge and talking with Hildebrandt, I can't help but wonder if Hildebrandt might not have had more sympathy with the following interpretation than would Bethge. On Bethge's use of a stage theory see Eberhard Bethge, "Bonhoeffer's Pacifism: Some Comments by Eberhard Bethge," *Newsletter for the International Bonhoeffer Society for Archive and Research* (April 1978): 6-7; also see Andreas Pangritz, "Sharing the Destiny of His People," in *Bonhoeffer for a New Day*, ed. John W. de Gruchy (Grand Rapids: Eerdmans, 1997), 258.

6. *"Schwärmertum"* is the term of derision used by mainstream church authorities to refer to a variety of "radicals." It is usually translated as enthusiasts or fanatics. I imagine some similar slur was intended when Bonhoeffer was accused of "reviving legalism and monasticism." See Eberhard Bethge, *Dietrich Bonhoeffer: Man of Vision, Man of Courage,* trans. Eric Mosbacher et al. (New York: Harper & Row, 1970), 410. It is also interesting to note that Bethge feels compelled, in commenting on *The Cost of Discipleship,* to distance that book from "the peaceful backwater of the Pietists . . . [and] the other-worldliness of the Enthusiasts, neither of which remain in touch with reality" (Bethge, *Dietrich Bonhoeffer,* 378).

7. It has struck me for years that Bonhoeffer, by this interpretation, was the perfect embodiment of Reinhold Niebuhr's influential views on Christian pacifism. For critiques of Niebuhr's views see John Howard Yoder, "Reinhold Niebuhr and Christian Pacifism." *The Mennonite Quarterly Review* 29 (April 1955): 101-17 and Mark Nation, "Those Damned Pacifists: On the Horns of Niebuhr's Dilemma," in *Church Divinity 1990/1991,* ed. John H. Morgan (Bristol, IN: Windham Hall Press, 1991), 30-45.

8. G. Clarke Chapman, "What Would Bonhoeffer Say Today to Christian Peacemakers?" in *Bonhoeffer's Ethics: Old Europe and New Frontiers,* ed. Guy Carter et al. (Kampen, The Netherlands: Kok Pharos Publishing House, 1991), 226. Chapman is here speaking of the "price to Bethge's defense [of his understanding of Bonhoeffer's pacifism]."

cused narrowly on the question of pacifism as typically understood. An abbreviated version of this was published in 1991.[9] John Yoder wrote a letter to me
responding to the published version. Though he was appreciative, he expressed
critiques. One of them concerned "the simplicity with which you equate pacifism with moral absolutism."[10] I knew what he meant.[11] The following is my
attempt to offer an alternative construal of Bonhoeffer's pacifism, one provoked by Yoder's comment. Though I doubt seriously that what follows would
have satisfied John Yoder's exacting standards, nonetheless I hope it gives
honor to the man from whom I have learned so much, including this way of
reading Bonhoeffer and his pacifism.

Introduction

While writing this essay I asked a British coworker here at the London Mennonite Centre what she knew about Dietrich Bonhoeffer. She stated two things: he
was a pastor and he participated in a plot to kill Hitler. This squared with my
previous experience. Usually if someone knows anything about Bonhoeffer it is
that he was involved in these conspiracies. At academic conferences as well, if
one is discussing social ethics or the question of the use of violence, one can almost be assured that if Bonhoeffer's name is evoked, it will be because he was
involved in a plot to kill Hitler.

Of course, when asked, many also know that Bonhoeffer wrote *The Cost
of Discipleship* and *Life Together*.[12] And yet, when it comes to offering scholarly
reflections on the social ethics legacy of Bonhoeffer, these writings are often
largely ignored. Instead "responsibility" becomes the interpretive key, responsi-

9. Mark K. Nation, "'Pacifist and Enemy of the State': Bonhoeffer's 'Straight and Unbroken Course' from Costly Discipleship to Conspiracy," *Journal of Theology for Southern Africa* 77
(December 1991): 61-77. In this essay on Dietrich Bonhoeffer I argued basically two points.
First, using Larry Rasmussen's definition of pacifism, I argued that Bonhoeffer was probably
never a total pacifist, though his position was probably closer to pacifism than to any other position available to him on the use of violence. Second, I argued that he held this position rather
consistently from approximately 1930 or 1931 to the end of his life.

10. Letter from John H. Yoder to Mark Nation, 24 February 1992.

11. Larry Rasmussen had quite effectively used Yoder's critique of Barth as a way of criti-
cizing Bonhoeffer's aversion to moral principles in his *Dietrich Bonhoeffer: Reality and Resistance* (Nashville: Abingdon Press, 1972), 149ff. Yoder's more recent essay, "'Patience' as Method
in Moral Reasoning: Is an Ethic of Discipleship 'Absolute'?", in this volume, 24-42, is an incisive
response to the notion that pacifism, or a discipleship ethic, is peculiarly absolutist.

12. Dietrich Bonhoeffer, *The Cost of Discipleship*, rev. ed., trans. R. H. Fuller (New York:
Macmillan, 1959); *Life Together*, trans. John W. Doberstein (New York: Harper & Bros., 1954).

bility as it is defined by involvement in a conspiracy and illuminated by phrases like "arresting the wheel."[13]

On one level this essay could be seen as a retrieval. It is a retrieval of what was central to Bonhoeffer in thinking about social ethics, including the issue of the use of violence. Ernst Feil once stated that "[*The Cost of Discipleship*] is of no little significance for the study of Bonhoeffer's Christology" despite the fact that "not much attention has been paid to this fact."[14] So, likewise, *The Cost of Discipleship* is of "no little significance" for the study of Bonhoeffer's social ethics and views about violence, despite the inattention to this fact.

What I hope to demonstrate is that if one is to understand the theological and social ethics of Dietrich Bonhoeffer it is a mistake to ignore *The Cost of Discipleship*. *Cost* was not "merely" a devotional work for Bonhoeffer. Nor did it represent a position he outgrew when he entered the "real" world of responsibility as a Niebuhrian analysis might suggest. Rather, the thought in *Cost* represents a trajectory Bonhoeffer's life and thought followed from approximately 1931 to the end of his life. Given this fact, it is hardly adequate to make some vague concept such as "responsibility," linked to tyrannicide, the heart of the social ethics legacy of Bonhoeffer. Rather Jesus Christ, Christian community, and discipleship are the key terms for Bonhoeffer when describing what it means to be Christian in the world.

On a second level this essay is an attempt to take Bonhoeffer even more at his word than I did in my earlier essay. That is to say, Bonhoeffer said he was a pacifist at various times, but articulated his understanding of this most fully in *The Cost of Discipleship*. He specifically reaffirmed the thrust of that book in a letter from prison.[15] And, furthermore, it was in prison that he said, "I'm firmly convinced — however strange it may seem — that my life has followed a straight and unbroken course, at any rate in its outward conduct."[16]

On a third level I am taking a cue from Bonhoeffer, one I should have noted more fully before from Rasmussen. Larry Rasmussen says:

13. E.g., see John D. Godsey and Geffrey B. Kelly, eds., *Ethical Responsibility: Bonhoeffer's Legacy to the Churches* (Lewiston, NY: The Edwin Mellen Press, 1981); Robin W. Lovin, *Christian Faith and Public Choices: The Social Ethics of Barth, Brunner, and Bonhoeffer* (Philadelphia: Fortress Press, 1984), ch. 6; Wayne Whitson Floyd and Charles R. Marsh, eds., *Theology and the Practice of Responsibility: Essays on Dietrich Bonhoeffer* (Valley Forge, PA: Trinity Press International, 1993); Andreas Pangritz, "Sharing the Destiny of His People," in *Bonhoeffer for a New Day*, 269.

14. Ernst Feil, *The Theology of Dietrich Bonhoeffer*, trans. Martin Rumscheidt. (Philadelphia: Fortress Press, 1985), 78.

15. Dietrich Bonhoeffer, *Letters and Papers*, enlarged ed., trans. Reginald H. Fuller et al. (New York: Macmillan, 1971), 369.

16. Bonhoeffer, *Letters and Papers*, 272.

what counts [for Bonhoeffer] is the formation of the self into Christ's form, formation occurring in communion with the living Christ; furthermore, and decisively, the testing of Christian action is referred to the self's preparation for receiving Christ's concrete command. What really matters for ethics happens in character formation.[17]

Bonhoeffer himself says this in the essay intended to be a programmatic introduction to his book *Ethics*, "Ethics as Formation":[18]

It is not by astuteness, by knowing the tricks, but only by simple steadfastness in the truth of God, by training the eye upon this truth until it is simple and wise, that there comes the experience and the knowledge of ethical reality. . . . The point of departure for Christian ethics is the body of Christ, the form of Christ in the form of the Church, and formation of the Church in conformity with the form of Christ.[19]

This is Bonhoeffer's way of affirming in a formal way not only what he had articulated in his book, *The Cost of Discipleship*, but what had been the focus of his life up to and including this time. Discipleship, conformity to Christ, in his own life, situated within the life of the church, was his preoccupation. That preoccupation did not change in the last stage of his life. There is a consistency throughout, just as he claimed.

In order to establish my thesis I will focus first on the themes that are central to *The Cost of Discipleship*. Next I will look at how these same themes are prominent in the life and writings of Bonhoeffer beyond this book, including a brief look at the disparity, real and imagined, between *Cost* and themes mentioned or developed in *Ethics* and *Letters and Papers from Prison*, and embodied in his life. The concluding section offers interpretations which respect both the consistency of Bonhoeffer's teaching and the extreme nature of his context.

Discipleship: The Book

It is not primarily the purpose of this paper to establish that the book *The Cost of Discipleship* itself is central among Bonhoeffer's writings. Rather it is the larger claim that the convictions most fully articulated in *Cost* represent the

17. Rasmussen, *Dietrich Bonhoeffer: Reality and Resistance*, 158.
18. Hans Pfeifer, "Ethics for the Renewal of Life: A Reconstruction of Its Concept," in *Bonhoeffer for a New Day*, 140.
19. Bonhoeffer, *Ethics*, 65, 84.

convictions that were most central to Bonhoeffer's life and thought from approximately 1931 to the end of his life. And, further, it is the claim that these convictions were, for Bonhoeffer, inseparable from his views on social ethics.

However, since *Cost* does represent the clearest exposition of these convictions, it is important that we deal first with the book itself. And here a few comments need to be made before I turn to its contents. First, it is important that we remember that, contrary to the opinion of some, *Cost* was not a book that arose out of the events of 1933.[20] As Bethge reminds us: "It might be said that in 1932 not only were the basic tendency and basic questions underlying *The Cost of Discipleship* already in existence in a complete form, but the answers had also been formulated."[21] Again, according to Bethge, "It was [Jean] Lasserre who provided the first impulse for his great book *The Cost of Discipleship*."[22] This "first impulse" began during Bonhoeffer's year at Union Theological Seminary in 1930-31, during which time he was friends with the budding pacifist Jean Lasserre, with whom he also lectured on pacifism.

Second, it is important to note that nothing preoccupied Bonhoeffer more during his brief life than the Sermon on the Mount and the writing of *Cost*.[23] As has been mentioned, his preoccupation began in 1930 or 1931.[24] The first notes for the book were made in 1934 while Bonhoeffer was in London. The actual writing was done between 1935 and 1937.[25] Of course this means that the writing was done while he was director of the seminary (first at Zingst, then) at Finkenwalde. Therefore, much of the writing was originally done for presentation as lectures. But, according to Bethge, even long after the book was published in 1937, i.e., at least as late as the spring of 1940, Bonhoeffer's "theology and his language still resembled what was to be read in his *Cost of Disciple-*

20. For a good discussion of the context from which *Cost* came and its significance see Bethge, *Dietrich Bonhoeffer*, 368-79.

21. Bethge, *Dietrich Bonhoeffer*, 377.

22. Bethge, *Dietrich Bonhoeffer*, 112. See Lasserre's disavowal of any deep influence in Geffrey B. Kelly, F.S.C., "An Interview with Jean Lasserre," *Union Seminary Quarterly Review* 27 (Spring 1972): 149-60; cf. F. Burton Nelson, "The Relationship of Jean Lasserre to Dietrich Bonhoeffer's Peace Concerns in the Struggle of Church and Culture," *Union Seminary Quarterly Review* 40 (Spring & Summer 1985): 71-84. I must say that Lasserre's disavowal clearly strikes me as simply a case of modesty. For it is clear that Bonhoeffer was close friends with Lasserre during his time at Union Seminary in 1930-31. And it is clear that his preoccupation with the Sermon on the Mount and with pacifism began about the time he became friends with Lasserre, the only obvious influence in that direction in his life at that time.

23. Bethge speaks of Bonhoeffer's "perpetual concern with the Sermon on the Mount." (Bethge, *Dietrich Bonhoeffer*, 298).

24. See also Bethge, *Dietrich Bonhoeffer*, 141, 153-56, 158.

25. Bethge, *Dietrich Bonhoeffer*, 377.

ship and *Life Together*."[26] And, finally, it must be kept in mind that toward the end of his life, in a letter of July 21, 1944, Bonhoeffer said that he could ". . . see the dangers of [*The Cost of Discipleship*], though I still stand by what I wrote."[27]

Since *The Cost of Discipleship* is a well-known work it is not necessary to attempt a summary of its entire contents. Rather what I want to do in the next few paragraphs is to point to some of its central themes — Jesus Christ, the church, and discipleship — suggesting that these central themes were central not only in *Cost* but in Bonhoeffer's life and thought generally, including his social ethic.

First, the centrality of Jesus Christ. On the very first page of *Cost* Bonhoeffer refers to Jesus Christ as "the sole object of it all." Or as he puts it a little later: "Beside Jesus nothing has any significance. He alone matters."[28] And this is not an ethereal Jesus. This is the Jesus "who came to the publicans and sinners, the weak and the poor, the erring and the hopeless." It is also important to note that at the outset of *Cost* Bonhoeffer is pursuing the existential meaning of Jesus: "What did Jesus mean to say to us? What is his will for us today?"[29] This is only a slightly different version of the more famous statement in his letter from prison about "who Christ really is, for us today."[30] *Cost* represents for Bonhoeffer an antidote to an abstract Christology, i.e., a Christology divorced both from the Jesus of the Gospels and the current life of the church.[31] "Revival of church life," says Bonhoeffer, "always brings in its train a richer understanding of the Scriptures."[32]

Bonhoeffer was convinced, as is obvious in *Cost,* that a new look at Jesus and the Sermon on the Mount in the Scriptures could bring such revival. And thus the whole of *Cost* is Bonhoeffer's attempt to recapture the richness of the life and teachings of Jesus of Nazareth, the One who is central within the Scriptures, the One Christians confess to be the incarnate Word of God. But, of course, Bonhoeffer also thought it important that Christians confess that the Lord is risen and alive today. "The body of the exalted Lord is also a visible body in the shape of the Church." This visibility is evident, says Bonhoeffer, partly through the preached Word and the Sacraments. One might expect this way of putting it from a German Protestant theologian. However, that is not all, says Bonhoeffer.

26. Bethge, *Dietrich Bonhoeffer*, 580.
27. Dietrich Bonhoeffer, *Letters and Papers from Prison*, 369.
28. Bonhoeffer, *The Cost of Discipleship*, 37, 63.
29. Bonhoeffer, *The Cost of Discipleship*, 41, 37.
30. Bonhoeffer, *Letters and Papers*, 279.
31. For a direct statement regarding this concern see Bonhoeffer, *The Cost of Discipleship*, 63-64.
32. Bonhoeffer, *The Cost of Discipleship*, 37.

> The Church needs space not only for her liturgy and order, but also for the daily life of her members in the world. That is why we must now speak of the living-space *(Lebensraum)* of the visible Church. The fellowship between Jesus and his disciples covered every aspect of their daily life. . . . This common life bears living testimony to the concrete humanity of the Son of God.[33]

Though Bonhoeffer will, with justification, argue that this last point is not absent from Luther, clearly it was not emphasized by Bonhoeffer's contemporaries who were Lutheran theologians. But it was because of this conviction that Bonhoeffer had the other emphases I now mention.

Bonhoeffer could not discuss Christ without discussing the sociality of Christ, viz. the church. With the first line of *Cost*, Bonhoeffer reveals his concern with the church: "Revival of *church life* always brings in its train a richer understanding of the Scriptures."[34] This line signals that the whole book will be for and about the life of the church. Remember *Cost* was published while Bonhoeffer was teaching seminarians. And as Bethge has said, this book "was to become Finkenwalde's own badge of distinction."[35] Bonhoeffer clearly had the life of the church in mind when he wrote *Cost*. But just in case that point was missed, he wrote two chapters with the title, "The Visible Community." "The followers are a visible community; their discipleship visible in action which lifts them out of the world — otherwise it would not be discipleship. And of course the following is as visible to the world as a light in the darkness or a mountain rising from a plain."[36] Or, again,

> The member of the Body of Christ has been delivered from the world and called out of it. He must give the world a visible proof of his calling, not only by sharing in the Church's worship and discipline, but also through the new fellowship of brotherly living.

If this is not clear enough, he sets the church over against the world.

> Let [the Christian] remain in the world to engage in frontal assault on it, and let him live the life of his secular calling in order to show himself as a stranger in this world all the more. But that is only possible if we are visible members of the Church. The antithesis between the world and the Church must be borne out in the world.[37]

33. Bonhoeffer, *The Cost of Discipleship*, 278, 284. See also 277-304.
34. Bonhoeffer, *The Cost of Discipleship*, 37, emphasis mine.
35. Bethge, *Dietrich Bonhoeffer*, 369.
36. Bonhoeffer, *The Cost of Discipleship*, 132.
37. Bonhoeffer, *The Cost of Discipleship*, 289, 297.

As has already become obvious, it is the visibility of the church, this "brotherly living," this antithesis between the world and the church, which is connected to our third theme, discipleship. Needless to say, discipleship is emphasized in *The Cost of Discipleship*. However, it should be noted for anyone who has not read *Cost* that Bonhoeffer, as a good Lutheran, continually struggles to retain a robust sense of the grace of God. And although the book is wonderfully infused with a sense of the grace of God, Bonhoeffer's accent is elsewhere. He was convinced that grace had been emphasized at the expense of faithful obedience to the gracious God. "Grace alone does everything, they say, and so everything can remain as it was before." What this notion leads to, says Bonhoeffer, is "cheap grace."

> Cheap grace is the preaching of forgiveness without requiring repentance, baptism without church discipline, Communion without confession, absolution without personal confession. Cheap grace is grace without discipleship, grace without the cross, grace without Jesus Christ, living and incarnate.

On the other hand:

> Costly grace is the gospel which must be *sought* again and again, the gift which must be asked for, the door at which a man must *knock*. Such grace is *costly* because it calls us to follow *Jesus Christ*. It is costly because it costs a man his life, and it is grace because it gives a man the only true life.[38]

And this pursuit of costly grace is not a mere abstraction for Bonhoeffer. He illustrates the kind of behavior and attitude it leads to throughout the book. Among other things it includes renouncing revenge, loving enemies, being meek, pursuing mercy, raising up the oppressed, bearing testimony to the truth, living with few material possessions, and a willingness to suffer persecution and rejection for the sake of righteousness.[39]

This brief recounting of the basic themes of *The Cost of Discipleship* is perhaps not particularly controversial. The more difficult tasks remain. The first is to establish that these themes were not peculiarly central to *Cost* but rather were central for Bonhoeffer throughout the whole of his life and thought. The second task, which I will leave for the last section, is to wrestle with why *The Cost of Discipleship* and the thought it represents are not seen as more central to Bonhoeffer's

38. Bonhoeffer, *The Cost of Discipleship*, 46-47.
39. Though in some ways the argument for this understanding comprises the whole of the book, see esp. Bonhoeffer, *The Cost of Discipleship*, 133, 156-71, 192-201, 289.

social and theological ethics legacy. First, then, a discussion of the enduring themes offered through the narrative of Bonhoeffer's life.

Discipleship: Beyond the Book

It is not necessary for the purposes of this essay to attend to the details of Bonhoeffer's writings before 1931.[40] For it was apparently in 1931 that Bonhoeffer underwent transformations in his approach to Christian theology and certain Christian practices. Bonhoeffer himself says that before this point he "had not yet become a Christian."[41] Among the changes Bonhoeffer experienced after becoming a Christian were that he went regularly to church, engaged in systematic meditation on the Bible, spoke of the practice of oral confession, more frequently quoted the Sermon on the Mount "as a word to be acted upon," had an apparent piety, saw the revival of the church and its ministry as his supreme concern, and "suddenly saw as self-evident the Christian pacifism that [he] had recently passionately opposed."[42] It is neither possible nor necessary to ascertain what it was that precipitated Bonhoeffer's transformation. What we do know is that it came either at the end of his time in the U.S. or soon thereafter and that he subsequently threw himself into the Sermon on the Mount and the writing of what became *The Cost of Discipleship*.

Though there were many ways in which Bonhoeffer expressed his understanding of discipleship, certainly peace was a dominant expression. In a lecture at a Czechoslovakian youth peace conference in the summer of 1932, Bonhoeffer made one of his numerous statements on behalf of peace. He said:

> War in our day no longer falls under the concept of struggle because it is the certain self-annihilation of both combatants. It is in no way to be re-

40. This is not to suggest that there are no intellectual or lifestyle continuities before and after Bonhoeffer's "conversion" around 1931. There, of course, are. A number of ideas that were quite important to Bonhoeffer later were expressed first in his two dissertations. The importance of community and the sociality of Christ and the desire to hold act and being together found first expression in his dissertations. However, given that there are continuities, these concepts will be covered in what will be discussed here. Where there are discontinuities we will take Bonhoeffer at his word that his approach to theology has undergone a significant shift.

41. It is impossible to be certain when this transformation happened. From the available evidence it appears not to have happened before 1931, and 1931 appears to be the most likely candidate. For the evidence see Bethge, *Dietrich Bonhoeffer*, 153-56; Geffrey B. Kelly and F. Burton Nelson, eds., *A Testament of Freedom* (New York: Harper San Francisco, 1990), 444-50.

42. Bethge, *Dietrich Bonhoeffer*, 153-56.

garded as an order of preservation in the light of revelation, simply because it is so destructive. The power of annihilation extends both to the inner and the outer man. . . . War today, and therefore the next war, must be utterly *rejected* by the church. . . . Nor should we be afraid of the word pacifism today.[43]

About a month later, at another youth conference at Gland, Bonhoeffer struck the same note. He said:

The church renounces obedience should she sanction war. The church of Christ stands against war for peace among men, between nations, classes and races. But the church also knows that there is no peace unless righteousness and truth are preserved. . . . But it must be a struggle out of love for the other, a struggle *of the spirit, and not of the flesh.*[44]

About the same time Bonhoeffer also delivered a lecture to the German Student Christian Movement in Berlin, entitled *Christ and Peace (Christus und der Friede).* Here, in this brief address he includes the emphases on Jesus, the church, and discipleship in ways clearly foreshadowing *The Cost of Discipleship.* First he comments about how, once again, "worldly courts of justice" have failed in establishing peace. He says Christians should not be particularly surprised and should realize such courts have no absolute authority. "There is only one authority, the one who has spoken in a binding way on this question, and that is Jesus Christ. . . . For the simple reader, the Sermon on the Mount says things that are entirely unmistakable." And later: "So long as the world is without God, there will be wars. For Christ, rather, it is a matter of our loving God and standing in discipleship to Jesus in whom we are called with the promise of blessedness to become witnesses for peace." In case he has not yet been explicit enough, Bonhoeffer goes on:

The command, "you shall not kill," and the Word "love your enemy," are given to us simply to obey. Every form of war service, unless it be Good Samaritan service, and every preparation for war, is forbidden for the Christian. Faith that sees freedom from the law as a mere arbitrary disposal of the law is only human faith in defiance of God. Simple obedience knows nothing of the fine distinction between good and evil. It lives in the discipleship of Christ and does the good work as something self-evident.

---

43. Dietrich Bonhoeffer, *No Rusty Swords,* ed. Edwin H. Robertson (London: Collins, 1970), 166.

44. Bonhoeffer, *No Rusty Swords,* 183.

He also responds to the typical question about love for enemies being valid only for personal, face to face relationships:

> What is sin for an individual is never virtue for an entire people or nation. What is proclaimed as the gospel to the church, the congregation, and thereby, the individual Christian, is spoken to the world as a judgment. When a people refuses to hear this command, then Christians are called forth from that people to give witness to peace. Let us take care, however, that we miserable sinners proclaim peace from a spirit of love and not from any zeal for security or from any mere political aim.

And, finally: "The weapons in this conflict with the enemy of the gospel are faith and love, which is purified by suffering. How much greater this than the conflict for mere earthly goods."[45]

On April 7th, 1933, the German government issued the Aryan Clauses, which forbade those of Jewish origin to hold state office. This directly affected the church, since pastors worked for the state. Under this legislation Jewish Christians would be forbidden to work for the church. Bonhoeffer was one of the first in the Confessing Church movement to speak out on this question. But not only did he speak out early, he also spoke out for Jews qua Jews and not just for Jews who were a part of the church. Many leaders in the church never spoke out on behalf of all Jews. In an essay Bonhoeffer said that the church should act in three ways for the Jews in general. First, it should ask the state whether its actions are legitimate given the character of a state. Second, it can aid victims of any abuses by the state. And, third, it can engage in direct political action when that becomes necessary, i.e., "jam a spoke in the wheel."[46] These were ways for the church to act for Jews in relation to the state. For the church itself, however, the impact of the Aryan Clauses was a serious theological matter. Bonhoeffer boldly declared that "the church cannot allow its actions towards its members to be prescribed by the state." He argued:

> What is at stake is by no means the question whether our German members of congregations can still tolerate church fellowship with the Jews. It is

45. Kelly and Nelson, *A Testament of Freedom*, 99-101. In a lecture given November 19, 1932, Bonhoeffer gave another lecture, entitled "Thy Kingdom Come," in which he spelled out in more detail the tensions between church and world and how both relate to the Kingdom of God. See "Thy Kingdom Come: The Prayer of the Church for God's Kingdom on Earth," in *Preface to Bonhoeffer: The Man and Two of His Shorter Writings*, ed. John D. Godsey (Philadelphia: Fortress Press, 1965), 27-47.

46. Bonhoeffer, *No Rusty Swords*, 221; the whole paper is on pp. 217-25. For context see Bethge, *Dietrich Bonhoeffer*, 206-10.

rather the task of Christian preaching to say: here is the church, where Jew and German stand together under the Word of God; here is the proof whether a church is still the church or not.[47]

In the summer of 1933 Bonhoeffer gave a series of lectures on Christology in a seminar at Berlin University. Though of course there is much of interest in these lectures, I can only mention some of the most salient points.[48] First, from beginning to end the Christology which Bonhoeffer articulates is an engaged, existential Christology. He speaks first of Christ *pro me* then, later on, of Christ *pro nobis*. Second, and related, is Bonhoeffer's focus on the sociality of Christ, the presence of Christ within the church.[49] And, finally, Bonhoeffer wants to avoid the liberal splitting of Jesus and Christ. The church only knows Jesus as the Christ. The Christ of faith is the only historical Jesus we know. These three christological themes are present in a variety of ways in most of Bonhoeffer's writings. We will return to this in the last part of the essay.

On October 17, 1933, Bonhoeffer moved to a German parish in South London, where he served as pastor for the next year and a half. "His deepest commitment at this time . . . was to his reflections on the Sermon on the Mount and on 'discipleship.'"[50] During this time, Herbert Jehle, a pacifist, often visited him. They discussed Gandhi and pacifism. The fruit of his intense study of the Sermon on the Mount included sermons preached in London, a deepening of his desire to study with Gandhi, as well as work on *The Cost of Discipleship*.

Bonhoeffer's ecumenical activity also continued while he was in London. Among other things he attended the ecumenical Youth Conference at Fanö, Denmark at the end of August, 1934. On the second day Bonhoeffer spoke on the theme, "The Universal Church and the World of Nations." The manuscript of the

47. Bonhoeffer, *No Rusty Swords*, 223, 225. One response Bonhoeffer (and Martin Niemöller) made to the Aryan Clauses was to issue a formal "Declaration" responding to the Clauses as they affected the ministry of the church, a declaration that became a call to form the Pastor's Emergency League (244-45).

48. The lectures are published as Dietrich Bonhoeffer, *Christ the Center*, trans. Edwin H. Robertson (New York: Harper San Francisco, 1978). For discussion of the lectures see Jaroslav Pelikan, "Bonhoeffer's *Christologie* of 1933," in Martin E. Marty, ed., *The Place of Bonhoeffer* (New York: Association Press, 1962), 145-65; Ernst Feil, *The Theology of Dietrich Bonhoeffer*, 74-76.

49. Of course this continues a theme begun in his first book, *Sanctorum Communio*, published in the U.S. as *The Communion of Saints*, trans. R. Gregor Smith (New York: Harper & Row, 1963).

50. Bethge, *Dietrich Bonhoeffer*, 256; see also Wolf-Dieter Zimmermann and Ronald Gregor Smith, eds., *I Knew Dietrich Bonhoeffer*, trans. Kathe Gregor Smith (London: Collins, 1973), 77-103.

lecture is missing. According to Bethge, in this lecture, Bonhoeffer, for the first time "declared that there could be no justification for war, even where that war was defensive."[51] In a sermon on the same topic, also given at the Fanö conference, Bonhoeffer made some very strong statements on behalf of peace. "Peace on earth is not a problem, but a commandment given at Christ's coming."

> There shall be peace because of the church of Christ, for the sake of which the world exists. And this church of Christ lives at one and the same time in all peoples, yet beyond all boundaries, whether national, political, social, or racial. . . . For [Christians] know that whoso is not able to hate father and mother for his sake is not worthy of him, and lies if he calls himself after Christ's name. These brothers in Christ obey his word; they do not doubt or question, but keep his commandment of peace. They are not ashamed, in defiance of the world, even to speak of eternal peace. They cannot take up arms against Christ himself — yet this is what they do if they take up arms against one another!

His next statement indicated both Bonhoeffer's realism and his awareness of the thought and activities of Gandhi.

> There is no way to peace along the way of safety. For peace must be dared. . . . Peace is the opposite of security. . . . Peace means to give oneself altogether to the law of God. . . . Battles are won, not with weapons, but with God. They are won where the way leads to the cross. Which of us can say he knows what it might mean for the world if one nation should meet the aggressor, not with weapons in hand, but praying, defenceless, and for that very reason protected by 'a bulwark never failing'?[52]

The group discussions at Fanö, led by Bonhoeffer, were principally concerned with the universal nature of the church and the question of conscientious objection.[53]

On three occasions between the late 1920s and 1934 Bonhoeffer gave thought to visiting Gandhi in India. In 1934 he secured an invitation to visit Gandhi's *ashram.* Bonhoeffer hoped to visit at the end of 1934. There is no question but that his interest in being with Gandhi was intricately connected with his involvement with the Sermon on the Mount. As Bethge says:

51. Bethge, *Dietrich Bonhoeffer,* 311.
52. Bonhoeffer, *No Rusty Swords,* 285-86.
53. Bethge, *Dietrich Bonhoeffer,* 314. Bonhoeffer also helped to pass two resolutions — one for conscientious objection, one against nationalism — at Fanö (Bonhoeffer, *No Rusty Swords,* 289).

Bonhoeffer was motivated by the desire to witness the experiment along the lines of the Sermon on the Mount as exemplified by Gandhi — namely, the purposive exercises and the Indian methods of resistance to a power that was regarded as tyrannous. . . . What he sought was a prototype for passive resistance that could induce changes without violence. His quest concealed an unacknowledged anxiety that the church struggle might become an end in itself and remain satisfied with reiterated confessions and ceaseless activity. What he was aiming at, therefore, was a means of combating Hitler that went beyond the aims and methods of the church struggle while remaining legitimate from a Christian standpoint.[54]

However, for a third time, Bonhoeffer's visit was not realized. For when he first received the invitation, there was urgent business to attend to in relation to the London congregations. And when that was finished he was needed to begin a seminary training program back in Germany.

From 1935 until 1940 Bonhoeffer's time and energy were devoted mostly to the training of ministers for the Confessing Church movement. For two and a half years that training was done formally at the seminary at Finkenwalde. For the remaining time, except when Bonhoeffer was out of the country, the training was done through his appointment with a group of churches.

During the time at Finkenwalde Bonhoeffer was devoted to the theme of discipleship.[55] Not only was that preoccupation finally to issue in the book, *The Cost of Discipleship,* in 1937, but it also shaped Bonhoeffer's own life and the way in which he structured the life of the seminary community. To many, the rigorous discipline established for the daily life of the community seemed more like a monastery than a Protestant seminary. Along with normal study, meals, and recreation, each day was comprised of morning and evening common prayer, antiphonal repetition of the psalms, readings from other portions of Scripture, choral singing, Gregorian chants, and a half hour of silent meditation on a passage of Scripture.[56]

Bonhoeffer also established an inner community within the seminary for those who chose to participate in it. In addition to the other disciplines already mentioned, this "House of Brethren" required its members to adhere uncompromisingly to the Sermon on the Mount, participate in regular oral confession, and share their financial resources with one another.[57]

54. Bethge, *Dietrich Bonhoeffer,* 332.
55. Bethge, *Dietrich Bonhoeffer,* 341.
56. Mary Bosanquet, *The Life and Death of Dietrich Bonhoeffer* (New York: Harper & Row, 1968), 152.
57. Bethge, *Dietrich Bonhoeffer,* 379ff.

Bonhoeffer was criticized for the "monastic" lifestyle he required for the seminary and the House of Brothers. And there is no question but that he was attempting to form the disciplined community that he believed the church should always be, but especially would need to be in order to live faithfully in the difficult context of the Third Reich. For, contrary to what some critics believed, Bonhoeffer never saw the church or the Finkenwalde experiment as ends in themselves. Rather the discipline was ultimately to make them fit for service for God and others, to engage in "'the most inward concentration for the service of others.'"[58]

Bonhoeffer also continued to speak out on behalf of the "pacifism" he espoused. On March 16, 1935, military conscription was introduced in Germany. In May, Hitler made a speech relating to military service. The Finkenwalde students and their director heard the speech over the radio. Most of them were enthusiastic, wondering when their time to serve would come. Bonhoeffer had a different response. He suggested "that conscientious objection was something a Christian ought to consider."[59] The majority of the seminarians disagreed with him. And they undoubtedly did not agree with the two pacifists whom Bonhoeffer invited to speak at the seminary — Herbert Jehle, a physicist, and Hermann Stöhr, secretary of the German Fellowship of Reconciliation, a religious pacifist organization.

When the Chamby Youth Conference was held in 1935, Bonhoeffer did not attend. However, he did send a memorandum to propose some topics for discussion. Among them were conscientious objection and "the use of coercion, its right and its limitations."[60] In June and July of 1935, Bonhoeffer wrote an article entitled "The Confessing Church and the Ecumenical Movement," in which he asked the Ecumenical Council "whether it will speak a word of judgement about war, race hatred and social exploitation, whether through such true ecumenical unity of all evangelical Christians among all nations war itself will become impossible."[61]

In 1936 Bonhoeffer drafted a catechism. Among the questions in the catechism were questions about war: "How should the Christian act in war? There is no plain commandment of God on this point. The Church can never bless war or weapons. The Christian can never take part in an unjust war. If a Christian takes to the sword, he will daily pray to God for forgiveness of the sin and pray for peace."[62]

58. Bethge, *Dietrich Bonhoeffer*, 387.
59. Bethge, *Dietrich Bonhoeffer*, 352.
60. Bethge, *Dietrich Bonhoeffer*, 394.
61. Bonhoeffer, *No Rusty Swords*, 338-39.
62. Bethge, *Dietrich Bonhoeffer*, 144.

In April of 1937, Bonhoeffer prepared some notes on war and peace for the ecumenical conference to be held in Oxford in July. Among other things he said, "The Church of Christ must affirm this message [of peace] before the whole world. . . . The church may never surrender this world-wide commission, as it is contained in the Gospel, to anyone. . . . The church, then, appeals to Christendom and to the nations for peace."[63]

Beginning in the summer of 1937, Bonhoeffer's relationship with the church began to change. If we include the international church, the ecumenical church, his relationship had begun to change the previous year. For in 1936, according to Bethge, Bonhoeffer no longer expected much from the ecumenical movement.[64] But within Germany itself the government began more aggressively to attack the church in the summer of 1937. In July, Martin Niemöller, pastor at Dahlem and leader of the Confessing Church movement, was arrested, to be held for eight years. Shortly thereafter Niemöller's assistant and Bonhoeffer's close friend, Franz Hildebrandt, was arrested. On September 28 the doors to Finkenwalde were closed by the government as well. As Bethge puts it, by the fall of 1937 it "had become quite impossible to serve the Confessing Church while remaining within the law."[65]

Though these external threats to the life of the Confessing Church were serious, Bonhoeffer was more bothered by the internal failures of the church. These became especially apparent in 1938. This was the year, according to Bethge, when "the Confessing Church reached its lowest point."[66] On April 20, 1938, all pastors on active duty were required to take an oath of allegiance to the Führer. Bonhoeffer's name did not appear on a list of pastors; therefore he did not have to refuse to take the oath. Bonhoeffer was ashamed of the Confessing Church for, by and large, affirming the oath, especially when it already knew how difficult things were for the Jews and when the threat of war against Czechoslovakia became more apparent.

Two other events were to expose "the Confessing Church's commitment to nationalism." First, in late September of 1938, a liturgy was produced for the Confessing Church in which there was "an uncommonly daring confession of guilt . . . calling on the congregation to pray that the immediate threat of war might be averted." Second, at the same time, "a letter became public that Karl Barth had written from Basel to his colleague in Prague, Professor Hromadka, encouraging the Czecho-Slovaks to vigorous military resis-

63. Bonhoeffer, *The Way to Freedom*, ed. Edwin H. Robertson, trans. Edwin H. Robertson and John Bowden (London: Collins, 1972), 147-48.
64. Bethge, *Dietrich Bonhoeffer*, 462.
65. Bethge, *Dietrich Bonhoeffer*, 484.
66. Bethge, *Dietrich Bonhoeffer*, 501.

tance."[67] The government and the bulk of the Confessing Church responded quite negatively to both.

Following on the heels of these events was the "Crystal Night," on November 9, 1938. The Confessing Church was, by and large, silent in the face of these thousands of acts of terrorism against the Jewish population. Bethge says that "in that evil year Bonhoeffer began to separate himself from the rear-guard actions of the defeated remnants of the Confessing Church."[68]

To the man who had just a year earlier finished the manuscript of *The Cost of Discipleship,* silence in the face of terrorism against Jews was too much. To the man who had only very recently once again called on the church to love its enemies and be willing to suffer for its faithfulness to Christ, this was too much.[69] In March of 1939, Bonhoeffer left Germany mainly to avoid the compulsory military service to which men of his age were liable that year.[70] In June Bonhoeffer came to the U.S. for the second time. Many wanted this exciting young German theologian to stay. But he could not. He left New York after less than a month.

> I must live through this difficult period of our national history with the Christian people of Germany. I will have no right to participate in the reconstruction of Christian life in Germany after the war if I do not share the trials of this time with my people.[71]

Bonhoeffer's basic thought seemed unaltered at this point. In fact, in a conversation with Paul Lehmann shortly before leaving New York, Bonhoeffer confirmed specifically that he continued to embrace "pacifism" in the face of the possibility of revolution against Naziism.[72] According to Bethge, up through the spring of 1940 Bonhoeffer's "theology and his language still resembled what was to be read in his *Cost of Discipleship* and *Life Together.*"[73] However, the context into which Bonhoeffer returned was different. On August the 23rd of 1939, Bonhoeffer finished his final term with the ordinands at seminary. Though his official relationship to the church remained intact through 1943, his last direct work done on behalf of the church was done in 1940, when he took three pastoral journeys on behalf of the Council of Brethren. Severe re-

67. Bethge, *Dietrich Bonhoeffer,* 510.
68. Bethge, *Dietrich Bonhoeffer,* 512.
69. See, e.g., his sermons in early 1938 on "Christ's Love and Our Enemies" and "The Secret of Suffering," in Kelly and Nelson, *A Testament of Freedom,* 299-303, 304-8 respectively.
70. Bethge, *Dietrich Bonhoeffer,* 543.
71. Dietrich Bonhoeffer, *The Way to Freedom,* 246.
72. Lehmann, quoted in Rasmussen, *Dietrich Bonhoeffer: Reality and Resistance,* 58.
73. Bethge, *Dietrich Bonhoeffer,* 580.

strictions were soon placed on Bonhoeffer's public communication. In the autumn of 1940 he was forbidden to preach or give public speeches; the following March he was forbidden to publish.[74]

Now that Bonhoeffer could no longer speak publicly and had no church to work with or for which to train ordinands, he turned to "the only functioning community of which he could still feel a part, his family with its network of allies and friends."[75] One member of his family, Hans von Dohnanyi, worked for *Abwehr,* a military intelligence agency. Bonhoeffer joined *Abwehr* both because he could avoid the military draft by being in it and because a number of the men working in it were plotting the overthrow of the Hitler regime.

Often in discussions of this last phase of Bonhoeffer's free existence attention is focused on the violence, intrigue, and tyrannicide connected with Bonhoeffer's involvement in the conspiracy. Though we should not ignore these components of the efforts to overthrow the Hitler regime, we nonetheless should not overstate them. To begin with, Bonhoeffer's own role in the conspiracy was certainly not central; his central activities involved using his international contacts to let the world beyond Germany know there were those within Germany who opposed Hitler.[76] Furthermore, in his careful analysis, Larry Rasmussen has made it clear that virtually all of the conspirators were against acts that were either illegal or violent except as a last resort. Some were opposed to the use of violence altogether. Several of the scenarios for the overthrow of Hitler involved the use of no violence, unless things got out of hand and there was resistance.[77]

During 1941 and 1942, Bonhoeffer was also involved in a small rescue operation, called "Operation Seven," in which twelve to fifteen Jews were saved. His involvement in this operation may have led to his arrest.[78] In any event, on April 5, 1943, Bonhoeffer was arrested. The next two years were spent in prison, where, on April 9, 1945, he was executed.

During Bonhoeffer's last few years of freedom he wrote portions of what he hoped would become a book on ethics. While in prison he also wrote numerous letters. It would be good to provide a full discussion of *Ethics* and *Letters and Papers from Prison* in the light of Bonhoeffer's life and writings from

---

74. Bethge, *Dietrich Bonhoeffer,* 590, 599-602, 634.

75. James Wm. McClendon, Jr., *Systematic Theology, Vol. 1: Ethics* (Nashville: Abingdon Press, 1986), 203.

76. Bethge, *Dietrich Bonhoeffer,* 626ff.

77. Rasmussen, *Dietrich Bonhoeffer: Reality and Resistance,* 174-211.

78. Bethge, *Dietrich Bonhoeffer,* 649-51; 687.

1931 to 1943. I cannot do that here. However, let me make a few brief comments.[79]

First, anyone who was following Bonhoeffer scholarship in the 1960s and 1970s should be wary of sloganizing from Bonhoeffer's later writings. For instance, sometimes one would hardly have guessed that Bonhoeffer's fellow prisoners described him as a man of profound faith and deep prayer from the way in which "religionless Christianity" and other terms were thrown around in the 1960s.[80]

Second, we do well to remember the incomplete nature of these writings. From prison Bonhoeffer said of *Ethics* that "my ideas were still incomplete."[81] He also said about some of his writings from prison that they were "mainly critical; and so I'm looking forward to getting to the more constructive part."[82] Since they were incomplete and, in some instances at least, imbalanced, it is at best risky and at worst distorting to place too much emphasis on specific concepts from either set of writings, especially concepts that seem inconsistent with the basic thrust of his life or earlier writings.[83]

Third, within *Ethics* and from *Letters and Papers* there is at least as much to affirm the basic message of *The Cost of Discipleship* as there is to raise questions about it. For instance, in *Ethics* Bonhoeffer says that "testimony to Jesus Christ, is inseparably bound up with Holy Scripture."[84] He says that the "form of Christ is one and the same at all times and in all places."[85] He says that the "Sermon on the Mount is there for the purpose of being done."[86] And he speaks of individual Christians and the church being conformed to Christ.[87] Furthermore, he says

79. I have discussed both books at some length, albeit with a specific focus in my earlier paper, "'Pacifist and Enemy of the State,'" 36-41. I also almost wholeheartedly concur with the critique of Bonhoeffer's ethical method in Rasmussen, *Dietrich Bonhoeffer: Reality and Resistance*, 149-73.

80. For testimony of fellow prisoners see Zimmermann and Smith, eds., *I Knew Dietrich Bonhoeffer*, 222-32.

81. Bonhoeffer, *Letters and Papers*, 129.

82. Bonhoeffer, *Letters and Papers*, 393.

83. Three things seem apparent to me as I read *Ethics*. First, Bonhoeffer is working against dominant contemporary modes of understanding ethics. Second, he is searching for new categories and a new language with which to formulate ethics. And, third, in the midst of wrestling with new formulations, he is attempting to reaffirm that to which he is already committed. Needless to say, it is difficult even for someone as brilliant as Bonhoeffer to be precise when wrestling with new ideas, on the go, and in fragments. Therefore, one must approach such articulations with appropriate tentativeness.

84. Dietrich Bonhoeffer, *Ethics*, ed. Eberhard Bethge (New York: The Macmillan Co., 1965), 294.

85. Bonhoeffer, *Ethics*, 84.

86. Bonhoeffer, *Ethics*, 43.

87. Bonhoeffer, *Ethics*, 81, 83, 247.

that "according to Holy Scripture, there is no right to revolution; but there is a responsibility of every individual for preserving the purity of his office and mission in the *polis*. . . . [I]t is an integral part of his life in sanctification, and it arises from obedience to the Lord of both Church and government."[88] Quotations such as these are not at all difficult to find in *Ethics*. And, as I said, they clearly seem to affirm the same kind of thought that exists in *Cost*.[89]

Furthermore, it is from prison that Bonhoeffer reaffirms what he has written in *The Cost of Discipleship*.[90] And there are the words from the conclusion of his proposed "Outline for a Book," written around the same time:

> The church is the church only when it exists for others. To make a start, it should give away all its property to those in need. The clergy must live solely on the free-will offerings of their congregations, or possibly engage in some secular calling. The church must share in the secular problems of ordinary human life, not dominating but helping and serving. . . . In particular, our own church . . . will have to speak of moderation, purity, trust, loyalty, constancy, patience, discipline, humility, contentment, and modesty. It must not under-estimate the importance of human example (which has its origin in the humanity of Jesus and is so important in Paul's teaching); it is not abstract argument, but example, that gives its word emphasis and power.[91]

Now, of course, had Bonhoeffer lived, no one knows what would have come of many of the ideas he expressed in his writings from prison. Nonetheless, it is worth noting that there is nothing in these statements to indicate that Bonhoeffer had become some sort of "realist" who had outgrown the notions he had expressed at Finkenwalde or in *The Cost of Discipleship*.

Discipleship in a World Full of Nazis

If I am right that the thought embodied in *The Cost of Discipleship* was determinative for Bonhoeffer, then why is his social ethics legacy portrayed otherwise? Why is it that discipleship is not viewed as central to his whole *life*, rather than simply a preoccupation of one book? And why is it that we — pacifists and

88. Bonhoeffer, *Ethics*, 351.
89. This is not at all to suggest that there are no statements in other directions. Clearly there are. In fact, a part of my point is precisely that it is unclear what Bonhoeffer would have said about certain subjects in a completed *Ethics*. (For data for the other directions see, e.g., Bonhoeffer, *Ethics*, 214-61 and Rasmussen, *Dietrich Bonhoeffer: Reality and Resistance*, 32-73.)
90. Bonhoeffer, *Letters and Papers*, 369.
91. Bonhoeffer, *Letters and Papers*, 382-83.

nonpacifists alike — do not take him at his word that he continued to stand by the discipleship (and the pacifism) articulated in *The Cost of Discipleship* until the end? There are a number of reasons.

The first stems from what leads Larry Rasmussen to refer to Bonhoeffer as a "radical contextualist."[92] Bonhoeffer's contextualism is most obviously and bluntly stated in a lecture he gave in Barcelona in 1929, before his "conversion." In that lecture he said "there are no actions which are bad in themselves — even murder can be justified — there is only faithfulness to God's will or deviation from it."[93] He also justified a nationalistic approach to war in this lecture.[94] As Bethge says, "excessively nationalistic statements such as occur in his Barcelona addresses henceforward never crossed his lips."[95] However, it is true, as Rasmussen says, that "a rejection of the teachings of the Sermon on the Mount as timeless principles carries through uninterruptedly. And his ethic remains radically contextualist . . . although it becomes far more christocentric than here."[96]

However, it is important to note that it was not only *after* his strong pronouncements on peace, or his authorship of *The Cost of Discipleship*, or *after* his claim to be a pacifist that he had embraced a "radical contextualism." From beginning to end Bonhoeffer embraced what could be described as a contextualist approach to ethics. Not long after Barcelona Bonhoeffer's thought does become "far more christocentric." However, even with that, as Larry Rasmussen has said, Bonhoeffer engaged in a great deal of caricaturing of the need for solid moral guidance in order to make room for a free Christ.[97] Rasmussen appropriately asks: "How does Bonhoeffer 'test the spirits' so as to distinguish between Christ's concrete command and false guidance, and between 'conforming' acts and malforming ones?"[98] Indeed, how does Bonhoeffer know he ought to be for peace rather than for war, for the Jews rather than against them? If one reads back through the narrative in this essay one can see how: he looks at the Jesus of the Scriptures, proclaimed by the church, that leads to discipleship. The claim by the church is that the sovereign God has made himself known in Jesus

92. Rasmussen, *Dietrich Bonhoeffer: Reality and Resistance*, 153.

93. Bonhoeffer, *No Rusty Swords*, 41.

94. This part of the lecture is excluded from *No Rusty Swords*, but may be found in Rasmussen, *Dietrich Bonhoeffer: Reality and Resistance*, 96-98.

95. Bethge, *Dietrich Bonhoeffer*, 92.

96. Rasmussen, *Dietrich Bonhoeffer: Reality and Resistance*, 99.

97. Again, for an excellent critique of Bonhoeffer's method see Rasmussen, *Dietrich Bonhoeffer: Reality and Resistance*, 149-73. For an illuminating parallel critique, upon which Rasmussen draws, see John H. Yoder, *Karl Barth and the Problem of War* (Nashville: Abingdon Press, 1970): 47-50, 57-81. For one way to reflect on Bonhoeffer's perceived problem see John H. Yoder, "'Patience' As Method in Moral Reasoning" in this volume, 24-42.

98. Rasmussen, *Dietrich Bonhoeffer: Reality and Resistance*, 155.

Christ. Bonhoeffer's life and writings, narrated in this essay, demonstrate that his life and constructive writings outstripped his theory in this regard.

The reason why this radical contextualism in relation to Christ is so important is that if one can disconnect Christ from the Jesus of the Gospels (as Bonhoeffer argued against in both *Christ the Center* and *The Cost of Discipleship*), then one can much more easily ignore the claims of the biblical Christ so powerfully articulated in *Cost*. One can then replace that Christ with some abstraction such as "responsibility" and fill that abstraction with our contextual content rather than deriving that content from the biblical Christ. To that we now turn.

Especially this side of Reinhold Niebuhr, responsibility is a key term in relation to social ethics for Protestant ethicists. This side of Niebuhr's polemic against pacifists, many assume that pacifism and responsibility do not mix.[99] However, this will not fly with Bonhoeffer and, in fact, trades on a stereotype of pacifism. It needs to be born in mind, e.g., that it was while he was in the midst of his deepest reflections on the Sermon on the Mount that Bonhoeffer wrote the following remarks in response to recent legal discrimination against the Jews.

> All this means that there are three possible ways in which the church can act toward the state: in the first place, as has been said, it can ask the state whether its actions are legitimate and in accordance with its character as state, i.e., it can throw the state back on its responsibilities. Second, it can aid the victims of state action. The church has an unconditional obligation to the victims of any ordering of society, even if they do not belong to the Christian community. "Do good to all people." In both these courses of action, the church serves the free state in its free way, and at times when laws are changed the church may in no way withdraw itself from these two tasks. The third possibility is not just to bandage the victims under the wheel, but *to jam a spoke in the wheel* itself. Such action would be direct political action, and is only possible and desirable when the church sees the state unrestrainedly bring about too much or too little law and order.[100]

---

99. For an incisive critique of Niebuhr see John H. Yoder, "Reinhold Niebuhr and Christian Pacifism," *The Mennonite Quarterly Review* 29 (April 1955): 101-17; also see my critique of Niebuhr's use of the term "responsibility" in Nation, "Those Damned Pacifists," 39-40; for further on responsibility and pacifism see John Howard Yoder, "Peace Without Eschatology?" in Yoder, *The Royal Priesthood*, ed. Michael G. Cartwright (Grand Rapids: Eerdmans, 1994), 161ff.

100. Kelly and Nelson, *A Testament of Freedom*, 139, emphasis mine. The image of "jamming a spoke in the wheel" does not seem particularly different from the image of "arresting the wheel" that Bonhoeffer used in Tegel prison (Otto Dudzus in Zimmerman and Smith, *I Knew Dietrich Bonhoeffer*, 82). One image is intended to imply an action of stopping movement, the other is one of changing directions. Both imply political actions to affect public policies.

That many would imagine that pacifists would only be interested in the first two but not in the third option is a failure of their imagination, not an inadequacy of pacifism, Bonhoeffer's or otherwise.[101] He took many actions on behalf of peace and on behalf of the Jews while espousing pacifism. He spoke of jamming "a spoke in the wheel" on behalf of the Jews while he was still clearly espousing pacifism. And, of course, his desire to study with Gandhi was in order to effect changes in Germany "in a Christian manner."[102] All of these responsible acts, and others, were done and encouraged while Bonhoeffer was speaking in the idiom of *The Cost of Discipleship*.

A third reason many cannot accept Bonhoeffer as a consistent pacifist is that pacifism is often peculiarly linked to absolutism. And, therefore, after Bonhoeffer was involved in the conspiracy to topple the Hitler government, many felt the need to come up with a theory that explained Bonhoeffer in stages, thereby accounting for an absolutism that he came to abandon. But this is not necessary. John Yoder begins his essay, "'Patience as Method in Moral Reasoning" by stating

> It is not always meant as a term of abuse, but it is always inaccurate, when the views I represent are called "absolutist."
>
> > I do hold (a) that the authority of Jesus in moral matters is greater than that of other teachers, or of "reason," or of "intuition."
> > I do hold (b) that the prima facie burden of proof lies with those who would advocate exceptions to the general guidelines of Christian morality, rather than with those who advocate respecting them.
> > I do argue (c) that certain of the looser kinds of "situational" and "consequential" moral reasoning, and certain loose forms of exception-making which have been fashionable in the last generation are irresponsible.
>
> Yet none of these positions (a through c) can properly be called "absolutist," if that term is meant as a distinguishing characteristic. In each of those debates (a through c) the other value, which according to others

101. For theories about why pacifists can be activists see John Howard Yoder, *The Christian Witness to the State,* reprint edition (Eugene, OR: Wipf & Stock, 1997); John Howard Yoder, *Nevertheless,* 2nd ed. (Scottdale, PA: Herald Press, 1992); and Duane Friesen, *Christian Peacemaking & International Conflict* (Scottdale, PA: Herald Press, 1991).

102. For a suggestive discussion regarding how the Gandhian nonviolent resistance Bonhoeffer desired could have been effective in Nazi Germany see Mark Nation, "The Politics of Compassion: A Study of Nonviolent Resistance in the Third Reich," M.A. Thesis, Associated Mennonite Biblical Seminaries, 1981. Also see Gene Sharp, *The Politics of Nonviolent Action* (Boston: Porter Sargent Publisher, 1973) and Yoder's bibliography in Yoder, *Nevertheless,* 157-60.

should override my commitment, is no less subject to be called an "absolute."[103]

I believe Yoder's essay on absolutism is a rather devastating response to those who label his pacifism rooted in discipleship absolutist. But whether other readers agree with that conclusion or not, Bonhoeffer was never committed to a position he would have seen as "absolutist," despite the fact that he referred to himself as a pacifist.

A fourth reason why *Cost* and *Life Together* are often ignored in considering Bonhoeffer's social ethics legacy is that they are too "churchy." This is a mistake on several levels. On one level, to address the church is to address a community, a social entity. Besides, the Protestant church which Bonhoeffer addressed included a significant portion of the population in Germany. Even if one's view of "social ethics" is that it first has to deal with the larger society, to help the Protestant segment of the German people to learn what it meant to have Christian social relations would indeed have been "social ethics."[104]

On another level, as was mentioned earlier, and as is obvious from Bonhoeffer's life and writings, he always believed the church should be actively involved in the world. It was largely because the Confessing Church was so self-absorbed that he became disillusioned with it. It was not a new thought when he wrote from Tegel that "the church is the church only when it exists for others."[105] When Bonhoeffer was seeking to train a disciplined clergy at Finkenwalde he was not seeking "the seclusion of the cloister but the most inward concentration for the service of others."[106]

However, we are still not getting to the heart of Bonhoeffer's understanding of the church. I, as a pacifist, have often been asked: "What would you have done about Hitler?" And, of course, what the questioner has in mind is that any reasonable person would know that Hitler had to be stopped. Any reasonable person knows that ending tyranny sometimes entails the use of violence. Of course, what the questioner is often not conscious of, while asking the question, is that during World War II "reasonable" people ending up killing from thirty-five to sixty million people to "get rid of Hitler." That involved considerable fire bombing, the killing and maiming of millions and millions of civilians, and the dropping of two atomic bombs. What about Hitler? is one question to ask. However, that is not the central question from the legacy of Bonhoeffer. Rather,

103. Yoder, "'Patience' as Method in Moral Reasoning," in this volume, 24-25.
104. This is not to say that it would be unimportant or something other than social ethics if the Lutheran Church in Germany were much smaller.
105. Bonhoeffer, *Letters and Papers,* 382.
106. Bonhoeffer quoted in Bethge, *Dietrich Bonhoeffer,* 387.

the main question he would pose to us is: "What would you do with a church which chooses to go along with a government that systematically eliminates Jews, gypsies, and homosexuals, and mounts a war that would lead to the deaths of more than thirty-five million people?"

Yes, Bonhoeffer wrestled with the question about Hitler. But what preoccupied him was how to shape a Christian people that would embody discipleship seriously enough that an Adolf Hitler could not have his way with them. John Wilcken is right that "there is an ecclesiastical dimension to all of Bonhoeffer's thinking, even that which does not directly concern itself with ecclesiological themes. His theology can be rightly understood only if it is seen as produced within the church and for the church."[107] A church that would then give itself for others. A church that would have the courage to love neighbors *and* enemies.

"I'm firmly convinced — however strange it may seem — that my life has followed a straight and unbroken course," said Bonhoeffer. "Today [21 July 1944] I can see the dangers of [*The Cost of Discipleship*], though I still stand by what I wrote." When we read these statements from Bonhoeffer, made toward the end of his life, and when we look at the life he lived and the words he wrote, we can see an embodiment of the thesis of John Yoder's book, *The Politics of Jesus:* "The ministry and the claims of Jesus are best understood as presenting to hearers and readers not the avoidance of political options, but one particular social-political-ethical option."[108] Both *The Politics of Jesus* and *The Cost of Discipleship* were not primarily about pacifism.[109] They were, rather, about the claims of Jesus on our lives, lives to be expressed through discipleship in the context of the church, lives lived in service to the world.

Involvement in the conspiracy? This was hardly an easy choice for Bonhoeffer. But I am reminded of that wonderful quote from Peter Berger: "In a world full of Nazis one can be forgiven for being a Barthian."[110] Yes, and in a world full of Nazis, when the church has largely joined in the Nazi celebration, one may be forgiven for . . . for failing to live quite as one had written, yet more

---

107. John Wilcken, "The Ecclesiology of Ethics and the Prison Writings," in *A Bonhoeffer Legacy,* ed. A. J. Klassen (Grand Rapids: Eerdmans, 1981), 196.

108. John Howard Yoder, *The Politics of Jesus,* 2nd ed. (Grand Rapids: Eerdmans, 1994), 11.

109. I would think that both Yoder and Bonhoeffer could have resonated with the warning of Stanley Hauerwas that "to say one is a pacifist gives the impression that pacifism is a position that is intelligible apart from the theological convictions that form it. But that is exactly what I wish to deny. Christians are non-violent not because certain implications may follow from their beliefs, but because the very shape of their beliefs form them to be non-violent" (Stanley Hauerwas, "Pacifism: Some Philosophical Considerations," *Faith and Philosophy* 2 [April 1985]: 100).

110. Peter L. Berger, *A Rumor of Angels,* expanded ed. (New York: Anchor Books, 1990), 21. I don't fully agree with Berger's sentiments, but, nonetheless, love the statement.

fully in line with the Gospel than most of the rest of us, in similar, extraordinary circumstances, would have the courage to do.

More than anything else, Dietrich Bonhoeffer's life was given to shaping a disciplined church that was to live and proclaim the gospel of Jesus Christ in the midst of the world created and loved by God. Bonhoeffer did not want a church that was self-absorbed. He wanted to work within and for a church that appreciated and lived *The Cost of Discipleship,* even in the midst of an often violent world. Among other things, this focus led him to embrace what he referred to as pacifism. It was only after he received no support for his pacifism and concerns about nonviolent resistance; only after he was disillusioned with the Confessing Church and the ecumenical movement; only after he could no longer preach, teach, or publish that he turned to the conspiracy. And even then his own work was mostly that of trying to bring the war to a close with a little less violence. Ironically, despite perceptions, it was probably not his involvement in any conspiracy that got him arrested and therefore led to his death, but rather the saving of the lives of a few Jews. Even as he faced death this man was seen by his fellow inmate as "so devout and so certain that God heard his prayer."[111] Bonhoeffer's life and thought were captivated by Jesus Christ and his call upon our lives: *Nachfolge.* For Bonhoeffer, following after could never be divorced from a life shaped by the body of Christ and lived in the midst of the world. Thus for us to ignore *Nachfolge* as we formulate our social ethics in his light is to miss very much of the legacy of a life well lived.

For in the difficult, dangerous, ugly, violent world that was Nazi Germany, the life of Dietrich Bonhoeffer presented (and presents) a joyous, albeit polyphonic, portrayal of a life of faithfulness.

> God wants us to love him eternally with our whole hearts — not in such a way as to injure or weaken our earthly love, but to provide a kind of *cantus firmus* to which the other melodies of life provide the counterpoint. . . . Where the *cantus firmus* is clear and plain, the counterpoint can be developed to its limits. The two are "undivided and yet distinct," in the words of the Chalcedonian Definition, like Christ in his divine and human natures. May not the attraction and importance of polyphony in music consist in its being a musical reflection of the Christological fact and therefore of our *vita christiana?*[112]

Bonhoeffer's wondrous, polyphonic life simultaneously pointed us to the *cantus firmus* while embodying what Barry Harvey has called "the poetizing

---

111. Zimmermann and Smith, *I Knew Dietrich Bonhoeffer,* 232.
112. Bonhoeffer, *Letters and Papers,* 303.

memory of Jesus," which is to say "a nonidentical repetition which is both faithful to what is repeated *and* poetic, that is, which allows this memory to go on and on."[113] Thus were his discipleship — and the pacifism that flowed from it — richly textured and varied, faithful and yet evocatively poetic. Sometimes, I regret, deeply regret, that he did not live among us for a much longer time. But since that was not possible, the least we can do is to allow the memory of Jesus, embodied in Bonhoeffer, "to go on and on."

113. Barry Harvey, "The Wound of History: Reading Bonhoeffer after Christendom," in *Bonhoeffer for a New Day*, 88.

Tradition and Truth in Christian Ethics: John Yoder and the Bases of Biblical Realism

Grady Scott Davis

Reflecting on the state of theological ethics in 1981, James Gustafson wrote that "the radical Christian ethics of Yoder mark a substantive position for which there are many sound defenses; to opt against it is to opt against some fundamental claims of traditional Christianity." This, however, comes fast on the heels of Gustafson's remark that, despite its historical, biblical, sociological, and moral warrants, "I note Yoder's option here because it is the one most dramatically different from the option I shall pursue."[1] The attentive outsider, unaccustomed to the ways of Christian ethics, is likely to wonder what, with all those warrants, makes Yoder's a "radical Christian ethics," and why Christians would pursue anything else.

The knowledgeable, of course, will recognize Gustafson as the heir and representative of an important tradition in Protestant ethics, running back through H. Richard Niebuhr to Ernst Troeltsch. From this perspective those "fundamental claims of traditional Christianity" are the bailiwick of "Protestant sectarianism," of which "the Mennonites have come to represent the attitude most purely."[2] Only through their radical refusal to acknowledge the complexity of human existence have such sectarians been able to deny not only "the historical and cultural relativity of our reasoning and our decisions," but the "relativity of values that we must take into account in all our choices."[3] Thus when Gustafson writes that "the

---

1. James Gustafson, *Ethics from a Theocentric Perspective, Volume One: Theology and Ethics* (Chicago: University of Chicago Press, 1981), 75-76.

2. H. Richard Niebuhr, *Christ and Culture* (New York: Harper and Row, 1951), 56.

3. Niebuhr, *Christ and Culture*, 236-37.

human task is to decide what is the morally best possible course of events and state of affairs,"[4] he takes for granted an arena of relativity in which responsibility is only partially specified by Christian faith.

In order to participate fully in the work of the world it is important that faith be informed by the best available information about the world. Gustafson follows Troeltsch in asking whether "some traditional affirmations about God" are "incongruous with well-established data and explanations in science," extending this to the eschatological affirmations of Scripture. "We may not be able to say what the end will be," Gustafson writes:

> but, as Troeltsch stated, it will not be the Apocalypse of traditional Christian thought . . . if our perceptions of the Deity are in and through nature and human experience, and what is imaged is a divine governance of the world, then the biblical eschatological symbols or the contemporary Christian developments of them are not sustainable.[5]

Yoder's thought may be radical, in the sense of insisting firmly on the roots of Christian tradition in the biblical narrative, but this "biblical realism" requires adopting, as Gustafson earlier put it, "a norm which is found in a particular historical event rather than in 'nature' or in universalizable moral principles."[6] Such a realism can appeal only to a minority, and one which insists on confronting, rather than comprehending, the larger society and its concerns. Consequently it risks, like any "sectarian" movement, marginalization and ineffectiveness.[7]

That a biblical realism grounded in specific historical events may remain a minority position, or suffer marginalization by mainstream society, says little, however, about the credibility of its claims. In what follows I shall argue: (1) that Yoder's stance on tradition, knowledge, and truth are more subtle, and critically more sustainable than those of the tradition represented by

---

4. James Gustafson, *Ethics from a Theocentric Perspective, Volume Two: Ethics and Theology* (Chicago: University of Chicago Press, 1984), 302.

5. Gustafson, *Theology and Ethics,* 264, 268.

6. James Gustafson, *Protestant and Roman Catholic Ethics: Prospects for Rapprochement* (Chicago: University of Chicago Press, 1978), 67.

7. The church/sect distinction is a particularly burdensome legacy from Troeltsch, even when used, if it ever is, as a term of sociological art (Ernst Troeltsch, *The Social Teachings of the Christian Churches* [Louisville: Westminster/John Knox Press, 1992], I: 333-34). It fosters the sense that there is a Christian mainstream that is somehow independent of the story of Jesus and worthy of perpetuation simply because of the social status it has achieved. From the realist position developed in this essay such a stance is absurd. The issue is faithfulness to Christ, not to the various human institutions that may have struck out on paths of their own designing.

Gustafson; (2) that if Yoder is right about the gospel narrative then none of the physicists's findings tell in the least against the traditional doctrine of eschatology; and (3) whether or not Yoder is right about the gospel narrative, Gustafson's preference for the Reformed tradition tells us very little about the kinds of people we should be or the lives we should pursue. All of this, however, needs a bit of philosophical stage-setting.

The difficulty in getting clear about "realism" is compounded by its use in a number of contexts, none of which are easily commensurable. Those uses found in political theory, metaphysics, and the philosophy of mathematics form no part of the discussion to follow.[8] My purposes involve only those debates about realism centering on the theory of knowledge, some related issues in the philosophy of language, and specifically those arguments that concern themselves with the debate over "realism and relativism."

The distinction between "realism" and "relativism" is itself in need of a comprehensive history, which I will not attempt to provide here. But it is worth reflecting on the reason we might have for embracing or rejecting one or the other. Friends of relativism, when they can be found, are usually impressed by the diversity of ways that human beings organize their lives and the incommensurable accounts they give of the world's basic building blocks. Recognizing how broad the spectrum of practice and belief can be is liberating. Thus Evans-Pritchard writes that:

> in my own culture, in the climate of thought I was born into and brought up in and have been conditioned by, I rejected, and reject, Zande notions of witchcraft. In their culture, in the set of ideas I then lived in, I accepted them; in a kind of way I believed them.[9]

8. The canonical modern works on the issue of realism in mathematics may be found in Paul Benacerraf and Hilary Putnam, eds., *Philosophy of Mathematics: Selected Readings* (Englewood Cliffs, NJ: Prentice-Hall, 1964). A slightly less august, but still daunting collection for contemporary metaphysics is Michael Loux, ed., *The Possible and the Actual: Readings in the Metaphysics of Modality* (Ithaca, NY: Cornell University Press, 1979). Political realism, which is much closer to the background concerns of this essay, finds canonical form in Hans J. Morganthau, *Politics among Nations: The Struggle for Power and Peace* (New York: Knopf, 1967). It is worth being very clear about all of these senses, if for no other reason than the realism about moral epistemology I share with Yoder contributes mightily to the rejection of Morganthau's political realism. I don't know if Yoder holds any views about modal realism and possible worlds, or about the metaphysical status of mathematical entities. I may have once, but they have faded away into memories of graduate school. When arguments typically connected with one debate slide onto the grounds of another, however, confusion follows fast.

9. E. E. Evans-Pritchard, *Witchcraft, Oracles, and Magic among the Azande* (Oxford: Oxford University Press, 1976), 244.

The ability to enter into the lives of others is, for Evans-Pritchard, crucial to understanding their culture and its components. If this means sharing their beliefs, "in a kind of way," then we should do so; the alternative is ignorance or worse.

The ranks of realism are filled, by and large, by those who fear that too much identifying with the thoughts and practices of others risks aiding and abetting the most outrageous beliefs and behavior, running the gamut from witchcraft and non-Western medicine to the political horrors of the death camp and the hospital. Protecting against this is not simply a philosophical, but a moral, duty. In the debates that characterized the 1960s and early 1970s, realists of varied stripes hoped to establish either a scientific standard of rationality, perhaps along the lines of Popper, or, as Martin Hollis put it, "*a priori* elements which are not optional."[10] While those debates have, for the most part, simmered down, relativism continues to provoke political dismay. Thus Thomas McCarthy, discussing Richard Rorty's claim that there is no philosophical way to refute "apologists for Nazism, Stalinism, or the Inquisition," writes that:

> If he means that we might well fail to convince or convert them, he is obviously right, but that says nothing about the validity of racial theories, dialectical physics, or torture as a method of arriving at truth. If, however, he means that the arguments for their beliefs are as strong as the arguments against them, he is obviously wrong.[11]

That Rorty is wrong McCarthy fails to demonstrate; that he is "obviously" wrong is false. Part of the problem with McCarthy and other of Rorty's critics is their failure to recognize how specific Rorty's attack on truth and rationality as "regulative ideals" has been. The arguments he adduced early on in support of Kuhn were directed against those who insisted that "we must

10. Martin Hollis, "Reason and Ritual," in *Rationality*, ed. Bryan Wilson (Oxford: Basil Blackwell, 1970). Bryan Wilson's anthology continues to be a superior place to begin looking at this issue. After that it becomes almost impossible to manage the various related versions of the debate. One strand runs through analytic philosophy of science and revolves around names like Hempel, Kuhn, Feyerabend, Popper, and Putnam. In analytic epistemology the debate comprises, among others, Chisholm, Harman, Lehrer, and Alston. In the philosophy of language the central names are Davidson, Dummett, Rorty, and Putnam. Though it has since become an issue in itself, Richard Rorty, *Philosophy and the Mirror of Nature* (Princeton: Princeton University Press, 1979), particularly chapters 3-7, comes closest to bringing it all together. A brief reflection on his many contributions to the debate may be found in Hilary Putnam, *The Many Faces of Realism* (La Salle, IL: Open Court, 1987).

11. Thomas McCarthy, "Ironist Theory as a Vocation: A Response to Richard Rorty," *Critical Inquiry* 16 (1990): 644-55.

see scientists as 'in touch with external reality' and therefore able to reach rational agreement by means not available to politicians and poets."[12] Here Rorty is not denying anything that the working scientist is likely to say. The objects of his criticism are, first, the view that the "reality" with which scientists deal is somehow different from that of politicians and poets and, second, those philosophers who identify "realism" with the uniquely philosophical task of laying out the conceptual foundations for the shape that reality must take.

Applying the same arguments to political philosophy, Rorty, not surprisingly, gets the same results. Nobody that we would seriously think worth arguing with doubts that Hitler was a murderous sociopath or that six million Jews, along with several more million Gypsies, homosexuals, and various other undesirables died as part of the direct implementation of his murderous policies. But nothing the philosopher can produce by way of argument can render it impossible that "Hitler might be seen as in the right and the Jews in the wrong."[13] The ubiquitous philosophical Nazi, that intellectual catamite ever ready to subvert an argument, will always object that this or that premise has not been proved, or that different scientists have achieved results that cast doubt on some crucial matter of fact. When Rorty writes that "we *know* that we are the good guys and the Nazis are the bad guys," only to insist that "the trouble is, of course, that this same sort of knowledge-claim is made, in all sincerity, by the bad guys, and we shall never have any resources available that will not be equally available to them,"[14] he is not denying that we are the good guys. He is denying that there can be higher-level philosophical theory that will prove our claim to knowledge over theirs. Nor will political theorists, sociologists, or culture critics discover such a theory. When they reach for the universal they encounter exactly the same obstacles as the more traditional philosophical establishment. The argument is not about Hitler, it's about what philosophy can do.

Rorty's attempt to characterize himself as an "ironist" probably causes more trouble than it is worth. Clifford Geertz's strategy of calling his position "anti anti-relativism"[15] is not likely to fare much better, nor is John Yoder's recent attempt to distinguish "between relative relativism, which is morally imperative in a multicultural world, and absolute relativism, which denies ulti-

12. Rorty, *Mirror of Nature*, 342.

13. Richard Rorty, "Truth and Freedom: A Reply to Thomas McCarthy," *Critical Inquiry* 16 (1990): 633-43.

14. Rorty, "Truth and Freedom," 639-40.

15. Clifford Geertz, "Anti Anti-Relativism," in *Relativism: Interpretation and Confrontation*, ed. Michael Krausz (Notre Dame: University of Notre Dame Press, 1989).

282

mate accountability."[16] A simpler way to stake out the territory is the imperial one of claiming a minimal realism and then challenging all comers. This, in any event, is the path chosen by Donald Davidson, who writes that "the truth of an utterance depends on just two things: what the words as spoken mean, and how the world is arranged. There is no further relativism to a conceptual scheme, a way of viewing things, a perspective." From this he concludes, first, that any coherence theory of truth must be consistent with this minimal account of correspondence, and "second, a theory of knowledge that allows that we can know the truth must be a non-relativized, non-internal form of realism."[17] Davidson's "minimalist attitude toward truth"[18] takes it as obvious that truth is far and away the clearest of our epistemic notions. This is a point captured by Tarski sixty years ago, when he embraced Aristotle's characterization of truth as "to say of what is that it is, or of what is not that it is not."[19]

A little reflection suffices to see how this is both the least and the most that needs to be said about the concept of truth. Anything less would fail to make clear the connection between what we say and what we are saying it about. To say anything more is superfluous or unintelligible. What would it mean for a theory of truth to be true, after all? "The world is everything that is the case,"[20] for example, either repeats Aristotle's point or introduces some strange mystical entity, "the world," that is somehow distinct from the various things about which we speak truly. To talk of truth as "idealized warranted assertability," as Putnam seems inclined to do, reverses the direction of clarity. We are typically much clearer about what it means to speak the truth than what would count as a warrant, real or ideal. Replacing the clearer with the obscure is a sure path to philosophical bankruptcy.[21]

16. John H. Yoder, "Meaning after Babble: With Jeffrey Stout Beyond Relativism," *Journal of Religious Ethics* 24: 125-39.

17. Donald Davidson, "A Coherence Theory of Truth and Knowledge," in *Reading Rorty: Critical Responses to Philosophy and the Mirror of Nature,* ed. A. Malachowski (London: B. Blackwell, 1990), 122. The publishing history of this essay requires some comment. According to Davidson, the original was given in Stuttgart in 1981 and subsequently published in Germany. Rorty offered a response, to which Davidson replied, in 1983. Davidson's original and Rorty's response appeared in 1986 in a volume devoted to Davidson. The version provided by Malachowski contains further reflections by Davidson, dated 1987. This seems the fullest account of the matter so far.

18. Davidson, "A Coherence Theory," 135.

19. Alfred Tarski, *Logic, Semantics, Metamathematics: Papers from 1923-1938* (Oxford: Oxford University Press, 1956), 155 n. 2.

20. Ludwig Wittgenstein, *Tractatus Logico-Philosophicus* (London: Routledge and Kegan Paul, 1922), 1.

21. Davidson, "A Coherence Theory," 136.

Davidson's is a form of realism in the most minimal, and the only intelligible, sense. It takes it as obvious that the true statements we are in a position to make give us a picture, albeit partial, of the way the world is. This is a minimalist realism in at least two senses. For while we "take the objects of a belief to be the causes of that belief,"[22] this neither specifies the composition, physical or otherwise, of those objects, nor does it indicate how, precisely, we came to know about them. This point is crucial. Davidson's realism is neutral as regards "the pitcher is on the windowsill," "my mother loves me," and "the Lamb who was slain was worthy to receive power."[23] The first is a report about what I see when I look up from the keyboard; the second would require a rather long account of how we learn and apply concepts like love, as well as some specifics of family history. The last is a claim about which Yoder and I disagree. Since I do not believe in any gods, I *ipso facto* do not believe that the god of Abraham, Isaac, and Jacob chose Israel from among the peoples, that the story of Israel displays Yahweh's providential design for humanity, or that there is an annointed one who will bring to fulfillment that story. Consequently I am not inclined to believe "that Messiah has been placed by God above and not within the cosmology and culture of the world."[24] But the disagreement is a direct function of the realism we share.

Furthermore, the fact that we disagree says absolutely nothing about our individual reasonableness, much less the reasonableness of the belief about which we disagree. Unlike Troeltsch and Gustafson, I don't see how anything like modern radioastronomy could render incredible the thought that:

> The throne of God and of the Lamb will be there, and his servants shall worship him; they shall see him face to face, and bear his name on their foreheads. There shall be no more night, nor will they need the light of lamp or sun, for the Lord God will give them light; and they shall reign for evermore. (Rev. 22:3-5)

The words combine to generate well-formed sentences in English. These sentences are part of an intelligible, albeit difficult, narrative, and the fact that I don't know exactly by what mechanisms these events are to be brought about does not differentiate them from the claims made by astrophysicists for black holes and the big bang. Not only that, but it seems perfectly reasonable that anyone who believes that "these words are trustworthy and true," should be

22. Davidson, "A Coherence Theory," 132.
23. John H. Yoder, "'But We Do See Jesus': The Particularity of Incarnation and the Universality of Truth," in Yoder, *The Priestly Kingdom: Social Ethics as Gospel* (Notre Dame: University of Notre Dame Press, 1984), 61.
24. Yoder, "'But We Do See Jesus,'" 60.

taking whatever steps are necessary to "wash their robes clean," and avoid finding himself locked out among the "dogs, sorcerers and fornicators, murderers and idolaters, and all who love and practice deceit" (Rev. 22:6, 24-25). What will, in the end, make one of us right or both of us wrong is the way things turn out, but only some very shaky theories of rationality or investigative method would accuse either of us of irrationality.

This, of course, was Rorty's point. Davidson's approach to language and interpretation requires that "an interpreter must so interpret as to make a speaker or agent largely correct about the world,"[25] but any particular belief, even the ones we care most about, may be false, and there is nothing to be had by way of a philosophical theory that will render those beliefs immune from criticism or rescue them if they are false. The faith of the Christian and the way his beliefs hang together may be subject to criticism, but not in the simple ways envisioned by Ayer's positivism or the liberal relativism of Troeltsch.

Nonetheless, the skeptic is inclined to wonder "why couldn't all my beliefs hang together and yet be comprehensively false about the actual world?" It is one thing to admit "that it is absurd or worse to try to *confront* our beliefs, one by one, or as a whole, with what they are about," but this "does not answer the question nor show the question unintelligible."[26] Davidson's response comes in two steps. First, as Davidson has insisted on numerous occasions, there is "the interdependence of belief and meaning."[27] For my beliefs to be comprehensively false would mean that most of what I was inclined to say about the world would have to come out wrong from the perspective of someone whose beliefs were comprehensively true. But the question would then arise as to how that epistemically fortunate fellow could interpret my talk. For instance, Davidson notes, "If you see a ketch sailing by and your companion says, 'Look at that handsome yawl', you may be faced with a problem of interpretation." The obvious move is to assume that your friend has simply misused a technical term (leaving as a last resort the chance that you have done that). This is not the only possibility, of course; you may share the dictionary definitions of yawl and ketch, and he may simply have failed to notice the placement of the masts. "But," writes Davidson, "if his vision is good and his line of sight favourable it is even more plausible that he does not use the the word 'yawl' quite as you do, and has made no mistake at all about the position of the jigger."[28] Notice that, in order to resolve the interpretive question, it may be necessary to elicit information from your companion. After discussing the terms,

25. Davidson, "A Coherence Theory," 133.

26. Davidson, "A Coherence Theory," 123.

27. Donald Davidson, "On the Very Idea of a Conceptual Scheme," reprinted in Davidson, *Inquiries into Truth and Interpretation* (Oxford: Oxford University Press, 1984), 195.

28. Davidson, "Idea of a Conceptual Scheme," 196.

comparing angles of vision, considering glare and approximate distances it will usually be possible to resolve the dilemma, but only if both interlocutors agree on most of the background conditions. Were your fellow sailor to hold "comprehensively false beliefs," each attempt to draw him out would create yet another interpretive problem, not least of which would be how you managed to be floating together on open water. Rather than concluding that he held false beliefs, you would be systematically undermining your ability to interpret his noises at all. If this problem persisted it would become more and more difficult to attribute any beliefs at all to this individual. Rather than conclude that his beliefs were false, you would be forced to conclude that he spoke no comprehensible language.

To imagine that we ourselves might be comprehensively mistaken flounders on the fact that our beliefs, true and false, are the product of our interactions with the world. "We must," Davidson insists, "take the objects of a belief to be the causes of that belief. And what we, as interpreters, must take them to be is what they in fact are."[29] Languages are the products of human creativity, but in order to function as engines of communication they must be able to record and report our interactions with the rest of the world. It doesn't much matter whether we use "tree" or "arbol," but it matters quite a lot that "el arbol se cayó en la selva" is true if and only if the tree fell in the forest, and that the events which prompt the Spanish speaker to say the one are the same that would lead me to say the other. "Communication begins," as Davidson puts it, "where causes converge: your utterance means what mine does if belief in its truth is systematically caused by the same events and objects."[30] Because our beliefs are caused by events and objects, and because we must interpret the language of any mature speaker so that most of his beliefs coincide with most of ours, the prospect of global skepticism is reduced to a philosophical chimaera.

Since we are typically uninterested in the bulk of our beliefs, this does not help us answer any particular questions. It does not even tell us very much about our knowledge of the world, for while we may rest assured that most of everybody's beliefs are true, nothing has been said about justification, the mini-

29. Davidson, "A Coherence Theory," 132.
30. Davidson, "A Coherence Theory," 132. Throughout, Davidson takes it for granted that a complete account of communication would have to take into account the way in which particular statements are indexed to time and place. In the course of an actual life a tree falling on the banks of the Orinoco might prompt Juan to utter the Spanish sentence, while a redwood falling in northern California might prompt me to come forth with the English. But this is not relevant to the larger argument here. It should not be necessary to remark that none of this denies the obvious facts that people lie, make mistakes, tell jokes, produce literature, and the like. All of these complex practices depend, for their possibility, on the ordinary communicative use of language to report beliefs based on our experiences of the world.

mal third condition for knowledge.[31] Davidson is quick to point out that he has said nothing in particular about "the canons of evidential support (if such there be)."[32] Nonetheless, once the problem of truth, and with it global skepticism, has been disposed of, certain aspects of justification go as well. It is not clear that science, for instance, even if it had a method, would be in any privileged place for justifying many of my beliefs. My mother's affection, for example, does not stand in need of any scientific test. The idea that the language of perceptions, emotions, intentions, and desires can, in principle, be translated into the neurochemical language of brain processes is of very little interest here, since it will either provide some string of symbols that translate into what I would normally mean by "my mother loves me," or risk disconfirmation by the body of my evidence for the truth of that claim.[33] Nor is it clear what a scientific investigation of Yoder's eschatological expectations might amount to.

The fact is that only a few of our most interesting beliefs fall into the domain of the physical sciences. The reason for this is that most of our interesting beliefs are about ourselves and other people, and while we are physical beings, and thus subject to the laws of nature, we are also rational self-movers and consequently hard to capture under any but the simplest of nomological generalizations.[34] Not only that,

31. Until the 1960s analytic theory of knowledge took as its starting point the idea that to make a knowledge claim was to assert that something was a justified true belief. In a paper that William Alston has called "the shortest article to be heard round the world," Edmund Gettier posed the question of whether we needed a fourth condition for knowledge or a much more restricted account of justification. At no point has anyone, to my knowledge, suggested dropping one of the classic three conditions. Therefore, the literature on "Gettier problems" and related issues does not affect the argument that follows. Keith Lehrer (*Knowledge* [Oxford: Oxford University Press, 1974]) is a particularly clear and generally compelling account of the epistemological scene and the impact of Gettier problems. More recent bibliography, along with systematic critiques of Lehrer, may be found in Alston, *Epistemic Justification: Essays in the Theory of Knowledge* (Ithaca, NY: Cornell University Press, 1989).

32. Davidson, "A Coherence Theory," 134.

33. Richard Rorty, "Mind-Body Identity, Privacy, and Categories," reprinted in *Materialism and the Mind-Body Problem,* ed. David Rosenthal (Englewood Cliffs, NJ: Prentice-Hall, 1971).

34. Davidson calls his position "anomalous monism" and it has provoked extensive comment and criticism. Davidson's "Thinking Causes" (in *Mental Causation,* ed. John Heil and Alfred Mele [Oxford: Oxford University Press, 1993]) is a recent restatement of the position, followed by a number of responses. Attempts, by economists and political scientists among others, to provide formal game-theoretical models for human behavior have had very limited success. Alasdair MacIntyre suggests some important reasons for this in *After Virtue,* 2nd ed. (Notre Dame: University of Notre Dame Press, 1984), 89-105. I have, in a rather different context, tried to expand on MacIntyre's suggestions in my "Bosnia, the United States, and the Just War Tradition," in *Religion and Justice in the War over Bosnia* (New York: Routledge, 1996), 93-99.

but human nature, such as it is, turns out to be extremely malleable. Although Davidson's arguments fairly eliminate the grounds for any plausible form of philosophical relativism, the recognition of human diversity that entranced some relativists and horrified the would-be realists remain a fact of our social consciousness. "What looks like a debate about the broader implications of anthropological research, is really a debate about how to live with them," notes Geertz, who goes on to deplore as an exercise in self-deception the attempt of the "anti-relativists" at "placing morality beyond culture and knowledge beyond both."[35] The various attempts to provide foundations for knowledge and morality that demonstrate certain forms of practice and belief to be irrational, abhorrent, and preferably eradicated are more likely to be attempts to shore up their own teetering sense of cultural security.

Nonetheless, there remain some thinkers convinced that foundations are there to be had for securing philosophical epistemology. Responding to arguments by Keith Lehrer and Fredrick Will, William Alston formulates "minimal foundationalism" in terms of the distinction between "mediately" and "immediately" justified beliefs, where a mediately justified belief is derived from other beliefs that are themselves either immediately justified or part of epistemic branches that ultimately depend on immediately justified beliefs.[36] At the individual level, "each person has a set of immediately justified beliefs," which are justified "by experience, by self-evidence, or whatever."[37] Immediately justified beliefs, which serve as the foundation of knowledge, do not carry with them the notion of certainty or incorrigibility, hence, according to Alston, they avoid the criticisms of those notions offered by Lehrer and Will. Since foundationalism "must be attacked in its most defensible, not its most vulnerable, form," Alston concludes that foundationalism remains a viable option.[38]

Alston defends foundationalism as an alternative to coherentism, and defends an "evaluative" concept of epistemic justification over against a "deontological" one.[39] Of interest here are the examples Alston gives of immediate

35. Geertz, "Anti Anti-Relativism," 15, 32.

36. William Alston, "Has Foundationalism Been Refuted?" reprinted in Alston, *Epistemic Justification*, 42-43.

37. Alston, *Epistemic Justification*, 11.

38. Alston, "Has Foundationalism Been Refuted?" 56.

39. William Alston, "Concepts of Epistemic Justification," in Alston, *Epistemic Justification*, 97. The ultimate thrust of Alston's project need not concern us. For a detailed discussion of Alston's article "Has Foundationalism Been Refuted?" and of the critics to whom he is responding, see Jeffrey Stout, *The Flight from Authority: Religion, Morality, and the Quest for Autonomy* (Notre Dame: University of Notre Dame Press, 1981), 25-36. In the intervening years it appears that Alston's project in epistemology has been closely related to his project in the philosophy of

knowledge. "If," he writes, "I am justified in believing that my watch is on the desk because of my visual experience, or if I am justified in believing that $2 + 3 = 5$ because it is obvious to me that this is the case, these are examples of immediate justification."[40] In the case of sense experience, Alston has earlier suggested, "the fact believed is itself an experience of the subject," while in examples of self-evidence "we can take the *way* the proposition appears to one, variously described as 'obviously true', 'self-evident', and 'clear and distinct', as the ground on which the belief is based."[41] But consider the case of $2 + 3$. Alston is correct that our recognition of this is in some sense immediate, but precisely the sense of immediate becomes clear when we contrast $2 + 3$ with $215 + 388$. Perhaps some of us are so accustomed to adding that 603 pops immediately to eye or tongue, but I, at least, have to think about it for a minute, and some people, I imagine, don't feel quite comfortable unless they write the problem out. The natural explanation for this lies in the way we learned to do sums. First we were taught to count, then taught to associate the numbers with the numerals, and after that, drilled in simple sums, perhaps through grouping pictures of kinds of objects. Only then did we proceed to more complex sums, which we were taught could be aligned in columns, carrying over tens and so on.[42] Through drill and daily practice what a five-year-old finds difficult, and achieves only through steps, becomes for most of us second nature.

It is less frequently noted, at least by philosophers, that we acquire our perceptual skills in much the same way, hand in hand with our linguistic ones.[43] The

---

religion, which has much in common with that associated with Alvin Plantinga and Nicholas Wolterstorff (cf. their *Faith and Rationality: Reason and Belief in God* [Notre Dame: University of Notre Dame Press, 1983]). The "logical apologetics" of these moves in philosophy of religion contrast in important ways with Yoder's account of knowledge. At heart, this is a protectionist strategy designed to secure intellectual legitimacy and allow its adherents to bracket their religious beliefs so that they can engage the collective activities of the society as a whole. Though I don't intend to argue it here, this seems to be part and parcel of the "detheologizing" of the voice of theology Stout associates with Gustafson (see Stout, *Ethics after Babel: The Languages of Morals and Their Discontents* [Boston: Beacon Press, 1988], 167-86).

40. Alston, *Epistemic Justification*, 11.

41. Alston, "Concepts of Epistemic Justification," 106-7.

42. I am relying here on two years of reviewing the homework of my own kindergartner and first grader, taking it pretty much for granted that the method is similar in Richmond, Roswell, and Rochester. The continuity of teaching methods with those of Renaissance Italy may be gathered from Paul F. Grendler, *Schooling in Renaissance Italy: Literacy and Learning, 1300-1600* (Baltimore: Johns Hopkins University Press, 1989), 154-55 for primers and hornbooks; 311-19 for merchant skills in the vernacular curriculum).

43. One philosopher who has stressed this point, and made explicit the connection with the cognitive abilities of children, is Nelson Goodman in his *Problems and Projects* (Indianapolis: Bobbs-Merrill, 1972), 57-79.

perceptual abilities of newborns are both extremely rudimentary and begin developing practically from birth. As parts of a complex world governed by physical laws, the random or instinctive movements of infants provoke regular physical responses. In some unfortunate situations they are put in harm's way before their perceptual mechanisms are sufficiently developed, but if they survive and are provided extensive stimulus by adults, newborns rapidly begin to mimic sounds and gestures, learning to produce recognizable phonemes and ultimately words in the second six months of life.[44]

By two, babies are beginning to produce rudimentary sentences on a regular basis, to achieve specific ends. They are learning to apply color words, to pick out types of object, and to describe the environment in ever greater detail. Our assessment of their perceptual abilities cannot be separated from their linguistic ones. If, for example, a four-year-old complains that the iced tea is too salty, we may suspect some confusion, though the paternalistic "you mean sweet, don't you?" is not the end of the matter. If we compare her tea with our own there are many possibilities. We may find them indistinguishable, in which case we might try further questions to see what's going on. Is the tea more salty than the apple? Yes? Is it more salty than the honey? Maybe we do have a confusion of terms. On the other hand, maybe her tea is salty. This may point us in the direction of a dangerous product mispackaging or, perhaps, a brother-in-law with an underdeveloped sense of humor. In some, comparatively rare, instances, we may finally turn to an explanation in terms of physiology.

By the time children enter kindergarten they are beginning to fine-tune their language to conform to the grammatical norms of their social environment. They are also becoming atuned to the complexities of their sensory environment. Thus the five-year-old, coming in from play, correctly identifies by smell the tomato sauce simmering on the stove, sees, to his despair, the avocado nestled among the pears and bananas, and expresses yet again his feeling that his father's taste in music is defective. "Normal mastery of a language," which usually comes

---

44. The various qualifications built into this scenario are designed to accommodate various subpar forms of infant care. For instance, mature palates recognize four basic tastes: sweet, salty, sour, and bitter. These are apparently undeveloped in newborns, as evidenced by the fact that the accidental substitution of salt for sugar in hospital formula has no impact on the sucking reflex. Undetected, babies consume life-threatening and occasionally fatal amounts of salt in hospital nurseries (Daphne Maurer and Charles Maurer, *The World of the Newborn* [New York: Basic Books, 1988], 81). At another level, lack of extended individual attention to otherwise healthy newborns retards recognition and linguistic skills, a problem frequently encountered in adoptees from China and Eastern Europe that have been warehoused for lack of paid staff. Placed in standard homecare situations with mature adult caregivers, development typically catches up, but this resilience is not inexhaustible. Witness the rare "wildboy" cases and the sadly less rare instances of childhood deprivation and abuse.

well before the end of grammar school, involves, as Chomsky puts it, "not only the ability to understand immediately an indefinite number of entirely new sentences, but also the ability to identify deviant sentences and, on occasion, to impose an interpretation on them."[45] The same is true for the mastery of sensory experience. Even the mature adult can, with practice, develop new olfactory and taste abilities. To move from domestic sparkling wine to quality Champagne, for instance, can be a revelation. With regular, though moderate, practice new levels of discrimination may reveal subtle differences between Veuve Cliquot and Taittinger or Moët and Perrier Jouet. This may also lead to cultivating a new vocabulary, though it is perfectly possible to bring previously learned terms to bear, as with "fruity" and "nutty." With time and habit those previously unknown tastes and aromas may become so well-known that it appears "obvious" that your host is serving the Veuve Cliquot nonvintage Brut.

Beyond the facts of linguistic and perceptual mastery, however, we need nothing further by way of linguistic theory, "Humboldtian" or otherwise, to address the epistemological issue.[46] The self-evidence and obviousness that characterize what Alston calls "immediate" beliefs is a function of language acquisition, training, and practice. This means that the presuppositions and practices which support that training are crucial to developing the mastery that makes particular perceptions and beliefs obvious or self-evident to one group, in situations that remain opaque and inarticulable to others. This, not some self-contained "conceptual scheme" or "form of life," is what Wittgenstein was pointing to in distinguishing people who "are transparent to us" from those with whom "we cannot find our feet."[47]

A similar recognition, when asked "in what sense can the Jesus story be reported as true for non-Palestinians," prompts John Yoder to insist that Christians do see Jesus.[48] Confronted with a variety of arguments that do not simply question the truth of Christianity, but are disposed "to box in the claims of Christian witness," some are tempted to make peace with modernity by embracing some strategy that either qualifies or relativizes the claims of the church.[49] But this would be a mistake. Neither the claim that we need "a common denominator language" nor "the fear that what we used to believe can all be explained reductionistically by some causation language,"[50] amounts to a

---

45. Noam Chomsky, *Current Issues in Linguistic Theory* (The Hague: Mouton, 1964), 7.

46. Chomsky, *Current Issues*, 24-25.

47. Ludwig Wittgenstein, *Philosophical Investigations*, 2nd ed. (Oxford: Basil Blackwell, 1958), II: 223.

48. Yoder, "'But We Do See Jesus,'" 50.

49. Yoder, "'But We Do See Jesus,'" 47-49.

50. Yoder, "'But We Do See Jesus,'" 47.

compelling argument for abandoning the claims of the Gospel message. The claims of modern science and Western political power cannot in the end change the fact that "reality always was pluralistic and relativistic, that is, historical."[51] In just the same way, the proclamations of the various religions are particular, made in history, and subject to critical analysis.

There is nothing more foundational for an individual's immediate beliefs than the tradition, or in some cases traditions, that have shaped his language and perceptual skills. This is what a number of thinkers are attempting to capture in talking about the "narrative component to epistemology." On one hand, human beings are creatures of nature, endowed with various senses that biochemically register the inpact on various receptors of the world at large. This sets limits on the malleability of the individual and makes it necessary, as Aristotle put it, to distinguish between what we can choose and what we can wish.[52] On the other hand, humans more than other animals have developed the ability to interpret their environments, share those interpretations, and elaborate projects of individual and corporate action that may substantively transform the world and themselves, leading to new occasions for interpretation and action. As they rear their children, human parents naturally impart to them whatever accounts of the world and its parts are *au courant*.

An older, and for the most part clearer, account of this process, comes not from "narrative ethics" or "narrative theology," but from the philosophy of science. Discussing a drawing, N. R. Hanson writes that:

> A trained physicist could see one thing in fig. 8: an X-ray tube viewed from the cathode. Would Sir Lawrence Bragg and an Eskimo baby see the same thing when looking at an X-ray tube? Yes, and no. Yes — they are visually aware of the same object. No — the *ways* in which they are visually aware are profoundly different. Seeing is not only the having of a visual experience; it is also the way in which the visual experience is had.[53]

The immediate belief prompted by a visual experience is not simply a matter of physiology and photochemistry. It depends crucially on a specific local version of the material, made of objects and events that have a particular identity within the practices of its inhabitants. Because they are engaged in particular projects to specific ends, some objects and events will be central and other rele-

51. Yoder, "'But We Do See Jesus,'" 59.

52. Aristotle, *Ethica Nicomachea*, trans. W. D. Ross (Oxford: Oxford University Press, 1925), 1111b.

53. Norwood Russell Hanson, *Patterns of Discovery: An Inquiry into the Conceptual Foundations of Science* (Cambridge: Cambridge University Press, 1958), 15.

gated to the margins. Some parts of the world will be attended to with great care and others only occasionally noticed. Thus I, for instance, go on oblivious to the march of the constellations through the night sky while the ancient agriculturalist cannot do the same with impunity. Should he plant too early or too late he would risk the welfare of family and friend.

In the laboratory, as Hanson puts it, "the visitor must learn some physics before he can see what the physicist sees,"[54] but the same is true of any arena of investigation, including ethics. Consider a typically dense remark of Paul Ramsey's on conscientious objection. "The 'right' of pacifist conscientious objection," he begins:

> can be granted for the fostering of the consciences of free men only because in national emergencies there are a sufficient number of individuals whose political discretion has been instructed in the need to repel, and the justice of repelling, injury to the common good. No political society can be founded on a principle according *absolute* rights to possibly errant individual consciences.[55]

This is a particularly vivid example of what I have elsewhere called Ramsey's "Augustinian ethics."[56] "Political society" here emerges out of the murderous context of fraternal strife, what Augustine called the "earthly city" and Hobbes the "state of nature." The everchanging components of the earthly city are each, in Augustine's way of putting it, "a gathering of rational beings united in fellowship by a common agreement about the objects of its love."[57] The proper function of political society is to promote and protect the common good and to this end it establishes magistrates and endows them with the authority and means of coercion necessary to secure that good.

What makes Christianity different, for Ramsey, is the advent of a new form of love, which prohibits "the direct killing of any man, as an end in itself or as a means of preserving the life that a Christian should love far less than he loves God and his neighbor in God who stands before him in the guise of a robber or a murderer."[58] Christian love demands that the neighbor be accorded

54. Hanson, *Patterns of Discovery*, 17.

55. Paul Ramsey, "Selective Conscientious Objection," in Ramsey, *The Just War: Force and Political Responsibility* (New York: Scribner, 1968), 93.

56. G. Scott Davis, "'Et Quod Vis Fac': Paul Ramsey and Augustinian Ethics," *Journal of Religious Ethics* 19, 2 (1991): 31-69.

57. Augustine, *De Civitate Dei Contra Paganos*, ed. and trans. W. M. Green et al. (Cambridge, MA: Harvard University Press/Loeb Classical Library), book XIX, ch. 24.

58. Paul Ramsey, *War and the Christian Conscience: How Shall Modern War Be Conducted Justly?* (Durham, NC: Duke University Press, 1961), 45.

more than merely natural respect; God loves all lives equally and enjoins believers to do the same. As Ramsey reads Augustine, when faced with the robber or murderer the Christian must lay down his own life rather than protect it at the cost of his malevolent neighbor's. But while private self-defense is rejected, the Christian cannot ignore the claims of his neighbors. Because "the existing political authority has the responsibility for that combination of wills or agreement as to goods necessary to the earthly life," the Christian citizen who "finds himself called to responsible action" is obliged to do his part in protecting the common good.[59]

Ramsey takes it as obvious, as does Augustine, that promoting the common good requires the exercise of deadly force. Not only that, but the authorities will on occasion need to issue some coercive threat in order to secure the help of the citizenry in repelling assault. If, but only if, the bulk of the citizenry is willing, in extremes, to take up arms, then the authorities may allow a minority to opt out, for personal or sectarian reasons. But this is very clearly special permission, which must be sought from the authorities and which may, in dire circumstances, be withheld. For the individual to assert himself against the good of the community is "a radically non-political and an ultimately inhumane viewpoint." It is ultimately, for Ramsey as for Augustine, unchristian.[60]

To distinguish the political from the nonpolitical, the humane from the inhumane, or the Christian from the unchristian is, tacitly or not, to signal a commitment to a particular story as embodying in its general shape the norm of this kind of life. These stories, and the habits of action and perception necessary to acting in accord with them, are transmitted and sustained over time by traditions. But it would be a mistake to assume that traditions are simple,

59. Ramsey, *War and the Christian Conscience*, 39. In addition to the essay mentioned above, I develop Ramsey's account of Augustine and the just war tradition in my *Warcraft and the Fragility of Virtue: An Essay in Aristotelian Ethics* (Moscow, ID: University of Idaho Press, 1992), chapter three.

60. Ramsey, "Selective Conscientious Objection," 93. Ramsey's Augustinianism undergoes subtle changes over his career. In one of his last works, discussing Stanley Hauerwas, Ramsey writes that "at least, the possibility of war is an essential part of the stories we tell ourselves of our eventful past, challenges and triumphs or failures, the heroes we honor, our monuments, institutions, laws, and national holidays. Yet he wishes to deny that this means that as the people of God we live also in an earthly city. . . . Here in Hauerwas's appropriation of Jesus Christ we can begin to see some of the things the chief pastors and teachers of the church should find ways of saying to the churches — if they mean or meant to speak up for pacifism" (*Speak Up for Just War or Pacifism: A Critique of the United Methodist Bishops' Pastoral Letter "In Defense of Creation"* [University Park, PA: Pennsylvania State University Press, 1988], 37-38). Ramsey's discussion of Yoder, however, is by and large negative in its conclusions, while eirenic in embracing the peace churches (see 96-123).

sealed, or set in stone. Once we have acknowledged the inescapably historical component in knowledge and ethics it becomes, to paraphrase a paraphrase, history all the way down.

Like all things historical, traditions are fluid and subject to change. In the history of Christianity the year 311 is "epochal."[61] While Eusebius eventually felt the need to bring his *Ecclesiastical History* down to the ultimate triumph of Constantine, it had originally ended with the words of Galerius's edict of toleration, "that Christians may exist again and build the houses in which they used to assemble," where

> they will be bound to beseech their own god for our welfare, and that of the state, and their own; that in every way both the well-being of the state may be secured, and they may be enabled to live free from care in their own homes.[62]

The new story is not unique to Eusebius. "A feeling of triumphant happiness," as Marrou puts its, "is evident throughout the fourth century from Lactantius to St. Augustine." Delivered seemingly at one stroke from their persecutors, "a rather premature theology of history went so far as to base an argument on this unexpected, miraculous success of the Gospel. The Christians of this period had, as we should say today, the feeling of moving in the direction of history."[63] In one sense Eusebius, Lactantius, and Augustine are correct. The Gospel is miraculous and Christians, like everybody else, are part of God's providence. But the theology of history to which Marrou alludes goes further. Augustine in particular argues that having inherited the mantle of empire, it is now the responsibility of the church to support its members in exercising the responsibilities of empire. Thus he could write to Boniface in 418 that it is not "impossible to please God while engaged in active military service." As long as Boniface seeks peace and does not abuse his power or give in to bodily temptations, maintaining the public order is his responsibility. It is "necessity, therefore, and not your will," Augustine reassures him, that slays the rebel and the barbarian invader.[64]

From Yoder's perspective this version of the gospel story is not merely

---

61. John H. Yoder, "The Constantinian Sources of Western Social Ethics," reprinted in Yoder, *The Priestly Kingdom*, 135.

62. Eusebius, *Ecclesiastical History* (Cambridge, MA: Harvard University Press/Loeb Classical Library, 1929, 1932), VIII, 17, 9-11. The place of Eusebius in the creation and history of Christian historiography is sketched suggestively in Arnaldo Momigliano, *The Classical Foundations of Modern Historiography* (Berkeley: University of California Press, 1990), 132-52.

63. Jean Danielou and Henri Marrou, *The Christian Centuries, Vol. I: The First Six Hundred Years* (London: Darton, Longman and Todd, 1964), 291.

64. Augustine, *Epistles*, trans. J. G. Cunningham, in Nicene and Post-Nicene Fathers, series 1, vol. 1, ed. Philip Schaff (Grand Rapids: Eerdmans, 1979), letter 189, paras. 4, 6.

premature, however, it is a failure of faith. This is not to say that Augustine thought of himself as betraying the church. But for Augustine the distinction between the church and the world "had become invisible, like faith itself." As a result, "the order of redemption was subordinated to that of preservation, and the Christian hope turned inside out."[65] From the earliest days of the church there were the same tensions, interpretive differences, and occasions for conflict that operate in any human community. Yoder insists, discussing the status of women, for example, that even "in the first century an original vision of equality soon came to be modified by less revolutionary interpretations of the Gospel setting in which subordination made sense."[66] What distinguishes Yoder from both contemporary relativists and various theologians of liberation, however, is his strict realism. If the story of Israel is true, and if Jesus taught a new ethic of discipleship, then faithfulness demands that believers do what they can to ascertain the nature of his teaching and make every effort to bring it to life. Otherwise, it is tempting to ask, what is the point?

In the first edition of *The Politics of Jesus,* Yoder considered six possible answers to that question:

(1) What hints Jesus provided have, in any event, to be revised for a non-interim society;
(2) his peasant message fails to speak to our complex social organization;
(3) Augustine was correct in recognizing an obligation to exercise responsibility in the larger society;
(4) Jesus' "ahistorical" message was primarily about the inner self;
(5) Jesus' message proclaimed "radical monotheism," thus relativizing all human ethics;
(6) Jesus was not concerned with message, but with sacrifice and redemption.[67]

In the second edition Yoder adds the following:

(7) The Bible is an important text, despite the fact that there is no consensus on whether *any* historical message can be recovered;
(8) the diversity of texts and traditions in the canon present too many historical messages;

65. John H. Yoder, "The Otherness of the Church," reprinted in Yoder, *The Royal Priesthood: Essays Ecclesiological and Ecumenical* (Grand Rapids: Eerdmans, 1994), 57.
66. John H. Yoder, *The Politics of Jesus: Vicit Agnus Noster,* 2nd ed. (Grand Rapids: Eerdmans, 1994), 192.
67. Yoder, *Politics of Jesus,* 5-8.

(9) what humanity needs are the ahistorical messages provided by reading from the perspective of various genres;

(10) whatever message Jesus might have had must be qualified by those associated with the other members of the Trinity;

(11) the real message of the Gospel is forgiveness, however badly we behave.[68]

The first thing to notice is that none of these positions is at odds with the "realism" I have appropriated from Davidson. They all point to other facts about Jesus, God, or ourselves that make it either impossible or inappropriate to vest much weight in the gospel message. Positions 5, 6, 10 and 11, for instance, locate the "real work" of God in activity independent of Jesus' earthly career. Items 4 and 9 identify ethical reflection with autonomous human nature and the need for spiritual guidance. The limits of historical reconstruction surface in 7 and 8, along with the odd maxim that if something cannot be done, attempting it is irrational.[69] Finally, 1 and 2 collapse into 3, which amounts to registering a preference for the story that motivates Augustine and Ramsey over that discerned by Yoder.

A second point to notice is the relative weakness of any of these claims considered independently. The claims that Jesus' message is "ahistorical," directed toward the "inner self," or primarily about forgiveness, for example, must confront a genuine embarrassment of riches in the amount of discussion Jesus and Paul are portrayed as lavishing on social life in a community constituted by those who claim to have heard the gospel. This is the point generally missed by critics of *The Politics of Jesus*. In a very puzzling remark, for example, Thomas Ogletree notes that "the ethical creativity of the Synoptic authors resides chiefly in their accounts of discipleship," only to conclude that "there is only slight interest in the import of the Christian message for the economic and political arrangements of the time."[70] Yoder's point is that the "accounts of discipleship" throughout the New Testament are not merely creative, they are revolutionary. They are grounded in the belief that Jesus is the Messiah, that his message is one "of revolutionary subordination, of willing servanthood in the place of domination," and that those who accept that message are faced with

---

68. Yoder, *Politics of Jesus*, 15-18.

69. This is different from the reasonable maxim that if you believe that something is impossible, then it is irrational to attempt it, though even here St. Benedict counseled his monks to "accept the command meekly and obediently" and if their superior should insist to "do as told, trusting in God's help" (*Rule*, ch. 68). What may appear futile to a secular historian may look less so to one possessed of the theological virtues.

70. Thomas W. Ogletree, *The Use of the Bible in Christian Ethics* (Philadelphia: Fortress Press, 1983), 116.

the task of "finding how in each role the servanthood of Christ, the voluntary subordination of one who knows that another regime is normative, could be made concrete."[71] Life in the church is the process by which the consequences of accepting this task are worked out.

Yoder is quite precise about what this means for those who would be disciples:

If the cross defines agape, it denies:

    a. that "one's own" family, friends, compatriots, are more to be loved than the enemy;

    b. that the life of the aggressor is worth less than that of the attacked;

    c. that the responsibility to prevent evil (policing Neighbor B) is an expression of love (it is love in the sense of a benevolent sentiment but not of *agape* as defined by the cross) when it involves the death of the aggressor;

    d. that letting evil happen is as blameworthy as committing it.[72]

To adopt these positions is scandalous because it amounts to rejecting both pagan justice and the vision of Christian responsibility embodied in Augustine and Ramsey.[73] This does not imply that aggression is a good thing, or that people should take more than their due, but it does signal the resolve to relinquish recourse to deadly force in protecting the innocent. Here everything depends upon the truth of the gospel message. If it is not true that Jesus is the Messiah, who has triumphed over the powers, then the innocent are being abandoned to no good end. If Jesus is what the church takes him to be, however, then following him is what we are called to do. But if voluntary subordination is the norm, it is a cosmic one, and it remains so regardless of social organization. If this is not "a comprehensive social ethic in the sense of twentieth-century Christian ethics,"[74] then something has gone wrong with contemporary Christian ethics.

The question is not, first and foremost, whether Christian Scripture provides a ready-made plan for ameliorating the effects of poverty, or any other social problem. All problems arise in particular historical communities and contexts, and it would be unreasonable to assume that specific programs can be generated in advance of the problems. Yoder's concern is to determine whether or not the biblical narrative comprises the attempts of the early community to

71. Yoder, *Politics of Jesus*, 187.

72. John H. Yoder, "Peace Without Eschatology?" reprinted in *The Royal Priesthood*, 164.

73. Davis, *Warcraft and the Fragility of Virtue*, 36-49.

74. Ogletree, *Use of the Bible*, 117.

be faithful to its calling as the church of Jesus the Messiah. His biblical realism, with its insistence on the binding nature of Jesus' call to discipleship on those who hear and accept it, is tied closely to what we might call the logic of lordship.

If following the call to discipleship requires foresaking human justice, then it cannot legitimately reside in merely human grounds. Only if Jesus is lord of all creation is it possible to follow him in good conscience. But what does it mean to be lord?

One way to think about lordship is in terms of the law. The lord is whoever can legitimately exercise the power of law in a particular domain. But law, as Herbert Fingarette puts it, is a confrontation of wills, not of bodies:

> The difference is this: if I grab you and hold you, I am exercising power over your body, but if I give you an order, the immediate object of my power is your will. Instead of being subject to bodily force, you are to act of your own will as I order you to act.

The law, it turns out, requires both obedience and

> the power to disobey. This paradox necessarily holds true of God's laws, too. God may command us to act in certain ways. In doing so He exercises His dominion over our will. But this exercise of dominion, if it is to make any sense, implies that He does not physically compel us.[75]

This, however, gives rise to further puzzles. If, for example, the subordinate refuses to obey, then the lord is forced to constrain his subject. Otherwise the order was nothing more than a request and there is no law. But if the superior is bound to act in order to maintain the reality of the law, it would seem "that the dominator's hand is forced; the logic of the enterprise dominates the dominator," a situation in which "paradox intensifies when we assume that God's central relation to us is expressed in terms of His Will or Law. Then even the Almighty is bound by this necessity intrinsic to law. He has no option."[76] Something like this, it would seem, underlies the traditional doctrine of divine justice.

On the other hand, given that the law defines humanity's relation to God, compliance must "make a difference." If anyone claims that his moral identity is defined by his relationship to God, then acting in terms of what he

---

75. Herbert Fingarette, "The Meaning of Law in the Book of Job," reprinted in *Revisions: Changing Perspectives in Moral Philosophy*, ed. Stanley Hauerwas and Alasdair MacIntyre (Notre Dame: University of Notre Dame Press, 1983), 259-60.

76. Fingarette, "Law in the Book of Job," 261.

takes to be the divine will must be connected with some expectations as consequences. Otherwise, he would be forced to assume "the odd proposition that God has in reality no will one way or another as to whether the subject shall act rightly or wrongly! If He does not have any will in this regard, why should we? We are left with nonsense."[77] But this should be familiar. Fingarette has diagnosed the problem at the heart of Niebuhr and Gustafson. "What looks at first glance like a very refined ecumenical openness," as Yoder will come to put it, "actually constitutes a firm formal bias against those views which hold that there is such a thing as *binding* revelation, valid knowledge, or a firm moral imperative."[78]

Fingarette goes on to argue that Job, driven to despair by the unintelligibility of a righteous God punishing a righteous man, comes ultimately to realize "the irrelevance of the concept of law in relation to God." This might seem to run up against Yoder's understanding of discipleship, but in fact it makes even clearer the conceptual preferability of his account of the Christian story to that of Augustine and Ramsey. In the story of Israel, God displays his willingness to take seriously the meaning of the law and to punish even his chosen people. Nonetheless, the words of Elihu to Job, that "your wickedness touches only men, such as you are; the right that you do affects none but mortal man," remain true, leading Fingarette to conclude that "God's justice, or whatever it is, is not a matter of law, because human obedience or disobedience does not touch Him but only human beings." Suffering is not punishment for an affront against God, but rather "the experience of the finitude and fallibility of personal will, and also, in the perspective of human morality, of its ultimate impotence and defeat." Whatever salvation or intercession may come from outside requires that "we have learned the essential wisdom that consists in abandoning hope in our personal power to make things as we will them to be."[79] Fingarette's conclusion echoes Augustine's charge that pagan virtues are

77. Fingarette, "Law in the Book of Job," 262.

78. John H. Yoder, "How H. Richard Niebuhr Reasoned: A Critique of *Christ and Culture*," in Glen H. Stassen, D. M. Yeager, and John H. Yoder, *Authentic Transformation: A New Vision of Christ and Culture* (Nashville: Abingdon Press, 1996), 81. The publishing history of this essay may someday receive a chapter of its own. The preface to Stassen et al. describes it as "an essay which was originally written in 1958 . . . and circulated for decades only in mimeographed form" (11). The copy in my files is a xerox of "text for Stassen/Hauerwas editing process" and describes itself as "draft of May 1986 for further criticism." The headnote indicates that "the first outline of the material being reviewed here was drafted in 1962." While much of the final version remains the same, there have been some interesting rearrangements, expansions, and qualifications. It would be an unfortunate loss to purge those older copies in favor of what will, no doubt, become the textus receptus.

79. Fingarette, "Law in the Book of Job," 264-66.

"puffed up and proud, and so must be reckoned as vices rather than as virtues." The irony is that it fits the tradition of Niebuhr equally well.[80]

Resolving the question between Yoder and Ramsey moves in a rather different way.[81] In a recent attempt to sketch the development of early Christian thought about war, the authors warn against "the disastrous assumption which, rejecting or ignoring critical hermeneutics, assumes that NT and early Christian belief and practice are normative, at face value, for contemporary Christian life."[82] This, however, is not quite Yoder's point. The fundamental claim is that the message of Jesus is normative, "not because Jesus told us to . . . but because God is like that."[83] It is important to be faithful in interpreting Scripture because it is there that the Christian claims to learn most clearly what God is like. This is neither a fundamentalist claim about biblical inerrancy nor a scholarly claim about reconstructing the historical Jesus. It does, however, signal the belief that the Lord revealed himself most clearly in a particular historical context, that the Bible read as a whole provides various accounts of the attempt to work out what it means to be a follower of the Lord, and that an important component of faithfulness to that enterprise lies in according those accounts a

---

80. Augustine, *De Civitate*, book XIX, ch. 25. Though it has not been a theme central to this essay, Yoder's critique of fundamentalism is also highlighted by Fingarette's remarkable essay. Niebuhr's relativizing results in a *tabula rasa* on which the Protestant liberal can inscribe whatever agenda, with whatever method, seems called for by current social problems. It is no accident that the work of sociologists, social psychologists, biologists, medical researchers, and economists is heavily represented in the social ethics of Niebuhr, Gustafson, and those influenced by them (cf. Gustafson, *Ethics and Theology*, chs. 7-8). The biblical literalist achieves a clean slate by wiping away the complexities of history and the Christian traditions and claiming not only the text, but direct empowerment to interpret it. An illuminating example of some of the consequences is the fractious history of evangelical Protestantism. Mark Noll's *The Scandal of the Evangelical Mind* (Grand Rapids: Eerdmans, 1994) is an account by a critical insider. See particularly chapter 5. To use the language of Fingarette, fundamentalists and relativists both are like Job's friends, "smugly self-satisfied in their assumption that they already possessed all the truth and so could invent realities to fit their theory. They showed neither integrity nor humility in this regard. They were in bad faith before God" ("Law in the Book of Job," 272).

81. This could just as easily be termed the conflict between Tertullian and Augustine. Yoder frequently couples "Tertullian and Origen" in contrast to "Ambrose and Augustine" in sketching the way in which "the view of Christians on the morality of violence in the public realm was reversed" (*The Priestly Kingdom*, 74). Although I am inclined to think Yoder is correct about this, I am not primarily concerned here with the details of scriptural and patristic thought and am not inclined to allow that debate to obscure the philosophical points being made.

82. Robert J. Daly, *Christians and the Military: The Early Experience* (Philadelphia: Fortress Press, 1985), 2.

83. John H. Yoder, *The Original Revolution: Essays on Christian Pacifism* (Scottdale, PA: Herald Press, 1977), 51.

privileged place in contemporary Christian attempts to continue the project of faithful living.

When Yoder turns to the biblical text he typically asks what is discovered there that is distinct or even unique. Thus in discussing Paul on the powers, Yoder writes that "subordination to these Powers is what makes us human, for if they did not exist there would be no history nor society nor humanity." Life in the world, as Fingarette might put it, inevitably comes up against insurmountable difficulties, whether in the guise of hostile rulers, vicious colleagues, or metastasizing cells. This everyone knows, but Paul realizes that if "God is going to save his creatures *in their humanity,* the Powers cannot simply be destroyed or set aside or ignored. Their sovereignty must be broken." By willingly taking on humanity and then refusing to exercise their kind of power, "even to save his own life," he showed that it was possible to escape them. "Here," Yoder insists, "we have for the first time to do with someone who is not the slave of any power, of any law or custom, community or institution, value or theory."[84] Unlike the Stoic or Epicurean, who seeks either detachment from the powers or equanimity in a chaotic world, Christ achieves freedom.

Liberated from late medieval and modern assumptions about Paul, a contemporary reader can discern throughout the Pauline corpus a concern to establish and reiterate this fact. Thus Paul's thought does not turn on liberating grace over and against the killing law. Rather, "the basic heresy he exposed was the failure of those Jewish Christians to recognize that since the Messiah had come the covenant of God had been broken open to include the Gentiles." On Yoder's reading, the issue is how the disciples of Christ are going to live in witness of the freedom demonstrated in his death and resurrection, and Paul's answer, along with that of the other distinctive theological visions of Scripture, is that the church is "to be a new and inexplicable kind of community of both Jews and Christians."[85] This is a community where each is subject to the other and none make recourse to the destructive powers of this world.

If we contrast this vision of the church to that of Augustine, classically expressed in *The City of God,* Yoder's question is simple. Does the move to an "invisible church," whose membership can only be recognized in the heavenly church triumphant, mark a development of or a movement away from the new social order preached, for example, by Paul and the author of Luke? One way to answer this is to ask how the competing positions allocate authority in decision making. When Ramsey, for instance, considers the work of the moralist in society, he finds it essential to "separate procedurally between the task of moralists

---

84. Yoder, *Politics of Jesus,* 144-45.
85. Yoder, *Politics of Jesus,* 216.

and church councils and the task of the statesman." The statesman is in charge of the welfare of the community, and even when his character or knowledge may be deficient

> the statesman is still the magistrate and the church is the church, whose business it is to comment *in moral terms* on *the moral issue* in public questions and thus to guide and form the conscience of the statesman, whose business it is to know and judge the facts.

If the true church is an invisible entity, recognized only in heaven, then the earthly church should accept its status as one among many subgroups within society. Each group has its proper activity and thus its proper authority. To step outside its jurisdiction threatens the safe working of the whole. "If moralists or church councils," writes Ramsey, "arrive at conclusions that depend on the facts being thus and so, and not otherwise, then the role of the statesman in knowing the facts and finally determining a moral course of political action would be invaded."[86] Churches and moralists must know and keep their places.

This does not mean, for Ramsey, that citizens are commanded to follow their political leaders blindly; "every citizen must make up his part of the public-policy decision. He is a lesser magistrate."[87] His jurisdiction, however, is limited, and he must refrain from invading the jurisdiction of another. Specifically, he must acknowledge that the statesman is in command of political strategy. That superior magistrate is advised by "military planners" trained in "strategic analysis," which "is probably more highly advanced in the United States than in any country in the world."[88] Strategists determine the most effective way to achieve an end; moralists may comment upon whether the end and the means to it are just. If the moralist determines that some policies are wicked, it is his duty to deplore them and perhaps counsel other citizens to revoke the authority of their leaders. But the moralist's authority does not extend to matters of fact. "The private individual," Ramsey concludes, "can in good conscience will what his government wills in the matter of deterrence," so long as the government does not espouse direct attack, even under duress, on noncombatants. Neither the private citizen nor the moralist has standing to determine whether "disproportionate combatant damage" or "disproportionate," though legitimate, "collateral death and destruction" will in fact achieve the hoped-for deterrence.[89]

---

86. Paul Ramsey, "Again, the Justice of Deterrence," reprinted in Ramsey, *The Just War*, 337-38.

87. Ramsey, "Justice of Deterrence," 338.

88. Ramsey, "Justice of Deterrence," 344.

89. Ramsey, "Justice of Deterrence," 361.

Ramsey rightly locates the difference between himself and a thinker like Yoder in the fact that "the Christian pacifist may be right, and the just-war Christian may be wrong."[90] This is not, however, all that can be said on the matter. Yoder may, for example, point out that by according authority to the various experts who study the workings of earthly power, the statesman accepts the dominion of those powers and attempts to work with them. There are, the "realistic" statesman insists, facts about how politics works, and it is his responsibility to act on the basis of those facts. This, however, is the reasoning of Ananias and Sapphira, and is subjected to one of the least ambiguous judgments of Scripture (Acts 5:2-5). Followers of Augustine embrace the contemporary equivalent of "the Roman legal tradition," as opposed to "the simple language of the Gospel," because they, like the saint, are "willing to grant that this simple language would be written off as irrelevant."[91] Yoder can admit that this language may be irrelevant to the world, but it cannot be irrelevant to the church, for "the definition of the gathering of Christians is their confessing Jesus Christ is Lord."[92] If discipleship involves confession, and if what Christians confess is rooted in the gospel story, then it seems bizarre, if not incoherent, to maintain that working out the requirements of the Christian story means giving up the language of that narrative where we claim to learn best what God is like.

For Yoder to insist that "we can only have gospel social ethics if we let confession and non-confession make a difference," and that "we can only be doing gospel social ethics if we are telling the story of Jesus,"[93] does not amount to a proof that Ramsey's version is a falling away from the faith. It is not clear what "proof" would mean in such a context. But this does not mean there is no fact of the matter. One goal of this essay has been to call into question the various relativisms that would deny, on methodological grounds, the possibility of truth claims grounded in an account of the biblical narrative. In the process I suggested that there was no credible foundation for philosophical epistemology that could eliminate recourse to one or another tradition in articulating our beliefs. Furthermore, if we characterize traditions in terms of the narratives that shape the ways they organize and deliberate about action, it turns out that we do not have a choice between "narrative ethics" and some other way of proceeding; the issue is *which* narrative forms our thinking and whether, if we are so disposed, we can remain faithful to it.

90. Ramsey, "Justice of Deterrence," 361.

91. Yoder, *The Priestly Kingdom*, 75, 79.

92. John H. Yoder, "Why Ecclesiology Is Social Ethics: Gospel Ethics Versus the Wider Wisdom," reprinted in Yoder, *The Royal Priesthood*, 108.

93. Yoder, "Ecclesiology Is Social Ethics," 109.

The claims of all traditions are claims about the way the world is, and depend for their truth on that world. But the adequacy of those claims only emerges in the very long run; in the interim, adherence to one or the other is a matter of complex and humanly unpredictable individual and social pressures. One way of talking about the Christian response to those pressures is in terms of "faithfulness." It is in faith that the Christian proclaims Jesus is Lord, but it requires self-criticism to stay focused on what the gospel means, and self-criticism requires realism about the possible gap between contemporary practice and the vision that inspired it. As Fingarette put it, "those who think doctrine and administrative structure constitute law fail to understand that when such vision ceases to inspire the people, the best legal institutions become corrupted."[94] For Yoder this means living constantly with the belief that Jesus, as Lord, has absolute power over creation. Without him there is no way to avoid the suffering and despair that are central to the experience of human finitude. If he chooses to convert even the most recalcitrant instead of exercising that power every Christian knows him to possess, his love is remarkable. But I must still, as a matter of logic, live as though I stood under the power of that command, hopeful that my failures will be forgiven.[95] The nonbeliever denies the existence of the Lord, which if true renders faith tragic. The Augustinian identifies the lordship of Jesus with pagan justice, which renders faith either pointless or capricious. The Niebuhrian identifies the lordship of Jesus with local human deliberation, which is either self-deception or idolatry. "The real issue," as Yoder rightly puts it, "is not whether Jesus can make sense in a world far from Galilee, but whether — when he meets us in our world, as he does in fact — we want to follow him."[96]

94. Fingarette, "Law in the Book of Job," 273.
95. Fingarette, "Law in the Book of Job," 262.
96. Yoder, "'But We Do See Jesus,'" 62.

THE OTHERNESS
OF THE CHURCH

The Believers Church
in Theological Perspective

James Wm. McClendon, Jr.

John Howard Yoder was a scholar and indeed a scholar's scholar — his influence is even more felt through other scholars' use of his work than through his own extensive teaching career. This paper, originally prepared for a Believers Church Conference in Hamilton, Ontario, in October 1996, has been rewritten to show the influence of John Yoder upon it as well as upon the concept of the Believers Church as he helped develop it in conferences from the "first" in Louisville, Kentucky, 1967, to this recent one at McMaster Divinity College. At Hamilton, Yoder stepped down as chair of the continuing committee for all these conferences. As will become clear, the present paper grew in large measure from his ongoing contribution. It is thus a fitting addition to a *Festschrift* in his honor. On the other hand, this paper reflects my own interpretation of the ecclesial life Yoder has influenced. It grows from my perception of and participation in that life. Thus it begins with a personal testimony, and it ends in Scripture — moving between two poles of historic baptist life.

I

I grew into Christian faith in what many would call a "voluntary" church. This was the old original Baptist church in Shreveport, Louisiana, a Southern city that in my youth displayed many of the woes and joys of the American South. There I made my profession of faith and was baptized in the years between the two World Wars. We young Christians in that church were taught to value liberty: we were told that Baptists had played a major part in gaining religious liberty in the United States and elsewhere; we could see for ourselves that our own participation was freely chosen, not something prearranged for us by our parents or by any others; we were taught, also, that we had an obligation to defend others' liberty of worship including their liberty to abstain from worship. We were free to be Baptists; they were free not to be, free even to be Methodists or whatever else they would. Later I would learn that our liberty and that of our neighbors was not quite so absolute as it then seemed; yet in those early years it was like the truth of the Bible itself, unquestionable — indeed, it *was* the truth of the Bible: Did not John 8:32 say, "And ye shall know the truth, and the truth shall make you free"?

Even then, though, the voluntariness of a voluntary church had its limits. No one in Shreveport supposed that a group of us, or even a church full of us, could do as we liked in any case. "Voluntary" didn't mean that someone who wasn't a member in good standing could barge in and vote in a church business meeting. "Liberty" didn't mean that whoever was preparing the Lord's Supper could fill those little glasses with wine from the liquor store rather than the customary grape juice from the grocery store. In fact, someone made that very experiment once at our church, and the consequences were not at all happy! We were committed to voluntarism, but that was only one among several commitments as strong or stronger.

Still, that boyhood church seems remarkable to me. I have reported only a fragment of its common life, which was far richer than I have said. Partly this was because of the worship: our pastor, M. E. Dodd, had a truly catholic gift for it — he brought to our services a sense of the holy; he brought a way with words that drew on King James English and complemented it with Tennessee eloquence; he knew how to draw our large congregation into one body of wonder, prayer, and praise. All this took place in a lovely domed worship space that modestly echoed Saint Sophia of antiquity. Partly, too, our church life was richer because everybody then seemed to learn the Bible: we Baptists (and Methodists and Presbyterians, too) could quote it even if many of us lacked the skill to locate the chapter and verse of our quotations. Our church was richer, too, because we shared a pervasive sacramental life, though we did not call it that: the rites of baptism and the Lord's table were observed in such a way that at least one Louisiana youth would never be able to forget whose child he was. Moreover, our religion was richer because it was strongly related to Shreveport politics and government and culture: when there was a question of government that would within its limits be fair to all people, or a question of saloons that threatened the health and livelihood of the city's weaker members, or a question of a college that would provide education for young women, we knew in each case the side our church would be on. In summary, our church in its time and place was broad gauge. It was strongly evangelistic; it was persistently educational; it was richly sacramental; it presented itself as a seamless whole. When I learned in that church to defend the voluntary church, I was learning a rationale that I would later define (with John Yoder) as truly "catholic."[1]

But was our church not only catholic but voluntary? Certainly so, if that meant we consented to be the Christians that we were. In that sense, though, the membership of every church in our town, every church in North America, was and is voluntary: no tax to support a state church; no law constituting us Lutherans or Buddhists or Catholics or Baptists. In North America those old battles had long ago been fought and won. If that is all "voluntary" meant, it has no present use and we can move on to other matters. Contrariwise, if by "voluntary" any mean to deny the influence of others' lives upon their own, that is simply mistaken: I owe what I now am, including my so-called "free" choices, to a variety of influences and conditionings that make me so; beneath all these influences, as I believe, are the everlasting arms of divine election and divine providence. Our spiritual ancestors were not stupid folk; they did not use such high and holy words as "voluntary church" lightly and unadvisedly; we must take care to see what they meant if we are to mean anything useful by such words now.

Earlier in our century, theologian Harris Franklin Rall, in search of a way to characterize his own Methodists, contrasted "gathered church" and "given church." In eighteenth-century England the given church was the existing, institutional Church of England spread in its parishes across the land; the gathered church was the class meetings and open-air exercises of the Wesleys and their followers. Harvard historian George Williams, in a 1991 essay, agreed with Rall that the gathered/given distinction might be used to analyze not only eighteenth-century England but other ecclesial situations. For the Radical Reformers the given church was either Roman Catholic or it was the new state churches of the Magisterial Reformers; in both these cases the radicals found the given church deficient, and their response was gathered churches others called Anabaptist, communities that were in the words of Walter Klaassen "neither Catholic nor Protestant."[2] Williams found still other uses of "given" and "gathered." Over against the Old Roman church of late medieval times stood the magisterial Protestant churches themselves; Lutherans and Reformed then

---

1. James Wm. McClendon, Jr. and John Howard Yoder, "Christian Identity in Ecumenical Perspective," *Journal of Ecumenical Studies* 27 (Summer 1990): 561-80.

2. Walter Klaassen, *Anabaptism: Neither Catholic Nor Protestant*, rev. ed. (Waterloo, ON: Conrad Grebel Press, 1981).

were "gathered" from the given Roman church. The church of Pentecost, on this way of reckoning, was both given and gathered: as constituting a new divine beginning, it was God's gift, the given church; yet it was a community gathered from Israel and from the existing nations with their many tongues and myths.[3]

One of the advantages of this given/gathered classification is its flexibility. While Troeltsch's well-known typology seems to make the church type forever church, leaving the Anabaptists forever a sect, the given/gathered scheme of classification allows what had been the gathered church in one era to become the given church of another. The radical people called Methodists, forming a gathered church in eighteenth-century England, found themselves in mid-twentieth-century America worshiping in stately urban edifices, though often, by that century's end, those same buildings were less than a tenth filled on Sunday morning, thus replicating the deserted architectural monuments of the English mother church: once more, gathered church had become given church on the way to becoming gathered church again. The same was true of the radical Baptists of New England and the South: these dissenters of the early eighteenth century who had forsaken the stately meeting halls of colonial America to gather elsewhere for hot revival preaching and soul-shaking song found themselves two centuries later lonely in their neoclassical piles. For these folk "gathered" had become "given" once more, while the newer Christian phenomena were charismatic churches or house-churches or still other movements.[4]

So the gathered/given terminology is flexible, but flexible labels may be faulty — if the teams change their names too often, how can the fans stay loyal? If we are committed to a gathered church, does it cease to deserve our loyalty when its mansions grow more stately? Are we no longer Baptists if we do not worship in brush arbors? For me, the term "gathered church" bears an ongoing witness: the passive "gathered" declares that it is not we but God who gathers: the church is called out before it can call others; it is gathered before it is missionary. Thus we rightly cling to "gathered" as one of our names, though we admit we have changed greatly.

Such considerations apply *mutatis mutandis* to the concept of the voluntary church. Like "gathered," "voluntary" was a word first applicable to congregations for whom the existing structures had failed. Such dissenters turned deliberately to more faithful ways, building communities that could fulfill the Great Commis-

---

3. George Huntston Williams, "The Believers' Church and the Given Church," in *People of God: Essays on the Believers' Church,* ed. Paul Basden and David S. Dockery (Nashville: Broadman Press, 1991).

4. Williams, "Believers' Church," 329f.

sion, fellowships to stand clear of the state and its authority, assemblies that read the Bible with opened eyes, obeyed biblical commands, and practiced gospel solidarity with other believers. Their freedom was not a good or goal in itself or in isolation from the gospel; freedom was exactly a part of that good news. Such revolutionary dissent has recurred in Christian history, and what is meant by "voluntary" in one case or another must be determined empirically.

- *Hutterites* or *Hutterian Brethren* turned away from the capitalism and attendant militarism they saw overtaking Europe: they *volunteered* to experiment with collective ownership unprotected by any sword.
- *Swiss Brethren* forsook control of Christianity by their state government: they *volunteered* to convene churches not authorized by the city council.
- *Waldshut,* a town in South Germany, led by its parish priest, gave up a corrupt clerical religion: following Balthasar Hubmaier , they *volunteered* a new pattern of life and thought summarized in his "Eighteen Theses" (see Pipkin & Yoder, 1989).
- At *Schleitheim* radical believers abandoned previous attempts to go it alone and *voluntarily* formed a unity, sealed in the atoning blood of Christ (their motif was *Vereinigung,* at-one-ment)[5] that embraced a distinct way of living including daily home Scripture reading and a weekly Lord's Supper.
- Terrible experience of government by militant saints (at Münster) led many North German and Dutch baptists to renounce the use of force: led by a genius elder named Menno Simons, these radicals *voluntarily* formed communities of such peaceable stability that they have survived to this hour as Mennonites.
- Meantime, radical Christians in England and newfound America shared similar renunciations and *volunteered* similar experimental communities of life and faith, giving rise to people pejoratively called (Ana)baptists but by themselves just *Baptists.*

More broadly all these were called Anabaptists or Baptists, for in the course of nearly three centuries most of them had turned back to believer's baptism. They had recovered the primitive incorporative act, deliberate on the part of candidate and community alike. As a practice, it fit them well, because like the risky life of faith that followed, baptism required the wholehearted (and once immersion was reinstituted, the whole-bodied), i.e., voluntary, participation of each.

5. Cf. John Howard Yoder, trans. and ed., *The Legacy of Michael Sattler* (Scottdale, PA: Herald Press, 1973).

Then came the early seventeenth century, and here a great rift, unnoticed by some, makes our story less smooth than the one I learned in that Shreveport church long ago. Up until the early 1600s, the term "voluntary," like the term "gathered," usefully designated several episodes in radical history, though it meant something rather different in each case. Starting at about 1650, however, there is a profound change in the intellectual and social weather. This vast rift issued in the Enlightenment, and its consequences remain to this day. There now appeared (1) a new sense of the human self, called *individualism*, (2) a new, science-oriented way of construing human speech that among other effects *segregated religious utterance*, and (3) a new way of doubting much that we know, retrospectively dubbed *foundationalism*. Here again, some care with words is required: if with historians we call this enduring cluster of mental habits "modernity," we must not confuse it with the religious term "modernism," which was only one of the forms modernity took. In course of time, significantly, modernity also took shape as fundamentalism.[6]

The impact of this new, *modern* way of thinking is illustrated by the struggle over the human will that occurred in the Baptist denominations. What chiefly distinguished the two main sorts of English Baptists from one another involved the freedom of the unregenerate human will. The "Short Confession of Faith in XX Articles" of 1609, composed at Amsterdam in about 1609 by John Smyth (frequently called the first English Baptist), denies any "sin of origin or descent" because all sin is "actual or voluntary," and it affirmed that "men of the grace of God are able . . . to repent," while alternatively they are able to resist the Holy Spirit.[7] A generation later (1644) the (first) London Confession of the Particular Baptists held the contrary: "All since the Fall are conceived in sinne, and brought forth in iniquitie" (Article IV) and "Faith is the gift of God wrought in the hearts of the elect by the Spirit of God" (Article XXII) without the least mention of human ability.[8] This difference was explicit. Of course, similar struggles were occurring at about this time in other Christian camps, notably among the Reformed in Holland: The Synod of Dort (1619) rejected the attempt of the Arminian Dutch Reformed to take the path the General Baptists had already followed. These struggles are still with us today: note that they arose in new cultural weather, in a modernity that gave these conflicts over the human will a definitive role they had not had in earlier baptist centuries.

6. Nancey Murphy and James Wm. McClendon, Jr., "Distinguishing Modern and Postmodern Theologies," *Modern Theology* 5 (April 1989): 191-214.
7. William L. Lumpkin, compiler, *Baptist Confessions of Faith*, 2nd rev. ed. (Philadelphia: Judson Press, 1969), 100f.
8. Lumpkin, *Baptist Confessions*, 157-63.

Much that was thought and said about the "voluntary" church in the period from 1650 onwards is shaped by this new climate of thought. New thoughts are conceived by new men (for they conceived their human nature differently from their predecessors), they are declared in a new language (for the very grammar of religious utterance had changed), and they are argued or proposed with a new dread, the terror of uncertainty (for the era of philosophical foundations had arrived). The old labels, Baptist, Mennonite, Brethren, and the like, persisted into this new era, but now these terms were applied to a people divided on two sides of a crevice the wider changes had opened. Modernity was an earthquake rumbling across the world and opening vast fissures in earth's crust. Some baptists found themselves on one side of that fissure, some on the other, though both endured the same modernity. The chief areas in which differences appeared were the freedom of the will (already mentioned) and the nature of Scripture. The former difference issued in the continuing struggle over Calvinism from that century to the present; the latter would erupt in the fundamentalist-modernist controversy. Neither side of either battle could do full justice to baptist convictions; neither side could express the original vision that had made baptists baptists, and neither side was in good position to make the believers church truly the believers church.[9] Baptists (large or small b) might by the grace of God survive the modern era, 1650 to our own time, but only with great difficulty could they be baptists in it.

II

This long unsuitability of the present age to baptist (or radical biblical) existence is central to what I have to say, so I mean now to give three concrete examples of the difficulties some faced. (I will follow this with a sign of hopeful change.) For John Leland (1754-1841), a Virginia Baptist preacher, liberty, the realm of the voluntary, could be argued in Jeffersonian fashion by appealing to self-evident principles. While Jefferson had written in the draft constitution of 1776 that "We hold these truths to be self evident . . . that all men . . . are endowed by their creator with inherent and inalienable rights,"[10] his Baptist political ally John Leland proclaimed church freedom in a 1791 work titled *The*

9. James Wm. McClendon, Jr., *Ethics: Systematic Theology Volume I* (Nashville: Abingdon Press, 1986) and *Doctrine: Systematic Theology Volume II* (Nashville: Abingdon Press, 1994).

10. Quoted in Garry Wills, *Inventing America: Jefferson's Declaration of Independence* (New York: Random House, 1978), 374.

Rights of Conscience Inalienable.[11] Leland put forth this claim of inalienable rights not in the first instance as essential biblical teaching (which of course it was not) but as an apologetic device to argue for liberty for nonestablished churches in the new United States. Yet what began as external apology addressed to the political order inevitably became, in the minds of many Christians, doctrine proper and timeless; they no longer distinguished this apology from essential Christian teaching. Thus E. Y. Mullins's 1908 book, *The Axioms of Religion*, took the Leland line again, arguing that Baptist principles were simply self-evident.

Whether baptist truth is discovered in the pages of Scripture or looked up in a philosopher's table of self-evident axioms matters a good deal both to Christian doctrine and to political theory: for example, an appeal to the rights of the *individual* conscience (this was Leland's appeal) provides no adequate defense of the children of pacifist Mennonites or Hutterites who seek to live on the land in communities free from military conscription; by individualizing the claim of the kingdom of Christ, the axiomizers willy nilly diminished it.[12]

This brings up my second example, the modernist-fundamentalist struggle in Canadian life early in the twentieth century. (Similar examples abound in the United States and elsewhere.) Thomas Todhunter Shields (1873-1955) was for many years the highly gifted pastor of Jarvis Street Baptist Church in Toronto. Self-taught, exact, and eloquent, Shields is known for his vigorous (and divisive) attacks on McMaster College, the predecessor of the present university. He believed it had not stayed true to the faith of its founders. His leadership in the Baptist denomination opened rifts that in some cases remain unhealed even now. Representing his fundamentalist position as the faith once delivered to the saints, Shields placed ultimate reliance on the infallibility of Scripture (later theorists would call this biblical inerrancy), and he related the remainder of his theological convictions to it. Thus he defended the truth of the Bible (and his own doctrinal preaching) on ground that was itself neither biblical nor self-evident, namely his theory of infallibility. By the theory, though, he could indeed validate his teaching in a satisfactorily modern fashion.

Mark Parent has shown in an interesting article that the English-born Shields came quite late in his ministry to this distinctive (and in Shields's version, divisive) view of Scripture. It was the person and work of Jesus Christ that had founded Shields's early theology, and not until after the First World War

---

11. H. Leon McBeth, ed., *A Sourcebook for Baptist Heritage* (Nashville: Broadman Press, 1990).

12. On Leland see Michael Broadway's forthcoming dissertation from Duke University Press.

did he begin to change. Earlier he had declared that the Bible is not to be regarded as a textbook of science, but is "solely a textbook treating of sin and salvation."[13] Similarly, typology, not biblical literalism, dominated Shields's early reading of the Old Testament. By 1922, however, he had begun the course that shaped the rest of his career: now for him "the first principle was the inspiration and authority of the Scriptures, and it was only in the second instance that there came an insistence upon the essential deity of Jesus."[14] One cannot but wonder if the militancy Shields had brought to promoting Canada's war on Germany in 1914 had turned, a decade later, into a war against German literary and biblical scholarship. In any case, as Shields proclaimed in 1930, the Bible "could not be more utterly unlike every other book had it literally dropped from the skies."[15] In the end, Shields's broad evangelicalism narrowed to this foundational inerrancy, so that the talents of one eloquent Baptist leader were used only to support an ever-shrinking constituency of withdrawn fundamentalists.

Contrast the thought of another Canadian Baptist, Douglas Clyde Macintosh (1877-1948). Born in Ontario, Macintosh was savingly converted as an adolescent (as he would later say, he then made the "right religious adjustment" to God).[16] After graduating and teaching for a time at McMaster in Toronto, Macintosh went on to earn his doctorate at Chicago in its modernist heyday. In 1909 he was called to teach in the Yale Divinity School, where he served out a long career as professor of systematic theology. Macintosh as a Baptist was strongly attached to the Bible, but his ultimate line of theological defense was not scriptural infallibility, which he rejected, but the religious experience of each believer who had made a "right religious adjustment" in the experiences of sin and grace. Thus he invoked what was for him a scientific criterion, an indefinitely repeatable empirical experiment, to validate the truth of Christianity in a modern, i.e., a foundational, fashion. In his case, philosophical interest and training led him early to seek a foundation (which he found in experience), and then gradually to widen it, recovering in the process more of the biblical and evangelical faith of his childhood. Toward the end of his life Macintosh set out to write a three-volume theological work that would deal in successive volumes with social religion (1939), personal religion (1942), and finally a summary

13. Mark Parent, "The Irony of Fundamentalism: T. T. Shields and the Person of Christ," *Fides et Historia* 26 (Fall 1994): 46, quoting an 1899 Shields sermon.

14. Parent, "Irony of Fundamentalism," 47, 49.

15. Parent, "Irony of Fundamentalism," 54.

16. Douglas Clyde Macintosh, *Theology as an Empirical Science* (1919; Arno Press, 1980), 41 and passim; also in Vergilius Ferm, *Contemporary American Theology: Theological Autobiographies,* vol. 1 (New York: Round Table Press), 277-322.

theology that would encompass both. Regretfully, the third volume never appeared.

Thus the foundation satisfactory to one side was mutually rejected by the other, even though both sides shared many believers church practices. My argument is simply that their strategies were each based on the intellectual culture of their day, which demanded a self-evident epistemic foundation; in attempts to meet this need they were indistinguishable. Yet their unity in baptist convictions was split by the yin and yang of these opposed modernities.[17]

This paves the way for my third example of the vicissitudes of the voluntary church, the recent bitter conflict in the *Southern Baptist Convention*. Prior to the battle, as sociologist Nancy Ammerman has shown, most Southern Baptists belonged in neither of the camps that would come to be labeled moderate-liberal and fundamentalist-conservative. Then in the early 1980s a fundamentalist minority set out purposefully to capture the machinery of the annual Convention. The ensuing battle forced the majority who had merely occupied the middle ground to take one of the two sides; in the end the fundamentalists gained political control of the Southern Baptist Convention with its vast ecclesial bureaucracy.[18] Noteworthy in this complex, dark struggle is the appeal the winners made to biblical inerrancy. The beauty of inerrancy was not that it offered hermeneutical guidelines (for it did not)[19] but that it made Scripture a *foundation* for knowledge — the very sort of foundation that the modern period demanded for all its reasoning. Ammerman, after describing the fundamentalist victory, writes that "while 'modernity' might be the long term victor in the [American] culture, this institutional segment of the culture [the Southern Baptist Convention] had been reclaimed by a fundamentalist movement."[20] Her judgment, though, needs correction at this point. The fundamentalist movement *is* a modern movement; it is a *phenomenon of modernity*, so that fundamentalism's victory reflects modernity's triumph even more than a moderate outcome could have done.

Now consider this: the Alliance of Baptists, an organization formed to resist the fundamentalist capture of the Southern Baptist Convention, in 1987 is-

17. For the philosophical expansion of this theme, see Nancey Murphy's *Beyond Liberalism and Fundamentalism: How Modern and Postmodern Philosophy Set the Theological Agenda* (Valley Forge, PA: Trinity Press International, 1996).

18. Nancy Tatom Ammerman, *Baptist Battles: Social Change and Religious Conflict in the Southern Baptist Convention* (New Brunswick, NJ: Rutgers University Press, 1990).

19. Cf. Humphreys's article, "Biblical Inerrancy: A Guide for the Perplexed," in *The Unfettered Word: Southern Baptists Confront the Authority-Inerrancy Question*, ed. Robinson B. James (Waco, TX: Word Books, 1987).

20. Ammerman, *Baptist Battles*, 252.

sued a declaration of principles or "Covenant." (It was a time, they declared, "when historic Baptist principles, freedoms, and traditions need a clear voice.") The first two elements of this new Covenant[21] were commitment to the freedom of the individual and the freedom of the local church. Here again in the Southern Baptist struggle, foundational *principles,* namely freedom and the voluntary principle, self-evident to Thomas Jefferson and his intellectual children, were invoked in protest by believers church people as they confronted a new given church, the newly conquered Southern Baptist Convention.

III

Already, though, there are signs of hope. Some felt that these attempts of their fellow political moderates failed to confront the deeper difficulties. Thus in 1997 some young Baptists working in Southern U.S. university settings drafted a declaration, "Re-Envisioning Baptist Identity: A Manifesto for Baptist Communities in North America." In the spirit of the preceding analysis of modernity, it warned against "two mistaken paths" that imperiled Baptist life. Concretely, the mistaken paths were those of the now hardened opponents in the late Southern Baptist controversy: those who would "shackle God's freedom to a narrow biblical interpretation," opposed by those who would "sever freedom from . . . the community's legitimate authority." These were the two versions of modernity just noted. The politics of separation had failed to settle the deeper issues because in important ways the two sides were alike mistaken, and the "baptifesto," as it was called, summoned both sides to recognize and renounce the underlying "idolatry" that had caused the theological war.

This document is interesting because it moves away from the kind of modernity that has so far kept all kinds of baptists (and not just Southern Baptists) from their true business. The theological battles over human nature and its freedom and over the Bible and its divine and human status were predestined by the *Zeitgeist;* this battleground was staked out by modernity itself, and if modernity is at last ending, baptists may soon hear one another again.

Two new-old features pervade "Re-Envisioning": its New Testament saturation together with its allusions to the earliest baptists give it some shelter from the heavy weather of modernity (it escapes, to be concrete, the triple alternatives of foundationalism *or* skepticism, of biblical literalism *or* private inter-

---

21. Walter B. Shurden, *The Baptist Identity: Four Fragile Freedoms* (Macon, GA: Smyth and Helwys, 1993), 85.

319

pretation, of social individualism *or* social collectivism).[22] It says that each of these alternatives is idolatrous; like stone idols each of them is dead. Thus not "voluntarism," a term preempted by modernity in its several forms, but the older concept of liberation or liberty is its opening theme — the liberty of free churches. This freedom, like the exodus from Egypt, constitutes an escape; specifically, the churches may escape the dying assumptions of the present age. But the way into the future requires burying the idols.

Positively, "Re-Envisioning" offers five "affirmations," each introduced by an italicized slogan explained in the paragraphs that follow it. As befits a time of crisis, the slogans mean to challenge complacency. They are intended to startle minds, not settle them. In brief, the five affirm:

1. *Bible study* in **reading communities** rather than private interpretation or supposed "scientific" objectivity.
2. *Following Jesus* as the call to **shared discipleship** rather than expressing a (foundationalist) theory of competent souls.
3. *A free common life in Christ* in **gathered, reforming communities** rather than withdrawn, self-chosen, or authoritarian ones.
4. *Baptism, preaching, and the Lord's table,* **powerful signs that seal God's faithfulness** rather than mechanical rituals or mere symbols.
5. *Freedom without coercion* **as a distinct people under God** rather than relying on political theories, principalities, or powers.

Each motto names a standard baptist practice (here *italicized*). Each then takes a cue from the New Testament and earliest baptist life to "re-envision" that practice (here **bold**). Modern alternatives of the left and right are then explicitly rejected.

The practices are not novel; they have persisted for baptists through good days and bad, through premodern and modern times. In my own words, they are shared Bible study (we are a people of one book), an evangelism that summons into a new communal life, a divine fellowship shaped by remembering signs that reclaim the biblical story, and thus a countercultural, counterpolitical church. These practices have been supported by all sides right through the modern period, yet no side could adequately protect this heritage. One wing could not freely practice Bible reading because it had adopted a modern theory of inerrancy; another could not because it had adopted modern, private interpretation. One sort of baptist could not freely practice evangelism because it supposed outsiders had no free will; the other could not because outsiders

---

22. Murphy and McClendon, "Modern and Postmodern Theologies."

had an inviolate human right of privacy. One understanding failed to baptize and to gather at the Lord's table because of its individualism; the other failed because of its collectivism. The authoritarian side could not practice the politics of Jesus; neither could the individualist side. I do not suppose that the authors of "Re-Envisioning Baptist Identity" have overcome all these modern difficulties at a stroke, but they point a hopeful way. It is a way, as their title suggests, that will require some rethinking, some re-envisioning.

In particular, *biblical study* is related to what John Yoder with others calls the Rule of Paul: the claim of 1 Corinthians 14 that when believers meet, each brings a contribution.[23] These contributions will not be identical, will not be in the same tone of voice, will not come from the same authoritative commentaries. Harmony comes not from ministerial authority but comes when at the Spirit's behest contributors aim to build up the church (1 Cor. 14:26-29). As the "baptifesto" puts it, "When all exercise their gifts and callings, when every voice is heard and weighed, when no one is silenced or privileged, the Spirit leads communities to read wisely and to practice faithfully the direction of the gospel."

The biblical *priesthood of all believers* grows from practicing the way of Jesus: it is not that each of us makes his or her way to God independent of all the rest of us; rather such priesthood means we are members one of another in Christ. "Re-Envisioning" puts it positively (we are priests one to another, confessing faith and fault to each other in the church) and then adds a negative: "We reject all accounts of freedom that construe faith as a private matter between God and the individual or as an activity of competent souls who inherently enjoy unmediated, unassailable, and disembodied experience with God." It rejects "identifications of the priesthood of believers with autonomous individualism."

The biblical *practice of church* as lives bound together is undergirded in this document by the practices (not the abstracted doctrines) of believers baptism and called-out, table-gathering church membership. Granted, the baptifesto challenges those who visibly lack these practices (will they not consider regaining them?), but before that it challenges any of its own who too confidently assume they already have them. Thus baptists must "close off nominal Christianity in our own ranks. [The baptifesto] is only second a gesture toward other traditions and communities to the end that they might make disciples of those whom they baptize."

This declaration has most trouble, I think, in saying what it intends about

---

23. John Howard Yoder, *The Priestly Kingdom* (Notre Dame: University of Notre Dame Press, 1984), 22, and *The Fullness of Christ: Paul's Vision of Universal Ministry* (Elgin, IL: Brethren Press, 1987).

church and state in Western society. It yearns to show that there is a *kind of liberty* that, just because it follows Jesus, cannot be content with modern church states and surviving state churches. Nor can followers of the crucified be content with current Western institutions such as the culture-church as a social bulwark or civil religion as the state's underlying myth. Its authors intend to say all this clearly, forcefully, and biblically, while at the same time affirming the obligation to support others' freedoms as well as our own, yet they have not easily reduced these to the brief space of two columns. I am glad of what it says: "The disestablishment of the church is constitutive of its identity as God's called-out community which foreshadows the coming reign of God as does no other community." Yet I wish it might have been more explicit, for example, about the peacemaking task of Christ's church (a lifelong task for John H. Yoder), or about the peoplehood that constitutes their wider community.

IV

It is time, then, to ask a hard question: If "come out from among them" is typically the path of the voluntary or gathered church, if this sort always says no to some given ecclesial home in order to say yes to a freshly gathered church, will such a church not repeatedly fall into heresy and schism? What is to keep such a fluid and evolving movement oriented to the wholeness of Christian faith? Protestants have their *sola gratia* and Catholics their *magisterium;* what have we radicals to keep us integral and true? Is the call to radical protest a call to isolation and to *Schwärmerei,* fanaticism? For answer, I turn to a passage in Ephesians, 4:1-16, that I believe points to the Christian future. This passage opens with a celebration of the great confessional unities: one body, one Spirit, one hope, one Lord, one faith, one baptism (4:4-6). It concludes with an appeal for growth "completely into Christ, who is the head" (4:15 NJB). Yet I will begin with a famous but hard-to-translate verse in the center: Ephesians 4:13. In NJB this reads:

> . . . until we all reach unity in faith and knowledge of the Son of God and form the perfect Man, fully mature with the fullness of Christ himself.

Here "perfect Man" is the striking term. The gendered word is unacceptable to the translators of the New Revised Standard Version, who when they reach the Greek word *andra* simply pass over it, recognizing that *anēr* is not *anthropos,* not "man" in the sense "human being": Ephesians has the distinctively male Greek word. Yet I think the New Jerusalem Bible, though it boldly translates as

322

"Man," misleads as well, for it suggests that this "perfect Man" is only God's holy people. In truth we face here a translator's puzzle. Markus Barth, in the Anchor Bible commentary on Ephesians, argues for a quite different reading. The main verb in the verse, he points out, is "come" or (as in NJB) "reach" — the Greek *katantao* means to arrive at a given point, or sometimes "to meet a person." In every use of this verb, Barth writes, "movement is presupposed." But who or what is it that makes a journey to encounter a *perfect male human being?* In answer, Markus Barth suggests two images from the ancient world. The first envisions

> a festival procession that is under way in solemn fashion for a solemn purpose. Those partaking in the cortege go out to meet a very important [traveler, who will bring] them bliss, joy, security, and peace.[24]

Such a cortege might, for example, go out to receive a king as he approached a city. Psalm 68, just quoted in Ephesians, describes such a royal procession. There is also another possibility: the movement might be that of a bridal party going outside the walls to welcome the approaching bridegroom. Both sorts of solemn march were social customs in Paul's day and both would be familiar to the first readers of Ephesians. Barth tells us we need not choose between them, since in Psalm 45, again in the Song of Songs, and in the rites of many ancient cultures as well, the two sorts of procession, marital and political, were actually combined: the city provided a bride for the approaching king. Barth adds that the movement of the procession toward the Expected One was matched by his own approach to them. Then he reminds us that

> the "coming of the Lord" is fundamental to the life, faith, confession, worship of the [early] church. The saints pray, "*maranatha*, [our] Lord, come!" (I Cor 16:22; Rev 22:20). The hoped-for coming of Jesus Christ is usually called his "parousia" (I Thess 4:15-17; Matt 24:27, etc.).[25]

Here, in brief, is the direction of the believers church in the "coming" century — indeed, its true or proper direction in any century from first Advent to last Advent. We are to move together toward the full knowledge of the *huios tou theou*, the Son of God — so says Ephesians 4:13. When that last, full meeting comes, and only then, will our goal be reached. But all is not then ended, for as Markus Barth points out,

24. Markus Barth, *Ephesians: Volume II, Translation and Commentary on Chapters 4-6,* The Anchor Bible, Vol. 34A (Garden City, NY: Doubleday, 1974), 484-96; the quotations are from 485.

25. Barth, *Ephesians: Volume II,* 486f.

just as a king or bridegroom, by his advent and through his meeting with those expecting him, fulfills the hope and changes the status of many, so according to Eph 4:13 does the Son of God, the Perfect Man, the Messiah. He makes his people participants in his perfection and riches. All that is his becomes theirs. The transformation of the many, effected by the meeting with [this unique] Man, is in this case distinct from a gradual improvement. It resembles a sudden change comparable to the effect of forgiveness and sanctification.[26]

Paul in Romans calls this still-awaited "sudden effect" glorification. When that comes, the assets of the Coming One will be bestowed upon the citizens or upon the bride, so that (in the language of Ephesians) the Messiah himself is perfected by incorporating his people into himself, one Christ. Thus the New Jerusalem Bible and the New Revised Standard Version are not all wrong, even though their translations are deficient, for finally what they proclaim will also come true — they have simply jumped ahead of the writer of Ephesians to reach the final stage![27]

In just what is that great and sudden change in the people of God to consist? Ephesians has already answered. For 4:13 serves as the center, the fulcrum, by which we may understand the entire passage, 4:1-16. What the apostle urges in the verses before and after it discloses the changes already under way in the lives of those who have joined the cortege and are moving outside the city walls to meet their coming Prince. None of these ongoing changes is independent of the Coming One's presence and his help: he whom we are to meet is quietly, as if incognito, already present in our midst. Consider these expected changes as Ephesians lists them.

First, there is *the binding character of Christian ethics.* Israel was set free from bondage in order to observe God's law; not set free to ignore the Ten Words. God's messianic people must now "make fast with bonds of peace the unity which the Spirit gives" (4:3 Revised English Bible). So the theme of unity, which runs through Ephesians, is linked here with other still-to-be-realized Christian themes. It is linked to peace, so little acknowledged in Christian history save by a few radicals, it is linked to the acknowledgment of the Spirit that is being recovered by Pentecostals for us all, it is linked to bondage or servanthood, which is the old Anabaptist way of the cross. So — if it plans to march to meet the coming One in the solemn procession of verse 13 — the "voluntary" church now must look well to Christian unity, to peacemaking, to Spirit-giftedness, to suffering servanthood.

26. Barth, *Ephesians: Volume II,* 487.
27. Barth, *Ephesians: Volume II,* 495.

This demand is preceded in Ephesians by the seven unity themes of Christian doctrine: one body, Spirit, hope; one Lord, faith, baptism; one Father God "over all and through all and in all" (4:6 REB). Later Christians have read these seven to reflect the holy Trinity: God the Spirit, God the Lord or Word, and God the Father. Certainly what these verses bring out is that the radical church that marches to meet its Savior must be *a church holding fast the treasure of biblical doctrine:* the Bible is a treasure of faith as well as a treasure of practice; the story the Bible tells is God's own story, told as God pleases to tell it.

There immediately follows this *a doctrine of ministry* suitable for an assembly marching to meet its bridegroom-king. Our Catholic and Protestant forebears quarreled over orders of ministry — twofold ministry, threefold ministry, and the like. Ephesians knows nothing of this, but it does distinguish two categories of ministry: an equipping or training ministry functionally divided into *apostles* (who plant churches), *prophets* (who declare God's truth), *evangelists* (who make certain we do not remain an ethnic enclave but share our good news), and *pastor-teachers* (who instruct and guide each flock).[28] Ephesians then places a greater emphasis upon the second category, the full ministry of the saints, "God's holy people," equipped by these just-named preparers and trainers (4:12 NJB). Here the Yoderian theme is the abolition of the "laity," the rejection of supposed Christians who receive without any felt need to give. It displays members of "a church without laymen and priests":[29] no special privilege accrues to the first, helper category, who are only *servi servorum dei,* servants of the servants of God.

Now to the final three verses of our paragraph, where we meet the *organic doctrine of church* that coheres with this futuristic vision. I quote the English translation made by my Swiss guide Markus Barth:

> [14]"No longer are we to be babes, tossed by waves and whirled about by every doctrinal gust, [and caught] in the trickery of men who are experts in deceitful scheming. [15]Rather by speaking the truth in love we shall grow in every way toward him who is the head, the Messiah. [16]He is at work fitting and joining the whole body together. He provides sustenance to it through every contact according to the needs of each single part. He enables the body to make its own growth so that it builds itself up in love.

Is that the shape of the voluntary church in the "coming" century? After all that has happened in our era — our experiment with modernity, our awesome science, our terrible wars, our broken human compacts, our empty hu-

---

28. Yoder, *The Fullness of Christ.*
29. Barth, *Ephesians: Volume II.*

man hearts — are we to turn back in the end to such well-worn words as these that speak of the great coming parousia, back to a passage that points toward an ethics, a doctrine, a practice of ministry, back to a community preparing for a coming day — the day when, though we know not when, he comes? Are the heirs of the radicals destined to become part of the welcoming cortege or (as we say in our jargon) members of the committee that will go to meet this Coming One, meet him lest he reach our national walls, reach our ghetto walls of pride and privilege, reach our very souls' walls and find us unready for the Great Day?

Meeting in the Power of the Spirit: Ecclesiology, Ethics, and the Practice of Discernment

Gayle Gerber Koontz

For who can learn the counsel of God?
Or who can discern what the Lord wills?

We can hardly guess at what is on earth;
and what is at hand we find with labor;
but who has traced out what is in the heavens?
Who has learned your counsel,
unless you have given wisdom
and sent your holy spirit from on high?

The Wisdom of Solomon 9:13, 16-17

In his small book, *Body Politics,* John Howard Yoder named decision making by open dialogue and consensus as one of five central practices of the church. This practice of "meeting in the power of the Spirit" or "the rule of Paul," he suggested, might even be called a sacrament of the church — in its root meaning as an action of God "in and with, through and under what men and women do."[1] Incorporating the freedom of all to speak in a consensual deci-

1. John Howard Yoder, *Body Politics: Five Practices of the Christian Community Before the Watching World* (Nashville: Discipleship Resources, 1992), 73. For a more scholarly treatment of

sion-making process is a flexible and practically focused method of Christian moral reflection, one which I will refer to in this essay as the practice of community discernment.[2]

While Christian "discernment" has long been of interest to those attuned to the interrelationship of ethics and spirituality, it is receiving renewed attention from scholars examining the "practices" of the church. Discernment appears, for example, among the subjects treated in *Practicing Our Faith*. Frank Rogers there writes that discernment "makes intentional a process of reflection on and participation with God's Spirit as the fundamental context in which we live and make choices."[3] Such a practice is an ethical practice — a process of moral evaluation involving character, principles, values, modes of reasoning, interpretation of facts, decision-making structures and procedures — in response to concrete, often messy situations. But it is also a spiritual practice. For those who desire the Word of Christ to be determinative for ethics, that Word must be discerned. Such discernment involves creative interaction of the spirit of Christ and followers of Christ in response to specific situations.

But how is discernment to be done? What encourages this creative interaction of Spirit and situation in ethical decision? How can it go wrong? What makes discernment a "virtuoso" rather than a "flatfooted" performance, borrowing terms from James Gustafson?[4] Frank Rogers makes some suggestions. But in the concluding chapter to *Practicing Our Faith,* Dorothy Bass and Craig Dykstra suggest ongoing exploration of particular expressions of Christian practices as a way of learning from each other. How has a particular community shaped a practice? How does it help us participate in the activity of God's Spirit? How do we evaluate it ethically? Where has it hurt or oppressed? How has the community practicing it learned from it? In the spirit of this invitation, and having an appreciation for comments based on "thick description," I would

this point see "Sacrament as Social Process: Christ the Transformer of Culture," *Theology Today* 48 (April 1991): 36-39.

2. Yoder uses the term "discernment" more specifically in relation to one step in another of the five practices he outlines — the practice of reconciliation or "binding and loosing." In that process, based on Matthew 18, "discernment" begins with two or three and expands only as necessary into a full-blown community discernment process. Because the theological conviction that the Holy Spirit moves in the process of discerning conversation overlaps in both cases, in other Mennonite writings the term "discernment" appears both in relation to "binding and loosing" and in reference to decision making by open dialogue and consensus (or by some mixed process that involves both voting and consensual procedures).

3. Frank Rogers, Jr., "Discernment," in *Practicing Our Faith,* ed. Dorothy C. Bass (San Francisco: Jossey-Bass Pub., 1997), 117.

4. James M. Gustafson, "Moral Discernment in the Christian Life," in *Norm and Context in Christian Ethics,* ed. Gene Outka and Paul Ramsey (New York: Scribner's, 1968), 26.

like to offer one example of the practice of community discernment in a Mennonite context for ongoing reflection.

I have chosen to focus on community rather than individual discernment since Anabaptist-Mennonites, particularly in the Swiss tradition in which John Howard Yoder was rooted and from which context he spoke, had special interest in the practice of decision making in the community of believers or "meeting in the power of the Spirit." As a result there are some theoretical as well as practical resources from this tradition at our disposal. Community discernment has also been practiced by some groups of Christians in religious communities as widely different as Catholics and Quakers, which provides further perspective in evaluating Mennonite practice.

The narrative of "The Campus Guest" which follows is based on a series of events which took place in Indiana in the early 1980s in the church institution where I teach, the Associated Mennonite Biblical Seminaries.[5] The situation involves a stranger who pressed the limits of hospitality at the seminaries, a guest who challenged foundational community values. As background to the narrative it is important to know that "Assembly" refers to a structure which included all members of the seminary community — not only faculty and students but also their spouses, not only presidents and development personnel, but also secretaries and maintenance workers. The Assembly met occasionally to discuss and decide matters of import to the whole community and annually chose a coordinating committee, which provided leadership.

The Campus Guest

Tom Strong came to the campus of the Associated Mennonite Biblical Seminaries in northern Indiana on January 18, 1982.[6] He was not a member of a

5. In January 1994 the seminaries were incorporated as one Associated Mennonite Biblical Seminary. In the 1980s although there were separate boards, presidents, and fundraising procedures, there was one dean and the faculty and student body carried little sense of separate seminary identity. To avoid grammatical awkwardness I may occasionally refer to the Associated Seminaries as one "seminary."

6. In the following narrative the name of the "guest on campus" has been changed. The rest of the story is intended to be historically accurate. In preparing this account I am indebted to David L. Myers who chose to write a student paper shortly afterwards, for which he interviewed a number of people involved ("An 'Uninvited Guest': A Case Study of [name of guest] Visit to AMBS Using Force-Field Analysis and Change Theory." Unpublished student paper in Conflict Management course, Associated Mennonite Biblical Seminaries, December, 1982). Records from the seminary archives, conversations with several faculty members, and my own selective memories of the event (I was a member of the congregation which helped to host Tom

church. Earlier in the month in New York he had met a middle-aged single social worker, an active member of a Mennonite congregation in a town near the seminaries, when she joined a street demonstration for better social welfare programs in the City. Attracted by her ethical commitment, her compassion for the poor and her missionary welcome, he decided to follow her to Indiana. When she discovered upon his arrival that Tom had assumed he could simply move in with her, she appealed to her congregation for assistance. Other church members provided initial hospitality and introduced him to the community, including giving him a tour of the seminaries.

Indicating interest in the peace tradition of the seminaries and ambivalence about his previous involvement in the military, Tom said that he would like to return to campus and attend some classes. He talked with several professors who gave him permission to visit some of their second semester classes, which he then began to do. After several weeks Tom began to "wear out his welcome" as a guest. He made it increasingly clear that he valued freedom absolutely. He did not tolerate authority and indicated that he was philosophically committed to anarchism. One professor who had agreed to his attendance in class on a day-by-day basis as long as class size permitted it, reported that "at first Tom seemed to make some pointed comments which were good" and made students think about their commitments. But then he began to dominate class discussion or spoke at inappropriate moments. During one of those times the professor told Tom that "this is a time to remain quiet" and he did so.

His unorthodox views and the way they challenged the status quo intrigued several students who talked with Tom informally in the lounge and on campus. Some made allowances for him because he was a stranger, a seeker, a street person. Several women reported to other students that they did not feel comfortable or safe around Tom since they felt that he read their normal campus "friendly" behavior as sexual invitation. As February came to a close, faculty began to express growing uneasiness with the situation and the sense that "the dean should clean this up." One staff person suggested that the business committee should handle the situation because this committee "is responsible for the grounds and the buildings; also for security and trespassing." Some students, who got wind that the faculty might "try to get rid of Tom," expressed grave concern about this attitude which seemed inconsistent with Christian care for those who are socially marginalized.

On March 1, faculty meeting participants (a group which ranged from

---

and taught an initial course at the seminaries that year) contributed to the narrative. Most of the faculty members who participated in the 1982 decisions are no longer active at the Associated Seminaries.

twenty-one to twenty-four people during this period and which regularly included the president and dean as well as six or so "administrative faculty" and two student representatives) addressed the situation of the "visitor" in their scheduled meeting. Concern was expressed that "some of the basic levels of difficulty in his life be addressed in a caring, confronting way." The faculty and staff decided that the guest should meet with a group consisting of the dean, a member from the congregation which was hosting the guest, and the two pastoral counselors at the seminaries. The action noted further, "that he be gently but firmly informed that he may not attend classes, pending a recommendation from the above group. In the meantime, he is invited to apply for admission, with a view toward possible matriculation in the fall semester."

On March 3 Tom submitted an incomplete application form signed with an "X" to the registrar.

The appointed group met with Tom on March 4. No agreement was reached in a highly volatile meeting. Tom was extremely angry, shouted and cursed at the dean, the representative authority figure. Following the emotional heat of this exchange, the presidents decided that Tom's growing influence "was enough." Day-to-day administrative attention to the relationship with Tom shifted to one of the president's offices and the situation "became an Assembly issue."

After reporting the outcome of this meeting to the faculty on March 8, the faculty agreed "that the visitor not be allowed on campus any longer." The faculty did not act on how to implement this decision. The following procedure was considered: if Tom continued to go to class, the dean would follow and ask Tom to leave. If Tom refused, the dean would dismiss the class. An administrative faculty member, who felt that it was necessary to "deal more drastically with Tom," argued that this procedure gave too much power to Tom since he could effectively cancel classes, and this idea was dropped.

Tom continued to come to classes. One professor reported the faculty action and asked Tom to leave the room. He refused. During the next class session Tom made the case for his view for the entire hour. After class the professor told Tom that he could not use the entire hour without "the whole class participating in deciding how the hour should be used." The professor also began to feel "increasingly ambivalent about the amount of time I was devoting to him." Another professor did not want to "make a case of it in class" and permitted Tom to attend in spite of the faculty action. He reported that Tom "behaved well." He wondered if asking Tom to leave wasn't going against the grain of Christian community.

A member of the development staff, growing increasingly impatient with the situation, felt that "Tom was a schizophrenic" and that "we don't have the gifts here to deal with [Tom]." He was also concerned that far too much administrative time and energy were being given to Tom. "The president is running behind on other things that would have pushed the Kingdom further ahead than [dealing with] Tom." Energies spent on Tom were "out of proportion with the benefits that could have been realized had the same amount of energy been spent elsewhere." He felt that quick, direct action like calling in the police should have been taken much sooner.

A number of students who learned of the March 8 faculty action that Tom no longer be allowed on campus questioned this action and felt that students should have been drawn into the decision-making process much earlier. Student gossip channels passed along the idea that faculty and administration were contemplating police action and questions were raised about the compatibility of such action with commitment to Christian peacemaking and nonviolence. One student indicated that he felt the administration and faculty had an overblown sense of Tom's dangerousness and said "ideas like carrying Tom off campus seemed motivated by defensiveness." Tom in conversation with students shared his conviction that all systems will eventually resort to force or violence if pushed. In various settings he also made it clear that he would cooperate with students but not with administrators.

A female student reported privately that "if someone were looking in from the outside, then Tom's behavior with women wouldn't 'objectively' seem that bad — prolonged hugs, some kissing." She noted that some of the women students' eroding sense of security was based on the fact that Tom did not follow commonly observed boundaries in the community. "This had a personal effect on me," she said. "Could I sit in the lounge and relax or did I have to worry about Tom coming in?"

On March 10 the president met with Tom to address three issues: (1) matriculation procedures for class participation, (2) a public statement by Tom regarding appropriate relationships with seminary women, and (3) Tom's seeing a therapist which could be arranged by the seminaries. Tom agreed to respect procedures for class participation and to make a public statement regarding commitment to appropriate relationships with seminary women. No agreement was reached on the third issue.

The same day the Assembly coordinating committee decided to call a special assembly regarding Tom so that the entire seminary community would be clearly informed and have a voice regarding subsequent actions. The following day Tom met with the committee and agreed to publicly announce in the special assembly the first two agreements he had made with the president.

On March 12, the day the assembly had been scheduled, Tom met with a member of the student executive one-half hour before the meeting and informed her that he would not be able to follow through with the previously agreed upon commitments.

The special assembly lasted for two and a half hours. After some heated debate the group accepted a motion which affirmed the normal matriculation procedures for Tom (three nos, some abstentions). In addition the group offered and considered various options for further response to Tom. The president met with Tom and informed him that because he had failed to follow through with agreed-upon commitments that the relationship between Tom and the seminaries had to change fundamentally. The president indicated that the Administrative Committee and the Assembly Coordinating Committee would be meeting to discuss appropriate action.

The committees met on March 15 and considered four options: (1) police action for removing Tom from campus, (2) carrying Tom off campus, (3) having an "escort" follow Tom wherever he went while on campus, (4) a "ban of silence" directed toward Tom by the entire seminary community. The group agreed on a combination of the third and fourth options, which reflected a substantial consensus at the March 12 Assembly meeting. In the meantime the president had also been able to contact a family member of Tom's. The family member did not want to be further involved with Tom, but indicated that there was a history of emotional illness, a pattern of Tom forcing institutions to "put him out," and that Tom was more likely to be verbally than violently aggressive.

Later that day when Tom was informed of the committees' decision, he replied, "This is kid's stuff. They've put me in prisons and all of that. The heavier you get, the worse I'll react — heavier and heavier. I'll be coming to campus tomorrow."

The following day, March 16, the two committees informed students and faculty in closed session about their proposed action, explaining the definition and rationale for the ban and escort. Their written statement noted:

> During the past weeks our community has been seeking to relate constructively to Tom Strong. Unfortunately, he has confirmed that he will not make commitments, or follow through with responsible action; he has repeatedly refused requests which faculty have made of him; he has refused to give any indication of cooperation, and that he did again in extended meetings and conversations with him this weekend and Monday. He has over these weeks instilled anxieties in both staff and students.
>
> Because of his past history of manipulation of institutions in which he has provoked them to request his eviction by the police (we have references to document this) [we] are requesting the following alternate pattern of action be respected. . . .

333

1. We are appointing an escort to accompany Tom on the campus at all times. The purpose of this will be to encourage silence in classes and to restrain unwelcome advances to women students.
2. We ask for the imposition of a ban of silence toward Tom on campus. Both faculty and students are requested to ignore Tom's presence and his speeches, whether in class or elsewhere.

Tom has been informed of this course of action.

At the conclusion of the noon meeting regarding the ban, Tom came into the room. Everyone immediately, without any word of direction, folded their chairs and left the room without speaking.

March 18, Steve, a member of a local Mennonite congregation, arrived on campus to serve as Tom's "escort." Steve was encouraged to dialogue with Tom (he needed a "conversational outlet"), and if necessary remind others in the community to uphold the ban. The president told Steve that no physical force should be used.

On March 22 Tom came (uninvited) to a faculty meeting. He was asked to leave, and finally did so when a faculty member left with him. After ten or fifteen minutes Tom returned to the meeting and again was asked to leave. He refused saying, "I won't leave. I want to know people. I'm not well known enough." The chair adjourned the faculty meeting, but it was announced in German, a language which Tom did not understand, that the group would reconvene in another location.

The ban was consistently observed between March 16 and the beginning of spring break on April 4. Steve reported in retrospect that Tom respected the overall approach of the ban and had no desire to make waves about it. Tom planned to "weather it out" thinking that people intellectually agreed with the ban but emotionally would not be able to continue it and that gave him hope. Steve also said, "Tom didn't like the silence. He seriously considered leaving many times. He said he couldn't function if no one talked with him." He was puzzled and disarmed by the community response.

March 31 the president met with Tom for lunch off-campus, listened to some of his concerns and volunteered to give him a ride to the East Coast, where Tom had come from, when his family drove there for spring break. The president asked for a response by April 2.

On April 2 Tom informed the president by phone that he would not be traveling east with him. Tom did not return to the campus after that.

The president later learned from people who had been hosting Tom that on April 12 he was arrested for disorderly conduct and resisting arrest and taken to the county jail. From there he went to the area Veteran's Administration Hospital where he had made an appointment to undergo testing. Upon release the hospital gave him a bus ticket to South Bend, Indiana, and suggested that he go to the city rescue mission. There has been no further contact between Tom and the seminaries.

Theological Convictions and Community Discernment

The story of the campus guest illustrates in a striking way the *inseparability of theology and ethics* in Mennonite thought and practice. The narrative helps us see how theological convictions, and more specifically convictions about the nature, purpose, and shape of the church, shape Christian ethical reasoning and the practice of moral discernment. Consider, for example, how ecclesiology shapes ethics

- through the structure and leadership of the discerning community
- through the processes of decision making adopted
- by influencing what the community identifies as a moral issue
- by privileging certain principles and norms in discernment
- by influencing the character (virtues) of individuals in the community and the character of the community itself
- through the biblical texts and other narratives and memories selected and appealed to in the worship life and in the ethical imagination of the community.

To focus this more clearly, it is helpful to consider the implicit theology — convictions about the interrelationships of Christology, ethics, and ecclesiology — which undergirded and guided the practice of moral discernment as the seminary community responded to the campus guest. These convictions initially led to the formation of the structure known as the Assembly and influenced the type of leadership and the procedure for decision making that the community adopted for a period of years. These convictions encouraged the community to identify the forceable removal of Tom from campus as a "moral problem" and to accept nonviolence as a weighty moral principle. They influenced the development of values and virtues in the community, ones that could tolerate and sustain a slow-moving, sometimes unwieldy, broadly inclusive process of decision. They provided the framework for selecting biblical texts and historical memories (which included shunning or the ban) that were recalled in the ongoing worship, educational, and practical life of the seminaries from at least the 1960s to the 80s.[7]

7. During this period John H. Yoder was influential as a theologian, colleague, and teacher. He was a younger member of a creative group of seven Mennonite leaders who in the

Mennonite seminary leadership in these years took both Scripture and the believers church tradition seriously as they engaged in theological reflection. Their theological framework assumed a strong and vital connection between Christology, ecclesiology, pneumatology, eschatology, and ethics.[8] Like Christians in many other denominations, theological leaders at the seminaries accepted God's gracious and reconciling forgiveness in Christ as foundational, recognized that God's coming reign of peace, justice, and mercy oriented new life in Christ, and believed that God's Holy Spirit comforts and guides followers of Christ. But their reading of Scripture in tandem with believers church perspectives colored teaching and worship in several, quite particular ways.

Christology and Ethics

Rather than stressing the saving action and grace of God (which was assumed), teaching at the seminaries tended to emphasize the believer's response — profound commitment to follow Christ in life. This continued the *strong connection between Christology and ethics* characteristic of the Anabaptist Mennonite tradition. Jesus was not only a savior from sin and evil but an example of right living for contemporary Christians. In particular they gave attention to the ways in which Jesus, in the midst of his great passion for righteousness and healing, chose not to retaliate evil for evil but broke patterns of hostility and violence with forgiving love. Confessing that Jesus is the Christ meant taking up

fifties published a number of *Concern* pamphlets for the purpose of the renewal of the church. In this interaction the seeds of two later books, *The Fullness of Christ* and *Body Politics,* grew. Yoder wrote an influential early piece arguing that Anabaptism offers an "entirely different view of the Christian life, of the work and nature of the church, and fundamentally also of the meaning of redemption." "The Anabaptist Dissent: The Logic of the Place of the Disciple in Society," in Concern Pamphlet Series, No. 1 (privately published by a group of seven Mennonites, June 1954, copies in the Associated Mennonite Biblical Seminary library collection, Elkhart, Ind.) In addition he published an essay on binding and loosing (in Concern Pamphlet Series, No. 14, February 1967), 2-32, and emphasized leadership based on gifts.

8. Mennonite theologian Marlin Jeschke illustrated some of these interconnections when he wrote that ". . . it has been widely held that one might receive forgiveness but not necessarily a new nature, or that one might receive spiritual life but not undertake church membership, or that one might receive forgiveness of sin but not the gift of the Holy Spirit, or again, that one might accept church membership but not regeneration. The above-mentioned dimensions of life in the church are not, however, optional. They must all be held together in a balanced total unity." Jeschke, "Discipline and Discernment," in *The Believers' Church in Canada* [addresses and papers from the Study Conference in Winnipeg, May 15-18, 1978], ed. Jarold K. Zeman and Walter Klaassen (Winnipeg, Manitoba: Mennonite Central Committee [Canada], 1979), 112.

the form of life of Jesus and adopting a pattern of the age to come. It meant regeneration through the power of the Spirit, a new ethical life. And it meant a new social life. Membership in the church involved incorporation into a community of reconciliation.

This provided the ground for a community ethic and educational culture which among other things was earnest about discipleship, was familiar with the notion and procedures of moral discipline in the church, and which embraced pacifism and peacemaking as a way of community life.[9]

Christology and Ecclesiology

Reading Scripture in tandem with believers church perspectives, theological leaders at the seminaries further *forged a strong connection between Christology and ecclesiology,* a position also characteristic of the Anabaptist-Mennonite tradition. John E. Toews wrote in 1989 that Protestantism and evangelicalism in general have taught that "the church is an afterthought; it is not integral to Jesus' proclamation of the kingdom. Christology and ecclesiology are not explicitly linked. Biblical scholars continue to write volumes on Christology that say nothing about the church."[10] Toews's pithy essay attempted to make explicit an implicit Mennonite theological understanding of the essential relationship between Christ and the church. This understanding founds and motivates the practice of community discernment.

Toews examined Matthew 16:17-19 for the way in which it brings together two classic messianic themes — the cosmic rock and the messianic building.[11] He argues that both illustrate that the mission of Jesus is integrally bound up with the creation of the church. Jesus is to gather the end-time people of God on the rock so that he may save and protect them. Jesus is to build a new temple, a new creation where God will dwell in a new and powerful way

---

9. According to the *Mennonite Encyclopedia,* the most influential book to date related to Christology by a twentieth-century Mennonite theologian is likely John H. Yoder's *The Politics of Jesus.* It adopts current emphases on Jesus' humanity and his ethical significance and argues that Jesus' life, calling of alternative community, teaching, and crucifixion are normative for Christian ethics. See article on "Christology" by Marlin E. Miller, *Mennonite Encyclopedia V* (Scottdale, PA: Herald Press, 1990), 149.

10. John E. Toews, "Christ the Convener of the Church," in *Jesus Christ and the Mission of the Church: Contemporary Anabaptist Perspectives,* ed. Erland Waltner (Newton, KS: Faith and Life Press, 1990), 34. See also C. Norman Kraus's much more extended treatment of Christology from a modern interpretation of Anabaptism, *Jesus Christ Our Lord: Christology from a Disciple's Perspective* (Scottdale, PA: Herald Press, 1987).

11. Toews, "Christ the Convener of the Church," 38.

among his people. In addition, Toews demonstrated how New Testament images of atonement are rooted in community and in all cases carry the theme that the saving work of Christ creates a people. As a pioneer, captain, firstborn and head, Jesus is pictured in relation to a people. "Baptism into Christ means baptism into the people of whom he is the head, not primarily initiation into a personal relationship with Christ."[12]

"The challenge facing Mennonite churches," Toews concluded, "is to recover and expand our historic theology of the church as an authentic discipling and disciplining community" and to formulate an understanding of Christ as one who builds community and integrates individuals into communities of healing and meaning.[13]

Among other things this theological orientation provided vision for and supported commitment to developing structures, leadership, and process for community (rather than primarily individual) patterns of moral and spiritual discernment.

Community Discernment as an Essential Practice of the Church

The theological perspective described above assumed that "binding to God entails also that members of the church bind themselves to *each other* under God."[14] Within the Anabaptist tradition this included clear commitment to give and receive exhortation and counsel, to practice mutual aid and reconciling initiatives, to engage in service and discernment of gifts, and to seek together the will of God through the interpretation of Scripture.

For particular congregations or communities of believers "seeking together the will of God" implied an intentional process of discernment through which they could come to know the mind of Christ for specific questions or situations. Community discernment was basic to ethics. As Art Gish noted, "Distinguishing between right and wrong, good and bad, is the work of God mov-

12. Toews, "Christ the Convener of the Church," 52.

13. Toews, "Christ the Convener of the Church," 54-55. The theological orientation at the seminaries, drawing on Scripture and the believers church tradition, respected both the individual (*voluntary* membership in the church; *choosing* to follow Christ, freedom to *dissent*) and the Christian community (*community* of discipline, *body* of Christ, *mutual* aid). In the context of American Protestant religious culture, much of which was highly individualistic, serious teaching about the role of Christian community in the life of faith, even balanced with an appreciation for individual conscience and dissent, appeared as heavy emphasis on community.

14. Harry Huebner and David Schroeder, *Church as Parable: Whatever Happened to Ethics?* (Winnipeg, Manitoba: CMBC Publications, 1993), 159.

ing through the whole body. . . . Ethical decisions are to be made in relation to the Christian community."[15]

The practice of community discernment, as it was envisioned by seminary leaders, was rooted in the biblical witness and rested on interpretation of a number of texts and themes. Most common references were to the authority of the church to bind and loose and the promise of Jesus that his Spirit would be with those gathered in his name for that purpose (Matt. 18:15-20). It was emphasized that Jesus used the term *ekklesia* only two times, both of them in connection with the practice of binding and loosing, a practice which was interpreted to include both discernment and discipline.[16] They appealed as well to the witness of the decision-making process of the early church in Acts 15 ("It seemed good to the Holy Spirit and to us"), the abiding presence of Jesus through the Holy Spirit described in John 14–17, and many other passages dealing with decision, testing, examining, and interpreting.[17]

Understood to be a "mandate given to the church," discernment was envisioned as "a corporate process of sorting out some matter of controversy, seeking a solution to some problem, resolving some conflict, or finding an answer to some question."[18] It involved "disciplined listening to others in the Christian community, for the Spirit of Jesus lives within believers and speaks in a human voice."[19] It assumed that discussion under the Spirit of Christ was "just as 'spiritual' as preaching and no less central to the congregation's life."[20]

A further assumption was that the Scriptures stood at the center of the process of discernment. As faculty member Leland Harder put it, "Christ is our authority, but the Bible is the only place where we meet the historical Jesus. The

---

15. Arthur G. Gish, *Living in Christian Community* (Scottdale, PA: Herald Press, 1979), 96.

16. Gish, *Living in Christian Community,* 94. Ralph Lebold, "Decision Making," *Mennonite Encyclopedia V* (Scottdale, PA: Herald Press, 1990), 220, also notes that binding and loosing is not only a mandate to practice church discipline but a decision-making model for the church.

17. For more background on the biblical basis of this practice see Leland Harder, *Doors to Lock and Doors to Open: The Discerning People of God* (Scottdale, PA: Herald Press, 1993), 51-53; Marlene Kropf, "Discerning God's Voice: Spiritual Discernment in Mennonite Congregations," address given in 1991 (Elkhart, IN: Mennonite Board of Congregational Ministries, 1995), 4; John Rempel, ed., "Congregational Discernment" in *Minister's Manual* (Newton, KS: Faith and Life Press, 1998), 217-23. Luke Timothy Johnson has done the most extensive and helpful work I know of on the process of discernment in the book of Acts. See *Scripture and Discernment: Decision Making in the Church* (Nashville: Abingdon Press, 1983, 1996).

18. Harder, *Doors to Lock,* 17.

19. Kropf, "Discerning God's Voice," 7.

20. J. Lawrence Burkholder, "The Peace Churches as Communities of Discernment," *Christian Century* (September 4, 1963): 1074.

Holy Spirit is our guide, but the Bible is the connecting link between the Spirit's work and the Lord of the church."[21]

But while Scripture was central and essential, neither was it sufficient for interpreting the will of God. Writing for a study conference in the late fifties, a well-known Mennonite leader summarized a view of the relation of Christ, church, Scripture, and Spirit which became influential in teaching and learning at the seminaries:

The mind of Christ is most assuredly discerned when the body of Christ by the Scriptures, the illumination of the Spirit, and the exercise of mutual charismatic gifts seeks the will of her Head. The Spirit, the Scriptures, and the functioning of gifts bestowed in the church are interacting elements which together constitute the authority of the church in union with the living Christ. This is because they constitute the power to discern His will.[22]

Not Scripture alone, not the individual interpreter of Scripture, but the discerning church in union with the living Christ guides Christian ethics.

The Seminary as a Discerning Community

The Associated Seminaries as an organization was neither a "congregation" nor a "church" given the authority to discern God's will for the church. It was an institution created by the church for a specific and more limited purpose — the education of pastors and other leaders primarily for the Mennonite church. But as an institution of the church, the seminaries functioned within the framework of the church and the theological tradition which founded and nurtured it.

In the late 1960s a faculty study articulated a model for theological education based in the Free Church tradition.[23] The faculty came to the conclusion "that not only the content but also the context of the curriculum must be shaped by our theological convictions."[24] Those theological convictions fo-

21. Harder, *Doors to Lock*, 55.
22. Richard Detweiler, "The Authority of the Church — Its Nature and Location" in *The Nature of the Church*, 41. From a study conference sponsored by the Mennonite General Conference at Laurelville Mennonite Camp, September 24-25, 1958. In the Associated Mennonite Biblical Seminary library holdings, Elkhart, Indiana.
23. The full report of the study process by Ross Bender was published as *The People of God* (Scottdale, PA: Herald Press, 1971).
24. AMBS Catalog, 1987-89, 113. This theological education statement was included in the seminaries' catalog from the completion of the faculty study through 1989.

cused on ecclesiology and included the ideas that the "people of God" are a discerning community, a ministering community, a worshiping community, a witnessing community, a disciplined community, and a worldwide fellowship. Each of those convictions, it was suggested, had curricular implications as well as a role in shaping the context of theological education.

From this foundation, the expectation, structures, processes, and leadership for the practice of community discernment arose. Dean Ross Bender was quite explicit in noting that "the task of spiritual discernment is the fundamental task of the church and that the seminary, being a seminary of the church, shares in this task."[25] While the seminaries had a specific mission, narrower than that of the church, it had a shared general calling with the church. "The seminary is not only a community which reflects; it must also be a community which acts in response to the will of God and which thus participates in the renewing activity of a renewing God."[26] That responsibility required discernment with respect to the particular decisions with which the seminaries were charged.

Given this framework it was natural to ask, "What does it mean for the seminary to be a discerning community?" The creation of the Assembly was an attempt to respond in terms of community structure. Assembly meetings and leadership were open to any member of the community, making it possible for any member of the seminary community to take an active role in shaping decision making.[27] Marlin E. Miller, one of the presidents of the seminaries when Tom arrived on campus in 1982, later wrote in another context about the "alternative community of moral discernment." Who participates in the discerning community? he asked. Are decisions made only by leaders? Experts? Those existentially caught? Miller responded that the emphasis on Christian community as the place of moral discernment and decision making means that all persons "who have made a common commitment to Jesus Christ assemble to determine the way through the maze."[28] The Assembly structure sought to make this possible.

25. Ross T. Bender, "Seminary and Congregation: Communities of Discernment," *The Mennonite Quarterly Review* 39 (July 1965): 164.

26. Bender, "Seminary and Congregation," 180.

27. Marlene Kropf, in her 1995 address, repeats the importance of any member participation for the discernment process; "Discerning God's Voice: Spiritual Discernment in Mennonite Congregations" (Elkhart, IN: Mennonite Board of Congregational Ministries, 1995). There were decisions, of course, which were clearly the responsibility of the seminary boards and not the Assembly, but the Assembly could offer weighty counsel even in such matters, especially in influencing the views of the presidents, dean, and students who met regularly with the Boards.

28. Marlin E. Miller, in *Bioethics and the Beginning of Life*, ed. Roman J. Miller and Beryl H. Brubaker (Scottdale, PA: Herald Press, 1990), 205-6.

In its statement about discernment, the faculty stressed that the discerning of which they spoke was not solely an intellectual activity, but "involves the interplay of critical reflection with that kind of purposive action which issues from the response of obedience to the will of God." This suggested that the educational program must not only involve critical reflection but "must involve each member in the experience of Christian community."[29] The intention of the seminaries was not only to think about, but to actually become a discerning community.

Ecclesiology, Ethics, and the Practice of Discernment

While there are many details of the narrative about the campus guest that evoke comment regarding ethical decision making and the practice of discernment, I would like to offer several general proposals which have emerged from my own reflection on this situation and to invite further conversation.

1. Ecclesiology is for ethicists (not just for systematic theologians and those working in the practical ministry fields). To speak with rather than past each other, ethicists from Mennonite and other Christian traditions must attend to their assumptions about the nature, purpose, and shape of the church. For in a variety of ways in different contexts, ecclesiology profoundly shapes ethics.[30]

The practice of discernment described above illustrates more clearly than pacifism often does, the foundational character of ecclesiology for "believers church" ethics. Mennonites have been intriguing to some in the ecumenical Christian community because of their historically rooted, ongoing commitment to pacifism and peacemaking. The strong tie Mennonites have welded between the gospel of Jesus Christ and a ministry of reconciliation both in theology and practice has earned the denomination's reputation as one of the "historic peace churches." But the tendency to quickly focus on pacifism (as an attractive ethical option, a passive irrelevancy, or a radical ethical irritant) in contemporary theological conversation with members of this tradition, misses the fact that more foundational for Mennonite ethics than "peace" is ecclesiology and pneumatology. Focusing more clearly on the relevance of ecclesiology for ethics may enhance cross-denominational conversation.

2. There is room and need for creative work dealing with ethics for church institutions. If John H. Yoder is correct in asserting that Jesus is politically rele-

29. AMBS Catalog, 1987-89, 114.
30. Those who stand in the believers church tradition especially notice this because our particular ecclesiology has been a minority one.

vant,[31] that is, that the Christian gospel offers guidance for the conversion of social units toward the mind and spirit of Christ, examining the practices of church institutions should help us to see and evaluate how this is taking place. Christians considering the process of ethical transformation have tended to focus either on the transformation of individuals or on the transformation of society (political or economic or secular) rather than on the transformation of groups of Christians — in congregations or in those hybrid organizations we call church institutions. Our conversion narratives are either personal or broadly social.

The interdisciplinary approach to the study of the church known as "congregational studies" has begun to address this lacuna with respect to Christian congregations; it has the potential to gather valuable data for ethical reflection. But it seems to me that there is much that could be learned by attending more carefully to the ethical issues faced by Christian organizations and institutions. How are the issues addressed and resolved? How do they go about decision making? What norms and values are priorities as they proceed? What difference do their Christian commitments make? What impact does the theological tradition(s) in which they stand have? How might the "character" of the institution be identified and described and how does it reflect the character of Christ? How does "community character" affect the moral choices the institution must make?

3. Community discernment is a neglected and potentially empowering Christian practice. It appears to me that the practice of community discernment has been neglected in several ways. First, *as a method for Christian moral reflection* it has largely been ignored by Christian ethicists. Usually ethicists assume that an individual thinker or agent (shaped by her surrounding communities of course) is the *locus* of ethical reflection and decision. Even much of the current published material on Christian discernment focuses on the individual who engages in discernment or the way in which the community assists or influences the individual in moral discernment, rather than on the practice of community decision and discernment itself.

Failing to understand community discernment and its function as an ethical method, leads critics to characterize Mennonite ethics as "biblicist" (an application of biblical principles and norms in a straightforward and wooden way), or narrowly "christocentric." A deeper understanding of the practice of

---

31. See John Howard Yoder, *The Politics of Jesus* (Grand Rapids: Eerdmans, 1972, 1994). Rebecca Chopp, paraphrasing Iris Marion Young, reminds us that the "political is the entire realm of human decision making: cultural meanings, institutional structures, social habits, all that humans in some way decide, shape, or form collectively" (Chopp, *Saving Work* [Louisville: Westminster/John Knox, 1995], 62).

moral discernment recognizes that in this ethical method the Word of God for particular situations emerges through the power of the Spirit weaving together facts, feelings, norms, virtues, values, and reasoning from many sources in the unfolding conversation of a community that is facing a decision.

The narrative of the campus guest is particularly useful, I think, in demonstrating the flexibility of this method of proceeding in relation to situations that involve conflicting principles and decisions. In this situation the explicit community norms of hospitality to strangers and nonviolence were in tension with implicit norms of justice (what is fair to students?) and stewardship (what is our responsibility in fulfilling the mission of the seminaries?). The resolution (employment of shunning) was an imaginative employment of an historical practice, designed only for use *within* the voluntary community of believers, to a situation involving someone who was not a member of the community. In this way the resolution drew upon but moved beyond "tradition." Further, the resolution preserved and brought into a more "fitting" balance all four of the values or principles which had been thrown into disarray by the challenges Tom posed. (1) It was possible to resume the educational mission of the seminaries.[32] Justice and stewardship were served. (2) The seminary community continued to offer some limited hospitality to Tom through the escort and through contact by the president off-campus. (The seminary community might, however, have pursued this value further by more explicitly recognizing its connection to the larger church and by sharing its "sense of responsibility" for Tom with the larger Christian community. Seminary representatives might have more aggressively followed up contacts with the congregation who had helped host Tom or with other organizations whose mission would have more clearly called them to continue a supportive relationship with Tom.) (3) Shunning represented a strong expression of power. But it was an expression of power acceptable within the framework of Mennonite ethics and did not compromise commitment to the vocation of peacemaking.[33] Neither did it require the community to employ physical violence in response to Tom. This option was unforeseen early in the process, when it appeared to many that the principles of hospitality and nonviolence would need to be sacrificed for the principles of justice and stewardship.

32. My own view, shared by some others involved, is that ironically the educational mission of the seminaries continued forcefully when the "normal" educational process was interrupted by Tom. The way in which the community responded to the situation was for many the most significant theological education experience of the semester.

33. Shunning in congregational settings functioned as a "last resort" step following significant attempts to work with someone who did not accept the values or counsel of the congregation of which they were a member. Most members of the seminary community had no personal experience of the practice of shunning.

In addition, this method of proceeding permitted time for the character of the community as a whole to be tested and expressed thoughtfully in relation to an ethical dilemma. (What kind of seminary do we want to be? What does it mean for us as a seminary community to follow Christ?) Calling in the police did not seem to be "in character" for the community given its understanding of the character and mission of Jesus. Nor was passive nonresistance in character. Theological and ethical debate exploring the implications of "nonresistance" in relation to "nonviolence" had been part of the teaching and learning agenda for years. Though a way through the dilemma with Tom was unclear as the March 12 meeting drew near, somehow in the process of debate and gossip, testimony and misunderstanding, administrative leadership and spoken dissent, the creative power of the Holy Spirit moved the community toward a decision that for a variety of reasons "seemed good to the Holy Spirit and to us."[34]

"Meeting in the power of the Spirit" as an "ethical method" is not appropriate for all settings and situations. It does not represent *the* normative approach for all Christian communities of decision. But it is an option to be seriously considered and evaluated by those who make the study of Christian ethics their profession.

Second, *as a practical mode of decision making for smaller groups* (a practice which has taken different forms in different denominational contexts), community discernment has been overlooked as a valuable and employable model for Christian reflection and decision. Part of this may be due to existing theological frameworks; there may be no vision or categories for community discernment. Part of this may be due to historical and personal factors; there may be no practical experience of or trust in community discernment.

In any case, the strong spirit of individualism which has permeated North American culture and Christian moral life in this setting is clearly inhospitable to community-oriented models of moral discernment. J. Lawrence Burkholder, attempting to make a case for community discernment in a *Christian Century* article in 1963, lamented that individualism is so strong and discernment of the body so vague "that the local church generally squanders its collective power potential." Consensus is seldom sought, participants do not assume discussions will lead to binding commitments, controversial issues are avoided, and the idea that dialogical give and take can be an instrument of the Holy Spirit is not valued.[35]

34. John H. Yoder, in "Sacrament as Social Process," 43, notes that in the "apostolic model" of decision making it is not necessary to choose between consequentialist and deontological modes of reasoning or to prefer story or virtue. He wrote, "They would have seen no reason to choose among those incommensurate kinds of reasoning; why not use them all."

35. Burkholder, "The Peace Churches as Communities of Discernment," 1073.

But with vision and commitment, community practices can be built and shaped. Trust in the value of a process can grow through its employment. The events reflected in the narrative of the campus guest indicate what can happen when a Christian institution takes such a process seriously.

As a particular historical embodiment of community discernment, of course, the seminary process can be faulted at many points. For example, in relation to understandings of discernment influenced by the Catholic tradition, the community spent too little time in prayer seeking to discern what spirits were moving in the situation and naming and releasing the attachments and interests which moved or blocked individuals and the community at specific points. In relation to the understandings of discernment developed by Quakers, there was inadequate space for silence, "waiting on God." In relation to Anabaptist models, Scripture played an indirect rather than a direct part in the process of discernment.[36] Further, the campus culture which had developed some of the virtues which support peaceable relations and careful discernment (listening to others, gentleness or defenselessness, humility, encouragement, suffering love) was lacking in some other virtues important in community discernment (being comfortable with public conflict as a necessary part of discerning conversation, readiness to speak the truth in love.) The ponderous nature of the participatory process and the high value placed on patience in relationship to strangers and "enemies" meant that some of the women who felt vulnerable in Tom's presence had to bear the burden of insecurity and fear for a longer period of time as the process of discernment unfolded than would have been the case had there been quick administrative action to remove Tom from campus. Further, as an application of the theological idea that the Holy Spirit may speak to the community through anyone, the campus guest example falls short. While the Assembly structure permitted "everyone" to speak, everyone did not speak. Introverts seldom speak in large plenary sessions. Women tend to speak up less quickly than men. Meetings (even those which go on for two and a half hours) cannot go on forever.

Nevertheless, this imperfect, in some respects flatfooted, practice of discernment *was* an example of a social group in the process of being transformed by the Spirit of Christ. Adoption of the Assembly structure, for example, in spite of its limitations, did permit an unusual amount of participation in moral decision making by a wide range of women and men in the seminary commu-

36. It could be argued that this may be acceptable for a seminary community which regularly studies Scripture outside of the Meeting, but it might not be adequate for some other "Anabaptist" organizations.

nity.[37] This structure might be one example of what Larry Rasmussen referred to as "community democracy," a style of governance which "depends on shifting leadership, high levels of member participation, the capacity of its organizers and troublemakers to see through the dominant ways of doing things, and a collective ability to offer alternatives." Recommending Jesus as the model for "life-giving governance" of which "community democracy" is an example, Rasmussen wrote that "rather than shaping his followers into the usual hierarchy of power, Jesus constituted his community around power turned upside down."[38] The Assembly structure was an attempt to make concrete such "power turned upside down."[39]

While the model had its shadow sides, it was designed to make room for the possibility that the Spirit of Christ might speak not only through those who stood within the ordinary power structures of the community — faculty and administration — but also through prophets who might be standing on the margins of these structures. Indeed, the Assembly structure and process of decision making permitted time and space for a number of students to question what they perceived to be moral shortsightedness on the part of administration or faculty. While dissent can still be suppressed in subtle ways in practice, the structure and decision-making process invited alternative voices to listen carefully to each other, to be open to change, and to be surprised by the emergence of something unforeseen as the Spirit moved in the process of discernment.

In this process, "hanging on" to the commitment to follow Christ as a community required time and discourse which permitted an ethical possibility to emerge (shunning) which would not have emerged had the community quickly compromised its commitments to nonviolence and hospitality and re-

---

37. Even Tom attended the major session of the Assembly.

38. Larry Rasmussen, "Shaping Communities," in *Practicing Our Faith*, 123-25. Letty Russell supports Rasmussen when she calls Christians to refuse the temptation of the "pinnacle complex" (Jesus' temptation) and work "to transform the pyramid so more persons gain access to the structures of decision making." Russell, "Good Housekeeping," *Feminist Theology: A Reader*, ed. Ann Loades (Louisville: Westminster/John Knox, 1990), 237. It could also be argued that such a structure is more just. Marion Young proposes that justice in a community has to do more with procedural issues of participation in deliberation and decision making than it does with distribution of goods and services. See Rebecca S. Chopp, *Saving Work*, 63.

39. The Assembly structure was disbanded in 1990 when the two seminaries reviewed its structure in the process of becoming one corporation. Reasons for the change included complexity of structures and time required for community processing of issues, the fact that the seminary community was fragmented by growing numbers of part-time, off-campus students, and the unfamiliarity and discomfort of some newer faculty members from other educational institutions with the unusual structures and consensual decision-making procedures the Assembly represented.

sorted to removing Tom from campus. Not only the specific content of the norms and character of the community, but also the discernment process itself, fostered the development of an alternative way of expressing power which was consistent with the community's understanding of the character and call of Christ.

Along with its limitations, and employed in appropriate settings, the practice of community discernment has the potential to release the power of the Spirit of Christ in the midst of concrete moral discernment and decision. As an approach to moral decision making, it encourages a Christian community to bring all of its resources to bear on a significant issue it faces, trusting that through open conversation God can indeed transform earthen vessels — both individuals and communities — slowly, persistently, painfully, gracefully — toward the image and likeness of Christ.

Sorting the Wheat from the Tares: Reinterpreting Reinhold Niebuhr's Interpretation of Christian Ethics

Michael G. Cartwright

It is no secret that John Howard Yoder's book *The Politics of Jesus*[1] "influenced a whole generation of radical Christians in the U.S.A."[2] Also important, if not as well documented, is Yoder's influence on Christians in the "mainline Protestant" churches, especially as the latter have confronted what amounts to the disestablishment of mainline American religion.[3] Perhaps the greatest lesson Protestants have learned from Yoder is that there are *alternatives* to the "modernist" hermeneutic that has dominated Christian ethics in twentieth-century America.[4]

That Yoder intended to challenge the presumptions of what he called the "modernist" hermeneutic of mainstream ethics[5] in *The Politics of Jesus* is clear to anyone who reads the essay entitled "The Possibility of a Messianic Ethic" (ch. 1 of *The Politics of Jesus*). There Yoder identified three theses which served

1. John H. Yoder, *The Politics of Jesus* (Grand Rapids: Eerdmans, 1972).

2. Ched Myers, *Binding the Strong Man: A Political Reading of Mark's Story of Jesus* (Maryknoll, NY: Orbis Books, 1988), 460.

3. For one of the most recent examples, see Stanley Hauerwas and William H. Willimon, *Resident Aliens: Life in the Christian Colony* (Nashville, TN: Abingdon, 1989).

4. Numerous Christian ethicists have testified to the impact Yoder's work has had on them. For example, James William McClendon begins the preface of his *Ethics: Systematic Theology*, vol. 1 (Nashville, TN: Abingdon, 1986) by saying that the experience of reading Yoder's *The Politics of Jesus* "changed my life" (7).

5. In the footnotes of his discussion, Yoder notes that the works of H. Richard Niebuhr and Reinhold Niebuhr exemplify the modernist approach to ethics.

to ground the claim of the irrelevance of Jesus to contemporary social ethics. Against the backdrop of these propositions, Yoder's discussion of the sixfold claim of Jesus' irrelevance, and the resulting shift to "common sense" as the bridge to a reconstructed social ethic, serves as a kind of intellectual therapy whereby his readers come to see the logic of their own thinking. In so doing, Yoder calls upon his readers to consider whether they have prematurely resolved the question of Scripture and ethics.

But it would be a mistake to think that Yoder's agenda in *The Politics of Jesus* was determined by his criticism of the modernist hermeneutic in mainstream Christian ethics, although some readers have alleged that Yoder's negative argument looms larger than his exegesis. Of course, Yoder was aware of the fact that his book would be read at several levels. In fact, in the preface to *The Politics of Jesus* Yoder noted that "at the deepest level" his study could be understood as "an exercise in fundamental philosophical hermeneutics."[6] Obviously, not all readers are able to follow the argument at that level, although they may find that Yoder's study raises questions that they cannot answer without engaging in the hermeneutical struggle. The primary significance of *The Politics of Jesus* — at least for most American Protestant readers — has not derived from Yoder's exegetical arguments (as provocative as they are!) nor from Yoder's positive argument for a "bridge" between Scripture and ethics. Rather, Protestants are indebted to Yoder for having identified some of the *a priori* assumptions that we would have to give up if we were to move beyond "modernist" hermeneutics.

Ironically, many of these assumptions have their historical origin in the context of sixteenth-century disputes with the Anabaptists, a legacy of which most Protestants are content to be ignorant. What few readers of *The Politics of Jesus* realized, then or now, is that Yoder's preparation for writing that book began almost twenty years earlier, as a graduate student at Basel. In fact one of Yoder's first publications was an essay on "Modern Theological Thought and Its Criticism of Nonresistance" (1953), later published under the title of "Reinhold Niebuhr and Christian Pacifism" (1955).[7] Shortly thereafter, Yoder would complete his graduate study in the history of sixteenth-century Protestant reformation.

Over the years, Yoder's dissertation[8] and subsequently published histori-

---

6. Yoder, *The Politics of Jesus*, 5.

7. John H. Yoder, "Reinhold Niebuhr and Christian Pacifism" *Mennonite Quarterly Review* 29 (April 1955): 101-17. Also published as Church Peace Mission Pamphlet #6 (Scottdale, PA: Herald Press, 1968).

8. John Howard Yoder, *Täufertum und Reformation in der Schweiz: I. Die Gespräche zwischen Täufern und Reformatoren 1523-1538.* Schriftenreihe des Mennonitischen Geschichtsvereins, no. 6 (Karlsruhe: Buchdruckerei und Verlag H. Schneider, 1962).

cal studies of the "dialogues" between the Swiss Anabaptists and the magisterial reformers[9] have contributed to renewed recognition of the ecclesiological dimensions of the hermeneutic of the early Swiss Anabaptists.[10] In fact, throughout his career, Yoder has drawn on the results of his early research as an historical theologian,[11] but most readers have not recognized how central Yoder's historical scholarship is to his ethical analysis.

In this essay, I want to call attention to some connections between these two aspects of Yoder's work, connections which are not as widely known as they should be. And I will do so in the course of offering an interpretation of Reinhold Niebuhr's "interpretation"[12] of Christian ethics. As will be obvious, my analysis of Niebuhr's hermeneutics draws upon Yoder's historical studies of the Anabaptist-Reformed dialogue, but it also arises out of my own reassessment of Niebuhr's work in conjunction with Yoder's critique of mainstream ethics.

My argument proceeds in three steps. First I will summarize the main features of Niebuhr's argument in *An Interpretation of Christian Ethics* and Yoder's assessment of Niebuhr's critique of pacifism. Second, I will call attention to the Reformed patterns of Niebuhr's interpretation of Christian ethics which Yoder's work as an historian of Anabaptist-Reformed dialogues would have prepared him to recognize. Finally, I will show how Niebuhr's "interpretation" replicates aspects of the sixteenth-century Reformed hermeneutic, particularly as displayed in Niebuhr's reading of the parable of the wheat and the tares. Indirectly, I also hope to show that Yoder's historical analysis of sixteenth-century polemics is a critical factor in his contributions to ecumenical Christian ethics and hermeneutics.

---

9. John Howard Yoder, *Täufertum und Reformation im Gespräche: Dogmengeschichtliche Untersuchung der frühen Gespräche zwischen Schweizerischen Täufern und Reformatoren*, Basler Studien zur Historischen und Systematischen Theologie, vol. 13 (Zurich: EVZ-Verlag, 1968).

10. Perhaps the best single essay on the topic is Yoder's "The Hermeneutics of the Anabaptists" *Mennonite Quarterly Review* 41 (1967): 291-308. Reprinted in *Essays in Biblical Interpretation,* ed. by Willard Swartley (Elkhart, IN: Institute of Mennonite Studies, 1984), 11-28.

11. See for example, Yoder's article "The Turning Point of the Zwinglian Reformation" *Mennonite Quarterly Review* 32 (April 1958): 128-40, and "The Evolution of the Zwinglian Reformation," *Mennonite Quarterly Review* 43 (Jan. 1969): 95-122. The latter article is a translation and adaptation of one chapter of Yoder's *Täufertum und Reformation im Gespräche.*

12. Because my argument is not limited to Niebuhr's book, *An Interpretation of Christian Ethics,* I have chosen to refer to Niebuhr's "interpretation" of Christian ethics as a way of indicating that I am discussing the hermeneutical aspects of Niebuhr's position in the broader sense.

I

Almost thirty years before Paul Lehmann called attention to the hermeneutic character of Christian ethics,[13] Reinhold Niebuhr wrote *An Interpretation of Christian Ethics*.[14] As the title suggests, Niebuhr is not oblivious to hermeneutic issues. But unlike Lehmann, Niebuhr did not think the ecclesial context was significant for interpreting Christian ethics. In fact, in retrospect, the most notable feature of Niebuhr's study is the remarkable absence of "church" as a concept. As I will argue, this absence is closely related to the political allegory which undergirds Niebuhr's "interpretation" of Christian ethics.

Of course, the most obvious feature of *An Interpretation of Christian Ethics* is Niebuhr's trenchant criticism of the political naïveté and shallow theology of liberal/pacifist ethics, a critique which would be restated and intensified a few years later in Niebuhr's famous essay "Why the Christian Church Is not Pacifist" (1940). A considerable portion of Niebuhr's critique in the first two chapters of the book involved his own use of Scripture to attack his opponents' rather shallow appeals to the ideals of Jesus. Throughout, Niebuhr attacked biblicist appeals. In fact, he was no less severe in his condemnation of naive appeals to Scripture by liberal pacifists than he was in castigating conservative warmongers.

Against both forms of biblicism, Niebuhr argued a transcendent interpretation, which he regarded as *biblical* insofar as it manifests the "mythical truth" of "prophetic" religion (35).[15] Significantly, this conception is anchored in Niebuhr's use of the Old Testament[16] to explicate biblical eschatology and "the realm of redemption." Niebuhr's dialectical argumentation in this book added much to the emerging modernist consensus even as it lodged an ironic critique

---

13. Paul Lehmann, *Ethics in a Christian Context* (New York: Harper and Row, 1963), 29.

14. *An Interpretation of Christian Ethics* originated as the substance of Niebuhr's Rauschenbusch Memorial Lectures at the Colgate-Rochester Divinity School in 1934, and was then published in book form by Harper Brothers (1935). In the preface to the 1956 edition Niebuhr himself notes the significance of this fact stating that "it was meant to express both the author's general adhesion to the purposes of the 'Social Gospel' of which Rauschenbusch was the most celebrated exponent, and to spell out some of the growing differences between the original social gospel and the newer form of social Christianity. *The differences consisted primarily in making a sharper distinction between justice and love*" (8, emphasis mine). Subsequent references to this work will be made parenthetically in the text.

15. As he states, "In genuinely prophetic religion the God who transcends the world also convicts a sinful world of its iniquities and promises an ultimate redemption from them. The realm of redemption is never, as in rational and mystical religion, above the realm of living history, but within and at the end of it" (35).

16. Niebuhr offers citations from the Psalms as well as from Isaiah 40 and 45 in support of his depiction of the Hebraic worldview which informs "prophetic religion."

at certain uncritical features of the "modern mind,"[17] especially where the latter manifested a naive optimism. Niebuhr agreed with Rauschenbusch et al. that Jesus' ethic was rooted in "prophetic religion" (43), but against Rauschenbusch and the "social gospel," Niebuhr insisted on the *priority* of the transcendental dimension of Jesus' ethic:

> The ethic of Jesus does not deal at all with the immediate moral problem of every life — the problem of arranging some kind of armistice between various contending factions and forces. It has nothing to say about the relativities of politics and economics, nor of the necessary balances of power which exist and must exist in even the most intimate social relationships. The absolutism and perfectionism of Jesus' love ethic sets itself uncompromisingly not only against the natural self-regarding impulses, but against the necessary prudent defenses of the self, required because of the egoism of others. It does not establish a connection with the horizontal points of a political or social ethic or with the diagonals which a prudential individual ethic draws between the moral ideal and the facts of a given situation. It has only a vertical dimension between the loving will of God and the will of man. (45)

Here Niebuhr adroitly redefines "prophetic religion" in such a way that Rauschenbusch would hardly recognize as "prophetic" the elements of Jesus' teaching which Niebuhr emphasizes. But even more importantly, Niebuhr firmly situates Christian ethics within a modernist hermeneutic, thereby defining the limits of using Scripture in ethics within the categories of the modern age.

For example, in "The Ethic of Jesus," the second essay in *An Interpretation of Christian Ethics,* Niebuhr gives a detailed explication of the "impossibility of the ethical demands" of Jesus for the "natural man in his immediate situations" (50). Typical of Niebuhr's use of Scripture in conjunction with his ethical argumentation is his commentary on Matthew 7:11:

> "If ye then, being evil, know how to give good gifts unto your children, how much more shall your Father which is in heaven give good things to them that ask him?" This passage is significant because Jesus, true to the insights of prophetic religion, not only discovers symbols of the character of God in man's mundane existence, in the tenderness of parents to their children, but also because he sees this symbol of God's love among "evil" and not

---

17. See for example the first essay of *Interpretation of Christian Ethics,* "An Independent Christian Ethic," esp. 13.

among imperfect men. The contrast in prophetic religion is not between perfection and imperfection . . . but between good and evil will. (45-46)

Thus, Niebuhr argues, "infra-moral aspects of nature" are used by Jesus as "symbols of the supra-moral character of divine grace," but *not* as a basis for "transmuting" social relationships (46).

Once again Niebuhr shifts the ground of scriptural use by classifying Jesus' teachings. Thus, what is significant about Jesus' teachings is *not* that he called for confrontation with social institutions but that Jesus "understood" the real significance of "good and evil will" in human history. Obviously, the connection of Jesus' teachings with his life, ministry, death, and resurrection is irrelevant for Niebuhr at this point. Rather, as Niebuhr charts his way through carefully selected sayings of Jesus' Sermon on the Mount, he focuses on issues in relation to "pride" and "egoism," in addition to the misplaced "self-assertion" and "self-love" of individuals. Significantly, nowhere in this book is the "ethic of Jesus" commended by Niebuhr as an ethic for modern Christian communities.

In fact, Niebuhr is insistent in pointing out how greatly Jesus' ethic conflicts with "prudential" impulses. Thus, Niebuhr invokes his famous distinction between the "religious" (vertical) justification for Jesus' rigorous teaching and the kind of "socio-moral" (horizontal) justification that he finds lacking in such teachings as "love your enemies" (Matt. 5:43) and "forgive, not seven times, but seventy times seven" (Matt. 18:23). With these formal classifications in place, Niebuhr harshly criticizes the "liberal Church" for its misguided attempt "to elaborate the religio-moral thought of Jesus into a practical sociomoral or even politico-moral system" (52) contending that the effect of such efforts is to blunt the "penetration" of Jesus' transcendent (vertical) moral insights. Thus, Niebuhr contends that "horizontal" justifications of the Social Gospel cannot be found in such Jesus sayings as "love your enemies" and "forgive, not seven times, but seventy times seven."

> When, for instance, liberal Christianity defines the doctrine of non-resistance, so that it becomes merely an injunction against violence in conflict, it ceases to provide a perspective from which the sinful element of all resistance, conflict and coercion may be discovered. Its application prompts moral complacency rather than contrition, and precisely in those groups in which the evils which flow from self-assertion are most covert. This is the pathos of the espousal of Christian pacifism by the liberal Church. . . . (52)

By no means was it an accident that Niebuhr's ultimate claim concerning the limits of Jesus' religious ethic is couched in the critique of pacifism. But what is more important for the story I am sketching in relation to Niebuhr's use of Scripture is the *methodological* distinction introduced by Niebuhr based on his dialectical account of "prophetic religion" cast in terms of a single (vertical) religious reference — "the will of God . . . defined in terms of all-inclusive love." With this hermeneutical lever in place, Niebuhr can announce his pivotal conclusion:

> The ethic of Jesus may offer valuable insights to and sources of criticism for a prudential social ethic which deals with present realities: but no such social ethic can be directly derived from a pure religious ethic. (55)

Niebuhr's follow-up discussion of "the ethical problem of rewards" serves simply to shore up his claim about the "non-prudential" character of Jesus' ethic. Jesus' demands for an "absolute obedience" cannot be understood outside the framework of his eschatological perspective. Therefore, Jesus' ethic is *irrelevant* to Christian ethics in the twentieth century *except* as a transcendent criticism.

Although Niebuhr does refute the claim that Jesus had an "*interimsethik*," this denial only functions to reinforce the sense in which the "eschatological element" serves as the *basis* for the ethic of Jesus. Thus, Niebuhr asserts that the ethical demands of Jesus "proceed from a transcendent and divine unity of essential reality, and their final fulfillment is possible *only* when God transmutes the present chaos of this world into its final unity" (59). Noting that the "logic of this thought" is obviously apocalyptic in provenance, Niebuhr concludes:

> Placing the final fulfillment at the end of time and not in the realm above temporality is to remain true to the genius of prophetic religion and to state *mythically* what cannot be stated *rationally*. If stated *rationally* the world is divided between the temporal and the eternal and only the eternal forms above the flux of temporality have significance. To state the matter *mythically* is to do justice to the fact that the eternal can only be fulfilled in the temporal. But since myth is forced to state a paradoxical aspect of reality in terms of concepts connoting historical sequence, it always leads to historical illusions. (59, emphasis mine)

Thus, according to Niebuhr, the "mythic" structure of Christian "truth" must be freed from the subsequent "historical illusions" of the church in order for the transcendent significance of "prophetic religion" to be properly appreciated.

> The historical illusions which resulted inevitably from this mythical statement of the situation in which the human spirit finds itself do not destroy the truth in the myth. . . . Nevertheless, it must be admitted that the ethical

rigor of the early church was maintained through the hope of the second coming of Christ and the establishment of his Kingdom. (60)

As any seminarian can attest, by this point in Niebuhr's argument, the reader is entangled in so many *formalist* distinctions (infra-moral vs. supra-moral, religious [vertical] vs. socio-moral [horizontal], prudential ethic vs. eschatological ethic, mythical vs. rational truths, etc.) that countering the logic of his argument on this final point appears hopeless.

More to the point, given all the formal distinctions Niebuhr has drawn, the significance of this final step in his argument is easily missed. For with this step, Niebuhr effectively moves the *locus* of Christian ethics *outside* the context of the church as a historic community. Niebuhr concludes the chapter on "The Ethic of Jesus" with a fascinating double-edged critique of the two previous Rauschenbusch lectures.[18] Regarding each as competing "interpretations" of Christian ethics, Niebuhr contends:

> Both interpretations flow from the same illusion of liberalism, that we are dealing with a possible and prudential ethic in the gospel. In the one case [Charles Clayton Morrison] its unqualified application is recommended in spite of the fact that every moment of our existence reveals its impossibility. In the other case [Shirley Jackson Case], necessary compromises are regarded merely as adjustments to varying ages and changing circumstances. The crucial problem of Christian ethics is obscured in either case. (62)

Niebuhr's contention that he is offering a superior account to Morrison and Case is more than clever rhetoric. But the principal reason for this claim has very little to do with conflicting interpretations of Jesus' ethics. The real issue for Niebuhr is human *sin*. In the 1956 preface to *An Interpretation of Christian Ethics,* Niebuhr confirms this judgment:

> The social gospel was that part of the liberal movement which had a sense of responsibility for social justice. It thought it could exercise that responsibility by insisting that love was the law of life in all and not merely in personal relations. It usually neglected that aspect of human behavior which St. Paul describes as "The law in my members, warring against the law that

18. As noted in the preface to the 1956 edition, the substance of Niebuhr's *Interpretation of Christian Ethics* originated in his Rauschenbusch lectures for the year 1934. The two previous Rauschenbusch lectures were given by Charles Clayton Morrison (at that time editor of *The Christian Century* and a prominent pacifist), subsequently published as *The Social Gospel and the Christian Cultus,* and Shirley Jackson Case, subsequently published under the title of *The Social Triumph of the Ancient Church.*

is in my mind." It was, in short, rather oblivious to the power and persistence of self-regard in both individual and collective terms. (8-9)

Niebuhr's well-known claim that there is and must always be a difference between the possibilities of "moral man and immoral society"[19] is here specified in terms of the "war within" the individual Christian. The prominence of this conception of sin structures Niebuhr's understanding of the conflict between the individual and social "levels" of morality. Thus in the concluding chapter of his book *Moral Man and Immoral Society,* Niebuhr argues:

> A realistic analysis of the problems of human society reveals a constant and seemingly irreconcilable conflict between the needs of society and the imperatives of a sensitive conscience. This conflict, which could be most briefly defined as the conflict between ethics and politics, is made inevitable by the double focus of the moral life. One focus is in the inner life of the individual, and the other in the necessities of man's social life. From the perspective of society the highest moral ideal is justice. From the perspective of the individual the highest ideal is unselfishness.[20]

Given this "individual versus society" structure of Niebuhr's vision of both ethics and politics, the larger societal context ultimately determines the hermeneutical possibilities for his ethic. For Niebuhr, there is no mediating possibility, for no alternative community can stand outside this dialectic structure of politics. There is (and can be) no possibility for effective subversion of the political by the ethical even (or especially) within religious communities.[21]

In the end, what Niebuhr has to account for in order for his argument to be consistent is not simply the seeming incongruity between the teachings of Jesus and contemporary Christianity, but the political situation of the church as well. This aspect of Niebuhr's "interpretation" of Christian ethics is

19. See the title of his earlier book, *Moral Man and Immoral Society: A Study in Ethics and Politics* (New York: Charles Scribner's Sons, 1932). An oft-cited summary of his argument is taken from the concluding paragraph of the first chapter (p. 22): "The dream of perpetual peace and brotherhood of human society . . . is a vision prompted by the conscience and insight of individual man, but incapable of fulfillment by collective man."

20. Niebuhr, *Moral Man and Immoral Society,* 257.

21. At one point, Niebuhr appears to suggest a different view only to reinscribe this "religious" possibility within the individual/society dialectic. See *Moral Man and Immoral Society,* 81: ". . . the full force of religious faith will never be available for the building of a just society, because its highest visions are those which proceed from the insights of a sensitive religious conscience. *If they are realized at all they will be realized in intimate religious communities, in which individual ideals achieve social realizations but do not conquer society*" (emphasis mine).

not present in *An Interpretation of Christian Ethics,* and is only partially present in *Moral Man and Immoral Society.* But this does not mean that Niebuhr did not find a biblical basis for this aspect of his "interpretation" of Christian ethics. Indeed, as I will argue shortly, there is reason to believe that Niebuhr's conception of politics was derived from a single verse in the New Testament.

II

Yoder's first published response to Niebuhr appeared shortly before *An Interpretation of Christian Ethics* was to be reissued. Although Yoder's essay focused primarily on the "Why the Christian Church Is Not Pacifist" essay, his discussion of Niebuhr's ethic was sufficiently broad to encompass the major features of Niebuhr's argument in *An Interpretation of Christian Ethics.*

Significantly, Yoder did not attempt to deny much of Niebuhr's criticism of modern liberal pacifism. Indeed Yoder indicates agreement with several features of Niebuhr's argument. Yoder's primary disagreement with Niebuhr stems from the latter's conception of redemption, particularly with respect to the doctrines of resurrection, the church, and regeneration, each of which was identified as "works of the Holy Spirit." In each case, Yoder's disagreement with Niebuhr's interpretation of Christian ethics takes the form of noting the *absence* of particular Christian doctrines from Niebuhr's ethic.

For example, Yoder calls attention to the fact that the concept of the church is missing from Niebuhr's ethic. He comments that the only time the word "church" is used, is to "criticize the medieval synthesis of Catholicism." In Yoder's view this is a significant lacuna in Niebuhr's interpretation of Christian ethics. Indeed it is the crucial issue.

> For the body of Christ differs from other social bodies in that it is not less moral than its individual members. If being a perfectly loyal American, a free mason, or a bourgeois, identifies a man with that group egoism in such a way as to make him less loving than he would be as an individual, the contrary is true of being a member of Christ. Thus the thesis of *Moral Man and Immoral Society* falls down in the crucial case, the only one which is really decisive for Christian ethics.[22]

In the same context, Yoder comments that this omission is particularly surprising in light of Niebuhr's interest in history: "In the Bible, the bearer of the

---

22. Yoder, "Reinhold Niebuhr and Christian Pacifism," 115.

meaning of history is not the United States of America, not Western Christendom, but a divine-human society, the church, the body of Christ."[23]

The following year Yoder offers a more extended discussion of the *eschatological* character of the meaning of history in his essay on "Peace Without Eschatology?"[24] Once again, Yoder insists that the eschatological covenant community is the *locus* of the "meaning of history":

> The ultimate meaning of history is to be found in the work of the church. (This relationship of Christ's suffering to His triumph is also stated in Philippians 2; the centrality of the church in history in Titus 2 and 1 Peter 2.) The victory of the Lamb through His death seals the victory of the church. Her suffering, like her Master's, is the measure of her obedience to the self-giving love of God. Nonresistance is right, in the deepest sense, not because it works, but because it anticipates the triumph of the Lamb who was slain.[25]

Here we see glimpses of themes that recur in *The Politics of Jesus,* where Yoder specifies the relationship of ecclesiology and eschatology for Christian ethics. Also the emphasis on the church's participation in the suffering of the "Lamb's War" is a theme which arises out of Yoder's Anabaptist-Mennonite heritage.

In dramatic contrast to Niebuhr's "interpretation" of Christian ethics, Yoder argues that "only a clearly eschatological viewpoint permits a valid critique of the present historical situation and the choice of action which can be effective." And the viewpoint Yoder espouses — "peace with eschatology" — is based upon a very different construal of New Testament eschatology than that described in Niebuhr's *An Interpretation of Christian Ethics.*

> The New Testament sees our present age — the age of the church, extending from Pentecost to the Parousia — as a period of the overlapping of two aeons. These aeons are not distinct periods of time, for they exist simultaneously. They differ rather in nature or in direction; one points backwards to human history outside of (before) Christ; the other points forward to

---

23. Yoder, "Reinhold Niebuhr and Christian Pacifism," 115.

24. Although Yoder mentions Niebuhr's work only at the end of this essay (84) it is clear from the context that he regards Niebuhr's ethical position as characteristically "peace without eschatology."

25. John H. Yoder, "Peace Without Eschatology?", a paper presented to a Theological Study conference at Heerenwegen, Zeist (The Netherlands) in May 1954, reproduced as a pamphlet in the *Concern* pamphlet series. I am quoting from *The Original Revolution* (Scottdale, PA: Herald Press, 1971), 61, where it was included as the third chapter under the title "If Christ Is Truly Lord."

the fullness of the kingdom of God, of which it is a foretaste. Each aeon has a social manifestation: the former in the "world," the latter in the church or the body of Christ.[26]

This difference in the way in which Yoder and Niebuhr perceive the relationship of the church to the world in conjunction with the eschatology of the New Testament is not without precedent. Indeed, this difference also cropped up in the debate between the Anabaptists and the Swiss Reformed Councils at Bern in 1538.[27] The primary focus of that earlier debate was the Anabaptist practice of "binding and loosing" or "the ban" (Matt. 18:15-20). The Reformed party argued against the ban, based upon an interpretation of the Bible that stressed the continuity of the Old Testament with the New. In contrast, the Anabaptists made a radical distinction between the two testaments, thereby emphasizing the importance of "binding and loosing" as a dominical practice.

This debate became polarized when the Reformed preachers appealed to the parable of the wheat and the tares to justify the slow progress being made in improving the moral life of the church. The Anabaptists responded that in their judgment the parable did not teach the toleration of wickedness within the church. Apparently, the disagreement boiled down to different readings of Matthew 13:30 — "Let good and evil both grow until the harvest" — in relation to Jesus' allegorical interpretation (Matt. 13:37-43). The Reformed party read Matthew 13:30 as a warrant for refraining from the use of the ban for the purpose of church discipline. In so doing, they implicitly interpreted the church as being in the same situation as the "field" of the parable.

The Anabaptists objected that the "field" in the parable was the world, *not* the church. For them, Matthew 18:15-20 was the practice by which the church could be distinguished from the world, and any church which could not be separated from the world could not be the true church. By contrast, the Reformed party was hesitant to apply the ban to members of the church because they were concerned that they might "uproot" someone from the church who might eventually find grace before God if they remained. On this point, the Anabaptists regarded the Reformed party as inconsistent: the Reformed party advocated tolerance in dealing with sin in the life of the church, yet these same leaders advocated persecuting (including killing) Anabaptists.

26. Yoder, "Peace Without Eschatology?" 55.

27. I am indebted to Ervin Schlabach's dissertation on "The Rule of Christ Among the Early Swiss Anabaptists" (Ph.D. diss., Chicago Theological Seminary, 1977), 231-48. Schlabach's discussion closely parallels the summary of the proceedings of the debate found in *Quellen zur Geschichte der Täufer in der Schweiz*, ed. Martin Haas (Zürich: S. Hirzel, 1952-1974), vol. 4, 108-57.

As the debate proceeded, the Reformed party made a formal distinction between "sin" and "offense," arguing that the ban had been given for use in cases of offense (as judged by the pastors alone), whereas the magistrates should be given the task of dealing with serious sins or crimes. From the Anabaptist perspective, the Bern pastors simply did not have confidence in the congregational process as described in Matthew 18:15-20.

Finally, the Reformed party invoked a distinction between the "visible church" and the "invisible church" and a parallel distinction between an "inward ban" and an "outward ban." They accused the Anabaptists of confusing the two kinds of bans, and thereby collapsing the visible church into the invisible church. In response, the Anabaptists rejected the substitution of this dualism for their distinction between church and world.

As others have pointed out, as far back as Augustine's *City of God* this kind of Neoplatonic dualism has been used to transpose the historical schema of *aeons* into an ahistorical or *superhistorical* dualism. In every case, the net result is to diminish the sense in which the church is a *concrete, identifiable, salvific community*.[28] Therefore, embedded in the Anabaptist-Reformed dialogue is a profound difference in the vision of the church in relation to the meaning of history, not to mention the different hermeneutics of these communities.

None of this information would have surprised John Howard Yoder at the time he was responding to Niebuhr's ethic. Indeed, Yoder's graduate research covered these and other dialogues between the Anabaptist and Reformed parties between 1523 and 1538. When he read Niebuhr's *Interpretation of Christian Ethics,* he would have recognized the familiar pattern of formalist distinctions. In 1538, Heinrich Bullinger had appealed to the transcendent significance of the rule of faith and love to rule out the practice of "binding and loosing" (Matt. 18). And as Yoder also discovered, under Bullinger's tutelage,[29] the Reformed pastors claimed that the teachings of Jesus were not normative in matters of church discipline. After all, they argued, the circumstances of life in first-century Palestine were obviously different than sixteenth-century Europe. In particular, now Christians — not Romans — were in charge.[30]

Although the list of reasons is not as fully developed in 1538, the trajectory is fairly clear. These arguments for the irrelevance of the ethics of Jesus are

---

28. Gerhard Lohfink, *Jesus and Community* (Philadelphia: Fortress Press, 1984), 5.

29. Heinhold Fast and John H. Yoder, trans. and eds., "How to Deal with Anabaptists: An Unpublished Letter of Heinrich Bullinger," *Mennonite Quarterly Review* 33 (April 1959): 83-95.

30. Schlabach, 248, following *Quellen zur Geschichte der Täufer in der Schweiz*, 157.

roughly the same as those which Yoder identifies as characteristic of "main-stream ethics" in the first chapter of *The Politics of Jesus*. More importantly, for my purposes, they are arguments which form the basis of Reinhold Niebuhr's "interpretation" of Christian ethics.

III

At about the same time that Yoder was completing his initial research on the Anabaptist-Reformed dialogues of the sixteenth century, Reinhold Niebuhr could be found preaching sermons on the topic of "The Wheat and the Tares." What is striking about these sermons is not only the fact that they bear close re-semblance to the Swiss Reformed arguments represented at Bern in 1538, but also that the argument is strikingly similar to the argument in Niebuhr's book *An Interpretation of Christian Ethics*.

In order to substantiate this claim, I will begin with an outline of the claims made in Niebuhr's relatively late sermon on "The Wheat and the Tares."[31] Then, I will try to show how this same set of claims can be discerned in *An Interpretation of Christian Ethics*, particularly in the final chapter "Love as Forgiveness." Finally, I will show how this allegorical reading can be linked to Niebuhr's argument in the chapter on "The Ethic of Jesus," thereby forming the basis of Niebuhr's interpretation of Christian ethics.

In the opening words of his sermon, Niebuhr extolls the importance of

---

31. Reinhold Niebuhr, "The Wheat and the Tares," sermon from the Union Theological Seminary Collection, Richmond, VA transcription by the author from audio-tape #N-665. I am grateful to Mrs. Ursula Niebuhr (widow of Reinhold Niebuhr) for permission to use a tran-scription of the sermon in this study. Transcript page numbers refer to my own transcription of this sermon. Subsequent references to this work will be made parenthetically in the text. It has proved impossible to identify the exact date and location of this sermon. Internal references to political events (exchange of barbed comments between Khrushchev and Eisenhower) suggest a date between 1956 and 1960.

Niebuhr preached on this text on other occasions as well. Robert McAfee Brown notes that "Niebuhr preached an earlier version of 'The Wheat and the Tares' one summer to the farming community at Heath, Massachusetts, winning over the congregation with the opening comment, 'This sermon may be good theology, but it is certainly bad agriculture.'" Robert McAfee Brown, "Acknowledgments" to *The Essential Reinhold Niebuhr: Selected Writings and Addresses*, ed. Robert McAfee Brown (New Haven, CT: Yale University Press, 1985), vii.

For an example of a similar — although I would argue a substantially different — treat-ment of this text from Matthew's gospel, see the sermon by the same title in Ursula Niebuhr's collection, *Justice and Mercy* (New York: Harper and Row, 1974), 51-59. The latter sermon is also included in *The Essential Reinhold Niebuhr*. It was preached on 28 February 1960 at Union Theological Seminary, New York.

this "precious eschatological parable" from Matthew 13 because "it could correct many errors which come out of other emphases in Scripture."[32] Niebuhr does not explicitly identify the "errors" he has in mind. However, many of his comments do reflect interchurch disputes of the Reformation era, particularly the Anabaptist-Reformed dialogues of the 1530s.

In the course of the sermon, Niebuhr enlists the support of the Old Testament prophets for the purpose of discussing the "meaningfulness of history" as a crucial characterization of what he calls "biblical faith." Just as in *An Interpretation of Christian Ethics*, a particular understanding of the significance of New Testament eschatology is proffered. But in this context Niebuhr explicitly says that at the heart of the Christian view of history, he sees a *theodicy*. According to Niebuhr, Christians should understand the "central affirmation of the New Testament" to be "the fact that *nobody* can come before God in history and be justified." In fact, it is this insight which makes it possible to have a quite different eschatology: "According to the New Testament eschatology, history does not culminate in the triumph of good over evil but in the growth of good and evil" (3).[33] In the last phrase, Niebuhr can be seen to be grounding *both* his conception of biblical eschatology and the meaning of human history in a single verse: "let both [wheat and tares] grow together until the harvest" (Matt. 13:30).

Several features of the sermon are worth noting before proceeding with more specific analysis: (1) Niebuhr is juxtaposing his own view of theodicy (and eschatology as well) against the naive nineteenth-century liberal faith in progress; (2) several different references exhibit Niebuhr's sympathy to Jewish struggles to understand Christian confidence in the face of an "unredeemed world";[34] (3) at several points Niebuhr speaks quite personally, beginning with a description of his own pilgrimage toward a mature view of the meaning of history.

> I remember what satisfaction I took when I discovered what everybody knows — that the nineteenth century view was wrong. So I saw these Christ/Antichrist passages of the New Testament and [said] there you have it — this is how history really is. (4)

32. Note the strong parallels between the sermon and the last chapter of *An Interpretation of Christian Ethics*, "Love as Forgiveness," 201-13. Those scholars wanting to contend that there is a maturity in the "later Niebuhr" not found in his earlier writings should ponder the strong lines of continuity in Niebuhr's realist ethic. Although it is probably not possible to discover an answer at this point in time, it is interesting to ponder the close proximity of Niebuhr's sermon to the time of the "preface to 1956 edition" of *Interpretation*.

33. This claim already suggests that Niebuhr is not attending to particular claims about eschatology held by non-mainline Protestant churches.

34. Note that Niebuhr nowhere countenances the possibility that the Church might be the kind of alternative community which can bear witness to God's redemption.

Still further, Niebuhr notes the influence of Rosenstock-Huessy in leading him to see how "the Protestant Reformation put a new quirk to this [development]" in reaction to Roman Catholicism (4), "[b]ecause what we find in the Reformation was a very alarming thing," namely the church of Christ warring with itself via the accusations of the Antichrist. Niebuhr concludes rather ruefully, "And how I rejoiced at the truth of them — [or] what I thought was the truth of them" (5).

> What I did not see . . . was that the ultimate evil was a reason for the destruction of the Good rather than and not the denial of the Good. And it was probably right to say that narcissism was the Antichrist as Catholicism conceived it and that communism was the Antichrist as Catholicism conceived it. That's right too, in its context. (5)

After noting the regrettable "history of the religious wars" in the sixteenth and seventeenth centuries, Niebuhr concludes this first part of the sermon with the observation that "the whole history of the conception of Antichrist is rather pathetic" (6).

Having disposed of the legacy of Christian polemics with this rhetorical aside, Niebuhr moves on to give a sketch of world history, noting with obvious glee what an illusion it is to claim that the Kaiser [Wilhelm] or King Charles I or the Czar [Nicholas of Russia] is [or was] "the final form of evil." Then Niebuhr opines: "Haven't our fathers made themselves silly for long enough with their rather implausible Antichrists?" (7)

> Would that we could go back to this profound verse in scripture — the parable of the wheat and the tares. And it is quite different than the other eschatological parables. It doesn't say that there isn't a *specific* form of evil, it only says that in history good and evil are so mixed up that you make the judgment at your hazard. (7)

Thus, argues Niebuhr, "Good and evil *both* grow . . . [therefore]," citing Matthew 13:30, "let both grow until the harvest" (8-9).

One additional feature of Niebuhr's sermon is worth noting at this point. In a personal comment, Niebuhr humorously admits that he "never paid much attention to this parable" because as a "young guy growing up in the corn country [Nebraska]," this parable "outraged my agricultural intelligence" (7).[35] But

37. Niebuhr notes that the farmers he worked with that summer "weren't under any illusions about the wheat and the tares. . . . [A]ll of agriculture means a war against the terrorist for the sake of the wheat or for the sake of the corn. This is outrageous to say 'wait until the harvest days. . . .'"

then Niebuhr goes on to use this image to discuss the relationship of freedom and evil in human history, saying that "this is exactly the situation we are in . . . in the whole history of the world."

> And how can we say that there is an *explicit* form of evil and a *specific* form of good? *All we can say* is that Scripture was right in the first place when it says that "Good and evil both grow" in history for the simple reason that freedom grows. And in human freedom you always have the capacity for good or evil. . . . (8; emphasis mine)

With typical dialectical brilliance, Niebuhr has woven a tapestry of human history,[36] in this case basing his exhortation on a single verse of this parable of "the wheat and the tares."

In the conclusion of the sermon, Niebuhr draws three moral lessons from his reflections on this parable: (1) "How can we say that there is an explicit form of evil and a specific form of good? All we can say is that good and evil both grow. . . ."; (2) "We would be most evil if we *pretend* to be most good"; and (3) "We are in history and we have to know also . . . we are not gods but men. As men we make our judgments. As men and *not* gods we will await the final judgment" (9).

Much could be said about Niebuhr's interpretation of this parable. But for my purposes the most noteworthy aspect of this sermon is the way in which Niebuhr is using Scripture, and the close parallels which exist between this sermon and Niebuhr's early book *An Interpretation of Christian Ethics*. Could it be that the *implicit* authorization for Niebuhr's "interpretation" of Christian ethics can be found in this parable? Or more precisely, is it possible that Niebuhr's "interpretation" of Christian ethics is based upon his reading of a single verse (Matt. 13:30)?

If the answer to these questions is yes, then it would be very ironic for at least two reasons. First, as I have already noted, Niebuhr strongly condemns the naïveté of liberal and pacifist exegesis of Scripture in the service of their rival "interpretations" of Christian ethics.[37] But second and more importantly, it would

36. Niebuhr himself often used the image of the loom on which "the fabric of history is woven." See his editorial "The Unity of History," *Christianity and Crisis* 2 (4 May 1942): 1. There also the connection between Niebuhr's vision of the unity of history and the issue of war is made quite explicitly.

37. For a particularly trenchant critique of the biblical exegesis of liberal theologians, see "Why the Christian Church Is Not Pacifist." But of course, Niebuhr thinks the parable of the wheat and the tares offers a *different* case as he notes at several points in his sermon. The naturalistic setting and its commonsensical orientation of the parable lend themselves nicely to Niebuhr's empirical predispositions.

be ironic because (as I have shown) this is precisely the text which the Swiss Reformed pastors used to refute the Anabaptists in their debate at Bern (1538).

It may seem unfair to use one of Niebuhr's sermons as the basis for a critique of the hermeneutical basis of his ethics, but in Niebuhr's case there is no strong sense in which the rhetoric of his sermons differs from the modes of argument in his major theological and ethical works. Indeed, one of the most telling reviews of the Gifford Lectures suggested that the broad-ranging *The Nature and Destiny of Man* (1940) was not so much the work of a scholar as it was the work of a "preacher expounding the Word in line with his private revelation. . . ."[38]

Furthermore, given the fact that the *wirkungsgeschichte* of the parable of the wheat and the tares encompasses the history of the "invisible church"[39] concept, we cannot avoid asking if there is a relationship between Niebuhr's "interpretation" and the Protestant tradition in which he was formed.[40] That Niebuhr would have resisted attempts to pigeonhole him as any kind of Protestant "traditionalist" is obvious, but it is also important to note the ways in which Niebuhr's own exegetical praxis consistently stands *with* Augustine, Luther, and Calvin and *against* those movements and traditions which are aligned historically with Donatus, Menno Simons, and Pilgram Marpeck. That is to say, there is a real argument about the "goods internal to the practice"[41] of

38. Prof. Robert Calhoun's review of Niebuhr's work as quoted in Richard Fox's *Reinhold Niebuhr: A Biography* (New York: Pantheon, 1985), 203-4. Calhoun, who was renowned for his erudite lectures on the history of Christian theology, objected to the selective way in which Niebuhr mined the Christian tradition, and went so far as to say that "on its historical side this book cannot be taken seriously."

39. The term "invisible church" has a long history with too many twists and turns to recount. Here I will simply note its relationship to the magisterial Reformation's debates with the Anabaptists in the sixteenth century and its parallels in St. Augustine's great work *The City of God*, where the two cities exist in overlapping relationship. Comments by St. Augustine regarding "the parable of the wheat and the tares" have certainly influenced subsequent discussions of the "invisible church." For particular references, see *The City of God* (New York: Modern Library, 1950), Book XX, particularly section 5, ". . . a divine judgment in the end of the world," 714-16; and section 9, "What the reign of the saints with Christ for a thousand years is, and how it differs from the eternal kingdom," 725-28.

40. As is well-known, Niebuhr's father was a pastor in the German Evangelical Synod of North America (later to become the Evangelical Reformed Church of America, and subsequently to merge with the Congregational Church to form the United Church of Christ). Niebuhr was ordained in this denomination and served a parish in Detroit, Michigan, before taking the position at Union Theological Seminary in New York.

41. Here I am adopting this phrase from Alasdair MacIntyre's account of practical reason in his book *After Virtue: A Study in Moral Theory*, 2nd ed. (Notre Dame: University of Notre Dame Press, 1984), 222-25, especially 222, where MacIntyre discusses the importance of conflict or ongoing argument for specifying the goods internal to the practice of a "living tradition."

Christianity reflected in this text and its various ecclesial performances. Niebuhr is not only a participant in this ongoing argument, he *reflects* particular forms which the argument has taken. In this respect, it does not matter whether Niebuhr actually knew the provenance of the arguments he employed in his interpretation of Christian ethics. Indeed, it may be that the fact that Niebuhr could employ such arguments without knowing their history is the best proof of how deeply they are embedded in mainstream ethics.

More precisely, Niebuhr's use of the parable of the wheat and the tares reflects his defense of a particular conception of the church. Thus, when Niebuhr wrote his famous manifesto "Why the Christian Church Is Not Pacifist"[42] on the eve of the United States' entrance into World War II, what was at stake was an "interpretation of Christian ethics," which is structured by a particular vision of the church that is itself allegorically depicted for Niebuhr in the parable of the wheat and the tares. An examination of other occasional writings also supports this contention.[43] Further confirming this impression is the fact that another sermon by Niebuhr, "The Providence of God,"[44] based on Matthew 5:43-48, makes use of many of the same images, illustrations, and arguments[45] as those found in the above-cited sermon on "The Wheat and the Tares."

42. Originally privately circulated as a pamphlet, it was quickly published as the first essay in a collection entitled *Christianity and Power Politics* (New York: Charles Scribner's Sons, 1940), 1-32.

43. See the essay "Can the Church Give a Moral Lead?" in the collection *Essays in Applied Christianity* (New York: Meridian Books, 1959), 90-92, where Niebuhr notes, "If we claim to possess overtly what remains hidden, we turn the mercy of Christ into an inhuman fanaticism." Similarly, Niebuhr's first *published* article, "The Attitude of the Church Toward the Present Moral Evils," *The Keryx* 1 (February 1911), addresses quite similar questions. Clearly, this is an issue which Niebuhr addressed in a consistent way throughout his career.

44. Reinhold Niebuhr, *Justice and Mercy,* ed. Ursula Niebuhr (New York: Harper and Row, 1974), 14-22. The sermon was preached at Union Theological Seminary in New York on February 3, 1952. Significantly, Niebuhr read Matthew 5:43-48 as a testimony to moral truth: "A non-moral nature is made into the symbol of a transmoral mercy." Thus, it is to be understood as a testimony of God's universal "providence" and not an exhortation to "love our enemies" as such.

45. Note the parallel use of Psalm 73. More explicit in this context is Niebuhr's admiration for the integrity of Stoicism as a moral philosophy. There is the same insistence on the "fragmentary character of human morality" and the strong sense that freedom in history must be qualified by humility before the God who justifies us in the midst of our own evil. Thus, Niebuhr once again proclaims (22):

> We must not deny that there is a kind of religion that enhances the ego and gives it an undue place in the world. But from the standpoint of our faith we should take our humble and contrite place in God's plan of the whole, and leave it to him to complete the fragmentation of our life.

But to return again to Niebuhr's earlier study *An Interpretation of Christian Ethics*, it is no mere coincidence that the final chapter of that study bears a striking resemblance in both language and argument to the aforementioned sermon. That essay, "Love as Forgiveness," offers a revised account of "forgiveness" in contrast to the pacifist stress on forgiveness. There we discover Niebuhr's denunciation of historic Christianity, which he notes often "succumbs to the parochialism of the human heart and lends itself to the sinful inclination of human groups to make themselves God" (210).[46]

In that same essay, Niebuhr also provides what may have been his most graphic — if not his most definitive — statement of how he understood the dialectical relationship of "prophetic religion" to Christianity and Western civilization:

> It may be that the insights of a prophetic religion may qualify and mitigate the cruelties of the social struggles through which we are passing to a greater degree than now seems probable. It is comforting to know, nevertheless, that if this should not prove true, the truth of prophetic religion, *and of Christianity in so far as Christianity is truly prophetic,* must survive the tempests of a dying civilization as an ark surviving the flood. At some time or other the waters of the flood will recede and the ark will land. (212)

What is most fascinating about this passage and the argument which follows it is the fact that Niebuhr admits that his interpretation of Christian ethics as "prophetic religion" does involve a kind of *discipline,* but the discipline which is invoked is *not* that of the church as a "contrast society,"[47] but rather the church as the "ark" which "generate[s] the vitality of any culture and age" in the face of the forces of anarchy. Once again the focus is on human sin, and the meaning of history is cast within a view of divine Providence based on a theodicy, a theodicy which I would argue is most explicitly stated in Niebuhr's sermon on "the Wheat and the Tares."

Thus, this very modern Augustine who on the one hand challenges the "children of God" to contribute spiritual "vitality" to the dying civilization of Western culture, also warns that they must beware of the two greatest evils: "the impiety of making themselves God and the cruelty of seeing their fellow men as devils because they are involved in the same pretension."[48] This is as close as

---

46. Niebuhr, *Interpretation of Christian Ethics*, 210. Again note the similarities between this statement and the ending of Niebuhr's sermon on the wheat and the tares.

47. Here I invoke the phrase employed by Gerhard Lohfink in his study of *Jesus and Community*, op cit.

48. These are the final words of Niebuhr's *An Interpretation of Christian Ethics*, 213.

Reinhold Niebuhr ever came to offering an explicit ecclesiology, but what we have is really Niebuhr's account of how "prophetic religion" can keep the remnant of Western civilization afloat, indeed *must* do so if history is to have any meaning at all. As such the church is but an instrument, an "earthen vessel" which serves, like all other human institutions in that dark sea called human history.

According to Niebuhr's "interpretation" of Christian ethics, the most discipline that can be exercised in the church is that minimal *ordering* which keeps the crew at work keeping the ark afloat in the seas of anarchy. Any more discipline, any more coherence of purpose would suggest the illusion that Christians are something other than fallible human beings perpetually haunted by sin and the knowledge that before God "no man can be justified in human history." This conclusion would seem to bear out Yoder's claim that the Christian doctrine of redemption is "consistently slighted" in Niebuhr's ethics.[49] For Niebuhr, the theodicy of the wheat and the tares serves to eliminate the necessity of ecclesiology by interpreting politics realistically as the limited but necessary sphere of order in a world in which all social relationships, including the church, are tainted.

Niebuhr implicitly acknowledges other interpretations of Matthew 13:24-30, but he never attempts to enter into dialogue with these interpretations. They simply serve as counterpoints to his dialectical arguments. More to the point, however, Niebuhr omits any reference to Jesus' "interpretation" of the parable in Matthew 13:36-43 (one of the few allegories found in the Gospels which is explicitly attributed to Jesus).[50] Given the fact that Niebuhr drew three moral lessons from the parable *sans* the Matthean allegory, I would argue that this omission is very significant.

In particular, Niebuhr never notes the fact that in that allegorical interpretation attributed to Jesus, there is no confusion about the "explicit form of evil" and the "specific form of good": the field is the world and the good seed means the sons of the kingdom; the weeds are the sons of the evil one . . . the harvest is "the close of the age." Niebuhr apparently ignored this intertextual reading of the parable. Instead, he interprets the parable as a portrayal of a *futurist* eschatology of the "final judgment" or "transcendent" judgment, in rela-

---

49. Yoder, "Reinhold Niebuhr and Christian Pacifism," 115.

50. It should be noted that the allegory attributed to Jesus by Matthew is thought by most historical critics to be an addition or a redaction by the Matthean editor/author. E.g., see Joachim Jeremias, *The Parables of Jesus*, 2nd rev. ed. (New York: Charles Scribner's, 1963), 77-79. For a different view see David Hill, *The Gospel of Matthew* (Grand Rapids: Eerdmans, 1972), 228-29.

tion to which "our partial meanings and our fragmentary judgments and purposes" are thoroughly relativized.[51]

But of course, that is *not* the only way in which the parable of the wheat and the tares has been interpreted in the history of exegesis. What Niebuhr has done is to inscribe his own favored — but no less *biblicist!* — reading of the parable of the wheat and the tares based on the suggestive phrase, "let both grow until the harvest" in his "interpretation" of Christian ethics. Thus, what in earlier eras Augustine did in opposition to the concerns of the Donatists, and Bullinger did to the Anabaptists, Niebuhr does to the various other "interpretations" of Christian ethics.

In the preceding analysis of Niebuhr's sermon, I have tried to demonstrate the connection between Niebuhr's interpretation of Christian ethics and the Reformed Protestant argument against the Anabaptists in the sixteenth century. I have argued that like the Reformed pastors, Niebuhr's interpretation of Christian ethics is based on a narrow reading of the parable of the wheat and the tares, a reading which in turn supports assumptions about the primary significance of the political order. I have *not* tried to argue that Niebuhr's agenda is at all points the same as that of the Reformed pastors. Indeed, the social circumstances of the two readings are very different even if some of the assumptions about political order are the same. Nor have I argued that my interpretation of Niebuhr's interpretation of Christian ethics accounts for all aspects of his argument. In these respects, my discussion is limited to the hermeneutical features of Niebuhr's interpretation of Christian ethics.[52] I have also tried to restore the contested argument that is implicit in Niebuhr's interpretation of Christian ethics, an argument which derives from the Anabaptist-Reformed dialogues that Yoder analyzed in his dissertation. Having reconstructed the argument, I think we are in a better position to evaluate the historical rootage of Niebuhr's hermeneutic as well as the hermeneutical significance of Yoder's response.

51. Niebuhr, "Wheat and the Tares," 9. Significantly, the illustration Niebuhr uses to convey this point is an ironic comment on cold-war rhetoric: "One of the things I find so worrisome when I read the speeches of Mr. Khrushchev and Mr. Eisenhower is that they sound so much alike. . . . This is the situation we are in. We are deeply involved in the flux of history."

52. Given more space, I would argue that Niebuhr's conception of politics and his theodicy of the wheat and the tares are rooted in the Augustinian dualism of the letter and the spirit, a conception of biblical interpretation which implicitly excludes the ecclesial context. See chapter one of my dissertation, "Practices, Politics and Performance: Toward a Communal Hermeneutic for Christian Ethics" (The Graduate School of Duke University, 1988). There I also argue that the basis of the Anabaptist "communal hermeneutic" can be specified in the practice of "binding and loosing" as described in Matthew 18:15-20.

For Niebuhr, there can be no social embodiment of Christianity in history because history has not changed after the life, ministry, death, and resurrection of Jesus. Ultimately, for Niebuhr, the Lordship of Christ is *beyond* history, not within history. But for Yoder and the Anabaptist tradition, what took place in the life, ministry, death, and resurrection of Jesus altered history. Indeed, according to Yoder, the Lordship of Christ is what *defines* history, from the Christian perspective. This means that Christian ethics is eschatologically focused and the church is the community which bears witness in the world that the end has come.[53] Thus, we have two different narrative typologies, and two different "interpretations" of Christian ethics based on very different conceptions of the relationship of the church, and eschatology, and the meaning of history.

What no one appears to have noticed up to the present is that Niebuhr's own "interpretation" of Christian ethics is supported by an *allegory* based on the Reformed tradition's reading of the parable of the wheat and the tares. Whether Niebuhr's allegorical exegesis reflects the "political unconscious"[54] of twentieth-century American culture is a question beyond the scope of this essay, but there can be no doubt that Niebuhr's interpretation of Christian ethics is structurally opposed to Yoder's interpretation of the "politics" of Jesus. This hermeneutical conflict also reflects the problem of hermeneutics in contemporary American Christian ethics.

Conclusion

In retrospect, it is unfortunate that Reinhold Niebuhr never responded to Yoder's essay on "Reinhold Niebuhr and Christian Pacifism" or Yoder's other critical discussions of mainstream ethics. In charity to Niebuhr, perhaps we should consider the possibility that he simply did not know about Yoder's work.[55] But if the preceding discussion of Niebuhr's "interpretation" of Christian ethics is any indication, in all likelihood Niebuhr would have been no more

---

53. For a fuller discussion of these claims, see John H. Yoder, "If Christ Is Truly Lord," in *The Original Revolution* (Scottdale, PA: Herald Press, 1971), 52-84.

54. Here, I invoke the phrase made famous by Fredric Jameson in his book by the same title: *The Political Unconscious: Narrative as a Socially Symbolic Act* (Ithaca, NY: Cornell University Press, 1981).

55. Whether Niebuhr actually read Yoder's essay is not known, but it is clear that Niebuhr did receive a copy of Yoder's essay on "Reinhold Niebuhr and Christian Pacifism." Irvin Horst, the editor of the series of pamphlets in which Yoder's essay appeared, sent Niebuhr a copy. Niebuhr sent Horst a terse acknowledgment of receipt, with no reference to the content of the essay.

willing to consider Yoder's challenge than Bullinger and company were willing to consider the Anabaptist argument in the sixteenth century.

To his credit, John H. Yoder never stopped working to establish the groundwork for dialogue between Anabaptists and other Protestants, despite the fact that his efforts were often met with silence. More recently, there have been signs that mainstream Protestants not only have taken Yoder's work more seriously, but are now more interested than before in dialogue with the Anabaptist tradition. Over the past two decades, Yoder and Richard J. Mouw[56] have engaged in an ongoing discussion of issues which have prevented dialogue between their traditions, thereby laying the basis for a renewed Anabaptist-Reformed dialogue.[57] There is reason to hope the dialogue will continue on a broader front in the years to come.

In any event, we can be grateful for Yoder's efforts. Not only has Yoder taught mainline Protestants to read Niebuhr within the context of "modernist" hermeneutics, he also pinpointed the ecclesiological, eschatological, and historical issues that were at stake in mainstream ethics. In that sense, Yoder the historian of Christianity paved the way for Yoder the Christian ethicist, and both created the possibilities for renewed ecumenical dialogue about the use of Scripture in Christian ethics.[58]

56. Mouw is a philosophical ethicist and a member of the Christian Reformed Church who teaches at Fuller Theological Seminary.

57. Richard J. Mouw and John H. Yoder, "Evangelical Ethics and the Anabaptist-Reformed Dialogue" *Journal of Religious Ethics* 17 (Fall 1989): 121-37. This essay extends the discussion that began in 1985 with an exchange in the *Theological Students Fellowship Bulletin:* Yoder, "Reformed Versus Anabaptist Social Strategies: An Inadequate Typology" (May-June 1985): 2-7; and Mouw, "Abandoning the Typology: A Reformed Assist" (May-June 1985): 7-10.

58. I am grateful to L. Gregory Jones and Stanley Hauerwas for comments and criticisms in response to an earlier draft of this essay.

Love Your Enemies: The Church as Community of Nonviolence

Jane Elyse Russell, OSF

Introduction

Little did I guess, when I signed up for John Howard Yoder's Radical Reformation seminar in 1973, how deeply John's outlook on ecclesiology and ethics would affect the rest of my religious and intellectual life. A Franciscan sister who had been active in the post–Vatican II renewal of my religious congregation, I found myself unaccountably fascinated by the "believers church" or "sectarian" movements we studied in that seminar. I was astonished at the similarities between Peter Waldo and Francis of Assisi. I was appalled to learn how the reforming energies of Waldo, Conrad Grebel, and the others were lost to the Catholic Church, through whatever combination of their stubbornness and the intransigence of the church authorities of their times.

As the reader may surmise, I did not and do not agree with every move made by the radical reformers or every point argued by John Howard Yoder; nonetheless, I have found my Franciscan/Christian conscience repeatedly challenged by the witness of this tradition. Since that initial encounter, I have taken whatever opportunities have come my way in scholarship, teaching, or congregational leadership to explore and expand the points of contact I sense between the "believers church" position and the most vital currents within the Catholic tradition.

- My dissertation focused on "four Catholic movements [in the postconciliar Church] with an Anabaptist parallel."

- When I teach ecclesiology I include a sympathetic presentation of early Anabaptism.
- As a campus minister, I directed the Rite of Christian Initiation of Adults in two parishes over twelve years, seeking to maximize that rite's potential to form new Catholics as committed disciples.
- I have encouraged sister- and brother-Franciscans to view our way of life "according to the form of the holy Gospel" as not really one *option* among many, but as the path every Christian is meant to walk.[1]

Because John Yoder encouraged all these endeavors and more with his persistent questions and memos, I offer as my contribution to his Festschrift one of these bridge-building efforts. In it I assert — to a Franciscan audience[2] and through them to the wider church — that the call to peacemaking and nonviolence is not just a piece of the Franciscan charism but an essential part of the Christian life itself. I further inquire, if the practice of nonviolence was and is an essential dimension of our Christian life, what features or practices in the church are necessary to sustain such a stance?

$$*\qquad*\qquad*$$

Most people know that the Franciscan tradition includes a call to peacemaking, to being people of nonviolence. Doesn't the "Peace Prayer" commonly attributed to Francis begin, "Lord, make me an instrument of your peace"? My challenge today is to remind you how Franciscan peacemaking is rooted in the more basic call to Christian discipleship, and to explore what that might mean for the larger church to which we belong.

We could begin by asking which of the following two statements by Christian churchpeople best represents the teaching of Jesus:

> [Our] teaching begins in every case with a presumption against war and for peaceful settlement of disputes. In exceptional cases, determined by the moral principles of the just-war tradition, some uses of force are permitted. Every nation has a right and duty to defend itself against unjust aggression.[3]

---

1. See, besides the present essay, my "A Holy Newness: The Franciscan Movement as a Leaven for Renewal of the Church," *The Cord* 46 (November-December 1996): 287-99.

2. This essay was first presented to the 1996 Franciscan Federation Conference in Atlanta, Georgia.

3. National Conference of Bishops, *The Challenge of Peace: God's Promise and Our Response* (Washington: USCC, 1983), Summary, I.A.1-2.

One should . . . not protect the gospel and its adherents with the sword, nor themselves. . . . True believing Christians are sheep among wolves, sheep for the slaughter. They must be baptized in anxiety, distress, affliction, persecution, suffering, and death. They must . . . reach the Fatherland of eternal rest, not by slaying their bodily [foes], but by mortifying their spiritual enemies. They employ neither worldly sword nor war, since with them killing is absolutely renounced. Indeed they do not defend themselves — unless we were still under the old law. . . .[4]

What do you think?

The first statement is what Catholics expect a church to say. It is taken from the U.S. Bishops' pastoral, *The Challenge of Peace.* The second statement is startling, strange, and impractical — but arguably bears a more direct relation to Jesus' words on the use of force, as summarized in the Sermon on the Mount (Matt. 5–7; Luke 6:20-49).

The long history of the Christian church shows periods sometimes more, sometimes less faithful to Jesus' teaching on peace, forgiveness, and nonviolence. While the U.S. Bishops' peace pastoral takes significant steps toward rehabilitating the path of nonviolence (about which more later), it primarily speaks out of "just war" logic. I think Christians today are searching for a simpler, more direct form of faithfulness than the just war tradition provides. How can we walk the path of nonviolence and unmask the illusory logic of violence, especially we who say in our Third Order Regular Rule (no. 20), "let the sisters and brothers be peaceful"?

In this quest, I would like to recall examples of churches and groups which *have* taken the mandate of nonviolence seriously, and examine what that looks like in practice. I will sketch for our review the church of the first three centuries, the patterns of Francis and the early Franciscan movement, and the early Swiss Anabaptists whose Mennonite descendants are counted among the historic peace churches.

Then we can look at Catholic teaching in our time and bring it into dialogue with these examples. I hope that the combination of past and present voices will give clues as to how our church could live the Gospel of peace more consistently, and how such a church could help to change the world.

First, the historical question: What does the church look like when it takes the call to nonviolence seriously?

---

4. Conrad Grebel, *Letter to Thomas Müntzer,* trans. J. C. Wenger (Scottdale, PA: Herald Press, 1970), lines 182-91.

JANE ELYSE RUSSELL, OSF

1. The Church of the First Three Centuries

Having grown up in a military household, I was astonished to learn in graduate school that the church in early years followed literally Christ's words about nonviolent love.

For example, the second-century Didache, the "Teaching of the Twelve Apostles," begins its moral catechism with a near-verbatim repetition of the most challenging passages from Matthew's Sermon on the Mount:

> The Way of Life is this. . . . [B]less those that curse you, and pray for your enemies; besides, fast for those that persecute you. For what thanks do you deserve when you love those that love you? Do not the heathen do as much? For your part, love those that hate you; in fact, have no enemy. . . .
>
> When anyone gives you a blow on the right cheek, turn to him the other as well, and be perfect; when anyone forces you to go one mile with him, go two with him; when anyone takes your cloak away, give him your coat also; when anyone robs you of your property, demand no return. You really cannot do it. Give to anyone that asks you, and demand no return; the Father wants His own bounties to be shared with all.[5]

A number of Protestant and Catholic scholars have pointed out a strong orientation toward nonviolence in the New Testament and in the church of the first three centuries. Richard McSorley, SJ, has summarized *The New Testament Basis of Peacemaking*. Donald Senior calls "enemy love" "Jesus' most scandalous teaching," and affirms that it was "a capital part of the New Testament."[6]

Catholic exegete Gerhard Lohfink shows that the church maintained, into the third and fourth centuries, its distinctive New Testament form as a "contrast-society" defying the norms of the surrounding pagan world. Christians formed a close-knit "fraternity" among themselves, calling each other by the family titles of "brother" and "sister," and taking care of one another in time of need.

Christians refused to participate in many aspects of the pagan culture, such as the shows or the public banquets. A key part of their Christian uniqueness was living without violence or domination, as Christ had mandated and

5. *The Didache* (Or, *The Lord's Instructions to the Gentiles Through the Twelve Apostles*), in *Readings in Church History*, vol. 1, ed. Colman J. Barry, OSF (Paramus, NJ: Newman Press, 1960), 25.
6. Donald Senior, "Jesus' Most Scandalous Teaching," in *Biblical Reflections on "The Challenge of Peace*," ed. John T. Pawlikowski, OSM, and Donald Senior, CP (Wilmington, DE: Glazier, 1984), 55-69.

modeled. The question of "whether, and under what circumstances, a Christian could perform *military service* disturbed the Christian churches into the fourth century."[7] Although "in the border provinces threatened by attack there was more willingness to compromise on this issue . . . ," in Rome itself, as witnessed by the Church Order of Hippolytus in 215 AD, "a baptized soldier had to promise not to perform executions or swear military oaths" in order to be accepted into the church.[8]

Tertullian thought that, unlike John the Baptist who allowed soldiers to continue their military service (Luke 3:14), "the Lord, in disarming Peter, thenceforth disarmed every soldier."[9] This line became a virtual slogan in the third-century church.

Origen of Alexandria also argued against Christians fighting with the sword. As a priestly people, they should fight instead "as priests and worshipers of God," i.e., through their prayers. Origen saw the church as performing "its specific service to the world (its priesthood) only in absolute nonviolence."[10]

The discussion about violence did not arise only in the pastoral counseling of soldiers, but formed part of the whole apologetic and evangelistic portrayal of Christianity. Christian preachers loved the prophecy in Isaiah 2:4:

> And they shall beat their swords into plowshares,
> and their spears into pruning hooks;
> nation shall not lift up sword against nation,
> neither shall they learn war any more.

The church fathers considered this prophecy fulfilled. The word of the Lord *had gone forth from Jerusalem* (in the apostolic preaching), and the nations *were beginning to stream in* to join the new people of God. The eschatological state of nonviolence and peace, prophesied by Isaiah, had become a reality in the church. Numerous patristic authors made this point; for example, Justin wrote in his *Apology* that "we who once killed one another, [now] not only do not wage war against our enemies, but, in order to avoid lying or deceiving our examiners, we even meet death cheerfully, confessing Christ."[11] What the apologists argued in writing, ordinary Christians by the hundreds and thousands

7. Gerhard Lohfink, *Jesus and Community,* trans. John P. Galvin (Philadelphia: Fortress Press, 1984), 168.

8. M. Hengel, quoted in Lohfink, *Jesus and Community,* 168f.

9. Tertullian, *On Idolatry,* quoted in Lohfink, *Jesus and Community,* 169.

10. Origen, quoted in Lohfink, *Jesus and Community,* 170.

11. Justin, *Apology,* quoted in Lohfink, *Jesus and Community,* 173.

demonstrated in accepting martyrdom to "confess Christ," the nonviolent one.[12]

Multiple texts from Justin, Irenaeus, Tertullian, and others make the same argument, from the nonviolent suffering of Christians to the fulfillment of the Isaiah prophecy, and thence to the messiahship of Jesus. The life of nonviolence was no peripheral issue, but a central part of the Christian duty to witness to Christ. While peace might not have come in fullness, it had appeared through those of every nation who accepted Jesus as Messiah, and followed his command and example of "turning the other cheek."

If the early church, by and large, actually lived the nonviolent ethic for centuries, what features of church life made this possible? From the sources, I would highlight four points:

1. A strong conviction of salvation received, of living in the "end times" through God's gift in Christ Jesus. They did not live according to the logic of the world, because the "present age" had been replaced by a new age with its own inner logic of grace.
2. Adult baptism, committing people to this way of life only after a strenuous catechumenate. (Although there is evidence of infant baptism from the late second century on, the baptism of adult catechumens predominated into the fourth century.)
3. Strong and frequent community interactions, to maintain the distinctive Christian convictions. The Didache urged Christians to "seek daily contact with the saints to be refreshed by their discourses" (ch. 4).
4. Pastoral leaders, starting with Paul and Peter and the other apostles, who led by example for the good of the community, rather than commanding with an authority based on coercion. The norm for this "servant leadership" was preserved in Mark 10:42-45:

> You know that those who are recognized as rulers over the Gentiles lord it over them, and their great ones make their authority over them felt. But it shall not be so among you. Rather, whoever wishes to be great among you will be your servant; whoever wishes to be first among you will be the slave of all. For the Son of Man did not come to be served but to serve and to give his life as a ransom for many.[13]

Although we can't presume that this norm was always perfectly fulfilled, the fact that it is passed on as a saying of Jesus suggests a real expectation that this

12. Ronald Musto, *The Catholic Peace Tradition* (Maryknoll, NY: Orbis, 1986), 40.
13. See also parallel verses in Matthew 20:25-28 and Luke 22:24-27.

type of leadership would prevail. St. Paul exemplified this style, in that he usually argues to persuade rather than simply issuing decrees.[14] In addition, the large numbers of apostles, deacons, and bishops who accepted martyrdom along with brother and sister Christians shows the readiness of Church leadership to live the noncoercive Gospel they proclaimed.

In summary, the vivid eschatological faith, adult commitment, strong community interactions, and servant leaders of the early centuries sustained a martyr church, which witnessed to the nonviolent Christ even to the point of giving their own lives.

What changed this pattern?

It's clear that adherence to the ethic of nonviolence changed rapidly as Christianity found toleration and legal status within the Roman Empire. Ronald Musto, who has traced "the Catholic peace tradition" over centuries, puts the fourth-century transition this way: "Born out of opposition to the prevailing value structure and nurtured in persecution, the church of the martyrs now suddenly became an accepted, favored religion and would soon be an official religion of the state. The alliance of Christian church and Roman empire produced changes in both."[15]

The Constantinian church assimilated to the empire which was embracing it. It developed a stake in preserving the Christianized empire from its foes — and began compromising its nonviolent origins, as Ambrose and Augustine baptized the "just war theory."[16]

2. The Franciscan Movement

Although Musto describes a steady parade of protests against the general acceptance of violence in succeeding centuries, I will note only two historical examples: the Franciscan movement, and the Swiss Anabaptists of the sixteenth century.

Musto affirms that Francis of Assisi "came closer to living a life of total pacifism than any other medieval figure."[17] The Francis who once dreamed of battlefield glory was *disarmed* in conversion, to become a man of peace, an ambassador of reconciliation. "Peace" was the greeting on his lips, whether in the towns of Umbria or when he went unarmed to convert the sultan. His many

---

14. See Lohfink, *Jesus and Community,* 115-20.
15. Musto, *Catholic Peace Tradition,* 46.
16. See Musto, *Catholic Peace Tradition,* 47-50.
17. Musto, *Catholic Peace Tradition,* 83.

writings, and the stories in his biographies, "are filled with references to the need for peace, the reconciliation of enemies, forgiveness, and to suffering evil rather than inflicting it."[18]

Musto points out that Francis' attitude of peacemaking and his embrace of poverty are closely connected, as they had been for earlier medieval "poverty movements." As Francis once said to the Bishop of Assisi, "If we had property, we should have need of arms to defend it." Or, to quote one startling section in the Earlier Rule (the *Regula NonBullata*):

> The brothers should beware that, whether they are in hermitages or in other places, they do not make any place their own or contend with anyone about it. And whoever comes to them, friend or foe, thief or robber, should be received with kindness. (RegNB 7:13f.)

This is an amazing image, to receive robbers with kindness! It sums up so much of Francis' thought. If we own nothing, and don't cling to things we use, we won't need to fight with anyone over anything. Such simplicity makes possible an attitude of *peaceableness* toward all.

The attitude of peace and nonresistance to evil is spelled out further in Francis' *Admonitions*, and in chapters 14 and 16 of the early Rule, with ample quotes from Christ's Sermon on the Mount and missionary discourses. Francis exhorts in the Rule, "All the brothers . . . should remember that they gave themselves and abandoned their bodies to the Lord Jesus Christ and for love of Him they must make themselves vulnerable to their enemies. . . ." (RegNB 16:10f.).

The Franciscan movement had a tremendous impact on the laity, as we know. The 1221 Rule for the Third Order, drawn up by Cardinal Ugolino on the basis of Francis' earlier version, commands the secular brothers and sisters to "be reconciled with their neighbors and to restore what belongs to others." It explicitly forbids members "to take up lethal weapons, or bear them about, against anybody."[19] Think of the effect of such a rule when embraced across the social classes in a feudal society!

Musto reports that an outgrowth of the mendicant orders and their tertiaries was a great surge in popular peace movements in the thirteenth century, which interrupted crusades and political wars with spontaneous demonstrations of people seeking alternatives to violence. Though we hear more about

---

18. Musto, *Catholic Peace Tradition*, 83.
19. Quoted in Marion A. Habig, *St. Francis of Assisi: Writings and Early Biographies. English Omnibus of the Sources for the Life of St. Francis*, 3rd rev. ed. (Chicago: Franciscan Herald Press, 1972), 171.

the Crusades, Musto maintains that the growth of the tertiaries and the peace movements actually involved greater numbers of people.[20]

We can identify features in the Franciscan communities to match those I pointed out in the early church:

1. Certainly Francis and his followers had a strong conviction of salvation received, of living in a new era through God's gift in Christ Jesus. Living by the words of the Gospel led Francis naturally into the life of nonpossessiveness, of forgiveness, of vulnerability and the reconciliation of enemies. It is all there in the Gospels and Epistles, for one who embraces Christ and tries to live by his words.

2. An adult commitment was required, a voluntary conversion in response to the preaching of repentance by Francis and his friars.

3. Clearly the friars and poor ladies, and the tertiaries as well, developed strong and frequent community interactions, which served to maintain their distinctive Franciscan/Gospel convictions.

4. Again we can see an ideal of *servant leadership* in the Order of Friars Minor and in the Rule of St. Clare. Francis describes the general and provincial leaders as "ministers and servants of the other brothers," in the mode of Christ who came "not to be served but to serve."[21] Clare similarly envisions the abbess as an approachable servant of her sisters (Rule, ch. 14, 16).

3. A Peace Church in the Radical Reformation

The Anabaptist movement is less familiar to a Catholic audience, but gives us a classic picture of the church as a community of nonviolence.[22] On this issue, the "historic peace churches" — the Anabaptists or Mennonites, the Quakers, and the Church of the Brethren — have much to teach us.

The evangelical Anabaptist movement arose in Zurich, Switzerland, among followers of reforming preacher Ulrich Zwingli. Conrad Grebel, Felix Manz, and others broke with Zwingli over the pace of reform. Against Zwingli's

20. Musto, *Catholic Peace Tradition*, 84f.

21. Matthew 20:28, quoted in Regula NonBullata 4 and Admonitions 4.

22. I know of very few treatments of the Free Church tradition from a Catholic perspective; but see Michael Novak, "The Free Churches and the Roman Church," *Journal of Ecumenical Studies* 2 (1965): 426-47, and Kilian McDonnell, "Church Order and the Ontologizing Function of Liturgy," in *Worship* 44 (November 1970): 528-40. See also Daniel Liechty, ed., *Early Anabaptist Spirituality,* in the Paulist Press Classics of Western Spirituality series (1984).

wishes, they began implementing a simpler Lord's Supper, withholding their infants from baptism, and ultimately — after concluding that their "sprinkling" as children was no authentic baptism — rebaptizing one another.

These "Anabaptists" (rebaptizers), as the movement was called by opponents, comprised various streams and ideas. One question on which they disagreed was whether or not the times called for Christians to take up arms to bring in the reign of God. Thomas Müntzer in Germany advocated this; the Zurich Anabaptists believed otherwise. Their letter to Müntzer contains the stirring affirmation of Christian nonviolence in the face of suffering which was quoted above.[23]

One regional meeting to resolve disputed issues produced a consensus statement, the "Brotherly Union of a Number of Children of God Concerning Seven Articles."[24] This "Schleitheim Confession" fills in other dimensions of what a nonviolent church "looks like." Its seven articles include the following teachings:

1. Baptism: to be given only to "those who have been taught repentance and the amendment of life and [who] believe truly that their sins are taken away through Christ . . . ; hereby is excluded all infant baptism, the greatest and first abomination of the pope."
2. The Ban: members "who have given themselves over to the Lord, to walk after [Him] . . . and still somehow slip and fall into error and sin," should be "warned twice privately and the third time be publicly admonished before the entire congregation according to the command of Christ" (Matt. 18).
3. The Breaking of Bread: to be done only among those beforehand "united in the one body of Christ," through baptism.
4. Separation from "the wickedness which the devil has planted in the world": "we have no fellowship with them, and do not run with them in the confusion of their abominations." (Modern Catholics tend to be jarred by this one, especially since the wickedness meant "all popish and repopish works and idolatry, gatherings, church attendance, winehouses," etc. All such things are considered "flatly counter to the command of God." Strange as it sounds to us, the idea of separation from people and behaviors not of God does have a scriptural basis, in 2 Corinthians 6:17

---

23. See note 4.

24. Translated in John H. Yoder, *The Legacy of Michael Sattler* (Scottdale, PA: Herald Press, 1973), 34-43. The South German Michael Sattler is considered the principal author of the consensus statement.

and Revelation 18:4ff.) They anticipate a later article here, with a reference to violence. In the pursuit of separation, "Thereby shall also fall away from us the diabolical weapons of violence — such as sword, armor, and the like, and all of their use to protect friends or against enemies — by virtue of the word of Christ: 'you shall not resist evil.'"

5. "Shepherds in the church of God": "shall be person[s] according to the rule of Paul (1 Tim. 3:7)." "The office of such a person shall be to read and exhort and teach, warn, admonish, or ban in the congregation, and properly to preside among the sisters and brothers in prayer, and in the breaking of bread. . . ." We see here the standard ministries of the word, of governance, and of liturgical leadership; contrary to Catholic practice, however, these shepherds are discerned locally. There is even a reference to their possible martyrdom: "But if the shepherd should be driven away or led to the Lord by the cross, at the same hour another shall be ordained to his place, so that the little folk and the little flock of God may not be destroyed. . . ."

6. The Sword: "an ordering of God outside the perfection of Christ." That is, it has its place. "It punishes and kills the wicked, and guards and protects the good . . . and the secular rulers are established to wield the same. But within the perfection of Christ only the ban is used for the admonition and exclusion of the one who has sinned, without the death of the flesh. . . ." If this viewpoint had prevailed in the church and society, there would have been no Inquisition, no burning of heretics, and no wars of religion!

This article from Schleitheim insists that Christians really are not to use the sword, even "against the wicked for the protection and defense of the good, or for the sake of love." As reasonable as the defense-of-others motivation sounds, the brethren at Schleitheim did not allow it because it would go against the command and example of Christ, who deals with a sinner only through words of love and warning. "Since Christ is as is written of Him, so must His members be the same." As John Howard Yoder has summarized it, the essence of the Christian vocation is to follow Christ precisely at the point of his novelty.

In terms of the practices of church life which can sustain an ethic of nonviolence, the picture which emerges from the Schleitheim Confession and other early Anabaptist documents displays features like those I highlighted in the early church and the Franciscan movement:

1. A lively conviction of salvation renewed in their times, of living in the "end times" through a new eruption of God's grace in Christ Jesus. The

sense of present grace was nurtured by diligent searching and straightfor-ward obedience to the scriptural word of God.

2. Adult baptism, committing people to this way of life only upon under-standing and acceptance of the Gospel. The church community was *not* coterminous with the whole society, as it was considered to be in medi-eval Christendom.

3. Strong and frequent community interactions, sharing Scripture and prayer, simple meals and earthly goods when needed.

4. Pastoral leaders chosen locally for their wisdom and Gospel convictions, who led by example for the good of the community.

Deep Christian faith, adult commitment, community support and ser-vant leaders willing to face martyrdom all seem to be features necessary to the development and sustaining of a church witnessing to the nonviolent way of Christ.

4. Toward an Ecclesiology of Nonviolence for Today

I have sketched outlines of three different eras/groups which believed that em-bracing Christ meant following his way of peacemaking and vulnerability. If we had time, we could extend the survey into the present and look at groups like the Catholic Worker or Pax Christi, to hear from contemporary Catholics who believe that the call to nonviolence is not an option but a mandate for Chris-tians. Lacking that kind of time, I will briefly assess the official status of nonvio-lence in our church today, and point to resources for an "ecclesiology of nonvi-olence."

Vatican II's Pastoral Constitution, *Gaudium et Spes,* called for "an evalua-tion of war with an entirely new attitude" in the modern era (art. 80). It is the first official statement to validate the possibility of a conscientious objection to bearing arms (art. 78 and 79). Although it affirms the tradition of the limited just war, it rejects certain developments of modern warfare such as the doctrine of deterrence, the arms race, and the use of modern weapons for "the destruc-tion of entire cities or of extensive areas along with their population" (art. 80). Musto lauds *Gaudium et Spes* for these advances, which "opened the door for a gradual discarding of the just-war tradition."[25]

Almost twenty years later, the U.S. Bishops' peace pastoral, *The Challenge of Peace,* was a further development in Catholic theology and yet a disappoint-

---

25. Musto, *Catholic Peace Tradition,* 191-93.

ment to many who wanted a clearer statement. Musto accents the positive, calling it a "revolutionary . . . synthesis of and compromise between the just war and pacifist traditions within Catholic history":

> For the first time in American Catholic history pacifism and "active nonviolence" are seen as both evangelical imitations of Christ and legitimate means of serving the *political* community, . . . means of Christian action as legitimate as military defense in the service of the nation (pars. 73-77). In the last analysis . . . the bishops admit that nonviolence "best reflects the call of Jesus both to love and to justice" (par. 78). . . .[26]

Even so, the bishops do not go so far as to repudiate the fifteen-hundred-year habit of speaking from within the logic of empire and earthly calculations of "reasonableness." The long and complex document reaffirms the just war doctrine as a basis for moral evaluations of national policy. Based on just war considerations, the bishops agree with Pope John Paul II that "in current conditions 'deterrence' based on balance, certainly not as an end in itself but as a step on the way toward a progressive disarmament, may still be judged morally acceptable."[27]

The bishops' ten-year anniversary statement, *The Harvest of Justice Is Sown in Peace*, continues the uneasy compromise between these two traditions; however, in light of events such as the successful nonviolent revolutions in the Philippines and in Eastern Europe, the document does grant "new importance" to nonviolence and raise "new questions" about the just war theory.[28] Slowly, perhaps, we are inching back as church toward radical faithfulness to the nonviolent Christ![29]

What clues can we derive toward an *ecclesiology of nonviolence* from the contemporary voices as well as from our historical examples?

John Dear, SJ, offers an interesting "ecclesiology of nonviolence" in his book, *The God of Peace*. He gives us a picture — the church as community of peacemakers — without telling us how to get there. He knows what the church should *not* be: "Instead of modeling itself on imperial Rome, the Church needs to be transformed into a community of nonviolence. . . . The Church is not supposed to be dominating, powerful or hierarchical."[30] His strongest positive

26. Musto, *Catholic Peace Tradition*, 261-64.

27. John Paul II, "Message to U.N. Special Session 1982," no. 3; quoted in *The Challenge of Peace*, par. 173.

28. National Conference of Bishops, *The Harvest of Justice Is Sown in Peace* (Washington: USCC, 1994), part I.B.

29. Musto says that the evolution of American Catholic thought on war and peace "is a classic model of the dynamic of change and dialogue within the Mystical Body" (238).

30. John Dear, *The God of Peace: Toward a Theology of Nonviolence* (Maryknoll, NY: Orbis, 1994), 108.

points are examples such as a nonviolent base community in the Philippines and the witness of courageous leaders like Martin Luther King, Jr., and Oscar Romero.

Although the peace pastoral, as we saw, speaks from the just war framework of the Constantinian church, it also recognizes a less "established," more countercultural ecclesiology in Avery Dulles's vision of the church as the "community of disciples."[31] Because this view of the church could support a more prophetic nonviolent ethic, I quote at length the bishops' presentation of it:

> It is clear today . . . that convinced Christians are a minority in nearly every country . . . including nominally Christian and Catholic nations. In our own country we are coming to a fuller awareness that a response to the call of Jesus is both personal and demanding. . . . To be disciples of Jesus requires that we continually go beyond where we now are. To obey the call of Jesus means separating ourselves from all attachments and affiliations that could prevent us from hearing and following our authentic vocation. To set out on the road to discipleship is to dispose oneself for a share in the cross (cf. Jn. 16:20). To be a Christian, according to the New Testament, is not simply to believe with one's mind, but also to become a doer of the word, a wayfarer with and witness to Jesus. This means, of course, that we never expect complete success within history and that we must regard as normal even the path of persecution and the possibility of martyrdom.
>
> . . . In order to remain a Christian, one must take a resolute stand against many commonly accepted axioms of the world. To become true disciples, we must undergo a demanding course of induction into the adult Christian community. We must continually equip ourselves to profess the full faith of the Church in an increasingly secularized society. We must develop a sense of solidarity, cemented by relationships with mature and exemplary Christians who represent Christ and his way of life.

Notice how this vision of the church echoes our pacifist examples:

1. It shows an awareness of living by a logic contrary to that of the present age, in that disciples "take a resolute stand against many commonly accepted axioms of the world." (However, some would charge that the bishops are using worldly logic when they endorse [even conditionally] the use of lethal force.) Certainly we all need to learn more about the nonvio-

31. *The Challenge of Peace,* IV.A (nos. 274-78, pp. 85f.), following ch. 1 of Avery Dulles, *A Church to Believe In* (New York: Crossroad, 1982). Dulles's chapter was itself based on a passing reference to the People of God as "the community of the disciples" in John Paul II's *Redemptor Hominis,* no. 21.

lent means of conflict resolution (*Challenge of Peace* nos. 221-30) as a whole new kind of logic, which has already had more practical success than most people realize.

2. This vision recognizes the need for adult commitment: true disciples must "undergo a demanding course of induction into the adult Christian community." Those who have worked with the Rite of Christian Initiation of Adults (RCIA) like to think of that process as the requisite "demanding course of induction." But how much training in the Christian obligation to peacemaking is included in the average parish RCIA program? And what can be done for the majority of Catholics who "complete" their Christian catechesis in their early teens? The bishops' pastoral challenges all who lead the Catholic community to find better means for adult Christian formation — especially to capture the ongoing learning process of discipleship, which "requires that we continually go beyond where we now are."

3. The pastoral calls for strong community interactions: "a sense of solidarity, cemented by relationships with mature and exemplary Christians." This laconic comment, like the previous element, invites extensive pastoral strategies for implementation, to make it real.

4. The quotation above does not speak explicitly about servant leaders, but affirms that every disciple must "dispose oneself for a share in the cross," and "regard as normal even the path of persecution and the possibility of martyrdom." Dulles's essay, in passages not quoted by the bishops, suggests a modest view of church leaders as "mature and faithful disciples" not different in essence from their brother and sister disciples.[32] It could perhaps be said that the very form of the peace pastoral — developed through a process of hearings and multiple drafts, and written in a style of exhortation rather than command — represents a return to more of the servant style of leadership than has been common in the Catholic hierarchy.[33]

Thus, the U.S. bishops' peace pastoral offers tantalizing hints of evolution toward a more countercultural "community of disciples" and martyrs, even while speaking in the familiar magisterial mode to nations and world leaders.

Overall, I have no neat conclusions, but have offered some hints toward new ways to think about our church. While this conference aims to strengthen

---

32. Dulles, *A Church to Believe In*, 11f.

33. John Linnan, CSV, endorses this view. See his "Perspectives on Church in *The Challenge of Peace*," in *Biblical and Theological Reflections on "The Challenge of Peace,"* 167-80.

our commitment as Franciscans to the nonviolent ways of Francis and of Jesus, the call to be peacemakers is in fact addressed to *every* Christian. Only when our church as a whole lives out a vivid eschatological faith, with "a demanding course of induction into the adult Christian community," strong interactions with other mature Christians to sustain us, and leaders who are more servants than hierarchs — only then will we become a true peace church. Perhaps we Franciscans, in dialogue and cooperation with the heirs of the Anabaptist tradition, can help lead the way into such a renewed Catholic church!

TERTIUM DATUR

History, Theory, and Anabaptism:
A Conversation on Theology
after John Howard Yoder

Stanley Hauerwas and Chris K. Huebner

SH: To start, we need to make clear why we are doing our paper as a dialogue. Basically, I am just tired of doing papers on John. But more important, I think a dialogue is appropriate given the way John worked. That is, he always responded as concretely as he could to a specific assignment. In other words, his work was always a dialogue. He never wanted to do anything that was self-generating. That was true even of *The Politics of Jesus* and the essays in *The Original Revolution.* None of his books were attempts to develop some freestanding intellectual project. And I think that is absolutely crucial for understanding the character of his work. He never wanted to work systematically if that meant needing to have a secure starting point. He did not have a place to begin because he was always responding in a community, which makes his work extraordinarily free-ranging. That, of course, also means his "position" is hard to put together. And that is the reason I thought that this kind of dialogue might make some sense.

CH: But at the same time, you have to be careful of making the claim that dialogue is *the* appropriate genre to understand Yoder's work. Because that is just another version of the kind of methodologist assumption — that his work has to be limited to this particular form rather than that — that he would reject.

SH: That's right. I also thought — given the fortunate character of your being here, as a young Mennonite who grew up under the influence of Yoder, unavoidable given your father's education of you — that it would be wonderful to hear your kind of reflections about the influence of John in juxtaposition to me, coming out of the mainstream, admittedly ambiguously so, and my thoughts about the shaping of John on my life.

CH: I suppose that for me there is a sense that theology somehow "begins" with Yoder, I think because that was all I ever knew, both growing up, since that's what my Dad was teaching and was teaching us, and then when I got to Canadian Mennonite Bible College, where theology always included his work. So that became the "grid" through which everything else had to be sifted.

SH: It is interesting when you say that theology for you begins with Yoder. From the kinds of Catholic sensibilities which I obviously have, that immediately throws up red flags. Such a claim makes it sound as if you can begin with Yoder without attending to the Christian tradition. Although of course there is a sense that for theology to begin with Yoder means you cannot begin with Yoder, since he is so tradition-determined.

CH: Well of course you cannot distinguish the Yoder that I say my understanding of theology "began with" from the larger context of the Mennonite/Anabaptist narration of the Christian tradition that I just grew up in.

SH: Right. Did it ever occur to you to call that "limited"?

CH: No, not until a lot later. And by then I had a response.

SH: What was the response?

CH: Just the kind of thing that Yoder taught me, namely that for such a perspective to be called "limited" is to accept the standard types of categorizations — between church and sect or withdrawal and presence — that can be called into question.

SH: One of the things that I have wondered about is when you have a giant like Yoder, which I think is not an inappropriate description, he can stop you from going on. There is so much there to take in that it takes a long time to receive it. And I am sure that you need to go on. Do you have any sense of that?

CH: When you say that Yoder is a "giant," I almost get the sense that this might be another difference between your experience or reception of his work and mine. For you he came along and changed your life because of the way he put things. But I didn't know there was any other way to put things, so I never really realized he was such a giant until much later.

SH: I think it is interesting to reflect on why I read Yoder sympathetically. He knew that I had been taught to read sympathetically, given my training at Yale. Of course, Yale taught sympathetic reading because that "proved" that Yale was "superior." I was not trained well enough at Yale, however, because I came to believe that Yoder was not just another position "to understand," but rather that he was right. I am sure that I came to that judgment partly because I am a Methodist and a committed sanctificationist. Moreover, I had learned from Barth, that that entailed christological commitments that simply had to be there for a proper understanding of theology. But I was unable to put it all together. Reading Yoder put it all together for me. I think I say in *The Peaceable Kingdom* that I wanted to be a sanctificationist and a Niebuhrian, but knew that you could not consistently do so given the kind of social ethics that the Niebuhrs, and in particular Reinhold, represented. I think that was one of the reasons that I was able to read Yoder sympathetically. I have always worried, though, whether I really want to be nonviolent. I really think nonviolence is the way we must be as disciples of Christ, but I have always worried whether my own commitment to nonviolence is not part of being such a "contrarian."

CH: Let's think about that in terms of Yoder's last book, *For the Nations* and your *Against the Nations,* which his book is obviously at least rhetorically a response to. When you get into the arguments, it becomes clear that his "for the nations" stance does not mean that he is entirely in favor of the nations or that he somehow generally affirms what the nations are doing, and your "against the nations" stance does not mean "let's go and destroy them."

SH: Right.

CH: And when you get into the actual positions represented there, they sound, at least to me, very similar at many crucial points. So one is tempted to think that maybe the difference between Yoder and yourself is merely rhetorical. But then again what Yoder has taught us is that those "rhetorical" differences often make all the difference.

SH: I'm not sure I understand that.

CH: If the substance of your position, say, in *Against the Nations,* and Yoder's in *For the Nations* is roughly the same, in the sense that it is not the case that you are against the nations in a way that contradicts or is the opposite of his being for them, then one obvious way of resolving the apparent contradiction is to suggest that he is just putting the same thing in a rhetorically different manner, which is to deny that there is really that much substantial difference between you. But then he is going to come back, and I think rightly in some senses, and say that those rhetorical differences are quite significant after all. Or to put it differently, I doubt that he would ever qualify "rhetorical difference" with the word "merely."

SH: John can be for the nations because he was never intellectually and ecclesially tempted to be in control in a way that that would capture the imagination. But I have to be against, because I come from a tradition that has thought that there is no alternative to being in control. Of course that is not quite true. When I say I come from such a tradition, I do not mean to say that I come from that tradition given my class and ecclesial background. It was only the pretension of a Yale education that would have given me that presumption of being in control.

CH: So coming from that establishmentarian standpoint, to be "against the nations," so to speak, throws things for a loop in a way that calls into question the whole church-sect dichotomy, which is the same thing that Yoder is trying to do by being "for the nations" coming from the opposite standpoint that he comes from.

SH: That is exactly right. I think it works that way. Which is one of the reasons I thought it might be useful for us to have this conversation. My polemical style is meant to make my work dramatic. And I do not apologize for that. But it can make some overlook the "constructive" side of what I am trying to do. Constructively, the heart of my work is to think christologically in a manner Yoder taught me. In seminary I had taken a course with Hans Frei, in which we read the classical christological developments plus modern Christology. One of the things that impressed me was how the liberals of the eighteenth and nineteenth centuries emphasized the life of Jesus. I had not read Yoder at all at that point, but I thought there was something right about that. And it had to do with my Methodist sanctificationism. The teachings of Jesus ought to matter. And yet at the same time I wanted to be thoroughly orthodox, both trinitarian and christologically. When I read *The Politics of Jesus* Yoder helped me see why you cannot separate the life of Jesus from cross, resurrection, and ascension, and why the challenges facing the church require the later christological displays that we now associate with the development of Catholic Christianity. So it was crucial for me that Yoder teaches us to see that discipleship is internal to christological display. Moreover, when you see that connection you also realize that you cannot avoid social location — which would be another way to say church — for thinking about what kind of community is capable of sustaining the continual concrete display of the life of Jesus. Of course, some think that what Yoder gives you is Jesusology, not Christology. But that is really a profound mistake.

CH: You would accept that depiction as long as it is just another way of saying that we need to keep Christology concrete, would you not? And in fact Yoder uses the term Jesusology positively in precisely this sense.

SH: That is right. The difficulty here is that I think I have the greater stake in wanting to say that God never lets the church go wrong in what it says positively about Jesus than John did. That is, I think some account of infallibility is necessary.

CH: But at the same time you have to try to disentangle what the church is saying from what the state or the world is forcing onto it or somehow saying through the church. Or at least that is where Yoder comes in.

SH: Right. That's right.

CH: He would probably accept what you say about the church as long as it is clear that you are talking about the "true church" in some sense, and then make the argument over against the infiltration of the world into the church with Constantinianism.

SH: Again that seems right. But such discriminations are hard. You can say that when the church separated orthodoxy from discipleship, as perhaps was the case for later readings of Nicaea — I do not believe that Nicaea would ever separate trinitarian claims from discipleship — but Nicaea can underwrite that separation once you get it. So John, I suspect, wanted to relativize or make less central the development of doctrine than I do.

CH: Or at least put it into a larger social and historical context.

SH: And that is perfectly appropriate, because John has a stake in rewriting the history of doctrine, as in his *Preface to Theology,* a book we can hopefully get published.

CH: I suppose one of his crucial points is that the history of theology is best understood in terms of different histories, and in fact often conflicting histories, rather than history in the singular. If it makes all the difference, for Yoder, whether the meaning of history is rooted in the world, the state, or the church, through God, then it comes down to (in a way that is not unlike MacIntyre) a question of competing histories. So I think that you are right that he has a stake in rewriting the history of doctrine in order to overcome the Constantinian assumptions that have been written into other versions of that history.

SH: In that sense, though, Yoder is in the kind of bind Milbank exemplifies. On the one hand, he claims to be against metanarrative. And yet the way to oppose the Constantinian reading seems to require something like a metanarrative. He provides it every once in a while in outline, and I think he's right to provide it.

CH: In a way I think so too. But can we, or should we, make a distinction in talking about Milbank and Yoder on metanarrative? It almost seems that Yoder offers a continuous rewriting of history — whenever you definitively state that this *is* the way it was, then you have probably made a mistake. But Milbank has a lot more confidence in his metanarrative than Yoder. So Yoder appears to focus more on the constant process of narration and re-narration itself rather than on the actual narrative produced.

SH: Right. It was not by accident that John re-narrated Christianity's relationship to Judaism. And it is brilliant stuff. But you wouldn't necessarily see Milbank committed to that re-narration in that same way. That is the reason why it is going to be so fascinating to see the comparison between Yoder's and O'Donovan's understandings of the relationship between Christianity and the Jews. John says — and I learned it all from John — that God sent Christians into the world so that Jews might live in a manner that makes Christ's life, cross, and resurrection intelligible. Now there is nothing odd about that for John. If God is God, why should you be surprised that the promised people end up living the way Christians should have lived? So interestingly enough, Christian unfaithfulness, by becoming worldly in the Constantinian sense, makes the Jews possible. And therefore we know from the Jews that it is possible to live the way Jesus made possible. If you want a metanarrative, there you have a big-time metanarrative. And it also has everything to do with what John calls "biblical realism," which he never developed in terms of a theory, but rightly so. He is a textual reasoner the way the Jews are textual reasoners. He never was without text.

CH: You started this all by referring to Frei's course on Christology. Having now just brought up biblical realism, maybe this is a good time to ask whether, or in what sense, you take Yoder's christological work to be different than Frei's and how that all ties into the larger idea of narrative. Yoder does not make a big deal about biblical realism as a technical term that can stand on its own. But it seems to me that there is a sense in which it overlaps with Frei's idea of how the biblical narrative constitutes that which is real — the "world" in the larger metaphysical sense of the term — that Christians are called to embody. Yet Yoder wants to distance himself from basing theology on the category of narrative that one finds in Frei, or maybe more from later followers of Frei than Frei himself.

SH: I think John would have used the category of narrative if it was useful to make clear what he wanted to say. But I think that his worry about narrative — and I suspect his worry about my use of narrative — would be that such an approach might suggest that you need prior philosophical sets of considerations into which you discover the significance of Israel or Jesus. He was just not going to let you do that. And I am very sympathetic with that worry. The difficulty is how you contextualize — to use Yoder-like language — the servant's ministry of speaking to those who are "outside," who are not initiated into the practices of the church in a manner that helps them appreciate what your claims are about. I have never employed the category of narrative or the anti-foundationalist moves as an apologetic strategy. Yet it can very quickly become that.

CH: Do you think Frei did that in the way that later theologians, such as Placher and Thiemann, who claim to continue his project, appear to do a lot more significantly?

SH: I think such developments are quite mixed. I think Hans was so shaped by Barth and his reading of Barth, as Yoder was, that he was almost reduced to silence. Barth can do that to you. Hans tried to find ways to make what he had learned through those readings of Barth shape other readings. He did that through his account of identity ascriptions, and those kinds of questions, and that led him to certain claims about the importance of narrative. But I think that Hans and the whole "Yale school" were far too irenic to really do theology the way Yoder did. Of course you take big academic losses to come out where Yoder and I came out.

CH: I guess another way of putting my question is as follows. You have said that there is a tension in Yoder between his biblical realism, on the one hand, and his hermeneutics of peoplehood, on the other. But might it not be objected in response to that claim, and on behalf of Yoder, that when you argue that this is a tension, you are forcing his references to biblical realism and the text into some reified account of the text or into some kind of dualism between the text and everything else or between the text and the community that is exactly what he is trying to overcome?

SH: That seems to be a fair account. I think finally all John can say is, "Look, I do not have a theory, but don't you find this convincing?" And the answer is, "Yes, I find it very convincing." He gives a better account of more possible readings than I think anyone else has given, while avoiding the mistakes founded on theories of Scripture required by the Protestant Reformation. I think that is the only answer that John has. There is no way that you can ever cut off possible future readings, and John knew that.

CH: I guess he never does offer a "final reading."

SH: That's right. Give him another alternative and he will have a response to it. Of course, one of the reasons that John's readings are so compelling is that he had unbelievable intellectual powers. And yet I think it would be a mistake to focus just on those intellectual powers in terms of the imagination that was unleashed in Yoder. I think that his imagination had everything to do with being Mennonite. In other words, just like I do not want to separate Martin Luther King, Jr., from the black church, I think it would be a real mistake — despite some of John's antagonism to the Mennonites — to think that he would have been possible without the Mennonites.

CH: Can you articulate that more specifically?

SH: I think one of the things I really do not know is the significance of what I think of as "the hidden years." Where and how did John learn all this stuff? For example, after having recently read *Christian Witness to the State*, a book he wrote in 1964, you said that so many of his characteristic moves are already there. How did he get on to everything so early? It must have had to do with battles that were going on in Mennonite life in Goshen and the Concern group and what he was learning in Europe during those years. All of that is hidden to most of us. It would just be fascinating to do a kind of archaeological study on Yoder's early years. I used to think that it must have been something like this: the Harold Bender generation rediscovered the Anabaptist texts and the Yoder and the Kaufman generation became the theologians that the texts made possible. But it is now clear to me that this is a false reading, because Yoder and Kaufman were so critical of the Harold Bender generation. Or there may be some truth to such an account, but not much. John spent all that time as a historian of the Anabaptist sources. That is what he really cared about.

CH: Maybe what Yoder and Kaufman, coming out of the Concern group, discovered in a more significant way was history or historical location. I guess Bender was a historian, but the necessity of historical articulation for theology itself seems to be a subsequent development achieved in very different ways by both Yoder and Kaufman.

SH: In that sense, I think John was shaped by European academic culture, which still accepted a strong distinction between theology and history. And he tended to be much more respectful of historical methodology than I am. But I don't think you can understand him if you separate his work as a historian, even though he always claimed to be an amateur, from his work as a theologian. When he did historical work he often was doing theology, and vice versa. Just through the explication of the texts of the Anabaptists, he was trying to make them determinative for shaping our ways of living. But I have not read all of his historical work, I have to say. I've read some. I have read the book on Michael Sattler. But there is so much more.

CH: Have you read his dissertation?

SH: No. But even if I had, I do not think that it would help us understand how he understood the interrelationship of his work in history with his theology. Indeed, I suspect that even he could not provide such an account.

CH: You mean in the sense that he was too close to it?

SH: He would always say "it is careful historical work." Of course one believes in careful historical work. But I always thought that behind "careful historical work" was the presumption that there was a kind of objectivity that I simply do not believe in. But he did believe in such objectivity. Of course that also needs to be qualified, because he certainly did not believe that something called "history" existed in and of itself, that is, separate from social context.

CH: So his is a different kind of objectivity than the sort of standard sense of the term. If you do the work in the right ecclesiological context, he would always say that God is going to make it come out right.

SH: Which brings us back to the question of the sources of his imagination. I think John thought he had to read so-called "Roman Catholic sources." But he was much more amenable to the Fathers, I think, than the Middle Ages. I don't think John read much in Aquinas, for instance.

CH: It certainly doesn't come up much.

SH: It almost never comes up. So he wanted to say, "I have to read your sources, because they are my sources too." But then John could say to the Catholics, "If you are really going to be Catholic, you need to read Sattler. He is part of your history too." I think he is dead right about that. The problem with Catholicism is that Catholics have not read the Anabaptists as Catholics. Hopefully now some Catholics will take account of Yoder.

CH: Is there nobody in the Catholic theological world that is doing that kind of accounting? You would think there is, especially given his presence at Notre Dame.

SH: I don't know. At Notre Dame they are currently talking about how to replace "the Protestant theologian." I was there when John was appointed to teach full-time at Notre Dame. In fact, I was one of those urging that John be hired. But I remember clearly in his discussions about coming to Notre Dame that John did not come as a Protestant ethicist.

CH: That would be to give up the game.

SH: It would have been exactly to give up the game. He always put it that "I can come to Notre Dame because they want to have a representative of the church's nonviolent witness," and that "I am willing to be there as part of their peace studies commitment." That was always how he understood his vocational commitment to Notre Dame. He did not come to be the "Protestant ethicist."

CH: I guess his work in the Kroc Institute is a witness to that.

SH: As well as the courses he taught. It would be very interesting to look at the courses he taught. I doubt that he ever taught a course in Protestant ethics.

CH: But he did do the Radical Reformation.

SH: That would be completely consistent with his understanding of his role at Notre Dame.

CH: I am just thinking back again to the point on the imagination. And I guess the way you would probably put it is that you cannot separate Yoder's intellectual or cognitive powers from the kinds of virtues that were embodied by him through the larger Mennonite church community. And he does make a big deal about patience as method or as methodological non-coercion, especially with respect to letting others speak and sort of letting things go the way they are going to go.

SH: I learned from John — I oftentimes feel I learned everything from John —

why you cannot separate argument from moral context. He taught me that careful argument is an alternative to violence. John always assumed that. And it does require patience. One of the other things I also learned from John was a kind of nonjudgmentalism. And I think that has become very much a part of me. I know people think I'm terribly judgmental. But it never occurs to me to make negative judgments about people who are in the military, for example. I assume, firstly, that they never knew there was an alternative. Even if nonviolence is a theoretical possibility about which they might have heard, they have never seen it embodied. So how would they know that they have an alternative to military service? Secondly, I assume that they may have known the alternative and that they are conscientious participators, which certainly is to be honored. John taught me that and I try not to forget it. But he had a capacity for suffering fools that I do not. And I don't compliment him on that. I think he suffered fools far too much. It had to do with his understanding of being a guest. At Notre Dame he always thought he was a guest. Therefore you always put the absolute best face on whatever is going on. I thought at times that this came close to being stupid, I have to say. There is a kind of irresponsibility to such a stance. I am hesitant to talk this way, because that is what the mainstream always says. But in the departmental politics concerning, for example, appointments to be made, he would merely clarify. He would never say what he wanted.

CH: He would always let others set the agenda first, and then respond to it.

SH: From my perspective that did not seem to be taking up his citizenship in the department.

CH: I suppose you could argue that such a restriction of one's participation to mere response and clarification is to take the Radical Reformation stance as a position of response and make it normative in a way that he did in obviously very good ways, but in a way that could be problematic in certain cases as well.

SH: Well I think it was. I always thought John should have been much more forceful in naming the kind of people for which we ought to search. Of course our difference on these matters could be attributed to different personal styles. But I am about community building too. And if you are about community building, you must have strong views. Not everybody needs to have views as strong as I do about everything. But I think that John always deferred, and I did not always like it. And I wondered how significant that was, i.e., whether these were kind of "personal" matters or whether it really indicated deep intellectual differences between us.

CH: But I suppose you could say that representing your views forcefully, as you put it, is to let the mainstream or the establishment off the hook too easily, in a way that his more subtle ways of going after it are perhaps more permanent. On the one hand, they might be easier to brush aside, because his voice is not as "loud" as that of others, but on the other hand maybe his views are not so easily brushed aside, whereas loud voices are often simply ignored because they are offensive. So it might be suggested that his being more subtle in that sense may actually allow his views to remain on the table after the original argument is long over.

SH: John's strategy was "letting them roll over you," and through your own truth-saying over generations, you may win.

CH: Right. He would always let the mainstream destroy itself rather than take some sort of preemptive strike and try to destroy it. And he would let it destroy itself by exposing inconsistencies, incoherences, questioning the categories, and presenting alternative histories and readings. But would you say that this represents a deep intellectual difference between the two of you?

SH: Though I should like to imitate him, I also want to influence those around me in a more direct way than John did. I have a stake in trying to make Duke Divinity School faithful to what I regard as the central vision of Methodism and evangelical Catholicism. And I can't stop trying to do that. John could be much more forceful in other contexts. In a Mennonite context he was really forceful. He was as combative as he could be. My presumption is that there is no context that is not my context. Of course that's because I do not have a community in the same way he had. I think that had to do partly with the way he dealt with just war. He let just war advocates have the first word. He would let them roll over him and point to the inconsistencies. I think that towards the end of his life, however, John became much more aggressive and self-referential. Thus the footnotes in *For the Nations* where he says "I did that there." I think that was a kind of impatience, saying "people have not read me."

CH: Or he seems to have been starting to say that while others think they are making an original point, he actually said it earlier.

SH: I really like that he was beginning to do that. He was also getting much more forceful about the incoherencies of just war. I think he was beginning to say, "Look, you people are telling me that this is just a set of tests, and you're not the least bit willing to institutionalize them." If that is the case, then he is going to say, "that's it, we can't talk this way." But I am not sure John ever adequately took up one of the issues in just war that Ramsey always pressed. John tended to take on those people who said that just war and pacifism are really in the same ball game insofar as you presume that violence bears the burden of proof. What O'Donovan and Ramsey — and O'Donovan learned it from Ramsey — are saying is that nonviolence does not have priority, but that justice does. And coercion is intrinsic to the nature of justice.

CH: But the obvious comeback on behalf of Yoder is that that is just to start with a conception of justice, which then you read things like Jesus' life, death, and resurrection back into. And Yoder's point was that the only place you can start is with the life, death, and resurrection of Jesus, which you can *then* call justice. And he can then argue that such justice will be nonviolent and noncoercive because that's what Jesus' life, death, and resurrection were.

SH: To be sure, that is what he should say, but he did not spell it out as well or as often as I think was needed. I don't know where he really entered into those discussions. You might be able to see that in the reflections about punishment that he has beginning with his conversation with Girard [in the Internet collection]. Because the crucial issue that Ramsey and O'Donovan have always been concerned about is not distributive notions of justice, which underwrite some extraordinary violence that liberals try to justify, but just basic forms of redress. You've killed; redress. You've stolen; redress. The crucial issue is to conceive of how we, as Christians, can embody a form of justice as punishment that we owe the aggressor.

CH: Well, on that level I don't think he would have any problems talking in terms of justice, though it appears that Ramsey and O'Donovan have an account of justice that is somehow prior to Christology.

SH: That may be right. That is certainly the way to put the issue. Of course, the question is also whether liberal regimes can even provide a coherent account of justice. But that is the kind of point John seldom explores. Indeed, John was never as interested in or thought necessary the kind of critique of liberalism that I have been talking about developing. And I think I know the reason why. John thought that any kind of critique of liberalism required you to have an alternative. And he didn't.

CH: I think, however, that he would probably object to the strategy of rejecting liberalism *as such*. His response to you and MacIntyre might be that you cannot give the kind of totalizing rejection of any kind of politics without begging a lot of important questions. You have to look more at the specific practices themselves. So, for example, he was willing to take democratic forms of communication more seriously than other aspects of liberalism.

SH: But this raises another set of questions. John never, that I know of, in any public context came out and said how the interconnections between abortion, assisted suicide, and sexual promiscuity are all developments of liberal political theory and practice. And he should have been — and I use this term with commendation — as moralistic about those matters as he was about nonviolence. He needed to show that nonviolence is interconnected with those developments. We live in a society that aborts its children, and we live in a society that is sexually promiscuous, and we live in a society that has no way of talking about greed in any serious way. It is not accidental. They are all interconnected to the fact that we live in a society that does not have the slightest commitment to nonviolence. Now John did not seem to be deeply concerned about that.

CH: It seems like he always took his polemic against violence to be more wide-ranging, and thus a more direct route to providing an alternative to unjust social structures. So that if you can articulate the kind of politics and practices that a world of nonviolence requires, then you will have gone a long way to answering those other, more "issue oriented," questions. But if you start with the other questions like abortion and greed, then it is easy to take a big leap over the sort of substructure and other crucial practices that underlie them.

SH: Of course all this about interconnectedness having to do with the developments of liberal political and economic practices would need to be defended. But I suspect that John thought that would be too much of a legislation for the wider world. He might at most spell out such interconnections for the life of the church, which then would be a witness for the world.

CH: Just as he often limits his ethics to telling Christians what to do, as in his claim that Christian ethics is for Christians.

SH: Right, as in his lectures on marriage.

CH: Yes, and in refusing to pay certain taxes and those kinds of matters. I guess that is a more ad hoc way of making the type of rejection or criticism of liberalism that both you and MacIntyre want to make in a more a thoroughgoing manner.

SH: But I am not sure that is entirely satisfactory. I think John always worried about my attraction to theory even if it took the form of critique of theory. I don't know that "worried about" is the right locution. He just did not think he needed to be concerned with theory. He didn't need it for what he was doing, but I suspect that somebody needs it, which of course relates to you. How do you go on after Yoder?

CH: Well the hard part is to refrain from depicting and arguing in favor of his rejection of theory without turning that into another kind of theoretical discussion. And that is something with which I struggle. To the extent that anti-foundationalist arguments are often just another form of foundationalism, I suspect that to call Yoder's position "anti-theory" is not quite right either. What he is always going to refrain from is simply representing or defending the contrary position, because of his suspicion of dualisms or polarities. So if you would characterize his work as anti-theory, that might be giving the-

403

ory too much credit. But he is anti-theoretical to an extent, if you compare his work to, say, Paul Feyerabend's "methodological anarchism" in the philosophy of science. But I think the point he rightly makes against the anti-theorists, even if not directed explicitly at them, is that you have to be careful not to turn theory and anti-theory into another dualism through which you then articulate your position.

SH: I suppose his distrust of philosophy in general is the distrust of any separation of a saying from who said it. And the "who's saying" implicates not just this or that person, but the historical context his or her interests are serving and so on. I remember I once read a book by Robert Grant that claimed most of the early Christians were really a kind of rising bourgeoisie and therefore that they were not the urban poor who had nothing to lose. And I asked John what he thought of it, and he said, "Well then it's all the more remarkable that they preserved these documents which were clearly against their self-interest." He was never put off by any of that kind of contextualization.

CH: Right. I suppose that for Yoder the deep problem with most of the discussion of anti-theory would be that they are carried on in abstraction from the politics that embody it. So, for example, Feyerabend makes the point that his methodological anarchism should not be taken as a defense of any kind of political anarchism. But Yoder would never let a sort of "methodological" discussion of anti-theory stand on its own as others do. And it then turns out that the primary question is one of looking at the kind of politics in which you are embedded. And that is why I think MacIntyre becomes a lot more interesting to look at in comparison with Yoder, because he certainly shares a suspicion of theory, or at least of "strong" theory, and will always embed it in a particular kind of political community.

SH: But it takes a lot of theory for MacIntyre to re-embed in that way. Which brings us back to what we talked about early on, namely that Yoder is always writing under assignment.

CH: Right.

SH: I mean that is a politics that has everything to do with the substance of his position. He was lost without an assignment. He actually said that. There is a paper in this Internet collection that he delivered down in Bloomington, Indiana. And all they gave him as an assignment was to talk about the earthly and the celestial Jerusalem.

CH: It wasn't enough to go on?

SH: No. But he did it, because the Jews had asked him to do it. But there is a kind of postscript at the end that says "I don't think they liked it." It was the anti-defamation league, and it was certainly all right for them not to like it.

He had tried to respond in a situation where he had not received enough specification about what the agenda might be, and he ended up imposing his agenda.

CH: I suppose in that sense that it will always be a matter of contingency. I mean it is probably fine if some conversations don't get off the ground.

SH: I can almost hear him say, "Of course!" And that is why it may be hard for the significance of what John has done to be recaptured by others. Because how do you recapitulate those contexts? It is almost impossible to recapture them. So now you reread Yoder noncontextually, which puts the burden on you and the young Mennonites or others who care to carry it on.

CH: Obviously you think that Yoder is a tremendously significant figure on the contemporary theological scene. Which brings us back to the question of continuing Yoder's "project" that we talked about earlier. How would *you* think about going on after Yoder? Or what might it look like — I don't want to say "to do something more 'constructive,'" because that begs a lot of important questions — but to move on after Yoder without simply repeating everything that he did, as he did it? Or is that even an intelligible question?

SH: I think it is. And I think the first answer would be to give a "Yoderian" answer, which is, "I haven't got the slightest idea." But it is an intelligible question. I think what John would have said is that it is just going to depend upon historical contingency. As the mainstream churches continue to die — not that they are going to die entirely — I think Yoder will become increasingly intelligible. And as the dying of the mainstream churches forces conversation with the Jews about how to endure over centuries without being in power, that aspect of John's work will become more important. And as Christians rediscover the political significance of everyday acts of kindness, everyday acts of cooperation necessary to sustain, for example, a place of worship, I think that John will be a resource for us. But he certainly would not want to close off the next question, the form of which he would not anticipate.

CH: So I guess we are caught between knowing that it is important to ask what it looks like to do theology after Yoder, and knowing that if we try too hard to make that history come out right, we just repeat the same kind of Constantinianism that he was always trying to rescue us from.

SH: That is right. And to school yourself against trying to make past answers insure the future. John never did that. But it is hard to avoid. Can you think of anything we haven't covered that we would want to discuss?

CH: One thing that would be interesting to consider on these matters of history and political contextualization is the point you have made in other contexts about what you take to be Yoder's failure to take seriously somebody like Kovesi, and his account of moral notions and "thick" descriptions. And despite the fact that in a sense he makes those kinds of moves all the time, Yoder seems to have no interest in getting into those kinds of arguments that lead into accounts of the virtues and related matters. I suppose this is connected to the point you were making earlier about the interrelationship between abortion and other liberal social and political practices.

SH: I think he would look at anything he thought he needed. If you could convince him that he needed Kovesi, he would read him. We obviously never convinced him of that. I also think that that partly has to do with John's mental powers.

CH: You mean that he did not need to rely on the work of other people?

SH: He did not need to rely on other people in the way that I do. It had to do with his mental powers and with being a Mennonite. He was never tempted to philosophical mistakes, such as the attempt to provide explanations, in the way that many of the rest of us were tempted. He did not need to be schooled out of that. I was oftentimes stunned when I was reading some philosophical text, and I would say something like, "John, I just figured something out." And he would say "Of course." It would never occur to him that there was any problem.

CH: But at the same time, he was interested — at least he had been more recently — in taking someone like Jeffrey Stout seriously. So you would think that with respect to the kind of Wittgensteinian materialism that emphasizes social and cultural rootedness — in a way that sounds like a lot of his points, at least in the piece on H. Richard Niebuhr and even, as I was reading yesterday, already in *Christian Witness to the State* — there is room to clarify his position on those matters against a more "establishmentarian" use of those ideas in just the same way he did more recently with respect to Stout on relativism and pluralism and related matters.

SH: I am very tempted to play John Howard Yoder at this point. And he would say "Well yes, Chris, if it's helpful to you then you do that. And if that's a conversation you need to have, then you do it that way." It was just not a conversation that he necessarily needed to have.

CH: Well, fair enough. I guess that is the only way he really could respond.

SH: He never tried to develop a "position." I think John was genuinely exploratory. I do not think, for example, that he thought Christian nonviolence necessarily committed him to always avoiding certain kinds of coercion. I think he was open to the possibility of wondering, say, "Let me see, what would it mean for a big group of people to hold a violent person down under certain conditions?"

CH: Sure. But every time he did consider it, he came up with the same answer, namely that coercion would be problematic.

SH: It would be problematic. But then he says in *Christian Witness to the State*, "Well, if a person in one of our communities feels called to the police function of the state, let him bring it to the community and lay it before us." I don't think he thought that you could preclude the possibility that the answer might be, "under these conditions, OK."

CH: Right. If he did preclude it, then that would be the kind of "starting from scratch" or the kind of foundationalist or methodologist response that he always taught us to avoid.

SH: The question always put to me is "your church doesn't exist." Did John ever address that question that you know of?

CH: Sometimes you got the sense of his being afraid that his church was overdetermined in the Constantinian sense. Or at least that the Mennonite churches in Ohio and northern Indiana that he was more familiar with have too great a confidence in themselves that then becomes problematic for knowing what they are all about. And then he was always interested in raising questions regarding self-understanding and the nature of discipleship for the church itself. And pushing larger conversations that at least in certain cases they would not have thought of on their own.

SH: David Shank, who had worked with John in Europe, talked at the funeral about a meeting of the Concern group in Amsterdam, which I never knew about. Apparently John had written a paper on Bender, which I have never read, in which John went after Bender with a ferocity that he later thought was maybe not useful. I bet he never took it back, but he may have felt bad about it. But Shank said that John accused Bender of wanting to turn the Mennonites into a denomination. That was an extraordinarily illuminating remark for me, because John was right. Bender was about turning the Mennonites into a denomination. The "Anabaptist vision" was an attempt to provide "marks" for the purpose of defining a denomination. I had just assumed that the Mennonites were a denomination. But when Shank said that I suddenly realized that John didn't assume that. John thought you were a movement. How or whether you institutionalize a movement then becomes very important. So that meant John always knew his church could be the Franciscans for a while, and so on and so on. But then one of the things that worries me about John is not the old charism vs. institutionalism debate, because I think that is a false dichotomy. But the crucial question then is "How do you pass it on?" I think John defended a free church ecclesiology, though that may put the matter in too conventional a form. But he certainly thought, as Mennonites always thought, that leadership must be responsive to particular communities. And there is no reason that Catholics can't do that too. But then the question becomes how do you institutionalize inner communion between particular communions. He was not necessarily against bishops in that regard either.

CH: I suppose that just to the extent that you make carrying on your sole concern, or even one of the more significant concerns of the community, you lose the sense of what it means for the church to be the church in the way that he was always articulating it. If the church *is* the church, it will carry itself forward. Or rather God will ensure that it continues.

SH: But I think John would not say — not simply because it would be impolite — that the whole Catholic sacramental system correlative to the priesthood was unfaithful.

CH: I am not sure. But you mention Bender's "marks" of the church. It would be interesting to consider these in light of Yoder's five practices of the church that come up again and again, for example in *Body Politics*. I guess what needs to be examined is how to distinguish his articulation of those five practices that make up the body politics of the church from the normativity of certain marks which are used as a reference, with the primary purpose being self-continuation. To fail to do that would be to give in to just the kind of Constantinian temptation again of trying to make history come out right in a way that denies the "agency" of God.

SH: I guess he would say that. But surely there is the issue of faithfulness — just like you want to know how to produce future Chris Huebners. I mean that's not unfaithful, is it?

CH: No, it's not. What else am I going to say? But that cannot be the primary aim is, I guess, how he would always respond.

SH: That's true. It cannot be the primary aim. Because you will not produce future Chris Huebners if such a production is your primary aim. You can only produce Chris Huebners when you subject your life and their life to God's Kingdom. That, I think, is what John thought and lived. When all is said and done he thought that what mattered was God.

CH: Exactly.

SH: Let's end it on that.

Theology in the Mirror of the Martyred and Oppressed: Reflections on the Intersections of Yoder and Cone

J. Denny Weaver

I. Introduction

As a tribute to John H. Yoder, the "father" of modern Free Church and Christian pacifist thought, this essay will use a lens focused by Yoder's work to examine the writings of James H. Cone, the "father" of black theology. While Yoder's thought critiques what black theology considers white theology, scholars have not put black theology in conversation with theology influenced by Yoder. The following begins that conversation.

Like Yoder, Cone poses an alternative to the inherited theology of Christendom. Focusing on ecclesiology, Christology, and atonement, the discussion to follow will show that while black theology and a theology shaped by Yoder's assumptions have some potential points of divergence, they also share substantial common ground and should recognize each other as theological kinfolk with parallel and intersecting interests. Putting them in conversation will also show that black theology and a theology shaped by nonviolence are not special-interest enterprises of limited scope. Rather each represents a particular perspective from which to proclaim a message of universal significance.

II. Nonviolent Critique of Christendom Theology: A Synopsis

Yoder's multifaceted critique of the Constantinian ecclesiology of Christendom is well known. He also raised questions concerning Nicene-Chalcedonian, creedal theology, and Anselmian atonement theology. Under the influence of these impulses,[1] one of my efforts in recent years has been to show more specifically how the classic formulas reflect the perspective of the Constantinian and post-Constantinian church in which they became the accepted norm, and then to articulate formulations of Christology and atonement that specifically reflect the New Testament narrative of Jesus and thus constitute faithful alternatives[2] to the classic formulations of Christendom.

The classic christological formulations of Nicaea and Chalcedon — "one substance with the Father," "truly God and truly man" — are not wrong in themselves. In fact, if one assumes the philosophical system and the worldview in which they were articulated and if one asks the questions they answer, they are likely the best answers to the questions. However, when viewed from the New Testament perspective of Jesus who rejected the sword, these formulas have noticeable deficiencies as statements of core theology. These formulas identify ontological categories to which Jesus belongs, but they lack reference to the particularity of Jesus that appears in the New Testament's narrative. Identifying Jesus in terms of abstract categories of humanity and deity allows one to claim Jesus without acknowledging and being shaped by his life and teaching, in particular his rejection of the sword. Such designations allow one to confess or affirm Jesus Christ without being Christ-like or *Christ*ian. In other words, these formulas reflect a marginalization of ethics from christological understanding or ethics that express convictions that do not stem from the particularity of Jesus.

Similar observations and conclusions apply to the several versions of satisfaction atonement, which developed from its first full articulation in Anselm's *Cur Deus Homo?* (1098). Some version of satisfaction has been the prevailing atonement image since the medieval church. For Anselm, Christ as man offered

---

1. That is, while I understand my efforts to follow in the footsteps of John H. Yoder, I make no claim that he would have agreed with or endorsed all of the following.

2. "Alternative" is used here to mean one option among two. It does not imply a priority of Christendom's theology nor allow Christendom's theology to define the parameters of the discussion. Rather the intent is to be specific to the narrative of Christ, so that that specificity makes a difference in the way Christians — Christ-identified people — live in the world. See, for example, John H. Yoder, "A People in the World," in *The Royal Priesthood: Essays Ecclesiological and Ecumenical*, ed. Michael G. Cartwright (Grand Rapids: Eerdmans, 1994), 81 n. 19.

his death to the Father to satisfy the debt owed by humankind because of sin, while at the same time Christ as deity satisfied the debt since only God himself could satisfy the debt. Atonement thus answered a question about the relationship within the godhead, namely why Christ was both God and man.[3] This offer of compensation that turned away the wrath of a wrathful God became for Luther "a submission [of Christ] to the punishment required by a criminal offence of public character." As reshaped by Luther and other reformers after him, "Christ as God consigned his manhood to penal punishment" whereas in Anselm "Christ the man offered his godhead as compensation."[4] In either of these cases, Jesus' death satisfies a requirement emanating from God, and the sinner who accepts Jesus' death escapes the debt owed or the deserved penalty and is thus reconciled to God. In either version, atonement consists of an abstract, legal transaction between God and the sinner, which takes place beyond the realm of history, and without reference to any particularity of Jesus other than his sinless death. It results in the sinner's salvation, but does not change the ongoing life of the saved individual.

Abelard (1079-1142) proposed what has come to be called the moral influence theory, which most books on the history of doctrine consider an alternative to the satisfaction theory. In the moral theory, the death of Jesus responds to the distorted image sinners have of God. They perceive God more as a harsh judge than a loving Father. When the Father gives his Son to die, the death of Jesus then demonstrates God's supreme love for sinners, who consequently cease rebelling and turn toward God when God's love is perceived. Although more intrinsically inclined toward an ethical dimension than the satisfaction theory, the moral influence motif still focuses on the death of Jesus and it fails to make use of any particular aspect of the life or teaching of Jesus.

These atonement formulas portray salvation apart from the life of the saved person; ethics and the particularity of Jesus in the New Testament narrative are separated or marginalized from the heart of the theological equation. Parallel to the christological formulas, this conceptualization of atonement allows one to claim salvation in Christ while neglecting, abandoning, or rejecting Jesus' teaching and example on the sword. These formulas allow one to claim Christ without being Christ-like or *Christian*.

Extending Yoder's analysis of the Constantinian church, I have argued that the classic christological and atonement formulas and images reflect the outlook of that church, which came to identify the cause of the reign of God —

3. John Bossy, *Christianity in the West: 1400-1700* (Oxford: Oxford University Press, 1985), 5-6.
4. Bossy, *Christianity in the West*, 93-94.

the course of God's providence — with the progress of the social order. The emperor ordained Christianity as the official and required religion of the empire, but the teaching and life of Jesus did not fundamentally reshape the way emperors ruled. This empire acknowledged Christianity as the official and required religion, but continued to oppose the other — the enemy — with the sword just as it had when the so-called pagan religions constituted the empire's official faith. It is such an understanding of Christianity that can and does underlie the formulas of Nicaea, Chalcedon, and Anselm as core formulations of Christian faith. There was no specific agenda to develop a "pro-sword" theology. Statements of the formulas that became classic Christology are obviously found prior to the councils of Nicaea and Chalcedon. However, when Christians and the early church had evolved so as to accommodate the sword, the formulas that became official reflected the change.[5] They were compatible with an ethics derived from the exigency of the empire rather than the particularity of Jesus.

My reconstruction of atonement and Christology begins with a historicized restatement of Christus Victor atonement imagery that is anchored in both ends of the New Testament. The symbolism of Revelation makes the book a multifaceted statement of Christus Victor imagery. The historical antecedents of those symbols make clear that the confrontation of the reign of God and the reign of Satan has occurred in the historical arena, and involved Jesus Christ and his church (the earthly manifestation of the reign of God) and the Roman Empire (the earthly symbol or representative of all that is not under the rule of God). The book of Revelation thus depicts the cosmic and eschatological dimensions of the historical confrontation between Christ and his church and Roman Empire. At the other end of the New Testament, the Gospels portray the same confrontation between the representative of the rule of God,

---

5. In defense of the classic formulas, some writers have argued that the classic christological formulas received no substantial shaping by the coincidence of their development within the church of the so-called Constantinian shift described by John H. Yoder, and it has been claimed that finding the formula in a pre-Nicene writer invalidates the argument for the link between formulas and ecclesiology. However, these arguments neglect to consider that the Constantinian shift happened in evolutionary fashion, that its beginnings are apparent already in the second century, and that its culmination is indeed later than Constantine. Finding an early version of the classic formula thus actually testifies to the evolutionary nature of the shift, and arguing that the Nicene-Chalcedonian formulas became widely accepted only later than the time of their proclamation further underscores that they reflect the church identified with the empire rather than the New Testament narrative of Jesus. I would further suggest that denying a substantial link between the classic formulas and the church in which they developed runs counter to the assumptions of social history and of much recent historical work, which would place great stress on understanding any given formulation in terms of its context.

namely Jesus, and everything and everyone that is not under the rule of God. These reconstructions of what I call a historicized Christus Victor is then also a narrative Christology, that needs the particularity of Jesus. It is this particularity that shows how God's rule confronts evil and that reveals the nature of God's reign in history. To be reconciled to God — to be saved — means to become part of that story of the reign of God made visible by Jesus that stretches from creation to the eschaton.[6] Since Jesus makes present the rule of God, it is clear that God's rule confronts evil nonviolently.

My religious roots are in the minority pacifist Mennonite tradition, rather than in the so-called mainline Christian tradition. "Discipleship" — following Jesus — was one of the operative words as I was growing up. The stories and the vivid illustrations in *Martyrs Mirror*,[7] one of the most prominent literary identifying marks of the Anabaptist-Mennonite tradition, underscore the marginal social location. A woman tied to a ladder, with a man's back serving as a fulcrum for the ladder as she is pushed into the flame; a mangled body on the ground, hands bound behind its back, as a reluctant executioner takes repeated whacks to sever the head; a man about to be pushed backward into a wine barrel full of water and drowned by immersion; a man being sawed apart, as a perpetrator holds aloft a dripping arm severed above the elbow, while another perpetrator saws on a knee — such illustrations from *Martyrs Mirror* give reality to the fact that the tradition of my religious roots originated as the perceived enemy of the majority Christian voices in the sixteenth century, who became the fathers of the majority Protestant tradition in North America.

Standing in such a historically marginal location, even when the modern

6. For glimpses of this evolving reconstruction of non-Constantinian theology, see J. Denny Weaver, "Christology in Historical Perspective," in *Jesus Christ and the Mission of the Church: Contemporary Anabaptist Perspectives,* ed. Erland Waltner (Newton, KS: Faith and Life Press, 1990), 83-105; J. Denny Weaver, "Atonement for the Non-Constantinian Church," *Modern Theology* 6 (July 1990): 307-23; J. Denny Weaver, "Christus Victor, Ecclesiology, and Christology," *Mennonite Quarterly Review* 68 (July 1994): 277-90; J. Denny Weaver, "Narrative Theology in an Anabaptist-Mennonite Context," *Conrad Grebel Review* 12 (Spring 1994): 171-88; J. Denny Weaver, *Keeping Salvation Ethical: Mennonite and Amish Atonement Theology in the Late Nineteenth Century* (Scottdale, PA: Herald Press, 1997), ch. 2.

7. Thieleman J. Van Braght, *The Bloody Theater of Martyrs Mirror of the Defenseless Christians* (Scottdale, PA: Mennonite Publishing House, 1950). This book first appeared in Dutch in 1660. It was published as a reminder to acculturated Dutch Anabaptists not to forget their roots, and has been reprinted numerous times in several languages. An introduction to *Martyrs Mirror,* with a brief selection of stories and reproductions from the remaining 30 of the 104 original copper plates that supplied illustrations for the 1685 Dutch edition, is John S. Oyer and Robert S. Kreider, *Mirror of the Martyrs: Stories of Courage, Inspiringly Retold, of Sixteenth-Century Anabaptists Who Gave Their Lives for Their Faith* (Intercourse, PA: Good Books, 1990).

descendents no longer suffer the consequences depicted in *Martyrs Mirror* illustrations, allows one to construe the world differently than does the majority tradition. When those roots in the pacifist Mennonite tradition were cultivated by John H. Yoder's seminal analysis of Christendom ecclesiology and Jesus' rejection of the sword, I saw a biblical image of Jesus with different emphases than the mainstream theology, and I perceived some characteristics of classic Christology and atonement that had not been apparent to the majority of Western Christians. Specifically I was impressed by the absence of explicitly ethical content in the classic formulas. In response I sought to articulate alternative formulations that specifically reflected the nonviolence of the politics of Jesus.[8]

Several elements of this personal sketch are important for what follows. One is the way that standing in a supposedly marginal religious tradition enabled or perhaps forced me to see the Bible and classic theology in a light different from the majority. A second element is the specifically Christian character of this newly articulated theology; it develops out of or in conversation with the New Testament picture of Jesus. Another element is the particular critique of the classic formulas, namely that the abstract nature of the classic categories enabled a Christian theology that accommodated the sword. A fourth element is the linking of the classic formulas to the Constantinian and post-Constantinian church. And a fifth element is the specific reconstruction of atonement growing out of Christus Victor. These elements all return in other forms in the discussion to follow.

Under the stimulus of John H. Yoder's thought I had made these observations and developed the approach to atonement and Christology outlined above before I encountered the thought of James Cone in a systematic way. When it came, the encounter with Cone was very significant. It changed once again the way in which I envisioned a Christology and atonement that reflected the politics of Jesus.

III. James H. Cone and Black Theology

In *God of the Oppressed*,[9] James Cone describes his theological roots in the African-American experience, particularly in the soil of the Macedonia African Methodist Episcopal Church in Bearden, Arkansas. One dimension of the

8. This phrase is meant to refer to John Howard Yoder, *The Politics of Jesus: Vicit Agnus Noster*, 2nd ed. (Grand Rapids: Eerdmans, 1993).

9. James H. Cone, *God of the Oppressed*, rev. ed. (Maryknoll, NY: Orbis, 1997).

black experience was exclusion from Christianity as practiced by white folks. The white church in Bearden affirmed faith in Jesus Christ but excluded blacks socially as well as from Sunday morning worship. These white folks considered themselves good peopie since they did not engage in rapes or lynchings of African Americans, and many attended church regularly and considered themselves faithful servants of God. Yet they did everything in their power to define black reality. They taught that "God created black people to be white people's servants," which meant that blacks were "*expected* to enjoy plowing their fields, cleaning their houses, mowing their lawns, and working in their sawmills." Black people were also expected to attend segregated schools, sit in the balcony at the movies, drink from a "colored" water fountain, and much more. When blacks got out of their "place," that is, objected to their subservient status, it meant being beaten by the town cop and spending time in jail.[10]

In contrast to the exclusion and suppression experienced from the white church, the Macedonia A.M.E. Church filled Cone with feelings of and aspirations for freedom. "Through prayer, song, and sermon, God made frequent visits to the black community in Bearden." They received reassurance of God's concern for their well-being and safety. And as God's Spirit visited their worship, they "experienced a foretaste of their 'home in glory,'" a sample of the eschatological reality of the otherworldly home identified with heaven.[11] Quite obviously, the experiences of African Americans in the African-American community differed from the experiences of the Anglo Americans who lived in a predominantly white society. Cone's experience as a black theologian began in the black community and in the black church, so that for him black theology is shaped by the reality of what it means for the black church to live in a "society dominated by white people."[12]

The black church is determinative for black theology. The shared history and culture provide a sense of community. The black church provides a worship tradition, a music tradition, and a preaching tradition, all of which shape black theology and find expression in it both in form and in content. For obvious examples of the black church as a resource in Cone's theology, note the development of perspective between his *A Black Theology of Liberation* and the later *God of the Oppressed,* and the "testimony" of *My Soul Looks Back.* Cone's experience in the black church clearly locates him within a particular perspec-

10. Cone, *God of the Oppressed,* 2-3, emphasis Cone's. See also James H. Cone, *For My People: Black Theology and the Black Church* (Maryknoll, NY: Orbis Books, 1984), ch. 1.

11. Cone, *God of the Oppressed,* 1.

12. Cone, *God of the Oppressed,* 4.

tive from which he reads the Bible and does theology.[13] Naming that African-American perspective also identifies the white church as a particular perspective within which to read the Bible and do theology.

Given these differing particular perspectives, it should not come as a surprise that when black people and white people read the Bible, they perceived it differently. As explained by Cone, white theologians built logical and abstract systems and debated abstract issues like infant baptism, predestination versus free will, or the existence of God. White preaching and white theology defined Jesus as a "spiritual Savior," who delivered people "from sin and guilt," with salvation largely a "spiritual" matter and separated from the concrete realities of this world. This salvation was compatible with slavery, and continued the kind of faith which accommodates assumptions of white superiority. For white theologians, oppression of black people has not been an important theological issue. With a few notable exceptions, they have debated abstract issues such as the relationship of Jesus' humanity to his deity, but have failed to describe relationships between Jesus, salvation, and concrete problems such as oppression or hunger. This theology reflects a society which does not perceive color — or the social conditions of people of color — as an important point of departure for theology.[14] Stated another way, much of theology by white theologians has separated or marginalized theology from ethics.

In contrast to an abstract idea of God and a spiritual savior, when African Americans read the Bible from within their history, Cone said, they saw a God involved in history, a God who liberated the slaves from Egypt and raised Jesus from the dead. With the Exodus, "Yahweh is disclosed as the God of history, whose revelation is identical with his power to liberate the oppressed." The stories in the Bible reveal that "Yahweh is the God of justice who sides with the weak against the strong." Blacks believed that since God the liberator had delivered Israel from Egypt, then he would also deliver blacks from slavery and oppression. The Jesus who reflects the God of Abraham, Isaac, Jacob, and the Exodus, can be nothing other than liberator. When blacks read the Bible, they did not find a docile Jesus teaching a spiritual salvation. Rather they discovered Je-

13. James H. Cone, *A Black Theology of Liberation*, C. Eric Lincoln Series in Black Religion (Philadelphia: Lippincott, 1970); *My Soul Looks Back* (Maryknoll, NY: Orbis Books, 1986). For another example of the black church as a formative theological resource and shaper of vision, see Cone's description of how the black church shaped the vision of Martin Luther King, Jr., and was the foundation for his embrace of nonviolence as the way to resist evil. James H. Cone, *Martin and Malcolm and America: A Dream or a Nightmare* (Maryknoll, NY: Orbis Books, 1991), 121-31. See also Lewis V. Baldwin, *There Is a Balm in Gilead: The Cultural Roots of Martin Luther King, Jr.* (Minneapolis: Augsburg Fortress, 1991).

14. Cone, *God of the Oppressed*, 42-52.

sus the liberator, calling his people to freedom and working for their liberation. The salvation Jesus brought was not merely a spiritual transaction, it was actual liberation from the conditions of oppression in which African Americans lived. Thus Cone calls liberation the essence of black religion, both in its content (the Bible's stories of liberation) and its form (as the preacher leads the congregation into moments of actual liberation in the spirit). Christian theology as interpreted by black theology specifically envisions salvation in concrete social terms, and is always a word about liberation of the oppressed.[15]

In Cone's analysis, the white reading of the Bible rests comfortably on the christological formulations of Nicaea and Chalcedon and Anselm's satisfaction atonement. "What are we to make of a tradition," Cone asks, "that investigated the meaning of Christ's relation to God and the divine and human natures in his person, but failed to relate these christological issues to the liberation of the slave and the poor in the society?" Whether or not one believes that the supposedly universally applicable theology of the Nicene-Chalcedonian tradition lost the essence of the gospel, Cone says, it is clear that African Americans have a different history and a different theological orientation, both as Africans and as Christians.[16]

According to Cone's analysis, in themselves the generic categories of "humanity" and "deity" of classic Nicene-Chalcedonian theology lack an explicit ethical content. This absence clearly set the stage for the development of a theology which supported the "church's position as the favored religion of the Roman State," and which did not address the conditions of the poor and the oppressed.

> Few, if any, of the early Church Fathers grounded their christological arguments in the concrete history of Jesus of Nazareth. Consequently, little is said about the significance of his ministry to the poor as a definition of his person. The Nicene Fathers showed little interest in the christological significance of Jesus' deeds for the humiliated, because most of the discussion took place in the social context of the Church's position as the favored religion of the Roman State.[17]

In consequence, "Christology is removed from history, and salvation becomes only peripherally related to this world." Cone locates this Nicene Christology in the social and political context of the church at the time of the Arian controversy. The Nicene Fathers in the time of Emperor Constantine were not slaves.

15. Cone, *God of the Oppressed*, 57-76.
16. Cone, *God of the Oppressed*, 104-5.
17. Cone, *God of the Oppressed*, 107.

Thus "it did not occur to them that God's revelation in Jesus Christ is identical with the Spirit of his presence in the slave community in the struggle for the liberation of humanity. They viewed God in static terms and thus tended to overlook the political thrust of the gospel."[18] Stated another way, this theology clearly separated theology from ethics. It finds its modern continuation in the spiritualized salvation noted in previous paragraphs. Thus white theologians could claim Jesus as defined by Nicaea and Chalcedon, claiming — correctly — to stand in the orthodox theological tradition, but at the same time owning slaves or continuing to participate in the oppression of slavery.

Cone's treatment of atonement notes the absence of ethics in the classic formulas, namely Anselmian satisfaction or substitutionary atonement and the moral influence theory attributed to Abelard. Cone emphasizes that reconciliation is "primarily an act of God." As such, it embraces the entire world, changing sinful human beings into new creatures. Former slaves, alienated from God, now have a new relationship to God — they are free and reconciled to God. "Fellowship with God is now possible, because Christ through his death and resurrection has liberated us from the principalities and powers and the rules of this present world." The point Cone stressed is that reconciliation has an objective reality that is linked to "divine liberation." Reconciliation with God happens "in history." It is "not mystical communion with the divine" nor a "pietistic state of inwardness bestowed on the believer." Thus "God's reconciliation is a new relationship with *people* created by God's concrete involvement in the political affairs of the world, taking sides with the weak and the helpless." Israel is God's people because God "delivered them from the bondage of political slavery and brought them through the wilderness to the land of Canaan. . . . Liberation is what God does to effect reconciliation, and without the former the latter is impossible. . . . Reconciliation is that bestowal of freedom and life with God which takes place on the basis of God's liberating deeds." Thus for Cone, "the objective reality of liberation is a precondition for reconciliation," and it is clear that "God's salvation is intended for the poor and the helpless, and it is identical with liberation from oppression."[19]

The link between liberation and reconciliation, which is clearly found in the New Testament, Cone said, has been cut for most of the history of Christian thought. He identifies a twofold cause of the separation: "the influence of Greek thought, and the Church's political status after Constantine." Greek thought led to "rationalism." The latter cause, namely the condition of the post-Constantinian church, "produced a 'gospel' that was politically meaningless for

18. Cone, *God of the Oppressed*, 181.
19. Cone, *God of the Oppressed*, 209-10.

the oppressed. Reconciliation was defined on timeless 'rational' grounds and was thus separated from God's liberating deeds in history." Definitions of atonement developed "that favored the powerful and excluded the interests of the poor."

Cone applies the critique specifically to both Anselm and Abelard. Anselm's soteriology was built on the divine-human Jesus of Chalcedonian Christology, depicting salvation in terms of a spiritual transaction with God which spoke neither to the social conditions of African Americans in slavery nor to the oppressive character of racism in modern society. As Cone says, Anselm answered the question about the necessity of the God-man "from a rationalistic viewpoint that was meaningless for the oppressed." It was "a neat rational theory but useless as a leverage against political oppression. It dehistoricizes the work of Christ, separating it from God's liberating act in history." A similar critique applied to Abelard. For Cone, what Abelard called an act of love "de-emphasized the objective reality of divine revelation," at the same time that Abelard "apparently failed to grasp the radical quality of evil and oppression."[20]

Cone's reconstruction of an atonement motif anchored in the concrete reality of history builds on Christus Victor, the classical theory given renewed visibility by Gustav Aulén. Cone notes that Christus Victor focused upon the "objective reality of reconciliation as defined by God's victory over Satan and his powers." While Aulén's method was "nonpolitical," Cone says, the classical theory itself offers an opportunity for contemporary theology "to return to the biblical emphasis on God's victory over the powers of evil." The classical theory serves modern theology when it is "radicalized politically," and liberation and reconciliation can be "grounded in history and related to God's fight against the powers of enslavement." That is, the powers confronted and ultimately defeated by the resurrected Christ include not only the powers of evil mythically expressed in the figure of Satan but "earthly realities as well." Such powers confronted by Christ in the cross and resurrection include "the American system," symbolized by government officials who "oppress the poor, humiliate the weak, and make heroes out of rich capitalists"; "the Pentagon"; the system symbolized in "the police departments and prison officials, which shoots and kills defenseless blacks for being *black* and for demanding their right to exist."[21]

20. Cone, *God of the Oppressed*, 211-12.
21. Cone, *God of the Oppressed*, 212-13.

IV. Theology-in-General: A Critique

For so-called mainline Protestantism as well as Catholicism, the formulations of Nicaea and Chalcedon and of Anselmian and Abelardian atonement images have functioned like a theology-in-general. That is, they have served as the unquestioned givens in Christology and atonement, as the accepted mainstream formulas that every Christian theology should acknowledge. They have been posed as the theology that is assumed true without the need to prove itself. This theology, as the assumed theology-in-general for all Christians, would not have a qualifier such as "black" — precisely because it was assumed to be the general theology that applied to all Christians.

From Cone's perspective, it is quite evident that the presumed theology-in-general is not really theology in general.[22] Nicene-Chalcedonian Christology, accompanied by Anselmian (or Abelardian) atonement, were formulations developed by churchmen who belonged to the ruling class. They developed theological formulations of salvation which separated theology from ethics or

22. The idea that every theology reflects and emerges from a particular context, and the idea that theology may speak with universal intent from this particular perspective are currents running through much of the writing of James Cone. For example:

"Theology is not universal language; it is *interested* language and thus is always a reflection of the goals and aspirations of a particular people in a definite social setting. . . . Theologians can learn much from the sociologists of knowledge. The latter . . . demonstrates convincingly the function of a social a priori in all thinking and thus refutes decisively the naïve assumption of many theologians who claim that God-ideas are objective and universal. Theologians must face the relativity of their thought processes: their ideas about God are the reflections of social conditioning; their dreams and visions are derived from this world." (*God of the Oppressed*, 36, 41)

"What theologians regard as the central issues of their discipline, therefore, cannot be separated from their place in society, from what they think, believe, and are seeking to do in society. Hence, the social location and interests of theologians must be critically evaluated in order to understand why they do theology the way they do, and why they advocate certain views and not others. This may appear to some professional theologians as a minor and self-evident point; but the vast majority of white theologians are not always honest about it, for they seem to do theology as if its definition and meaning, its issues and problems, are self-evident and need no discussion with those who are not a part of their theological club." (*For My People*, 29)

"The equation of theological identity of the AME Church with white Methodism means that the former has lost its distinct historical identity. If a creative and distinct Christian theology does not arise out of the historical struggle for justice, then from where does it come? The failure to recognize this obvious theological point can only mean that the theological perspective of many black leaders is derived from the dominant culture that thinks of its own particular values as universal." (*My Soul Looks Back*, 90)

allowed ethics to have a foundation other than Jesus. These formulations thus accommodated the dominance of the ruling class and neglected consideration of the oppressed. For Cone, this theology continues in more recent times in the assumed mainstream theology that accepts the status quo of the white power structure, the theology of those who claimed to be Christian but who also rationalized white superiority. It is the theology which accommodated the violence of slavery and still continues with a spiritualized salvation that does not challenge racism and oppression. It is a particular, qualified theology — white theology or oppression-accommodating theology or the theology of the ruling class and the status quo. From the perspective of the alternative theology discussed in section three, it is violence-accommodating theology. Its assumed status as the general theology that made it the theology of the numerical majority of Western Christian adherents served to camouflage its qualifiers or its particularity as the theology of the dominant class and the status quo.

However, in spite of the supposed theology-in-general's link to the dominant class, Cone does not reject the traditional language outright. He believes that "Athanasius' assertion about the status of the *Logos* in the Godhead is important for the church's continued christological investigations." While it is clear, he said, that the "*homoousia* question is not a black question," the Nicene assertion that Jesus is one with the Father and Chalcedon's claim that Jesus is both human and divine are both "implied" in black theological language. But had Athanasius been a black slave in America, Cone continued, "I am sure he would have asked a different set of questions. He might have asked about the status of the Son in relation to slaveholders."[23] The sketch developed in section two has a similar relationship to Nicene-Chalcedonian theology. It is not that the time-honored and longstanding formulas need to be rejected. They do not. In any case, conversation with it is a virtually inevitable component of any effort to construct Christian theology. The point is, however, that the credibility or validity of the new, specific theologies is not dependent on the extent to which they borrow from or are anchored in the presumed theology-in-general.

V. Particular Theologies

Thus, while not unaware of the significance of the traditional language of a supposed theology-in-general, Cone and other black theologians have worked diligently since the mid sixties to develop a theology — actually several sometimes competing theologies — shaped by the black experience of slavery and

23. Cone, *God of the Oppressed*, 13.

oppression. And although this theology has a qualifier, namely "black," its truth and its focus is not limited to African Americans. While it gives meaning to African-American history, this specific theology also has a strong message to the white community, namely to recognize the particular and specific nature of the theology that has served the white agenda, and to make the necessary and required changes in both theology and practice. Similarly, the sketch from section two also proclaims a message with universal scope, namely to point out the extent to which classic theology has accommodated violence of the sword, and to suggest changes in both theology and practice.

A significant cultural distance stands between Cone's roots and my roots, which gave shape to the particular theology sketched in section two. My roots are in the radical reformation of sixteenth-century Europe and the Mennonite community in North America whose specifically European ethnic roots have endured to the present (although now fast disappearing in the progressive Mennonite denominations). Cone has roots in Africa and in the experiences of slavery, oppression, and racism that African Americans endured in North America.

But in the midst of the different cultural roots and any number of differences one could point out between our theological programs, some striking parallels emerge. They are particularly striking to me because the conclusions expressed in the sketch of section two were clearly in place before I began any kind of systematic encounter with black theology in general and James Cone in particular. One parallel is simply that each of us had roots in a tradition marginal to the supposed normative, mainstream European theological tradition. From these supposedly marginal traditions there emerged a critique of the "mainstream" theological tradition with significant parallels. Both are explicitly Christian and, as such, both make use of the particularity of the Jesus in the New Testament.[24] I had stressed Jesus' rejection of the sword; Cone described Jesus as liberator. And from that awareness of the particularity of Jesus, both critiqued the categories of the classic formulas. When they are viewed from stances in the "margins," it is clear that the classic formulations use abstract categories, which separate theology from ethics and enable adherents to claim Jesus on the one hand while acting out an ethics that is not based on the particularity of Jesus. Both supposedly marginal analyses linked the loss of the New

24. There is a common root for this christocentric emphasis in the parallel reconstructions made by Cone and myself. I reflect the influence of John H. Yoder who studied with Karl Barth, while James Cone wrote his doctoral dissertation on Karl Barth. Cone also makes clear that since the original publication of *God of the Oppressed*, a "radical development" has taken place in his christological reflections. He no longer sees Jesus as "God's *sole* revelation. Rather he is an important revelatory event among many" (Cone, *God of the Oppressed*, xiv).

422

Testament narrative and the emergence of the abstract categories of classic thought to the change in the church symbolized by Constantine. And in their reconstruction of an alternative to the classic theology, both of the new theologies stressed narrative, and both anchored their soteriology in a reformulation of the Christus Victor atonement motif that was the dominant motif in the pre-Constantinian church.

VI. Impact of Black Theology

It was the influence of John Yoder that brought into focus the theological perspective of section two, and enabled the recognition of parallels just described. However, engagement with James Cone's work goes beyond a simple recognition of parallels. Since black theology is rooted in the black church, to encounter black theology means to take the black church seriously as the Christian church. As Cone's books make abundantly clear, his theology is Christian truth shaped by the black church. As such, black theology is not merely special pleading for an oppressed minority but a challenge addressed to all Christians, whether or not they acknowledge it.

Encountering James Cone and black theology altered my perspective on the material sketched in section two and brought sharper focus to at least three areas. First, seeing the parallel between Cone's critique and my analysis of the classic formulas gave clarity to the fact that the classic formulas and the theology built on the classic formulas do not constitute a theology-in-general. These formulas are not a theological given whose truth is assumed a priori, while the burden of proof falls unilaterally only on alternatives. In fact, the classic formulas and the theology shaped by them is a theology that reflects and speaks out of a particular historical context. That context is the church of Christendom, which identified itself with the Western social order. In this essay the two issues of the sword and racism exhibit how the theology of Christendom has accommodated the prevailing structures and values of the social order.

This recognition of the particular roots of any theology shifts the location of the burden of proof. Assuming the existence of a theology-in-general places the burden of proof on the qualified or specific theologies. However, acknowledging that there is no theology-in-general, only specific theologies, lays the burden of proof equally on all theologies. Thus, for example, it is not only black theology that has to validate its understanding of atonement shaped by the experience of slavery or its claim that the gospel means liberation. The presumed theology-in-general has an equal obligation to justify an image of atonement that reflects medieval feudalism or Greek ontological categories or a Christology that enables an ethics that ignores the particularity of Jesus.

Second, the engagement with Cone makes abundantly clear that the question of violence is not limited to the issue of pacifism and refusal of military violence, the dominant question of historic Mennonite peace theology. My initial foray into theology envisioned a theology which would not accommodate "the sword." However, slavery and racism and the enactment of white superiority are also forms of violence. So are poverty, sexism, and patriarchy. The list could continue. Engagement with James Cone and black theology makes clear that a concern for nonviolence must encompass a wide range of justice issues.

Third, recognizing that violence includes systemic forms of violence such as racism (as well as sexism and patriarchy, poverty, and more) makes painfully clear why the principle of nonresistance that shaped the peace teaching of my earlier years is an inadequate peace stance. Nonresistance comes from Jesus' words about not resisting evil in Matthew 5:39. This concept defined the historic Mennonite peace position for much of this century. Nonresistance, as a refusal to resist an evil act with another evil act, has meaning when one faces active aggression. It means little, however, in the face of systemic violence such as racism or poverty. In fact, not resisting in that context can acquiesce to the status quo and thus accept or enforce its systemic violence. Engagement with the activist, liberationist orientation of black theology shows that in order not to acquiesce to systemic violence, one who claims nonviolence must be willing to espouse active nonviolent resistance. And it is appropriate for the church founded on Jesus Christ as the one who makes visible the reign of God in history to be the locus of such nonviolent social change. If the church does not confront injustice, then it is not being the church. To be faithful to the gospel, the nonviolent church must be willing to support the liberation theme of the gospel according to Cone. To be reconciled to God is to join the struggle for liberation of the oppressed. James Cone was quite correct when he said

> There can be no reconciliation with God unless the hungry are fed, the sick are healed, and justice is given to the poor. The justified person is at once the sanctified person, one who knows that his freedom is inseparable from the liberation of the weak and the helpless.[25]

25. Cone, *God of the Oppressed*, 214. In critique of Cone's assertion that liberation is the message of the gospel, womanist writers such as Delores Williams (*Sisters in the Wilderness: The Challenge of Womanist God-Talk* [Maryknoll, NY: Orbis Books, 1993], 20-21, 143-61) have noted that in the biblical story, the oppressed and abused do not always experience God's liberating power. The paradigmatic example is Hagar, who finds divine support in the wilderness

424

VII. Violence

Early black power advocates made a point of saying that blacks rejected white calls for nonviolence. To reject that call for nonviolence, however, is not necessarily to advocate violence. Cone wrote with great passion about the "white theologians and preachers who condemned black violence but said nothing about the structural violence that created it," and who quoted Jesus' sayings about loving enemies and turning the other cheek "but ignored their application to themselves."[26] From a black perspective, it was one more instance of white folks trying to define the reality of black folks. And in that context, denying white calls for nonviolence and asserting that blacks should liberate themselves "by any necessary means" was as much a statement that blacks will define their own reality as it was an assertion of violence. Further, Cone distinguished nonviolence from self-defense. Cone called self-defense a "human right," and asserted that white people should not tell black people what means they may use to confront racism. And he asserted that nonviolent "resistance" was "the only creative way that an African-American minority of ten percent could fight for freedom and at the same time avoid genocide" during the era of the Civil Rights Movement.[27] Finally, Cone argued that one cannot absolutize the nonviolence of Jesus, even if we could be completely sure of the biblical evidence. To make what Jesus did an infallible guide would mean being "enslaved to the past."[28]

At this point, I can indicate some points where my approach might diverge from that of Cone. With regard to his point about the biblical evidence for Jesus' nonviolence, I might ask whether Cone can be as certain as he is that the New Testament narrative placed Jesus on the side of the oppressed when he allows modern form criticism to challenge that same narrative at another point, namely on Jesus' rejection of violence.[29] I could also disagree with Cone on some other aspects of the question of violence. And in a related area, further

---

through Yahweh's angel (Gen. 16:7), and whose survival comes through following the command of the angel to return to the exploitative relationship with Sarai and Abram (Gen. 16:9). It is also necessary to say that from the perspective of John H. Yoder, liberation is not the normative dimension of the politics of Jesus. While suffering is never normative, on occasion one may be called on to endure suffering when human liberation action is not possible rather than resort to violence. If one assumes that liberation or liberating action is always possible because the essence of God's activity is liberation, the assumed causal link between God and liberation can become a source of appeal for violence to achieve liberation.

26. Cone, *My Soul Looks Back*, 44.

27. Cone, *For My People*, 45, 58; Cone, *Martin and Malcolm*, 303.

28. Cone, *God of the Oppressed*, 204.

29. Cone, *God of the Oppressed*, 204-5.

analysis might raise an ecclesiological question, namely whether Cone's understanding of the relationship of the church (as faith community) to oppressed social groups opens the door to another version of the Constantinian temptation that his theological analysis challenged so effectively.[30] At this point, however, the conversation need not fall into such debates. A very productive and mutually enriching discussion can develop around analysis of the forms of violence and oppression that we encounter at all levels in the world around us, and then about appropriate responses to resist violence and to achieve liberation.

I also believe that much could be learned about nonviolence from the African-American community, which in the course of the struggle to survive and overcome oppression has learned a great deal about how apparent weakness can confront strength and effect change. I note only one example. Early in 1984, five armed inmates escaped from a Tennessee prison near where Louise Degrafinried, a seventy-three-year-old African-American grandmother, lived. When her husband let the cat out early in the morning, one of the escapees pointed a shotgun at him and forced his way into the house. But once inside, the elderly woman simply told him: "Young man, I am a Christian lady. I don't believe in no violence. Put that gun down and you sit down. I don't allow no violence here." The man looked at her a moment, and then complied. She made breakfast for the young man, comforted him, and prayed with him. When the police arrived, she told the prisoner to let her do the talking. Then she went out to meet the police, who descended from their cars with guns drawn. "Y'all put those guns away," she said. "I don't allow no violence here. Put them away. This young man wants to go back." They complied. And she told her husband to escort the young man out to the car. The police applied handcuffs and led him away. This account is even more striking when compared to that of two other of the escapees. When they encountered a couple barbecuing in their back yard, the husband went into the house for a gun. When he returned, the escapees shot him and took his wife hostage, releasing her the next day.

William Willimon eventually recounted these stories in *Christian Century*.[31] However, when it happened, Mrs. Degrafinried had her proverbial fifteen minutes of fame. I saw her interviewed as a guest on the morning news show of one of the national TV networks. Because she had captured an armed

---

30. For John Yoder's discussion of such questions, see his "The Racial Revolution in Theological Perspective," in *For the Nations: Essays Public and Evangelical* (Grand Rapids: Eerdmans, 1997), 97-124.

31. William H. Willimon, "Bless You, Mrs. Degrafinried," *Christian Century* 101 (14 March 1984): 269-70. A similar story is told in Langston Hughes, "Thank You, M'am," in *The Best Short Stories by Negro Writers: An Anthology from 1899 to the Present*, ed. Langston Hughes (Boston: Little, Brown, 1967), 70-73.

prison escapee, the media called her a heroine — but she did not fit the mold they had prepared for her. I enjoyed the visible perplexity of the usually confident and unflappable TV host. Rather than using the almost universally assumed method of guns and violence to subdue violence, she had captured apparent strength with seeming weakness. The host tried several questions, groping for some understanding, but her action and her answers fit no category and no heroic models in his experience. The host had obviously never read John H. Yoder's *What Would You Do?,* in which he talked about "another way out" as one of the possible responses to a violent attack.[32] I am certain that the African-American tradition in North America could supply many such stories, and provide a clear testimony for the efficacy of nonviolence for North Americans with the faith to see it.

VIII. Theological Reconstruction

This essay suggests the need for theological reconstruction. Section two sketched a reconstruction specifically influenced by Jesus' rejection of the sword; James Cone's reconstruction of Christian theology was shaped by the African-American experience. Acknowledging that there really is no theology-in-general, as noted in section four, creates the freedom to contemplate new constructions of theology. As Christians we can look with new and fresh eyes at the story of Jesus. Without a perceived need to use the language of the presumed theology-in-general, we can begin to construct theology which genuinely reflects the liberating story of Jesus rather than the several ways that supposed theology-in-general has contributed to exploitation and oppression. One need not apologize nor feel marginalized or displaced from the mainstream for developing theology that does not pass through the juncture of supposed theology-in-general, whether that newly specific effort is black or feminist or womanist or peace church theology. At the same time, calling for the construction of specific theologies is not a relativistic acceptance of every theology. After all, as both Yoder and Cone remind us in different ways, it is from the particularity of Jesus that each specific theology ultimately gauges its truthfulness and to which they return to consider points of difference.

Stated more specifically for the peace churches, this analysis of theology-in-general and specific theologies has quite clear implications for the development of a theology that reflects peace. That peace and freedom depend on vio-

32. John H. Yoder, *What Would You Do?: A Serious Answer to a Standard Question* (Scottdale, PA: Herald Press, 1983), 27-28.

lence is the strongest unquestioned given in the United States national self-understanding. That is the principle learned from United States history, with 1776 as the foremost, foundational example. An anecdote can illustrate the pervasiveness of the assumed link between violence and freedom. My school once conducted "Junior Orals," a kind of leisurely oral interview of all third-year students. In the bicentennial year of 1976, I asked all eight students who faced my interview panel this question: "What would have happened if there had been no war in 1776?" All day, in virtually identical words, as though reading together from the same script, all but the last student answered, "I guess that we would still be oppressed by the British." The students' answer shows quite clearly how pervasive is the faith in violence of the United States. My short — and probably impatient answer — was, "Well, what about Canada?" Although the eighth student gave a different answer, it was really eight for eight who believed that "we" would still be oppressed by the British. (I learned later via the grapevine that the last student who gave a different answer had heard an earlier interviewee talk about "J. Denny's question" — and thus she knew how to feed me an answer that would make me happier.)

For peace church theology as for black theology, there should be a clear sense that theology which accommodates violence of any stripe differs from theology which does not. In different ways, the specific theologies consulted in this paper acknowledged that defining Jesus in the abstract categories of Chalcedon has allowed Christians to claim Jesus while simultaneously accommodating violence and exploitation condemned by the specific narrative of Jesus. If there truly is a "connection between thought and social existence," to use James Cone's words, then the connection between life and theology, and between Jesus' life and our Christian theology, cannot be the same for those who accommodate violence and those who do not. Cone writes, "The life of a black slave and white slaveholder were radically different. It follows that their thoughts about things divine would also be different, even though they might sometimes use the same words about God."[33] If rejection of violence is truly intrinsic to the gospel of Jesus Christ, then I can paraphrase Cone to say, "The life of a violence rejectionist and a violence accommodater are radically different. It follows that their thoughts about things divine would also be different, even though they might sometimes use the same words about God."

It should not surprise anyone that a theologian of the peace church and a theologian of the black church should want to construct a differently oriented theology from that theology which accommodates violence. To dispute such efforts because they seem to be an unnecessary departure from a received tradi-

33. Cone, *God of the Oppressed*, 9-10.

428

tion with presumed authority is to work out of the assumption that there is a theology-in-general. Such a challenge fails to recognize that there is a connection between thought and social location or social existence; it fails to recognize that theology developed within a social context that accommodates violence can and will differ from theology which refuses to accommodate violence. May God grant us the wisdom and the courage to abandon the idea of theology-in-general, to grasp the particularity of Jesus, and to listen to the specific theologies that can strengthen our resolve to develop specifically liberating and peaceful theology.

Theological Orthodoxy and Jewish Christianity:
A Personal Tribute to John Howard Yoder

A. James Reimer

I. A Tribute

I've lived intellectually with John Howard Yoder for at least thirty years. I've gone to bed with him, woken up with him in the morning, dragged him to class with me regularly, argued with him over dinner, travelled with him on trips, and accompanied him to concerts. I've taken him as arsenal into "enemy" territory (foundationalists and Constantinians in "Yugoslavia," Germany, and Toronto). It's been a virtual cohabitation, with all the resulting domestic squabbles and quarrels that come with the territory. In this posthumous Festschrift for Yoder, I pay my personal tribute to this man by sharing with readers the ups and downs of my life with an intellectual sphynx, whom I will always remember as that bearded figure on crutches.

Sometime in the late 1950s, I first heard Yoder speak in my home congregation — the Bergthaler Mennonite Church, Altona, Manitoba. I don't remember what he said but I was impressed. Since then I have heard him on numerous occasions, read virtually all of his books, and within the past two years spent hours in conversation with him. While I never had him as a classroom teacher (I didn't follow the usual Mennonite seminary route in my education career), he has been my teacher in every other sense and has permanently shaped my Mennonite self-understanding. I developed a "love-hate" relationship with his thinking, and found that within Mennonite circles I tended to be critical of him, seeking emancipation from his "claustrophobic" grip on me. In non-Mennonite circles I discovered him to be most useful for debate and Mennonite

430

apologetics. It's too early to tell what the nature of his future legacy for the Mennonite church and the larger Christian community will be. He leaves a weighty one — of that there is no doubt.

I recall, while studying at Union Theological Seminary, New York, in 1971-72, trying to come to terms with Yoder's reading of our Mennonite heritage in that bastion of Niebuhrianism. That year I wrote a paper on "Mennonite Nonresistance in the Light of Reinhold Niebuhr's Critique of Pacifism" for Robert Handy, who in a written evaluation of the paper responded: "I happen to know John Yoder and respect him very much; I was somewhat surprised to find him using the 'middle axiom' concept, usually related to the realist, responsible society, ecumenical ethics of Oldham and Bennett." Niebuhr had died a year earlier but his presence was palpable in teachers like Roger Shinn, with whom I took a course on "Conflict and Reconciliation," and to whom I gave a copy of Yoder's just-published *Nevertheless: The Varieties of Religious Pacifism*.[1] Shinn had been a major and company commander in Europe in World War II, been captured by the Germans, and held the Reinhold Niebuhr Professorship in Social Ethics at the seminary. One of the texts he assigned was Frantz Fanon's *The Wretched of the Earth*, which introduced me to the powerful psychological nature and need for violent revolt by oppressed peoples.[2] During that year I wrote to Yoder, at the time president of Goshen Biblical Seminary, telling him I was working on a paper on Niebuhr vs. Anabaptists/Mennonites and asked him to send me "any relevant material especially . . . [his] thought and work on the subject." He replied promptly, sending me some texts and advising me how to get other material, with the words: "If you come up with any conclusions which you think are convincing, I would be grateful for the privilege of seeing a carbon of your paper." I never sent him my paper. With Yoder one had the sense that he had already thought of all the arguments — to disagree with him was either not to have understood him or to have gone over to the other ("apostate") side.

A normal objection to Yoder's nonviolent alternatives to solving conflict was, "They don't work!" His characteristic reply: "They haven't really been tried." This begged the question, of course, of how hard one would have to try before establishing that nonviolent options did in fact not work. In the final analysis, the power of Yoder's prophetic word lay not in the effectiveness of various strategies but in their fidelity to what he took the Jesus message to be. He had an admirable assurance of the rightness of his reading of the biblical mate-

---

1. John H. Yoder, *Nevertheless: The Varieties of Religious Pacifism* (Scottdale, PA: Herald Press, 1971).
2. Frantz Fanon, *The Wretched of the Earth* (New York: Grove Press, Inc., 1963).

rials and history. He gave the impression of one who had never substantially changed his mind on anything. I have often wondered whether Yoder could have written once what his teacher Karl Barth wrote three times for the *The Christian Century* on "how I have changed my mind."[3] Despite his rejection of universal, rational truth claims as in classical foundationalism, his razor-sharp logic always seemed to me to presuppose some foundational rationality implicitly, if not explicitly. He had a way of logically disarming the "opponent" that seemed irrefutable. It was a style of argumentation that placed a premium on consistency, and he was usually able to show how the "opponent" was being inconsistent in one way or another. His book *When War Is Unjust: Being Honest in Just War Thinking*[4] is one of the most impressive examples of this way of arguing. It was an approach that left many a reader and listener on the defensive, at times highly effective, at other times greatly alienating. Whether alienating or convincing, it was a witness to the truth of Jesus Christ that could not be ignored in ecumenical circles. He left no doubt that a commitment to "Jesus as Lord" was the heart of his intellectual and ethical project.

My own occasional uneasiness with Yoder's "uncompromising" theological-social ethic may have been at least partly due to my being a Canadian Mennonite and the progeny of Dutch/Prussian/Russian Mennonites (my great-great-great-grandfather was the founder of the *Kleine Gemeinde* church in Russia in 1812, and my ancestry moved to Manitoba in 1874), rather than of American Swiss Mennonite. There are important historical differences between the two streams of Mennonites that have significant theological-ethical ramifications. Despite the many migrations within the Dutch/North German Mennonite stream through the centuries, there was a greater tendency among the "northerners" (in Europe and in Canada) toward "assimilationism" of various kinds, particularly among those who stayed behind during periods of mass migrations. This is most dramatically evident, of course, in the Dutch Mennonite story, but is present in subsequent periods of acculturation in Russia and in Canada. Many Swiss Mennonites assimilated into American culture but more often than not it appears they left the church in the process. It is not surprising, therefore, that a theological, ethical, and ecclesiological recovery of Anabaptist-Mennonite distinctives in this century, which would highlight the differences between the descendents of sixteenth-century Anabaptists and other mainline Christian groups, would emerge from within the American, Swiss Mennonite

3. Karl Barth, "How I Have Changed My Mind: 1928-38," "How I Have Changed My Mind: 1938-48," "How I Have Changed My Mind: 1948-58." Collected and reprinted in Karl Barth, *How I Changed My Mind* (Richmond: John Knox Press, 1966).

4. Yoder, *When War Is Unjust: Being Honest in Just War Thinking* (Minneapolis: Augsburg Publishing House, 1984).

tradition rather than my Canadian stream. This renewal movement emphasized the distinction between Christian community and civil society as it was
experienced within the largest imperial power in the world. Most Canadian
Mennonites, although they benefited greatly from the Swiss Mennonite renewal movement, never had the same passion about noncomformity, partly for
historical reasons, partly for contextual reasons. Canada was not a superpower
and the special multicultural fabric of Canadian society gave a different color
to the relationship of Mennonites to the wider culture in Canada. As I look
back on my own religious, ethnic upbringing in the village of Altona, Manitoba, I note that, true, we were an ethnic enclave, surrounded by the English,
German Lutherans, French Catholics, native Canadians who lived in nearby re-
serves, and a few Jewish families. The primary distinguishing factor, however,
was our language (a Low German, High German, Dutch, Russian amalgam)
and distinctive eating habits. As I think of it, our worship services and theology
were not that different from German Lutheranism, both in form and content.

I knew Mennonites were pacifists but the rest of my theology was a mix of
conservative and evangelical Protestantism, shaped just as much by my experience with Interschool Christian Fellowship and American-style revivalism as
Anabaptist theology. As a challenge to this frame of mind I encountered Bender
and Yoder in my years at Canadian Mennonite Bible College. They had a strong
impact but never totally convinced me. There were other theological and philosophical streams to my education that modified my reading of Bender and
Yoder. It always seemed to me that Yoder was "right" in a limited sphere of life
and knowledge, but that his thought could not provide a comprehensive foundation for many other areas of reality and human existence — music and the
arts, to give just one example. There were also theological and philosophical issues to be dealt with that were not exclusively or even primarily ethical in nature — e.g., existential meaning in the face of personal suffering and death, or
the numerous issues raised by science and cosmology. Questions of the
wherefrom and whereto of cosmic reality and human existence, I continue to
believe, are not to be defined in moral-ethical categories as exhaustively as
Yoder's work suggests. And even within ethics, the parameters of Yoder's ethics
are not large enough to include many of the frontiers of modern ethical dilemmas in the area of risk analysis, biomedical research, and cloning that my colleague Conrad Brunk is working on for Canadian government agencies.

My first serious intellectual engagement with Yoder's theological-ethical
thought was in the early 1970s, with issues arising out of his 1964 *The Christian
Witness to the State*. I still think this is one of Yoder's best books, in that it lays
out in simple and graphic terms his own neo-Schleitheimian view of the
church and state in contrast to the views held by other traditions. Reading

chapter seven of this book, "The Classic Options Graphically Portrayed," in which he contrasts his own proposal with the medieval Roman Catholic, Lutheran, Calvinist, Liberal, Niebuhrian, Jehovah's Witness, and Amish-Mennonite views, was an eye-opener for me.[5] There were two main "revelations" I received from this book: one, the notion of "middle axioms": that (1) rights, freedom, justice, equality language can be used by the church in its communication to larger society in a way that does not compromise its own christological norm of unconditional love *(agape)* and that (2) while Christians always fall short of the christological standard, "sin" can never be systematically factored in as a relevant variable for Christian ethics the way Reinhold Niebuhr did it.[6] The first I found theologically helpful; the second continues to give me difficulty. It has always seemed to me that Yoder did not allow adequately for the human fallibility of individual Christians as well as the Christian community. I grant that the fact of "sin" (the "is" of sin) ought not to be built into one's ethic in such a way that it anticipates and excuses sinful behavior (virtually functions as an "ought"). But I do believe that "sin" is a theologically relevant category for doing Christian ethics: particularly in how we understand the God-given role of religious, social, and political institutions in a post-lapsarian world. When his new, expanded edition of *Nevertheless: Varieties of Religious Pacifism* appeared in 1992, I was curious whether in his chapter on "The Pacifism of the Messianic Community" (which represents his own view) he might have modified his thinking on sin in the church from the time of the first edition in 1972. I discovered a slight modification. What he adds is a brief allusion to individuals even within the Messianic community being "moral cripples": "Being crippled," he says, "I am unashamed of needing a crutch; and most of us are moral cripples."[7] This is an admission of a sort, but it is "biological" metaphor which in my view does not adequately address the continuing "moral-volitional" nature of fallenness even amongst the "saints." What Yoder, and here he remains our prophetic guide, resisted is compromising the public witness of the church by too easily slipping into existential excuses. The above "moral cripple" reference is immediately followed by the assertion: "Yet the social meaning of a peace witness is far more fundamental than that. The existence of a human community dedicated in common to a new and publicly scandalous enemy-loving way of life is itself a new social datum. A heroic indi-

5. Yoder, *The Christian Witness to the State* (Newton, KS: Faith and Life Press, 1964), 60-73.
6. Yoder, *Christian Witness*, 66, 72.
7. Yoder, *Nevertheless: Varieties of Religious Pacifism*, rev. ed. (Scottdale, PA: Herald Press, 1992), 135-36. On one of my car trips with Yoder, in October 1996, I asked him about this addition in the "Messianic Community" chapter. He expressed amazement at how carefully I had read him but did not really shed further light on the issue.

vidual can crystallize a widespread awareness of need or widespread admiration. However, only a continuing community dedicated to a deviant value system can change the world."[8]

One of my first public critiques of Yoder's thought came in a 1983 article, "The Nature and Possibility of a Mennonite Theology." In that essay, I placed Harold S. Bender, Robert Friedmann, Yoder, and Gordon Kaufman on a theological continuum in which they share some common assumptions about the world, the church, and theology; assumptions which stand in tension with classical Christian thought. What they all have in common, I suggested, is a suspicion of metaphysical-ontological thought in favor of historical-ethical categories. This puts them, I proposed, within the modern Enlightenment project. If I had to rewrite that essay, I might well highlight more the differences among these four thinkers than I did at the time. I would also want to acknowledge to a greater degree the theological "orthodox" or "neo-orthodox" aspects particularly of Bender's and Yoder's thought. However, my basic thesis still holds.

I argue that Yoder, like Bender and Friedmann before him, and the more radical historicist Kaufman, prefers a "prophetic-eschatological" reading of the Judeo-Christian tradition to a "priestly-sacramental" one.[9] In his polemic against liberal and political realists (Niebuhrians), on the one side, and pietistic existentialists on the other, he interprets the gospel essentially in "social-political" terms — i.e., as a nonviolent way of living in this world which presupposes the lordship of Christ. Jesus' message is a political one, albeit a politics of a different kind (one premised on nonviolent relationships). This is the basic thesis of his best-known book, *The Politics of Jesus*.[10] My quarrel with Yoder in that article is not so much his strong emphasis on the gospel as a historical-political-ethical message, but the virtual eclipse of what I call the sacramental, mystical, cultic, metaphysical, and ontological dimensions. This historicist, anti-metaphysical orientation makes Yoder's thought less critical of our age than he intends it to be — it in fact buys into modern historicism. In that 1983 article I also cite passages from his *Preface to Theology*[11] in which he, like

8. Yoder, *Nevertheless*, 136.

9. A. James Reimer, "The Nature and Possibility of a Mennonite Theology," *The Conrad Grebel Review* 1 (Winter 1983), 40-46.

10. Yoder, *The Politics of Jesus* (Grand Rapids: Eerdmans, 1972).

11. Yoder, *Preface to Theology: Christology and Theological Method* (Goshen Biblical Seminary). Distributed by Cokesbury Bookstore, Old Building, Duke University, Durham, NC 27708. At his lecture on "The Politics of Jesus Revisited" (March 14, 1997), I asked him how existential questions of meaning figure in his social-political perspective on Jesus' theology. While not excluding the existential dimension, he made light of it by suggesting that I and Woody Allen had time to indulge in such preoccupations but most people in the world do not have that luxury.

Kaufman, identifies with the Hebraic view of things over against the Hellenistic and later Greco-Roman views in a way which positively links that Hebraic view with modern historicist thought. In his separating of "Athens" and "Jerusalem" he has much in common with Tertullian of the second century, but in his linking "Jerusalem" with modern historical thinking he parts company with classical thought. The ancient ecumenical creeds, particularly in their trinitarian affirmation, represented a coming together of "Athens" and "Jerusalem" that I believe to be important for Christian theology and ethics. I find this perspective lacking in Yoder's thought as well as in others of the so-called "non-foundationalist" school of theology.

My own theological project has been largely shaped by my growing interest in the classical imagination, especially as it developed in the encounter between Jewish-Christianity and Greco-Roman culture, and the trinitarian and christological debates of the Patristic period. It has come to be my firm conviction that in the context of this encounter and these debates, a distinctive Christian doctrine of God emerged that is *foundational* for later Christian thought and ethics. The critical issue for Christians, and in particular for Mennonites in the "Free Church" tradition, is the "Constantinian" problem. The question quite simply put is: Can the development of classical Christian orthodoxy be distinguished from the Constantinianization of the church (usually assumed to be the fall of the church by those in the believers church stream)? It is at this point that I have done some of my most serious engagement with three of Yoder's texts: *The Priestly Kingdom; Christian Attitudes to War, Peace, and Revolution;* and *Preface to Theology.*[12] For many years I have taught a course on "War and Peace in Christian Thought," both at Conrad Grebel College and at the Toronto School of Theology. Two staples of my textbook diet in this course have been the *The Priestly Kingdom* and *Christian Attitudes.* Where I have found Yoder one of the most stimulating debating partners in this course is around the question of "Constantinianism." Since most of my students come from what Yoder would call "Constantinian" traditions — Catholics, Orthodox, Lutherans, Anglicans, so-called "mainline" Protestants of various stripes — Yoder's Constantinian thesis usually gets me a lot of intellectual mileage. I have found, however, the "Constantinian shift" axiom in Yoder's thought ("axiom" in the sense that the specter of "Constantinianism" is an evil ghost that hovers behind virtually every sentence Yoder writes, a bit like Schleiermacher was the unseen enemy behind everything Karl Barth wrote) to be both right and troubling.

12. Yoder, *The Priestly Kingdom: Social Ethics as Gospel* (Notre Dame: University of Notre Dame Press, 1984); *Christian Attitudes to War, Peace, and Revolution: A Companion to Bainton* (Goshen Biblical Seminary, 1983); *Preface to Theology.*

In two of my published writings I spar with Yoder on this issue. One is "Trinitarian Orthodoxy, Constantinianism, and Theology from a Radical Protestant Perspective." In this essay I try to show how, despite Yoder's respect for what the early church theologians did with the Trinity at Nicea and with Christology at Chalcedon, he has a fundamental suspicion of this so-called postbiblical *Hellenistic* development and its link to imperial power. It is for Yoder a departure from biblical narrative into metaphysical-ontological thinking: "If we call into question the acceptance of *Hellenistic* thought forms which are foreign to the way the Bible thinks, which don't fit with the *Hebrew* mind, or with the *modern* mind either for that matter, then again we have to challenge whether it does us much good."[13] I try to establish that theological orthodoxy as it developed in the first five centuries stands in fundamental continuity with the Scriptures, that it went beyond the Scriptures in formulating a uniquely Christian doctrine of God. Furthermore, classical trinitarian orthodoxy need not be identified with sociopolitical Constantinianism but can function as a critique on all forms of "Constantinianism" and is, in fact, a necessary framework and grounding for Christian ethics.[14] In a subsequent essay, "Towards a Theocentric Christology: Christ for the World," I go further in defending a more pluralistic reading of the Constantinian period.[15] The Constantinian problem challenges all of us, emerging as the consequence of successful missionary activity as it tries to deal with the problems of relating Christian faith to culture. It was not a monolithic "apostate" phenomenon. There was a multiplicity of responses to this challenge in the third, fourth, and fifth centuries (Tertullian, Eusebius of Caesaria, Lactantius, Salvian, and Augustine, to name only a few). It is not helpful to demonize this whole era. Doing so not only does an injustice to the diversity of the period (is bad history) but robs us of creative possibilities for engaging culture and politics in our own era. That something went seriously wrong with the Eusebian type of "political theology" in the Constantinian court is undeniable. But to label the whole of the fourth century

---

13. Yoder, *Preface to Theology,* 140 (italics mine), as cited in Reimer, "Trinitarian Orthodoxy, Constantinianism, and Theology from a Radical Protestant Perspective," in *Faith to Creed: Ecumenical Perspectives on the Affirmation of the Apostolic Faith in the Fourth Century,* ed. S. Mark Heim (Grand Rapids: Eerdmans, 1992), 139. I am more and more of the view that we make too much of the difference between the Hebraic-biblical view and the Hellenistic-biblical-postbiblical view. They have much in common with each other, more than either has with modern and postmodern worldviews.

14. Reimer, "Trinitarian Orthodoxy," 148.

15. Reimer, "Towards a Theocentric Christology: Christ for the World," in *The Limits of Perfection: A Conversation with J. Lawrence Burkholder,* ed. Rodney J. Sawatsky and Scott Holland (Waterloo, ON: Institute of Anabaptist-Mennonite Studies, 1993), 95-109.

era as apostate, thereby closing the chapter on all other so-called "mainline" traditions — Orthodox, Catholic, Anglican, Protestant — simply won't do.[16] And this leads me to the central topic of this essay: What about "theological orthodoxy" as it developed in the first five centuries in its relation to early "Jewish Christianity" as Yoder understands it?

II. Messianic (Diaspora) Judaism

In March 1997, Conrad Grebel College and the Toronto Mennonite Theological Centre invited Yoder to give a series of lectures in Waterloo and Toronto. Two of the lectures dealt with a theme that seemed to be of increasing interest to Yoder toward the end of his life: diaspora Judaism and its relevance to Christianity, particularly the believers church tradition.[17] Yoder's reading of the biblical and early church's theological development is a serious challenge to my own defense of theological orthodoxy. I devote the following pages to an exposition of Yoder's view as expressed in these lectures, and in his book *For the Nations*, with my response.

Jews as Non-non-Christians

In the lecture, "Judaism as a non-non-Christian religion" (a typical Yoder turn of phrase), Yoder makes the case that early Christianity was a voluntary form of Judaism, a messianism within Judaism that led to the Christian movement. From the second century onward, mainstream Christianity has been anti-Jewish, at first in the form of the theory of supercession, and by the fourth century, outright antagonism and political ostracism, frequently manifesting itself in expulsions of Jews, forcing them into ghetto culture. The Jew came to be viewed not as honest "non-Christian," but as "infidel," responsible for "deicide." Responses by Christians in turn have varied from missionizing Jews, ignoring

---

16. Reimer, "Theocentric Christology," 103-7.

17. Yoder gave the following presentations: March 12, a lecture on "Tolstoy" to my "Modern Christian Thought" class; March 13, a public lecture on "The Politics of Jesus Revisited" at Emmanuel College, Toronto School of Theology; a conversation with Mennonite doctoral students and friends on "The Jewishness of the Free Church Vision" at the Toronto Mennonite Theological Centre; March 14, a faculty forum on "Judaism as a Non-non-Christian Religion," at Conrad Grebel College, to which faculty of the University of Waterloo Religious Studies Department were invited; and another public lecture on "The Politics of Jesus Revisited" in the Conrad Grebel College chapel.

them, giving them a permanent priority in the plan of God, to a post-holocaust biblical perspective in which any explicit Christian proclamation to the Jews is rejected. For Yoder, the gospel is a message of reconciliation between Jew and Gentile, two peoples becoming one, the rejection of all coercion in matters relating to faith and civil governance of churches, as the Radical Reformation understood it.

Jesus, himself a Jew, was not anti-Jewish; and in those areas where he differed from other Jews, he was "well within the parameters of tolerable diversity which the Judaism of the time could support, and which Judaism today can support. The same is true of the nonviolence or the nonresistance of Jesus."[18] Similarly, Paul was fully Jewish even in his mission to the Gentiles, a mission which he saw as related to the coming of the Messianic age. Only a Jew could have believed that the Messiah had come. Paul's mission in a Gentile city always began from the synagogue. Only in the second century did Gentile minority groups begin separating church from synagogue. For some eighty years after Pentecost, synagogues were open to Messianic believers. The churches were in effect "messianic synagogues" that did not split off communion with Jewry. Ethically (as in the rejection of violence) non-messianic Jews acted the way Christians did at the time. Only later did non-messianic Jews come to be known as Jews and messianic Jews as Christians. Jews became through this process an ethnic enclave which ultimately led to Zionism: The *"abandonment of missionary perspective on the part of Judaism is an adjustment not to the Gentile world but to Christianity,"* says Yoder.[19]

For this reason, the fall of the church, which has frequently been associated with Constantine in the fourth century, really begins already in the second century: "The 'apologists' like Justin Martyr, who reconceived the Christian message so as to make it 'credible' to non-Jewish culture, whether to philosophers or religious people or practical or powerful people, detached the message of Jesus from its Jewish matrix and thereby transposed it into an ahistorical moral monotheism with no particular peoplehood and no defenses against acculturation."[20] In this process the church lost the globalness of its message, the Torah (law) as grace, and diaspora life as suffering servant. It was these elements that the Radical Reformers set out to retrieve.

18. Yoder, "Judaism as a Non-non-Christian Religion" (Shalom Desktop Publishing, 1996), 118.

19. Yoder, "Judaism as a Non-non-Christian Religion," 121.

20. Yoder, "Judaism as a Non-non-Christian Religion," 119.

Christianity as a Jewish "Free Church" Movement

In the second of the lectures mentioned above, "The Jewishness of the Free Church Vision," Yoder makes the connection between messianic Judaism, or the early Jewish-Christian community, and the believers church tradition more specifically.[21] He calls the "free church" a "renewal movement within Jewry." For two centuries, Christianity and Judaism were overlapping circles, with a small segment of non-messianic Jews and some Gentiles outside. Origen and later Chrysostom, notes Yoder, still preached on Sunday to those who on Saturday had worshiped in the synagogue (13 n. 22). He repeats the claim that the "christianizing of Judaism" resulted in the abandonment by Jews of their missionary vision and the division of Jews into an ethnic Jewish minority and a Christian establishment. Modern Zionism is the culmination of this process, with the synagogue becoming in effect one more "church" in North America, and the State of Israel modeling itself on Western thinking — the state no longer a believing community, but as individualized as in the West.

The magisterial Reformers were critical of medieval unfaithfulness — wrong turns in the development of the papacy and in the doctrines of salvation and the sacraments:

> The deviation they deplored had not taken place before the sixth century, since these 'Reformers' did not intend to abandon the great creeds of the fourth and fifth centuries, or the achievements of Constantine, Theodosius, and Justinian in creating the Christian Empire. The 'radicals' of the Reformation on the other hand dated the 'fall' earlier, beginning at the latest with the persecution of dissenters at the order of Constantine, and perhaps much earlier at the death of the last apostle. *For our purposes the exact date does not matter, but we are learning something about how to define the substance of the loss. The first dimensions of the loss to become visible are precisely those traits of early Christianity tied to the Jewishness of the Gospel.* (3, emphasis added)

Yoder blames the "apologetes" (at least partially) for this loss of Jewishness, in their changing the faith into an "ahistorical moral monotheism" in order to make it more palatable to Gentile culture.

21. Yoder, "The Jewishness of the Free Church Vision," lecture given at Toronto Mennonite Theological Centre, Toronto School of Theology, on March 13, 1997. First presented as the third lecture in the Bethel/Earlham series, Richmond, April 30, 1985. Minimally revised as of May 1996. Some of my comments are taken from notes I made for myself on Yoder's verbal comments that went beyond the written text itself. Subsequent citations of this lecture will be inserted into the body of the text.

Exilic Jewish identity defined by the synagogue made it flexible and able "to live without central administration." When this diaspora notion was lost with the separation of the "church culture" from the "synagogue culture," Western Christianity looked to Rome for centralized identity. The Radical Reformation was a return to a "synagogue-free-church" model.

> Thus in prinicple, the issues raised by the radical reformers (Hus and Cheltschitksy, Sattler and Marpeck) were transpositions of the old Jewish identity agenda, now restated as an intra-Christian critique. *The anticlericalism, the anticentralism, the warning against antinomianism, the rejection of national-governmental control of the churches, which had marked earlier Christianity, were rooted jewishly just as truly as was the nonviolence of the free churches.* (4, emphasis added)

What Judaism and Radical Reformation have in common include seeing God as continuing agent of critique and historical change more than sanctification of a static present, unembarrassment about their particularity and minority status, derivation of group identity from a book more than clergy and ritual, and a distinctive and serious moral commitment (although sixteenth-century free churches did not transcend the anti-Semitism of their age, and contrasted too easily between the Old and New Testaments).[22] The Jewish-Christian schism was not part of Jesus' or Paul's vision for the coming Rule of God, and Yoder infers in the latter part of his lecture that reconciliation between Judaism and Christianity is the way to religious renewal: "The recovery of our sense of the Jewishness of original Christianity and especially of free church renewal should give a second wind to the forces of renewal. Whether the impact be commonality or dialogue, confession or guilt or joy in reconciliation and common witness, to restore the recognition of the sister communion might just call Christians back to their roots as the free church minorities in the West have been failing to do" (8-9).

Yoder is unapologetic in his particular reading of the Jewish story — making "Heschel [more representative] than Ben Gurion, Arnold Wolf than Meir Kahane, Anne Frank than Golda Meir" (12). It is appropriate particularly within the Jewish story to identify this particular stream of inner-Jewish

---

22. Yoder, "The Jewishness of the Free Church Vision," 4-6. Yoder goes on in his text to identify more specifically some sociological similarities between the historic Mennonite and Jewish experience which are interesting but not relevant for my purposes here. One particularly interesting thing he does say is that "Mennonites have seldom been thoroughly or riskily pacifist. Certainly their peace position does not enter as deeply into their spirituality and self-understanding as is the case for Friends" (6).

thought, he says, because "there is not, as for most other ethnic communities and most 'nations,' any one central authority within the community to define from what perspective it must be read" (10). It is this latter point, namely Yoder's reading of the Jewish story, that we consider in the final part of this section of the present essay, and for that we look particularly at one essay in Yoder's most recent book, *For the Nations*, "See How They Go with Their Face to the Sun."[23]

Diaspora: Jewish and Christian Paradigm

Yoder consciously entitles his most recent book *For the Nations* to correct what some have incorrectly labelled his "sectarian" or "against the nations" stance.[24] This, Yoder claims, is not a change of conviction but was always his view; namely, "that the very shape of the people of God in the world is a public witness, or is 'good news,' for the world, rather than first of all rejection or withdrawal."[25] This witness to the nations is best understood, according to Yoder, in the words of JHWH through Jeremiah: "Seek the peace of the city where I have sent you" — that is, witnessing as a diaspora living amidst foreign peoples.[26] For Yoder, the time of Jeremiah and Constantine represent two ancient turning points more significant than the Reformation or the Enlightenment for clarifying the Christian faith. The one (Jeremiah) symbolizes the birth of a new concept of "believing community" and the other (Constantine) the apostasy of that diaspora vision.

In Chapter 3, "See How They Go with Their Face to the Sun," Yoder develops most fully this Jeremian turning point. Citing God's command to the Jewish people in Babylon, "Seek the welfare of the city where I have sent you into exile, and pray to the Lord on its behalf, for in its welfare you will find your welfare" (Jer. 29:7 RSV), Yoder defends the view of Jewish writer Stefan Zweig that the scattering of the Jews was the beginning of a new divine mis-

---

23. Yoder, "See How They Go with Their Face to the Sun," in *For the Nations: Essays Public and Evangelical* (Grand Rapids: Eerdmans, 1997). While the other two Jewish essays we have considered above stem from an earlier period in Yoder's thinking, this one was first presented on September 23, 1995, at Loyola Marymount University, Los Angeles.

24. The title *For the Nations* appears to be a conscious contrast to Stanley Hauerwas's book, *Against the Nations: War and Survival in a Liberal Society* (Minneapolis: Winston Press, 1985).

25. Yoder, *For the Nations*, 6.

26. Yoder, *For the Nations*, 3.

sion. It represented God's negative judgement on monarchy and the start of a "fresh prophetic mandate, of a new phase of the Mosaic Project."[27] Diaspora (the "Joseph paradigm") was not a brief detour after 586, but a model for normal Jewish existence for the next millennium and a half. Babylon, not Jerusalem, becomes the cultural center of world Jewry until the Middle Ages. What has come to be known as "canonization," the process of selecting a manageable body of defining literature, is what helps to give the scattered community its identity (55ff.). Other markers of identity are the Torah, rabbinate, circumcision, and the synagogue. The transition from a temple culture to a synagogue culture was, for Yoder, "the most fundamental sociological innovation in the history of religions . . ." (71) — a shift from centralized authority to dispersed communities of believers. It is this synagogue culture which continues in earliest Christianity:

> Messianic Judaism in the first century, which we now call 'Christianity,' went from here with no basic change as far as social structure and worldview are concerned. 'Christians' (most accurately described for the first generations as 'messianic Jews') modified the synagogue pattern only slightly by their openness to non-Jews, and by their love feasts; the lay, book-centered, locally managed format of the synagogue remained. When the synagogue polity came later to be overshadowed among Christians by sacerdotalism and episcopacy, that represented a fall back into the pre-Jeremian patterns of Hellenistic paganism (71 n. 48).

God's judgment on Constantinian and neo-Constantinian Christianity is, thus, the same as it was on the pre-Jeremian imperialistic-monarchical Jewish culture. The intent of God in the prelapsarian world was heterogeneous "nonfoundational" diversity. The sin of "Babel" is the attempt by the human community to absolutize and homogenize itself, and the punishment of dispersion of tongues is really a blessing — the demonstration of God's initial primeval ordination of multiplicity and diversity. The people of Babel, says Yoder, were the first foundationalists (62-63). The later scattering of the Jews into dispersion was therefore a continuation of God's initial "nonfoundationalist" purpose. What would never have occurred to the "polyglot Jews" at home in Babylon

> was to try to bridge the distance between their language world and that of their hosts by a foundationalist mental or linguistic move, trying to rise to a

27. Yoder, "See How They Go with Their Face to the Sun," 53. Subsequent citations of this essay will be given parenthetically in the text.

higher level or dig to a deeper one, so that the difference could be engulfed in some *tertium quid,* which would convince the Babylonians of moral monotheism without making them Jews, and to which the Jews would yield without sacrificing their local color. They did not look for or seek common ground. (73)

III. Another Reading of the Jewish Story

Yoder admits that his is not the only reading of the Jewish story, even within Judaism. In response, I draw here on an alternate reading by my colleague John W. Miller, a specialist in Hebraic literature who has published extensively in the area.[28] Miller is a contemporary of Yoder's, and, with Yoder and five other American Mennonites, spent time studying and doing voluntary service in postwar Europe in the 1950s. They published a small periodical called *Concern,* and were known as the "Concern Group."[29] Miller's theological stance on the role of the state in society, and the relation of the church to the state, is markedly different from that of Yoder, as is his reading of Israel's story.

Canonization and the Transition to Synagogue Culture

Miller agrees with Yoder that it was probably during the exilic period that Jews began the "canonization" process — the collection of a body of authoritative literature from their history for purposes of identity. Where he disagrees with Yoder is on the role of the Jewish establishment in Jerusalem in compilation and dissemination of the Jewish scriptures. In a letter to Herbert Klassen, Miller finds Yoder's "pejorative brushing aside of the whole second temple period as

28. A few of his publications are *Jesus at Thirty: A Psychological and Historical Portrait* (Minneapolis: Fortress Press, 1997); *The Origins of the Bible: Rethinking Canon History* (New York: Paulist Press, 1994); *Reading Israel's Story: A Canon-history Approach to the Narrative and Message of the Christian Bible,* Background Essays for Teachers in the Blenheim Bible Study Program (Kitchener, ON).

29. For a recent history and dialogue with members of this group, see *The Conrad Grebel Review* 8 (Spring 1990). I was involved in the special event to which all seven original members of the "Concern Group" were invited for conversation and reflection. Interestingly, Yoder decided not to attend. All those in attendance agreed that Yoder had probably been the most influential figure in articulating the concerns of the group. John Miller has openly acknowledged his "change of mind" on a number of issues since that time, including his critical distancing of himself from the position maintained by Yoder at a number of significant points.

portrayed in Ezra and Nehemiah" to be "mind-boggling."[30] While, according to Miller, we know little about exactly how and when synagogue culture began, "John's notion that the canon and synagogue arose without there being any centralist organization is ahistorical and fantastical." Miller believes that some kind of center at Jerusalem did continue to play an important role in the religious life of the Jewish community after the exilic period, thereby in effect relativizing the normative nature of the diaspora as Yoder sees it.

Jews and the Nations

Miller's much more fundamental disagreement relates to his view of the role of the Jews in witnessing to the nations. Miller takes particular issue with Yoder's claim in "Face to the Sun" that it would never have occurred to Jews in Babylon to attempt to mediate in a foundationalist way between their world and that of their hosts, to seek common ground, that "Jews knew that there was no wider world than the one their Lord had made and their prophets knew the most about" (73). According to Miller, Yoder is simply wrong on this point: "The Jews (through their scriptures) did seek to locate their story within the wider world story, and in Genesis 1–11 ascribe a very clear place to the nations (and to the role of the nations) in God's postdiluvian will for the world. It is of this that Paul speaks in Romans 13, a text which John dislikes and marginalizes (as he dislikes and marginalizes Genesis 9)." Miller agrees with Yoder that God calls Israel and the church to be a blessing to the nations of the world as a covenanted, believing people rather than a state. Where Yoder falls short is in not seeing this blessing in the context of the whole of creation and history. For Miller, the God of Creation, the God who "sovereignly guides all nations, charging them with responsibility for protecting human life," is the same God as revealed in Christ. Yoder "advocates a universal pacifism that does not feel responsible for making history come out right. These ideas and ideals have become normative for many modern Mennonites. This is not, however, what the Bible teaches, nor what Mennonites have believed historically." According to Miller, the diaspora and the Jerusalem scholarly community told the Jewish story (law and prophets) in the setting of the Creation story at one end and the Wisdom writings at the other. The Genesis story (creation [Genesis 1 and 2], fall [Genesis 3], building of cities and involvement in skills and trades [Genesis 4ff.], increasing fragmentation, chaos, and account of various nations [Genesis 9–11]) is an attempt to understand the Jewish experience theologically in the larger context of the

30. John W. Miller, Letter to Herbert C. Klassen, 3 March 1998.

nations. God is seen as a God of all nations, not just of the Jewish nation; Adam and Eve were not only the ancestral parents of the Jews but of all humans; and the promise to Abraham that his descendents would become a great nation [with a special covenant] is for the blessing of all nations. Messianic expectations have to do with how this will happen. It is true, as Yoder says, that an important paradigm shift took place in the second temple period, when the synagogue throughout the diaspora becomes important (a type of "believers church" is born), but the synagogue does not displace the temple, and there is always a hope for restoration of the temple — Babylon is never considered to be the exclusively normative symbol.[31]

IV. What About Classical Theological Orthodoxy?

What are the implications of these two different readings of the Jewish and early Jewish-Christian tradition for "theological orthodoxy" as defined by the classical period of Christianity? Yoder is rather selective in his choice of a slice of Jewish experience (diaspora synagogue culture, the "Joseph" paradigm), and making that normative not only for the whole of Judaism but also for the whole of Christianity. Is this a comprehensive enough picture of the Jewish story, and the Christian narrative as it has developed over the millennia? Miller recognizes the importance of the "scattered-exilic" model but places it within a broader, global, national and international vision. Yoder, it is true, sees the role of exilic Jewish culture as seeking the blessing of the host nations, although he never, in my view, satisfactorily shows how that blessing is actualized in concrete situations. Yoder was a non- if not anti-foundationalist long before the present postmodern disenchantment with foundationalism. He idealizes decentralized diversity, and is suspicious (he would call this being realistic) of all institutional centers of power and authority. Yoder reads this anti-foundationalism back into the prelapsarian intent of God in Creation. One wonders where the ontological and theological grounds for ultimate unity and reconciliation lie in Yoder's theological ethic. Miller, on the other hand, gives more weight to a type of what I would call theological foundationalism (although he doesn't use the term) existing at the very heart of Creation. God's intent for the human race, from the beginning, is not fragmentation, diversity, diaspora and exile, but unity. The theological foundation for this in both Jewish and Christian thought is the one God of the Jews, Christians, and all nations. Ultimately, the difference between Yoder's and Miller's vision is the relation between "exilic" culture (both for Jews and Christians) and larger global,

31. John W. Miller, conversation with author, 26 March 1998.

world culture. For Miller, the same God is at work in both, using different means to achieve God's divine purpose with the nations. For Yoder, because exilic culture is ethically and politically normative, it is not clear whether and how God is at work outside that alien community. If exile and diaspora are the norm, how is a unified vision ever possible?

More specifically, does the logic of Yoder's position not finally end up being incompatible with the trinitarian councils of Nicea and Constantinople, and the christological definition of Chalcedon? He does say in *The Politics of Jesus:*

> To deal with the many ways, ebionitic and docetic, of avoiding the normativeness of Jesus, would call for a different kind of study from the present one. Such questions are of a dogmatic, not exegetical character, and would need to be encountered on that level. . . . If we were to carry on that other, traditionally doctrinal kind of debate, we would seek simply to demonstrate that the view of Jesus being proposed here is more radically Nicene and Chalcedonian than other views. We do not here advocate an unheard-of modern understanding of Jesus; we ask rather that the implications of what the church has always said about Jesus as Word of the Father, as true God and true Man, be taken more seriously, as relevant to our social problems, than ever before.[32]

In this passage Yoder implies that the early church was right in rejecting the "heretical" reductions of Jesus either on the human side (ebionitic) or the divine side (docetic), and that his own challenge to take Jesus' normativity for ethics seriously presupposes classical orthodoxy, and is in fact strengthened thereby. After carefully examining his writings on Jewish Christianity, however, I am not so sure. They seem to confirm my earlier suspicions. In these lectures he seems more radically restitutionist than ever. He suggests that the fall occurred not in the fourth century but in the second century with the apologists and the consequent loss of the early Jewish-Christian paradigm. The fall now occurs at the point where the Hebraic-Christian and Greco-Roman worldviews encounter each other in a creative synthesis.

What does one do with the success of the missionary movement to the Gentiles (the Greeks and the Romans)? Is this shift from synagogue to church, from Hebraic monotheism to Christian trinitarianism (the rejection of Greco-Roman dualism or polytheism), truly to be seen as the fall of the Christian vision? Yoder rightly identifies and denounces the tragic nature of the historic split between Judaism and Christianity, and the consequent anti-Semitism. But in emphasizing the continuity between the early Christian community and the messi-

32. Yoder, *The Politics of Jesus*, 105.

anic diaspora community of the Jews, does he not underestimate the discontinuity that sets in immediately with the emerging success of the missionary movement as we find illustrated already in Acts 15 (the giving up of the critical ceremonial marks of Judaism even in the diaspora)? Is one not finally faced with some radically new developments in the Christian understanding of God that include the move toward Nicea and Chalcedon, incorporating both Judaism and Hellenism in a new third way?[33] It seems to me that theologically there are complex issues present already in the New Testament writings that Yoder's thesis does not adequately address. To claim that in the first five hundred years following the death of Christ a new "religion" with a distinctive "doctrine of God" evolved surely does not necessarily entail supercessionism and anti-Semitism.

The theological inadequacy of Yoder's thesis also applies to his rather univocal identification of the Reformation Radicals with the free church movement of messianic Judaism and the early Jewish-Christian community. This strikes me as an ahistorical approach to the rather heterogeneous social and intellectual origins of the Anabaptists in late medieval society (not to mention historic Judaism and early Christianity). He is right in noting some sociological and ethical parallels between the Radicals of the Reformation and early Jewish Christians (really messianic Jews, according to Yoder), and between later Mennonites and Jews. But are there not some profound theological differences that Yoder avoids? Aside from the *heterogeneity* of the Anabaptist movement, are there not significant theological-anthropological differences that stem from the rise of the modern world, which provide the context of the rise of the modern Free Church tradition? Voluntaristic-nominalistic assumptions shape the Radicals' view of individual freedom and responsibility in a way quite foreign to the classical period.[34] Noble and prophetically important as Yoder's political-ethical agenda is, in the end it shortchanges critical theological insights central to the Christian tradition. More than that, the central theological affirmations found in classical orthodoxy are needed to undergird the very moral and ethical claims to which Yoder witnesses so singularly.

33. It is interesting that Wolfhart Pannenberg, who laments the avoidable divisions that occurred in Christian history as a result of Chalcedon in 451, the East-West split in the eleventh century, and the Reformation, says, "Some divisions are certainly necessary, i.e., in cases of apostasy from faith in Jesus Christ. Primitive Christianity had to separate itself from Judaizing and Gnostic errors, and the early church from Arianism." *Systematic Theology: Volume 3* (Grand Rapids: Eerdmans, 1998), 411.

34. For a critical look at the influence of nominalism on Balthasar Hubmaier's anthropology see my chapter, "The Adequacy of a Voluntary Theology for a Voluntaristic Age," in *The Believers Church: A Voluntary Church*, ed. William H. Brackney, Studies in the Believers Church Tradition (Kitchener and Scottdale: Pandora Press and Herald Press, 1998), 135-48.

Deuteronomic or Constantinian: What Is the Most Basic Problem for Christian Social Ethics?

Gerald W. Schlabach

> For the LORD your God is bringing you into a good land, . . . a land where you may eat bread without scarcity, where you will lack nothing. . . . You shall eat your fill and bless the LORD your God for the good land that he has given you. Take care that you do not forget the Lord your God. . . . When you have eaten your fill and have built fine houses and live in them, and when your herds and flocks are multiplied, and all that you have is multiplied, then do not exalt yourself, forgetting the LORD your God, who brought you out of the land of Egypt, out of the house of slavery, who led you through the great and terrible wilderness, . . . to humble you and in the end to do you good. Do not say to yourself, "My power and the might of my own hand have gotten me this wealth."
>
> Deuteronomy 8

If one knows John Howard Yoder mainly as a leading spokesperson for Christian pacifism, and reads only that subset of his writings which directly engages issues of war, peace, and church-state relations, one might conclude prematurely that for Yoder and for anyone who follows his lead, Constantinianism must be the single most basic problem for Christian social ethics. This much is clear: in Yoder's reading of church history and social ethics, Constantinianism is not simply a fourth-century phenomenon but is emblematic for a thorough-going and oft-repeated Christian unfaithfulness. The dubious changes in Christian thought and practice that allowed churches to become the official re-ligion of the Roman Empire, apparently capped a slow and subtle renunciation of Jesus' messianic mission. That mission was to bring God's reign through the nonviolent cross of suffering service, not the sword of domination — through a qualitatively new community, not through empire — by embodying God's reconciling justice, not by imposing the world's retributive justice.

Such a reading certainly offers a trenchant heuristic device.[1] Nonetheless, sole preoccupation with Constantinianism entails a serious oversight if not a misunderstanding, with implications for both the pastoral agenda and the pro-phetic witness of the church. After all, to define Constantinianism as the core problem for Christian social ethics is to concentrate our ethical reflection on the effort to avoid evil and unfaithfulness — rather than the challenge of em-bracing the good in a faithful manner. No Christian ethic can neglect evil, of course, nor underestimate its seductions. But we may misunderstand both if we fail to notice that the occasion (though not the source) of temptation is first of all the good itself.[2]

We would do better, then, to understand Constantinianism as only the most prominent instantiation of an even more basic problem, which bears with it an even more subtle temptation. This is the temptation of which Deuteron-omy 6–9 warned God's people, and which arose precisely because they *were* God's people. Composing late in Israel's monarchy but projecting their warn-ing back across the Jordan and into the mouth of Moses, the Deuteronomic writers did not doubt that God had wanted to give their once-oppressed people a land in which to prosper securely. Nor did they question their identity as the

---

1. After all, those theologians, bishops, and ordinary believers who have favored one Constantinian settlement after another throughout church history would hardly *say* they had renounced the cross of Jesus Christ. But the device of Constantinian analysis may be all the more necessary in order to show how Christians have renounced the authority of Jesus' nonvio-lent teachings simply by placing them at the margin of Christian theology, and betrayed the meaning of Jesus' cross simply by domesticating it into a solely metaphysical, ahistorical trans-action. Cf. John Howard Yoder, *The Politics of Jesus*, 2nd ed. (Grand Rapids: Eerdmans, 1994), 4ff. and 15ff.; John Howard Yoder, *For the Nations: Essays Public and Evangelical* (Grand Rapids: Eerdmans, 1997), 4-5 n. 11.

2. It would be possible to proceed from a discussion of why orthodox Christian theolo-gies have rejected Manichaeism and all other systems of ontological dualism as heresy. One could then review the Augustinian argument that evil is a privation of good rather than a sub-stance, which means that evil acts are always parasitic upon the good that God created. In con-versation with Yoder's thought and those he has influenced, however, it seems appropriate to orient my argument more strictly in the biblical narrative.

450

people whom God had called into covenant. Even so, God's very gift had brought with it the highest moment of danger. For the day in which they seemed most fully to have entered the land and appropriated God's gift was actually the moment when they had proven most likely to forget the Lord, to trust and credit their own power, or to use their selective memory of God's gracious deliverance as irrevocable validation for them to possess the land in any way they chose.

This Deuteronomic juncture, then, presents God's people with an even more fundamental challenge than the Constantinian juncture. The Deuteronomic problem is the problem of how to receive and celebrate the blessing, the *shalom*, the good, or "the land" that God desires to give, yet to do so without defensively and violently hoarding God's blessing. The Christian community will neglect this challenge to its peril; the church's ethicists will render a poor service if they contribute to that neglect.

The Limits of Anti-Constantinianism

Whether Yoder himself interpreted Constantinianism as *the* most basic problem for Christian social ethics, or simply left this impression inadvertently, is unclear.[3] Certainly he argued throughout his career that many of the most serious temptations Christians face are ones that involve decisions to embrace the state, its protection, its sword, and its idolatrous claim to be the primary source of social creativity or even to *be* God's very reign. If this recurring temptation bears the name of the fourth-century Roman emperor Constantine who legalized and favored Christianity, a single astute politician was hardly its source.

---

3. In the preface to *For the Nations* — the last book he published before his death — Yoder stated his belief that "the two ancient turning points represented by Jeremiah and Constantine have become . . . the two most important landmarks outside the New Testament itself for clarifying what is at stake in the Christian faith," and went on to make explicit his intention that *For the Nations* add an interpretation of "the Jeremian shift" to his longstanding argument "about the difference Constantine makes" (8-9). This statement represents a recognition that simply to critique Constantinianism — as important as that is — does not by itself produce an adequate Christian ethic. I regret, of course, that Yoder's death precludes conversation with him over the relationship between the Deuteronomic juncture and the Jeremian shift. My emphasis on the former may only be a procedural difference with Yoder, not a substantive one, for I first set out to compare problem and problem (Constantinian and Deuteronomic temptations), rather than problem and solution (Constantinian and Jeremian shifts). The reader will find my own argument also moving toward a stress on the Jeremian way of living in the world as an exile community that nonetheless seeks the shalom of the nations in which it finds itself.

451

For if Constantine's policies do mark a watershed in church history, his importance is still one that was conferred *upon* him at the time by bishops and other
Christian leaders such as the church historian Eusebius. Constantinianism
then really consists of all the reasons they did so — trends that were already in
place before Constantine and rationalizations that only a minority of Christians have resisted since. Yoder and his students have identified various reasons
— a general acculturation that slowly made it seem normal to imagine Christian sons and brothers as soldiers, loss of ethical rigor in favor of doctrinal
rigor, and the easy assumption of Christians with growing access to power that
they had a responsibility "to make history come out right."[4]

One thing all of these explanations for church-state accommodation
have in common is their attempt to trace backwards toward some basic mistake or cluster of mistakes — a point at which early Christians began to fall
into temptation. If the fourth or third centuries do not adequately explain
Constantinianism, then developments already in the second or first century
may do so. Or perhaps one must delve deeper still, into the very pages of the
New Testament canon where many discern early signs of hierarchical
institutionalization in the Pastoral Epistles, or patriarchy in Paul, or anti-
Jewish polemics in John. Of course it might be hard to conclude such digging
without eventually questioning the apostolic wisdom of calling Jesus "Lord"
and thus vindicating the language of dominance, or wondering why Jesus
himself compared God with an oppressive landowner. Such genealogical trac-
ing will either have to end somewhere, or implicate God for so foolishly risk-
ing incarnation as a vulnerable servant within the messy business of human
history.

The point here is not to vindicate the authority of scripture,[5] nor is it to
hedge the authority of post-canonical tradition against every possible indict-
ment for fundamental mistakes and outright unfaithfulness. The so-called
church fathers who pastored a fledgling Christian movement into new cultures
throughout the Graeco-Roman world surely made mistakes and committed
sins. The formative theologies they created in the process and sought to consol-
idate into the rough consensus of orthodoxy must therefore remain subject to a
reassessment that will ask how their more serious mistakes and sins may have
skewed their theological legacy. No, the point here is simply that the effort to

4. John Howard Yoder, *The Royal Priesthood: Essays Ecclesiological and Ecumenical*, ed.
Michael G. Cartwright (Grand Rapids: Eerdmans, 1994), 152-57, 198-203.

5. We do well to think of the Bible itself according to what Allen Verhey, an ethicist in the
Reformed tradition, has called a "Chalcedonian consensus" between the Word of God and human words. See *The Great Reversal: Ethics and the New Testament* (Grand Rapids: Eerdmans,
1984), 169-74.

root out Constantinianism will eventually yield diminishing returns unless we correct an oversight in our understanding of the relationship between faithfulness and temptation. We misconstrue the Constantinian temptation unless we attend not just to how unfaithfulness and evil may surely lead to further unfaithfulness but also to how faithfulness itself, and even the good that God gives, may become the occasion for temptation.

Yoder might have agreed. His best-known book, *The Politics of Jesus*, strongly implies that some ways of being tempted are better than others.[6] Yoder argued that even though Jesus ultimately rejected the option of violent revolution that the Zealots of first-century Palestine presented to him, it tempted him far more than did other options — precisely because he was being faithful to God's messianic calling to proclaim a new jubilee that was good news to the poor. As Aristotle has taught Stanley Hauerwas to say, "The brave necessarily know fears that cowards never experience."[7] Likewise, Christians may sense some temptations precisely *because* they have faithfully begun to follow Christ on a path that others have not.

Furthermore, when Yoder addressed his own Mennonite community, especially during the first half of his career, his interests often lay somewhere that was logically and sociologically prior to Constantinianism. In essays of the period, Yoder regularly employed lessons that the German theologian Ernst Troeltsch had drawn from church history early in the twentieth century when he wrote his magisterial work, *The Social Teaching of the Christian Churches*.[8] Such lessons served to warn Mennonites about ways in which rural settledness, economic prosperity, social complacency, and ethnic self-containment could lead it to duplicate Constantinian dynamics on a small scale.[9] A small Christian community of believers committed to structuring its life together according to Jesus' law of love — a Troeltschian "sect," that is — could change into something more like an institutional "church" or *kirche*, which had accommodated itself to the sub-Christian ways by which society generally employs wealth and

---

6. Also see John H. Yoder, *The Original Revolution: Essays on Christian Pacifism*, Christian Peace Shelf (Scottdale, PA: Herald Press, 1971), 13-33.

7. Stanley Hauerwas, *The Peaceable Kingdom: A Primer in Christian Ethics* (Notre Dame: University of Notre Dame Press, 1983), 8, 121. Cf. Aristotle, *Nicomachean Ethics*, 3.6.

8. Ernst Troeltsch, *The Social Teaching of the Christian Churches*, trans. Olive Wyon (Chicago: University of Chicago Press, 1981).

9. The most important example is probably his "Anabaptist Vision and Mennonite Reality," in *Consultation on Anabaptist-Mennonite Theology: Papers Read at the 1969 Aspen Conference*, ed. A. J. Klassen (Fresno, CA: Council of Mennonite Seminaries, 1970). Yoder argued here that ethnically defined Mennonitism was not really Anabaptist at all but a "small Christendom . . . a *Corpus Sulum Christianum*, a small Christian body, a Christian corpuscle."

power.[10] Yoder's use of Troeltschian analysis underscored, if nothing else, his recognition that Constantinianism always begins before there is some Constantinian settlement proper — that some other problems always arise before some emperor presents his tempting offer.

What Yoder may not have so clearly recognized is that this chronological priority reflects a logical priority, the priority of the Deuteronomic juncture over the Constantinian one. After all, for North American Mennonites or *any* human community to have sought to enjoy a measure of peace, economic security, and communal integrity was not in itself a sin. Such a desire in fact reflects the human need for God's promised *shalom* — that full-bodied Hebrew conception of peace, justice, and well-being in every dimension of life. Nor was it a sin to have actually enjoyed some measure of this *shalom*, at least insofar as enjoyment was one fruit of faithful proclamation of — and living response to — a gospel announcing God's peaceable, reconciling work in all relationships. To enjoy some measure of *shalom* does not preclude temptation, of course; instead it easily becomes the occasion for more subtle temptation. This means that although Constantine should represent to us the wrong *way* to embrace God's promise of liberation, *shalom*, and blessing in all of life, we must not forget that God *does* want to free, heal, and bless even if, in blessing, God risks the possibility that God's people will abuse God's gift. Our most basic problem, then, is the Deuteronomic challenge of receiving and celebrating God's gift without oppressing, violating, and hoarding in new ways.

Failure to recognize this more basic problem than Constantinianism not only leads us to misconstrue the relationship between faithfulness and temptation but leads to other misunderstandings.

On the one hand, focusing mainly on Constantinianism leads us to overinterpret church history yet undervalue some of its deeper lessons. If the central challenge for faithful Christians is seen as avoiding anything that might lead to Constantinian compromise, this notion easily beguiles believers in the peace churches and other dissenting traditions into thinking that a firm renunciation of church-state alliances and use of the sword is *sufficient* to avoid

---

10. To be sure, Yoder also noted ways that typologies in this church/sect genre can lock ethical reflection into categories that render the teachings, cross, and politics of Jesus something other than normative; see John Howard Yoder, "How H. Richard Niebuhr Reasoned: A Critique of *Christ and Culture*," in *Authentic Transformation: A New Vision of Christ and Culture*, ed. Glen H. Stassen, Diane M. Yeager, and John Howard Yoder (Nashville: Abingdon Press, 1996), 41-43; Yoder, *For the Nations: Essays Public and Evangelical*, 3-4. Still, into his final years Yoder continued to recognize a certain validity to Troeltschian analysis by marching his graduate students at the University of Notre Dame through Troeltsch's tome.

Constantinianism. Renunciation on this basis then sets up a we/them reading of church history that depends on evidence that "they," the mainstream Constantinian Christians, have become the fallen church, in order to uphold the self-identity that "we" enjoy as the presumed faithful church. Never mind that this we/them reading ignores the prospect that even the "faithful" church always is and always has been fallen, too. To underestimate the common Deuteronomic problem that Christians all face prior to the Constantinian one actually is to make us more vulnerable to both. For we fail to see that the central pastoral challenge *is* that of learning to live "in the land" — celebrating without hoarding God's blessing, loving God without neglecting love of neighbor, loving neighbors without failing to welcome strangers and love enemies, all while ensuring that the liturgy and piety needed to sustain these practices do not inadvertently distract from them.

Meanwhile, the same we/them interpretation of church history easily leads anti-Constantinians to turn a deaf ear to the wisdom that has in fact emerged from "classical" theology as done within "mainstream" parts of the Christian tradition. One does not have to agree with the conclusions Reinhold Niebuhr reached in one of his most famous anti-pacifist essays in order to agree with him that Christianity offers more than merely a new law or ethic of love. Instead, wrote Niebuhr, it "measures the total dimension of human existence" and announces that "there is a resource of divine mercy which is able to overcome a contradiction within our own souls, which we cannot ourselves overcome."[11] We begin parting with Niebuhr when we insist that divine grace is empowering, not just merciful — transforming, not just forgiving. Nonetheless, the teaching, liturgy, sacraments, and spirituality of the larger Christian tradition can remind pacifists of what they may learn too late if they seek to follow Christ and form communities of love through their own efforts alone: *God's grace must sustain discipleship.* We love because God first loved us. We need God's grace even to receive rightly God's gifts and respond faithfully. Prophets, too, need pastors.

On the other hand, overlooking the common temptation to misuse even God's gifts may allow Christians in the all-too-Constantinian mainstream to turn their *own* deaf ear to the prophetic challenge of those who would resist every Constantine and refuse every sword. God's unmerited offer of salvation and God's gracious blessing hardly constitute a blank check for *every* possible way of appropriating God's gifts and putting them to use, nor are they a vindication of our favorite national, tribal, economic, or ecclesiasti-

---

11. Reinhold Niebuhr, "Why the Christian Church Is Not Pacifist," in *Christianity and Power Politics* (New York: Charles Scribner's Sons, 1940), 2.

cal causes.[12] The rightness of doctrine, the presence of the Holy Spirit in the church, the authenticity of apostolic succession, the grace in sacraments, the reality of healed lives among ordinary believers, the communion of saints, and the wisdom of pastoral care do not necessarily mitigate that most basic and subtle temptation to appropriate unfaithfully and ungratefully the very goods that God has given. Becoming clear about this will actually allow anti-Constantinians to pose their prophetic challenge to other Christians more poignantly and normatively.

There is even something right about the vision of Christendom — as that *societas* in which right relationship with God is rightly ordering and reintegrating every relationship and all of life. Although Yoder's followers have rarely noticed, the Christendom vision is itself a vision of *shalom*. If we see the Deuteronomic rather than the Constantinian juncture as presenting our most basic challenge, we can insist just as strongly and even more clearly than we have, that *historic* "Christendom" represents a premature effort to grasp through faithless violence at the fullness of life that is God's to give fully at the eschaton. In other words, peace churches should be able to witness even more forcefully and prophetically to the Constantinian "mainstream" if they do *not* view it as utterly fallen. For it is precisely because orthodox Christianity has gotten some things quite *right* that its misappropriation of God's gifts for limited, selfish, tribal, and non-catholic ends is so much the greater *scandal* to God's saving purposes in history.

Neither mainstream nor dissident Christian traditions can be complacent, according to this view. For if Constantinianism is *not* the most basic problem for Christian social ethics, then both are more clearly forewarned. The warning to mainstream traditions recapitulates the one that Israel's prophets struggled to drive into stubborn ears: gracious chosenness does not preclude judgment but renders it more serious. Meanwhile, the warning to dissenting traditions is this: they are hardly exempt from temptation because they renounce Constantine, and in fact become more vulnerable to it by neglecting their more basic temptation.

The Primacy of the Deuteronomic Juncture

If the juncture that Deuteronomy 6–9 describes is most critical for Christian social ethics, warrant for this claim comes from the artifice by which the

---

12. The logic of unmerited favor would seem to render this needless to say, yet the historical record demands that we do say it.

Deuteronomic writers presented their warnings. By taking their words back across the Jordan to Moses, they addressed patterns that had and would recur across various historical contexts.[13] Though the writers obviously could not have known that those patterns might continue within a community that would eventually consider itself a "New Israel," their own artificial foresight converges with our own hindsight. For at the hinge of history, there is this: according to Luke 4, Jesus himself resisted each of the devil's temptations by orienting himself according to Deuteronomy 6–8.

The continuous and underlying challenge that this Deuteronomic juncture clearly exposed had been intrinsic since the call of Abraham. How is a people to celebrate God's blessing, in a land that God had promised, while enjoying God's gift in such a way that other nations too might find a blessing in the life of this people? Abraham and Sarah died possessing no more than a burial plot in the land of promise. Yet the "Yahwist" who told much of their story made clear that walking in "the way of the Lord" had already made them a blessing to other nations.[14] That fact alone already posed the question: What kind of possession and which way of living in the land best allows God's people to fulfill God's calling most fully and faithfully?[15]

13. "These are the words that Moses spoke to all Israel beyond the Jordan — in the wilderness, on the plain . . . in the land of Moab [where] Moses undertook to expound the law. . . ." (Deut. 1:1, 5; 9:1f.). As a circle of reformers in Israel's late monarchy set out to rework more ancient texts in a way that would sharpen their contemporary relevance, the writers and redactors depended on the mantle of Moses' authority. Certainly that is the first reason they recrossed the Jordan editorially. By Deuteronomy 8, however, their artifice was proving instructive in other ways, for it gave them a platform from which to envision as many as six historical settings: the "house of slavery" in the land of Egypt (8:14); the "great and terrible wilderness" where God had tested and humbled their people (8:2-6, 15-16); the setting "today" on the banks of the Jordan (8:1, 11, 19); the time of God-given prosperity in a "good land" (8:1, 7-10); the time of growing complacency in which they might "exalt [themselves], forgetting the Lord" (8:11-14, 17-19a); and the prospect "that you shall surely perish" (8:19b-20). Of these six, the setting across the Jordan offered the most crucial perspective on all the others, for it was the place where God's people had retained a sharp memory of oppression, liberation, and need for God, where the law at Sinai and the testing of the wilderness had refined this memory, and where they had stood with keenest hope for the fullness of God's promise. Of the other five settings, however, the contrary one in which God's people were in danger of forgetting all this, exalting themselves and trusting in their own power, was most pressing and in fact most current.

14. Hans Walter Wolff, "The Kerygma of the Yahwist," trans. Wilbur A. Benware, *Interpretation* 20 (April 1966): 131-58.

15. When the Hebrews later asked God for a king so that they could be like other nations even if this meant rejecting God as their king and defender (according to the Deuteronomistic historian[s] or redactor[s]) this new juncture and its consequences may have been ominous in more obvious ways, but the monarchy was only one especially prominent and dubious answer to the problem of how to live in the land and enjoy the liberation God had promised.

Subsequent to Deuteronomy and the exile of which it warned, Israel would again face this question — and the debate it produced became the cauldron into which Jesus of Nazareth would enter.[16] As John Yoder taught us, Jesus injected an option that was "original" yet faithful to voices in Israel's debate that had nearly gotten lost. This "original revolution" and the "politics of Jesus" effected a new kind of peoplehood through a new way of entering into the land. Henceforth, the "land" would be a redemptive community life that was not finally tied to any actual terrain, nor to the kind of tribal or national defense that always excludes some whom God is calling out "from every tribe and language and people and nation" to make into "a kingdom and priests serving our God, and [thus] reign on earth" (Rev. 5:9-10). In fact, the way to enter this "land" and "reign" was through the nonviolent suffering service of which Isaiah's disciples had once spoken, wherein God's scattered people fulfill Jeremiah's exhortation to seek the *shalom* of the cities in which they find themselves, and at last share the blessing of Abraham among all the nations of the earth.

Jesus' inauguration of a "new community" did not exempt this community from analogues to Israel's Deuteronomic juncture, however. As the early church struggled to balance the evangelical thrust toward inclusion with the need for church discipline and a clear moral witness,[17] it was negotiating one dimension of its own Deuteronomy-like challenge. Already in the first generation, Christians had to discern how God would have them rework pre-Christian social relationships (1 Cor. 11:17f.; Philemon), organize their own institutional life (1 Cor. 12–14; 1 Tim.; Titus), and weigh the demands of family life (1 Cor. 7). Such questions came to a head as the second and third generations grappled with the delay in Jesus' return. The watershed that every Chris-

16. Return from exile was a new exodus liberation, but the terms that allowed the exiles to reenter the land were messy and remained subject to geopolitics. The exclusionary ethnic policies of Ezra and Nehemiah offered one argument on how to live in the land; the story of God's frustration with Jonah and mercy even toward cruel Nineveh voiced a protest. The Maccabean insurrection against foreign rule argued with its swords that religious integrity required national independence and territorial integrity; a growing Diaspora argued with its feet that Israel might not need territory to be a people. The Zealots who kept the Maccabean dream alive, the Pharisees who developed voluntary communities, the Sadducees who compromised with imperial realities, and the Essenes who started over in isolated enclaves, all continued the debate.

17. In Ephesians 2, for example, the affirmation that Christ has broken down the dividing wall between Jew and Gentile comes with a reminder that God's grace had called all of them out of a deadening life of "trespasses and sins," "desires of flesh and senses," and "wrath," in order to walk in the "good works, which God prepared beforehand to be our way of life." The breaking down of ethnic and cultural walls did not mean that the new community could or should dispense with moral boundary markers.

tian movement begins to face in its second and third generation reflects the church's own most critical version of the juncture that Deuteronomy articulates.[18]

To be sure, Christians have needed to rework — and yet maintain — their eschatologies in order to negotiate this juncture. Strikingly, the early Christian document that most clearly reflects the problems of second-generation Christianity also reflects clearly the need for some new eschatology. The charismatic layman who recorded a series of visions and prophetic exhortations called *The Shepherd of Hermas* in Rome in the early second century was probably a freedman who had experienced economic upward mobility thanks in part to his Christian lifestyle.[19] Now he grappled with the temptations of prosperity, his children's indifference to the faith, conflicts of loyalty between business partners and the Christian community, and the growing worldliness of some church leaders. In urging himself and others to remain faithful, Hermas combined moral exhortation or *parenesis* with an apocalyptic genre.[20] The central image in Hermas's apocalyptic sections was that of a tower which must be completed before the end could come. Christians were its stones and must fit together rightly, else God could not complete the tower. God was in fact extending time so that more could repent — a second time if necessary. Still, doubts about whether any more than two repentances were possible, along with the apocalyptic genre itself, served to sustain a sense of urgency.

Hermas's eschatology is not canonical, of course, in either a literal or fig-

18. Biblical scholars and social ethicists have rightly seen a watershed or perhaps even a trauma in the experience of second-century Christians as they sought to come to terms with the delay of the Parousia. However, when the standard account has implied that the lesson of the delay is that "this changes everything" — so that Christians of no generation after the first need assume that Jesus' ethic of nonviolent discipleship applies to them except in paradoxical ways — that account has missed the Deuteronomic point.

19. Scholars of early Christianity have debated whether *The Shepherd of Hermas* had multiple authors, but even those who argue for multiple authorship recognize that the document reflects a coherent set of communal concerns representing a distinct social segment within the Christian community of Rome during the first half of the second century. See Carolyn A. Osiek, *Rich and Poor in the "Shepherd of Hermas": An Exegetical-Social Investigation*, Catholic Biblical Quarterly monograph series, no. 15 (Washington, DC: Catholic Biblical Association of America, 1983), 14; Carolyn Osiek, "The Genre and Function of the Shepherd of Hermas," *Semeia* 36 (1986): 113-21; James S. Jeffers, *Conflict at Rome: Social Order and Hierarchy in Early Christianity* (Minneapolis: Fortress Press, 1991), 106-20.

20. This rare combination of genres is itself telling, insofar as *parenesis* tends to be socially conservative as it passes down the moral common sense of a community, while apocalypse conveys a heightened sense of urgency and demand for moral change. The combination indicates Hermas's need to maintain an eschatological tension even as the church found itself settling in for a longer haul than it had expected.

urative sense, but his problem might as well be. Family life, freedom from slavery, a measure of economic prosperity, and charisms allowing for a greater role in the Christian community — these are God's gifts. Yet we cannot appropriate them rightly without orientation from God's ultimate purposes. Pacifism alone would hardly ensure a proper eschatological tension; when third-century apologist Origen defended Christian refusal to participate in warfare and civic offices against charges from the pagan critic Celsus, his assurance that Christians were helping the emperor in battle more by praying than by fighting (*Contra Celsum,* 8.73) was in crucial ways more "Constantinian" than the later just war formulations of Augustine. Ironically, it was Augustine who has required theologians ever after to discern the life of the Christian community within a field of eschatological tension, lest Christians settle too complacently into any land.

Augustine's most fateful move was to rationalize ecclesiastical reliance upon imperial sanctions against Christian schismatics in a vain attempt to realize mutual love in the body of Christ.[21] The legacy he thereby left is all the more tragic because it undermined the message of his great contribution to ecclesiology. Augustine reminded the church that its earthly pilgrimage could *never* be entirely settled but must always involve an eschatological tension. In writing the *City of God* during the last two decades of his career, Augustine actually undercut Eusebian optimism about the possibility that official status for the church could ever really mean "Christian times" for the empire, as some church leaders were saying.[22] In his account of the "two cities," Augustine insisted that while on pilgrimage within the earthly city, citizens of the heavenly city must keep clear that they only dare use (not find joy in) temporal goods, and must not place their hope or loyalty in the proud, pretentious, and earthly city that had built itself upon love of domination and of self. The challenge for Christians, then, was to see themselves as Jeremiah's exiles, called to seek the peace of the city in which they found themselves while remaining loyal to another homeland built on true peace, in love for God and neighbor.[23]

Augustine's eschatologically informed ecclesiology did not provide defin-

---

21. See chapter four of Gerald W. Schlabach, "For the Joy Set Before Us: Ethics of Self-Denying Love in Augustinian Perspective," (Ph.D. diss., University of Notre Dame, 1996).

22. See especially the first four chapters of R. A. Markus, *Saeculum: History and Society in the Theology of St. Augustine,* 2nd ed. (Cambridge: Cambridge University Press, 1988).

23. Augustine, *City of God,* 19.26. Intriguingly, both Augustine and Yoder, in their very different ways, ended their long reflections on the role of the church in the world by returning to Jeremiah's injunction to the exiled Hebrews in Babylon (Jer. 29). Cf. Yoder, *For the Nations: Essays Public and Evangelical,* 8-9, 51-78.

itive answers about *how* to live in the land as a pilgrim people. In part, he left the question unanswered because the inexorable dynamic of pilgrimage and the eschatological tension of exile render *every* answer tentative, partial, and situational in the best sense of the word. For another part, he obscured the answer by his own recourse to violence, which tempted him to do what his own deepest theological intuitions might have rendered impossible — to grasp at the fullness of God's peaceable end before its time, as though it were not after all a gift of grace. What Augustine nonetheless did make clear is that the fundamental challenge of the Deuteronomic juncture had not gone away.

Augustine had at least posed the right question again, even while his problematic answers underscored the warning of Deuteronomy to "take care." Together with Hermas but more than any other "church father," Augustine reminds Christians that they cannot negotiate the Deuteronomic juncture without retaining a vital sense of eschatological tension.[24] For even when — and especially if — the eschaton is delayed, Christians must beware of complacency; they must articulate their gospel in a way that applies redemptively to this "land" and this life in time. Yet as soon as they begin living out God's promise of redemption in life and time rather than placing their hope only beyond history, they must live in that very "land" which God gives, in a way that nonetheless sustains a tension with landedness and temporality itself.

Of course Augustine, Origen, Hermas, and, for that matter, the Pastoral Epistles, may also seem to symbolize the trends that allowed the church to ally with Constantine. But to say only that can be misleading. Constantine remains a major temptation and a false answer but is not, finally, our primary problem. Life is our problem. The first of God's gifts is the very goodness of creation, and though sin has intervened, God's saving restoration of life and the good of right relationship actually re-poses the question: How is the faith community to anticipate the temptation and avoid the unfaithfulness that will find an occasion in God's very gift? *How to live rightly in "the land?"*

The Agenda of Christian Social Ethics

Once we recognize that the greatest occasion for temptation is the very good that God gives, the links between a number of difficulties in Christian social ethics start to come into focus. Just as Deuteronomy 8 brought together a perspective on virtually every phase of Israel's history, few issues in Christian social

---

24. Here again, we learn from Yoder. See, for example, "Peace Without Eschatology?" in *The Royal Priesthood*, 143-67.

ethics do not somehow converge within the church's own version of the Deuteronomic juncture. To meet at this juncture does not require Christians of historically divergent traditions to agree from the outset on their answers to the problem that it poses, but chiefly to agree that it might allow them to debate their differences more fruitfully.

Still, my argument so far may require agreement on two methodological implications and it will now proceed by way of a third: (1) Insofar as critiques of Constantinianism either support or depend upon a "fall of the church" paradigm for interpreting church history, they tend to be dysfunctional — not just for ecumenical debate,[25] but also for ethical discernment within those churches that historically have defined themselves over against some "fallen" mainstream Christianity. (2) Inasmuch as good itself is the most important occasion for temptation, one can never assume an *inexorable* link between some present unfaithfulness or moral dilemma and some prior theological mistakes or ethical blunders. To be sure, no idea may enjoy a genealogy pure from self-interest and will to power; there are better and worse theologies; hermeneutics of suspicion have a place. Nonetheless, suspicion is not disproof; *post hoc* does not always mean *procter* sin. Theology and ethical reflection done within a "Constantinian" church are not necessarily wrong all the way down. Some positions that nonpacifist "Constantinian" churches have taken historically are surely controvertible, yet still represent efforts to respond to the right problems.

These two implications clear the way for us to act constructively upon the suggestion that (3) all who have received life in the name of Christ share a common agenda to debate and discern. I will outline this agenda as a series of paired concerns that must stay in conversation with one another in order for Christians to negotiate how they will live in "the land" and appropriate the good that God gives. Inevitably I will hint at the direction I believe this conversation might best proceed, but my larger argument does not stand or fall on whether the reader would quickly agree to go the same direction. For now my argument, after all, is simply that any Christian community that would be faithful will have to answer to both poles of each tension — sooner or later, one way or another. Thus, ethical debates within and among Christian communities will prove most fruitful if we face our common agenda outright, as charted below.

25. To cite ecumenism as a self-evident value would be question-begging in this context.

Landedness and Diaspora

Some readers may object that I have equivocated by speaking both figuratively and literally of the challenge to live rightly "in the land." Other readers may be positively uneasy about making ancient Israel's occupation — of *inhabited* land, cities, houses, cisterns, vineyards, and olive groves that others had built and planted (Deut. 6:10-11) — such a fundamental source for Christian ethical reflection.[26] But the relationship between figurative "land," actual land, and the *shalom* God promises is precisely what requires discernment. Ever since Jesus closed his inaugural speech in Nazareth by extending God's promise of good news and jubilee to Gentiles (Luke 4:16-27), Christianity has represented an argument with the more exclusionary and landlocked tendencies within Judaism (cf. Deut. 7:1-6). The point here is not that Deuteronomy 6–9 offers the last word on how to live in any land or kind of "land" but simply that it poses a problem we cannot avoid.[27] Christianity's Jewish roots run through the Diaspora all the way back to the mixed society of Galilee; Christian eschatology in turn looks forward to a continuing exile among many nations. Thus, we have resources for discerning peaceable relationships to land, and the overlapping communities that might live in a land, without recourse to conquest or Constantine.

But let us be clear: we do no favor to any dispossessed people if we think of land only in a figurative rather than an earthy sense. That European Christians have identified God's cause with their lands, taken others' land, and abused both, means only that we are doubly or triply irresponsible if we now embrace the urbane delusion of those who consume the products of late industrial society while pretending not to be in relationship with the land at all. Those of us who are theological intellectuals may be able to read the Exodus abstractly as a journey into "freedom" or "history" rather than into an actual land,[28] but human rights are

26. This might seem to vindicate violent conquest from the start, after all, or even to give it divine sanction. Bloody struggles for control of land in Bosnia, Rwanda, and Palestine may make us jittery about using "the land" as a figure, allegory, or motif.

27. Historical-critical readings of the Bible may actually provide some help, insofar as Israel's actual occupation of Canaan was less of the conquest that the book of Joshua portrays and more of a social revolution from within, by which dispossessed Canaanites found a coalition, hope and identity with Hebrews who had come through their exodus. A careful reading of the Hebrew Scriptures will find various ways in which God's promise of land was sometimes fulfilled without exclusive territorial control. A respectful reading of Judaism will note ways in which God's promise of communal blessing has been fulfilled even in Diaspora.

28. I have heard the poet-farmer Wendell Berry cited as making this point both about the alienation of urbane intellectuals from land and agriculture, and about the true nature of the Exodus.

more basic, less abstract, and most earthy for those who need them most. If Constantinian *ways* of living in the land are what have left us uneasy about speaking to this question, then we should *both* renounce Constantine *and* demonstrate positive models for dwelling in the land without ejecting other inhabitants.

Liberation and Responsibility

The fact that many of us continue to benefit from oppressive ways of controlling land and exploiting its resources surely makes it dicey to criticize or advise those who now fight for their share.[29] Still, one message of Deuteronomy is that it may yet be possible for the poor and the rich to meet imaginatively back across the Jordan to share experiences and wisdom from both sides. To look for perspective on *that* side of the Jordan is to exercise a "preferential option" for those who are making an exodus and longing for a fuller taste of the fruit of a promised land. Even so, the warning obtains: "Take care." Sooner or later any successful social movement or revolution must institutionalize the changes it proposes. However difficult it is to anticipate the challenge of managing social institutions while struggling for liberation, the way a people or community "enters into the land" will inevitably condition the way it dwells there. Success will thrust the challenges of responsible management even upon revolutionaries.

One kind of case for nonviolence begins, then, with the Deuteronomy-like warning to take care — but so does another kind of case for social responsibility. A restorationist impulse has often accompanied the formation of historic peace churches. The idea is that if only the church could return back to the other side of the Constantinian divide, it might be able to start over and cross the Jordan some other way, so to speak. And in fact, the imaginative move that the authors of Deuteronomy made would support the idea that the Christian community too will find a privileged perspective on its entire history by transposing its moral imagination to a point back near its beginning. Even as peace churches argue that the Constantinian way of "living in the land" has been wrong, however, they must eventually take on the challenges not only of faithful critique, but of faithful settling, faithful institution-building, and faithful management of community life. They cannot expect their critique to be credi-

29. The challenge that national liberation movements in the so-called Third World presented to Christians of the so-called First World during the 1960s through the 1980s may *seem* to have receded, but only that. In any case, global environmental challenges present the problem in new forms. Those with doubts about the ways their own societies have exploited the earth hope other societies will not repeat their environmental mistakes, even as they sense they may not have the moral credentials to press their warnings.

ble if they bring a principled suspicion to all institution-building, or to all exercise of authority by leaders called to focus communal life, or to all forms of discipline. If the only alternative that peace churches, free churches, and other reform movements within Christianity have to offer is a perpetual starting over with primitive forms of face-to-face community, then they are admitting that they really have no idea how to live long in the land that God would give them. And they should not be surprised if mainstream "Constantinian" Christians dismiss their witness as little more than an effort to avoid the most basic problem of Christian social ethics.

Peaceableness and Policing

Once a social movement or a church has begun to enjoy some good gift, it finds that it now has something to conserve and protect. So if the community has not anticipated its Deuteronomic juncture, it arrives there flat-footed, unprepared for the occasion of its greatest and most subtle temptation. It has prospered. It experiences a certain security. And if some of its members — its children, its aged, its infirm — inevitably remain more vulnerable than others, that vulnerability seems to justify protective measures, perhaps in the name of love for these neighbors. Even a pacifist community can find itself dependent upon someone else's policing efforts, or find it needs to develop its own. Before we attribute this dynamic either to inevitable moral compromise or to intractable moral tensions from life within a society that does not share Christian convictions, let us notice that the matter has deeper roots: "Prosperity" and "security" are legitimate (if partial) translations of the word *shalom*.

To be sure, preachers have abused the term "prosperity" and politicians have abused the term "security." They have been able to do so, however, precisely because these *are* goods that God desires to give to all peoples, and for which all peoples long. The question for Christian ethicists is not *whether* but *how* God's people are to treat them. Once again, our root challenge is to discern *how* to live in the land of God's promise in a peaceable way, a way consistent with our conviction that the land is in fact God's gracious gift rather than a property of our own seizing. The argument of Christian pacifists against lethal forms of coercion — particularly when the case for policing serves to rationalize forms of "national defense" that are more nationalistic than defensive — begins with the recognition that because God in Christ has refused to consign any one or any people to the permanent status of enemy, *neither may we*. A community that embodies this argument would rather renounce its present claim upon God's gift of *shalom* than deny the love of enemy that God has shown to it by calling it together as a community of reconciliation even "while we were enemies" (Rom. 5:6-11, especially v. 10). For it believes that to "protect" God's gift of *shalom* in a way that excludes others from its possibility, is in fact to lose God's gift in another way.

Implicit here is the reminder that Christians will discern how to live in the land by the light of their eschatology.[30] Obviously, not all communities that have borne the name of Christ have agreed on how to negotiate their paths between the call to live peaceably and the desire to preserve, protect, or police that life. A mere few paragraphs cannot adjudicate the historic debate between pacifist and just war traditions. What all must remember, however, is that the life of Christian communities does not cease being one of eschatological exile, just because Christians are now living in this world's land longer than either their first-century mentors or some first-century imitators have expected. The "not yet" in the eschatological life of the church may well mean that Christian pacifists must recognize the need for some form of policing and accept the challenge of developing nonlethal sanctions and nonviolent civil defense. Even so, the "already" of eschatological life means that the church can hold lightly to the goods that God gives in this life, and stake its life together on its trust that historical existence does not limit the Giver's promise. Although the just war ethicist may disagree, he or she should not be able to do so without confronting a Christian version of the Deuteronomic warning: if "the land" into which Christians have entered is a reconciled catholic community drawn from all tribes and nations, then we must "take care" lest we forget the nonviolent cross that wrought our own exodus into this land, and so find ourselves living in some *other* land, by attempting to defend it now in some *other* way.

Discipline and Hospitality

The most workaday versions of Deuteronomic temptation are those that arise from within the church's own life. Gaining clarity on how to live in the land does not eliminate the need to judge between behaviors and ways of life. Rather, such clarity already implies the judgment that some moral patterns are better than others — more conducive to human thriving because they are more compatible with God's intention for God's creation and people. And yet it has been

30. The argument is of course akin to Yoder's own (see note 24) but akin also to more recent observations by the Roman Catholic moral theologian Lisa Sowle Cahill in *Love Your Enemies: Discipleship, Pacifism, and Just War Theory* (Minneapolis: Fortress, 1994), 5, 12, 176-77, 231-32, 244-45.

the judgment of the Christian community that its way of life and identity include a fundamental commitment to welcome strangers and outcasts who may (paradoxically) challenge its identity or fit uneasily into its own community life. Thus, the Christian community fulfills its calling only when it practices both discipline *and* hospitality. For the path of faithfulness runs between the twin temptations of rigid exclusiveness and the kind of careless inclusiveness that would erode its identity altogether.[31]

Current debates over homosexuality seem most intractable precisely when discipline and hospitality are pitted against each other rather than embraced as the very creative tension that Christian communities must live through in order to discern a faithful sexual ethic. For of all human communities, this community especially requires both a disciplined corporate life that witnesses to its vision of the life God intended for human beings *and* a hospitality that welcomes the presence and the challenge of those who struggle to live up to the standards inherent in that vision — or who represent another vision entirely. On one hand, then, those who urge the church to recognize monogamous same-sex relations will be convincing only if they make their case in such a way that they reaffirm the right and responsibility of the Christian community to uphold moral standards compatible with its witness and vision. On the other hand, those who urge the church to reject such relations will be convincing only if they demonstrate the kind of thoroughgoing hospitality that has sat long with those who would challenge them with stories of pain, struggle, and grace.

In any case, this highly contested matter provides only the most current and pressing example of the creative and underlying tension between discipline and hospitality that is inherent in the calling of the church. A congregation confronts the tension in a small but hardly trivial way when it weighs the relative need for "contemporary Christian music" that might appeal to diverse social classes or new generations, and older hymns that sustain continuity with longer and deeper Christian traditions. Missionaries face it in a hundred ways when they seek to present the Christian message as good news that makes claims upon its hearers — even as it requires its proclaimers to respect their dignity, their cultures, their worth, and their best religious insights. In none of these cases will we find the path of faithfulness by suppressing one pole of tension, but only by embracing the tension itself.

And so with each of the poles of tension that together define the chal-

---

31. I have addressed the paradoxical identity of the Christian community more extensively in "Beyond Two- Versus One-Kingdom Theology: Abrahamic Community as a Mennonite Paradigm for Engagement in Society," *Conrad Grebel Review* 11 (Fall 1993): 201-5.

lenge of living in the land that God gives. This is the basic agenda of Christian social ethics.[32]

Conclusion: The Unfinished Task of Normative Ecclesiology

The challenge and the agenda here are not new. Yet they may seem to be original insofar as preeminent Christian ethicists have avoided the search for a normative ecclesiology. That evasion has not always been obvious, but then, evasions evade. To identify the Deuteronomic juncture as critical for faithfulness does comprise an admission that in some ways Ernst Troeltsch and followers such as H. Richard Niebuhr were right: the church's journey through what sociologists have since called a "sect cycle," and the difficulty that the second or third generation of a religious movement has in maintaining its founders' fervor and vision, very nearly define the most basic and recurring problem of Christian social ethics. Still, Troeltsch and H. R. Niebuhr were ambivalent at best or evasive at worst on whether it is legitimate to propose a normative ecclesiology at all.[33] Troeltsch claimed to have reached his conclusions only after genuine inductive research,[34] but his suppositions favored a normative churchly stance that sought harmony and synthesis in a unified civilization. When H. R. Niebuhr refined Troeltsch's typology he claimed that "no single Christian answer" could negotiate the "enduring problem" of "Christ and culture,"[35] yet he constructed his own typology so as to favor his final "Christ transforming culture" type.

32. Perhaps we must recognize one final tension — the paradoxical tension between "living in tension" itself and the need of Christian communities to settle on normative decisions that represent their best effort to be faithful to Scripture, tradition, and the pastoral needs before them. They do well to recognize humbly that history is not over and they will yet need to converse hospitably with new strangers amid life situations no community or tradition can fully anticipate. But the professional ethicist in turn does well to recognize this: the task of charting how ethical conversations might best proceed cannot substitute for actually proceeding *as* faith communities with those conversations, nor for finally coming down somewhere in each field of tension, on specific questions, in specific times and places. The point is simply that when a congregation or church body *does* come to the end of a discernment process and takes a stand, accountability to both poles of each tension will make their stand a more solid not a weaker one.

33. See Duane K. Friesen, "Normative Factors in Troeltsch's Typology of Religious Association," *Journal of Religious Ethics* 3 (Fall 1975): 271-83, and John Howard Yoder, "How H. Richard Niebuhr Reasoned: A Critique of *Christ and Culture*," in *Authentic Transformation*, 41-43.

34. Troeltsch, *Social Teaching*, 20.

35. H. Richard Niebuhr, *Christ and Culture* (New York: Harper and Row, 1956), 2, cf. 231-32, 255-56.

We should accept the Troeltschian project, then, but only by turning it inside out.

In other words, we should make normative arguments overtly rather than covertly. We should reopen the possibility that the biblical narratives suggest their own "type" of social ethical posture, and we should let the typologies of Troeltsch and Niebuhr fall where they may.[36] One of Troeltsch's subtexts was that sect-type churches were shortsighted, that mixed-type churches (which incorporated both sectarian and churchly elements) were inherently unstable,[37] and so all churches tend eventually to settle into patterns of churchly establishment.[38] But if we start building our "types" by asking how Christian communi-

36. This is in the spirit of what I take Yoder to have meant when he called his approach "biblical realism."

37. When Troeltsch attended to what in his typology were mixed types, he consistently described them as though some law of nature rendered them unstable, like free electrons that must quickly join with one molecule or another. Troeltsch was sure that Luther's experiments with congregational polity and "believers church"-style meetings of the faithful within the institutional church were merely temporary expedients during a time of uncertainty and apocalyptic ferment; they were not, say, a lost opportunity (*Social Teaching*, 487-89; 511-12). Concerning Methodism — an example of a mixed type if there ever was one — Troeltsch described its separation from the established Anglican Church as inwardly *"inevitable"*: "For this body, like the Moravian Church, belonged essentially to the sect-type and not to the church-type, in spite of its earnest desire to remain inside the Established Church. Indeed, its own nature *forced it*" to do so. Only with the prosperity and flagging zeal of succeeding generations did the Methodist movement "become less and less of a sect and more and more of a Church, or, rather, a number of churches" (721-23, emphasis added; on the Moravians themselves, see the pages just prior). It is illuminating to compare this deterministic language with Troeltsch's portrayal of Luther. According to Troeltsch, Luther was hardly even *conditioned* by social forces, much less "inevitably" determined. Rather, "in this instance the religious idea was clearly the primary and dominant impulse" (see 465-66, 476). In contrast, Methodism was at first "inevitably" sectarian because its primary aim was not religious but social — "to awaken the masses" who were deteriorating morally under England's new industrial capitalism (721).

38. A more thoroughgoing analysis of Troeltsch's work — such as Duane Friesen has carried out in his article on "Normative Factors in Troeltsch's Typology" — would need to recognize that in his search for a "synthesis" Troeltsch *was* in fact proposing a normative ecclesiology. His Constantinian preference was for an established church-type Christianity that would provide worldly civilization with an otherworldly dimension. Not without compromise could this kind of Christianity incorporate the prophetic dimension from sectarianism or the transcendent dimension from mysticism, but the normative case for compromise was precisely that it was as close to synthesis as any church can come in history. One can reply to Troeltsch in three ways. First, as Friesen has shown, Troeltsch's normative claims are generally covert and at odds with his claim to have reached his conclusions only after "genuine" inductive research (*Social Teaching*, 20). Second, attempting an integrated account of the complex impulses that spring from the Christian gospel may be legitimate, but Troeltsch's kind of "synthesis" so eases the tension of Christian eschatology that it can hardly be the synthesis it

ties have responded to the challenges of Abraham, Jeremiah, Deuteronomy, and Jesus — or if we see someone like Augustine as reopening rather than closing off the post-canonical conversation about how to live as a pilgrim people — then what will most interest us in the Troeltschian project will be the very possibilities that it has tended to obscure.

In order to negotiate the Deuteronomic juncture, after all, the Christian community may well be called to be exactly what Troeltsch could only label a mixed type, or called to transform "culture" in countercultural ways that Niebuhr's typology tended to delegitimize. Thus, the Christian community must be *kirche*-like in its inclination to enjoy and celebrate God's gift together, yet *sect*-like insofar as it understands that gift to be a qualitatively different social existence. It must be *kirche*-like in its disposition to make its life available to the world as a people that "enters the land," yet *sect*-like in its refusal to protect its gains by erecting violent military defenses. The possibilities that Troeltschian typologies hid become more intriguing if we see their project as a reflection of the Deuteronomic challenge that we must accept — but only a dim reflection.

*　　*　　*

If my argument leaves no one altogether happy, perhaps that is inevitable. Since one lesson is that divergent Christian traditions must take one another's challenges quite seriously, the argument *should* leave no one unchallenged. While conversing mainly with Yoder and other interpreters of his anti-Constantinian legacy, nothing I have written should let Constantinians rest easy. If anything, the primacy of the Deuteronomic juncture and the tensions it allows us to chart can offer a framework to beat the mainstream tradition of Christian social ethics at its own game, where, as Stanley Hauerwas once protested, "The one with the most inclusive typology wins."[39]

And if my conclusion leaves no one with a tidy sense of closure, perhaps that too is fitting. Since another lesson is that any normative ecclesiology must anticipate tension for as long as the church continues its pilgrimage through history, the argument suggests a paradox: Christians can live rightly in the "land" that God gives only if they sustain a tension with landedness itself. Rec-

claims. Third, if a historical survey such as Troeltsch's is to inform a normative ecclesiology adequately, it must attend precisely to those historical examples that Troeltsch would have to call mixed types, but that are especially intriguing because they may in fact break out of Troeltsch's typology entirely.

39. Stanley Hauerwas, "The Testament of Friends: How My Mind Has Changed," *Christian Century* 107 (28 February 1990): 214.

ognizing our shared Deuteronomic problem — how to live in the land that God gives without abusing God's very gift — brings no easy comfort to *any* tradition without a corresponding discomfort.

Comforting to mainstream traditions, and discomforting to dissenters, is the message that, like it or not, we are all in this together. Like it or not, those of us in dissident traditions dare not see ourselves as immune from the challenge *and the call* to live faithfully in the "land" through time, simply because we renounce Constantine. Thinking we are immune will only make us more vulnerable to the temptations that find occasion in God's blessing, more resistant to the grace that enables us to be faithful and forgives us when we fail, and less likely to appropriate God's blessing in grateful and responsible ways.

Ethicists from mainstream traditions can say "we told you so" if they like, but here is the bargain: to recognize that the problem of Deuteronomy is the most basic problem for Christian social ethics will also be comforting to dissenters in *other* ways, and discomforting to the mainstream. For it underscores the message that the free church tradition already embodies by its dissent from the institutional unity of historical Christendom. This message is that the task of discerning a normative ecclesiology in its full sociological sense has been violently suppressed at worst, and remains sadly unfinished at best.

Perhaps it must remain unfinished until the end. If so, that is the normative claim which the Deuteronomic warning imposes upon all ecclesiology. Do enter the land, for God desires to grace you with good. Yes, *do*. But live there with the care and lightness that recognizes all land and all good as *gift*. As Hermas would say, the tower is not yet completed. As Augustine would add, no earthly tower of our own making is true or stable enough to become a worthy home. And of course the writer of Hebrews said it first, citing the obedience of Abraham, Sarah, and all those witnesses who have "looked forward to the city that has foundations, whose architect and builder is God" (11:10). It is they who are really the ones who can tell us *all*, "We told you so."[40]

40. A number of readers, as well as participants at the Associated Mennonite Biblical Seminary forum where I delivered an early version of this paper through the Marpeck Lecture series, have offered helpful comments and encouragement. Among them, I wish especially to thank my colleagues Loren Johns and Rachel Reesor, John Richard Burkholder, Todd Whitmore of the University of Notre Dame, and Stanley Hauerwas of Duke University. Finally, my colleague J. Denny Weaver has been a key conversation partner in recent years, and I am indebted to him for goading me to think through these issues more clearly, even when we have differed sharply.

Supplement to "A Comprehensive Bibliography of the Writings of John Howard Yoder"[1]

Compiled by Mark Thiessen Nation

Introduction

Anyone looking at this bibliography could quite legitimately ask: If the earlier bibliography was "comprehensive" then why was a supplementary bibliography of this length necessary or even possible within only two years after the publication of the first? There are several reasons. First, John Yoder, apparently, was regularly, though not quite systematically, cleaning out his files the last half dozen or so years of his life. As he did so he would keep a stack of stuff to mail to me. When he had collected what he perceived to be a sufficient quantity he would send them to me. The last few years I received an average of more than one envelope per week. I received four envelopes after he died! All of this is to say, in written notes or by sending me the actual text, John was constantly informing me of something he had recently written or revised, or of something older that he had recently rediscovered. Thus, to the end of his life — and beyond — I was, with his help, adding entries to the bibliography.

Second, some of the entries here are ones which John did not want me to

---

1. This bibliography is intended as a supplement to: Mark Thiessen Nation, "A Comprehensive Bibliography of the Writings of John Howard Yoder," *The Mennonite Quarterly Review* 71 (January 1997): 93-145. A slightly revised version of this (with corrections and additions) was published as Mark Thiessen Nation, *A Comprehensive Bibliography of the Writings of John Howard Yoder* (Goshen, IN: Mennonite Historical Society, 1997). It is referred to below as the *MQR* bibliography.

include in the earlier bibliography. Out of respect for John I did not include them. I have still not included items that are of a confidential nature. However, there are other items which he thought uninteresting or trivial which I have now included. Most of the items listed for the 1940s and 1950s, for example, John would not have included. Some of these I knew about before, others have come to light since his death. Of course John's youth and other contextual matters need to be kept in mind if one reads these papers, but I thought others should know about them. I have also decided to include a few letters that are John's responses to public academic discussions of his thought, responses that expand on points he had made elsewhere. John had not wanted to include letters in the original bibliography.

Third, during the last stages of completing the earlier bibliography my wife and I were in the process of moving to and settling into a job in London, England. Sometimes, partly because of the busyness generated by this move and partly because of working with various versions of my bibliography, some entries were inadvertently omitted. (One of the most embarrassing omissions was *Mennonite Quarterly Review* editor John Roth's essay on Yoder's "The Anabaptist Vision and Mennonite Reality." I knew about John Roth's essay. I still don't know how it was left out.)

And, fourth, a comment about entries about John's work by others. Most of these entries in the *MQR* bibliography and in this one were discovered through my own research rather than with John's help. Many of the new entries included here testify to the ongoing influence of John's work (as well as to the wonders of e-mail). Others are included now for various reasons. One of the complicating factors is that in Mennonite theological discussions John Yoder's voice often plays a role. How significant does that role need to be to deserve inclusion in this listing? You can see what my judgments have been. However, after discussion, I am sure I could be persuaded to include others or drop some of the ones I have included.

I have no illusions that the *MQR* bibliography plus this supplement equal the "really, really comprehensive bibliography." That is partly because I am certain there are still some accidental omissions. No doubt I have also misplaced one or more of a multitude of notes about bibliographical matters which John has sent me over the last decade. But mostly I know these bibliographies are not completely comprehensive because, as I write this, a process has still not been decided upon for dealing with John's literary estate. There are masses of files — unpublished papers, letters, and memos — that have to be sifted through. Without question there will be entries to add to the bibliography from these files, despite the fact that, over the last six years or so, John seemed to be attempting to send me everything he had ever written. I am confident that these two bibliographies together list everything major by John Yoder and that they are more than adequate for enabling scholars to make an accurate assessment of the incredible contributions John Yoder made through his voluminous writings over the course of more than fifty years.

Anyone wishing to contact me about Yoder's writings:

Mark Thiessen Nation
London Mennonite Centre
14 Shepherds Hill
London N6 5AQ
England

E-mail: Mark.TNation@BTInternet.com
Or: menno@compuserve.com
Fax (International) 44-181-341-6807
Phone (International) 44-181-348-5124

Bibliography Supplement

Writings by John Howard Yoder

1940s

"Job 1946," "Cycle," "Surface Tension," "Retort in Kind to Retort Unkind," "P-38," "Night Plane - Chapter of Man Faces Infinite." Poems in an untitled, mimeographed booklet of poetry, compiled by Jacob Suderman, faculty member, Goshen College, 1946.

"The Nature of Religious Liberty." *The Goshen College Record* (April 9, 1946).

"Behold the Lilies — Do They Organize?" (editorial). *The Goshen College Record* (April 22, 1947).

"Crown Hill Church." Ca. 1947, 4pp.

"History and Evaluation of Pietism." 1947, 31pp.

"The History of the General Conference Church at Sterling, Ohio." Ca. 1947, 6pp.

"In Case You Wondered" (editorial). *The Goshen College Record* (May 20, 1947).

"Mennonitism — Church or Complex?" (editorial). *The Goshen College Record* (February 11, 1947).

"Now That It's Been Asked" (editorial). *The Goshen College Record* (February 25, 1947).

"Of Means and the End" (editorial). *The Goshen College Record* (March 11, 1947).

"One or the Other" (editorial). *The Goshen College Record* (June 7, 1947).

"Questions for Now, Forever." *The Goshen College Record* ("*Special 1947 Commencement Supplement*").

"Questions for Now, Forever." *Maple Leaf* (Goshen College Yearbook 1947), 112-13.

"The Swiss Mennonite Churches of Southern Wayne County." A paper written for H. S. Bender course, "Mennonite History," Goshen College, second semester, 1947, 29pp.

"Investment." *Youth's Christian Companion* 30 (July 3, 1949): 625, 632.

1950s

"Histoire de la Fondation du Foyer Mennonite," in *Almanach Mennonite du Cinquantenaire 1901-1951* (Montbéliard: Publications Mennonites, 1951), 74-76.

"'Reflections on the Irrelevance of Certain Slogans to the Historical Movements They Represent' or 'The Cooking of the Anabaptist Goose' or 'Ye Garnish the Sepulchres of the Righteous.'" Paper typed by Yoder on the last day of a meeting of Mennonites in Amsterdam, April 15-26, 1952, 3pp.

"Addendum" [to "The Cooking of the Anabaptist Goose" — name given to this untitled paper by Paul Toews]. Further reflections on the themes of the paper, "The Cooking of the Anabaptist Goose," July 27, 1952, 5pp.

"Report on Meeting on Relation of Nonresistance to Discipline in Mission Congregations in French-Speaking Europe." Report written by Yoder, summarizing a meeting held on March 11 at Valdoie, France, 1954, 4pp.

"The Theological Basis of the Christian Witness to the State." Longer study prepared in March 1955, of which the briefer Puidoux paper (below) is a résumé.

"The Theological Basis of the Christian Witness to the State." A paper distributed in preparation for the Puidoux Theological Conference, August 15-19, 1955 (two parts: "The Reign of Christ over Church and State" and "Ethics for the State"); issued as "Work Paper No. 9" by Mennonite Central Committee, 12pp. (portions published as "The Theological Basis of the Christian Witness to the State" — see *MQR* bibliography under 1978).

[Untitled Chapel Talk on Matt. 19:16-26]. Presented at Goshen College, Goshen, IN, November 1956, 6pp.

"The Ecumenical Movement and the Faithful Church," *Gospel Herald* (January 15, 1957): 49-51; (January 22, 1957): 77-78; (January 29, 1957): 100, 117-18; (February 5, 1957): 125-26; (February 12, 1957): 150-51, 165; (February 19, 1957): 172, 189.

"Le Peuple de Dieu et le Monde selon la Bible." *Christianisme Social* (Paris) (April 1957).

"Der Staat im Neuen Testament." *Der Mennonit* (July, September, October, December 1957).

"The Church and the World." Lecture at Goshen College Theological Workshop, August 18, 1958, 13pp.

"Theological Basis of Christian Pacifism." Lecture at a Fellowship of Reconciliation summer camp, Green Lake, WI, August 19-22, 1959, at least 11pp.

1960s

Review of *Le Martyrologe Protestant des Pays-Bas du Sud au XVIme Siècle* by Alphonse Verheyden. *The Mennonite Quarterly Review* 34 (October 1960): 314-15.

"A Case Study: Missions and the Colonial Mentality." Intended for use in *The Encyclopedia of Modern Christian Missions,* 1961, 13pp.

"Proposals to New Approach to Conversation on the War Issue." Memo to Historic Peace Church Continuation Committee, April 1962, 6pp.

"The Christian's Responsibility to the State." *Ontario Peace Bulletin* (November 12, 1963): 2, 6-7 (published as a supplement to *The Canadian Mennonite* as well as distributed separately by the Conferences of Historic Peace Churches).

"Toward a Sifting of Faith from Culture." *Mennonite Life* (January 1964): 36-39.

"Prospectus for a Conference on the Concept of the Believers' Church." Unpublished paper, ca. May 1966.

"Gospel and Revolution." Sermon, August 7, 1966, 8pp.

"Anabaptist Origins in Switzerland." In *An Introduction to Mennonite History,* edited by Cornelius J. Dyck, 26-35. Scottdale, PA: Herald Press, 1967.

"Persecution and Consolidation." In *An Introduction to Mennonite History,* edited by Cornelius J. Dyck, 36-43. Scottdale, PA: Herald Press, 1967.

"A Summary of the Anabaptist Vision." In *An Introduction to Mennonite History,* edited by Cornelius J. Dyck, 103-11. Scottdale, PA: Herald Press, 1967.

"Checklist of the Functions of the Church." Commission on Church Organization, April 10, 1967, 4pp.

"A Plea for a Broader Conception of Evangelical Unity." 1967, 4pp.

"Nasty Noel" [under the pen name, Henderson Nylrod]. *Concern* 16 (November 1968): 2-3.

"The Possibility of a Messianic Ethic." Lecture given at the Chicago Society of

Biblical Research, The Lutheran School of Theology, Chicago, April 27, 1968. (This became the first chapter of *The Politics of Jesus*.)

Memo to Peace Secretaries — Lapp, Hackman, Fast [regarding transition from Church Peace Mission to New Call to Peacemaking]. 1969, 4pp.

Review of *The Just War: Force and Political Responsibility,* by Paul Ramsey. *Religious Education* 64 (May-June 1969): 246-47.

"Memorandum: The Need for a Special Study Effort" [regarding alternatives to violence and war]. September 10, 1969, 2pp.

1970s

"Liberating Must Come First: Exodus Precedes Sinai." Elkhart, IN, 1972, 10pp.

"Salvation Is Nearer Now." A Bible Lecture at Prairie Street Mennonite Church, September 10, 1972, 7pp.

Review of *Anabaptists and the Sword* by James M. Stayer. In *Church History* 43 (June 1974): 272-73.

"Radical Christianity: An Interview with John Yoder." *Right On* (later *Radix*) 6 (February 1975): 1, 5, 11.

"Alternatives to Violence." South Africa Lecture Series, 1976, 12pp.

"Letter to John R. W. Stott" [regarding "Principalities and Powers"]. October 27, 1976, 3pp.

"Introduction" [in French]. In *The Origins and Characteristics of Anabaptism,* edited by Marc Leinhard, 3-9. The Hague: Martinus Nijhoff, 1977.

"Between Christ and Caesar: Quietism, Involvement, Or . . . ?" Lecture presented at a symposium on "Christian Mission Under Authoritarian Governments," sponsored by the Overseas Ministries Study Center, Ventnor, NJ, May 3-6, 1977, 31pp.

"Memorandum: Affective Resources for Singles." Memo to 'interested persons,' July 1977, 13pp.

"Aportes De La Historia: Frente A La Problematica De La Riqueza." A paper written for a study process conducted by Fraternidad Teologica Latinoamericana, Argentina, ca. 1978, 13pp.

"A Brief Footnote to Use When Discussing Affective Resources." Memo to 'anyone concerned,' Dec. 13, 1978, 1p.

"Letter to John R. W. Stott" [regarding "Principalities and Powers"]. June 28, 1978, 3pp.

"Letter to John R. W. Stott" [regarding "Principalities and Powers"]. December 7, 1978, 10pp.

"Letter to Philip Wogaman" [responding to Wogaman's characterizations of

Yoder in his 1976 book, *A Christian Method of Moral Judgement*, following a discussion of Wogaman's book at the Society of Christian Ethics
Meeting]. March 27, 1978, 9pp.

"Memorandum." Unfinished Menno Dialogue on human rights, April 1978,
2pp.

"A Project in Living Church History: The Maturation of an Apostolic Community." Memo to 'whom it may concern,' September 22, 1978, 3pp.

"The Church and Change: Violence and Its Alternatives." Lecture presented at
Annual Conference, South African Council of Churches, Hammanskrall,
July 24, 1979, 20pp. (This was mistakenly listed as given in 1978 in the
earlier bibliography. Also, John retyped it in the 1990s for possible publication; thus the difference in pagination from the earlier bibliography
listing.)

1980s

[Untitled response to Paul Deats's "Protestant Ethics and Pacifism," in *War or
Peace?*, edited by Thomas A. Shannon, Orbis Press, 1980]. More or less
the repeat of the substance of a letter sent to Deats, March 23, 1981, 7pp.

"Are You Ready to Change?" Homily presented at Votive Mass for Christian
Unity, Sacred Heart Church, Notre Dame University, January 24, 1982,
5pp.

"History and Hermeneutics." Contribution to a seminar on homosexuality at
the Associated Mennonite Biblical Seminaries, probably March 18-20,
1982, 8pp.

"Etudes Bibliques" [on Isaiah 2, Micah 4]. *Eglise et Paix* 3 (Avril 1983): 2-13.

"When the State Is God." In *Not By Might: Gospel Herald Sampler 1908-1983*,
edited by Daniel Hertzler, 108-9. Scottdale, PA: Herald Press, 1983.

"A New Attack at an Old Issue: Redefining Homosexuality." Memo to 'colleagues in ethics,' August 14, 1984, 4pp.

"A 'Peace Church' Perspective on Covenanting." This is the unpublished version
(with editorial comments) of a brief piece published in *The Ecumenical
Review* (July 1986). Ca. 1984, 5pp.

"If It's Not Broke, Fix It." August 9, 1985, 3pp.

Review of *Biblical Pacifism: A Peace Church Perspective*, by Dale W. Brown. In
The Mennonite (November 1986): 506.

"Theological Perspectives on the Dignity of the Secular." Lecture given at Faith/
Learning Conference, Bethel College Conference, April 1986, 10pp.

"The Nonviolent Component of the February (1986) Manila Revolution." Presented at the Joan B. Kroc Institute for International Peace Studies, November 9, 1987, 3pp.

"Peace Theology Miscellany #18: Modern War and the Law of Nations Preparation for the First Vatican Council." Notre Dame, September 1987, 8pp.

"Peace Studies Miscellany #20: The Laws of War in Modern Treaties." July 1989, 2pp.

1990s

"Peace Theology Miscellany #3: Conscientious Objection to Particular Wars: The Movement of 1965-75 and Its Prehistory." Notre Dame University, November 1990, 6pp.

"Response to James Sterba on 'The Reconciling of Pacifism and Just War.'" Conference of Philosophers for Peace, University of Notre Dame, September 22, 1990, 3pp.

Review of *Vision, Doctrine, War: Mennonite Identity and Organization in America, 1890-1930,* by James C. Juhnke. *Pennsylvania Mennonite Heritage* (October 1990): 47-48.

Ye-su Cheng-chih (Mandarin translation of *The Politics of Jesus*). Translated by Timothy Liau. Hong Kong: China Alliance Press, 1990.

"Antipedobaptism Revisited: The Radical Reformation." A syllabus supplement to the graduate course "Radical Reformation" offered at Notre Dame, Spring 1991, 3pp.

Review of *The Condemnations of the Reformation Era,* by Karl Lehmann and edited by Wolfhart Pannenberg. *The Mennonite Quarterly Review* (October 1991): 465 (Replacement of entry for *MQR* (October 1991) in previous bibliography; Yoder did not review *The Puzzles of Amish Life.*)

"The Impact of Jesus on the World." Lecture presented at Cornell University, Ithaca, NY, as part of a lecture series entitled "Representations and Realities," October 21, 1991, 11pp.

"War Revisited: The Radical Reformation." A syllabus supplement to the graduate course "Radical Reformation," Notre Dame, Spring 1991, 2pp.

"If I Were M. Nation How Would I Describe J. H. Yoder [on theological method]." Memo written to Mark Nation, from the London, England, Notre Dame campus, early December 1991, 4 pp.

La Irrupcion del Shalom. Mexico City: SERPAJ, 1991.

"Christologie et dissidence au sein de la Réforme zwinglienne." In *Jésus-Christ aux marges de la Réforme* edited by Neal Blough, 51-63. Paris: Desclée,

1992. (Corrects the similar *MQR* bibliography entry, under 1992 scholarly essays.)

The Politics of Jesus [in Japanese]. Tokyo, 1992.

"Peace Theology Miscellany #8: Conspectus of the Criteria of the Just War Tradition." January 1992, 9pp.

"Absolute Philosophical Relativism Is an Oxymoron." Unpublished paper, drafted after the essay, "Meaning After Babble: With Jeffrey Stout Beyond Relativism," [Journal of Religious Ethics 24 (Spring 1996): 125-39], June 1993, 3pp.

"Swiss Anabaptism." In *An Introduction to Mennonite History*, edited by Cornelius J. Dyck, 50-60. Third ed. Scottdale, PA: Herald Press, 1993.

"A 'Thicker' Frame of Reference for Girardian Analysis of the Roots of Punishment." Memo to 'people who know Rene Girard's perspective,' Notre Dame, February 10, 1993, 14pp.

"Regarding Nature." Drafted and circulated in connection with a Notre Dame course on the just war tradition, January 1994, 8pp.

"Responding to Stanley Fish Lecture Responding to George Marsden Book." Memo 'to myself and potential confidential eavesdroppers,' November 2, 1994, 4pp.

"Testing the Methodological Underpinnings of the Just War Logic: Can the Just War System Be Boiled Down to a Single Clear Logic?" February 14, 1994, 13pp.

"Chapter XIII: Jesus in Relation to the 'Socrates' Section (1)." Also available in "You Have It Coming: Good Punishment. The Legitimate Social Function of Punitive Behavior," [Shalom Desktop Publications, 1995], 1995, 4pp.

Translation of Michael Sattler, "The Congregational Order." In *Hutterite Beginnings: Communitarian Experiments During the Reformation*, edited by Werner O. Packull, 303-15. Baltimore, MD: The Johns Hopkins University Press, 1995.

"The Challenge of a Christian Vocation of Providing a Life for Lifers: A Request for Comment." Memo 'to whom it may concern' (originally written for Tobias Winright regarding life sentences in prisons), June 27, 1996, 3pp.

"Chronology of Martin Luther King, Jr. and Civil Rights." Chapter 9 of Chapters in the History of Religiously Rooted Nonviolence: A Publication of the Joan B. Kroc Institute for International Peace Studies, ca. 1996, 9pp.

"Confessing Jesus in Mission." The English original from which the Dutch translation, published as "Jezus belijden in de zending" [*Wereld en Zending* 24 (1996)] was made, March 1996, 7pp.

"Kann Man Fur Ein Anderes Jahrtausend Bereit Sein?" In *Die Theologie auf dem*

Weg in das dritte Jahrtausend: Festschrift für Jürgen Moltmann zum 70, edited by Carmen Krieg, Thomas Kucharz, and Miroslav Volf, 80-87. Munich: Christian Kaiser Gütersloher Verlagshaus, 1996. (Equals *MQR* bibliography entry for 1996, "Is There Such a Thing. . . .")

"Let Me Count the Ways." A listing of "the many images/dimensions of Jesus as pertinent to discipleship and particularly to the ethics of wealth and violence," February 2, 1996, 3pp.

"The Metaphors of Clan and Culture Do Not Work to Characterize the Problems Related to Moral Language's Being Community-Dependent." Thoughts redacted after the paper "Meaning After Babble: With Jeffrey Stout Beyond Relativism" [*Journal of Religious Ethics* 24 (Spring 1996), 125-39], 1996, 2pp.

"Pacifism." In *Dictionary of Ethics, Theology, and Society,* edited by Paul Berry Clark and Andrew Linzey, s.v. London/New York: Routledge, 1996.

The Politics of Jesus [in Arabic]. Cairo, 1996.

"Trinity Versus Theodicy: Hebraic Realism and the Temptation to Judge God." Incomplete draft, in response to an editor's invitation, 1996, 12pp.

"Backgrounds to Ethical Interpretation of the Bombing of Hiroshima and Nagasaki in Terms of the 'Just War Tradition,'" 1997, 6pp.

The Christian Witness to the State. Eugene, OR: Wipf & Stock Publishers, 1997 (reprint of 1964/1977 Faith and Life edition).

Review of *Confusions in Christian Social Ethics: Problems for Geneva and Rome,* by Ronald H. Preston. *Pro Ecclesia* 6 (Fall 1997): 496-98.

"Jésus-Christ et les apôtres ont encore quelque chose à nous dire: qu'allons-nous faire?" (2e partie) *Les Cahiers de Christ Seul* 1 (1997), 77pp. (This and the first part [listed under popular essays for 1996 in *MQR* bibliography] are together a translation of Yoder's book, *Body Politics.*)

"La Radicalité du Message de Jésus." *Cahiers de la Reconciliation* (Paris) 64 (1997): 3-9.

"'Patience' as Method in Moral Reasoning: Is an Ethic of Discipleship 'Absolute'?" August 1997, 16pp. [This is a revision of the *MQR* bibliography entry for 1992, "Methodological Miscellany, Moral Theology #1" (Published for the first time as chapter two of this book)].

"*The Politics of Jesus* Revisited." A lecture at Toronto Mennonite Studies Center, March 1997, 7pp.

"*The Politics of Jesus* Revisited." A lecture at Eastern Baptist Theological Seminary, November 4, 1997, 8pp. (Only slight revisions from earlier lecture at Toronto, above.)

"Practicing the Rule of Christ." In *Virtues & Practices in the Christian Tradition: Christian Ethics after MacIntyre,* edited by Nancey Murphy, Brad J.

Kallenberg, and Mark Thiessen Nation, 132-60. Harrisburg, PA: Trinity Press International, 1997.

Review of *Theology, History, and Culture: Major Unpublished Writings, by H. R. Niebuhr* edited by W. S. Johnson. *Theology Today* 54 (1997): 114-15.

"Christian Unity — The Way from Below." This was a lecture written by Yoder late in 1997, to be presented in January of 1998 as the Paul Watson Lecture, sponsored by the Gray Friars, San Francisco, California. Following Yoder's death, it was read by Mike Broadway at this event, 21pp.

He Came Preaching Peace. Eugene, OR: Wipf & Stock Publishers, 1998. (Reprint of 1985 Herald Press book by the same title)

To Hear the Word. Eugene, OR: Wipf & Stock Publishers, 1999. (More or less the same as the 1996 "Shalom Desktop" publication, listed in the MQR bibliography, entitled "How to Be Read by the Bible." This is a collection of mostly unpublished essays on how Yoder understands his own way of reading the Bible.)

Karl Barth and the Problem of War. Eugene, OR: Wipf & Stock Publishers, 1999? (This was under discussion when John died. It would be a reprint of 1970 book with the possible addition of one or more other essays by Yoder on Barth. Wipf and Stock were also in conversation with Yoder about publishing other unpublished or out-of-print material. Any or all of these projects may go forward.)

"The Power of 'Power' is a Power." ?, n.d.

"Spirituality to Build a Nonviolent World." Translation of an essay by José Aldunate, SJ, for use in Yoder's Notre Dame theology course, Voices of Non-Violence, n.d.

Writings about John Howard Yoder

Barrett, Lois, et al. "What I Learned from John Howard Yoder." *Mennonite Life* 53 (March 1998): 4-13.

Beck, Ervin. "The Politics of Rudy Wiebe." *The Mennonite Quarterly Review,* forthcoming.

Bruggen, door M. "Samenvatting van Christelijke authenticiteit en politieke verantwoordelijkheid. Een vergelijking van de theologische en ethische standpunten van John Howard Yoder en Reinhold Niebuhr." Doctoraalscriptie aan de Theologische Faculteit, R. U. Groningen, 1988.

Bruggen, door M. "Christelijke authenticiteit en politieke verantwoordelijkheid." *Doopsgezinde Rijdragen* (Amsterdam) 15 (1989): 151-53.

Brunk, Conrad G. Review of *For the Nations* by John Howard Yoder. *The Conrad Grebel Review* 16 (Spring 1998): 128-31.

Burkholder, John Richard. "Continuity and Change: A Search for a Mennonite Social Ethic." Pamphlet. Akron, PA: Mennonite Central Committee, U.S. Peace Section, 1977.

Burkholder, John Richard. "John Howard Yoder, 1927-1997." *The Mennonite Quarterly Review* 62 (April 1998): 116.

Burkholder, John Richard. "Mennonite Peace Theology: Reconnaissance and Exploration." *The Conrad Grebel Review* 10 (Fall 1992): 259-87.

Burkholder, John Richard. "A Perspective on Mennonite Ethics." In *Kingdom, Cross, and Community: Essays on Mennonite Themes in Honor of Guy F. Hershberger,* edited by John Richard Burkholder and Calvin Redekop, 151-66. Scottdale, PA: Herald Press, 1976.

Burrell, David B. "From a Colleague at Notre Dame." *The Conrad Grebel Review* 16 (Spring 1998): 101-2.

Bush, Perry. "Anabaptism Born Again: Mennonites, New Evangelicals, and the Search for a Useable Past, 1950-1980." *Fides et Historia* 25 (Winter/Spring 1993): 26-47.

Camp, Lee. "Restoration and Ecumenism in the Churches of Christ: A Rapprochement in John Howard Yoder." A paper presented as part of a panel discussion on "Like Leaven in Bread: The Influence of John Howard Yoder — As Both Theologian and Person — On Those Who Studied with Him," Society of Christian Ethics, January 1999.

Carter, Craig. "The Pacifism of the Messianic Community: Christology and Ethics in the Thought of John Howard Yoder." Ph.D. diss., The University of St. Michael's College, Toronto, Canada, 1999.

Carter, Craig A. "A Response to John Howard Yoder's Lecture 'The Politics of Jesus Revisited'." March 15, 1997, 3pp.

Cartwright, Michael. "Radical Catholicity: John Howard Yoder, 1927-1997." *The Christian Century* (January 21, 1998): 44-46.

Charles, J. Robert. "A Mennonite Colossus." *Global Perspectives* [Mennonite Board of Missions] 98 (1998): 1.

Culp, Daryl. "Anabaptists as Harbingers of Postmodernity? A Comparison of Yoder and Kaufman," A lecture presented at the conference, "Anabaptists and Postmodernity," Bluffton College, Bluffton, Ohio, August 6-8, 1998.

Davis, Grady Scott. "Pacifism as a Vocation." In *Virtues and Practices in the Christian Tradition: Christian Ethics after MacIntyre,* edited by Nancey Murphy, Brad J. Kallenberg, and Mark Thiessen Nation, 239-61. Harrisburg, PA: Trinity Press International, 1997.

Davis, Grady Scott. "Pacifism as a Vocation." In *Warcraft and Fragility of Virtue:*

An Essay in Aristotelian Ethics, 27-51. Moscow, ID: University of Idaho Press, 1992.

Deppermann, Klaus. "Die Strassburger Reformatoren und die Krise des oberdeutschen Täufertums im Jahre 1527." *Mennonitische Geschichtsblätter* 25 (1973): 24-41.

"Disciplinary Process with Yoder Concludes." *Gospel Herald* (June 18, 1996): 11.

Driedger, Leo, and Donald B. Kraybill. *Mennonite Peacemaking: From Quietism to Activism.* Scottdale, PA: Herald Press, 1994.

Edwards, George R. Review of *The Politics of Jesus: Vicit Agnus Noster,* by John Howard Yoder. *The Mennonite Quarterly Review* 48 (October 1974): 537-38.

Friesen, Duane. "Response to 'Mennonite Social Ethics and *The Politics of Jesus:* Continuity and Change' by David Schroeder." From MCC *Politics of Jesus* Colloquium [see Swomley, 1976 for details], 1976, 2pp.

Friesen, Duane. "Toward a Theology of Culture: A Dialogue with John H. Yoder and Gordon Kaufman." *The Conrad Grebel Review* 16 (Spring 1998): 39-64.

Fujiwara, Atsuyoshi. "[On Christ and Culture]." Ph.D. diss., University of Durham, Durham, England, 1999?

Grimsrud, Ted. "A Faithful Teacher in the Church." *The Mennonite* 1 (March 3, 1998): 8-9.

Hallahan, Kenneth. "The Social Ethics of Nonresistance: The Writings of Mennonite Theologian John Howard Yoder Analyzed from a Roman Catholic Perspective." Ph.D. diss., The Catholic University of America, Washington, DC, 1997.

Harder, Helmut. "The Pacifism of the Messianic Community." In *Mennonite Peace Theology: A Panorama of Types,* edited by John Richard Burkholder and Barbara Nelson Gingerich, 35-41. Akron, PA: Mennonite Central Committee Peace Office, 1991.

Harink, Doug. "The Anabaptist and the Apostle: The Politics of Paul According to John Howard Yoder." Paper presented to the Canadian Theological Society, Spring 1997.

Harink, Doug. "For or Against the Nations: Yoder or Hauerwas, What's the Difference?" Paper presented to the Canadian Evangelical Theological Society, June 1998.

Hauerwas, Stanley. "From a Friend, Former Colleague, and Fellow Ethicist." *The Conrad Grebel Review* 16 (Spring 1998): 98-100.

Hauerwas, Stanley. "Remembering John Howard Yoder." *First Things* 82 (April 1998): 15-16.

Heilke, Thomas. Review of *The Royal Priesthood: Essays Ecclesiological and Ecu-*

menical by John Howard Yoder, edited by Michael G. Cartwright. *Mennonite Life* (September 1997): 43-45.

Hershberger, Guy F. Review of *The Politics of Jesus: Vicit Agnus Noster,* by John Howard Yoder. *The Mennonite Quarterly Review* 48 (October 1974): 534-37.

Hillerbrand, Hans. Review of *Täufertum und Reformation in der Schweiz. I. Die Gespräche zwischen Täufern und Reformatoren 1523-38,* by John H. Yoder. *The Mennonite Quarterly Review* 39 (October 1965): 309-12.

Houser, Gordon. "With Jesus on the Low Road." *The Mennonite* 1 (March 3, 1998): 16.

Huebner, Chris K. "Can a Gift Be Commanded? Theological Ethics Without Theory by Way of Barth, Milbank, and Yoder." *Scottish Journal of Theology* (1999).

Huebner, Chris K. Review of *For the Nations,* by John Howard Yoder. *Scottish Journal of Theology* (1999).

Huebner, Chris K. "Mennonites and Narrative Theology: The Case of John Howard Yoder." *The Conrad Grebel Review* 16 (Spring 1998): 15-38.

Huebner, Chris K. "The Pacifism of Christian Discipleship as Changing the Subject. Or, How Not to Read John Howard Yoder." February 4, 1998, 13pp.

Hutchinson, Roger. "'Responding to Realism: Assessing Anabaptist Alternatives.' Roger Hutchinson Responds to Mark Neufeld." [Neufeld's article in *The Conrad Grebel Review* 12 (Winter 1994): 43-62]. *The Conrad Grebel Review* 12 (Spring 1994): 226-29.

Jordan, Laurel Macaulay. "What Parents and Teachers Can Learn from God and What I Learned from John Yoder: The Noncoercive Nature of Divine Sovereignty and Patience." A paper presented as part of a panel discussion on "Like Leaven in Bread: The Influence of John Howard Yoder — As Both Theologian and Person — On Those Who Studied with Him," Society of Christian Ethics, January 1999.

Kaufman, Gordon D. Review of *The Christian and Capital Punishment,* by John Howard Yoder. *The Mennonite Quarterly Review* 40 (January 1966): 65-66.

Kaufman, Gordon D. Review of *The Priestly Kingdom: Social Ethics as Gospel,* by John Howard Yoder. *The Conrad Grebel Review* 4 (Winter 1986): 77-80.

Keim, Albert N. *Harold S. Bender, 1897-1962.* Scottdale, PA: Herald Press, 1998, especially chapter twenty-one.

Klassen, William. "Another Perspective on 'Leadership, Authority and Power.'" *The Mennonite Quarterly Review* 72 (January 1998): 96-102.

Klassen, William. "John Howard Yoder and the Ecumenical Church." *The Conrad Grebel Review* 16 (Spring 1998): 77-81.

Klassen, William. "Theologian an Ecumenical Leader." *The Mennonite Weekly Review* (January 22, 1998).

Koontz, Gayle Gerber. "Evangelical Peace Theology and Religious Pluralism: Particularity in Perspective." *The Conrad Grebel Review* 4 (1996): 57-89.

Koontz, Ted. "'Nonresistance and Responsibility': A Review and an Assessment." In *Mennonite Theology in Face of Modernity: Essays in Honor of Gordon D. Kaufman,* edited by Alain Epp Weaver, 156-76. North Newton, KS: Bethel College, 1996.

Kraus, C. Norman. Review of *The Christian Witness to the State,* by John Howard Yoder. *The Mennonite Quarterly Review* 40 (January 1966): 67-70.

Krauss, Wolfgang. "Peace Church Theologian Dies." *Church and Peace* 15 (Spring/Summer 1998): 27.

Kroeker, P. Travis. "The War of the Lamb: The Eschatological Genealogy of Morals." Lecture presented at the conference, "Anabaptists and Postmodernity," Bluffton College, Bluffton, Ohio, August 6-8, 1998.

Loewen, Harry. "To John W. Miller: 'Schleitheim Pacifism and Modernity: Notes Toward the Construction of a Contemporary Mennonite Pacifist Apologetic,'" [Miller's article in *The Conrad Grebel Review* 3 (Spring 1985): 155-63]. *The Conrad Grebel Review* 3 (Fall 1985): 285-87.

McClendon, James Wm., Jr. "John Howard Yoder, 1927-1997." *Books & Culture* 4 (May/June 1998): 6-7.

Meyer, Mary Ellen. "From a Sister." *The Conrad Grebel Review* 16 (Spring 1998): 96-97.

Miller, John W. "By John W. Miller to Harry Loewen: Further Reflections on 'Schleitheim Pacifism and Modernity, Notes Toward the Construction of a Contemporary Mennonite Pacifist Apologetic.'" *The Conrad Grebel Review* 4 (Winter 1986): 74-75.

Miller, John W. "In the Footsteps of Marcion: Notes Toward an Understanding of John Yoder's Theology." *The Conrad Grebel Review* 16 (Spring 1998): 82-92.

Mitchell, Anne T. "Review of *The Politics of Jesus.*" Written for a class at, I believe, the Episcopal Seminary in Alexandria, Virginia, 1980, 5pp.

Nation, Mark Thiessen. "A Response to 'In the Footsteps of Marcion: Notes Toward an Understanding of John Yoder's Theology' by John W. Miller in *The Conrad Grebel Review* (Spring 1998)." Unpublished paper, September 1998, 2 pp.

Nation, Mark Thiessen. "Helping Us See Jesus: John Howard Yoder 1927-1997." *Anabaptism Today* 17 (Spring 1998): 17-20.

Nation, Mark Thiessen. "He Came Preaching Peace: The Ecumenical Peace Witness of John H. Yoder." *The Conrad Grebel Review* 16 (Spring 1998): 65-76.

Nation, Mark Thiessen. "John H. Yoder in a Postliberal Context." Unpublished essay written at Fuller Theological Seminary, Pasadena, CA, December 1991, 20pp.

Nation, Mark Thiessen. "Unlimited Catholicity and Radical Reformation: The Ecumenical Theological Ethics of John H. Yoder." Ph.D. diss., Fuller Theological Seminary, Pasadena, CA, 1999?

Nation, Mark Thiessen. "Whose Politics? Which Polity?: Yoderian Reflections on Communitarianism." Unpublished essay, 1994, 28pp.

Neufeld, Mark. "Responding to Realism: Assessing Anabaptist Alternatives." *The Conrad Grebel Review* 12 (Winter 1994): 43-62.

Neufeld, Tom Yoder. "Varieties of Contemporary Mennonite Peace Witness: From Passivism to Pacifism, From Nonresistance to Resistance." *The Conrad Grebel Review* 10 (Fall 1992): 243-57.

Neufeld, Tom Yoder. "We Have This Treasure in Clay Jars: A Meditation Given at the Memorial Service." *The Conrad Grebel Review* 16 (Spring 1998): 93-96.

Neville, David. "John Howard Yoder (1927-1997)." *Faith and Freedom: A Journal of Christian Ethics* (Australia) 6 (April 1998): 26.

Park, Joon-Sik. "The Church as Ethical Reality: A Critical Synthesis of H. Richard Niebuhr and John H. Yoder." Ph.D. diss., Southern Baptist Theological Seminary, Louisville, KY, May 1991.

Peachey, Paul P. "The Radical Reformation, Political Pluralism, and the Corpus Christianum." In *The Origins and Characteristics of Anabaptism*, edited by Marc Leinhard, 10-26. The Hague: Martinus Nijhoff, 1977.

Pfeil, Margaret R. "A Pacifist Pedagogy for Teaching the Just War Tradition: Nuanced Argument and Faithful Participation." A paper presented as part of a panel discussion on "Like Leaven in Bread: The Influence of John Howard Yoder — As Both Theologian and Person — On Those Who Studied with Him," Society of Christian Ethics, January 1999.

Price, Tom. "Theologian Cited in Sex Inquiry." *The Elkhart Truth*, June 29, 1992. (This article was followed by a series of five articles examining "allegations of sexual misconduct against noted theologian John Howard Yoder," written by Tom Price, staff writer, *The Elkhart Truth*, July 12-16.)

Reames, Kent. "Histories of Reason and Revelation: With Alasdair MacIntyre and John Howard Yoder into Historicist Theology and Ethics." Ph.D. diss., University of Chicago Divinity School, December 1997.

Reimer, A. James. "Mennonites, Christ, and Culture: The Yoder Legacy." *The Conrad Grebel Review* 16 (Spring 1998): 5-14.

Rich, Mark. "Jesus' Jubilee Movement as the Chief Exemplar of the Kingdom of God: A Paradigm for Christian Ethics." Ph.D. diss., Northwestern University, Evanston, IL, 1997.

Roth, John D. "Living Between the Times: 'The Anabaptist Vision and Mennonite Reality' Revisited." *The Mennonite Quarterly Review* 69 (1995): 323-35.

Sawatsky, Rodney J. "Leadership, Authority and Power." *The Mennonite Quarterly Review* 71 (1997): 439-51.

Sawatsky, Rodney J., and Scott Holland, editors. *The Limits of Perfection: A Conversation with J. Lawrence Burkholder.* Second edition. Waterloo, Ontario/ Kitchener, Ontario: Institute of Anabaptist and Mennonite Studies/Pandora Press, 1996.

Schipani, Daniel. "John Howard Yoder: Teacher of the World Church." *Courier* [A Quarterly Publication of the Mennonite World Conference] 13 (First Quarter 1998): 4.

Schlabach, Gerald W. "Anthology in Lieu of System: John H. Yoder's Ecumenical Conversations as Systematic Theology." *The Mennonite Quarterly Review* 71 (1997): 305-9.

Schweitzer, Wolfgang. "Diskussionsbeitrag zu dem Aufsatz von J. Yoder 'Von göttlicher und menschlicher Gerechtigkeit." *Zietschrift für Evangelische Ethik* 6 (May 1962): 181-84.

Shaffer, Thomas. "The Jurisprudence of John Howard Yoder." *The Legal Studies Forum* 22 (1998): 473-86.

Shaffer, Thomas L., John H. Robinson, editors. "H. Jefferson Powell on the American Constitutional Tradition: A Conversation (Special Issue)." *Notre Dame Law Review* 72 (1996): 11-88.

Shank, David A. "From a Long-time Friend and Mission Colleague." *The Conrad Grebel Review* 16 (Spring 1998): 103-5.

Shin, Won Ha. "Two Models of Social Transformation: A Comparative Analysis of Political Ethics of John H. Yoder and Richard J. Mouw." Ph.D. diss., Boston University, 1998.

Smyth, Thomas William. "Rudy Wiebe as Novelist: Witness and Critic Without Apology." Ph.D. diss., The University of Toronto's Centre for the Study of Religion, 1997.

Snyder, C. Arnold. *The Life and Thought of Michael Sattler.* Scottdale, PA: Herald Press, 1984, esp. 89-97.

"Some Excerpts from the Press" [covering Yoder's lecture, "The Christian Responsibility to the State"]. *Ontario Peace Bulletin* [Supplement to *The Canadian Mennonite* and distributed separately by the Conference of Historic Peace Churches] (November 12, 1963): 8.

Stassen, Glen H. "Concrete Christological Norms for Transformation." In *Authentic Transformation: A New Vision of Christ and Culture,* edited by Glen H. Stassen, 127-89, 286-94. Nashville, TN: Abingdon Press, 1996.

Stassen, Glen H. "A New Vision." In *Authentic Transformation: A New Vision of Christ and Culture,* edited by Glen H. Stassen, 191-268, 294-99. Nashville, TN: Abingdon Press, 1996.

Stassen, Glen H. "In Memory of John Howard Yoder." *Baptist Peacemaker* 18 (Spring 1998): 19.

Stayer, James M. "Anabaptist Nonresistance and the Rewriting of History: Or, Is John Yoder's Conception of Anabaptist Nonresistance Historically Sound?" A paper written in late 1974 responding to Yoder's "'Anabaptists and the Sword' Revisited," 17pp.

Stayer, James M. "Anabaptist Nonresistance and the Rewriting of History: On the Changing Historical Reputation of the Schleitheim Articles and the Four Hundred Fiftieth Anniversary of Hans Denck's *Concerning Genuine Love.*" A paper read at the Schleitheim Seminar, June 28-29, 1977, Goshen College, Goshen, IN, 27pp.

Stayer, James M. "Die Anfänge des schweizerischen Täufertums im reformierten Kongregationalismus." In *Umstrittenes Täuffertum 1525-1975,* edited by Hans-Jürgen Goertz, 19-49. Göttingen: Vandenhoeck & Ruprecht, 1975.

Stayer, James, Werner Packull, and Klaus Deppermann. "From Monogenesis to Polygenesis: The Historical Discussion of Anabaptist Origins." *The Mennonite Quarterly Review* 49 (April 1975): 83-121, esp. 94-100.

Steinfels, Peter. "John H. Yoder, Theologian at Notre Dame, Is Dead at 70." *The New York Times,* January 7, 1998.

Suderman, Robert J. and Bruno Epp, "The Witness of *Concern* Magazine." A paper written for the course, "Theology of Anabaptist Classics (Discipleship)," at the Associated Mennonite Biblical Seminaries (includes expanded listing of contents, indices, and evaluation), 1974, 55pp.

Swomley, John. "Response to 'Political Thought and *The Politics of Jesus*' by Richard Mouw." Unpublished paper presented at the Mennonite Peace Theology Colloquium, designed to respond to *The Politics of Jesus,* sponsored by the Mennonite Central Committee Peace Section, Kansas City, MO, October 7-9, 1976, 5pp.

Thomson, Jeremy. "The Recovery of the Community in Ecclesiology: Community and Authority in the Ecclesiology of John Howard Yoder." Ph.D. diss., King's College, London, England, 1999.

Toole, David. *Waiting for Godot in Sarajevo.* Boulder, CO: Westview Press, 1998, esp. chs. 7 and 8.

Waltner, Erland. "From a Neighbor and Former Colleague." *The Conrad Grebel Review* 16 (Spring 1998): 105-7.

Walton, Robert. "Was There a Turning Point of the Zwinglian Reformation?" *The Mennonite Quarterly Review* 42 (January 1968): 45-56.

Walton, Robert. *Zwingli's Theocracy.* Toronto: The University of Toronto Press, 1967, esp. 185-200.

Warneck, Wilfried. "John Howard Yoder and the Peace Church Movement in Europe." *Church and Peace* 15 (Spring/Summer 1998): 28-30.

Weaver, Alain Epp. "Options in Postmodern Mennonite Theology." *The Conrad Grebel Review* 11 (Winter 1993): 63-76.

Weaver, Alain Epp. "Parables of the Kingdom and Religious Plurality: With Barth and Yoder towards a Nonresistant Public Theology." *The Mennonite Quarterly Review* 72 (July 1998).

Weiss, David. "In Memory of John Yoder: Scholar, Professor, Friend." *The Observer* [University of Notre Dame student-run paper], January 27 1998, p. 9.

Weiss, David R. "Op-ed Ethics: the Newspaper Column as Ethical Genre for a Community in Exile, The Vocation to Interpret Christian Life to the Larger World." A paper presented as part of a panel discussion on "Like Leaven in Bread: The Influence of John Howard Yoder — As Both Theologian and Person — On Those Who Studied with Him," Society of Christian Ethics, January 1999.

Westmoreland-White, Michael L. "Obituaries: John Howard Yoder." *Prism* [the journal of the Evangelicals for Social Action] (March/April 1998).

Winright, Tobias L. "The Presumption Against Harm in Policing: Implications for the Debate About the Complementarity of the Just War Tradition and Pacifism." *Annual of the Society of Christian Ethics* (1998).

Wolterstorff, Nicholas. Review of *The Royal Priesthood* by John Howard Yoder. *Studies in Christian Ethics* 10 (1997): 142-45.

Wood, Philip. "The Politics of Anabaptism: An Anabaptist-Mennonite Political Theology." Ph.D. diss., University of Leeds, Leeds, England, 1999.

Contributors

Michael G. Cartwright is Assistant Professor and Chair of the Department of Philosophy and Religion at the University of Indianapolis, Indianapolis, Indiana. He is the editor of *The Royal Priesthood: Essays Ecclesiological and Ecumenical* by John Howard Yoder (Grand Rapids: Eerdmans, 1994).

Grady Scott Davis is Associate Professor of Religion and the Lewis T. Booker Chair in Religion and Ethics at the University of Richmond, Richmond, Virginia. He is the author of *Warcraft and the Fragility of Virtue: An Essay in Aristotelian Ethics* (Moscow, ID: University of Idaho Press, 1992).

Marva J. Dawn works for Christians Equipped for Ministry in Vancouver, Washington. She translated and provided a commentary of *Sources and Trajectories: Eight Early Articles by Jacques Ellul That Set the Stage* (Grand Rapids: Eerdmans, 1997).

Stanley Hauerwas is Gilbert T. Rowe Professor of Theological Ethics at Duke University, Durham, North Carolina. His most recent book is *Sanctify Them in the Truth: Holiness Exemplified* (Nashville: Abingdon Press, 1998).

Chris K. Huebner is a Ph.D. candidate in theological ethics at Duke University. He has published essays on the antitheoretical aspects of John Howard Yoder's theology.

Harry J. Huebner is Professor of Philosophy and Theology at Canadian Mennonite Bible College, Winnipeg, Manitoba. He is coauthor (with David

Schroeder) of *Church as Parable: Whatever Happened to Ethics?* (Winnipeg: CMBC Publications, 1993).

Reinhard Hütter was recently Professor of Christian Ethics and Theology at the Lutheran School of Theology, Chicago, Illinois, and is currently Professor of Theology at The Divinity School, Duke University. His most recent book is *Theologie als kirchliche Praktik: Zur Verhältnisbestimmung von Kirche, Lehre und Theologie* (Chr. Kaiser Gütersloher Verlag, 1997).

William Klassen is a Research Scholar at the École Biblique in Jerusalem. His most recent book is *Judas: Betrayer or Friend of Jesus?* (Philadelphia: Fortress Press, 1996).

Gayle Gerber Koontz is Professor of Theology and Ethics at Associated Mennonite Biblical Seminary, Elkhart, Indiana. Her Ph.D. dissertation, from Boston University, is entitled "Confessional Theology in a Pluralistic Context: A Study of the Theological Ethics of H. Richard Niebuhr and John Howard Yoder."

James Wm. McClendon, Jr., is Distinguished Scholar in Residence at Fuller Theological Seminary, Pasadena, California. His most recent book is *Doctrine,* the second volume of his *Systematic Theology* (Nashville: Abingdon Press, 1994).

Nancey Murphy is Associate Professor of Christian Philosophy at Fuller Theological Seminary. She has written on the relationship between theology and science, including (with George F. R. Ellis) *On the Moral Nature of the Universe: Theology, Cosmology, Ethics* (Philadelphia: Fortress Press, 1996).

Mark Thiessen Nation is a Ph.D. candidate at Fuller Theological Seminary, and director of the London Mennonite Centre. He is coeditor (with Nancey Murphy and Brad Kallenberg) of *Virtues and Practices in the Christian Tradition: Christian Ethics after MacIntyre* (Valley Forge, PA: Trinity Press International, 1997) and is currently completing a doctoral thesis on John Howard Yoder.

Ernest W. Ranly, C.PP.S., taught philosophy at St. Joseph's College, Rensselaer, Illinois before committing his life to working with the people of Peru through Misioneros de la Precosia Sangre.

Arne Rasmusson is Lecturer in Systematic Theology and Ethics at Kortebo School of Theology, Jönköping, Sweden. He is the author of *The Church as*

"Polis": From Political Theology to Theological Politics as Exemplified by Jürgen Moltmann and Stanley Hauerwas (Notre Dame: University of Notre Dame Press, 1995).

A. James Reimer is Professor of Religious Studies and Theology at Conrad Grebel College. He is author of *The Emmanuel Hirsch and Paul Tillich Debate: A Study in the Political Ramifications of Theology* (Edwin Mellen, 1989).

Jane Elyse Russell, OSF, is Provincial Councilor, School Sisters of Saint Francis, U.S. Province, Milwaukee, Wisconsin. Her dissertation, under John Howard Yoder at the University of Notre Dame, is entitled "Renewing the Gospel Community: Four Catholic Movements with an Anabaptist Parallel."

Gerald W. Schlabach is Associate Professor of History and Religion at Bluffton College, Bluffton, Ohio. He is the author of *To Bless All People: Serving with Abraham and Jesus* (Scottdale, PA: Herald Press, 1991).

Glen Stassen is Lewis B. Smedes Professor of Christian Ethics at Fuller Theological Seminary. He is the author of *Just Peacemaking: Transforming Initiatives for Justice and Peace* (Louisville: Westminster/John Knox Press, 1992).

J. Denny Weaver is Professor of Religion at Bluffton College. His most recent book is *Keeping Salvation Ethical: Mennonite and Amish Atonement Theology in the Late Nineteenth Century* (Scottdale, PA: Herald Press, 1997).

Tobias Winright is Instructor of Religion at Simpson College, Indianola, Iowa. His Ph.D. dissertation, from the University of Notre Dame, is entitled "The Challenge of Policing: An Analysis in Christian Social Ethics."